HIKING TRAILS

OF THE SMOKIES

GREAT SMOKY MOUNTAINS
NATURAL HISTORY ASSOCIATION
Gatlinburg, Tennessee

TRAIL NARRATIVES BY: Bill Beard, Carson Brewer, Woody Brinegar, Margaret Lynn Brown, Tom Condon, Donald E. Davis, Beth Giddens, Doris Gove, William A. Hart, Jr., Lance Holland, Steve Kemp, Charles Maynard, David Morris, Ted Olson, & James Wedekind.

EDITED BY: Don DeFoe, Beth Giddens, & Steve Kemp
DESIGNED BY: Christina Watkins
PROJECT COORDINATION BY: Steve Kemp
TRAIL PROFILE MAPS BY: University of Tennessee Cartographic Services Lab
EDITORIAL ASSISTANCE BY: Jo Hoy, Ken Hoy, & Lynne Davis
HISTORICAL RESEARCH BY: Margaret Lynn Brown & Donald E. Davis
PRINTED IN THE UNITED STATES OF AMERICA ON RECYCLED PAPER

2   3   4   5   6   7   8   9   10

ISBN 0-937207-15-2

Great Smoky Mountains Natural History Association is a private, nonprofit organization which supports the educational, scientific, and historical programs of Great Smoky Mountains National Park. Our publications are an educational service intended to enhance the public's understanding and enjoyment of the national park. If you would like to know more about our publications, memberships, and projects, please contact: Great Smoky Mountains Natural History Association, 115 Park Headquarters Road, Gatlinburg, TN 37738 (615) 436-7318.

For Carson Brewer and Don DeFoe.
From the likes of humans, the Smoky Mountains
will never have better friends.

ACKNOWLEDGMENTS

This book happened only because several dozen people were willing to work very hard on it, most for little or no compensation. Although the people listed below were obviously dedicated to creating a hiking guide, I think their greater motivation came from the mountains themselves. While working with these wonderful individuals over the last two years, I've noticed one common thread which unites them: all have strong feelings about the beauty of the Smokies and want somehow to give something back. With this book they have done so.

Adopt-a-Trail Volunteers
for reviewing trail narratives
Wayne Adams (Panther Creek)
Dave Allaben (Boogerman)
Ben Anderson (Thomas Divide)
Mary B. Blevins (Meigs Creek)
Carolyn Burchfield (Anthony Creek)
Diana Conn (Twin Creeks)
Laura Cunningham (Lumber Ridge)
Ray Davis (Schoolhouse Gap)
Wayne, Sylvia, &Bart Davis (Cucumber Gap)
Harold Draper (Curry Mtn.)
Walter Eskew (Middle Prong)
Annette Evans (Noland Divide & Greenbrier Ridge)
Mike Fanelli (Caldwell Fork)
Gideon Fryer (Scott Mtn.)
Susan and Chris Grant (Baxter Creek)
Gordy Gilbertson (Bote Mtn.)
Ronald S. Graves (Roundtop)
Sandy Gregory (Little River)
Phyllis Henry (Old Settlers)
Mary Jane Johnson (Meigs Creek)
Stan Johnson (Ace Gap)
Lee Knight (Boogerman)

Gene Latham (Rich Mtn. Loop)
Tom Little (Porters Creek)
Robert Lochbaum (Hannah Mtn.)
Howard McAnnally (Old Settlers)
Johnny Molloy (Miry Ridge)
Meredith Morgan (Lower Mt. Cammerer)
John Murphy (Turkeypen-Finley Cane)
Lou Murray (Cane Creek)
Dale Myers (Meigs Mtn.)
Craig Noland (Grapeyard Ridge)
Jim O'Brien (Chimney Tops)
Alvin & Dorothy Ownby (Lead Cove)
Joe Penland (Chestnut Top Lead)
Bob Perlack (Cove Mtn.)
Joe Pidhouriz (Ramsay Cascades)
Ann & Andy Richter (Little River)
Sarah Roberto (Hatcher Mtn.)
Linda M. Seals (Beard Cane)
Don Schmidt (West Prong)
Pat Schmidt (Anthony Creek)
William F. Smith (Gabes Mtn.)
Paul Threlkeld (Road Prong)
K.R. and Janice Tipton (Crib Gap)
Roger Tipton (Rainbow Falls)
Floyd C. Weeks (Gold Mine)
Arnold Williams (Hazel Creek)
Michael Wood (Little Bottoms)
Edward A. Wright (Alum Cave)

National Park Service/Natural History Association Staff
for assistance and cooperation
Karen Ballentine
Eugene Cox
Babette Collavo
Steve Kloster
Don DeFoe

Jason Houck
Lynne Davis
Annette Evans
Kris Carr
Tamara Johnson
Kitty Manscill
Terry Maddox
George Minnigh
Keith Nelson
Joel Ossoff
Carroll Schell
Keny Slay
Donna Shope
and Marianne Wightman

The Entire Tremont Staff of Summer 1993
for hospitality

Nye Simmons, MD
for writing the health and safety section

Other Publishers and Authors
for permission to use excerpts from their books
Carson Brewer
Elizabeth Powers
University of Tennessee Press

Cartographic Services Laboratory
for the trail profile maps
Will Fontanez—Head Cartographer
Douglas Cain
Brian Dibartolo
Steve Gordon
Charles LaFon
Louise Mathews

Trail Wheelers

for pushing a little wheel over long trails

Rob Andres
Tom Condon
Dave Fazzino
Curtis Heck
David Morris
Bill Clabough
Bill DeLozier
Dan Lawson
Gaynell Lawson
Craig Noland
Phyllis Henry
John Wilbanks
Kathy Shewell
Don Watson

CONTENTS

ABOUT THIS GUIDE

Our objective in creating this guide book was to compile detailed descriptions of every trail in Great Smoky Mountains National Park (excluding Quiet Walkways and Self-guiding Nature Trails) which is officially recognized and maintained by the National Park Service. Now that the initial work is completed, our goal is to keep the guide as accurate and up-to-date as possible through frequent revisions and reprintings.

From the beginning, we sought to emphasize in the text the park's rich natural and cultural resources. We assumed that if all hikers wanted to know was where the trail began, how long it was, and perhaps how difficult, then all they really needed was a topographic map. Our belief has been that the majority of those individuals who take the time to walk the valleys and ridges of the Smoky Mountains are naturally curious about what is, or what once was, around them.

To build the text, we carefully selected 15 remarkable individuals and bestowed upon them the title "hiker/writer." Of the 15, seven are authors of at least one book; five are authors or co-authors of other hiking guides; at least five have earned or are earning doctorate degrees; three have worked as park rangers; three have had their own newspaper columns, and all have given their time, energy, patience, and talent towards the production of this guide.

As much as was practical, we assigned hiker/writers to trails that fit their areas of personal expertise. James Wedekind, a working geologist and hydrologist in Oak Ridge, TN, covered trails with special geological significance. Carson Brewer, who is frequently employed by the Smoky Mountain Field School to lead groups to Mt. Le Conte, covered most of the Le Conte trails for us. Margaret Lynn Brown and Donald E. Davis, both of whom have Ph.Ds in history, wrote the narratives for many of the trails with the deepest cultural stories. Brown and Davis also compiled a "Trail History Notebook" of the whole park for other hiker/writers to draw from. Tom Condon, an interpretive ranger for the National Park Service in Cades Cove, and a former Teacher/Naturalist for the Great

Smoky Mountains Institute at Tremont, worked on most of the Cades Cove and Tremont area trails.

The binding of this book is Smythe sewn using real thread. This is the most expensive type of binding and the most durable. The paper is a #40 pound recycled stock; light enough to not be a burden on the trail yet strong enough to last for years. We chose an off-black ink to cut down on "show-through" on the lightweight paper.

Great Smoky Mountains Natural History Association, a private, nonprofit organization, worked closely with the National Park Service in the development of this book. The Park Service provided equipment, experience, and expertise, while the Association provided funding and publishing know-how. Funding for the Association comes from sales of books and other products at park visitor centers and from membership dues. Excess of revenues over expenses (profits) generated by the Association go back to Park Service projects.

Keeping this book as accurate and up-to-date as possible will be much easier with input from hikers in the field. If you have corrections, please send them to:

Hiking Guide Editor
Great Smoky Mountains
Natural History Association
115 Park Headquarters Road
Gatlinburg, TN 37738

SK.

USING THIS GUIDE

MAPS . . . .

This guide includes two types of maps: an all-park trail map and individual trail profile maps. The all-park trail map was developed from the official National Park Service "Great Smoky Mountains Trail Map" which has been for sale in visitor centers for several years. For the purposes of this publication, we have added over 40 trail names which do not appear on the regular map. Consequently, all trails listed in this book appear on the enclosed map.

The purpose of the all-park map is primarily for orientation and trip planning. The MAP KEY code which accompanies each trail narrative refers to the grid along the border of this map. Mileages between most trail intersections are also included. If you lose or wear out the enclosed copy, replacements are available for a small fee at most park visitor centers or by calling Great Smoky Mountains Natural History Association (615) 436-7318.

At least two commercial hiker's topographic maps (Earthwalk Press and Trails Illustrated) also include the grid which corresponds to our MAP KEY codes. They come in 1:62,500 scales and paper or plastic versions. The United States Geological Survey (USGS) maps referred to in the narratives are 1:24,000 scale (7.5 minute). All of these maps are available at park visitor centers or by calling GSMNHA at the number above.

The trail profile maps which accompany each narrative were designed to show how rigorous each trail is and to locate major landmarks and trail junctions. They are based on the best information available at the time of printing. Some minor discrepancies of distance and elevation may have occurred due to rugged terrain.

TRAIL NARRATIVES ·

Each trail narrative begins with a callout section like the one shown below. An explanation of each component follows here.

> **LENGTH**: 10.0 miles, from Fontana Lake to Noland Divide Trail.
> **HIGHLIGHTS**: 6 backcountry campsites, fishing along the creek.
> **CAUTIONS**: 4 unbridged creek crossings.
> **MAP KEY**: 6-7 F-G; USGS quads: Noland Creek, Bryson City, Clingmans Dome.
> **USE**: Horse and hiking trail.
> **TRAILHEAD**: Drive 8.0 miles on Lakeview Drive northwest from Bryson City. Take the access trail from the parking lot at the bridge over Noland Creek.

LENGTH: Indicates the total mileage of the trail from the beginning and ending points listed. This also shows which direction the narrative runs (*e.g.* from "Fontana Lake" to the junction with the "Noland Divide Trail.")

HIGHLIGHTS: Some of the trail's more notable traits.

CAUTIONS: Potential hazards.

MAP KEY: The number and letter codes refer to the grids on the side of the all-park map that comes with this guide. Topographic hiking maps produced by Earthwalk Press and Trails Illustrated use the same grid, or will soon. The "USGS quads" refer to 7.5 minute (1:24,000 scale) topographic maps produced by the United States Geological Survey. Maps may be purchased at park visitor centers and other locations. To order Smokies quads from Great Smoky Mountains Natural History Association by phone, call (615) 436-7318.

USE: If listed simply as "Hiking trail" no horses are allowed.

TRAILHEAD: Directions to the beginning of the trail. START-ING POINT is used if the trail does not start from a road (*e.g.* if it begins from another trail).

BACKCOUNTRY ETHICS

RULES & REGULATIONS · · · · · · · · · · · · · · · ·

1. You must possess a backcountry permit while camping in the backcountry.
2. Camping is permitted only at designated sites and shelters.
3. Use of rationed sites and shelters must be confirmed through the Backcountry Reservation Office.
4. You may stay up to three consecutive nights at a campsite. You may not stay two nights in a row at a shelter.
5. Maximum camping party size is eight persons.
6. Open fires are prohibited except at designated sites. Use only wood that is dead and on the ground.
7. Use of tents at shelters is prohibited.
8. Food storage: When not being consumed or transported, all food and trash must be suspended at least ten feet off the ground and four feet from the nearest limb or trunk, or shall be stored as otherwise designated. See Bears and You!
9. Toilet use must be at least 100 feet from a campsite or water source and out of sight of the trail. Human feces must be buried in a 6-inch-deep hole.
10. All trash must be carried out.
11. All plants, wildlife, and natural and historic features are protected by law. Do not cut, carve, or deface any trees or shrubs.
12. Polluting park waters is prohibited; do not wash dishes or bathe with soap in a stream.
13. Pets, motorized vehicles, and bicycles are not permitted in the backcountry.
14. Firearms and hunting are prohibited.
15. Feeding or harassing any wildlife is prohibited.

Maximum fine for each violation is $500 and/or six months in jail.

BACKCOUNTRY PERMITS · · · · · · · · · · · · · · · ·

The backcountry use permit is free but is required for all overnight camping in the backcountry. The system is designed to protect the park and its solitude, both the quality of the natural environment and the quality of your experience. The National Park Service is charged with protecting the Smokies for present and future generations to enjoy. The permit system is an attempt to enable you and others to love this wild place without loving it to death.

How to get your backcountry permit. You may self-register for a permit at any ranger station by following posted instructions, but your itinerary may require access to a public pay telephone, as explained below:

Some sites are rationed—see chart on enclosed map— because of heavy use. You must telephone our Backcountry Reservation Office to obtain permission for the use of those sites. Failure to do so invalidates your permit and puts you in violation of regulations and subject to a fine.

If your itinerary includes at least one rationed site, we encourage you to make advance reservations up to a month ahead of the trip's start. To do so, you must plan your trip before your call and indicate exactly which site you intend to occupy for each night of your trip. If no rationed sites are involved, you may simply obtain your permit via self-registration upon your arrival in the park.

The Backcountry Reservation Office is open 7 days a week, from 8 a.m. to 6 p.m. The telephone number is (615) 436-1231. If you are not staying at a rationed site or shelter, you do not need to call the reservation office.

The following rules relate to trip planning: 1. Maximum party size is eight. 2. You may stay no more than one consecutive night at a shelter, three consecutive nights at a campsite. 3. You must stay in designated sites and follow your identified itinerary.

In addition, certain courtesies help make the permit system work for all of us. 1. Do not reserve more space than you intend to occupy; to do so prohibits use by other backpackers. 2. Please call the reservations office to cancel any nights or spaces that become available because of changes in your plans.

As of summer, 1994, the following backcountry campsites are rationed and require advanced reservations. Reservations may be made up to a month in advance. Call (615) 436-1231. The office is open 7 days a week from 8 a.m. to 6 p.m.

Campsites #10, 13, 23, 24, 29, 36, 37, 38, 47, 50, 55, 57, 61, 71, 83. Plus all shelters.

MINIMUM IMPACT CAMPING . . . .

Park regulations are designed to protect the backcountry and its denizens, but you can do more. Your sense of pride in using the backcountry so that the next person doesn't even realize you have been there is most important. As you comply with and promote sound backcountry use practices, you also actively perpetuate the wilderness qualities that you find so attractive. Here is a checklist of minimum-impact backcountry use practices:

♦ Abide by all backcountry-use regulations. They are designed for resource protection. ♦ Use a stove to minimize tramping and destruction of vegetation resulting from collecting firewood. ♦ Keep your group small to preserve a sense of solitude. ♦ Avoid cutting across switchbacks to prevent destructive trail erosion. ♦ Carry a sleeping pad; do not use tree boughs. ♦ Help remove litter to clean up after thoughtless campers.

Questions are best resolved before you hit the trail. Please ask for help from park rangers if you need it. In summary, leave the backcountry as you would expect to find it.

If you would like to help the park with backcountry maintenance or resource monitoring, call our Volunteer Coordinator at (615) 436-5615 about how you can help.

Toilet Use

Improper human waste disposal creates one of the most disgusting conditions in the backcountry. Regulations require that human

feces be deposited in a six-inch-deep hole and covered with soil and that no toilet use occur within 100 feet of a camp or water source or within sight of a trail. Defecating behind a shelter or near a spring creates very unhealthy conditions. All sanitary napkins and tampons must be packed out. Do not bury them.

SAFETY & MEDICAL CONCERNS

STREAM CROSSINGS & WATERFALLS—Heavy rains—particularly in warm weather—cause swollen streams that may be unsafe to ford. Do not cross a stream unless you are sure you can make it. Also, make sure your pack can be discarded quickly, wear shoes to protect your feet, use a stout stick for extra support, and, if you loose your footing, float with your feet downstream to protect your head. Just walking near a stream, on moss- and spray-covered rocks, can be hazardous. In no case should you camp next to a stream swollen by high water. Waterfalls can be extremely hazardous; climbing on them has resulted in numerous fatalities.

DRINKING WATER—All water obtained in the backcountry should be treated before drinking to protect you from health hazards. The recommended treatment is boiling for one minute. Pump-style water filters may not remove certain bacteria or viruses but most now remove Giardia. Chemical disinfectants require very long contact times for the water temperatures found in the mountains. Do not drink untreated water!

Waterborne illness can be spread by viruses, bacteria, and Giardia, all of which are undetectable by inspecting the watersource. Your first hint of problems may be cramps, diarrhea, nausea, or vomiting. Viruses or bacteria may affect you within 12-24 hours; Giardia's incubation period is 7-10 days, giving you time to get home before severe cramps and diarrhea strike. Treatment usually requires a physician's prescription, and sometimes expensive testing to reach a proper diagnosis.

BEARS & YOU—Most hikers look forward to seeing a bear during their stay at the Smokies. Bears in the park are wild and unpredictable, but they have caused few injuries to people who followed reasonable precautions. In fact, only when bears have been fed or have taken unprotected food from humans do they tend to cause property damage or injury.

Encounters along the Trail. Remain watchful. If you are lucky enough to spot a bear, observe it from a distance—do not throw food or leave food behind for it to eat. When you stop to picnic, keep your food and pack nearby and maintain a watchful eye in the adjacent woods. Bears familiar with human habits can be sneaky. If a bear approaches, quickly gather all your supplies and retreat along the trail. Leaving food behind only encourages further problems. Report all bear incidents to a park ranger.

Encounters in Camp. The best way to avoid bears is not to attract them. Keep cooking and sleeping areas separate except in shelters. Keep tents and sleeping bags free of food odors; do not store food in them. A clean camp is essential for you and later campers; pack out all food and litter.

Proper food storage is required by regulation. Your cooperation benefits those who follow you. Where food storage devices are present, follow directions and make use of them. Otherwise, adhere to the following instructions.

Place all food (including trash) in your pack. Select two trees, approximately 10-20 feet apart, with limbs about 15 feet high. Using a rock as weight, toss a rope over a limb on the first tree and tie one end to the pack. Repeat this process with the second tree. Raise the pack about six feet via the first rope and tie it off. Then pull the second rope until the pack is suspended at least ten feet high and evenly spaced between the trees; it must be at least four feet from the nearest limb or tree trunk. Tie it off.

INSECT STINGS—Reactions to stings from yellowjackets, bees, and wasps range from minor local swelling to life threatening ana-

phylactic shock. Local pain and swelling are expected; in 24 hours the hand or foot may be swollen twice its size, and eyes may swell shut. The eye itself is not affected, only the eyelid, and vision is not in jeopardy. If stung on the hand, remove all rings immediately. Though alarming, the condition will resolve in 2-5 days. Benadryl, an over-the-counter antihistamine, is helpful. Redness and local warmth are common, and not necessarily due to infection. Itching and hives (welts, like big mosquito bites) are a more serious reaction which should have medical attention promptly. Give Benadryl or other antihistamines immediately if available. Respiratory distress, wheezing, and/or collapse are potentially life threatening; antihistamines may help but injectable epinephrine in a sting kit is usually needed. Seek emergency medical treatment immediately.

Honey bees leave their stinger embedded in the victim, often with the venom sac still intact. Carefully scrape the stinger out with a credit card, pocket knife, or fingernail. Attempting to remove it with tweezers frequently squeezes the sac, injecting more venom into the victim.

Prevention requires prior knowledge of the allergy. Allergy shots to minimize the reaction need to be taken for a long time before being stung to be effective. Prescription sting kits should be carried by any sensitive individuals but are no substitute for desensitization. Many stinging insects are attracted to bright colors, perfumes, and moving objects. Try not to run if possible. You will likely be ignored, or investigated and left alone. However, if you have just stepped on a nest, running may be the best choice. Multiple stings can make a person very ill without actual anaphylactic shock. In the United States, many more people die from insect stings than snake bites each year.

SNAKE BITES—There are copperheads and timber rattlesnakes within the park, but they are usually not aggressive, preferring to avoid human encounter. Most bites occur from stepping on an unnoticed snake, or when attempting to handle or play with the snake. Up to 22% or more of bites inject no venom. Prompt local pain and swelling signal injected venom, unless a rare bite directly into a vein has occurred.

Traditional field treatments using incision and suction, and constricting bands have been discontinued in the face of medical research to address the topic. The word is slow to spread even among health professionals. Unskilled attempts at treatment often lead to severe complications, worse than the bite itself.

Keep the victim calm, avoiding any unnecessary activity. Splint the extremity as though for a fracture. Send for help. If walking out is necessary, do so slowly, and with frequent rest stops.

A tourniquet cuts off circulation, increases tissue damage, and may lead to amputation. Ice can cause extensive tissue damage when used on envenomated tissue, and increased circulation to the area will occur when the ice is removed.

Small children and the elderly are at greatest risk of serious injury, adults and older children may require hospitalization, but are seldom critical. Death is rare, and even without treatment is extremely unusual in the first 24 hours after the bite. Even though the Smokies receive nine million visits per year, no fatality due to snake bite has ever been documented.

Avoid stepping over logs where a snake may be resting, and give any snake a wide berth. If you find yourself too close to a snake, avoid any sudden movement. A tongue darting at you is only the snake gathering scent to try to identify you, not a prelude to a strike. Don't put your hands where you can't see them when climbing or gathering firewood.

POISONOUS PLANTS—Learn to recognize poison ivy by its characteristic three leaf pattern. Vines may be difficult to identify, however, and any should be suspect. Playing or swinging on vines may be hazardous enough without adding the inconvenience of an itchy rash. Washing with soap and water within 30 minutes of exposure may be preventive; long sleeves and trousers will help. Smoke from burning poison ivy vines can cause the same rash, but all over you — don't throw vines on the fire.

BLISTERS—Prevention is much better than treatment. Two pairs of socks are preferable. The inner pair should be light and non-absorbent, to prevent excess moisture buildup next to your skin. The outer should be wool or wool-synthetic blend for cushioning, and its ability to hold its loft when damp from sweat. The two socks dissipate friction by sliding on each other, rather that transmitting it to the skin surface. High tech socks that "wick" moisture away from the skin are expensive, but repay huge dividends in comfort.

Tape or moleskin any high friction "hot spots" that you are prone to before the hike. Band-Aids bunch up too easily to be effective. If you feel a "hot spot" developing, stop to add padding (tape, etc.) before the blister is fully formed. Once formed, a small blister may be covered in the same way. Larger blisters tend to tear open: cleanse the area well with soap and water, and drain with a flamed needle at the edge of the blister. Cover with tape. At least you can maintain a cleaner environment and reduce the chance of infection.

ANKLE INJURIES—A twisted ankle can bring an outing to an abrupt halt. An audible snap usually signals a serious sprain (torn ligament) or fracture. Immediate first aid measures of ice may not be available and may be contrary to the goal of getting back to transportation at the trailhead. The decision to walk (limp) out or send for help is an individual one. If you can put weight on the ankle comfortably, then it is probably OK to walk out. The more one has to favor the ankle, the greater care must be taken. Don't lead with the injured foot, and pay special attention to foot placement. An assistant's feet may tangle with yours, resulting in another fall; use such help with caution. If excessive pain prevents weight bearing, determine if help is available. Taping is unlikely to help with the acute injury.

Those with weak ankles should favor heavy boots with adequate ankle support, and possibly a brace to wear in the boot. The slip-on variety sold in pharmacies and ace wraps offer no mechanical support; consult a physical therapist or orthopedic surgeon for the best available device, as well as strengthening exercises to reduce the chance of injury.

HEAT-RELATED ILLNESSES—Heat exhaustion is caused by water and salt depletion in a hot environment. Weakness, feeling faint, nausea with possible vomiting, headache, dizziness, and possibly fainting, alone or in some combination are frequent symptoms. Fever and confusion are usually absent. Muscle cramps may be present. The victim usually appears cool and clammy.

Heat stroke is a breakdown in the body's ability to regulate temperature. High fever, hot-dry skin (frequently but not always), and severe confusion or coma differentiate this life threatening condition from the milder heat exhaustion. Occasionally heat exhaustion symptoms precede heat stroke (20% of the time).

Prevention includes the use of cool, loose fitting clothing, frequent rest in a cool place, avoidance of direct sunlight, and drinking lots of fluids. Sweat losses of 2-3 quarts per hour are possible with exertion in hot surroundings. Certain drugs may affect sweat production or the way your body responds to heat stress. If it causes dry mouth, or blurred vision it may be a bad combination with heat; antihistamines should be avoided if possible. Check with your doctor ahead of time. High humidity further compromises your ability to stay cool. Drink enough fluid to maintain output of clear, dilute urine. Water is fine, or sports drinks diluted 50/50 with water.

Field treatment for heat exhaustion consists of cooling measures: removal of excess clothing, seeking shade, lying down, resting, and oral hydration. Drink cool liquids slowly and steadily. Too much too fast may cause vomiting and make matters worse.

Victims of suspected heat stroke should be cooled at once by whatever means is available. Drenching the clothing with creek water would be ideal, but any water will do. Send for help. This is a true medical emergency.

LIGHTNING STRIKES—Lightning can cause mild injury as well as respiratory and cardiac arrest. Victims suffering respiratory or cardiac arrest may be saved through prompt bystander CPR with no medical equipment available. The heart usually starts again on its own after a brief period of inactivity. Breathing may take longer to recover; prolonged mouth to mouth assistance has led to successful recovery. Don't give up! Instruction in those techniques is not possible here, but regularly sponsored courses are available from your local Red Cross, American Heart Association, and many hospitals. Emergency medical evaluation is prudent for any survivor of a lightning strike; those who feel "OK" probably are, but should be checked as soon as possible.

Lightning was traditionally thought to seek the highest point for discharge, but is more complex in its behavior. Sometimes it hits where no predictive factors can be identified. It is most active around the edges of thunderstorms, and may strike before the storm seems to be upon you. Seek shelter away from solitary trees, high trees, rock outcroppings, or overhangs. It is thought to jump the gaps of overhangs much like a spark plug. It may travel down tree trunks and "splatter," and may follow wire fence lines. If no shelter is available, lie down in a shallow depression, away from any conductive material, or streams of water.

HYPOTHERMIA—This is an extremely dangerous condition involving the lowering of the "core" temperature (the temperature of the body's vital internal organs) beyond the lower level of efficient metabolic function. This causes involuntary shivering in an attempt to generate heat by muscular activity. At this point the victim may say they "feel very cold," but be rational. Confusion and loss of muscular coordination soon follow without treatment. One of the first signs may be a companion falling behind or tripping often. The victim may behave and walk as though drunk, and may lose coordination of fine motor skills such as those needed to strike a match. With this or soon after comes mental confusion, sometimes accompanied by seemingly irrational behavior. Hypothermic victims may be so confused as to undress in freezing conditions, or hallucinate—and act upon that hallucination!

Hypothermia (or exposure) is brought about by a combination

of factors. Cold, wet, and wind are a potentially deadly combination even with temperatures in the 50s F. if you aren't properly prepared. Children, because of their greater ratio of surface area to weight, are especially vulnerable. At higher elevations in the park, there is a year-round potential for this to occur.

You lose heat through breathing, becoming wet, being exposed to wind, sitting on cold objects, and through radiant losses — the heat your body gives up to its surroundings. Prevention is aimed at those factors present on the day of your hike. Cotton is great for coolness in summer, but a disaster when wet and cold. Avoid blue jeans in the winter. Synthetic pile fabrics are best for dependable warmth. A wind and rain suit will do double duty in foul weather, offering added insulation against radiant losses. Avoid sitting on cold rocks or ground, and if possible breathe through a scarf or collar if you think you are getting in trouble. Be sure your head is covered as up to 40% of your heat loss can be from your head. In the winter, and transition seasons, take a sweater in case the weather turns, or you're caught out late.

Field treatment involves stopping further heat loss and warming the victim. Usually getting dry and warming with a hot drink are sufficient. More severe cases may require construction of an emergency shelter to warm the victim, but that is beyond the scope of this section.

PREVENTION—Many outdoor emergencies and too frequent fatalities arise from hikers ignoring basic park guidelines and common sense. Regardless of how small or large your group, tell a responsible person about your trip, and establish a check-in procedure. This person notifies park authorities if you are overdue. Keep your group together, and if a large group, designate a "sweep" person who will bring up the rear. No one falls behind this person. Pair off into a "buddy system," and keep track of your buddy. Stay on the trail. You won't be lost if you do, just "bewildered" for a bit. Get off the trail, and you can become truly lost in short order in the dense growth. You are then almost impossible to find from the trail — and the trails get searched first. If night finds you, stay put.

The chance of injury and becoming more lost increase dramatically. Hiking alone is dangerous; if you must do so, leave a detailed itinerary with someone, and then stick to it.

Take appropriate clothing with you in a rucksack. Rain gear is always necessary. An emergency space blanket is no larger than your fist until needed and weighs only a couple of ounces. A coach's whistle can be carried in your pocket or around your neck, is audible from far away, and may be used long after you have yelled yourself hoarse. All children should have one; kids can become lost on a "nature break". Waterproofed matches in a waterproof matchbox should be in the pockets of any outdoor traveler. Fires in undesignated sites are strongly discouraged, but may be needed in a crisis.

GETTING HELP—If you are faced with a situation where outside help is needed, don't panic. Take a few minutes to sit down and fully assess the situation and plan your actions. Write down if possible your location, the victim's name, and the suspected nature of the problem. In the heat of the moment, such essential information is often lost or confused. Also, this will help you focus clearly on the problems at hand. Plan your route to the nearest trailhead where help may be obtained, or back to your car as the situation dictates. Other passing hikers, or backpackers at backcountry sites may be of assistance. Seek the closest phone or ranger station. The general information number is 615-436-1200. 911 emergency service is also available in many areas.

With a little common sense and good judgment, the chances of your having anything but fun are remote. Proper planning will further reduce the likelihood of problems on your outing.

Safety and Health Concerns courtesy Dr. Nye Simmons and the National Park Service.

SMOKY MOUNTAIN WEATHER

Local weather forecasts are posted at park visitor centers. Forecasts for longer than 48 hours hence are generally inaccurate.

SPRING—March has the most changeable weather; snow can fall on any day, especially at the higher elevations. "Spring break" backpackers are often caught unprepared when a sunny day in the 70s F. is followed by a wet, bitterly cold one. Major blizzards have occurred as late as early April. By mid- to late April, the weather is usually milder.

◆

SUMMER—By mid-June, heat, haze, and humidity are the norm. Most precipitation occurs as afternoon thundershowers. Summer weather generally persists through mid-September. At the lower elevations, expect highs in the mid-80s and lows around 60°. Above 5,000 feet, the highs will be in the mid-60s and lows in the low 50s.

◆

AUTUMN—In mid-September, a pattern of warm, sunny days and crisp, clear nights often begins. However, cool, rainy days also occur. Most leaves have fallen in the high country by mid-October. The peak of fall color in the lowlands is late October. Dustings of snow may fall at the higher elevations in November.

◆

WINTER—Days during this fickle season can be sunny and 70° F. or snowy with highs in the 20s. In the low elevations, snows of 1" or more occur 1-5 times a year. At Newfound Gap, 69" fall on average. Lows of -20° are possible in the high country. Major snow storms often leave backpackers stranded at the high elevations, especially in Appalachian Trail shelters.

TEMPERATURES & PRECIPITATION

	Gatlinburg, TN, elev. 1,462'			Clingmans Dome, elev. 6,643'		
	AVG. HIGH	LOW	PRECIP.	AVG. HIGH	LOW	PRECIP.
Jan.	51°	28°	4.8"	35°	19°	7.0"
Feb.	54°	29°	4.8"	35°	18°	8.2"
March	61°	34°	5.3"	39°	24°	8.2"
April	71°	42°	4.5"	49°	34°	6.5"
May	79°	50°	4.5"	57°	43°	6.0"
June	86°	58°	5.2"	63°	49°	6.9"
July	88°	59°	5.7"	65°	53°	8.3"
August	87°	60°	5.3"	64°	52°	6.8"
Sept.	83°	55°	3.0"	60°	47°	5.1"
Oct.	73°	43°	3.1"	53°	38°	5.4"
Nov.	61°	33°	3.4"	42°	28°	6.4"
Dec.	52°	28°	4.5"	37°	21°	7.3"

SPECIAL EQUIPMENT CONCERNS

CLOTHING—The one essential piece of equipment for hiking in the Smokies is a rain jacket. Bring it along even on sunny days when there's not a cloud in the forecast. Sooner or later you'll be thankful you did.

During the cooler months, rain pants can also be a big help. In warm weather, however, they tend to lead to overheating.

If hiking in the high country between September and May, always carry warm clothing, including hat and gloves. Many a balmy morning has turned into a frigid, wet afternoon on Mt. LeConte or the Appalachian Trail.

FOOT WEAR—Truly water-proof boots can be a big plus in the Smokies. Not only will they keep your feet drier during rainy weather, but they also give you a little extra assistance when crossing shallow streams.

WATER FILTERS—Although somewhat expensive, a good water filter is a worthy investment for backpackers in the Smokies. Boiling all drinking water is quite time- and fuel-consuming and tepid water doesn't do much to quench thirst on a muggy summer day. Get one that filters Giardia since it may be present in any spring or stream.

CRAMPONS—Small, clip on crampons can be very helpful when hiking high elevation trails during cold weather. The Appalachian Trail and some trails to Mt. Le Conte are notorious for having long, ice-covered stretches due to seeps and springs.

SUGGESTED LOOP HIKES

DAY LOOPS . . . .

For a park with some 150 trails, the Smokies are not especially well-endowed with short loop hikes, that is, walks that allow hikers to end up in the same place they started without much backtracking. One reason for this is that most park trails were built from old wagon roads that existed prior to park establishment. Old roads, like new roads, tended to go from one place to another, not around in circles. Forthcoming are some of the Smokies' better day loops.

Cades Cove/Abrams Creek Area

Rich Mountain Loop: 8.5 miles
Starting Point: Beginning of Cades Cove Loop Road
See Rich Mountain Loop narrative

Rabbit Creek/Hannah Mountain/Hatcher Mountain/ Little Bottoms/Cooper Road trails loop: 8.2 miles
Starting Point: Abrams Creek Ranger Station
See Rabbit Creek Trail narrative

Cooper Road/Hatcher Mountain/Little Bottoms loop: 10.9 miles
Starting Point: Abrams Creek Campground
See Cooper Road Trail narrative

Abrams Falls/Hannah Mountain/Rabbit Creek trails loop: 11.1 miles
Starting Point: Abrams Falls Trailhead (Cades Cove Loop Road)
See Abrams Falls Trail narrative

Finley Cane/Bote Mountain/Lead Cove trails loop: 7.1 miles
Starting Point: Finley Cane Trailhead on Laurel Creek Road
See Finley Cane Trail narrative

Cosby/Greenbrier Area

Low Gap/Appalachian/Snake Den Ridge trails loop: 12.5 miles
Starting Point: Cosby Campground
See Low Gap Trail narrative

Cataloochee/Big Creek Area

Caldwell Fork/Boogerman trails loop: 7.4 miles
Starting Point: Caldwell Fork Trailhead, just past Cataloochee Campground
See Caldwell Fork Trail narrative

Deep Creek/Smokemont Area

Deep Creek/Loop/Indian Creek/Deep Creek trails loop: 4.2 miles
Starting Point: End of Deep Creek Road
See Deep Creek Trail narrative

Deep Creek/Indian Creek/Martins Gap/Sunkota Ridge/Loop/Indian Creek/Deep Creek trails loop: 11.6 miles
Starting Point: End of Deep Creek Road
See Deep Creek Trail narrative

Deep Creek/Indian Creek/Stone Pile Gap/Thomas Divide/Indian Creek Motor/Deeplow Gap/Indian Creek/Deep Creek trails loop: 10.2 miles
Starting Point: End of Deep Creek Road
See Deep Creek Trail narrative

Bradley Fork/Smokemont Loop trails loop: 5.7 miles
Starting Point: Smokemont Campground
See Bradley Fork Trail narrative

Elkmont/Tremont Area

Little River/Cucumber Gap/Jakes Creek trails loop: 5.1 miles
Starting Point: Little River Trailhead above Elkmont Campground
See Cucumber Gap Trail narrative

Fontana Lake/Twentymile Area

Appalachian/Lost Cove/Lakeshore trails loop: 12 miles
Starting Point: Fontana Dam
See Appalachian Trail narrative

Twentymile/Twentymile Loop/Wolf Ridge trails loop: 7.3 miles
Starting Point: Twentymile Ranger Station
See Twentymile Loop Trail narrative

Lakeshore/Tunnel Bypass trails loop: 2.8 miles
Starting Point: End of Lakeshore Drive out of Bryson City
See Goldmine Loop Trail narrative

Cades Cove/Abrams Creek Area

Rabbit Creek/Hannah Mountain/Abrams Falls trails loop.
Length: 11.1 miles (1 night)
Starting Point: Abrams Falls Trailhead on Cades Cove Loop Road
(see Rabbit Creek Trail narrative).
Campsite: #15
Comments: Relatively easy. Best during the cooler months. Lots of
piney woods. Can be done the opposite way to avoid creek crossing
at beginning of hike.

Rabbit Creek/Hannah Mountain/Hatcher Mountain/Beard
Cane/Cooper Road/Wet Bottom trails loop.
Length: 17 miles (1 night)
Starting Point: Abrams Falls trailhead on Cades Cove Loop Road
(see Rabbit Creek Trail narrative).
Campsites: 15, 11
Comments: Relatively easy. Best during the cooler months. Lots of
piney woods. Can be done the opposite way to avoid creek crossing
at beginning of hike.

Rich Mountain Loop/Indian Grave Gap/Crooked Arm Ridge trails
loop
Length: 8.5 miles (1 night)
Campsite: Rich Mtn. Shelter
Starting Point: Beginning of Cades Cove Loop Road (See Rich
Mountain Loop narrative).
Comments: Best to hike clockwise. Good views of Cades Cove.
Nice during fall color season or when mountain laurel blooms
(May-June).

Anthony Creek/Russell Field/Appalachian/Bote Mountain/Antho-
ny Creek trails loop
Length: 12.9 miles (1-2 nights)

Campsite(s) #10 (optional second night at Spence Field Shelter)
Starting Point: Cades Cove Picnic Area (see Anthony Creek Trail narrative).
Comments: A difficult climb to the Appalachian Trail; it's best not to try it with a backpack in one day. Great views. A classic summer outing.

Cooper Road/Little Bottoms/Hatcher Mountain/Cooper Road trails loop.
Length: 10.9 miles 1 night)
Campsite: #17
Starting Point: Abrams Creek Campground (see Cooper Road Trail narrative).
Comments: A good hike for the cooler months. Mostly low elevation pine-oak forests. One of the easier backpacking loops.

Elkmont/Tremont Area

Jakes Creek/Miry Ridge/Lynn Camp Prong/Middle Prong/Panther Creek/Jakes Creek trails loop.
Length: 16.7 miles (1-2 nights)
Campsite(s): #26 (1 night) #27 & #28 (2 nights)
Starting Point: Jakes Creek trailhead (see Jakes Creek Trail narrative).
Comments: Water for campers staying at Campsite 26 is 0.5 mile away. Campsite #28 is another option, but it is a horse camp. Pleasant hardwood forest for much of the route.

Clingmans Dome Area

Clingmans Dome Bypass/Appalachian/Welch Ridge/Jonas Creek/Forney Creek/Forney Ridge trails loop.
Length: 18.4 miles (2 nights)
Campsites: Silers Bald Shelter, #69
Starting Point: Parking area at end of Clingmans Dome Road (see Clingmans Dome Bypass narrative)

Comments: Ascent of Forney Creek Trail is difficult not only for its 4,000' of elevation gain, but also for its many challenging stream crossings. Appalachain Trail section has views, spruce-fir forest, pleasant beech gaps.

Forney Ridge/Springhouse Branch/Noland Creek/Noland Divide trails loop
Length: 18.5 miles, including road walking (1-2 nights)
Campsite(s): #62 (1 night) #64 & #61 (2 nights)
Starting Point: Parking area at end of Clingmans Dome Road (see Forney Ridge Trail narrative).
Comments: Ascent on Noland Ridge and Noland Divide Trails is long, steep, includes many wet stream crossings. Spruce-fir forest and Andrews Bald are highlights. You must walk 1.5 miles on Clingmans Dome Road to complete loop.

Deep Creek Area

Deep Creek/Martin Gap/Indian Creek/Deep Creek trails loop
Length: 13.3 miles (1 night)
Campsite: #58
Starting Point: End of Deep Creek Road (see Deep Creek narrative).
Comments: Campsites #57 or #59 may also be used. Pleasant streamside trails.

Deep Creek/Pole Road Creek/Noland Creek/Noland Divide trails loop
Length: 19.2 miles (2 nights)
Campsites: #58 & #61
Starting Point: End of Deep Creek Road (see Deep Creek Trail narrative).
Comments: This loop requires a side trip down to campsite #61 since Noland Divide Trail has no campsites. Highlights include pleasant stream scenes on Deep Creek and views from Noland Divide.

From Newfound Gap

Appalachian/Dry Sluice Gap/Grassy Branch/Sweat Heifer
Creek/Appalachian trails loop.
Length: 13.6 miles (1 night)
Campsite: Kephart Shelter
Starting Point: Newfound Gap parking area (see Appalachain
Trail narrative).
Comments: Big trees, great views.

Smokemont Area

Bradley Fork/Smokemont Loop trails loop.
Length: 5.7 miles (1 night)
Campsite: #50
Starting Point: Smokemont Campground (see Bradley Fork Trail
narrative).
Comments: Pleasant streamside walking on Bradley Fork, cultural
history. One of the shortest backpacking loops in the park.

Balsam Mountain Area

Rough Fork/Caldwell Fork/Hemphill Bald trails loop
Length: 13.7 miles (1 night)
Campsite: #41
Starting Point: Polls (Paul's) Gap (see Rough Fork Trail narrative)
Comments: Great views, big trees.

Cosby Area

Snake Den Ridge/Maddron Bald/Gabes Mountain trails loop.
Length: 17.2 miles (2 nights)
Campsites: #29 & #34
Starting Point: Cosby Campground (See Snake Den Ridge Trail
narrative).
Comments: Big trees, waterfalls, a classic Smokies adventure.

Big Creek Area

Big Creek/Swallow Fork/Mount Sterling Ridge/Baxter Creek trails loop
Length: 17.1 miles (2 nights)
Campsites: #37 & #38
Starting Point: Big Creek Campground (see Big Creek Trail narrative)
Comments: Big trees, waterfalls, great views. A grand adventure.

SHUTTLE HIKING

Having a second vehicle to park at the other end of the hike opens up a big world of opportunities for both day hikers and overnighters. If a second vehicle isn't available, you may wish to investigate a commercial hiker shuttle service. Other shuttles may also exist. Check at a park visitor center or local hiking store.

Greenbrier/Cosby Area
(615) 487-5081 or 487-2263

Gatlinburg
Happy Hiker (615) 436-5632
C & O Taxi (615) 436-5893

Big Creek
Kathy & Tom Oke (704) 648-3857

Fontana Lake
land shuttle: Charlie Watts (704) 479-2504
boat: Luther Turpine (704) 498-2211 x277

Bryson City
Safety Cab (704) 488-2486

"Everything was perfection, and the views fell in our laps."

—HARVEY BROOM
Out Under the Sky of the Great Smokies

ABRAMS FALLS TRAIL

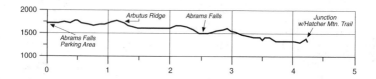

LENGTH: 4.2 miles, from the trailhead in Cades Cove to Hannah Mountain and Hatcher Mountain trails. (2.5 miles to Abrams Falls).
HIGHLIGHTS: Abrams Creek and Abrams Falls.
CAUTIONS: Do not climb on slippery rocks around falls.
MAP KEY: 2 D; USGS quads: Cades Cove, Calderwood.
USE: Hiking trail.
TRAILHEAD: Turn right onto unpaved side road between sign posts #10 and #11 on the one-way Cades Cove Loop Road. Side road terminates in large trailhead parking area.

The portion of this trail which goes to Abrams Falls has long been one of the most popular trails in the Smokies. Its trailhead is at the site of a former guest lodge operated by John Oliver in the 1920s. He was a direct descendent of John Oliver, the first white settler in Cades Cove (1818).

Abrams Creek, which borders the trail, and Abrams Falls were named for Cherokee Chief Abram. He lived in the village of Chilhowee at the mouth of Abrams Creek on the Little Tennessee River. This place is now buried beneath the waters of Chilhowee Lake.

The broad, heavily used path crosses Abrams Creek by bridge just beyond the trailhead. Abrams Creek drains Cades Cove and joins Mill Creek below the bridge. The sights and sounds of the creek enhance the pleasure of this walkway in all seasons.

Our wide path runs relatively level through rhododendron, not far from the picturesque stream. The Abrams Creek gorge has been formed by the abrasive power of waterborne sand and rock. The trail rises and passes over a low pine ridge. Then it descends to near stream level again. Up and down the path goes four times. The second rise is over Arbutus Ridge, named for trailing arbutus—one of the earliest blooming spring flowers. The trail crosses a dip in the crest of Arbutus Ridge at mile **1.0**. To the west, the tip of Arbutus Ridge balloons into a mile-round circle, around which the creek curves. When the leaves are down, one can view the beginning and end of this loop in the stream below, south and north.

This path provides excellent opportunities to see the underlying bedrock, which is Cades Sandstone. In the streambed it rises from the southeast to form strata that are worn away by waterborne sand and rock. Crossing Arbutus Ridge, the leading edge of the hairpin curve passes by sharply tilted Cades Sandstone outcrops.

At the falls, the 20-foot plunge is over the resistant ledge of this sandstone. It also appears in other places in the path. Beyond Arbutus Ridge, the trail rises again on the mountainside above the creek. Mountain laurel appears in these upper, dry slopes along with pines and oaks. The trail eventually runs above the falls and drops to Wilson Branch just beyond.

Abrams Falls is a delight to see, especially in high water. It flows over a bluff into a broad pool more than a hundred feet across. It's a picturesque place to pause and relax and absorb the sound of the falling water and the natural beauty of the pool and the falls. Beyond the falls, the trail continues on similar terrain for 1.7 miles to the ford in Abrams Creek at the intersection with the Hannah Mountain and Hatcher Mountain trails. The path runs the west slope of Abrams Creek Gorge through a mixed pine and hardwood forest. It descends to cross narrow hollows and small incoming branches and rises again. The ford is chancy at the best times and dangerous in high water.

Narrative by Woody Brinegar

ACE GAP TRAIL

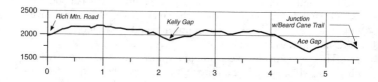

LENGTH: 5.6 miles, from Rich Mountain Road to Beard Cane Trail.
HIGHLIGHTS: Ace Gap, crossing of old railroad bed.
MAP KEY: 3D; USGS quad: Kinzel Springs.
USE: Horse and hiking trail.
TRAILHEAD: For those staying in Cades Cove, the easiest access is to drive up Rich Mountain Road to its end at the park boundary. This road can be reached via the Cades Cove Loop Road. For those traveling from outside the park, it is far easier to approach the trailhead through Dry Valley. Heading south on US 321, turn right after the Kinzel House Restaurant, a few miles west of Townsend. Follow this road to the Tuckaleechee Cove Methodist Church. Turn right here onto Old Cades Cove Road. This will take you through Dry Valley and to the park boundary at Rich Mountain Gap. At the gap, the Old Cades Cove Road runs headlong into the one-way Rich Mountain Road. A small area here provides parking for both the Ace Gap and Rich Mountain trails.

At the right of the trailhead is a sinkhole. To the left is a side trail to the entrance to Bull Cave, which descends almost vertically some 420', one of the deepest caverns in the southeast.

In the days before the park, Rich Mountain Road was used as a passage for cattle driven to the high Smokies for summer pasture. Those coming from some distance often spent the night in the gap and legend has it that one unfortunate bull slipped over the bluff to give the cave its name. Rich Mountain derives its name from the fertile limestone soil here.

At the start of the trail are some large oaks and the path here is heavily used. This is often the case at a parking area; visitors stretch their legs for a few minutes. Beyond that the path is far less traveled.

It's an easy trail running almost level, in and out around each of the ridge fingers extending out from the crest of the mountain. It's peaceful, not heavily used, disturbed only by the occasional explosion of a grouse ascending in rapid flight.

Above the trail the forest soon changes dramatically as the result of a forest fire in 1987 which burned the upper slopes of the ridge for more than a mile. The trail was the fire line, and the blaze occasionally reached it, but did not penetrate below. The most altered portion is a stand of bare pine trunks in a lush thicket of new growth. Arson was suspected as the cause.

Past the burned area is a white pine on the left of the trail with a lightning scar running the length of the trunk. A pitch pine, 30 inches in diameter, stands on the right just short of Kelly Gap. Its slightly bent trunk saved it from the Little River Lumber Company loggers when they harvested the timber over 80 years ago.

Kelly Gap is at **2.2** miles and is the location of Campsite #4 (Kelly Gap, 1,930'). The site has room for 4-6 tents and is used fairly often by horseback parties. If you had to choose between staying at site #4 or #7, #4 is probably the more pleasant. After swinging west around the bulge of a flanking ridge and then back again to the ridgeline, the trail comes in contact with a boundary line dirt road built by Laurel Valley developers in the late 1970s. The path nears this boundary road at three points.

Between Kelly Gap and the Beard Cane Trail there are a number of marvelous displays of pink lady's slippers in May.

At **4.7** miles Ace Gap is easily identified by the broad, old railroad bed which crosses here. Early in the twentieth century, Little River Lumber Company built a track up Davis Branch and across into the various hollows of the Hesse Creek drainage to reap the virgin forests of pine, oak, maple, poplar, and cherry. According to Gordon Wright, whose family's land borders the park here, Ace Gap was named by card playing timber cutters who gathered there to play cards in their free time. The company frowned on card playing in the mess hall and sleeping quarters because of property damage arising out of card game fights. Ace Gap was a peaceful site for cards.

In the gap is campsite #7 (Ace Gap, 1,680') a comfortable and level backcountry campsite but one with limited water nearby (there is a tiny stream 50 yards directly behind #7 through the woods). It accommodates two tents. From the gap the trail goes west on or near the ridgeline 1.4 miles to the junction of the Beard Cane Trail. It runs along Hurricane Mountain, so named because of a devastating storm early in the nineteenth century which mowed down a swath of trees on the mountain.

Views along the ridge are curtained off by summer foliage but are extensive in winter. Few outcrops are evident along this path, but the rock is Cades Sandstone, an extensive sedimentary formation extending from the north and west of Cades Cove to just north of this ridgeline. In Rich Gap, erosion has exposed the softer limestone.

Narrative by Woody Brinegar

ALBRIGHT GROVE LOOP TRAIL

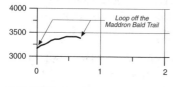

LENGTH: 0.7 mile, starting and ending at Maddron Bald Trail.
HIGHLIGHTS: Virgin forest.
MAP KEY: 9 D; USGS quad: Mt. Guyot.
USE: Hiking trail.

STARTING POINT: Hike Maddron Bald Trail for 2.9 miles from its trailhead on Laurel Springs Road. Continue straight at the junction where Maddron Bald Trail turns left.

This small loop off Maddron Bald Trail was named for Horace Albright, the second director of the National Park Service. Albright, a lawyer and conservationist, was an early advocate of a park in the Smokies, believing that national parks should be distributed around the country to serve more people. He helped mediate land condemnation conflicts, participated in the development of the park, and defied the efforts of Senator Kenneth McKellar of Tennessee to design a state line crest highway for the Smokies. He was also a good friend of

John D. Rockefeller, Jr. and gave him professional advice during 35 years of conservation philanthropy, including enabling gifts to the Smokies, Acadia, Shenandoah, Yellowstone, and at least 20 other parks. Albright deserves to have this beautiful grove named for him.

The narrow Albright Grove Loop Trail twists and rises along a small creek. The Eastern hemlock canopy overhead and the needle carpet provide an atmosphere even in winter that seems to require whispering. Tuliptrees, Fraser magnolias, and maples have grown into giants here, in a virgin forest that Champion Fibre Company once owned, but sold to the park commission after a condemnation suit.

Look for tree adaptation for supporting massive trunks. Beech trees send out buttress roots; silverbell trees bulge at the base; and Fraser magnolias extend roots that look like big toes. As the trail levels and starts down, look for a giant tuliptree on the left with a little spur trail made by admirers. To the right of the tuliptree are two American beech trees. A few yards farther down the trail stands the real giant of this trail, a tuliptree with a circumference of more than 25', or five to seven people stretching and grasping hands. However, this tree would no longer interest Champion Fibre. Its crown has been broken off, probably by lightning, and it lives with just a few lower branches. An elderberry shrub is thriving 50' up on the broken stump, and from the downhill side, you can see ferns and mosses growing up there. You don't have to go to the tropics to see epiphytes (plants growing high up on other plants) or buttress roots.

The trail descends past more big silverbells and Eastern hemlocks. In April, silverbell flowers carpet the trail. In fall, look for the light brown fruits about the size of an almond. Each fruit has four wings; it looks like it might be useful for the back end of a dart. Try to open one with your fingernail, and you will develop respect for the tooth strength of red squirrels.

The trail comes up to a ridge where a sign indicates a right turn. Look for a big Fraser magnolia to the left of the sign. It has a mass of stump roots, and some of them look as if they are impatient for the old tree to fall over. After passing a few more giant Eastern hemlocks and silverbells, the trail makes a rocky descent to the Maddron Bald Trail and a trail sign.

Narrative by Doris Gove

ALUM CAVE TRAIL

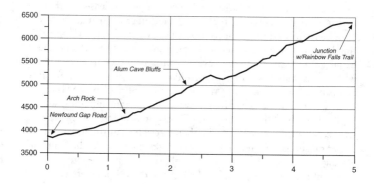

LENGTH: 4.9 miles, from Newfound Gap Road to Rainbow Falls Trail near the summit of Mt. LeConte.

HIGHLIGHTS: Arch Rock, Alum Cave Bluffs, old-growth forest, great views.

CAUTIONS: Exposed cliffs, ice in winter.

MAP KEY: 7 D; USGS quad: Mt. LeConte.

USE: Hiking trail.

TRAILHEAD: Drive 8.6 miles on Newfound Gap Road from Sugarlands Visitor Center (or 20 miles from Oconaluftee Visitor Center). There is a sign and several large parking areas marking the trailhead.

The Alum Cave Trail probably has the most spectacular scenery of any trail in the park. It boasts Arch Rock and Alum Cave Bluffs, dramatic landslide scars on the flanks of the mountain, excellent views of the West Prong of the Little Pigeon River gorge, and cove hardwood and highlands old-growth forest. Easy access makes it a popular trail.

The trail begins by crossing a particularly scenic flat stretch of Walker Camp Prong at Grassy Patch, the site of a warden's cabin built by Champion Fibre Company at the turn of the century, which was also the last settlement before the vast wilderness of the Smokies crest. Consequently, the cabin served as the base camp for early explorations. The old-growth forest at this elevation (over 3800') is a mix of yellow buckeye, Eastern hemlock, American beech and yellow birch, with a dense understory of 10-foot high rosebay rhododendron, dog-hobble, ferns and mosses.

Within 200 yards of the trailhead, you cross Walker Camp Prong and Alum Cave Creek on bridges. Alum Cave Creek enters on the right, and the trail follows it for about the next mile. Along this stretch you may notice the large boulders both in and alongside the creek. As hard as it is to imagine, the creek has moved these furniture-sized rocks just as it has transported grains of sand. Alum Cave Creek is noted for spectacular floods since it drains one of the steepest and most slide-prone slopes in the Smokies. When Mt. LeConte receives an occasional deluge on top of its normal 80 to 100 inch annual rainfall, this little creek must handle the extra load.

At **0.9** mile the trail crosses Alum Cave Creek, turns north and follows Styx Branch. This stream is named for the river to the mythological underworld and, coincidentally, it drains a high valley called Huggins Hell. There is no record of who "Huggins" was (although there was a Huggins family in Hazel Creek) but legend has it that a man named Huggins once declared he would "explore the area or go to hell trying." He was never heard from again, and is presumed to have suffered the latter fate.

The trail passes a dry wash choked with large boulders on the left. The boulders near the trail were left behind following a catastrophic cloudburst on September 1, 1951. In one hour four inches of rain fell. A wall of water surged through this spot and continued to Newfound Gap Road, washing it out in several places. Many of the rotten logs seen earlier are remnants of that episode.

Look uphill beyond the wash and notice a wall of logs and debris of recent origin. The Smokies continue to succumb to gravity, but in fits. On the evening of June 28, 1993, a deluge centered in Huggins Hell removed part of the mountain. A massive slide of soil, rock, trees, and water surged out of the hillside, taking a swath of the trail along with it. Trees toppled upstream, their foundations suddenly swept from beneath them. The slide spread above this point where the valley widened, and massive hardwoods stopped the catastrophic flow. Just ahead, you'll pass through the slide debris.

After crossing Styx Branch by foot bridge, you reach Arch Rock, a narrow passage in a steep slope, not an arch in the classic sense. The origin of this feature is often inaccurately attributed to the erosive power of Styx Branch cutting into the mountainside. While arches are often formed this way, Arch Rock is different. Notice the lack of rounding on the bottom and sides of the passage that would be expected in a stream bed. A stream flowing over slaty rocks will polish them smooth. But as you climb the stone stairs (smooth rocks for the stairs were brought in from the stream), you'll see that the rock in the passageway is jagged and sharp on all sides. The answer to how Arch Rock was formed is found further up the trail.

After crossing Styx Branch by foot bridge, the trail curves through thick rosebay rhododendron and old-growth hardwoods. The forest opens again at the 1993 slide. To the left is the tangle of tree trunks, rocks, sand, and gravel that used to fill the empty ditch on the right. The slide scoured the mountain to its bedrock skeleton, removing a section of mountain over 0.25 mile long and 20' deep. Jumbled soil and rock in the exposed sides of the ditch closely resemble the slide material, suggesting the material that fills these steep and narrow valleys was deposited in a similar grandiose fashion. Erosion here builds and destroys in an instant, then rests in biologic time, sprouting ferns and moss, rhododendron and hardwoods.

The trail climbs moderately up the side of Peregrine Peak, named for its former falcon inhabitants. At about **1.8** miles it leaves the forest and enters a thick heath bald. Heath in this case includes the smaller-leaved Catawba rhododendron, mountain laurel, and sand myrtle, which clings to the bare rock. A nice rocky spur known as Inspiration Point affords a view of the rugged valley below. Examine the rock and notice how much of it is pulverized as it crosses the trail. West across the gulf, the sheer rock cliffs on Little Duck Hawk Ridge are composed of the same rock as the bluffs at Alum Cave, just around the next bend.

All this rock—Arch Rock, Little Duck Hawk Ridge, and Alum Cave Bluffs—is called the Anakeesta Formation, named for rocks on Anakeesta Ridge located on the opposite side of the valley you just climbed out of. Anakeesta is Cherokee for "place of the balsams," referring to the native Fraser fir. But today Anakeesta means the fine grained contemporary of Thunderhead Sandstone, which forms the backbone of the main Smokies range. Unlike the Thunderhead, which came from sand deposits, the Anakeesta was originally oceanic mud. When the Smokies were being uplifted, as the continent buckled while colliding with Africa, the weaker mud was squeezed more readily than sand. The Anakeesta was squeezed between the more competent Thunderhead.

Of course, the Anakeesta is not mud but solid rock. When rock is forced to flow like toothpaste, it tends to change its original structure. This is what happened to the Anakeesta, and it bears the signature of intense deformation. Its jagged appearance is caused by the original layering in the rock intersecting the secondary fabric of squeezed rock called cleavage.

This structure, then, has more than one plane of weakness, which renders the Anakeesta more easily infiltrated by ground water and especially susceptible to the erosive action of freeze and thaw. Arch Rock was formed by this mechanism. Look across at Little Duck Hawk Ridge and notice the two "arches" through the ridge. Like Arch Rock, they were fashioned by freeze-thaw erosion.

The trail climbs steeply along the face of the mountain and reaches Alum Cave Bluffs 2.2 miles from the trailhead. You might notice the gunpowdery smell of the bluff before you reach it. Such large rock exposures are rare in the Smokies, and this one allows you to see the effects of mountain building on a finer scale. Notice that although most of the rock is sharp slate, there are thin lenses of sandstone as well. The lenses have been bent into tight folds, with slate squeezed all around them. In some places, the sandstone layers are stacked on top of one another. The sandwiching reveals how a more competent layer of rock (sandstone) behaves when it is engulfed by less competent material (slate) that is being deformed.

Alum Cave Bluffs also has a rich social history. The Cherokee claim that, as a boy, their great Chief Yanugunski (Drowning Bear) discovered the bluffs while tracking a bear. Dr. John Mingus and other early settlers started the Epsom Salts Manufacturing Company in the 1830's to exploit the bluff's minerals. However, there is no indication that actual mining ever occurred. During the Civil War, Confederate Colonel William Thomas, leading a group of soldiers composed mostly of Cherokees, built a road to Alum Cave Bluffs. Believing the minerals in the bluff, which include sulfides and salt-peter (substances essential to the manufacture of gunpowder), to be a vital strategic resource, he built a small stockade called Fort Harry near the Chimney Tops to protect his crude mine. Although there are no records of how much mining actually occurred, log hoppers and vats were still present in the early 1900s.

Alum Cave Bluffs marks the approximate half-way point in the trail. Leaving the bluffs, the trail passes an excellent view down the rocky spine of Little Duck Hawk Ridge. Climbing steeply, the trail swings around the ridge at a small side trail that leads several yards to Gracies Pulpit. This rocky promontory is named for Gracie McNichol, an early matron of Mt. Le Conte who is noted for climbing the mountain many, many times, including on her 92nd birthday. From the rocks there is a fine view of the Le Conte massif, rising above the valley of Trout Branch. You can see the four peaks comprising the Le Conte massif: West Point, Cliff Top, High Point, and Myrtle Point.

The trail descends 80' during the next 0.4 mile as it travels across an unnamed saddle, then climbs in earnest to the summit of Mt. Le Conte. The trail enters a grove of particularly healthy virgin red spruce in a distinctive uplands forest. At about **3.75** miles you will pass a slide (now overgrown with briars, yellow birch saplings, and mountain ash) where a switchback in the trail was washed away during heavy rains in the 1970s and again during December 1992. The trail was re-routed by installing the present stairs.

In its last mile the trail alternates between grassy scars of land-slides and red spruce forest. Above 6,000', dead Fraser fir dominate what once was a beautiful forest. A combination of the balsam woolly adelgid, which has infested the Fraser fir, and acid precipitation, which has sickened the red spruce, has almost removed the "spruce-fir" designation from the southern Appalachians. The forest now consists of red spruce, mountain ash, and an understory of dog-hobble, briars, and mosses.

Leaving the forest, the trail traverses the steep rock face below Cliff Top. This area receives little sunlight during the winter, and the trail is often covered with ice. The steel cables provide handholds in any weather, but especially in winter. Once the climb is over, you'll arrive at Cliff Top, one of the principal overlooks on Mt. Le Conte. It is a spectacular place. From the trail you can look down Trout Branch and across to the Chimney Tops. To the south, you can see beyond Newfound Gap to the Plott Balsams. Sugarland Mountain and Clingmans Dome dominate the skyline to the southeast. The peak itself is an area of slides, sand myrtle, and bare rock, which is noticeably different from that at Alum Cave Bluffs, but still part of the Anakeesta.

The trail swings around the mountain top, with views of Gatlinburg and Pigeon Forge; on exceptionally clear days you can even see downtown Knoxville, TN. Young Fraser fir grow all around you. Look for turtleheads in mid-summer, as well as bee-balm, monk's hood and yellow coneflower. The trail ends at a junction with Rainbow Falls Trail, a few hundred yards from Le Conte Lodge.

Employees at Le Conte Lodge commonly use Alum Cave Trail as their route to and from work, and they become proficient hikers over the season. The current record for leaving the Lodge, descending Alum Cave Trail, driving to Gatlinburg, purchasing beer, then returning is 3 hours and 45 minutes. Another Le Conte employee, on an emergency quest for popcorn and a newspaper, descended the trail in 1 hour 10 minutes, then completed the return trip in only 1 hour and 20 minutes. The Park Service, however, considers the Alum Cave Trail round trip to Mt. Le Conte a six to eight hour excursion, so you should devote a whole day to the hike, unless you're staying at the lodge or shelter.

Narrative by James Wedekind

ANTHONY CREEK TRAIL

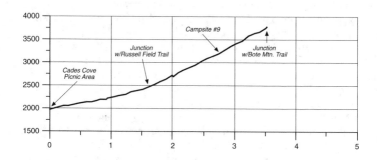

Cades Cove Picnic Area

Junction w/Russell Field Trail

Campsite #9

Junction w/Bote Mtn. Trail

LENGTH: 3.5 miles, from Cades Cove Picnic Area to Bote Mountain Trail.

HIGHLIGHTS: Anthony Creek.

CAUTIONS: Loose rocks in trail.

MAP KEY: 4E; USGS Quad Maps: Cades Cove, Thunderhead Mtn.

USE: Horse and hiking trail.

TRAILHEAD: At the back end of the Cades Cove Picnic Area. (Follow the signs to the picnic area from near the entrance to the Cades Cove Loop Road.)

Because of the quick access it provides to the high country surrounding Cades Cove, the Anthony Creek Trail is heavily used from spring to fall. This trail provides you the opportunity to reach Spence Field, Thunderhead Mountain, and Russell Field—all along the Appalachian Trail. But even better than all this, the Anthony Creek Trail brings you into contact with Anthony Creek itself. This rollicking mountain stream comes crashing and churning down from both Spence and Russell Fields.

The trail starts at the back end of the Cades Cove Picnic area. If you plan on staying in the backcountry overnight or hiking during a busy time, it is probably best to park either at the campground grocery store or the orientation shelter at the start of the loop road. Overnight parking is not allowed in the picnic area, and on busy weekends and in summer parking is gone by early morning. Both alternative parking areas are within easy walking distance.

The trail begins as an access road to a horse camp. A hemlock and rhododendron forest enclose the roadsides, greatly improving the hiking experience. Just over **0.25** mile into the hike you will reach an intersection with the Crib Gap Trail. This trail crosses Laurel Creek Road, providing access to the Schoolhouse Gap area. Continuing along Anthony Creek, you will immediately crest the hill and come upon the horse camp. Here, horseback riders can camp and keep their horses. On a busy weekend morning, this is a bustling place, as it no doubt was even in the days before the park.

Bill Cooper remembers taking his trained steer down to Bud Gregory's store here at the base of the trail in 1914. Bill was grazing cattle on Russell Field, as the cove people had done for almost 100 years. To get supplies up and down the mountain, Bill had trained the steer as a pack animal. The young steer could carry 3 bushels of meal plus needed groceries. But one time the steer refused to go, just "laid down, couldn't get up at all." Bill got an idea and "...got a handful of leaves and put on his tail and lit a match, set the leaves afire. He got up from there then."

The trail continues straight past the horse camp and again gets crowded in by the hemlock forest. Whenever the weather turns too hot to bear, always look for a hemlock forest. These trees love the cool, damp area of the sheltered little "hollers." Along Anthony Creek, Allnight Ridge to the east and Leadbetter Ridge to the west do the sheltering of this valley so narrow you can "holler acrost it," as one local once told me.

At about **0.5** mile you will cross Anthony Creek for the first time. Here is a fine wide bridge, easy for a horse or group of hikers to pass. The trail just beyond the bridge and to the right leads to the campground's water supply—no need to go exploring. There are just 3 old water tanks there. Continuing along 0.25 mile you will come to another unmaintained trail to the right. This trail winds its way around behind the campground until it reaches the horse concession's riding trails in about 2 miles.

Immediately over the rise, you will be crossing Anthony Creek again. Horse crossings can be done at the ford, but you can cross along a footlog with a handrail just 20' upstream. Be careful on wet days, the log can be quite slippery. In July, when the rhododendrons are in bloom, the view upstream is outstanding.

The trail now begins to climb more steeply. It will continue to climb until you reach Bote Mountain Trail, but always moderately. You will be climbing above Anthony Creek now. Listen to its song. From this point on the trail is rocky. Careful footing is a must.

A third stream crossing occurs at **1.25** miles with a fourth at **1.5** miles. The former is via a wide bridge, the latter along another footlog with handrail just upstream of the ford. This fourth crossing occurs just after passing a large tuliptree to the right. Not only is the tree impressive in size, but it is riddled with woodpecker holes. The woodpecker is actually the Yellow-bellied Sapsucker. This bird is aptly named. He bores small holes in a neat line to entice sap to flow. The bird then leaves to allow time for the sap to bleed out and insects to collect. Returning, the sapsucker laps up his feast of sap and bugs.

The fourth crossing actually takes you across the Left Prong of Anthony Creek. Just ahead is the Russell Field Trail to the right. Here you can choose to climb the small valley between Anthony and Leadbetter Ridges, finally ascending the latter to Russell Field. Our trail however continues straight between Anthony Ridge and Cold Water Knob. The trail now narrows and climbs through a more open cove hardwood forest. A third footlog with handrail awaits us at about mile **2.0.** This is the fifth and final crossing of Anthony Creek.

Along this section of trail an interesting plant can be found. The small leathery round leaves hugging the forest floor belong to partridgeberry. This amazing little evergreen has beautiful bright red berries seen from mid-summer through winter. It is not unusual to see last year's berries with this year's flowers in June. The partridgeberry is scattered all over the hillsides from here to campsite #9.

After an easy rockhop of a small spring branch, you will reach campsite #9 at mile **2.8.** This large campsite provides room for many small groups or two large groups. It lies along Anthony Creek, so water is close at hand, but remember always to treat it before use. The campsite is also open and spacious with many large trees including maples, birches, and cherries. Interestingly, in September and October the area is inundated with autumn coral root. This pale purple wild-flower is a saprophytic orchid. Having no chlorophyll, this plant gets its food from the roots of the trees around it.

From the campsite, the trail climbs another 0.5 mile to the junction with Bote Mountain Trail. This climb is the steepest and most strenuous. It also provides the best views, particularly in winter. From here you can catch glimpses back into Cades Cove. It must have been quite a view for the men of the Little River Lumber Company. From 1904 to 1907, the Little River Lumber Co. ran a portable mill up here to harvest these forests. The trees here are now second growth that will soon close the view.

After crossing a small spring, you will climb past a hillside of galax—the musky smelling plant along the ground—and onto Bote Mountain. From here a right will take you up 1.5 miles to Spence Field and some of the most spectacular views in the park. But do not forget Anthony Creek and the company it kept along the way.

Narrative by Tom Condon

APPALACHIAN TRAIL

INTRODUCTION

Of the 2,143 miles that comprise the Appalachian Trail, the Great Smoky Mountains account for 68.6 miles of it and boast not only the highest peak along the trail (Clingmans Dome, elevation 6,643') but also the longest continuous stretch above 5,000' (the 34 miles between Silers Bald and Cosby Knob). In addition to statistical distinctions, the A.T. offers hikers the many splendors of the whole park. If your route includes both high and mid-elevations, you can take in a fair share of the park's renown: more species of trees than in all of northern Europe, more species of salamanders than any other locale (one endemic), and many geologically interesting rock exposures, not to mention the abundance of wildflowers and panoramic views. While the section of the A.T. between Newfound Gap and Charlies Bunion is often crowded, the remote northeastern third of the Trail provides solitude.

The following A.T. segments are not organized for thru-hikers;

consequently, the direction and order of the accounts reflect the preferable routes for day hikers and backpackers. While reading the narratives, you might want to think of Newfound Gap as the focal point, the center of the park, if you will. This movement from Newfound Gap out toward the park boundaries enables you to walk downhill more than up, particularly if you embark on a hike of half the park's A.T. with either Clingmans Dome or Newfound Gap as your trailhead. For example, a walk from Newfound Gap to Davenport Gap (at the northeastern park boundary) entails climbing a total of 4,608' and descending 7,678'.

The A.T. is the only trail in the park marked by blazes; look for white rectangles painted on trees or rocks.

BG

APPALACHIAN TRAIL

NEWFOUND GAP TO CHARLIES BUNION

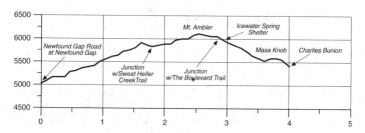

LENGTH: 4.0 miles, from Newfound Gap to Charlies Bunion.
HIGHLIGHTS: Panoramic vistas, rock outcrops.
CAUTIONS: Ice in winter, exposed cliffs, trail erosion.
MAP KEY: 8D; USGS quad: Mt. Le Conte.
USE: Hiking trail.
TRAILHEAD: Drive on Newfound Gap Road to Newfound Gap, 13.2 miles from Sugarlands Visitor Center or 16 miles from Oconaluftee Visitor Center. The trailhead is to the left of the overlook, at the end of the parking area near the restrooms.

The Appalachian Trail may be the best known trail in the park, but it is not one of the busiest. For the most part it lies deep within the park, far from easy access by day hikers. One segment of the A.T. is an exception: the 4.0 miles from Newfound Gap to Charlies Bunion. Here the trail is intersected by Newfound Gap Road, one of the prime tourist spots in the park.

This section of the A.T. was built in the fall of 1932 under the supervision of Sheridan West, a National Park Service engineer, and 22 crewmen. The crew began work on September 5 and finished October 6. All work was done by hand, using picks and shovels. According to park archives, this trail was the first development in the park for the benefit of the public and was built from the $509,000 allotted the park from the emergency relief bill passed in Congress in June 1931. The *Knoxville Journal* reported that when walking the trail, "gorgeous vistas of ridge on ridge of mountains burst upon the hiker or rider unexpectedly through openings in the trees."

The first 0.25 mile east of Newfound Gap is heavily traveled. The trail is along an easy slope and the coolness of the shady, mixed forest, the wide, firm-packed trail and the relief from the hundreds of milling, noisy people and cars crowding the gap are very inviting. Within 0.5 mile, though, most hikers have decided to return. After climbing gently and steadily from the gap, the trail ascends into a region dramatically affected by the balsam woolly adelgid. What was once a dense barrier of Fraser fir that made for a cool, dark hike with only occasional views is now a forest in transition. Thousands of skeletal, bare trunks dominate.

But even these features are temporary. In the newly opened slopes a wide variety of plants are taking advantage of the light even as the remains of the dead Fraser fir are rotting and falling out of the way. An active demonstration of successional growth is in progress. In the decades between the demise of the firs and the ascendance of whatever species come along to produce another forest canopy, we will have the consolation of many impressive views that were seen only in glimpses before.

Another plus for hikers in late summer will be the blackberries ripening alongside the trail. In the newly opened forest floor, thornless blackberries are an aggressive successor species and are thriving, in many cases choking out some of the less hardy grasses and ferns. Within 1.0 mile east of Newfound Gap, they are very noticeable. Of course, bears might also be tempted to dine on these fruits, so you might watch out for them. The thinning canopy now allows some impressive views both north and south. To the north you can see Mt. Le Conte, and the southern panorama encompasses the Oconaluftee River watershed.

At 0.7 mile, the trail comes to a sharp bend to the south as it skirts a ravine. This windy point catches any breeze that might stir and is a pleasant place on a hot day. The southern slopes of Mt. Le Conte are particularly visible along here. You reach the top of a ridge at 1.5 miles and find a grassy spot with a spur trail that leads a few dozen yards to a view north. The young hardwoods are large enough to screen the view somewhat, however. Unfortunately, this spot is also used as an illegal campsite, as the remains of recent fires and trash attest.

This section is also home to wild hogs. You may see a hog trap set off into the woods somewhere within the next mile or so. While you probably will not catch a glimpse of a hog, the destruction they cause by rooting for food will surround you. The areas that look like they have been churned up by a garden tiller are evidence of the problem.

The trail levels as it leads to the gap and intersection with Sweat Heifer Creek Trail at mile 1.7. Mud holes in the trail can be an obstacle in wet periods (most of the time!) and will be encountered through the next 1.5 miles. East of the junction, the trail begins a short, steep section. This is the steepest slope between Newfound Gap and Icewater Springs. Some excellent views into North Carolina are available in the lower part of the slope, and a pullout—grassy and wide with a view—provides a good excuse to pause and catch your breath.

The next landmark is the intersection with the Boulevard Trail at mile 2.7, a popular route to the summit of Mt. Le Conte. In another 0.2 mile, you reach Icewater Spring and shelter. The shelter itself is typical of those within the park with one exception: a compost privy has been constructed to help alleviate the impact of humans. This shelter is heavily used.

Along the trail to the north of the shelter, a couple of grassy areas have been extensively used as illegal campsites. A piped spring to the left could be considered the "original" Icewater Spring, since it once served the old shelter. Yes, the water is really cold. Unfortunately this spot is scarred by fires and fouled by trash, and the illegal tent sites are directly above the spring itself. Not a pleasant thought to consider as you draw water from the spring. A sign advising you to treat all water before using it is located at the shelter.

Descend steadily through a gully caused by millions of footsteps and seven feet of yearly rain. Hikers along this stretch sound like teams of shoed horses on cobblestones as they plod over slabs of silvery yellow slate and flaggy sandstone. 0.8 mile past the shelter, the trail leaves the red spruce, juvenile Fraser fir, and birch forest and changes abruptly to young second growth black cherry, yellow birch, American beech, and thornless blackberry. Swinging around from the shoulder of Mt. Kephart, the trail straddles the state line, and reaches a spectacular view of Charlies Bunion.

The sharp change in the forest is the result of two catastrophes; one natural and one man-caused. In their haste to clear cut Smokies timber, early twentieth-century loggers left the slash, or piles of brush and limbs culled from timber, in place. In 1925, a particularly vicious slash fire swept up the drainage of Kephart Prong, consuming over four hundred acres of woodland. The fire left the precipitous western escarpment of the Smokies void of vegetation. That was the initial, man-made catastrophe.

A natural event followed that created one of the most spectacular bluffs in the Appalachians. In 1929, a cloudburst scoured the veneer of soil from the exposed slopes, clogging area rivers with soil, rock, and trees from the denudation of the landscape. Local writer Horace Kephart, widely known for both his knowledge of outdoor lore and his acerbic wit, assembled a crew to survey the damage rendered by the storm. The hiking party included his friend George Masa, a photographer of some renown, and Charlie Conner, a local mountaineer. Undoubtedly awed by the destruction that exposed this new, craggy promontory in the Sawteeth Range, the group felt it required a name. Not one to repress levity, Kephart likened the knobby appearance of the cliffs to Charlie Conner's bunion.

While conducting research for his book *Strangers in High Places*, Michael Frome interviewed Charlie on the particulars of that day. Evidently, Charlie had no recollection of hobbling on a bunion resembling a rocky crag, but he did experience some sort of foot problem. Kephart, who promoted the establishment of the park (and conveniently sat on the committee for establishing place names), jumped at the opportunity to immortalize Conner and his ailment. Concurrently, he created the sort of place name that would forever lend itself to campfire storytelling. Incidentally, the small peak just before the cliffs is Masa Knob, a tribute to the third member of that day's group.

The craggy face of Charlies Bunion is unique among other expansive cliffs in the southern Appalachians. There is little resemblance between the Bunion's jagged, shattered face and the smooth granite walls of the Blue Ridge Mountains of North Carolina, or the rounded cliffs and overhangs in the gorges of the Cumberlands in Middle Tennessee. The scene would be more appropriate in the Rockies.

Since this place is easily reached from Newfound Gap, the rocks literally teem with day hikers on many weekends. A few careless ones have fallen to their deaths. The rock is shattered by deformation and dangerous to climb. Use caution exploring the Bunion.

Adjacent to the principal exposure lie several other cliffs. The view from these cliffs into the gulf created by Porters Creek is impressive. Brushy Mountain and Mt. Le Conte frame the valley on the west, and Porters Mountain stands to the north. Beyond Porters Mountain, the jagged peaks include Laurel Top, and Mts. Sequoyah, Chapman and Guyot. The peaks trace the main range of the Smokies, and the route of the A.T.

Why are the peaks here conspicuously rough and conical, and the ridges jagged and serrated, while most of the Smokies are rounded summits with long ridgelines? The answer is underfoot. Most of the Smokies express the character of dense, very hard, Thunderhead Sandstone. This rock, not easily worn by erosion, weathers smooth and round. The surrounding terrain mimics its spheroidal erosion. Look south into Bradley Fork Valley and notice the gentler landscape expressed by weathered Thunderhead.

The surrounding peaks appear radically different. They are founded on the slaty Anakeesta Formation. Pick up a piece of rock here or anywhere in a narrow band from the Chimney Tops to Pecks Corner and most will resemble gray slate. Some specimens contain small, dark mineral grains of biotite and chloritoid. The flat surfaces of the rocks are not the original layering of this deep ocean-derived rock, but cleavage surfaces. Look carefully and notice light and dark bands across the smooth cleavage faces. Those are the original bedding features. The intersection of the bedding and cleavage, with pervasive fractures, causes the rock to break into jagged pieces. These sharp, angular intersections in the rock reflect—on a larger scale—the shapes of the mountains. Arnold Guyot noticed this distinct formation when charting these previously unnamed peaks in the late 1850s. He aptly called them The Sawteeth.

Narrative by Bill Beard and James Wedekind

APPALACHIAN TRAIL

CHARLIES BUNION TO PECKS CORNER

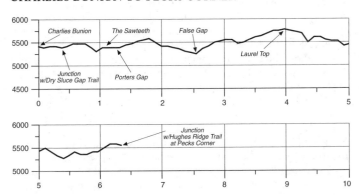

LENGTH: 6.4 miles, from Charlies Bunion to Pecks Corner
HIGHLIGHTS: Spectacular views from Charlies Bunion and The Sawteeth.

CAUTIONS: Exposed cliffs; rocky, eroded trail.
MAP KEY: 7-9 C-D; USGS quad: Mt. Guyot.
USE: Hiking trail.
STARTING POINT: Charlies Bunion, 4.0 miles east on the
Appalachian Trail from Newfound Gap.

The Appalachian Trail leaves the crowded rock of Charlies Bunion
and enters deep wilderness as it travels to Pecks Corner. This stretch
climbs and descends along numerous crags and gaps, largely through
upland virgin forest. Rocky spurs offer occasional views into both
Tennessee and North Carolina.

The trail descends to Dry Sluice Gap (5,376'). On the right, a trail
sign marks the junction with Dry Sluice Gap Trail, providing access
to Bradley Fork and Kephart Prong Trails. Past the gap, a spectacular
ridge aptly-named the Sawteeth leads toward Porters Gap. At places
the ridgetop is no more than 10 yards wide. (*For Sawteeth geology, see
A.T.: Newfound Gap to Charlies Bunion narrative.*) Views to the left
are of the rugged Porters Creek drainage where the park's only paper
birch trees grow in the ridge's shadow. The steep upper reaches of this
watershed produce powerful flash floods that regularly scour the
Porters Creek drainage. Ascend to a small sag called Porters Gap. At
an elevation of 5,400', on a 5,700' ridge top, this is not much of a gap.
After a short climb near the summit of Porters Mountain, descend to
False Gap at 5,233'. False Gap's name probably refers to the cryptic
sag back at Porters Gap.

An A.T. shelter cabin once stood at False Gap, but was dismantled around 1980. The shelter's foundation cut into a precariously
steep slope, and the steep trail to it eroded and became a ravine.
Respecting the prevalent erosion, the Park Service felt dismantling
the structure would help abate any further damage to the slope.

Climbing out of False Gap, you re-enter dense red spruce and pass
some fine views into Tennessee of rocky crags covered in sand myrtle
and mountain laurel. The trail swings around a knob and provides a
view of the North Carolina side. Next you skirt below the summit of
Laurel Top (elevation 5,907'), marked with a trail sign. Descend
steadily, passing many angular blocks of white quartz, and reach
Bradley's View at **4.9** miles. A blocky promontory of hard slate (still

the Anakeesta Formation), affords an excellent view of the upper Bradley Fork Valley, with steep hillsides covered with heath slicks and primeval forest. Hughes Ridge frames the valley to the east, and the heights of the Plott Balsams rise to the south.

On Hughes Ridge observe the abrupt change in the forest from mixed hardwoods and red spruce to pure hardwoods. This clear demarcation shows the point logged to by Champion Fibre Co. Champion relinquished these lands reluctantly. The company finally settled on a price after a bitter lawsuit, selling their massive holdings in the Smokies for over 350% of their purchase price only 11 years earlier.

A steep descent follows the very narrow ridge top. Notice the excellent trail construction. The Civilian Conservation Corps used hand labor to cut and place these flat stones to make a graded trail along this knife-edge ridge top. A cut through the rock a little further along may have served as a source for the stone.

The trail then climbs around Pecks Corner, skirting the summit, but gaining enough elevation to return to the upland forest and a beautiful grove of large red spruce. Around the end of Hughes Ridge, the trail passes several small springs, and reaches Hughes Ridge Trail. Pecks Corner Shelter is 0.2 mile down the Hughes Ridge Trail.

Narrative by James Wedekind

APPALACHIAN TRAIL

PECKS CORNER TO TRICORNER KNOB

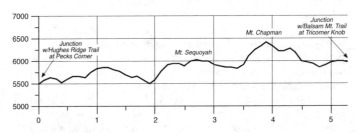

LENGTH: 5.3 miles, from Pecks Corner to Tricorner Knob.

HIGHLIGHTS: Views at Eagle Rocks, old-growth forest.
CAUTIONS: Exposed cliffs, isolated area.
MAP KEY: 9-10 C-D; USGS quad: Mt. Guyot.
USE: Horse and hiking trail.
STARTING POINT: A.T. at Pecks Corner (jct. A.T. and Hughes Ridge Trail).

Leaving Pecks Corner, the A.T. enters the heart of the Great Smokies wilderness. This region was never logged, and rarely visited until construction of the trail in the 1930s. The route follows the high Smokies crest and exceeds 6,000' elevation as it skirts the summit of Mt. Chapman.

Before the Civil War, the only persons documented to have visited this region of the Smokies were an 1821 survey crew. That party placed the boundary between Tennessee and North Carolina along the Smokies' crest. Even the Cherokee avoided travel through this rugged portion of the mountains, opting instead to cross at the lower gaps to the southwest. Realizing the dearth of knowledge about the southern Appalachians, Princeton geographer/geologist Arnold Guyot conducted the first exploration of the area in 1859.

After Guyot, few people returned to the area. Horace Kephart wrote in *Our Southern Highlanders* in 1913, "I know but few men who have ever followed this part of the divide"; he described it as "an uninhabited wilderness so rough that you could not make seven miles a day in it to save your life, even if you knew the course; and there is no trail at all." Construction of the A.T. in the 1930s opened this wilderness for the backpacker. Other than the A.T., there are no other trails in this wild area.

Past Pecks Corner, the trail climbs along an escarpment that breaks into Tennessee. The cliffs of Eagle Rocks rise above the trail. Note the familiar shamrock shape of the wood sorrel as the trail winds around the Carolina side of the peak. At 1.0 mile, reach the rocky bluffs of Eagle Rocks and a spectacular view.

The semi-enclosed gorge of Eagle Rocks Prong is framed by Woolly Tops Mountain to the west and Old Troublesome (an arm off Mt. Sequoyah) on the north. The entire valley is trail-less and always has been. Virgin upland red spruce and surviving Fraser fir mix downslope with yellow birch, American beech, maple, and cherry. Massive Eastern hemlocks and giant cove hardwoods (including tuliptree, cucumbertree, yellow buckeye, red oak, among others) thrive among the boulders on the valley floor.

When there are few hikers (which is rare) the next several miles are both eerie and serene. A moist duff of mosses, lichens, and ferns form a spongy mat on the forest floor. Often covered in fog and mist, the scene is reminiscent of the Olympic rainforest in Washington state.

The route descends into Copper Gap (elevation 5,490') then begins a steady climb of Mt. Sequoyah. The trail becomes more rocky with the ascent. Exposure of the Anakeesta Formation ends past Cooper Gap. North of here, massive beds of Thunderhead Sandstone are the foundation. Consequently, the mountains add girth and become less craggy, a change that reflects the more rounded weathering of the Thunderhead. In contrast, the slaty Anakeesta, which underlies the Smokies crest from here west to the Chimneys, forms steeper slopes and sharp peaks. Also note how the footing changes from flat slate that paves the trail like flagstone to angular rocks resembling crushed stone.

Mt. Sequoyah is named for *Sikwa'yi*, the inventor of the Cherokee written language. *Sikwa'yi* was born along the Little Tennessee River (now flooded as Tellico Lake) and lived in northern Alabama. To create his alphabet, he borrowed letters from English and German books (although he was illiterate in those languages) using them to denote syllables, rather than sounds. He printed the foreign symbols "as is," upside-down, or with added marks of his own, and created an alphabet for his people. The Cherokee learned Sequoyah's invention rapidly and began publishing The *Cherokee Phoenix*, a newspaper, in 1828. No man before, or since, is credited with creating an entire written language. Both this secluded mountain and the world's most impressive tree are honored with his name.

After topping out just short of the overgrown summit of Sequoyah (elevation 5,945') at **2.7** miles, the path follows a long descent to Chapman Gap. The trail then climbs again, passing below a mountain of the same name at **3.9** miles. At 6,417', Mt. Chapman is the fourth highest peak in the Smokies. Explorer Samuel Buckley named this mountain Mt. Alexander after an associate, but the Park Service later changed the name to honor Colonel David C. Chapman, often called the "Father of the Park." Chapman was an unflappable conservationist long before the term was widely used. A druggist by trade, Colonel Chapman braved both verbal and physical attacks to promote the park. As the first head of the Tennessee Great Smoky Mountains Park Commission, he aggressively challenged the major timber companies. However, Chapman also worked to evict mountain families from Cades Cove, and was maligned for those efforts. This mountain, which can either be calm and serene or buffeted by cold rain and snow, is testament to a man of similar contrasts.

After Mt. Chapman, you descend to Big Cove Gap, still well over a mile high. The trail continues through virgin woods and climbs toward Tricorner Knob. Guyot named this peak appropriately, for it is the junction of the main range of the Smokies with the largest transverse ridge, Balsam Mountain. However, Guyot lost his bearings here and thought the state line followed Balsam Mountain and Mt. Sterling Ridge instead of the accepted route over Mt. Guyot and Mt. Cammerer. You need only peer into the thick woods off the trail to understand his error.

Tricorner Knob Shelter lies beside the trail at **5.2** miles. The A.T. continues uphill 0.1 mile to an intersection with Balsam Mountain Trail, which leads 6.3 miles to Laurel Gap Shelter, and provides access to Straight Fork, Big Creek, and Mt. Sterling. The Tricorner Knob Shelter accommodates 12 people on wooden bunks. Treat the water from the spring, which flows in front of the shelter.

Nine miles from the nearest road, Tricorner Knob Shelter is the site of several rescues of hikers stranded by snowstorms. Hikers have spent nearly a week here waiting for drifts of up to 5' deep to melt. Winter backpackers should prepare for the worst and carry an ample supply of food.

Narrative by James Wedekind

APPALACHIAN TRAIL

TRICORNER KNOB TO LOW GAP

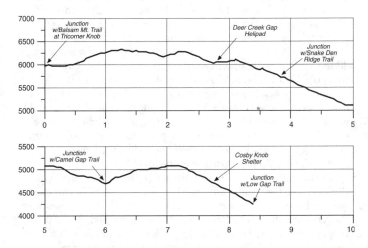

LENGTH: 8.4 miles, from Tricorner Knob to Low Gap.
HIGHLIGHTS: Views; old-growth forest.
MAP KEY: 9-10 B-C; USGS quads: Mt. Guyot and Luftee Knob.
USE: Horse and hiking trail.
STARTING POINT: Tricorner Knob, 15.7 miles north on A.T. from Newfound Gap.

Leaving the shelter at Tricorner Knob, the A.T. begins a gradual climb around Mt. Guyot. At 6,621', Guyot is the third highest peak in the eastern U.S., and the second highest in the Smokies. It holds the distinction, however, of being the highest mountain in the East that has no trail or road to its summit. Unlike the trammeled summits of Mt. Mitchell, Clingmans Dome, Mt. Le Conte or Mt. Washington in New Hampshire, few people enjoy the splendid isolation afforded atop Mt. Guyot.

Mt. Guyot is the central peak of a high massif that includes Tricorner Knob and Old Black. Their attendant side ridges—Guyot Spur, Pinnacle Lead, and Balsam Mountain—add to the mountains' girth. Guyot is curiously the coldest mountain in the Smokies, with an average temperature of 42.6° F. Le Conte is slightly warmer, at 42.8°. Anyone who has spent a sub-zero January night in the Tricorner Shelter will not doubt this claim.

Arnold Guyot was a Princeton professor of geography and geology during a period of enormous growth of those disciplines. Guyot left his native Switzerland in 1846 after having helped define the theory of continental glaciation (later known as the Ice Age) with his eminent colleague Louis Agassiz. While helping to establish what would become the National Weather Service, Guyot noted the complete lack of geographic knowledge of the Appalachians, especially in the South. He decided to devote himself to charting the largely unnamed, unexplored woodlands of the Smokies.

During the late 1850s, Guyot met naturalist and explorer Samuel Buckley, who had similar interests. Buckley first ascended this mountain, and named it for his new friend, Guyot. In 1859, Guyot enlisted the services of Robert Collins, noted highcountry guide and tollkeeper of the Oconaluftee Turnpike, to lead him along the Smokies' crest. Guyot and Collins carried a variety of bulky instruments; most important was a barometer to use as a crude altimeter. Guyot was masterful in his use of the barometer, and would camp on each high peak because the most accurate measurements were made at dawn. Guyot's measurements were amazingly precise when compared to those established by the U.S. Geological Survey many years later. He published the first map of the Appalachians about 1860. However, the manuscript was lost until 1929. By that time, most of Guyot's original names of the high places in the Smokies were forgotten and new names given. Guyot's accomplishments did not go entirely unnoticed, however. For besides this mountain, there are "Mt. Guyots" in Alaska, California, Colorado, and Utah.

The most striking features of Mt. Guyot are the stark boles of dead Fraser fir. As late as the mid-1970s, Guyot's summit was a dense stand of fragrant "balsam." Victims of the balsam woolly adelgid, the standing trunks generate an eerie mood. Thousands of the tiny adelgids bore into the trees, eventually killing them. Many young trees survive as part of the understory, but are attacked as they reach maturity when the adelgid is able to penetrate their bark.

Many red spruce do not appear healthy either. Their crowns are sparse, and many are dead. Biologists have found that growth of the spruce has slowed in the last several years. Scientists suspect that air pollution may be the problem.

As this section of trail nears its high point at 6,300', there are several small springs. The most reliable of these is Guyot Spring that rivals the large spring on Mt. Le Conte as the highest reliable water source in the Smokies. Past the spring is a manway that leads about 0.4 mile to the summit. The steep route is obscured by thornless blackberry and blowdowns, but passable. Guyot's summit is broad and forested, so there is solitude, but no view.

Continuing on, the A.T. enters a clearing, then skirts the summit of Old Black (elevation 6,370'). The name refers to the dark appearance of the mountain due to its dense conifers.

Next the trail descends into a large clearing at Deer Creek Gap (elevation 6,060') at **2.7** miles. The field is overgrown, but maintains a good patch of blueberry and thornless blackberry. This opening was caused by wildfire in 1924 that ravaged through the entire upper Big Creek watershed and burned to the summits of Guyot and Old Black. Such fires often followed logging operations. These scalded slopes became overgrown with briars and vines in later years, and were known as Hell Ridge. The next several miles of trail pass in and out of the old burn as you descend further to Yellow Creek Gap, and skirt the summit of Inadu Knob (elevation 5,940'). Inadu is the Cherokee word for snake, and presumably this mountain once harbored many. Do not expect to see many snakes at this elevation. The Snake Den Ridge Trail enters on the left at **3.7** miles at an outcrop of rippled sandstone.

Past Inadu Knob, the trail descends almost 800' in the next mile, tunneling through rosebay rhododendron much of the time. Many pieces of twisted metal are grim reminders of the crash of an Air Force F-4 jet on January 4, 1984. There were no survivors; the pilot and navigator evidently mistook their elevation and smashed into the mountain at a high speed. People as far away as Newport, Tennessee, reported hearing the thunderous explosion.

After skirting the summit of Camel Hump Knob (5,210'), the trail runs through low heath and sandstone ledges. The exposed ridge provides good views (south) of Balsam Mountain (Luftee Knob, at 6,234', is the prominent peak) across the Big Creek gorge. To the west are the heights of Old Black and Mt. Guyot. The pebbly sandstone is Thunderhead Sandstone, common throughout the Smokies.

At Camel Gap (elevation 4,694'), the trail passes through briars and mountain laurel, remnants of the Hell Ridge section. Camel Gap Trail ends here, having climbed 4.3 miles from the Big Creek Trail near Walnut Bottom. The forest now is wholly second-growth hardwoods.

You ascend sharply up Ross Knob and rejoin the ridge top and mature hardwoods. The trail angles southeast, away from the summit of Cosby Knob (elevation 5,160'). At **7.6** miles, you reach the side trail to Cosby Knob Shelter in a pleasant wooded glade, well off the ridge top. Bears are common here in summer, and resident skunks are overly tame. A reliable spring with strong flow serves as the headwaters to Rocky Branch of Big Creek. Past the shelter, the A.T. descends steadily 0.8 mile to Low Gap.

Narrative by James Wedekind

APPALACHIAN TRAIL

LOW GAP TO DAVENPORT GAP

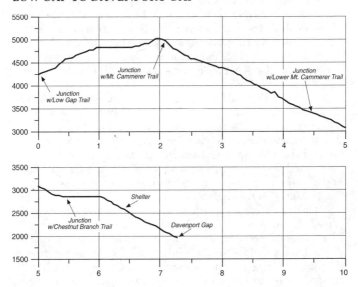

LENGTH: 7.3 miles, from Low Gap to Davenport Gap.
HIGHLIGHTS: Views, varied forest.
MAP KEY: 10-11 B; USGS quads: Luftee Knob, Hartford, and Waterville.
USE: Horse and hiking trail.
STARTING POINT Low Gap, accessible from Appalachian and Low Gap trails.

At 4,242', Low Gap is aptly named. This is the lowest elevation on the A.T. since Big Abrams Gap near Spence Field, 50 miles south! Low Gap is wide with many yellow birch and American beech trees. On the Tennessee side of the gap, Low Gap Trail descends steeply to

Cosby Campground. Low Gap Trail also leads into North Carolina, arriving at Walnut Bottom. The latter section receives heavy horse use and is badly eroded.

Incidentally, there are scores of "Low Gaps" in the southern Appalachians, and there were several in the Smokies when the park was established. To avoid confusion, the Nomenclature Commission dropped or renamed many duplicate names. They used some Cherokee words, but only chose those that were short, easy for whites to pronounce, or that "have a pleasant sound instead of harsh or meaningless ones."

Low Gap is a natural break in the Smokies' main range, and separates it from Mt. Cammerer. This break caused Professor Guyot to think that the state line ridge extended along Balsam Mountain, then to Mount Sterling. While often cited as a rare blunder by Guyot, Balsam Mountain and Mt. Sterling Ridge form a more continuous and prominent route than what was chosen as the state line by the early survey crews. Perhaps Guyot's mistake sought an "improvement" of the original survey.

Climbing out of the gap, the trail becomes noticeably more heavily used. At **1.0** mile, you reach the ridge top where the spur of Rocky Face Mountain meets the grassy summit of Sunup Knob. Walking is pleasant as the trail follows the nearly level ridge. Ahead are views of the rocky, side ridges of Mt. Cammerer. At **2.1** miles you reach the side trail to the summit of Mt. Cammerer, which leads 0.6 mile to the craggy pinnacle and old observation tower. Past the junction, the Smokies crest plunges into the Pigeon River gorge. The trail snakes its way along the crest on a moderate grade. At **2.2** miles the trail swings around the ridge at an outcrop of massive sandstone and conglomerate. The rock here is directly above the trace of the Greenbrier Fault, and dips steeply back into the mountain. Notice the quartz pebbles in the rock mixed with massive beds of sandstone. This rock is called conglomerate because of the variety of sand and pebbles of which it is composed. The rock above the fault is Thunderhead Sandstone, also found on Mt. Cammerer's summit and throughout the Smokies. Below the fault is the Elkmont Sandstone which is about 2 million years younger than the Thunderhead. The rocks are nearly identical here, so the actual trace of the fault is hard to define.

There is a fine view from these rocks of the Pigeon River Valley, and its confluence with Big Creek. The Black Mountains loom in the distance. These exposed rocks follow straight up the spine of the ridge back to the summit of Mt. Cammerer. Trailing arbutus, galax, wintergreen, mountain laurel, and blueberry thrive on this dry, sandy spur.

The trail leaves the ridge and descends into a moist hollow which shelters an Eastern hemlock grove among a boulder field. This hollow supports a variety of spring wildflowers (trout-lily, squirrel corn, spring-beauty, and trilliums) and a tasty crop of ramps. The trail switches back and remains in the wooded hollow that includes mature yellow buckeye, oak, and magnolia.

Boulder fields (also called block fields) like these are common below the steep summits in the Smokies. These large blocks of sandstone and conglomerate accumulated here around 20,000 years ago, during the Pleistocene Epoch. During this time of widespread glaciation to the north, these mountains were above tree line, in alpine tundra. Erosion of the exposed rocks was rapid and boulders settled on gentler slopes off the summits. Today, mosses, ferns, and flowers envelop the jumbled rocks, and their interstices offer hiding places for boomers (red squirrels), salamanders, wrens and other birds.

Passing back out of the woods, you skirt the heath bald along the ridge top, and continue to descend. A side trail on the right leads to a good spring in a rosebay rhododendron thicket. At **4.4** miles, Lower Mt. Cammerer Trail enters on the left, marked by a sign. This horse and hiking trail winds around the base of Cammerer to Cosby Campground.

The descent continues, now through a young second growth forest of red maple, tuliptree, various hickories and mountain laurel. At **5.4** miles, Chestnut Branch Trail enters on the right. It provides a shortcut to Big Creek Ranger Station. The trail levels alongside the ridge. In winter, if you turn around, you'll see a good edge-on view of Mt. Cammerer.

At **6.4** miles, you reach Davenport Gap Shelter on the left. The shelter is located in open woods at an old homesite. A good spring provides water and surely served the former residents. Less than a mile from the trailhead, this shelter is overused and often littered. It is often the scene of impromptu weekend parties.

Before the establishment of the park, many families lived in the Big Creek area and at Davenport Gap. For example, Fletcher Ford owned over 170 acres here, had an orchard, a five-room frame house, and two barns. The state gave him $3,850 for these holdings in 1930.

Davenport Gap honors William Davenport, the leader of the survey that finally established the state line through to Georgia in 1821. He also promoted use of the term "Smoky Mountains" concerning this range. Earlier reports usually referred to the Smokies as the Great Iron Mountains, and the Cherokee called them *unica*, meaning white. To settlers this word became Unaka or Unicoi. These names have been retained for the mountain ranges northeast and southwest of the Smokies, respectively.

The trail descends to Davenport Gap (elevation 1,975') at TN Highway 32 and NC 284. To the left, the road leads a dozen curvy miles to Cosby. Mount Sterling Village and Big Creek Ranger Station are over a mile to the right. You can reach I-40 by turning left at the Big Creek entrance to the park. By the way, it is best not to leave a car parked overnight at Davenport Gap. It is safer to leave cars at the hiker parking area at the Big Creek Ranger Station.

Narrative by James Wedekind

APPALACHIAN TRAIL

NEWFOUND GAP TO CLINGMANS DOME

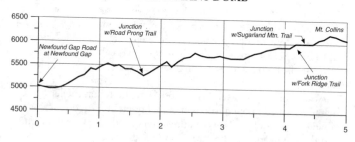

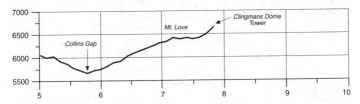

LENGTH: 7.9 miles, from Newfound Gap to Clingmans Dome tower.

HIGHLIGHTS: Highest elevation of entire Appalachian Trail.

CAUTIONS: Rocky trail after Mt. Collins.

MAP KEY: 6-8 D-F; USGS quad: Clingmans Dome.

USE: Hiking trail only.

TRAILHEAD: Park at Newfound Gap and cross Newfound Gap Road at painted crosswalk.

On September 2, 1940, President Franklin D. Roosevelt dedicated Great Smoky Mountains National Park at Newfound Gap. He had one foot in North Carolina and one in Tennessee, as you will have during much of this hike. The park was established in 1934, but formal dedication had been delayed because of other urgent political issues. It almost didn't happen in 1940 because of the mounting international crisis, which Roosevelt discussed in his dedication speech. On that Labor Day, thousands of people thronged Newfound Gap. Imagine how surprised a thru-hiker from Maine would have been.

Across from where Roosevelt spoke, the Appalachian Trail continues its route to Georgia. This section of the Appalachian Trail runs roughly parallel to Clingmans Dome Road, but the ridge top shields hikers from traffic noise for more than two-thirds of the hike.

From the Rockefeller Memorial, cross the entrance to the parking lot and then cross Newfound Gap Road. There is a pedestrian crossing, but don't count on cars to stop. Look for the A.T. trail sign. From here it is 1.7 miles to Indian Gap, 5.0 miles to Mt. Collins shelter, and 7.9 miles to Clingmans Dome. The trail drops beside a massive rock wall that supports the road, and there is a steep drop-off on the right. The A.T. is the only trail in the park marked by blazes; look for white rectangles painted on trees or rocks.

Mountain maple and witch-hobble line the trail. In spring, trout-lily and spring-beauty bloom here long after they have withered down the mountain. At a crumbling slate wall on the left, the trail starts a climb of 0.6 mile. Spruce trees of all sizes live here, but the large Fraser fir trees are dead, killed by a non-native insect, the balsam woolly adelgid. Young fir trees (with flat needles) look healthy, but you may find some with yellow or brown needles.

At the top of the rise, you can hear traffic noise for a while. Thornless blackberry patches crowd the trail, and bluebead lilies nestle in the moss. The trail crosses a fence that excludes wild hogs from a square of beech forest. You can walk up a stile made of grating, but the hogs, with their sharp hooves, cannot. In late April or May, the ground here is white with spring-beauty flowers.

The exclosure is about 150 yards wide. After you climb over the fence, the trail descends a steep section with roots, taking you back into spruce/fir forest. The first of many sets of log stairs helps on a steep spot. Then, after a switchback, the trail descends to Indian Gap and a view of the traffic. Road Prong Trail goes right to Chimney Tops Trail in 2.4 miles, and you can reach Newfound Gap Road in 3.3 miles. To continue on the A.T., cross to the lower right of the grassy area and look for the trail and a white blaze.

The climb out of the gap is about 0.8 mile, some of it on log steps. At the top, a large trailside tree has fallen, revealing its shallow root system and widening the trail. After another rocky climb, the trail switches back and runs through a ridge top area with silky grass and thornless blackberries (ripe in August or September).

At the top of the next rise, there are more tree skeletons and a vigorous undergrowth of small Fraser firs, mosses, and ferns. Twisty yellow birches grow here, and, as the trail starts down, a few catawba rhododendrons. The trail levels and crosses a log bridge over a tiny creek. From here to Mt. Collins, the trail design is good, with drainage ditches, water bars, logs across possibly muddy patches, and crosshatching on steps to prevent slipping. A note of caution, though: log water bars that slant across the trail can be slippery. Step over rather than on them.

After two small springs on the left, the trail reaches a high spot with a bench on the left and then descends to a junction with a connector to Clingmans Dome Road and Fork Ridge Trail. Just 0.2 mile farther is the junction with Sugarland Mountain Trail. From here it is 3.4 miles to Clingmans Dome. Sugarland Mountain Trail goes 12.1 miles along a ridge top to Fighting Creek Gap on Little River Road.

The junction has logs, a big quartz sitting rock, and blackberries, and it makes a good lunch or rest stop. Then you continue with the A.T. to the left. As you climb good log steps, you can see more dead trees than live ones, but after about 0.3 mile, the woods turn greener with more healthy trees and a rich understory of hobblebush and small American mountain ash trees. Pink turtlehead flowers bloom for most of the summer beside the trail. Soon the trail reaches the top of Mt. Collins, a high level ridge with good views. It was named for Robert Collins, who guided Guyot and other explorers in the 1850s. It was also here that Return Jonathan Meigs sighted a line to Blanket Mountain in 1802 to establish the northeast boundary between Cherokee and settler lands.

After Mt. Collins, the trail goes down a rocky, narrow, slippery section and then levels just above the highway. It then crosses the ridge, and traffic noise fades as you start a rocky climb. After switchbacks, the trail reaches the top of Mt. Love, named for a physician who explored this area with NC Senator Thomas Lanier Clingman. Then the trail crosses an open saddle from which you can see the Clingmans Dome radio tower, and you start the last rocky climb of this hike. It is twisty and narrow, with some big steps. You might hear voices from the lookout tower as you approach a final switchback surrounded by big spruces and firs. As you emerge from the woods and walk below the tower, people may peer down and wonder what sort of wildlife you are.

Clingmans Dome (elevation 6,643') is the highest point in the park and on the entire Appalachian Trail. Senator Clingman explored these peaks and insisted that this one, then called Smoky Dome, was higher than anything in the White Mountains of New Hampshire. Samuel Buckley made barometric measurements, determined some elevations, and named the highest point for himself. Then in 1858, Swiss geographer Arnold Guyot made precise and authoritative measurements. He named the dome after Clingman, who had helped to arrange his expeditions.

Turn left at the next A.T. sign and come out on the paved trail at the base of the tower. To the right, the paved trail goes down to the parking lot and restrooms in 0.5 mile.

Narrative by Doris Gove

APPALACHIAN TRAIL

CLINGMANS DOME TO SILERS BALD SHELTER

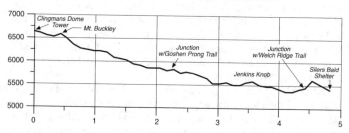

LENGTH: 4.8 miles, starting at Clingmans Dome parking area or tower and ending at Silers Bald Shelter.

HIGHLIGHTS: Views, grassy bald, southern limit of spruce-fir community.

CAUTIONS: A few steep, rocky spots.

MAP KEY: 6-7 E; USGS quads: Clingmans Dome, Silers Bald.

USE: Hiking trail.

TRAILHEAD: From Clingmans Dome parking area, hike the paved trail toward the Clingmans Dome tower and cut over to the A.T. near the summit. Or, find the Forney Ridge Trail (near the water fountain, to the left of the paved path to the summit). After 0.1 mile, turn right on the Clingmans Dome Bypass Trail and hike 0.5 mile up to the A.T.

On this trail, you really feel like you are walking on the spine of the world. It follows the ridge top, sometimes slipping to one side or the other. Some stretches are narrow and windy, others are broad, comfortable saddles, and still others have rocky outcrop slabs like the bony plates of a Stegosaurus dinosaur. The gray slabs and most of the boulders are Precambrian Thunderhead Sandstone that was thrust up to form these mountains. This sandstone settled in ancient oceans 500-600 million years ago, before there were hard-shelled animals to form fossils. It rested like a layer cake and hardened until continental collision with Africa shoved, folded, and cracked it into the tilted and irregular shapes you see today.

Dramatic changes occur today, also. As you go above 6,000' elevation, you see more and more tree skeletons standing tall and white. These are mostly Fraser fir trees, attacked by the balsam woolly adelgid. This aphid-like insect entered the park in the 1960s after being brought to North America from Europe. Although spruce and fir trees mix on these peaks, fir becomes more prevalent at the higher elevations. But half way out the trail to Silers Bald, at the Double Springs Shelter, spruces and firs disappear abruptly, and American beeches and yellow buckeyes take over the forest. This is the southern end of the spruce-fir range. Botanists theorize that, after the last interglacial period the climate and elevation around Silers Bald were ideal for American beeches, which dominated the forest and stopped the southern expansion of spruce/fir forest.

At 0.3 mile from the tower, you reach the junction with the Clingmans Dome Bypass Trail which has come up from the Clingmans Dome parking area. An American mountain-ash stands behind the sign, and there are some large Fraser firs to the right. You hike along a narrow ridge top with steep drop-offs and long views of Tennessee and North Carolina. The trail becomes rocky and descends to an open, grassy area with huckleberries, blackberries, and witch-hobble. It then alternates between grassy balds and spruce-fir woods as it dips to a saddle and then climbs to the peak of Mt. Buckley, named for Samuel B. Buckley, who measured peak elevations in the 1850s. Buckley named the highest peak, then called Smoky Dome, for himself. When Swiss geographer Guyot improved Buckley's measurements with more precise instruments, he named the highest peak after Thomas Lanier Clingman, a Civil War general, US Senator, Smokies explorer, and one-man public relations firm for North Carolina. Clingman had argued for years that the Smokies peaks were higher than White Mountain peaks of New Hampshire; Guyot proved him right.

After descending through more grassy areas, the trail drops off to the right of the ridge to a sheltered, moist forest with mosses and ferns and yellow birches. Rugel's ragwort grows here. This high-elevation plant has heart-shaped leaves and green/tan flowers that look like partly opened dandelion buds.

The trail is an easy dirt path with a few muddy spots, and, after a gradual descent, it intersects with Goshen Prong Trail at mile **2.2**. From here it is 10.4 miles down to the Little River trailhead at Elkmont.

From the junction, the trail goes over a small rise and descends 0.4 mile to Double Spring Gap. The shelter has 12 bunks and is surrounded by a flowery meadow where damage by wild hogs may be seen. Water is available from a spring just a few yards down into North Carolina (left). If you stand facing the shelter and look right, you see a hillside covered with spruce and fir; on the left, American beeches dominate with close, dark foliage. At the right rear corner of the shelter stands a tall yellow buckeye tree, and there are many buckeyes among the beeches.

The trail climbs out of the gap through rich beech woods on a good dirt trail with a few rocks. After a grassy summit (Jenkins Knob), it drops to the right of the ridge on a brambly and rocky section that could be slippery. From here on, the trail alternates between level, easy sections and short, rocky climbs. The bony and sharp mountain spine here is called the Narrows. The last level stretch has large, gnarled American beeches covered with shaggy lichens.

At a trail sign, Welch Ridge Trail goes left to meet Hazel Creek Trail in 1.8 miles, Jonas Creek Trail in 2.5 miles, and Bear Creek Trail in 6.5 miles —three ways to get to Fontana Reservoir. The Appalachian Trail continues right and starts a rocky, narrow, steep climb to the top of Silers Bald. After 0.4 mile of switchbacks and brambles, you haul out onto a wide grassy spot (elevation 5,607'). A large rock is blazed with the A.T. mark and with arrows.

The trail continues to the left through a dense patch of American beeches and crosses several open, grassy meadows. The Park Service does not maintain this bald, and the beech trees are creeping across the grass, low and bushy at first. For now, enjoy blueberries, blackberries, meadow wildflowers, and wonderful views of High Rocks to the southeast and Mt. Le Conte to the northeast.

After the last grassy spot, which has goldendrods, gentians, and cinnamon ferns, the trail drops off the bald and descends to the Silers Bald Shelter in a pretty gap at the headwaters of Fish Camp Prong of the Little River. There are 12 wooden bunks and a spring on the Tennessee side. From here, it is 2.6 miles to the next trail junction, Miry Ridge Trail, and 24.8 miles to the park boundary at Fontana Dam.

Narrative by Doris Gove

APPALACHIAN TRAIL

SILERS BALD SHELTER TO JCT. MIRY RIDGE

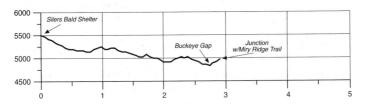

LENGTH: 2.9 miles, from Silers Bald Shelter to Miry Ridge Trail
HIGHLIGHTS: Beech forests, ridge walks.
MAP KEY 6 E; USGS Quad: Silers Bald.
USE: Horse and hiking trail.
STARTING POINT: Silers Bald Shelter, 4.5 miles south (west) of Clingmans Dome on the A.T.

This portion of the Appalachian Trail (A.T.) is a short and relatively level path through mostly beech forest. It begins at the Silers Bald

Shelter about 0.2 mile west of the bald's high point of 5,600'. A large rock in a small opening marks this spot. The A.T. continues down the rise through an open forest to the shelter. Nestled in a small clearing, this shelter is a good resting spot for backpackers from Clingmans Dome, 4.5 miles distant, or from Derrick Knob, 4.7 miles to the west. There is water on the Tennessee side of the trail approximately 200 feet down a small trail. The water is piped out of a spring, but should still be treated; animal signs are prevalent in this area. Like all A.T. shelters in the park, bears are frequent visitors, hence the fence across the front of the lean-to. Inside are two sets of benches capable of sleeping up to 12 people. There are also ropes hanging from the rafters to hang your food. No, not from bears, but from mice and skunks which also frequent the shelters.

For day hikers and backpackers passing through, the shelter is a nice place for lunch or a short break. The A.T. continues west through a young forest dominated by American beech and yellow birch trees. Occasionally, a larger pin cherry tree can be found. In late summer, the bears not at the shelters can be found up in these trees. Estimates by biologists claim a bear can put on up to three pounds per day when the cherries are ripe. Raise your eyes up occasionally, but do not miss the large Artist's Conk fungi slowly decomposing the dead beech trees.

At 0.5 mile, the trail begins to climb again. It is a moderate slope which quickly levels and drops once more. The trail will continue with these up and down spurts. Most will be moderate, but at mile 0.7, the crossing of Proctor Ridge will be more strenuous. Proctor Ridge is firmly planted deep in the Hazel Creek area of North Carolina. The ridge rises steeply before reaching the A.T. at an elevation of 5,200'. This area of the park was heavily logged in the early 1900s. Given time and protection, the hillsides are again forested.

Here along the Smokies' crest, logging gave way to grazing. Every spring, after the last snows, the local farmers would bring their cattle and hogs to the high country. They would graze them on the grasses and other plants during the summer. The fall mast production of acorns, chestnuts, and hickories would fatten the animals before being driven to market or back to the farm. Balds, like Silers, Spence, and Gregory, offered the best grazing, but all along the trail today you will find grasses and plants that would have fed many animals.

The trail drops again from Proctor Ridge and pushes westward past some large cherry trees. By mile **1.5**, you will start to notice some larger Carolina silverbells mixed in with the beech trees. In early June these trees are in full bloom. The blossoms are truly silverbells—small white bell-shaped flowers hang from the branches. After pollination, the petals drop, and mixed with those of the "sarvis" (or serviceberry), turn a summer's day into a winter scene. White petals cover the forest floor like a dusting of snow.

Continue along the A.T. as it rises and falls over small ridges. After a steep descent past two large silverbells with greatly swollen bases and root sprouts, the trail will level and then drop steeply again to Buckeye Gap at 4,817'. The gap is the half way point from Silers Bald to Derrick Knob. Stop for lunch in this small clearing surrounded by yellow birches, beeches, maples and of course yellow buckeyes. The headwaters of Proctor Creek are to the south of the gap. Water can be reached, but only after a steep drop.

The A.T. continues west by climbing steeply 100 feet in 0.1 mile to the Miry Ridge Trail. A right turn at this intersection will drop you down to Jakes Gap (4.9 miles) and the Tremont or Elkmont areas. Continuing straight along the A.T. will take you steeply up and over Cold Spring Knob and on toward Derrick Knob.

Narrative by Tom Condon

APPALACHIAN TRAIL

MIRY RIDGE TRAIL TO EAGLE CREEK TRAIL

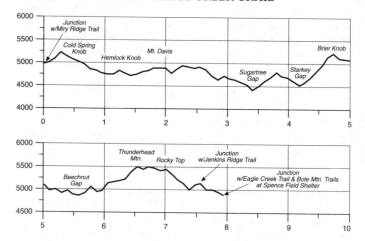

LENGTH: 7.9 miles, from Miry Ridge Trail to Eagle Creek Trail.
HIGHLIGHTS: Outstanding views.
CAUTIONS: Steep, slippery sections.
MAP KEY 6-4 E; USGS quads: Silers Bald, Thunderhead Mtn.
USE: Hiking Trail.
STARTING POINT: Jct. with Miry Ridge Trail.

From Miry Ridge to the Eagle Creek Trail junction is a long 7.9 miles. It involves very strenuous climbs and constant losses of altitude. Nearly everything you gain you will ultimately lose, except for the wonderful views and the experience of traveling one of the least hiked portions of the A.T. It is a challenge that many hikers neglect to take.

This trail section can be reached from Elkmont or Tremont via the Miry Ridge Trail or from Clingmans Dome via the A.T. Both of these approaches are more than 8 miles long. From either direction, you will be ascending Cold Spring Knob. When you reach the intersection of Miry Ridge and the A.T., you may wish to drop off Cold Spring Knob to Buckeye Gap. The gap is a nice open spot just 100 yards below the trail junction. The gap also has a small spring about 200 yards down a narrow path into North Carolina. You can fill up and rest up here before ascending the knob. Cold Spring Knob is a short (0.2 mile) steep (300') climb. Take your time and stop to enjoy the views. You will need to. From about halfway up the knob you will get some good views south into the Proctor Creek Valley of North Carolina or east to Clingmans Dome.

When you reach the top of Cold Spring Knob, you will pass a short flat area and then begin a descent toward the lower Hemlock Knob. This portion of the A.T., although it drops steeply at times, is a beautiful hike. You will be passing along a narrow ridge with great autumn through spring views of the valleys of both Tennessee and North Carolina. I like to stop occasionally and listen as the wind carries the sounds of the rivers up from far below. Shortly, you will reach an unnamed gap and begin to climb steeply again. Scattered in amongst the yellow birch and American beech are some Eastern hemlocks which give this knob its name. The climb up Hemlock Knob is thankfully very short and presently you crest the peak and begin to descend again. Up and down you will go for another half mile before starting a longer climb up Mt. Davis.

Mt. Davis is named for Willis P. Davis who was one of the founders of the Great Smoky Mountains Conservation Association. Willis and his wife Ann took a trip to the western U.S. in the summer of 1923. While out West, Mrs. Davis asked "Why can't we have a national park in the Great Smokies?" That question led the Davises to start a movement which would ultimately end with the dedication of Great Smoky Mountains National Park by Franklin D. Roosevelt in 1940. To honor her husband, who had died in 1931, Mrs. Davis asked to have a peak named for him. The Park Service felt so strongly about the Davises' devotion to the park idea that they named this peak for Willis and the ridge which climbs to it for Ann. Today we can rest here and thank these two special people for asking a simple question and then working to create a positive answer.

From the top of Mt. Davis, the A.T. drops quickly 400 feet to Sams Gap. Here you will reach the junction with the Greenbrier Ridge Trail. This trail drops along Davis Ridge to the Tremont area. A small spring 100 yards below will provide you with water if you are heading down the ridge. If you are continuing along the A.T., head over the small rise ahead to Derrick Knob Shelter for your water. The spring at the shelter is a bit nicer as it is piped right out of the hillside. Like all A.T. shelters in the park, Derrick Knob is a low stone structure capable of sleeping 12 campers. The shelter sits at the edge of the old Big Chestnut Bald. There is no bald here anymore, just a small opening around the shelter. A young beech forest is replacing the bald, although the grasses still remain as the dominant ground cover.

From the shelter, the A.T. continues its up and down habit. A moderate climb over a small ridge will lead you to a long, steep drop taking you to another gap and another climb. You will continue this pattern until you finally drop into Sugartree Gap at 4,435 feet at **3.4** miles. An old sign marks this spot as does the assortment of beeches, birches, oaks, buckeyes and of course some sugar maples.

After climbing up again, the trail levels and then gently descends from this unnamed crest. There are good views to the north of Devils Courthouse. Colonel Return J. Meigs named that steep ridge in 1797. While surveying the new Cherokee Indian Boundary, Colonel Meigs got a bit lost on this hillside. After several days, nearly dead from exposure, the Colonel stumbled upon a remote settler's cabin and was saved. To commemorate his struggle, he named the ridge the courthouse and one of its spurs the Devils Bench, where he must have felt he was judged.

This section of trail will not judge you too hard, but up ahead you will reach your hardest climb of the day. The A.T. drops down to Starkey Gap at 4,500', and then begins a very steep climb up Brier Knob (5,215'). In about 0.6 mile, the trail will climb more than 700'. This is a good place to take lots of short breaks and enjoy the views or the vegetation. The views, especially in the fall, are spectacular. On the Tennessee side you will look down Shut-in Creek and on into Wear Valley. The North Carolina view is down into Bone Valley.

Finally, you will pass the top of Brier Knob on the North Carolina side. You have now come **4.6** miles from Miry Ridge and finished the hardest climb. The trail continues 0.75 mile up and down, dropping moderately and then steeply to Mineral Gap. From here it is another climb up and over an unnamed ridge. This climb gives you some excellent views down along the Thunderhead Prong in Tennessee. On this tributary of Little River is a small cove known as New World. During the Civil War it provided refuge for an entire community. The people were so fed up with the constant bickering and raiding by Union and Confederate sympathizers that they packed up their entire community and moved to the small cove and started their "new world."

You will descend to Beechnut Gap at mile **5.5**. Like Sugartree Gap, this low spot is appropriately named. The area is surrounded by beech trees and only a short search should turn up the triangular beechnuts. If you have run out of water, this is a good place to shed your pack and follow the small trail down into Tennessee. A small spring exists here. It might be a good idea to stop and rest anyway, because the A.T. begins its final ascent of Thunderhead Mountain.

The climb up Thunderhead is steep in places, but generally only a moderate climb. It is also a short climb—only 0.8 mile from Beechnut Gap. The beech trees slowly give way to the rhododendrons. When the rhododendron completely dominates the trailside you will know you are near the top. Soon you will be standing by the benchmark indicating the highest peak in the western end of the park. At 5,527' above sea level and well above all the ridges around, you would expect a great view from the top, but there is not. The peak is covered in what is known as a heath bald—rhododendrons everywhere. A small stone pile allows you to climb enough to get your head above the shrubs and get a great 360 degree view of the park. Yet, if you walk just a short distance further, you can lie in a grassy field and enjoy a tremendous view of the Nantahala Mountains to the south and Cades Cove below.

This field on the flanks of Thunderhead is a great place to relax and recover from all the climbing. It will now be all downhill—well, almost all—to Spence Field and the shelter at the intersection with the Eagle Creek Trail. The A.T. continues across the field and ridge to a small rocky ridge appropriately called Rocky Top (5,441'). The sandstone outcrops and boulders strewn across this knob have been carved into for many years. Mother Nature did the first carving—rounding and smoothing the rocks. Later came the herders like Hop Harris and Red Waldron who indicated they were here more than 7 times from 1889 to 1920. Today occasional hikers stop and carve their name. The Natiional Park Service strongly discourages this practice as it often mars or destroys the area's historic significance.

The A.T. passes over another ridge and up to a second rocky out-cropping which could also be called Rocky Top. There are wonderful views from all these outcrops. Now the trail drops to a gap and for about 0.5 mile the views will be obstructed. From the gap the trail climbs one last knob. It then drops steeply to the eastern edge of Spence Field and the junction with the Jenkins Ridge Trail. Jenkins Ridge takes you across toward Blockhouse Mountain (5,470'), and down into some of the remotest parts of the Smokies.

To reach the Spence Field Shelter, you should continue along the A.T. through Spence Field. This large open area is just a shadow of its past. Today, at about 30 acres, it is the largest grass bald in the park, but when James Spence herded livestock here, the clearing was much more extensive. In the 1830s he cut and burned the surrounding for-est opening to create more than 100 acres of pasture. Time has undone his work and slowly the forest returns. Today the field is scat-tered with serviceberry or "sarvis" trees. These small trees have beau-tiful blooms in early spring —about the time that the circuit riding preachers would return for church "sarvices."

Climb now to the top of Spence Field and drink in the panoramic views. Pass over the top by the Bote Mountain Trail and proceed to the intersection with the Eagle Creek Trail. The shelter is about 0.25 mile down this trail, which takes you down to Fontana Lake in 9 miles. The shelter has a good water source nearby and 2 new bear boxes for food storage. Not only are the boxes designed to keep the bears out, they will keep the skunks and mice out too. It is probably still a good idea to hang your packs in the shelter as there are always a few mice who still associate packs with food.

Narrative by Tom Condon

APPALACHIAN TRAIL

JCT EAGLE CREEK TO DOE KNOB

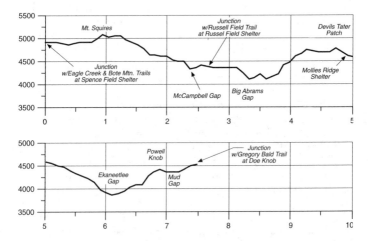

LENGTH: 7.5 miles, from jct. Eagle Creek Trail to Doe Knob
HIGHLIGHTS: Spence Field, ridge walking
MAP KEY: 3-4 E-F; USGS quads: Thunderhead Mtn., Cades Cove
USE: Horse and hiking trail
STARTING POINT: Eagle Creek Trail jct. on Spence Field

The trail rises gently through the west end of the extensive meadows of Spence Field and enters the beech forest of Mt. Squires. It's named for Mark Squires, an early leader promoting the Great Smoky Mountain National Park in western North Carolina.

At **1.0** mile the canopy opens into a picturesque acre of grassland known as Little Bald. Extensive views are afforded to the south and east. So inviting is this restful vista that few pass without pausing.

Steeply the path drops into McCampbell Gap, named for Robert McCampbell, who came to Cades Cove around 1850 seeking gold.

Unsuccessful with gold, he later found copper on the North Carolina side of the Smokies.

Rhododendron borders the path in places on the approach to Russell Field. Dr. Randolph Shields of Maryville advised that a Russell had lived and farmed there sometime in the nineteenth century. His principal crop was reported to have been potatoes. The Russell Field shelter with 14 sleeping spaces sits atop the backbone of Ole Smoky. Water is down the path on the Tennessee side. Along this path are a few blueberry bushes, ripening in August, and American mountain-ash trees which flower white in May and June and display clusters of brilliant red berries in August.

This is the middle of 3 shelters within 5 miles, Spence Field, Russell Field, and Mollies Ridge, with the most concentrated bunk space in the 450 miles between Springer Mountain, Georgia, and Damascus, Virginia. Because of their relatively easy access, use is heavy.

The path continues on the North Carolina side of the grassy, forested crest of Russell Field. Then it drops steeply through a yellow birch and beech forest to big Abrams Gap. Both this and Little Abrams Gap which comes next were named for Cherokee Chief Abram. Abram lived about 10 miles due west, as the crow flies, at Chilhowee Village, at the mouth of Abrams Creek on the Little Tennessee River (now covered by Chilhowee Lake).

It's a good climb up the Tennessee flank of Mollies Ridge. Legend has it that Mollie was a Cherokee maiden who died while searching for her true love, White Eagle, after he failed to return from a hunting trip. Naturally, she seeks him still on foggy and moonlit nights.

This crest is long and level dipping slightly at Devils Tater Patch. A more fitting name might be the Devils Hog Patch for these rooters keep the soil thoroughly tilled. Occasionally the hiker chances on these rooting machines. Sighting hogs displaying horizontal lines (a mark of the European boar) on their gray flanks is a thrill.

Mollies Ridge Shelter sleeps 14 and sits atop the ridge. It is buffeted by heavy wind and windswept rain and is often fogbound. Sometimes the fog is so thick you can drive in a peg and hang your pack, according to an old mountain saying. On the steep descent to Ekaneetlee Gap, the path has been worn into a foot-deep sluiceway, bordered by grass, then galax and trailing arbutus.

At 3,842' elevation, Ekaneetlee Gap is the lowest point on the long Smoky Mountain crest. It was the crossing of an ancient Cherokee trail from their eastern villages on the Oconaluftee River to other sites west and north of the Smokies. The gap forest is mixed hardwood with maple, cherry and yellow birch. It's one of a very few places on the crest of the Great Smokies where tuliptrees grow.

Ascending gently, the trail swings to the North Carolina side of the crest to bypass the summit of Powell Knob and hit Mud Gap. The largest tree here is a yellow buckeye, 40" across. Hogs often root the soil in this area.

The ascent to Doe Knob is fairly easy and this long summit is a broad and open woodland. The trail moves to the north side and drops slightly to the intersection with the Gregory Bald Trail, which continues west along the crest. The original Appalachian Trail continued in that direction, but in 1948 it was turned south at Doe Knob to cross the four-year-old Fontana Dam.

Narrative by Woody Brinegar

APPALACHIAN TRAIL

FONTANA DAM TO DOE KNOB

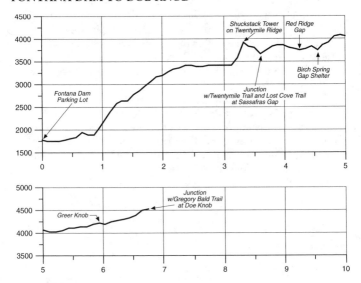

LENGTH: 6.8 miles, from Fontana Dam Road to Doe Knob
HIGHLIGHTS: Ridge running and the magnificent views from Shuckstack
CAUTIONS: Fallen leaves can be slippery on sharp ascent from trailhead to Shuckstack.
MAP KEY: 3 G-F USGS quads: Fontana Dam, Cades Cove.
USE: Horse and hiking trail.
TRAILHEAD: Beyond Fontana dam 0.6 mile on right fork of asphalt road. Look for Appalachian Trail sign.

Fontana Village is one of the major stopping places in the south for through-hikers (those going from Springer Mountain in Georgia to

Mt. Katahdin in Maine). They pick up mail, replenish supplies, eat restaurant fixin's, sleep on a soft mattress and rest up.

Fontana Dam, a couple of miles from the Village, rises 480 feet as the highest dam east of the Rockies. Built as a rush job during WWII with 3 shifts a day, 7 days a week, it was completed in 1944 to provide power for Oak Ridge National Laboratory and ALCOA.

There are parking areas short of the dam, and crossing by foot provides time to absorb this high bridge across the Little Tennessee River. To the right is the backed-up water of Fontana Lake, bordered on the north by the sharply rising slopes of the Smokies. To the left is the deep drop to the narrow band of river below.

Six-tenths of a mile beyond the dam the Appalachian Trail leaves the asphalt road and begins the zig-zagging ascent of the west fork of Shuckstack Ridge. There is parking space below the trailhead. Although graded, this path is sufficiently steep to require considerable energy. Earlier, the trail was far more demanding as it followed the ridgeline. When the path reaches the crest, in a number of places, traces of the old route are evident. In late fall the leaf-covered trail is rather slippery with dry or wet leaves. Losing your footing is a danger.

Views of the lake through the leaf curtain are available on occasion. When the foliage falls in late November, the horizon expands on the high trails. The closed forest tunnel opens into a broad array of the folds of the mountain beneath and above the path to the mountains beyond. November to April are favored months for some hikers in the high country.

Whereas the old trail went right over the peak of Little Shuckstack, it now skirts the upper flank and crosses to Shuckstack through the connecting gap. On the steep southern face of Shuckstack, the path is cut into a mud-colored rock bluff. The strata of this sedimentary formation, deposited in an ancient sea, have been tilted to the vertical with the seams clearly displayed. The more common rock along the upper trail appears as light gray bulges or out-thrusts of a harder sandstone fused by heat and pressure into the highly resistant bedrock of the mountain. Passing below Shuckstack peak the trail reaches the crest of Twentymile Ridge.

Magnificent views of rolling ridges in all directions are afforded from Shuckstack, 0.1 mile off the trail. To the north is the sweeping skyline of the Smokies. To the west are the Unicoi Mountains, including the prominent thrust of Hangover. Southward are the Snowbird and Nantahala Mountains, with the Appalachian Trail running the crest of the Nantahalas. The south end of the Blue Ridge Mountains lie to the southeast. It's a feast of mountains.

The fire tower is now gone, but the vistas remain from this cone-shaped upthrust. Don't pass it by.

Fontana Lake and Dam lie below this height with the narrow end of Cheoah Lake bumping the dam. The once picturesque Little Tennessee River is now but a stream of lakes, from beginning to end. From Shuckstack north to the Birch Spring Gap Shelter, the trail is a former road, once used to service the fire tower and to build the shelter. First, however, the trail descends to Sassafras Gap where the Twentymile Trail joins from the west and the Lost Cove Trail connects from the east.

The popular and accessible (**4.5** miles from Fontana Road) 12 person Birch Spring Shelter stands in a fairly steep draw 100 yards below the gap. A spring is quite near in an open, mixed hardwood forest of birch, basswood, white ash, black cherry, oak, maple and tuliptree. Some call it "The Hole" because of the sharp drop in and climb out. Blackberry vines border the trace above Birch Spring Gap which is 3,830' elevation.

Above the gap the trail levels somewhat on the ridgecrest until the ascent of Greer Knob begins. This knob was named for Andy Greer of Cades Cove who pastured his oxen there after the crops were in. One night, at the turn of the century, a storm hit causing the oxen and 15-20 head of cattle to huddle together. Lightning splintered trees and killed them all. The path skirts the west flank of this knob at a fairly level grade on a narrow, up and down route around stumps and rocks. It is not a 4' wide, graded trail, but a pleasant 1'-2' in breadth. There are a number of American chestnut sprouts along this knob-skirting path.

At Doe Knob the Appalachian Trail joins the crest of the Smokies and is met by Gregory Bald Trail.

Narrative by Woody Brinegar

BALSAM MOUNTAIN TRAIL

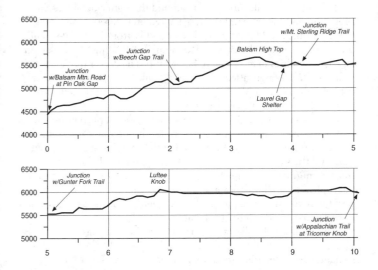

LENGTH: 10.1 miles, from Balsam Mtn. Road to Appalachian Trail at Tricorner Knob.

HIGHLIGHTS: Pleasant ridge walking, spruce-fir forest, rich historical significance.

MAP KEY: 10 C-D; USGS quads: Luftee Knob, Mt. Guyot

USE: Horse and hiking trail.

TRAILHEAD: Balsam Mountain Road at Pin Oak Gap. Access to the trailhead is via the Blue Ridge Parkway. Two and six-tenths miles south of Soco Gap, turn onto and follow the Heintooga Ridge Road 9.0 miles to its end at Heintooga Overlook. Here enter the one-way Balsam Mountain Road and follow 8.4 miles to Pin Oak Gap.

The Balsam Mountain Trail begins in Pin Oak Gap, through which cattle were once driven from Cataloochee to graze on the high, open areas of Balsam Mountain. Later, the Parsons Pulp and Lumber Company extended a logging railroad up Straight Fork through Round Bottom to Pin Oak Gap. This railroad spur continued almost to Pretty Hollow Creek, following a grade around the right side of Balsam Mountain and Mount Sterling Ridge. Civilian Conservation Corps (CCC) Company 2426, stationed at Round Bottom 1934 -1941, built the lower portion of the Balsam Mountain Trail. While Pin Oak Gap largely symbolizes man's positive labors, it has its darker history as well. In 1925, a disgruntled, terminated lumber company employee deliberately set fire to the forest near the gap. The fire burned all the way south to the Heintooga Overlook area.

The Balsam Mountain Trail offers a well-graded, pleasant mountain-top walk, ascending from northern hardwood forest into spruce-fir forest. While not difficult, the trail entails notable ascents to Ledge Bald and the slopes of Balsam High Top. From Laurel Gap to the trail's terminus at the Appalachian Trail, the ascent is gradual and offers pleasant walking. Because this is a popular route for horse parties, the hiker should be prepared for frequent muddy sections, requiring selecting a path on the trail margin.

The trail, which follows an old road to Laurel Gap, ascends steadily to reach the 5,184' crest of Ledge Bald at **2.0** miles. Ledge Bald is so named because of its proximity to a section of Balsam Mountain known as "The Ledge," which extends from around Heintooga to Pin Oak Gap. Ledge Bald is covered in second growth timber now; however, in earlier times the area was cleared and cattle grazed here. Floyd Woody recalled that Cataloochee residents and the Cherokee of Big Cove frequently met while ranging cattle on Ledge Bald. A Cherokee man named Jess Swinney sometimes spent the night with them. "And he was a great banjer picker," Woody said.

Elizabeth Powers, in *Cataloochee: Lost Settlement of The Smokies*, quotes Raymond Caldwell's description of the extent of grazing in the area. "My family ranged livestock in the Ledge...out near Pin Oak Gap, Heintooga, the Bald, the Big Swag, what we call Balsam Corner. Good plumb down toward the head of Round Bottom... Those were natural range in there. There was a lot of good grass..." The last grazing here was about 1936.

After an easy descent from Ledge Bald, Beech Gap, formerly called Big Swag, is reached at mile **2.2**. This gentle dip or "swag" in the mountains is indeed pleasant. Remnants of lush grass can be found here. In late summer and early autumn there is heavy growth of white snakeroot, a plant 1-4' tall with coarse toothed leaves and clusters of small white flowers. In earlier times, cows which grazed on this plant gave milk which caused "milk sickness," a sometimes fatal malady in humans. The Beech Gap Trail exits to the left, leading 2.5 miles to Round Bottom. Old railroad grades are noted on both the right and left sides of the gap. The grade to the left runs approximately 2.5 miles to end above the headwaters of Balsam Corner Creek and the grade to the right intersects with the rail grade from Pin Oak Gap after a mile. Families lived in shanty cars along these grades while logging was in progress. "The men logged and the women kept house," Eldridge Caldwell stated, according to Elizabeth Powers.

The trail ascends again beyond Beech Gap, passing below the summit of Balsam High Top before descending 0.3 mile to Laurel Gap and Laurel Gap Shelter. Laurel Gap Shelter is a stone, bear-proof structure situated in a pleasant grassy clearing. It sleeps 14 on wooden platforms, has a picnic table, fire pit, and fireplace inside. Water is available approximately 500 feet from the shelter along a path directly in front of it.

The trail climbs 0.2 mile beyond the shelter to the terminus of the Mount Sterling Ridge Trail. The Mount Sterling Ridge Trail leads right to the Swallow Fork Trail and Pretty Hollow Gap Trail at 4.0 miles and the Mount Sterling Trail at 5.4 miles. Straight ahead, our trail follows an easy grade around the slopes of Balsam Corner, reaching the Gunter Fork Trail at 5.2 miles. This trail leads 4.1 miles to Walnut Bottom. A sign at this junction warns hikers not to use this trail during times of high water and suggests the Swallow Fork Trail as an alternative. Formerly, a trail crossed near this point, connecting the rail grade on the Straight Fork side of the mountain with Gunter Fork and Walnut Bottom.

The trail ascends gradually toward Luftee Knob, alternating sides of the mountain as it climbs. The expanse of the Gunter Fork watershed spreads below on the right. To the left are views of Shawano Ridge with its ranks of sharp topped fir trees and Straight Fork Valley stretching far below. Rich spruce-fir forest extends along these summits. This forest is comprised of Fraser fir, red spruce, and a number of other trees such as American beech, yellow birch, red maple, hobble-bush and yellow buckeye. Not apparent today is the fact that the forest to the left—the Dan's Branch watershed—was largely removed in 1918-1919 by the Parsons Pulp and Lumber Company, except for the virgin spruce at the head of the stream. This rich beauty should not be passed hurriedly; rather, it should be savored as some of the best high country walking in the Smokies.

The trail reaches Luftee Knob at **6.8** miles and generally follows a 6,000' contour below the crest before continuing past Thermo Knob beyond. These two peaks were first measured by Swiss-born geographer, Arnold Guyot, in 1859. Guided by Robert Collins and his son, who lived near the Oconaluftee River on Collins Creek, Guyot reached the top of Balsam Mountain at a peak he called the Pillar, now known as Luftee Knob. Mr. Guyot was meticulous in making his observations and apologized for a "possible lack of accuracy within a few feet" on Luftee Knob because he was "interrupted by a storm while taking measurements." An accident to his thermometer led to the naming of Thermometer Knob, now known as Thermo Knob. Guyot named the next peak Raven's Knob which has since been changed to Mt. Yonaguska. What a struggle it must have been to penetrate these enchanted wilds to measure the high peaks of the Balsams and the main Smoky Mountain chain!

The trail continues on an almost level grade, offering a panorama of extensive fir forest with views of sharp-peaked Mount Hardison to the left of Mount Yonaguska. Mount Hardison is named for James A. Hardison, an original member of the North Carolina State Park Commission, a group promoting the formation of Great Smoky Mountains National Park. Mount Yonaguska was named for the Cherokee Chief Yonaguska, whose name translates to "Drowning Bear." The Oconaluftee, or Egwanulti Town Indians, as they were more accurately called, supported themselves by farming and selling livestock and ginseng to pioneer settlers. It was Yonaguska's adopted son, William Holland Thomas, and his son-in-law, Euchella, who were instrumental in allowing the Eastern Band to remain in North Carolina rather than following the Trail of Tears to Oklahoma. A few miles distant is Katalsta Ridge named for Chief Yonaguska's daughter, a noted pottery maker.

The trail turns sharply to the right in a pleasant gap between Mount Yonaguska and Mount Hardison at **9.3** miles. The abandoned Hyatt Ridge Trail used to terminate here. It once extended 9.5 miles to Round Bottom, but only the lower portion of this trail is maintained today. A portion of this trail existed even earlier as part of the Rosser Trail. This rugged trail began at Smokemont and crossed Hughes Ridge and Three Forks to reach Tricorner Knob. Our trail makes a final gentle ascent to reach the Appalachian Trail at **10.1** miles. The Tricorner Knob Shelter and water are 200 yards to the left.

Narrative by William A. Hart, Jr.

BASKINS CREEK TRAIL

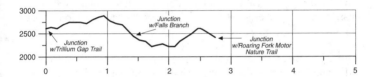

LENGTH: 2.7 miles, from Trillium Gap Trail to the middle of Roaring Fork Motor Nature Trail. (It's 1.5 miles one-way to the waterfall.)
HIGHLIGHTS: Baskins Creek Falls, solitude.
CAUTIONS: Steep, slippery manway to falls.
MAP KEY: 7 C; USGS quad: Mt. Le Conte.
USE: Hiking trail.
TRAILHEAD: Park on the side of the Cherokee Orchard Road just before the entrance to Roaring Fork Motor Nature Trail. Walk up Roaring Fork Motor Nature Trail (closed in winter) 0.2 mile to jct with Baskins Creek Trail. Turn left onto trail.

Mainly due to the cryptic nature of its trailhead, Baskins Creek Trail is rarely traveled. This is surprising since other waterfall destination trails in the neighborhood (Grotto Falls, Rainbow Falls) host hundreds (or even thousands) of hikers every day in summer.

From the jct. of Roaring Fork Motor Nature Trail and Baskins Creek Trail, a segment of the Baskins Creek Trail leads 100 yards to the right where it terminates into the Trillium Gap Trail. To the left (north) the Baskins Creek Trail weaves through an impressive forest of chestnut oaks, red maples, Northern red oaks, Eastern hemlocks, striped maples and large blackgums. Throughout the length of this route, there are also conspicuous outcrops of white vein quartz. These attractive minerals were created when massive slabs of bedrock were thrust westward as the Appalachian Mountains formed. As the rocks were bent, they often cracked and pulled apart. Hot, silica-enriched fluids moved through the fractures precipitating quartz.

At **0.2** mile, you climb an easy piney ridge with many trees killed by the native Southern pine bark beetle. Fire will probably be the next natural process to impact this slope, invigorating new growth of the fire-dependent Table Mountain pines which are common here. Partial views of Cherokee Orchard, Bullhead, and Mt. Le Conte are visible, especially in winter.

Descending steeply from the ridge toward Falls Branch, you pass through more pines and an abundance of mountain laurel. In late May and June, when the shrub's beautiful candy-stripped flowers bloom, this would be a good short walk to enjoy the event.

Cross Falls Branch on stepping stones at **1.0** mile, but if there have been recent rains, count on getting your feet a little wet. The trail now descends steeper still, down a short canyon dug by the rollicking branch. At several places the noisy stream has carved natural Jacuzzis in its bed, tempting hikers to take a trail-side dip on hot summer days. On the right, numerous handsome outcrops of Roaring Fork Sandstone are visible. The rock is named for the stream you'll hear roar near the end of this trail. Big blocks of white vein quartz are often associated with this type of rock.

At **1.2** miles, an unmaintained side trail takes off to the left. Sometimes this spur is marked with a sign reading "Baskins Cemetery." The wet, rugged, 0.2 mile spur snakes up to a small hillside cemetery with mostly unmarked stones.

Back on the main route, Baskins Creek Trail intersects another rugged spur to the left at **1.3** miles that is sometimes signed "Baskins Creek Falls ¼ mile." This spur leads past a rock pile and homesite in a broad, flat area beside the waters of Falls Branch. Tall, even-aged tuliptrees mark an old field. The route becomes steep, slippery and dangerous where it cuts down to the base of the falls. If you don't feel you can make the descent safely, don't even try it.

The falls pours over a substantial Roaring Fork Sandstone bluff 25-30' tall. It's a picturesque spot, with the tall trees, exposed rockface and splashing water. According to Park Ranger Glenn Cardwell, members of the tiny Baskins community (formerly located just downstream) used the falls for taking showers.

After treading carefully back to the main route, Baskins Creek Trail climbs steeply through a rhododendron tunnel, then doglegs down to a crossing of Baskins Creek. This is a somewhat difficult rockhop during much of the year, and you can count on getting your feet a little wet. Turn right immediately after the crossing, even though there is an old roadbed leading to the left.

Beyond the crossing, the trail follows Baskins Creek upstream through heavy rhododendron, then cuts over to an odd, dry gulch. The climb up the gulch is steep enough to raise a sweat in January, but you can stop frequently to admire the sizable chestnut oaks and Northern red oaks growing on the slope to the left. Topping the ridge, you will be able to hear Roaring Fork roar if its flow is high.

After a quick descent of the ridge, you come to the Bales Cemetery and trail's end at Roaring Fork Motor Nature Trail. The large cemetery is currently closed for restoration, but one grave stone visible through the fence reads

"MADE 1979 BY HIS GRAND SON HOMER BALES
CALEB BALES LIVED HERE AND RAISED 8 CHILDREN AND
DONATED BALES CEMETERY"

You can also hike to the falls from this trail head (1.5 miles), but starting from the other end is a bit more interesting of a walk.

Narrative by Steve Kemp

BAXTER CREEK TRAIL

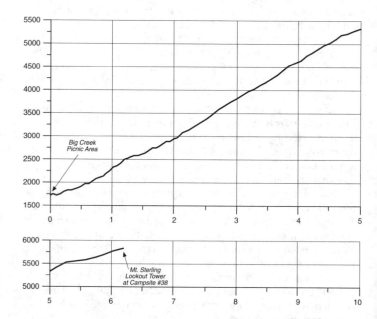

LENGTH: 6.2 miles, from Big Creek Campground to Campsite #38.
CAUTIONS: Steep, rocky trail.
MAP KEY: 11 B-C; USGS quad: Cove Creek Gap.
HIGHLIGHTS: Rock formations, virgin forest, Mt. Sterling Fire Tower.
USE: Hiking trail.
TRAILHEAD: Exit I-40 at Waterville, cross the Pigeon River, turn left, and drive 1.0 mile (part paved, part gravel) to the Carolina Power and Light plant. At a four-way intersection enter the park by going straight. At 0.2 mile, you come to Big Creek Ranger Station. Drive 1.0 mile to Big Creek Picnic Area (closed in winter) and hiker parking.

Six different lumber companies worked this land from the late 1800s to 1934, but this steep, rocky approach to Mount Sterling protected some of its old forest. The early companies tried to float logs down Big Creek, but boulders got in the way. A later company bought land, built a rail line in from Newport, TN, and Waterville, NC, and then sold out before cutting a single tree. The Cataloochee Lumber Company logged 100 million feet of lumber before going bankrupt in 1904. The Suncrest Lumber Company cut 1.5 million feet of spruce for the war effort (WW I, for planes) and then left the logs to rot. Raging fires in the 1920s burned not only logs and brush, but also logging equipment. Be careful. This mountain seems to have a way of fighting back.

Follow the trail through the picnic area to an elaborate foot bridge over Big Creek. After rainy weather, the water of Big Creek boils and thunders under this bridge, and a deep green pool waits on the far side. This part of Big Creek is not rock-hopper friendly.

Across Big Creek, Baxter Creek Trail turns right and runs between a cliff and the creek for 0.5 mile. Rosebay rhododendron and dog-hobble fill the shelf here. Christmas and maidenhair fern, hepatica, toothwort, foamflower, and wild ginger line the trail, especially in seeps from the cliff. The trail rises on a graded bench of packed dirt and a few stones, and you can see a large island in Big Creek to the right. After that view, Big Creek swings away, and you move out of the moist rosebay rhododendron bottoms into a young forest of tuliptree and American beech. The trail reaches the cliff top where slanted slabs of gray rock are decorated with pink and green lichens and lampshade spider webs. It crosses a draw, turns away from the cliff, and rises gradually through a more diverse forest of tuliptree, hickory, maple, flowering dogwood, and a few junior Eastern hemlocks. In 100 years or so, assuming continued government protection, these hemlocks will probably be the dominant trees. They dominated before the loggers came, and now they grow patiently, tolerating hardwood shade, while the tuliptrees frantically compete with each other overhead. Check back in a century.

A side trail on the right goes 0.25 mile to a large stone chimney on the bank of the creek. Beyond this point, as you move into a forest of larger trees, look for a giant gnarled American beech on the left and two big tuliptrees, one on each side of the trail. Then you walk through a large patch of ground pine that extends as far as you can see on both sides of the trail. This patch of clubmoss may be just a few plants with long, tangled root systems sending up shoots. Clubmosses and their relatives, the ferns, developed the first vascular tissue in plant evolutionary history; in other words, they invented a system to raise water from the ground and therefore to grow tall. Massive ferns and clubmosses covered the earth 300 million years ago, and their dead bodies make up much of the coal and oil we squander. Other vascular plants (trees and wildflowers, for example) later developed even better water transport systems, and ferns and clubmosses are understory reminders of ancient history. Clubmosses produce tiny dry spores that were once collected and used as ignition powder for fireworks and the flash for early cameras.

You will begin to hear Baxter Creek, and soon will cross a branch of it on elegant quartz stepping stones. Right after the creek, look for a large Eastern hemlock with many branches on the lower trunk. Most hemlocks grow straight up and shed their lower branches, making a log favored by loggers. This one may have saved itself by not conforming.

The trail becomes rocky, steep, narrow, and weedy as you ascend to cross the other branch of Baxter Creek. Right after the creek, you can see some fine Civilian Conservation Corps stonework on the down side of the trail. The walking becomes easier, but not for long. You soon start the serious climbing of this trail, which won't end until you reach the fire tower. As you climb, the landscape becomes a boulder field, and every boulder has a roof garden of sedum, moss, and ferns. The trees show a lot of ingenious adaptations to such rocky land: aerial roots, twisted trunks, counterbalanced branches. This may be a clue to some of the lumber companies' problems.

A few rocks support colonies of walking fern, which has thin, arrow-shaped fronds that grow long, threadlike strands from the tip, like the strand of cheese you get when you pull one piece of pizza away from the rest. The fern walks across rock faces by anchoring the tip of this strand in a pocket of soil and starting a new plant there.

Look for the leaves of putty-root orchids between the boulders.

They look like oval cutouts from crinkled dollar bills. The double bulb sends up a leaf in the fall and a flower stalk in late spring; they never see each other. This plant is also called Adam-and-Eve orchid, apparently because of the marriage-like union of the two parts of the bulb, but the separate careers of the flower and the leaf makes the Adam-and-Eve name appropriate even today.

After more climbing and another creek crossing, the trail turns away from Baxter Creek and rises to a small ridge overlooking Big Creek Valley. You can see Mt. Cammerer ahead and the power plant to the right. The trail rounds the end of the ridge in a rosebay rhododendron tunnel and then dips into moist coves and out to exposed ridges for a mile or so. One cove has great fractured slabs of rock and a beautiful cascade at a creek crossing. At about 2.0 miles, you climb to the second cliff of this hike, which juts out to the end of the ridge. The trail curves around in front of the cliff face on a good ledge and plunges into a new rhododendron tunnel. Fraser magnolias and striped maples grow in a break of the tunnel, which soon opens to a wide, comfortable ridge top. The ridge rises gently, but it will feel level compared to other parts of this trail.

When the ridge rises steeply, the trail curves left of the top into another rhododendron tunnel with black gum, sassafras, and sourwood trees standing straight among the tangled masses of rhododendron—another problem those loggers had to struggle through. Look for a huge American chestnut stump on the left in the tunnel and another big chestnut snag that leans dangerously over the trail.

The rhododendron tunnel gives way to a mature Eastern hemlock forest with little undergrowth. American beeches, Fraser magnolias, and silverbells stand among the hemlocks with tall, straight trunks and crowns above the highest hemlock needles.

The trail switches back again near a double-trunked chestnut snag and briefly becomes almost level. It meanders along a new ridge, through an alley of giant trees, mostly gnarled maples. The loggers probably didn't get this far up, though some of their fires may have damaged these ridges. As you leave the ridge top and pass into a quiet Eastern hemlock forest, you will see the first red spruces, probably small ones seeded from higher elevation. Here's a test to tell a spruce seedling from a hemlock or fir. Grasp a branch firmly as if you were shaking hands with it. Spruce needle ends are sharp enough to prick your fingers, while hemlock and fir feel soft. To confirm the identification, try to roll a needle in your fingers. The square spruce needles roll easily, while the flat hemlock or fir needles won't roll. At this elevation, spruce and hemlock grow together; the firs appear higher up.

At about **4.0** miles, the trail moves around the nose of a ridge and then climbs to an open saddle with a switchback. Three more switchbacks take you through a boulder field and several blackberry patches. These high elevation boulder fields were formed during the Pleistocene when extreme temperatures reached the southern Appalachians. Water seeped into bedrock cracks, and deep freezing broke off these boulders.

The trail continues along a ridge of quiet, mossy spruce-fir forest and then, becoming steep and rocky, climbs up three more switchbacks as if it were following a split rail fence. It straightens under a massive overhanging rock with a little cave on the left. After the rocks, the trail regains the ridge top and comes to a narrow side trail that leads to a spring. Baxter Creek Trail goes on straight (and up) for a little less than 0.5 mile to reach the grassy area with the Mt. Sterling Fire Tower and Campsite #38. This is a high (5,820' elevation) and usually cold campsite; it has room for 20 people and their horses. According to the back country reports, bears rarely visit this campsite; perhaps it's a long way up for them, too. You can climb six flights of the tower for good views. In the winter you can see the church of Little Cataloochee, perched on a ridge, if you look south-southwest. Clear days offer views of Mt. Cammerer, Max Patch, Clingmans Dome, Mt. Pisgah, and Mt. Mitchell. Look for a US Geological Survey benchmark at the base of the tower.

About 0.5 mile beyond the tower and campsite, Mt. Sterling Trail meets the Mt. Sterling Ridge Trail. This trail makes several connections in a remote part of the Smokies. One possibility is to make a loop with Walnut Bottom and Big Creek Trails for a long day hike or a two to three day backpacking trip.

Narrative by Doris Gove

BEAR CREEK TRAIL

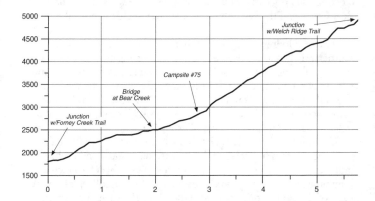

LENGTH: 5.8 miles, from Forney Creek Trail to Welch Ridge Trail.
HIGHLIGHTS: Old logging camp, scenic views.
MAP KEY: 5-6 F; USGS quads: Noland Creek, Silers Bald.
USE: Horse and hiking trail.
STARTING POINT: Hike 1.0 mile north from the Fontana Lake to end of Forney Creek Trail.

Bear Creek Trail begins from Forney Creek Trail at a trail junction 1.0 mile north of Fontana Lake. Bear Creek Trail angles left, crossing Forney Creek on a large motor bridge. Second-growth tuliptrees and mixed hardwoods are reclaiming this once heavily logged area. At the time the park was established, a man named Watson lived here, but it's unclear whether he built or took up residence in a cabin left by the Norwood Lumber Company.

Norwood Lumber Company owned and logged 17,000 acres of the Forney Creek drainage from Clingmans Dome to Silers Bald. Logging operations began in 1910 and continued until 1925. During World War I, the company cut red spruce that was used to manufacture airplanes, cutting some 40,000 board feet per day.

Bear Creek Trail follows the old railroad bed along Forney Creek for 300 yards before crossing Bear Creek on a wide auto bridge. After crossing the bridge, the railroad bed splits three ways. The spur up Bear Creek and the switchback to the left, which ascends Pilot Ridge, are both unmaintained.

The trail follows the graveled spur to the right and skirts the southern tip of Jumpup Ridge in a large, sweeping curve. Ascending the ridge through mixed hardwoods, the trail leaves Bear Creek and follows Forney Creek for a short distance. Rosebay rhododendron and dog-hobble are abundant along the steep banks. As the trail climbs the eastern slope of Jumpup Ridge, you reach Welch Branch at **0.3** mile, just above its junction with Forney Creek.

Continuing alongside Welch Branch, the trail passes through tuliptree, Eastern hemlock, and an occasional American beech. At mile **0.5**, the trail leaves Welch Branch in a switchback to recross Jumpup Ridge. The railroad can be seen at the switchback off to the right of the trail. It once crossed Welch Branch twice in a loop in order for the train to negotiate the turn. A large American beech tree stands in the switchback to the left.

As the trail moves around the ridge, it passes through large Eastern hemlocks, which quickly give way to a pine-oak forest. From **0.8** miles to **1.6** miles the trail follows the contours of the southwestern slope of Jumpup Ridge. The forest alternates from pine-oak with mountain laurel to tuliptrees, Eastern hemlock, and hardwoods.

The Norwood Lumber Co. made extensive use of inclines in its logging operations to help conquer the steeper slopes. These machines, also known as "Sarah Parkers," rode on a track laid along a cleared strip straight up a mountainside and pulled themselves up and down by means of a cable and a rotating drum. Loggers loaded timber at higher elevations, transported it via the inclines, and unloaded it down below. Here in the lower elevations, logs were usually skidded to the trail either by mule or horse teams or machine. Between mile **0.8** and **1.6**, you will notice the many ramps or grades that approach the railroad bed. Judging from their width and slope, they were probably used by teams to skid logs to waiting trains.

Returning to parallel Bear Creek at **1.8** miles, the trail moves through tuliptree and Eastern hemlock with rosebay rhododendron and dog-hobble along the creek. On the right, you'll see the remains of an old stove. This is the likely site of one of four logging cabins which stood in this area. Next, you cross Bear Creek on a narrow motor bridge at **1.9** miles. Just past the bridge, an old tub sits in another cabin site.

The trail travels along the right bank of Bear Creek to Poplar Flats, the recently established Campsite #75, located at **2.8** miles. Many tall, second growth tuliptrees now tower over the remains of the logging area. At the upper end of Poplar Flats, the railroad bed splits again with an unmaintained spur continuing along the right bank of Bear Creek. The trail follows the right spur in a large curve and begins a moderate climb. At the intersection, the remains of another stove are scattered beside the creek.

The top of Jumpup Ridge appears at **3.3** miles, where the trail turns north (left) to follow the ridge crest for 0.1 miles. At mile **3.4**, the trail cuts along the southwestern slope through a pine-oak forest. Views of High Rocks, up Bear Creek Valley, may be seen to the left.

At **3.6** miles you reach a gap where an unmaintained trail angles right to descend to Advalorem Branch, an oddly named creek since ad valorem refers to a tax based on a percentage of value. It is not known how this stream earned such a title. Just past the gap, the trail returns to the eastern slope of the ridge and continues a moderate climb. This open, mixed hardwood area has larger trees with galax beside the trail.

The trail reaches the crest of Jumpup Ridge at **5.0** miles. Then the trail follows the ridge crest before entering another gap at **5.3** miles. Here it returns to the western slope and enters an open hardwood forest of noticeably larger trees. The openness of the forest allows grass and mountain blackberries to crowd the narrow trail.

You reach Welch Ridge, elevation 4,890', at mile **5.8** and the trail ends at its junction with Welch Ridge Trail, which runs 6.5 miles right and northeast to the Appalachian Trail and the state line, or 0.7 mile left to High Rocks where a cabin and the foundation of a fire-tower remain. Great views to the south and east can be seen from High Rocks. In 1976, park employee Ray Dehart reported a mountain lion near High Rocks Tower.

Narrative by Charles Maynard and David Morris

BEARD CANE TRAIL

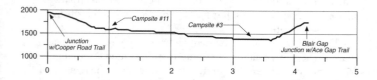

LENGTH: 4.2 miles, from Cooper Road Trail to Ace Gap Trail
HIGHLIGHTS: 3.5 mile trough between two mountains, fringed polygala and other spring flowers.
CAUTIONS: Hesse and Beard Cane creek crossings in high water.
MAP KEY: 2-3 D; USGS quads: Blockhouse, Kinzel Springs.
USE: Horse and hiking trail.
STARTING POINT: Cooper Road Trail, 4.9 miles northeast of Abrams Creek Campground.

Between the trailhead and Hurricane Mountain to the northeast, the Beard Cane Trail runs 3.5 miles on as straight a line as any trail in the Smokies. Yes, it wiggles a tad, but not much for a mountain trail.

Another feature is that the path descends, and ascends from a long, fertile trough between the parallel ridges of Hatcher and Beard Cane Mountains. This moist and shaded hollow displays a bumper crop of spring flowers, including the tiny beauty, fringed polygala. Only 2-5" high, it displays a picturesque reddish, winged bloom and is also known as gay wings and bird-on-the-wing. It flowers in May and is so small it's easily missed. A variety of trilliums also bloom here.

In the early years of the 20th century, the Little River Lumber Company cut the timber in this area and ran a narrow gauge railroad up the valley. Large tuliptrees, hemlocks, maples and oaks have reforested the land.

Beard cane is a cane that grows in places here and on the surrounding mountains, in low, moist spots. Dog-hobble and rhododendron are much in evidence and display their white blooms in May and June.

Near the trailhead on the south flank of Hatcher Mountain, the early pinkish-white flowers of trailing arbutus appear in March. The path crosses Beard Cane Creek over a dozen times as it swells from a small branch to a creek. Except during very high water, rock hopping works for all crossings. In wet weather this bottom-running path is water-logged and extremely muddy.

Campsite #11 (Beard Cane, 1,530') is reached **1.0** mile from Cooper Road Trail, in a flat, shaded area. Water is plentiful from Beard Cane Creek in wet weather, but not during the driest times.

Quite near the pleasant chatter of Beard Cane Creek, and not far from its junction with Hesse Creek, campsite #3 (Hesse Creek) is at mile **3.3**. Located in a level stand of hemlocks, it's a cool, comfortable setting for camping and sleeping. Beneath the thin veneer of soil and showing in a few places in the creek is the sedimentary bedrock of sandstone laid down in the Precambrian period.

At mile **4.2** you reach Blair Gap on Hurricane Mountain. The mountain is named for a devastating storm early in the 19th century which mowed down a large swath of trees.

Narrative by Woody Brinegar

BEECH GAP TRAIL I

ROUND BOTTOM TO BEECH GAP

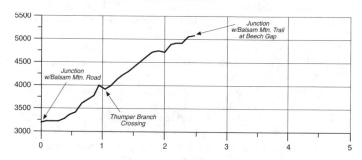

LENGTH: 2.5 miles, from Balsam Mtn. Road to jct. Balsam Mtn. Trail

HIGHLIGHTS: Pleasant stream at beginning, mature forest.

CAUTIONS: Unbridged stream crossing.

MAP KEY: D 10; USGS quad: Luftee Knob

USE: Horse and hiking trail.

TRAILHEAD: Round Bottom—Access to the trailhead is via Big Cove and Straight Fork roads which lead into Great Smoky Mountains National Park just beyond the tribal fish hatchery. You can access Big Cove Road from Highway 441, 1 mile south of Oconaluftee Visitor Center. Trailhead parking is 13.9 miles from the visitor center (3.8 miles from park boundary). Alternate trailhead access is 13.2 miles via the one-way Balsam Mountain Road which begins at the end of the Heintooga Ridge Road.

Round Bottom, the trailhead for the Beech Gap Trail—Sections I and II, is a beautiful, secluded spot nestled beside pristine Straight Fork. Despite the remoteness, the area has a rich history. Native Americans penetrated these wilds for eons, followed by pioneers who established small mountain farms.

Ira McGee built a mill on nearby Ledge Creek to grind corn. He also cleared the fields near the trailhead (known as the McGee Fields). In 1915 the railroad reached Cherokee and lines were extended into the Smokies, ushering in the logging era. One line extended from Ravensford to Round Bottom where it forked at McGee Fields. The main line continued up Straight Fork and the other up Ledge Creek through Pin Oak Gap into Haywood County.

The Parsons Pulp operation, which later became the Ravensford Lumber Company, removed about three-fourths of the timber from the Straight Fork watershed in the late 1920s through Round Bottom. Between 1934 and 1941 the Civilian Conservation Corps had a camp where Round Bottom Creek flows into Straight Fork. From this base, young men performed a variety of services including building the trails enjoyed by modern hikers.

Traveling north on Straight Fork Road, trailhead parking for the Beech Gap Trail II is located just before reaching the Round Bottom auto ford; however, limited additional parking for Section I may be reached by continuing through the auto ford 0.1 miles. For purposes of description, both segments of the Beech Gap Trail begin at the trailhead for section II.

An immediate fording of Straight Fork greets the hiker. This ford entails wading approximately 25 feet across the cement auto ford in water that is 4-6 inches deep during times of normal stream flow. Although this crossing is normally safe, it should be avoided during periods of high water. Beautiful stream vistas encourage a pause at this spot, particularly when trout are feeding on top water insects, as betrayed by their splash as they break the surface.

Continuing uphill past the ford, the trail begins on the left side of the road. It bears left and follows an old rail grade for 200'. The trail then turns sharply right and ascends gradually, then steeply through a small cove forested in birch, maple and tuliptree along a sometimes rocky surface. About midway through the cove the trail crosses a small unnamed stream which parallels it first on the right and then on the left.

At about **0.5** mile the trail switches left and ascends more gradually, passing galax and trailing arbutus along the trail margin. As the trail climbs, it passes through closed oak forest, comprised of several types of oaks, hickories and sourwood as well as other hardwoods. At about **1.0** mile the trail climbs around the headwaters of Thumper Branch, which refers to the "thumping chest," part of the distilling apparatus used to produce white liquor. Originally, this stream was called Stillhouse Branch by natives, but the name was changed as a result of a proposal by the North Carolina Park Commission Nomenclature Committee.

The trail crosses several wet areas at approximately **1.5** miles where springs flow across and in the trail for short distances. These places become quite miry as a result of regular horse use. In summer, these damp areas display especially nice stands of jewelweed or touch-me-not. Also, note areas of lush grass along the trail. In earlier times cattle, which were turned loose to graze along Balsam Mountain, roamed these slopes above Straight Fork.

The trail continues ascending toward Beech Gap, passing through forest with scattered Fraser fir and American beech trees, among others. At **2.5** miles the trail terminates in Beech Gap, a pleasant gap on the crest of Balsam Mountain. This gap, originally known as Big Swag, was once cleared for grazing by cattle and sheep. Later logging trains reached the crest of the Balsams and rail lines were constructed on both sides of the gap to facilitate removal of the rich timber. Evidence of these early rail grades is apparent on both sides of the gap. Laurel Gap is 2.0 miles to the left and Pin Oak Gap is 2.3 miles to the right.

Narrative by William A. Hart Jr.

Beech Gap Trail II

ROUND BOTTOM TO HYATT RIDGE

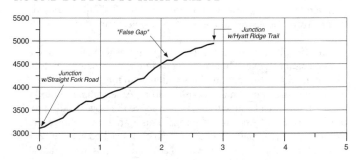

LENGTH: 2.9 miles, from Straight Fork Road to jct. Hyatt Ridge Trail.

HIGHLIGHTS: Pleasant stream at beginning, mature forest, excellent winter views of Balsam Mountain.

CAUTIONS: Unbridged stream crossing for those walking complete Beech Gap Trail.

MAP KEY: D 10; USGS quads: Bunches Bald, Luftee Knob.

USE: Horse and hiking trail.

TRAILHEAD: Round Bottom (See Section I for access details)

Round Bottom is the trailhead for the Beech Gap Trail—Sections I and II. The section I narrative contains a description of the historical aspects of the Round Bottom Area. Persons hiking the complete trail from Hyatt Ridge or Beech Gap should be aware of the Straight Fork ford. Normally, this crossing poses no difficulty; however, it should be avoided during times of high water. Section II of the Beech Gap Trail begins across from the parking area and is marked by a trail sign. The trail ascends above Straight Fork on a side-hill trail which offers several nice views of the stream. At **0.2** mile the trail passes through a stand of second growth tuliptree and continues its meanders around the contours of the slope. Some of the mountain folds contain small branches which flow downward over moss covered stones creating visually pleasing vistas. One such place is the stream crossed at **0.8** miles. These stream crossings, as well as other moist areas along the trail, tend to become miry with horse use. Also, it should be noted that many of these streams are not dependable water sources year round.

At **1.5** miles the trail ascends more steeply as it climbs around a pleasant sloping cove. There are several fine winter views of Balsam Mountain along this section. Also, a change in forest type will be noted reflecting mixed hardwoods including American beech and maple trees. Ahead you will see the sky above the ridge, leading to the expectation of "reaching the top." This is an illusion, however. What you see is actually a "false gap" which is reached at about **2.1** miles. Here the trail makes a switch back and ascends more gradually. This flat crest is an excellent resting spot.

The trail climbs gradually and ascends the slopes of Hyatt Bald. The bald is named for Ned Hyatt who cleared large fields on Hyatt Creek and who probably herded cattle on Hyatt Bald when it was cleared for grazing. The bald has since become overgrown with trees. At about **2.3** miles the trail crosses a relatively level ridge spur, passing several large oak trees before terminating at the Hyatt Ridge Trail at **2.9** miles. McGee Springs and the McGee Springs Campsite are 0.9 mile to the right. McGee Springs was named for Ira McGee who farmed near Round Bottom. The trail to the left connects with the Enloe Creek Trail and eventually terminates at Straight Fork Road.

Narrative by William A. Hart, Jr.

BIG CREEK TRAIL

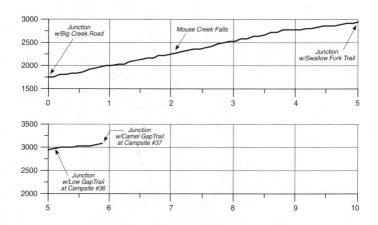

LENGTH: 5.9 Miles, from Big Creek Road to Camel Gap Trail.
HIGHLIGHTS: Historic area, beautiful creek walk, varied forest scenes.
MAP KEY: 11 B-C; USGS quads: Waterville, Cove Creek Gap, Luftee Knob
USE: Horse and hiking trail.
TRAILHEAD: Big Creek Picnic Area—Access to the trailhead via I-40: Exit I-40 at exit 451 (Waterville Road). Turn left after crossing the Pigeon River and proceed 2.3 miles to intersection. Continue straight ahead, passing Big Creek Ranger Station, to reach the trailhead at 3.4 miles.

The Big Creek Trail penetrates a large watershed and provides one of the most beautiful and interesting walks in Great Smoky Mountains National Park. Features which make the trail particularly worthwhile in any season are the continuous variety of stream scenes along the length of Big Creek, views of majestic ridges which flank the stream, and rich forest growth. Adding to Big Creek's appeal is its rich history. Understanding something of this history adds savor to walks in the basin.

From prehistoric times Indians passed the lower reaches of Big Creek, following a trail which led from near present-day Newport, Tennessee to trails in the Waynesville, North Carolina, area. Settlers, circuit riding preachers and livestock herders followed this route, and eventually pioneers carved out farms in the Big Creek wilderness. During the Civil War the area saw limited action from both Confederate and Union forces. Late in the 19th century the discovery of the area's rich forest resources ushered in an era of logging. The forest has reclaimed the slopes and Big Creek is becoming wilderness again; yet, signs of agricultural and logging activity remain.

Of all the influences on Big Creek's history, logging was perhaps the most significant. Because of its proximity to large mills and railroads, this was one of the first watersheds criss-crossed with logging railroads and it was completely cut over by the end of World War I.

The Crestmont Lumber company, operated by Champion Fibre, built its logging rail grades nearly to the crest of Balsam Mountain. Logs were transported back to the mill and dumped into a "tremendous pond" and held until being sent into the mill.

Crestmont, the site of logging operations, was located in the vicinity of today's trailhead parking. Portions of the mill's brick foundations are still visible. In addition to the mill, Crestmont had its own rail station and it was possible to enjoy passenger coach transportation to Newport before the rails were taken up about 1928. A company-owned general store at Crestmont supplied the needs of loggers and their families. It even had a soda fountain which dispensed lemonade and other drinks.

The site of the Civilian Conservation Corp's Big Creek Camp is across the road from the trailhead. Between 1933 and 1939, 100 young men constructed 40 miles of trail, three bridges across Big Creek, and the fire towers on Mount Sterling and White Rock (Mt. Cammerer). In fact, the Big Creek Trail was built originally as a motorway by the CCC.

The entrance road to the Big Creek trailhead passes the Big Creek Ranger Station at 0.2 mile. There is a small parking lot and pay telephone here. The Chestnut Branch Trail begins just past the Ranger

Station. The parking area for the Big Creek and Baxter Creek trails and the entrance to the tent camping area is reached at about 0.8 mile. The Big Creek Trail begins at a gated road uphill from the parking area.

The Big Creek Trail follows the road to Walnut Bottom, ascending steadily but gently throughout its length. Initially, the trail passes above the wooded bottoms beside the creek and eventually looks down upon the creek itself. Second growth tuliptree, scattered hemlock and maple, and sycamore trees with their mottled white trunks predominate. Good views of the ridges across the creek are possible along this segment. At about 1.0 mile, a faint trail leads steeply right to the Rock House, a natural store room in a large cylinder-shaped rock formation which is visible from the trail. This natural alcove was used as temporary shelter by early loggers.

To the left of the trail at 1.4 miles is the Midnight Hole. Here the waters of Big Creek flow between two large boulders and pour six feet into a large, deep, green pool nestled at the base of a high rhododendron covered bluff. This is an ideal place to enjoy the beauty of the stream and to observe trout in the depths of the pool. At 2.1 miles Mouse Creek Falls (a tributary of Big Creek) offers another excellent vista. The stream cascades approximately 20' over gray stone, creating a splash of white. The old logging rail grade which ascended Big Creek can be seen at the base of the falls.

At 2.2 miles the trail crosses Big Creek on a sturdy bridge at the head of a beautiful pool and joins the old logging grade which comes in from the left. The grade was blasted from solid rock here as in other places along the creek. At one such place known as Dead Man's Curve, a tragedy occurred. Six men working on a blasting crew had drilled a hole in the rock and inserted dynamite which became lodged before reaching bottom. When a worker used a crowbar to force it down, it exploded, killing four of the workers.

Past this point the trail passes a moss covered stone bluff covered by rhododendron. Thick patches of dog-hobble grow along the trail here, so named because it sometimes grows so thickly it proves an impediment to hunting dogs. Two of the largest boulders on Big Creek are passed at 2.4 miles. Beyond, there are many pleasant views of the stream. During low water the gray stone in the stream gives the water a steel gray appearance. At other times the stream appears blue-green.

At **2.8** miles the trail passes Brakeshoe Spring, which is a series of small rivulets running over mossy, gray stone. In 1919 the engineer of a logging train placed a locomotive brakeshoe into a depression in the stone. The water running over the gentle curve of the brakeshoe created a natural fountain from which the engineer paused to drink on his trips up and down the creek. Smoky Mountain hikers continued to enjoy the brakeshoe fountain for many years after the logging era ended. The brakeshoe disappeared from its niche sometime between 1974 and 1976, leaving only today's place name as a reminder.

The trail continues its gentle assent above Brakeshoe Spring, passing a variety of stream scenes. At **4.0** miles it crosses a small unnamed stream and then another at **4.3** miles that flows from Flint Rock cove. At **5.0** miles a sign marks the beginning of the Swallow Fork Trail which climbs left 4.0 miles to Pretty Hollow Gap on the Mount Sterling Ridge Trail. Beyond, the trail crosses Big Creek on a bridge to reach the Lower Walnut Bottom Campsite (hikers only) at **5.1** miles. This delightful area offers several campsites in a stand of buckeye trees on the right and in tall hemlocks on the left near the creek. Two steel poles at the site provide a place to secure packs from black bears which frequent the area.

Walnut Bottom was the site of a logging camp run by the Champion Fibre Company which housed loggers who cut timber on the upper reaches of Big Creek. According to historian Thomas Fetters, the doctor who served the Walnut Bottom Camp, Dr. McMahan, would load his "rail-bike" on an empty flatcar and ride up in the locomotive with the crew. The train of empty cars would be left there, and the loaded cars would be transported back to Crestmont. After he had seen the men in the long bunkhouses, Dr. McMahan placed his cycle on the track and rode the seven miles back downhill.

From a recreational standpoint, Walnut Bottom has been a source of enjoyment since the early 1900s. The T.N.C. Railroad (called the Peavine) held Sunday excursions to Crestmont for young people from Newport, Tennessee at the turn of the century. At the Crestmont Lumber Camp they took a logging train up Big Creek to Walnut Bottom. Young women brought white and sweet potatoes, fat-back and meal to fry fritters and bread. "After getting that far back in the mountains the young men went into the ridges to gather loads of ramps (a type of wild leek)," commented M. G. Roberts, a local historian for the *Newport Plain Talk*. "They brought them down to the girls to cook," according to Roberts.

"Yes they had coffee in their basket and brought sassafras bark to make tea. Some of the best fishermen in the party would catch trout and they stood a piece of bark near the fire and baked the fish on the bark. The girls enjoyed the compliments for the delicious meal. The boys enjoyed the partying and stealing a few kisses."

Just past the Lower Walnut Bottom campsite at **5.1** miles, the Low Gap Trail climbs right to reach the Appalachian Trail at Low Gap at 2.5 miles. At about **5.9** miles the trail ends at the Upper Walnut Bottom Campsite and junction with the Camel Gap Trail. The upper campsite is designated for both hikers and horse parties.

Narrative by William A. Hart, Jr.

BIG FORK RIDGE TRAIL

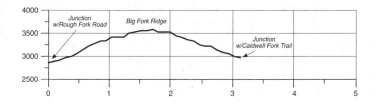

LENGTH: 3.1 miles, from Rough Fork Road to Caldwell Fork Trail.
HIGHLIGHTS: Good views.
CAUTIONS: Erosion in steep sections.
MAP KEY: 11 D; USGS quad: Dellwood .
USE: Horse and hiking trail.
TRAILHEAD: From I-40, take exit 20 (NC Highway 276) west to Cove Creek Road. Follow Cove Creek Road to Cataloochee Road. Drive to the end of the Cataloochee Road (past Cataloochee Camp-

ground and Ranger Station) and continue on the Rough Fork Road to the trailhead.

Built in 1935 by the Civilian Conservation Corps, the Big Fork Ridge Trail climbs over Big Fork Ridge, the main ridge separating the Rough Fork and the Caldwell Fork watersheds, and thus connects Rough Fork and Caldwell Fork trails. At its trailhead on the Rough Fork Road (0.8 mile from the road's intersection with the Cataloochee Road), the Big Fork Ridge Trail crosses Rough Fork by footbridge then, after a stately sycamore, skirts an open field. Just beyond lies an abandoned pasture—the site of Jim Caldwell's farmstead. White pines and tuliptrees are now slowly reclaiming these clearings.

Even though his farm is gone, Caldwell's legacy persists, for a creek and ridge both bear his name. Records state that James Caldwell owned 155 acres here, as well as a six-room frame house, barn, smokehouse, springhouse, chicken house, and wood shop, all of which he sold to make the park in 1930 for $5,800. The park preserved the springhouse and it now resides in the Mountain Farm Museum located at the Oconaluftee Visitor Center.

Soon, the trail enters a forest of red maple, Eastern hemlock, and white pine, with an understory of flowering dogwood. After the trail begins climbing, you encounter waterbars installed by the National Park Service to prevent erosion. Heavy horse use has resulted in severe erosion of steep sections, at times transforming the trail into a gulch. Next, you'll climb past huge Eastern hemlocks and enter a mountain laurel and rosebay rhododendron slick.

At 1.0 mile, after crossing three small rivulets, the trail bends to the right around a shaded northside slope; since little direct sunlight filters through, little undergrowth thrives. Soon the trail levels as you reach a brief knife-shaped ridge where you can hear Rough Fork far below. Coursing through Eastern hemlocks, you head downhill slightly. At one point, you walk between ecosystems: a dry ridge forest on the right and an increasingly dense forest to the left. Skirting a cove with many tall, straight tuliptrees, the trail crosses a small rivulet, then climbs slightly uphill through a rosebay rhododendron grove.

At 1.7 miles the trail reaches the top of Big Fork Ridge. Walking on a dry ridge among young Eastern hemlocks and striped maples, you may hear Red-eyed Vireos singing from the forest crown. Nearby, American chestnuts sprawl on the ground, victims of the chestnut blight. Circling a cove, the trail skirts left around the ridge, then proceeds downhill; Winter Wrens nest nearby. On the left stands a tree pocked with holes. These were bored by the Yellow-bellied Sapsucker who eats both the sap and the insects it attracts.

At approximately **2.0** miles, heading gradually downhill, the trail stretches along the ridge; sassafras thrives on this dry, sandy soil. Descending past a large Fraser magnolia (on the left) and stately Eastern hemlocks, the trail crosses a small seepage. Nearby, garter snakes, looking amazingly like sticks, may be sunning themselves. Be careful not to step on them.

Soon, to the left, the trail offers a good vista of the northern end of the Caldwell Fork Valley. An area of Eastern hemlock stumps testifies to the decisive effect of lightning. After passing a diagonal rockface, you enter an Eastern hemlock grove where a waterfall can be heard below and to the left. At **3.0** miles, the trail crosses Caldwell Fork on a long footbridge. A few hundred yards later, among white pines and Eastern hemlocks, Big Fork Ridge Trail reaches its junction with Caldwell Fork Trail. The latter's junction with McKee Branch Trail appears immediately to the right.

Narrative by Ted Olson

BONE VALLEY TRAIL

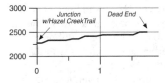

LENGTH: 1.8 miles, from jct. Hazel Creek Trail to trail's end.
HIGHLIGHTS: Hall Cabin, Bone Valley Creek, fern display.
CAUTIONS: 4 major and 1 minor unbridged stream crossings.
MAP KEY: 5 F; USGS quad: Thunderhead.
USE: Hiking and horse trail.
STARTING POINT: Hazel Creek Trail at Campsite #83.

The hike to the Bone Valley Trail is considerably longer than the hike on the Bone Valley Trail. The best access is to cross Fontana Lake via boat to Proctor, then hike 5.4 miles up Hazel Creek to reach Bone Valley. Boat shuttles are available from the Fontana Village Marina (800-849-2258). The Lakeshore Trail from Fontana Dam to campsite #84 (Sugar Fork) then up Hazel Creek avoids the need for a boat (12.9 miles).

This relatively short trail is well worth the effort it takes to get to the trailhead. From campsite #83, cross the wooden bridge over Bone Valley Creek and turn left and proceed upstream. Bone Valley received its name after a late spring blizzard in the 1870s. Lower valley farmers would herd their cattle to the mountaintop balds of the Great Smokies for summer pasture. The unfortunate fellow who had miscalculated the end of winter had his cows here when the snow hit. The cattle had no shelter and froze to death. Their bleached bones littered the valley floor for many years.

The trail approximately follows the narrow gauge railroad bed that Ritter Lumber Company's Shay locomotives plied to remove the timber treasures of Bone Valley watershed. Prior to the arrival of Ritter, Bone Valley and Hazel Creek saw some of the earliest commercial logging in the Smokies. Taylor and Crate built a splash dam on Bone Valley Creek and two more on Hazel Creek in the late 1800s. The ponds impounded by these dams were loaded with the finest tuliptree, magnolia, ash, and other logs that floated well. During "freshenings," rainy periods when the creeks ran high and strong, the dams would be opened in series, releasing their load of water and logs for the drive to the Little Tennessee River. Drovers in hobnail boots would follow the torrent and dislodge stuck or grounded logs. The logs were free-floated down the river to a log boom at Chilhowee, TN. From there they were rafted together and towed to the mill in Chattanooga, 200 miles from where they started.

The water at the first ford, like the three other main fords, is about knee deep under normal conditions. Raging water 2-4' deep can be encountered during and after storms and is very dangerous. Storms on the headwaters can cause flashfloods on the lower sections. The Rufus Hall Home was on the left of the trail just past the first ford. This house was occupied by a game warden in the 1930s.

Between the first and second fords, you will pass White Walnut Cove on your right. Veteran bear hunter Henry Posey recalls great bear hunting here and says the cove was loaded with grapes. Wild grapes not only supply crucial food for bears, squirrels, birds and other animals, they were also an important food for early settlers. Fox grapes (*Vitis labrusca*) have clusters of small, tart grapes and larger leaves. Muscadines (*V. rotundifolia*) have small leaves and very large grapes which drop as they ripen and are usually gathered on the ground.

After the third ford you will be traversing the grown-up fields of the Jesse Crayton Hall Farm. "Crate's" fields are remembered by former residents as being very lush and beautiful and "Crate" was well known for his fine herds of hogs and cattle. The wooded level land now supports a lush growth of several varieties of ferns with Christmas fern and wood ferns predominating. Soon you will cross Mill Creek. "Crate's" tub mill was located just upstream from here. Beebalm, a plant which has many medicinal uses and is a source of the antiseptic thymol, can be seen here in June and July.

Cross the main creek for the fourth time and arrive at the Hall Cabin. "Crate" and his wife, Mary Talitiga Dills, and 4 small children arrived in Bone Valley about 1877 and built this house shortly thereafter. The Park Service moved the cabin from its original location about 200' away. The cabin is the most remote historic structure in the park. Mary's garden of over one acre was located in the existing opening. A word of caution—many copperheads have been spotted here over the years.

The Hazel Creek area became famous in the 1920s and 30s as a sportsman's paradise and the Kress family of New York (Kress Department Stores) wanted in on the fun. They built a wonderful mansion, just to the south of the present location of the cabin, and furnished it in the style of a grand lodge complete with marble mantle pieces. The Kress house became a base camp for wealthy sportsmen who plied the waters of Bone Valley and Hazel Creek for rainbow trout. Non-native rainbows had been stocked after the devastation of the brook trout by the Taylor and Crate splash dams, mentioned earlier.

Just north of the cabin a trail through an impressive old-field stand of tuliptree and white pine leads about 0.5 mile to the Hall

Cemetery. "Crate" Hall and 18 other hardy souls are buried here. This is a wonderful spot to reflect on the tenuous life those settlers led in what author Horace Kephart called the "Back of Beyond."

Narrative by Lance Holland

BOOGERMAN TRAIL

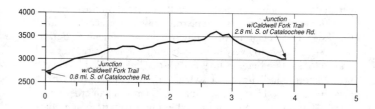

LENGTH: 3.8 miles, starting and ending at Caldwell Fork Trail.
HIGHLIGHTS: Old-growth forests, stone walls, views of Cataloochee Divide.
CAUTIONS: Stream crossings.
MAP KEY: 11 D; USGS quad: Dellwood.
USE: Hiking trail.
STARTING POINT: 0.8 mile from Caldwell Fork trailhead. From I-40, take exit 20 (NC Hwy. 276) west to Cove Creek Road. Follow Cove Creek Road to Cataloochee Road. On the Cataloochee Road, Caldwell Fork trailhead lies to the left between the campground and ranger station.

Boogerman Trail was named by Mark Hannah, a Cataloochee native, after "Booger" Robert Palmer, who lived nearby. Booger was the son of "Turkey" George Palmer, a legendary hunter who, according to his son, was able to "kill nine squirrels without missing a shot." As "Blind" Sam Sutton remembers it, Robert Palmer was just a schoolchild when a teacher in Big Cataloochee School asked him what he wanted to be when he grew up. "I want to be the Boogerman," he said. "Don't you want to be something else besides the boogerman?" asked the teacher. "No," he says, "That's what I want to be." The nickname stuck.

Because "Booger" Palmer, the former owner of this property, did not allow it to be logged, many huge trees grace Boogerman Trail, a side trail off Caldwell Fork Trail, and an excellent medium-length loop trail (6.6 miles). Intended exclusively for hikers, Boogerman Trail provides an interesting, challenging trail.

At the trailhead, you embark by crossing two small rivulets among dog-hobble and rosebay rhododendron. The trail climbs slightly uphill through an Eastern hemlock forest, its understory witch-hazel and striped maple; on the trail's banks are wood-sorrel, striped pipsissewa, and Christmas fern. Soon, the trail becomes rocky. As you continue uphill among large Eastern hemlocks and tuliptrees, look for ghost-like Indian pipe rising among dead leaves. This plant, lacking chlorophyll, feeds on rotting vegetation. Further up you encounter yellow birches and Virginia pines. At a break in the trees, Cataloochee Divide appears in the distance. Soon tall white pines tower over scrub pines; fallen needles perfume the air.

At approximately 0.5 mile the trail winds uphill around Den Ridge; Caldwell Fork roars below. While climbing, you see many dead American chestnut stumps. The trail continues through mixed hardwoods, including red maple and scarlet oak, along with some larger Eastern hemlocks. On the left, a large dead trunk stands; it is full of woodpecker holes, probably created by a pileated woodpecker and perhaps now the homes of owls and squirrels. At approximately 1.0 mile, Fraser magnolia and sourwood emerge. Sourwood, named for the acid taste of its leaves, is the park's largest member of the heath family. While still climbing up the ridge, you enter a grove of large Eastern hemlock, then wind around a small ravine filled with younger Eastern hemlocks. To the left are partial views of Cataloochee Valley.

By now the trail is rolling, yet generally level. A big white oak and tuliptree tower over the trail on the left. Soon you enter a white pine grove, its undergrowth consisting of trailing arbutus, striped pipsissewa, Christmas fern, and poison ivy. At approximately 2.0 miles, you cross Palmer Branch on a small log bridge, then enter an opening, the site of Robert Palmer's small farm. According to purchase records, "Booger" owned a three-room log house, two-room log house, four-stall barn, apple house, and spring house on 255.5 acres. In 1929, when the land was purchased for the national park, "Booger" was paid $5,375.

The trail continues slightly uphill through white pine and then a rich, mixed woodland of sizable Eastern hemlock, tuliptree, pignut hickory, oaks, and maples. To the right a small spring-fed rivulet carves out the earth, slowly forming its own valley. You might hear the drawn-out staccato call of the reclusive Yellow-billed Cuckoo, a New World member of the Cuckoo family.

Curving around a level part of the ridge, you enter a rhododendron thicket and cross five shallow spring-fed seeps. At one point, you see a partial view of Cataloochee Divide, with Caldwell Fork barely audible below. Spring to summer wildflowers include sundrops and larger purple-fringed orchids.

The trail climbs up a steep section among second-growth Eastern hemlocks, then heads downhill through much rotting American chestnut. Northern maidenhair ferns grow on the right. To the left stands a huge twin-trunk tuliptree—actually two 6' diameter trunks stemming from the same root system. Approaching Snake Branch at approximately 3.0 miles, you pass a stone wall. Approximately 100 yards long and 2' wide, this stacked stone wall has no mortar yet is so well-constructed it stands intact. Near the wall is a giant tuliptree, its hollow trunk so large a person can stand in it.

Following Snake Branch downhill, rock-hop across a large fast-moving fork, then walk downstream among large Eastern hemlocks and tuliptrees. Soon you rock hop across the creek again where another stone wall appears; though the upper half is collapsing, the lower half is intact. A third wall appears to the right, this one heading away from creek in an "L" shape. Then the trail enters an opening of ox-eye daisy, daisy-fleabane, tall meadowrue, and dwarf cinquefoil. After another rock-hop stream crossing, you enter a thicket of rosebay rhododendron, then emerge into a grassy clearing where a black walnut flourishes. A depression in the ground (to the left of the trail) marks the home site of Carson Messer; the notched American chestnut logs of his cabin are decaying. Perhaps the stone walls you passed earlier marked the perimeter of his land.

After stepping over a feeder stream overgrown with orange jewelweed, you enter a grove of white pines. At **3.8** miles you reach the junction with Caldwell Fork Trail. To return back to Caldwell Fork trailhead, walk 2.8 miles to the right.

Narrative by Ted Olson

BOTE MOUNTAIN TRAIL

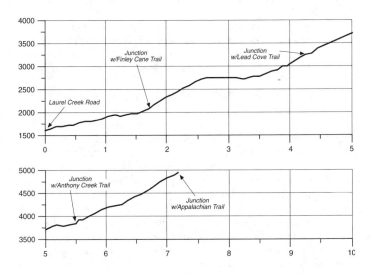

LENGTH: 7.2 miles, from Laurel Creek Road to the Appalachian Trail.

HIGHLIGHTS: Deeply banked, rhododendron flanked portion, incomparable Spence Field at trail's end.

CAUTIONS: Very rocky in places.

MAP KEY: 4 D-E; USGS quads: Wear Cove, Thunderhead Mtn.

USE: Horse and hiking trail.

TRAILHEAD: Laurel Creek Road, 3.4 miles from Townsend "Y." Park at the Schoolhouse Gap trailhead, 250 yards past the Bote

Mountain trailhead, on the right as you head toward Cades Cove. Walk back carefully beside the road to the Bote Mountain Trail.

This ridge trail has a long history as portions of it were used by James Spence for whom Spence Field was named and who lived and farmed there 6 months each year beginning in the early 1830s. In the 1850s, Isaac Anderson of Maryville used Cherokee labor to build a road up the ridge to the state line which follows the ridgeline of the Smoky Mountains.

Legend has it that the Indians selected this ridge rather than the one to the east as the best route for the road. They chose by voting (Cherokees reportedly were unable to voice the "V" sound). So they "boted" for Bote Mountain, and the other crest became known as Defeat Ridge.

Beginning in a cool, hardwood hollow, the road gently ascends for 1.2 miles to meet the drier ridgecrest at the junction of the West Prong Trail. It then runs the east slope of Bote Mountain in a gradual rise to connect each gap between the knobs of the ridge. A half mile above the Anthony Creek Trail junction is a turnaround where the CCC, Civilian Conservation Corps, improved roadway ceases.

For a time, in the late 1960s, the public was permitted to drive to this point making it a short walk to Spence Field. Beyond the turn-around, for 0.7 miles, the trail runs the west side of the ridgecrest and becomes a trough. It was dug by unnumbered thousands of cattle hooves going to and from the mountain meadows above during the years before the park. The soft soil beneath the thick rhododendron was worn through to the bedrock.

Walled in by mossy banks and rhododendron tunnels, it is delightfully picturesque anytime, but especially when gray clouds seep in for moist and gloomy companionship. It's a sluiceway, from rocky to very rocky, including sharply tilted bedrock of the Elkmont and Thunderhead Sandstone Formations.

Above this section, the path becomes the more standard graded trail. Yet, it's wider and passes through a yellow birch forest with paper thin curls of bark rolling out from the trunks.

As the path approaches the Appalachian Trail at the edge of Spence Field, it becomes extremely rocky. Spence Field is, to many, the most delightful spot on the long crest of the Smokies. It's a mountaintop meadow of thick grass, blueberry bushes, and serviceberry ("sarvis") trees, both of which bear ripe fruit in August. Bears feast here, breaking the limbs to reach the fruit. Blackberries also ripen in August. Views are splendid and include Cades Cove and Fontana Lake. Two miles east is Thunderhead, the most prominent summit of the Smokies west of Clingmans Dome. It has three peaks, including well known Rocky Top, the one nearest Spence Field.

Between the cove hardwood forest of maple, oak, black locust, and sourwood at the bottom and the yellow birch near the top, the forest changes from thick pine stands to pine-hardwood, to mostly hardwoods higher up. Maples and oaks are the dominant trees of the deciduous forests.

Though this is not the best of routes for wildflowers, the lovely yellow-fringed orchid grows midway between the trail junctions of the Finley Cane and Lead Cove trails in August. In the same area a lightning-caused forest fire occurred in 1987 which destroyed a good portion of a mile of forest canopy, especially on the east slope down to the Middle Prong of Little River. Thick, low level growth occurs here, as the trees send sprouts from the root-remains of a burned forest.

The Finley Cane Trail junction occurs on the right at **1.8** miles. This 2.8 mile trail from Laurel Creek Road serves as a leg of two popular triangular loops. One is of 7.1 miles and includes the Finley Cane, Bote Mountain, and Lead Cove trails.

The other loop is 9.3 miles and embraces the Finley Cane, Bote Mountain, Schoolhouse Gap and Turkey Pen Ridge trails. These are low elevation hikes, excellent for spring, fall, and winter walking.

Narrative by Woody Brinegar

THE BOULEVARD TRAIL

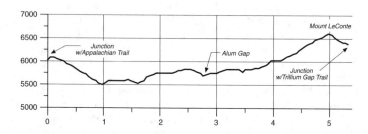

LENGTH: 5.3 miles, from the Appalachian Trail to the summit of Mt. Le Conte.
HIGHLIGHTS: Panoramic views, Anakeesta Knob, gradual climb.
CAUTIONS: Icy places in winter.
MAP KEY: 7-8 C; USGS quad: Mt. Le Conte.
USE: Hiking trail.
STARTING POINT: Drive to Newfound Gap and hike east (north) on the Appalachian Trail 2.7 miles.

A hiker shouldn't get overly warm on this trail, not even on the hottest day, for the altitude never drops below about 5,500' above sea level. It is a land of spruce and fir and high-altitude wildflowers.

The Boulevard Trail leaves the Appalachian Trail about 2.7 miles east of Newfound Gap and about 0.2 miles west of the A.T. shelter at Icewater Spring. It travels a rambling route northward on and near the crest of The Boulevard to Mt. Le Conte.

Five or 10 minutes after you start walking, you come to a small marker for the Jumpoff. You have a decision to make: do you take this side trip of approximately 1 mile round-trip? On a clear day, the view from the Jumpoff is good. Look southeast to Charlies Bunion and the Sawteeth and eastward to Mt. Guyot. Look down the great cliff you stand on and follow the valley of Porters Creek to Greenbrier. If you're doing a round-trip hike to Le Conte, you may want to save the Jumpoff for another day. But if it's well before noon and you intend to spend the night on Le Conte, you have plenty of time for the Jumpoff. A word of caution: people unaccustomed to Great Smokies trails may find the path to the Jumpoff rather rough.

Continuing on The Boulevard, you soon will cross a small stream, Walker Camp Prong. A 16-year-old Explorer Scout lost his life down this narrow little valley in February, 1970 during bitterly cold weather. Geoffrey Hague was hiking west on the A.T., toward Newfound Gap, with other Scouts. For some reason, he turned north on the Boulevard Trail while his companions continued on the A.T.. When he reached Walker Prong, he turned down it. Perhaps he intended to follow the stream down to the Newfound Gap Road. This might be a reasonable goal for a healthy 16-year-old in summer. But snow and ice made it impossible for Hague in winter. Searchers found his frozen body a few days later.

Pink turtleheads bloom near the stream in August. One of the most numerous wildflowers along this trail is yellow-flowered *Clintonia*. It blooms in May and June and produces blue berries in July or August. It grows thickly along many sections of the trail.

About 10 minutes after leaving the creek, you'll come to the first overlook from The Boulevard's crest. This one is to the east down into Porters Creek valley. Another 10 minutes will bring another overlook. Among the trees growing near it are pin cherry, American mountain-ash, Fraser fir, red spruce, and yellow birch.

At four or five places along this trail, you will see uprooted red spruces and Fraser firs. Look at the extremely shallow root system and you can understand why it is easy for strong winds to topple the trees.

Among the birdsongs you may hear up here are those of the Winter Wren, Veery, Dark-eyed Junco, American Robin, Chestnut-sided Warbler and Solitary Vireo. You may hear the gruff "cronk" of a Common Raven. If a small gray bird rises from the ground beside the trail and flutters away for a few feet, it's a junco. You usually can find her nest on the ground, partly concealed by overhanging grasses.

The high ridge you'll soon see up ahead and to your left is Anakeesta Knob, the high point of Anakeesta Ridge, which slopes down the west side of The Boulevard to Walker Camp Prong beside the Newfound Gap Road.

By the time you reach the crest of Anakeesta Ridge, just east of the Knob, you'll be ready for a rest. Sit there on a ledge of what's known as the "Anakeesta Formation." It's a bluegray, hard, slate-like rock. You've been walking on such rock since you crossed Walker Prong. It's called Anakeesta Formation, not because it occurs only on Anakeesta Ridge, but because it was here that geologists first defined its characteristics. You will notice rust-colored or yellowish streaks in some of the rock. This is iron pyrite, sometimes called fool's gold.

Lucinda Ogle of Gatlinburg tells a story about her late husband, Earnest, and others who were building the first road up the mountain to Newfound Gap. It was in the 1920s. One afternoon, they came riding their horses down the mountain and they were jubilant. They had discovered gold, they said. And they carried lumps of the ore in sacks on their horses. They had dug or blasted into Anakeesta Formation and found fool's gold.

Anakeesta Formation contains iron sulfide. When excavation (such as road construction) or a landslide exposes it to oxygen and fresh rain water, one of the precipitates of the chemical reaction is weak sulfuric acid. In the 1970s, a landslide on the southwest flank of The Boulevard, in the Huggins Hell area, released so much sulfuric acid into Alum Cave Creek that it lowered the pH of the water to the degree that trout could not live in it. The acid water either killed the trout or drove them down into Walker Camp Prong. It was years before trout returned to the stream in significant numbers.

Look to the northwest from the crest of Anakeesta at landslides on the south slope of Mt. Le Conte. After you walk a few more yards, still more slide areas will come into view.

From Anakeesta's crest, you descend quickly to Alum Gap, at about elevation 5,680', approximately 270' lower than the trail crossing of Anakeesta. Then comes the long, gradual ascent to Le Conte. You occasionally see Myrtle Point looming high ahead of you. Down to your left are the laurel slicks of Huggins Hell and the Alum Cave Bluffs area.

One of the plants you see blooming in middle and late summer along this portion of the trail is filmy angelica. It has fat pale green stems and clusters of white flowers tinged with green. Bumblebees love them. You also will see the yellow flowers of mountain St. John's-wort. You won't see either of these plants in the lowlands.

This trail doesn't take you into the south side of Le Conte, as you might think it would. Rather, it takes you on a curving route around the eastern side of the mountain. You pass under Myrtle Point and then turn west along its northern flank. The mountain is unusually steep here, though the trail grade is not. Landslides are common. Look along this portion of the trail for two uncommon plants, monk's hood and grass-of-Parnassus. Monk's hood has beautiful deep blue flowers atop a plant five or six feet tall. One clump of it grows on the lower side of the trail at a point where the trail takes a sharp left. Grass-of-Parnassus is a low-growing plant whose small white petals are veined with green.

Looking west along the northern slope of Le Conte, you see hundreds of dead trees standing like sticks. They are Fraser firs, killed by non-native balsam woolly adelgids.

You pass the marker for the side trail that leads 0.2 mile to Myrtle Point and move on to High Top (6,593'), marked by a pile of stones to the left of the trail. These were left by Mt. Le Conte boosters who want to make Mt. Le Conte higher than Clingmans Dome (6,643'). To achieve that goal, they must carry lots more rocks. Move downhill from here, down past the trail shelter in the clearing to on your left, then to the intersection with Trillium Gap and Rainbow Falls trails. You are at the end of the Boulevard Trail and there, just below you to the right, is the cluster of buildings that is Le Conte Lodge.

Narrative by Carson Brewer

BRADLEY FORK TRAIL

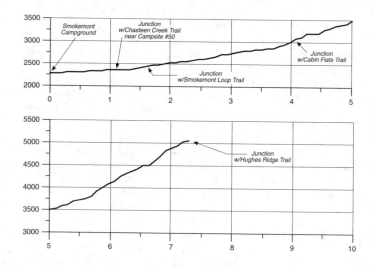

LENGTH: 7.3 miles, from Smokemont Campground to Hughes Ridge Trail.

HIGHLIGHTS: Pretty creeks.

CAUTIONS: Some rocky sections near the top.

MAP KEY: 8 E; USGS quads: Smokemont, Mt. Guyot.

USE: Horse and hiking trail.

TRAILHEAD: Enter Smokemont Campground from Newfound Gap Road. The trail starts at the far end of D Loop.

Bradley Fork Trail is an old road along the Bradley Fork of the Oconaluftee River. For the first 4.0 miles, the trail rises easily along the river; then it rises steeply up the side of Hughes Ridge for 3.3 miles. The lower part is used heavily by horses from Smokemont Riding Stable, but it is firm and well-graded, with a bridge at every creek crossing. It provides access to Hughes Ridge Trail, the Appalachian

Trail at Dry Sluice Gap, Cabin Flats Trail, and others.

The trail starts with Bradley Fork on the left and a high bank with dog-hobble and rosebay rhododendron on the right. As the trail rises, a connector from the horse stable merges from the right. Some hikers and perhaps some horses have made destructive shortcuts between the two trails.

The trail drops back to creek level with a mossy bench on the left and a spur trail to the water. After a brown cinder block pump house on the right, a utility road forks right, and Bradley Fork Trail continues straight into a forest of small trees and lush ferns and mosses. It alternates between open areas with tall weeds and thin forest of flowering dogwood, yellow birch, sycamore, and tuliptree. At 1.0 mile, the trail crosses a side creek on a wooden bridge and then reaches the junction with Chasteen Creek Trail at 1.1 miles. From here it is just 0.1 mile to Campsite #50, one of the easiest backcountry campsites to reach, and 4.0 miles up to Hughes Ridge.

After the trail sign, notice a creek overflow channel on the left. This is one of the many signs that Bradley Fork sometimes carries a lot of water. The trail rises a bit, with a sand bank on the right, and then enters thin woods. About 0.5 farther, it reaches the Smokemont Loop Trail, which provides a strenuous, scenic 3.8 mile route back to Smokemont Campground. The complete loop is 5.4 miles. From a bench on the left of the junction, you can see the log bridge that crosses Bradley Fork to begin the loop trail.

Bradley Fork Trail enters thin woods with ferns, but soon you see larger tuliptrees, sycamores, and yellow birches. Dwarf crested iris, foamflower, geranium, partridgeberry, yellow mandarin, hepatica, buttercup, violet, wood-sorrel, false Solomon's seal, and other spring flowers line the trail. Many small sweetshrub bushes grow here and may produce maroon, fruity-smelling flowers in April. Soon the trail comes to an open view of the fork and then runs along beside it. More wildflowers grow on both sides, but on the left several European weeds such as heal-all and broad-leaved plantain show that this area was settled and cultivated.

After a horse rail on the right, the trail runs between the fork and a rock bank. The next open section has white baneberry, Fraser's sedge, bellwort, and trillium to add to the spring wildflower list and a nice pool with boulders. Scarlet bee-balm blooms here in late summer.

Two sturdy bridges cross Bradley Fork where it splits to form an island. Look for log jams and other evidence of flooding on the island. Now Bradley Fork is on the right, and a moist bank on the left supports several Fraser's sedge plants. Look for their dark green blades all year and their powderpuff flowers in spring.

A long wooden bridge takes you across Bradley Fork again. Taywa Creek cascades in from the right. Bradley Fork is back on the left, and another large creek island shows signs of past flooding. As you continue along the fork, a drainage ditch appears on the right edge of the trail. It supports water striders, tadpoles, tall bee-balm, nettles, jewelweed, brook lettuce, and probably those midges that dive bomb your eyeballs in summer.

After the ditch, there is a stone wall on the right, and at mile **4.1** you come to a traffic loop with a bench, a "No Camping" sign, and a trail sign. Cabin Flats Trail begins here, going straight from the traffic loop. Bradley Fork Trail makes a sharp right turn and starts the climb to Hughes Ridge, 3.3 miles away. In the angle of the turn rests a sheep-sized, egg-shaped piece of quartz.

Bradley Fork Trail doubles back on itself for 100 yards and then swings left and rounds the end of a ridge. You can hear Bradley Fork below, but it is drier on the exposed ridges. The trail enters a creek valley and you can hear the falls and cascades of Taywa Creek hidden under masses of rosebay rhododendron and mountain laurel. Large Eastern hemlocks, tuliptrees, and Fraser magnolias line the trail as it becomes steeper. Soon you can see the creek in a lush ravine with several wind-thrown trees spanning it.

Two wooden bridges take you across the creek. At the second bridge, umbrella leaf, a spring flower related to may-apple, grows on both sides of the trail. At mile **6.0,** the trail becomes steeper, narrower, and rockier as it passes an overgrown traffic loop on the left. It turns left away from the creek and makes a right switchback into a hemlock grove. It then takes you through a boulder field, two more switchbacks, a weedy seep, and plenty of rocky climbing. Look for American chestnut saplings, witch-hobble, and red spruce trees as signs that you are near the top.

At the junction with Hughes Ridge Trail, you are 2.2 miles from the Appalachian Trail and 7.3 miles from Smokemont. If you turn right here, you could take Hughes Ridge Trail 3.0 miles to Chasteen Creek Trail and return to Smokemont in 5.1 more miles.

Narrative by Doris Gove

BRUSHY MOUNTAIN TRAIL

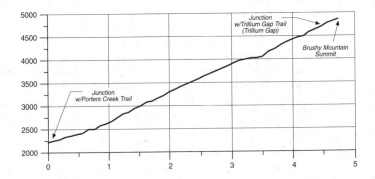

LENGTH: 4.7 miles, from Porters Creek Trail to summit of Brushy Mountain.
HIGHLIGHTS: Views, historic farm site, big trees, beech gap.
CAUTIONS: Small creek crossings, rocky sections.
MAP KEY: 8 C-D, USGS quad: Mt. Le Conte.
USE: Horse and hiking trail.
STARTING POINT: Walk 1.0 mile on the Porters Creek Trail to the start of the Brushy Mountain Trail.

Brushy Mountain Trail goes from Greenbrier Cove up to Brushy Mountain, a heath bald knob on a slope of Mount Le Conte. Heath balds, or laurel slicks, occur on high elevation, exposed areas with thin, acidic soils. The dominant plants are in the heath family: mountain laurel, rosebay rhododendron, sand myrtle, blueberry, and wintergreen. From a distance, this growth looks smooth; hence the name bald. On Brushy Mountain, the heath plants grow taller than most people and look brushy close up, but somehow the name Brushy Bald seems wrong.

At mile 1.0 from the Porters Creek Trail trailhead, Porters Creek Trail slips off to the left and Brushy Mountain Trail starts on the right. At this point there is also a side trail to an historic farm site, which used to be the Smoky Mountain Hiking Club cabin. The three buildings are reconstructed, but represent the community that thrived here until the 1920s. The John Messer barn, built about 1875, is a cantilevered barn, that is, the weight of the upper story is supported by beams extending out from a central box rather than corner posts or walls to the ground. Cantilevered barns are built more like toadstools than like toads, and they were often constructed with long, straight trees of this forest, especially tuliptrees and chestnuts. The Messer barn has four livestock paddocks as the central support, a rock foundation, locust logs at the base, and a shake roof.

Downhill from the barn, a stacked stone spring house straddles a small creek. The trail then rises to the cabin, passing two large umbrella magnolia trees, a patch of cardinal flowers (which bloom red in late summer), and a confused cluster of non-native boxwood. "Uncle Fred" Emert acquired this land from the Cherokees in the early 1800s, and it passed to John Ownby, then to John Whaley, and then to Pinkney Whaley, who cleared it for farming after the Civil War. In the 1890s, the Whaleys sold it to George McFall, who sold it to John Messer, who sold it in 1929 to the park commission. The Smoky Mountain Hiking Club reconstructed the buildings and built a nature trail in 1934. Club members, scout groups, and university classes used the cabin for several decades. The park now maintains the buildings.

The cabin is split-level with two large rooms and lofts and two fireplaces on one chimney. A rock patio near the upper room includes two mill stones. The Hiking Club has given up ownership and use of the cabin, and camping is not allowed there now, though the cabin and barn are open for people to walk through. The trail leading uphill from the patio joins the Brushy Mountain Trail.

To get to the official start of the Brushy Mountain Trail, return by the spring house and barn to the Porters Creek Trail. The trail ascends gently through Porters Flat, and you can see that this may have been excellent farmland once. Look for umbrella magnolias on both sides of the trail. These magnolias have some of the biggest leaves of any park tree, and the leaves have no lobes at the base of the leaf blade. As you proceed up the trail, Fraser magnolias, the ones with lobes, become more common and finally replace umbrella magnolias entirely. The trail drops to cross a small creek where you can find liverworts (they resemble soggy green cornflakes) growing on the rocks. In the woods on both sides of the creek are patches of young Eastern hemlocks all about the same size. Eastern hemlocks were here before the loggers and settlers; these young trees grow more slowly than tuliptrees or maples, but will probably again dominate this part of the forest.

A stone wall runs along the trail with its resident poison ivy vines. After crossing another trickle, you will see a trail to the right that leads down to the cabin. You ascend the valleys of Cannon and Trillium creeks, and then proceed up ridges of Brushy Mountain. The trail crosses a noisy but almost invisible creek and several house sites with chimney piles and foundation rocks. Hepatica, violets, foamflower, toothwort, anemones, wild geraniums, and many other flowers bloom along this trail in March, April, and May.

After the house sites and the end of the stone wall, look for a rock on the right with greenish rock tripe the size of a small Frisbee. Turn a piece of this giant lichen over and feel its black velvet underside.

You can hear Long Branch through the woods to the right, but the trail turns left and ascends. Shortly after the trail becomes rocky near a patch of Eastern hemlock trees, a faint, unmarked trail leads left to the fittified spring marked on the topographical map. When settlers lived here, this spring gushed intermittently, or had fits. Now it gurgles steadily but still produces a lot of water. It is marked by a rock cairn and walls on three sides. The water comes out from under rocks above and disappears under rocks below. It is hard to see the spring from the trail, but there is a large rock pile about 30 yards to the left of the Brushy Mountain Trail that can be seen just before the side trail appears.

The trail ascends steeply through a forest of silverbell, maple, striped maple, locust, and Eastern hemlock. Then it turns left and goes under a messy tangle of Dutchman's pipe vine, grape vine, Virginia creeper, and greenbrier. The main tree in the vine arbor is striped maple, with straight green trunks. At the end of the arbor, a big Fraser magnolia stands in a curve of the trail.

Around the end of a ridge the habitat is drier, and oaks, mountain laurel, large maples, sourwoods, and a few pines line the trail as you continue climbing. In open spots you can see across the valley of Cannon Creek. At the best viewing place, where there are big rocks on the right side of the trail, you can find Table Mountain pine, which distinguishes itself from other pines by growing wicked curved spines on the cone. Aside from the threat of falling cones, this ledge is a great place for lunch.

The trail rises to cross Trillium Branch on slippery moss-covered rocks. Look for a nurse log near the creek with yellow birch, rosebay rhododendron, mosses, and violets growing from the rotting wood. Across the creek is a patch of hobblebush on the left, a sign that you have gained altitude. This shrub grows best above 4,000'. Its white flowers appear in late April and May. In late July, its large heart-shaped leaves start to turn red or orange, and in winter, its light cinnamon velvet buds look warm on the coldest hiking day. Hydrangea, black cohosh, and clubmoss also grow near the creek. The trail then moves up through an old growth forest of giant Eastern hemlocks with a carpet of partridgeberries and an occasional patch of Indian pipe.

After passing an open, weedy area from a tree fall, the trail continues through dark Eastern hemlocks. Look for a boulder on the right with four mature hemlocks perched on it, reaching with their branches toward the light and with their roots back over the edge of the boulder to soil. Striped maple, rosebay rhododendron, and polypody fern have colonized cracks in the same boulder. The trail becomes somewhat rough and rocky with several switchbacks and occasional views of Brushy Mountain and Greenbrier Valley.

Once more the trail crosses Trillium Branch at a fine mossy waterfall. Shortly after the fall, grasses appear in the rocky trail, and the Eastern hemlocks give way to American beeches and a few silverbells. Asters and goldenrod grow among the grass clumps in the fall, and spring beauty carpets this area in the spring. At mile **4.5** you reach

Trillium Gap, a typical beech gap with two dominant plant species: American beech and grass. These two plants are better adapted than most to the constant wind that flows through a gap. At the trail junction stands a beech tree with an unusually large collection of initialed autographs and dates. The tree has also collected a horseshoe and holds it about five feet from the ground; it is a good hook for your pack while you rest.

Trillium Gap Trail goes left to reach Mount Le Conte in 3.6 miles. Straight ahead is the other branch of Trillium Gap Trail to Grotto Falls (1.6 miles), Roaring Fork Motor Nature Trail (2.8 miles), or Cherokee Orchard (5.1 miles).

To reach the top of Brushy Mountain, turn right at Trillium Gap and hike up an eroded, rocky trail that doubles as a stream bed through Eastern hemlock, rosebay rhododendron, and a few red spruce. The trail enters first a rhododendron, then a mountain laurel tunnel. Near the top, galax, wintergreen, and trailing arbutus line the trail, and as it levels out, other heath family plants appear: sand myrtle, blueberry, and huckleberry. Sand myrtle is a knee-high shrub with shiny, leathery evergreen leaves the size of sunflower seeds. It grows almost exclusively on high exposed knobs or ridges and produces tiny sweet-smelling white flowers in April and sometimes again in September.

The trail levels and provides great views for very tall people. But finally, you come to an opening (elevation 4,911') and can see the sharp rise of Mount Le Conte out of Trillium Gap and behind that, the backbone of the Smokies. From the Brushy Mountain heath bald, you can identify other heath balds on exposed ridges.

Narrative by Doris Gove

BULL HEAD TRAIL

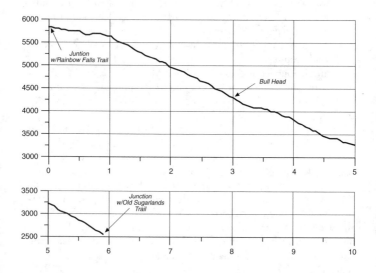

Juntion w/Rainbow Falls Trail

Bull Head

Junction w/Old Sugarlands Trail

LENGTH: 5.9 miles, from Mt. Le Conte summit at the Rainbow Falls Trail intersection to Old Sugarlands Trail.

HIGHLIGHTS: Spring wildflowers and fall colors.

CAUTIONS: Ice in winter.

MAP KEY: 7 C-D; USGS quad: Mt. Le Conte.

USE: Hiking trail.

STARTING POINT: The intersection with Rainbow Falls Trail, just under Mt. Le Conte's West Point. (Many hike up Mt. Le Conte by way of Rainbow Falls and return by the Bull Head Trail. This is why the Bull Head Trail is described here from the top down.)

The first high section of the trail offers good blooms in mid-summer; Turk's cap lily, for instance, along with crimson bee-balm and cutleaf coneflower. This same area in spring provides blooms of trout-lilies and spring-beauties.

If you aren't too busy looking at flowers, look across the valley of Le Conte Creek to the laurel hells and rock formations of Rocky Spur. You did lots of walking on Rocky Spur if you hiked up the Rainbow Falls Trail.

Though this trail meanders considerably, it runs generally westward from Le Conte's crest. As you look at Le Conte's northern profile, West Point is the westernmost peak you see on the crest. But nearly a mile west of West Point is another high peak. This is 5,818-foot Balsam Point. Fortunately for weary hikers, the Bull Head Trail doesn't cross the Balsam Point summit; it zigzags south of it.

After your skirt to the south of Balsam Point, you pass occasional lookout points where you can pause and gaze southward down into the valley of West Prong of the Little Pigeon and on across it to Sugarland Mountain and a portion of the main range of the Great Smokies.

Much of this route down the Bull Head Trail is flanked by heath vegetation. Heath plants in the Great Smokies include rhododendron, mountain laurel, mountain pieris, dog-hobble, flame azalea, trailing arbutus, sand myrtle, pinxter-bush, sourwood, and wintergreen. You will see many of these on this trail. At one point, you walk through a rhododendron tunnel for many yards.

At approximately the midway point of your hike, you come to the Pulpit. The Pulpit is a stone cairn built by men of the Civilian Conservation Corps when they constructed this trail in the 1930s. Nobody told them to do it. Somebody thought it would be a good idea, and enough others agreed to get the job done. They carried stones from far and near. The Pulpit is tall enough for those who stand on it to get a good look northward down into Le Conte Creek Valley. It's wide enough for two or three to sit on. So it's an excellent place to stop for lunch or a snack. For several yards along here, the trail is as nearly level as you find in the Great Smokies.

Growing and blooming along here are such trees and smaller plants as mountain laurel, mountain pieris, mountain pepper-bush, rhododendron, red maple, sourwood, wintergreen, galax, trailing arbutus, Table Mountain pine, and pitch pine. Mountain pieris is an uncommon shrub whose leaves you might mistake for those of mountain laurel. But they are slightly smaller and a little darker green than laurel leaves. The blooms look slightly like dog-hobble blooms. The trees and smaller plants growing here are typical of south-slope vegetation in the park.

Also, in this general area of the trail, you might be lucky enough to find yellow-fringed orchid blooms in August and pink lady's slipper blooms in May. In May, you also may find the blooms of both white and painted trillium.

The trails swings left (south) of the top of the Bull Head peak and then turns northward down the mountain in a series of switchbacks. This is the head of the bull, the profile you see from the north. It's not the head of a common domestic bull but the head of a wild buffalo bull. Some old-timers will show you the whole animal. They say Balsam Point is his shoulders, the crest of Le Conte is the body, and his tail is the Sawteeth (east of Charlies Bunion, on the main ridge of the Great Smokies).

On the north slopes of this route down the face of the bull, you find vegetation quite different from most of that near the Pulpit. Instead of pines and oaks and heath plants, there are trees such as Fraser magnolias, Eastern hemlocks, silverbells, yellow buckeyes, sugar maples, and basswoods. This is a cove hardwood forest. Some of the wildflowers that like such a forest differ from those that grow under the pines and oak. Black cohosh sends up its tall spikes of white blooms. A ropy vine called Dutchman's pipe climbs high in some of the trees. It has large, heart-shaped leaves and hard-to-find blooms that give it its name. Somebody who named it thought the bloom looks like an old Dutchman's crooked-stem pipe.

In two or three places along this section of trail, rock overhangs (they'd be called rock houses in the Cumberland Mountains) would provide storm shelter for a half-dozen or more hikers. Be warned, however, that some sources say you should avoid such rock overhangs during lightning storms. These shelters were formed when weathering caused huge chunks of stone to break out of the Thunderhead sandstone cliff and tumble down the slope. A great tangle of Dutchman's pipe is beside one of these.

The stretch of trail around the rock overhangs is especially good for wildflowers in April. You can count on seeing trilliums, hepatica, many violets, and other vernal friends.

The switchbacking finally ceases and the trail descends northward in a nearly-straight line to an intersection with Old Sugarlands Trail. To reach your car—if you parked at the Rainbow Falls Parking Area at Cherokee Orchard—turn right on the Old Sugarlands Trail and go slightly more than a half-mile to the orchard.

Narrative by Carson Brewer

CABIN FLATS TRAIL

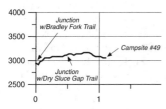

LENGTH: 1.1 miles, from Bradley Fork Trail to Campsite #49.
HIGHLIGHTS: Trestle bridge across Bradley Fork, old-growth forest.
MAP KEY: 8 D; USGS quad: Smokemont.
USE: Horse and hiking trail.

STARTING POINT: From the upper end of Smokemont Campground, hike up Bradley Fork Trail to an old traffic turnaround (4.0 miles). Bradley Fork Trail swings right and Cabin Flats Trail goes straight.

Cabin Flats Trail is a continuation of the gravel road along Bradley Fork. It curves around a rock face and then turns left to cross a rusty trestle bridge with new wood flooring and rails. From the middle of the bridge you can see dark, mossy creek rocks and impressive stone bridge foundations. Across the bridge, the trail turns left and then switches back to a rocky bench that rises above the creek. The angle of the switchback points to a massive tuliptree. People lived and farmed here and did some selective cutting, but this area escaped lumber company clear-cutting. This old-growth forest probably looks like it did when the Cherokees founded towns in this valley. As you continue up this trail, you see more giant tuliptrees and cucumber trees on the left and giant basswoods and yellow buckeyes on the right

nearer the creek. Mossy nurse logs support ferns, rosebay rhododendron and yellow birch saplings.

A log bridge with a handrail crosses a side creek. The large tree on
the left that you can touch from the footbridge is a basswood. After a
short stretch through Eastern hemlocks and rhododendron, you come
to the beginning of Dry Sluice Gap Trail, which climbs to the
Appalachian Trail in 3.8 miles. It goes left; for Cabin Flats, continue
straight.

The trail is level, quiet, and surrounded by giant trees. Jack-in-
the-pulpit, hepatica, violets, and foamflower bloom on the bank in
spring. After a slight rise and a possibly muddy seep, look down at
Bradley Fork to see a flood log jam—hundreds of trees piled and tangled.

Then the trail drops to creek level and turns right to run parallel
to the creek to Campsite #49. One tent site lies to the left and four
more to the right in a wide, flat weedy area. There is a tall pole for
hanging food bags and horse rails and stalls downstream from the last
tent site.

Narrative by Doris Gove

CALDWELL FORK TRAIL

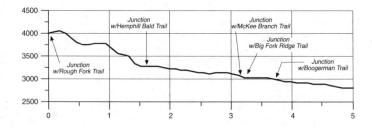

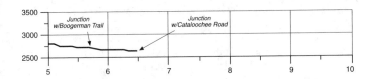

LENGTH: 6.5 miles, from Rough Fork Trail to Cataloochee Road. A reverse route is also possible.

HIGHLIGHTS: Excellent winter hiking trail, scenic stream valley, "Big Poplars."

CAUTIONS: Deep mud, wading.

MAP KEY: 11 E; USGS quads: Dellwood, Cove Creek Gap.

USE: Horse and hiking trail.

POLLS GAP TRAILHEAD: Take Heintooga Ridge Road north from Blue Ridge Parkway to Polls (Paul's) Gap. Follow Rough Fork Trail 3.5 miles to Caldwell Fork Trail.

CATALOOCHEE ROAD TRAILHEAD: From I-40, take exit 20 (NC-276) west to Cove Creek Road. Follow this road north and then west about 7.0 miles toward the Cataloochee Ranger Station. The trailhead lies to the left between Cataloochee Campground and Ranger Station.

Caldwell Fork is named for the second group of permanent settlers to reach the Cataloochee area. In 1841, Levi B. Colwell and his father James Colwell arrived in this valley from Madison County, NC. Eventually, the family began spelling their name "Caldwell," but it is still generally pronounced "Ca'well." Eldridge Caldwell, a grandson, described the primitive condition of his forebears' lives: "When they came in there, they just brought their rifle and their ax and their pot to cook in. So they practically lived on wild meat and fish."

Since Caldwell Fork Trail is both a hiking and horse trail, you should be prepared for deep mud in places. The most interesting way to experience this trail is to start it at its junction with the Rough Fork Trail, a direction that follows Caldwell Fork downstream, the ideal way to appreciate Caldwell Fork Valley's considerable natural beauty. Whatever route you select, you will have to arrange for transport back to your car unless you walk this trail as part of a 12-mile loop.

From its junction with Rough Fork Trail, Caldwell Fork Trail gradually descends into Caldwell Fork Valley through a beautiful forest of American beech, red maple, pignut hickory, American basswood, white oak, as well as many Eastern hemlocks. Since the latter species was the least commercially desirable tree, it is not surprising that individual Eastern hemlocks are often the biggest trees in second-growth forests. Loggers often left that species standing. Mountain people, though, did not overlook the Eastern hemlock and used its bark to obtain tannin for the tanning of leather and its branches for brooms.

Fortunately, giants of other species still exist in this valley. Pre-park loggers did not harvest all the larger hickories, oaks, and basswoods, as you will soon see. While the trail descends further into the valley, more undergrowth appears. At points, the trail becomes deeply and broadly furrowed, creating a muddy mess that many hikers avoid by stepping up on the bank. Unfortunately, this practice tends to further damage the flora beside the trail and erode its banks. After passing a small grove of virgin Eastern hemlock, you see the trail's first rosebay rhododendron and Fraser magnolia. Red-eyed Vireos nest in the trees above. To the right, looking like a dirty patch of snow, is a quartz outcrop, partially covered with moss.

Soon the trail passes old fence posts and a grassy area, reminding you of former human habitation. You move through a maple/hickory/tuliptree forest with an understory of striped maple and witch-hazel. Soon you'll notice, off to the left, some huge, centuries-old tuliptrees ("Big Poplars"). In summer months, the bases of these trees are muddy from horse traffic. Near here, in 1972, park ranger Bud Rice saw a mountain lion. Whether this reclusive mammal still lives in the park is not known, but the large deer populations in Cataloochee could support these cats.

Rejoining the main trail, you enter a thicket of mountain laurel and rosebay rhododendron (known locally as a "slick") and pass sweet birch, Eastern hemlock, and American beech as you near Caldwell Fork. On the right, next to the creek, is Campsite #41 and a hitching post for horses. A sign at the site reminds campers of the park's fishing regulations. These regulations are vital to maintaining healthy populations of fish because over fishing and habitat destruction nearly caused the disappearance of the only native fish, the brook trout. A pre-park resident of this valley, "Blind" Sam Sutton, remembered the large numbers of fish caught during the 1920s by vacationing fishermen. Sutton claimed that local people "wouldn't take off from work long enough to fish," but that "incomers" might "catch 'em by the hundreds."

Since the fork here is swift and wide, you cross by foot bridge then pass near young, dying white pines—evidence of the damage caused by the native Southern pine beetle. At **1.7** miles, the trail meets Hemphill Bald Trail. In the open area by the junction sign are wildflowers that flourish in disturbed soil—barren strawberry, hawkweed, wild strawberry, daisy, and red clover. Continuing on Caldwell Fork Trail, you cross Double Gap Branch on foot, then walk among white pines, red maple, and Eastern hemlock. Soon the trail leads downhill through thick rosebay rhododendron and runs alongside Caldwell Fork. A huge yellow buckeye grows on the right, identifiable by its scaly bark. Quite common in the Smokies, this tree possesses poisonous seeds and shoots which killed pioneer livestock. The Cherokee knew the seeds could be eaten if the poison were leached out and cooked away.

At one point, the creek below forms a scenic water slide, then snakes away behind rosebay rhododendron and mountain laurel. The trail here is level, its bank covered with wintergreen and galax. After moving through a cove hardwood forest, you enter a moist heath slick. Christmas ferns and Jacks-in-the-pulpit are some of the species capable of growing in such dense shade. The mellifluous song of the Winter Wren can sometimes be heard here. Further down the trail, common wood sorrel grows on a number of rotting logs.

Soon you cross 5'-wide Clontz Branch without benefit of a foot bridge. On this creek, a pre-park resident, Jim Evans, owned a house and blacksmith shop. According to old-timers, three Union soldiers are buried nearby. Two of them, Elzie Caldwell and Levi Shelton, are in one grave. They were killed April 1, 1865, by the notorious federal raider, Col. George Kirk, a Confederate deserter who was given a Union commission and headed a mountain guerrilla force out of eastern Tennessee. He and his 400 cavalry and 200 foot soldiers plundered Cataloochee and then advanced down Jonathan Creek into Waynesville, where they were finally driven back into Tennessee by a local confederate unit via Soco Gap. A small loop trail to the right leads to their graves.

At approximately **3.2** miles, you reach the junction with McKee Branch Trail, which ends at Purchase Gap and Cataloochee Divide Trail if you go right and 2.3 miles up. Approximately 150 yards later, a second junction, with the Big Fork Ridge Trail, appears. Persevering along Caldwell Fork Trail, you immediately cross McKee Branch on a footbridge.

Where McKee Branch flows into Caldwell Fork, Caldwell Fork School once stood, one of the three community schools in Cataloochee Valley; Big Cataloochee and Little Cataloochee also had their own schools. While children usually only attended school for five months from 8:30 to 3:30 because they helped with harvests, on Friday evenings, Caldwell Fork residents gathered to hear children recite poems and speeches. Another community building, a grist mill, once stood below Rabbit Ridge just across from where McKee Branch flows into Caldwell Fork.

At **3.7** miles you reach the first of two junctions with Boogerman Trail and simultaneously embark on a 2.0-mile portion of the hike memorable for its dozen stream crossings. Most of these are via foot bridges or logs; you will wade only twice through shallow feeder creeks. Good boots and foot placement will keep you dry. While all but the first of these crossings are over Caldwell Fork or its feeder creeks, the initial footbridge (broken in two at the time of this writing) spans Snake Branch, a creek beside which Sam Sanford once ran a farm outfitted with cabin, barn, smokehouse, shed, furnace, and springhouse.

The trail itself laces through rosebay rhododendron and mountain laurel beneath Eastern hemlock and yellow birch. The trail soon remains the only opening in unbroken forest, rendering its banks choice locations for new growth. They teem with young trees competing for sunlight. The view varies; sometimes the mature forest is obscured by dense rosebay rhododendron and dog-hobble. Two other note-worthy features: 1) a large Fraser magnolia clump consisting of one main trunk and roughly 50 shoots all stemming from the same root system, and 2) further along, a deep pool framed by a rock shelf and overhanging bushes—good trout habitat. The segment ends at **5.7** miles when it intersects once more with Boogerman Trail; look for the small waterfall in Caldwell Fork near this juncture.

After following Caldwell Fork for 0.5 mile, you veer away from it and enter a grove of white pines. Many have died and fallen, providing shelter and food for abundant wildlife. Poison ivy, Virginia creeper, ebony spleenwort, Christmas fern, and striped pipsissewa grow in the pines' shade, but you soon reach a clearing to the left and proceed through a hardwood forest. After passing under more white pines, you cross Cataloochee Creek on one last, long foot bridge over 25' in length and reputedly the park's longest log bridge. You reach Cataloochee Road at **6.5** miles and find the campground to the right.

Narrative by Ted Olson

CAMEL GAP TRAIL

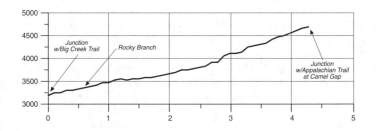

LENGTH: 4.3 miles, from Big Creek Trail to Appalachian Trail at Camel Gap.
HIGHLIGHTS: Pleasant forest scenes, scenic stream vistas.
MAP KEY: 10 C; USGS quad: Luftee Knob.
USE: Horse and hiking trail.
STARTING POINT: 5.9 miles up Big Creek Trail, past Walnut Bottom.

The Camel Gap Trail, formerly called the Yellow Creek Trail, begins at the junction with Big Creek Trail 0.2 mile east of Gunter Fork Trail. Eventually, the trail narrows and continues a short distance to a junction which is the common beginning of the Camel Gap and Gunter Fork Trails. These trails are well marked by signs and easy to locate. Signs warn the hiker planning to climb Gunter Fork to avoid this trail during high water in favor of the Swallow Fork Trail due to potentially dangerous crossings. The Gunter Fork Trail leads left 4.1 miles to the crest of Balsam Mountain and the Balsam Mountain Trail. The Camel Gap Trail continues straight ahead 4.2 miles to the Appalachian Trail at Camel Gap.

The Big Creek watershed was logged extensively early in the century with much of the timber being removed by the Crestmont Lumber Company between 1909 and 1918. Subsequently, a network of logging railroad grades was extended throughout the area, particularly on Swallow Fork, Gunter Fork and upper Big Creek. In fact, the Camel Gap Trail follows one of these logging grades to the very crest of the Smokies at Camel Gap. Imagine the sound of a steam locomotive slowly descending to the band mill at Crestmont, leading cars loaded with virgin timber, its shrill whistle echoing as it approaches.

The Camel Gap Trail climbs steadily along Big Creek and makes only one switchback before making a final ascent to Camel Gap and the Appalachian Trail at 4,694'. Because the trail follows an old logging grade, it is well engineered and offers a pleasant, gradual climb. Depending on the season, the trail offers the fresh green of spring foliage and a variety of spring wildflowers, the mature green of summer or the pastels of autumn when the forest is arrayed with gold, crimson, red and yellow. Regardless of the season, the trail provides magnificent stream vistas and a variety of forest scenes.

The trail ascends gently with good footing except where horse use has created muddy areas. Rocky Branch, fed by the spring at the Cosby Knob Shelter, is easily crossed at 0.6 mile. Beyond, the trail parallels the creek, sometimes at a distance and sometimes immediately beside it. There are several places beside Big Creek where the hiker can pause and admire the stream's beauty. The stream tumbles over solid stone in places, washes around large boulders, and flows in pleasant runs and pools. The stones which form the stream's bed seem scrubbed and clean giving the water an unusually clear, pristine appearance. With patient observation, trout may be seen feeding in pools.

The cove hardwood forest through which the trail passes nurtures a rich variety of trees, including yellow buckeye, yellow birch, American beech, maple, white basswood, and Eastern hemlock. Dutchman's-pipe may also be observed here. This woody vine, with leaves like valentine hearts, sometimes reaches 100' into large forest trees and may have a diameter of 4".

At **3.2** miles the trail begins a gentle switchback to the right to ascend away from the stream. Near this point, Yellow Creek joins Big Creek in a beautiful cove with an understory of rhododendron. Yellow Creek was closed to fishing in 1975 to protect its brook trout. However, in earlier times this stream was fished by mountaineers of the Cosby, TN area who favored the stream because of its abundance of trout. After crops were laid by in the summer, these men would cross the mountain and camp for weeks, consuming fried trout by the hundreds.

The trail ascends more steeply above the switchback and enters a northern hardwood forest. A fine stand of maple and Fraser magnolia will be noted along this segment. The large creamy white flowers of the Fraser magnolia appear in April or early May, before the tree's foliage is apparent. Its cucumber-like fruit is pinkish-red and may be found along the trail in August and September. Although the slopes are well forested, Balsam Mountain may be viewed from two limited vistas. Areas of thick catawba rhododendron can be seen on the crests of distant ridge slopes. These places called "laurel slicks" or "laurel hells" will appear pink when the rhododendron blooms in June.

Signs of early logging grades can be observed near the trail along its upper reaches. These spur lines allowed timber to be transported from rich stands on distant slopes to the main rail grade for transport to the mill at Crestmont. One of these spur lines extended approximately 5 miles around the headwaters of Yellow Creek, Deer Creek and Big Creek to the slopes of Mount Guyot. The old grades symbolize the hard work associated with the logging era, not to mention the inherent danger.

At **4.3** miles the trail reaches the Appalachian Trail at Camel Gap. The Snake Den Ridge Trail is 2.3 miles to the left, Low Gap is 2.4 miles to the right (west), and Cosby Knob Shelter is 1.6 miles to the right.

Narrative by William A. Hart, Jr.

CANE CREEK TRAIL

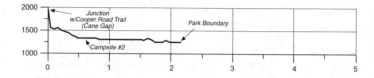

LENGTH: 2.1 miles, from Cooper Road Trail at Cane Gap to park boundary.
HIGHLIGHTS: Easy walking, cemetery.
MAP KEY: 2 D; USGS quad: Blockhouse.
USE: Horse and hiking trail.
STARTING POINT: Cane Gap, at jct. with Cooper Road Trail, 3.7 miles above Abrams Creek Ranger Station.

At Cane Gap, the Cooper Road Trail turns sharply right and the Cane Creek Trail goes ahead, slightly to the left. It is in good condition and soon drops into the Cane Creek bottoms (bottoms being lowlands along streams). In wet weather, the road is mushy and the crossings of Cane Creek may require wading. Usually, however, the crossings are easily made.

The old fields are in the second stage of reforestation, consisting mainly of Eastern hemlock and mixed hardwoods. A few Virginia pines from the first stage of reforestation remain standing or lie decaying on the forest floor.

At **0.6** miles, campsite #2 (Cane Creek) sits in a young hemlock forest, an open, restful location quite near the soothing murmur of

Cane Creek. The site receives only light use.

At **1.5** miles, the Buchanan cemetery sits on a rise under the canopy of two large maples. In 1885, the Buchanans began farming this 1,300 acre tract according to a *Maryville-Alcoa Times* article in July, 1978. However, the accessibility and fertility would indicate that it was settled and farmed earlier. In late June and early July you may see an uncommon shrub, mountain stewartia, blooming at the far edge of the woods around the cemetery.

The Buchanans grew most of what they needed on the land, with the principal crop being corn. Potatoes, beans, tomatoes, and most vegetables fared well in this and other coves in the Smokies.

It's an easy lowland walk through old farm fields reclaimed by cove hardwoods. Past the cemetery, the road use diminishes and the path narrows until reaching the park boundary at **2.1** miles, where it joins the land of Mountain Homes, Inc., private property.

The geology of this small valley is of Hesse and Nebo Quartzite, metamorphic rocks composed of the sedimentation and recrystallization of quartz sand. The Millers Cove Fault line runs through Cane Creek, but its path is not evident by change in vegetation or outcrops.

Notable mushrooms along this bountiful trail include *Lactarius indigo, Dentinum repandum, Lycoperdon pyriforme,* and *Sparassis crispa. Narrative by Woody Brineagar*

CATALOOCHEE DIVIDE TRAIL

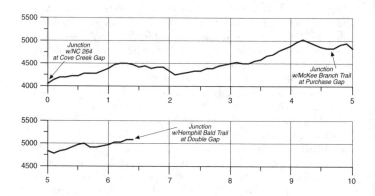

LENGTH: 6.4 miles, From Cove Creek Gap to Double Gap on Hemphill Bald.

HIGHLIGHTS: Spring wildflowers, good views.

CAUTIONS: Blackberry brambles in late summer, muddy patches.

MAP KEY: 11 D-E; USGS quads: Dellwood and Cove Creek Gap.

USE: Horse and hiking trail.

TRAILHEAD: I-40 to NC-276, exit 20, drive west to Cove Creek Road. Turn north on Cove Creek Road (also Old NC-284) and drive approximately 3.0 miles to Cove Creek Gap.

Cataloochee Divide Trail follows the crest of the Cataloochee Divide, whose ridge is also the park boundary. Consequently, the trail offers equally impressive views westward into the park and eastward toward the settled, agricultural areas adjacent to the park. The name "Cataloochee," derived from the Cherokee word "Gadalutsi," means "fringe standing erect" (referring to the trees on the spine of a ridge).

The trail begins by climbing through a grove of white pine, then through a mixed second-growth forest comprised of pignut hickory, black locust, striped maple, and black oak. It briefly heads downhill through mountain laurel and rosebay rhododendron, levels, and climbs through more second-growth forest. After passing near a large rock outcrop, the trail flattens along the boundary fence line. On the right is a large Northern red oak. A hardy species that thrives on the cool middle-elevation slopes of the Smokies, the Northern red oak was much prized by loggers, who wanted to turn the species into everything from furniture to fence posts. If not for the establishment of the park, this lovely oak would certainly have been logged.

At approximately **1.0** mile, the trail climbs. Below to the right is a lush cove, a good spot to look for black bear since the cove provides both food and shelter. Wading through waist-high colonies of white snakeroot, spotted touch-me-not, and false nettle, you continue climbing the narrowing ridge into an oak-maple forest. To the right, at one break in the trees, is a good view of Cataloochee Valley. Soon, on level ground, you enter a scrubby, grassy stretch where a variety of plants grow on the trail's banks—bracken fern beside flame azalea, whorled loosestrife beside Indian pipe and squawroot.

After a cow pasture, you pass huge American chestnut trunks (killed by the chestnut blight) that have fallen onto the fence; because it abuts unused land, the damaged fence has not been repaired. The trail continues along the fence line, passing wildflowers such as rue-anemone, white snakeroot, wild geranium, spiderwort, and goat's beard. Then, moving through a glade of rosebay rhododendron, the trail climbs through mixed second-growth oak/maple forest, with many dead chestnut trunks off to the right. You increasingly encounter smooth blackberry brambles, which hamper easy passage in late summer—long pants are necessary here.

At approximately **2.0** miles, a clearing appears on the left; it overlooks Cove Creek Valley, the Suttontown community, and U.S. Interstate 40. From there, skirting the edge of an old field, you pass a varied stand of trees (including black locust, American basswood, and black cherry) on the left, and then climb uphill through lush mixed second-growth woodland. Young mockernut hickories grow nearby. The trail heads slightly downhill and levels, rejoining the fence line, and a dirt road appears on the other side of the fence. This spot is Panther Spring Gap, named by early Cataloochee Valley settlers because of a local tale about a young girl being dragged away, screaming, by a panther. Although the panther (also called mountain lion and catamount) has long been considered extinct in the Eastern U.S. (excluding Florida, where the Florida panther is currently endangered), many unconfirmed panther sightings in the Smokies suggest otherwise. Whether these people have seen escaped zoo animals, released pets, or authentic wild panthers remains uncertain; but wildlife specialists think that the park could support a healthy population. Several of the alleged panther sightings occurred in the Cataloochee Valley, which certainly would be a likely place because the region is isolated and supports a large population of white-tailed deer.

Climbing uphill, you pass a huge white oak on the left then enter a mixed second-growth woodland comprised of red and striped maple, yellow birch, and American basswood. After coursing through a thicket of rosebay rhododendron and flame azalea, the trail rejoins the fence line and levels. Nearby, on the right, stands a huge, hollow yellow buckeye trunk, still putting out leaves. The trail swings left, meandering slightly uphill through lush woods around the upper edge of a cove. In this section, flowering dogwoods suffer from dogwood anthracnose, the recently discovered fungal blight threatening to destroy the park's dogwood population.

The trail returns to the park's boundary near mile 3.0, skirting a large shale outcrop. Now level, the trail follows the fence line along the edge of a large field—obviously not used as cattle pasture since common milkweed, daisy-fleabane, and fire pink abound. Entering a stand of Eastern hemlocks, the trail moves steeply downhill, providing, to the right, a good view of Cataloochee Valley. Soon you climb uphill through mountain laurel and enter another oak/maple forest. An old logging road appears on the left just past the fence.

At approximately 4.0 miles, the trail weaves in between three large yellow birches, one of which possesses big burls. Still climbing, the trail becomes clogged with false nettles; other spring wildflowers include spiderwort, fly poison, sundrops, wood betony, bluebead lily, and false Solomon's seal. At 4.6 miles (at Purchase Gap) the trail meets the McKee Branch Trail (a 2.3 mile walk to Caldwell Fork Trail). The Cataloochee Divide Trail continues slightly uphill along the park boundary fence line, then enters another oak/maple forest, with an understory of Juneberry (serviceberry) and young Eastern hemlock.

At approximately **5.0** miles, a stand of rosebay rhododendron forms a tunnel over the trail; then, just past a stand of Eastern hemlock, the trail suddenly becomes quite rocky, taxing the ankles. After entering a forest of yellow birch, red maple, yellow buckeye, and Eastern hemlock, the trail climbs on the right of a split-rail fence line (built by the Civilian Conservation Corps in the 1930s), then levels. This stretch of the trail offers good views to the left of Hemphill Creek Valley. Heading uphill, the trail soon passes The Swag, a private resort just off the park's boundary. Here, orange jewelweed and white snakeroot carpet the forest floor. Next, you walk downhill among rosebay rhododendron, Eastern hemlock, American basswood, and various oaks, then uphill among black locust and black cherry and more rhododendron. This section is eroded and muddy.

The trail rejoins the split-rail fence near mile **6.0**, and heads uphill. Dark-eyed Juncos and Blue Jays abound. Meandering downhill, you pass a cow pasture on the other side of the fence, then, at 6.4 miles, reach Hemphill Bald Trail at Double Gap.

Narrative by Ted Olson

CHASTEEN CREEK TRAIL

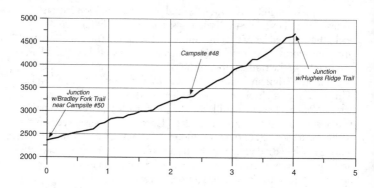

LENGTH: 4.0 miles, from Bradley Fork Trail to Hughes Ridge Trail.
HIGHLIGHTS: Waterfall, stream scenes.
CAUTIONS: Mud, steep and narrow trail.
MAP KEY: 8-9 D-E; USGS quad: Smokemont.
USE: Horse and hiking trail.
STARTING POINT: Hike Bradley Fork Trail 1.1 miles from Smokemont Campground.

Like many of the trails in the Smokemont region, this one has a dual nature: one end is relatively flat and wide on an old roadbed, and the other is steep and narrow as it climbs to Hughes Ridge. Chasteen Creek Trail's uniqueness derives from the depth and beauty of the creek valley through which it winds. The creek's course through fractured rock has resulted in a canyon with steep sides and a rushing, rock-filled waterway, providing lots of noise, white water, and cataracts.

Veering right from the junction with Bradley Fork Trail, you come immediately upon Campsite #50 (Lower Chasteen Creek, 2,360'), which is grassy and bounded by the creek and two trails. At this point the river is wider and slower than it will be further upstream. The first 1.0 mile of the trail presents a challenge to hikers since there is usually lots of mud. Occasionally the muddy stretches will be so long that avoiding it will be impossible. As the trail climbs, the mud problem ends.

At **1.2** miles a muddy and heavily used side trail veers left down to the creek and a hitching post for horses. A couple hundred feet beyond that, you'll see an impressive view of the creek and a particularly beautiful stretch of white water. As you return, please stay on the maintained trail, despite the temptation to avoid the mud and walk through the woods. Skirting the trail causes erosion, as you can tell by the handful of eroded gullies leading up the slope.

The trail steepens as it continues upstream, and trail wear from horse traffic drops markedly. For the next 1.5 mile, the trail plays tag with the creek. Sometimes it veers far from the water and the noise diminishes to a distant whisper. Other times it closes back to the creek, offering impressive views and noise. Photographers should be prepared for many photo opportunities, including the waterfall located on a small tributary which crosses under the roadbed on its way to the creek.

This lower section of the trail passes under some large trees. While none of them are old-growth, some of the Eastern hemlocks and tuliptrees have attained sufficient size to provide an open understory through which creek views are possible.

The roadbed ends at **2.3** miles. Not far beyond that point, you reach Campsite #48 (Upper Chasteen, 3,320'), a particularly attractive one situated between two creeks and under a dense stand of Eastern hemlocks. The ground is well drained and usually free of rocks and roots.

Above the campsite, you begin an arduous climb to Hughes Ridge. The trail is steep, rocky, and narrow as it switches back regularly. There are occasional open views of the surrounding ridges as the canopy thins along some of the drier sections. If you turn right at the trail junction with Hughes Ridge Trail, you descend 7.4 miles back to Smokemont; a left turn leads 4.7 miles to Pecks Corner on the Appalachian Trail.

Narrative by Bill Beard

CHESTNUT BRANCH TRAIL

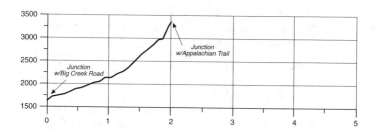

LENGTH: 2.0 miles, from Big Creek Road to Appalachian Trail.
HIGHLIGHTS: Old home sites, pleasant second growth forest.
MAP KEY: 11 B; USGS quads: Waterville, Hartford.
USE: Hiking trail.
TRAILHEAD: Big Creek Ranger Station.

The Chestnut Branch Trail is located approximately 150' from the large parking area at the Big Creek Ranger Station along the road to the Big Creek trailhead. A sign immediately before a bridge crossing Chestnut Branch marks the trail's beginning and indicates the Appalachian Trail is 2.0 miles and Mount Cammerer is 5.9 miles. The trail has generally good footing although several miry places and crossings of small streams make it occasionally soggy.

Chestnut Branch was once an old logging road used by many lumber companies that have cut timber in the area since the late 1890s. In the early 1930s, a trail described as a "fair class B trail" ascended a portion of the present route 4.7 miles to White Rock, now known as Mount Cammerer. Mrs. Zelphie Sutton, a member of one of the last two families to live on the branch, recalled that White Rock was known as "Old Mother." This name was locally applied to Chestnut Branch as well.

In terms of settlement along Chestnut Branch, Mrs. Sutton indicated there were about nine families living on the branch prior to park establishment. Near the bottom was the George Philips cabin.

Further up was the John Heilman place and the Hardy Sutton cabin and three outbuildings. Nearby was the Rufus Lindsey place, which consisted of a house, apple and chicken houses, a barn and a shed. Dee Leatherwood and Crow Hopkins also had houses along the Chestnut Branch Trail.

Life on a mountain farm was comprised of hard work. Mrs. Sutton's description of her labors is quoted by Joeseph Hall. "I've sawed a many, many hard day with my brother. I grubbed, split rails, and built fence."

The forest has now reclaimed the land and largely concealed the most obvious evidence of settlement on Chestnut Branch. However, signs of the past still remain and part of the enjoyment in walking this trail is identifying these vestiges. Rock walls, escaped English ivy, old fence posts, metal artifacts and even-age tuliptrees in old fields are ample evidence of former occupation. Also, the trail provides a convenient route to Mount Cammerer with its unique stone fire tower. A vista near the Mount Cammerer Trail provides an excellent view of the valley through which Chestnut Branch flows.

The trail ascends steadily at first through a hemlock forest. Occasional patches of partridgeberry, identified by its small round leaves and red berry, form a thick ground cover. Also, ground cedar will be noted near the trail. It extends on runners and is sometimes called "turkey's foot" by mountaineers.

After climbing steeply for 0.1 mile, the grade becomes more gradual for the next 0.7 mile. English ivy, escaped from an old homesite, borders the trail at one point. Chestnut fence posts and rock walls attest to early labors here. At 0.3 mile, the trail reaches a former clearing now grown up in tuliptrees. Note metal items such as old wash tubs at some of the home sites. The wash tub is probably one of the most common artifacts found at abandoned homesites throughout the Smokies. Such artifacts are completely protected by federal law. Do not disturb or remove.

At 1.1 miles the trail parallels the stream just past a homesite. Here a small, two-level cascade flows over mossy stones framed in rich rhododendron growth.

The trail becomes steeper and bears sharply right to ascend the ridge. A second switchback allows a more gentle ascent through a closed oak forest which presents a beautiful array of colors in autumn. Wintergreen, with its shiny green leaves, and trailing arbutus grow beside the trail here. Wintergreen was an old-time remedy, used as a diuretic. The trail approaches a tributary of Chestnut Branch and passes through heavy rhododendron growth in a narrow crease in the mountain folds. Four crossings of this tributary are made in a relatively short distance, followed by a short walk in the drainage itself, before leaving the stream.

At about **1.7** miles the trail passes through a tuliptree cove, once cleared for agriculture, and climbs steeply to the Appalachian Trail at **2.0** miles. Davenport Gap is 1.9 miles to the right (east), the Lower Mount Cammerer Trail is 1.0 mile left, and the Mount Cammerer Trail leading 0.6 mile to the fire tower is reached at 3.3 miles.

Narrative by William A. Hart, Jr.

CHESTNUT TOP TRAIL

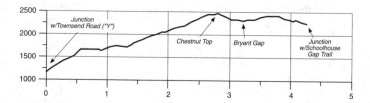

LENGTH: 4.3 miles, from Townsend "Y" to Schoolhouse Gap Trail.
HIGHLIGHTS: Spring wildflowers, winter views.
CAUTIONS: Poison ivy, no water along entire length.
MAP KEY: 4 D; USGS quad: Wear Cove.
USE: Hiking trail.
TRAILHEAD: Townsend "Y" (intersection Little River Road and Townsend entrance road).

Spring-beauty! Bloodroot, hepatica, trillium, toothwort, yellow-fringed orchid; these are words that you will be constantly repeating to yourself if you hike this trail in April. Chestnut Top is perhaps the most spectacular wildflower trail in the park. At least it's the most compact, for the greatest display is all within the first half mile. The trail bursts forth wildflowers throughout April and continues to a lesser degree right to September. There's just not enough room here to describe the variety. In one trip, I counted 36 species in bloom along the trail. There's no telling how many you could count.

But even after the fire pinks fade from view and the crested dwarf irises go to seed, keep walking this trail. It's a joyous walk whenever you can get to it. The trail winds up and along Chestnut Top Lead (lead is a local term for ridge) jumping back and forth from dry piney slopes to cooler mixed hardwoods. A fall or winter hike will offer excellent views across Turkey Pen Ridge and up the valley of the West Prong of the Little River to Thunderhead Mountain.

The trail starts at the Townsend "Y", a popular summer swimming hole and tubing spot. Although there are many parking places here, finding one can be difficult on a summer weekend. The path begins across the road from the "Y". It climbs steadily along a northeast facing slope. Try not to get too enthralled by the wildflowers and forget to watch the trail. There is a steep drop to the right—be careful here.

By summer the wildflower bonanza has faded and given way to the most feared plant in the park—poison ivy. Fear not, however, after 0.5 mile the trail turns onto a south facing slope, dries out and loses the ivy. Now you'll be walking through pines and chestnut oaks. No, the trail's name is not from these trees, but from the American chestnut, which once grew along these slopes. In fact, the oak gets its name from the chestnut, too. Although shorter and rounded, the oak's leaves somewhat resemble those of the American chestnut's.

The mighty American chestnut is no longer found here. It has been lost—lost to a disease from China. In the early 1900s, Chinese chestnuts were brought into New York City as ornamentals. With these trees came a fungus—*Endothia parasitica*—the cause of the chestnut blight.

Early settlers used the chestnut extensively. It provided food and money. The nuts could be harvested as they fell, sacked up and shipped off to Knoxville and other cities. The earnings from this crop were often called "shoe money," because it was usually used to purchase the children's shoes before the coming winter. Hogs could also be fattened on these protein and fat rich nuts. So too could people, as I'm sure many were.

Today, root sprouts keep the tree from extinction, giving hope to park managers and chestnut lovers alike. Resistance and revival might eventually come, but for now, as the tree matures the fungus attacks. Watch along the trail, you just might spot a young sapling struggling to keep the species alive.

The trail winds and climbs along the ridge, finally leaving the sounds of the Townsend "Y" and its summer traffic behind at **1.0** mile. Long, easy switchbacks continue for the next mile, taking you deeper into the hardwood forests. As you approach a sharp right bend at mile **2.0,** keep an eye on the pines to the left. Here you will see a bear "marker tree". This pine has been scratched and bitten by a large black bear. Nobody really knows why bears do this, but some think it involves marking territory. It may say to other bears, "I'm this big. I can mark this high. If you can't, you'd better stay out." This is only a warning to other bears, so you have nothing to fear as you enter his territory. If you do encounter a bear along the trail, do as my wife does — sneeze. Her sneeze once scared a young bear so much that he nearly ran into a tree as he tore off down the hillside.

Just up ahead you'll get a good view of Thunderhead Mountain and the Smokies crest. At 5,527', Thunderhead is the tallest peak in the western end of the park. The views will come and go now as the forest opens and closes.

Steadily climbing still at a 5% grade, you will reach the highest point by mile **2.8.** Now a short drop will put you at Bryant Gap. The Park boundary is just off the trail to the right. Views along this section go both ways. To the left is the park and the Smokies crest. To the right is Tuckaleechee Cove and Townsend.

The trail levels out for the next mile until its junction with Schoolhouse Gap Trail. Turning left here will take you 2 miles down to Laurel Creek Road, which runs between Cades Cove and the Townsend "Y". A right turn will bring you quickly to the park boundary at the southeast end of Dry Valley. Or, you just might wish to turn around and enjoy the quiet and beautiful 4.3 mile walk back to your car at the Townsend "Y".

Narrative by Tom Condon

CHIMNEY TOPS TRAIL

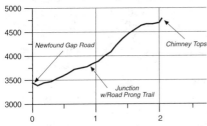

LENGTH: 2.0 miles, from Newfound Gap Road to the Chimney Tops.
HIGHLIGHTS: View from the top, big trees.
CAUTIONS: Steep trail, ice in winter, pinnacles at the top.

MAP KEY: 7 D; USGS quad: Mt. Le Conte.
ELEVATION CHANGE: 1,300'
USE: Hiking trail.
TRAILHEAD: Drive 6.7 miles south from Sugarlands Visitor Center on Newfound Gap Road (or 22 miles north from Oconaluftee Visitor Center). Look for a large parking area on the west side of the road between the lower tunnel and "the loop".

The Chimney Tops Trail is one of the most popular in the park because of its length and spectacular view, but it is a steady uphill hike and could be hazardous at the top. If there are several buses in the parking lot, you might want to choose another hike and do the Chimneys later.

This watershed was not as heavily logged as the Little River drainage just to the west over Sugarland Mountain, because of extensive private ownership and because land controlled by Champion Fibre Company was condemned for park purchase just in time to save its old-growth forest. Mary Brackin was born just below the Chimney Tops in 1889 and married Marshall Whaley at age 16. Throughout their marriage, she "put as much meat on the table as he did. I'd go up one hollow with a rifle and he'd go up another, and I'd come back with as many squirrels as he would."

From the parking area, hike down through Eastern hemlocks and listen as water noise replaces traffic. At the first bridge, across Walker

Camp Prong of Little Pigeon River, you see huge smooth boulders and a deep green pool downstream. At the other end of the bridge, on the right, is a Fraser magnolia with eight trunks. Look for its large lobed leaves. These deciduous magnolias, common up to 5,000', produce creamy white, pie-sized flowers in late April or early May and live only in the southern Appalachians.

The trail rises and crosses Road Prong, which joins Walker Camp Prong to form West Prong of the Little Pigeon River. The bridges are new and sturdy with three rails. Many spring wildflowers grow along the side, including trillium and hepatica. Later in summer, you will see bee-balm, jewelweed and Joe-Pye-weed. After the fourth bridge, about 0.9 mile from the trailhead, you pass the junction with the Road Prong Trail. Continuing right, the Chimney Tops Trail leaves the Road Prong behind, and, after a switchback, starts up a small creek valley. As the trail steepens, the rhododendron gives way to a mixed forest. Toothworts, foamflowers, and violets grow in the mossy bank. The creek valley becomes a ravine, with high ridges sheltering it.

Here you meet the stars and giants of this trail: yellow buckeye trees, the only palmately compound tree in the park—that is, each leaf has five leaflets extending from the leaf stalk like outstretched fingers. Look for a tree with those leaves, twigs that sit opposite each other on the branch, and bark with ripple patterns where the outer layer has peeled off. Because buckeyes grow in sheltered coves, and their seeds cannot germinate if they dry out, their presence indicates that this area was not farmed or logged extensively. Young buckeyes sometimes jump the gun and put out leaves in March, only to lose them in the next frost. But they have spare buds and can try again later. The flowers appear in May and look like a formal yellow-and-white corsage. In the big cluster of flowers, only one or two produce nuts, which fall in September. The nuts contain a poisonous narcotic alkaloid, and farmers moved their cattle away from buckeye coves in the fall. Indians made the nuts edible by roasting, grinding, and leaching out the poison. Squirrels either discard the poisonous part or are not affected by it.

Carrying a buckeye nut is said to give good luck, as long as you don't chew on it. Look for round, leathery capsules on the trail and break them open to reveal shiny mahogany brown nuts with a wood grain pattern. The nut will shrivel unless oiled. If you don't have any mink oil along, human oil will do: rub the buckeye along the side of your nose to bring out the rich mahogany color.

After a metal culvert, the trail becomes steep and rocky. The creek ripples down a mossy cascade on the right. Another creek comes in from the left, and after another metal culvert, the trail turns left to ascend a steep slope to a switchback. Please don't cut across this switchback—unauthorized trails cause erosion and habitat destruction. After the switchback, the trail ascends easily along Sugarland Mountain. Toward the top of the next ridge tall spruces branch over the valley. Next to a dead spruce is an opening with a view of Mount Le Conte. The trail descends and then levels along the top of a narrow ridge.

Facing you is a ridged, sloping rock pinnacle. Some people scramble up the rock face, but there is a safer path to the right with access to the top of the rock. If you are hiking with children, establish some safety rules before starting either route. Rocky handholds have been polished by sweaty hands until they shine like antique banisters. And these rocks qualify as antiques. They are part of the Anakeesta Formation, which is exposed in outcrops like this and Charlies Bunion. Anakeesta metamorphic slate is at least 600 million years old, laid down during the Pre-Cambrian Era.

From the top you can see another rocky hump farther along. Some hikers try to continue out to this rocky hump and beyond, although it is extremely dangerous to do so. Many injuries have occurred out there. The chimney holes are to the left of the rocks and should be viewed with extreme caution. The main shaft is big enough to fall into. Look back down onto Newfound Gap Road and across the valley to Mount Le Conte; the steep side of Sugarland Mountain appears opposite.

Narrative by Doris Gove

CLINGMANS DOME BYPASS TRAIL

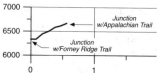

LENGTH: 0.5 mile, from Forney Ridge Trail to the Appalachian Trail.
HIGHLIGHTS: Views.
CAUTIONS: Ice in winter.

MAP KEY: 7 E; USGS quad: Clingmans Dome.
USE: Hiking trail.
TRAILHEAD: From Newfound Gap Road, drive 7 miles on Clingmans Dome Road to the Forney Ridge parking area at road's end. The trail begins at the jct. with the Forney Ridge Trail, 0.1 mile from the parking area.

This short trail is most often used as an access trail to the Appalachian Trail from the Forney Ridge parking area. If you want to avoid the crowds on the paved 0.5 mile trail leading to the observation tower at Clingman's Dome, this trail provides that option.

The trail begins after a 0.1 mile segment of the Forney Ridge Trail. At the junction, take a right turn uphill toward the A.T. To the left, Forney Ridge Trail descends toward the Forney Creek watershed and Andrews Bald.

Taking the trail to the A.T. provides you with some unexpected solitude in a busy section of the park since this trail actually receives little use. The slope is constant but gentle; the trail surface is rocky. Along the way, you pass some high elevation meadows off on the downhill slope. Tree cover quickly disappears because of dying Fraser firs, but you get some good views from the open areas. Don't be surprised to see deer along the way, especially if you're quiet as you walk.

The most pleasing feature of this trail occurs at its intersection with the A.T. about 0.3 mile west of Clingmans Dome observation tower. The junction is situated on a narrow, rocky ridge. To the north and west there are excellent views of Sugarland Mountain and the Elkmont region. In good weather, the crossroads makes for an appealing picnic spot since there are plenty of large rocks to sit on.

This spot is a favorite of mine because I once saw an immature bald eagle soar along summer thermals wafting up the mountain slope. The bird passed almost directly overhead, having flown up from the Fontana Lake area. I watched for 10-15 minutes as the air currents brought it closer and closer to the ridge.

While I can't guarantee eagle sightings, this short trail can make for a pleasant excursion. For a 1.4 mile loop you can combine it with the 0.3 mile from the A.T. to the tower and the paved trail back to the parking lot.

Narrative by Bill Beard

COLD SPRING GAP TRAIL

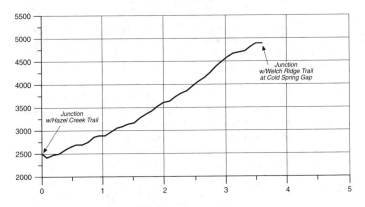

LENGTH: 3.6 miles, from Hazel Creek Trail to Welch Ridge Trail.
HIGHLIGHTS: Spring wildflowers.
CAUTIONS: Hazel Creek ford, rock hop stream crossings, badly eroded trail.
MAP KEY: 5 F; USGS quad: Tuskeegee.
USE: Horse and hiking trail.
STARTING POINT: Hike Lakeshore and Hazel Creek trails 6.7 miles north from Campsite #86 on Fontana Lake.

The Cold Spring Gap Trail is an important connector, leading from Hazel Creek to Welch Ridge Trail. It provides access to Forney Creek and the Appalachian Trail, receives steady use, and is badly eroded. The trail follows Cold Spring Branch for most of its length, crossing it many times without the luxury of foot bridges. With the added adventure of a wet ford of Hazel Creek, hikers should avoid this trail in winter or during high water.

The trail begins at the junction with Hazel Creek Trail and gently descends through pine and rosebay rhododendron toward Hazel Creek. The trail passes some rusted auto parts as it reaches the creek at **0.2** mile. Here the hiker (or horse!) must ford. Hazel Creek is about 20 yards wide at this point, but not very deep. It is best to try to step on the sandy bottom between the rocks, rather than on them. The deepest point is on the far side (as of this writing), and is 3-4' deep at full pool. Depending on the weather and time of the year, this crossing can be a refreshing interlude or a potential nightmare. Consider changing to lightweight shoes for the crossing.

After the ford, the trail climbs a switchback through old fields now sporting a crop of second growth tuliptree and woody vines. Then it joins the grade of an old logging railroad, which it follows most of the route. The trail passes the first of several home sites, then crosses Cold Spring Branch at **1.0** mile. A well-constructed rock wall suggests another home site before the trail climbs through a long switchback.

Another old logging railroad bed enters on the left after climbing away from the creek. The Cold Spring Branch drainage, like most of the Hazel Creek Valley, was logged by the W. M. Ritter Lumber Company. Between 1910 and 1928, Ritter logged 201 million board feet of virgin timber out of the valley via a standard gauge railroad all the way up the valley, with narrow gauge spurs up the branches. This section was one of those spurs that carried loggers and their axes and crosscut saws (called "misery whips") into the hills and later transported the massive hardwoods out.

Trail quality deteriorates as the grade steepens. The trail becomes very rocky, muddy, badly eroded, and occasionally "captures" small branches for short stretches. You also rock hop across Cold Spring

Branch several times as the ascent continues. The hiker must endure this neglected stretch for over 1 mile. A profusion of spring wildflowers along this perennially wet alluvial valley rewards the effort.

At **3.2** miles, the headwaters of Cold Spring Branch evolve from a rocky draw. This is a good source of water but not any colder than any other stream. Look for pink turtleheads in summer, but avoid the stinging nettles. The grade becomes even steeper, as the trail climbs to Cold Spring Gap on Welch Ridge. The trail is wide, rocky, and rutted in this last stretch.

At an elevation of about 4,600', this deep gap between Welch Bald to the south and High Rocks to the north once served as an important route for the early residents of Hazel and Forney creeks. As early as the 1830s, a transmountain road was planned to cross here that would connect the Little Tennessee and Tennessee valleys. The route often followed existing Cherokee trails, so this gap may have had an earlier significance. Portions of the road were built, but it was never completed.

The faint old manway to the right once was a maintained trail along Pilot Ridge down to Bear Creek. This route was abandoned in favor of Bear Creek Trail. You meet Welch Ridge Trail, which descends 7.3 miles from the A.T. near Silers Bald. To reach High Rocks, follow Welch Ridge Trail and a short spur left (west) 0.4 mile.

Narrative by James Wedekind

COOPER CREEK TRAIL

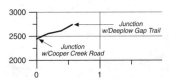

LENGTH: 0.6 mile, from Cooper Creek Road to Deeplow Gap Trail.
HIGHLIGHTS: Streams.
CAUTIONS: Unbridged stream crossing.

MAP KEY: 8 F; USGS quads: Smokemont, Whittier.
USE: Horse and hiking trail.
TRAILHEAD: Drive to the end of Cooper Creek Road, 3.0 miles from NC Highway 19. Watch for the turn-off sign from Highway 19 onto Cooper Creek Road.

This short trail is a connector between Cooper Creek Road and Deeplow Gap Trail. If you are hiking from Cooper Creek Road into the park, you will have to park on private property, so ask for permission and don't block any driveways. Walk up the road 0.1 mile past a steel cable barrier to the park boundary marked by a large locked gate.

Follow the rocky roadbed up the left (west) side of Cooper Creek. Since the creek itself is the park boundary, the right bank is private property. Rosebay rhododendron, Eastern hemlock and dog-hobble crowd the banks; oak, American beech, and other hardwoods populate the surrounding forest.

At **0.25** mile you will see a house across the creek and then notice that the trail and creek commingle on an old roadbed. In wet weather rock hopping is difficult, so you will need to get off the trail to your left to cross. The road turns right, but the trail continues left through thick rosebay rhododendron and dog-hobble, ending after crossing Little Creek at an old house site. Deeplow Gap Trail runs left 1.7 miles to Deeplow Gap and right 5.1 miles to the Newton Bald Trail.

Narrative by Charles Maynard and David Morris

COOPER ROAD TRAIL

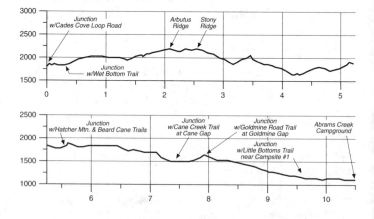

LENGTH: 10.5 miles, from Cades Cove Loop Road to Abrams Creek Campground.
HIGHLIGHTS: Redbuds in March, early April.
MAP KEY: 2-3 D-E; USGS quads: Cades Cove, Calderwood, Block-house, Kinzel Springs.
USE: Horse and hiking trail.
TRAILHEAD: Drive 4.3 miles on Cades Cove Loop Road from the beginning of the loop. Look for a trail sign on right and park on the left.

Cooper Road was once the main access to Cades Cove for settlers, farmers, and loggers. It is a well-established road, eroded deep into the hillside in some places, and still usable by park vehicles. Archeological evidence shows that humans lived in Cades Cove as early as 6,500 BC, and much of Cooper Road is a former Indian trail. Daniel David Foute, an early settler who owned much of the cove, improved the road in the 1830s for wagon transport to Maryville. The James Carson Iron Works, built on Kingfisher Creek in the 1830s, depended on the road, and Cades Cove farmers shipped apples, livestock, honey, lumber, and other products. In 1832, mail service came to Cades Cove. Charles Myers, whose family came to the cove in 1817, said in 1961, "We never were tied up in here and isolated like they might have you think. . . . For six years and a half I carried mail over these mountains and never missed a day. When I was eight I started going with my daddy peddling apples and driving cattle to market."

Cooper Road Trail angles across a series of sandstone ridges and has fewer tortuous turns than the other two old access roads, Rich Mountain and Parson Branch. From Cooper Road Trail, you can reach several other trails that run along ridge tops or along the creeks that drain the ravines. Just south of the road, and somewhat parallel to it, Abrams Creek cuts through the same ridges; it is the only drainage for Cades Cove.

Cooper Road Trail starts as an easy roadbed, with white pines, white oaks, tuliptrees, sourwoods, and red maples. Cades Cove Loop Road swings left and Cooper Road Trail swings right, so just a short hike takes you away from traffic noise. The soil is sandy and dry on the higher sections, and the area was heavily cut over by the Cades

Cove settlers. Vigorous growth of young trees covers the ridge tops and the valley bottoms are thick with rhododendron. At mile 0.3, there is a small sign for Wet Bottom Trail, which leads to Rabbit Creek Trail and the Abrams Creek parking area in 1.0 mile. This connector trail also intersects the path to the Elijah Oliver homestead.

The Cooper Road Trail continues straight through a stand of small white pines and a few small Eastern hemlocks and then rises out of Cades Cove to the first of many ridges. After a creek and a few muddy spots, the road cuts through a small gap and curves down to a creek ravine. It crosses the creek on a cement causeway and continues this pattern, with each ridge getting a little higher and steeper than the one before. On some of the steeper sections, the road has loose rocks; be careful when hiking on a leaf carpet in the fall. On each ridge you can see a clear vegetation pattern: rosebay rhododendron and Eastern hemlock along the creek thinning out and being replaced by mountain laurel and pines at the tops of the ridges. The other pattern is that some plants break the rules—a few laurels grow by the creek, or a healthy rhododendron stands near the top. At about 2.0 miles, the road zigzags in three sharp turns and then runs up and down some easy grades above a creek. Then it turns down to a creek draw. Christmas fern, partridgeberry, galax, little brown jugs, foamflower, violets, and Solomon's seal grow on the rocky bank. In spring, look for the pink twin flowers of partridgeberry. Each pair of flowers makes one fruit, which looks like a small cranberry with two blossom scars.

After crossing and following a creeklet, crossing a larger creek in a dip that may be wet, and going over two sandy ridge saddles, you climb a rocky, dry hillside to a gap and a junction (mile 5.6). To the left, Hatcher Mountain Trail leads to Little Bottoms Trail in 2.8 miles. (Abrams Falls is 4.7 miles.) Beard Cane Trail leads right to Ace Gap Trail in 4.2 miles. Cooper Road Trail continues straight on small ridge tops through white pine, red maple, red and white oak, and chestnut oak. At the bottom of a hill (mile 7.3), three boulders mark the junction with Cane Creek Trail, which leads to Campsite #2 in 0.6 mile and to the park boundary in 2.1 miles.

Cooper Road Trail turns left and climbs steeply out of the junction. Pussy toes, wintergreen, and trailing arbutus cover the road bank, and grasses and trees are getting established on the roadbed. At the top of the climb (mile **7.9**) is the junction with Goldmine Road, another early access to Cades Cove, which leads right to the park boundary and the Top of the World community in 0.8 mile. The elevation here is 1,750', and, except for one short climb up from a creek, it is downhill all the way to Abrams Creek Campground in 2.6 miles.

Cooper Road Trail descends gradually through scraggly woods. After a big white oak on the right with massive tangles of branches, the road drops more steeply to a cool ravine. It crosses a rocky creeklet and descends through hickory, pine, oak, and sassafras woods. A few Eastern red cedars grow here. These evergreens, so abundant elsewhere in Tennessee, are uncommon within the park boundaries. They grow at low elevation and usually on limestone, which underlies the sandstone of the ridges that you have been climbing. Redbud, which blooms in April and has smooth, heart-shaped leaves, also grows along this road because of the same conditions.

The trail crosses three more rocky wet patches, all parts of or tributaries of Kingfisher Creek, and then enters thick hemlock woods with a few tuliptrees. Backcountry campsite #1 (Cooper Road, 1,200') is on the left; from this direction you will see the stone fire rings before you see the official sign post. There is room for 10 people and 10 horses, and the site offers a pack hanging rope, three stone fire rings, and three small clearings as amenities. Kingfisher Creek runs behind the campsite, but in long dry spells, it may not have much water. Nearby blowdowns provide firewood.

Just beyond #1, at mile **9.6**, is the junction with Little Bottoms Trail, which leads left to Abrams Falls in 4.2 miles. Cooper Road Trail descends through Eastern hemlock, paw-paw, Fraser magnolia, and umbrella magnolia. In clearings from windthrow, small trees grow oversized leaves as they compete for space in the sun. Shrub yellowroot, bedstraw, violets, foamflower, cardinal flower, and little brown jugs grow along the road banks as the trail crosses and joins Kingfisher Creek for some rocky and possibly very wet sections. Maples, redbuds, devil's walking sticks, magnolias, white pines, and tangled American hollies form the mixed forest that alternates with stands of hemlock. To the left you can see a steep ridge that Little Bottoms Trail climbs to reach Abrams Creek, and as you hike around the nose of that ridge, you will see Abrams Creek down to the left. Then, at the gate (mile **10.5**), you will see Abrams Creek Campground. Abrams Creek Ranger Station and hiker parking are 0.5 mile further.

Cooper Road Trail provides access to several good day hike or overnight loops, and the following information may help you plan a trip or a car shuttle. To get to the Abrams Creek Ranger station from US 129, turn north onto Happy Valley Road, which is just east of the intersection of the Foothills Parkway and US 129. Drive 6.8 miles and look for a Park Service sign for Abrams Creek Ranger Station. The sign is on the left; turn right onto a narrow, winding road. Past the ranger station and the trailhead for Rabbit Creek Trail, another sign indicates hiker parking.

Wet Bottom Trail connector might also be useful for a loop hike. It starts 0.2 mile along Cooper Road Trail and descends 0.3 mile through thin woods to the Elijah Oliver Homestead path. Turn right, pass a large barn and two creeks. After a small wooded rise, look for an unsigned trail to the left in an open area, marked by a few rocks. This section twists through possibly muddy floodplain, past a hog exclosure and a spectacular patch of princess pine clubmoss. After a shoes-off crossing of Abrams Creek, you climb a steep bank to Abrams Creek parking area. An alternative, especially for wet or cold weather, is to follow the trail to the Elijah Oliver Homestead, take the path to Abrams Falls parking area (0.5 mile), and cross Abrams Creek on a bridge.

Narrative by Doris Gove

COVE MOUNTAIN TRAIL

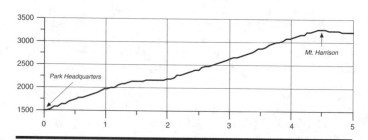

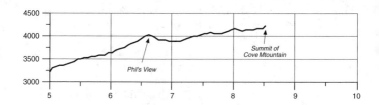

LENGTH: 8.7 miles, from Park Headquarters to summit of Cove Mountain.

HIGHLIGHTS: Seasonal views, waterfalls.

CAUTIONS: Hunting nearby.

MAP KEY: 6 C; USGS quad: Gatlinburg.

USE: Hiking trail.

TRAILHEAD: Park Headquarters complex. Entering the national park from Gatlinburg, TN on US 441, turn right (after approximately 1.5 miles) on an unmarked side road 150 yards before Sugarlands Visitor Center. Take the first left and park by the bridge. Walk across the bridge over Fighting Creek with the stone work on the sides. The trail starts on the far side of the bridge.

The Cove Mountain Trail offers a unique perspective into the struggles which face many of our national parks. But at the same time, it will give you an understanding of why these parks exist. It is a trail with two tales, or at least two sides. As you climb to the summit of Cove Mountain, to your left will be all that is good and special about the Smokies. There you will encounter birds, squirrels, and maybe even a bear or two in the wild. While to your right will be all the challenges. Along this trail, you will pass private homes, rental chalets, a ski resort, and a public hunting area. At the summit you will even find a fire tower remodeled to determine the types and quantities of poisons we all release into the air.

All around the "Trail Users" sign at the start of the route is a very interesting plant. This is Lycopodium or more commonly referred to as club moss or ground pine. These tiny evergreens are just one of many thousands of plant and plant-like species the park was established to preserve. To the park, these primitive organisms are as important as any tree or flower, bird or bear. It is the park's goal to save the ecosystem, not just a few isolated parts.

Pass on by the sign and continue on to Cataract Falls at **0.1** mile. This little 12 foot falls offers a cool, refreshing breeze on a hot summer day. The trail rock hops the creek and continues uphill past rhododendrons, hemlocks, and dog-hobbles. In May and June, look for the delicate white flowers of the latter. This small shrub gets its name from the early settlers who hunted in these mountains. Bear hunting in the 1800s was done with traps, guns, and dogs. When being chased by dogs, the heavy furred bears would charge into a patch of dog-hobble. They could get through with no problem, but the dogs would often get tangled, or "hobbled," by the leaves. Look closely at a leaf. If you rub your finger from base to tip, there's no big effect, but try it the other way. Ouch! Sharp, tiny teeth along the leaf margin cut into anything that passes the wrong way. Since these are evergreen, a smart bear could allude his pursuers by seeking out a patch of dog-hobble. You think bears are that smart?

Just ahead, Double Gourd Branch tumbles down through a worn fissure in some boulders and crosses the trail. Although small, the falls here is a very pretty cascade. The trail has been moderately climbing to this point. It will continue this way for the next 8 miles. Sometimes passing through warm pine-oak stands, sometimes passing beneath cooler hardwood forests. And even through rhododendron thickets like the one you find at mile **1.0**. Dry Pond Branch parallels the trail here for a short distance. The shade from the hillside and the moisture from the water make this a perfect place for rosebay rhododendrons. These large shrubs bloom with gorgeous white blossoms in early July, although some years are more spectacular than others. Early July is a nice time to be in a rhododendron jungle. Not only do you get to enjoy the blossoms, but you can escape the heat in this naturally air-conditioned forest. If you are here then, notice that the flowers have no odor and few insects visit them. These plants are pollinated by moths. The little yellow-green markings allow the moths a way to judge landings, while the sticky bracts around each flower keep crawling insects away.

Continue climbing moderately until at **1.5** miles you reach someone's backyard. You have now obviously reached the park boundary. You will now follow this to the summit of Cove Mountain. This house is an example of one of the biggest challenges facing the Smokies: development along the border. All this human activity puts more and more stress on the park and its resources. More visitors means more traffic and a greater amount of resources devoted to roads, parking areas, restrooms, garbage pickup, etc. Development around the park continues the never ending cycle. It's a challenge that the park struggles with every day. But it's a struggle we can all help reduce. By becoming more aware of our impact and helping others to do so, we all have the power to reduce the stress.

At mile 2.0, you will begin to pass under stands of dead pines. Look closely and you will see the tell-tale grooves left by the southern pine beetle on the underside of the bark. These native beetles have killed these pines, but at the same time they are helping the forest. They provide food for woodpeckers and ultimately allow more sunlight to the forest floor, helping the next generation of pines grow. Disturbances, like native insect infestations and fires, are part of a cycle which renews the forests. Further along this gentle climb, you will start to get views of Mount LeConte, especially in the winter. At mile 3.0, there is a larger opening through the trees to give you year-round views, but you've got to watch closely for it.

After passing a short spur trail to St. Moritz Road, Gatlinburg, you will begin a moderate climb up Holy Butt. Nobody seems to know why this place received such an unusual name, but it is worth contemplating as you continue uphill. At mile 3.5, you swing around the butt to face more of the development around the park. Look back and you will see the top of a chair lift for Ober Gatlinburg.

The trail continues to climb along another ridge, finally passing below Mt. Harrison and its ski lift. As you circle Mt. Harrison, you will catch one last glimpse of Gatlinburg, hear one last sound of civilization, and move away from the most developed of the park boundaries. The trail will still follow the park's edge, but the development now is only in the form of little-used jeep trails. From the small gap, the trail climbs gently around the head of Hickory Flats Branch. The stream starts well below the trail, so don't plan on water here. You have now begun the longest, steepest climb. You have come more than five miles and 1,600 feet, but the next 1.5 miles will see you climb more than 600 feet to a small ridge called Phils View. Although no record exists, it is believed that this point was named for the Smokies' first ranger—Phil Hough. Phil must have had great eyesight or the forest has grown since his time, for there is no view here today.

From Phils View, the trail drops along the ridge line to a small gap. From here you parallel an overgrown jeep trail for another mile until you reach a second gap. Here you leave the park briefly at an intersection with a more developed jeep trail. The Cove Mountain Trail continues straight ahead, climbing about 0.25 mile to the ridge line again. The trail then passes gently along a narrow ridge. During hunting season, you need to be a little more cautious here. For no longer are you bordered to your right by private land, but you are not completely within the park either. The land to your right is part of the Cove Mountain Wildlife Management Area. This land is heavily used to hunt deer, bear, and wild hog in season. It's not uncommon to hear gunshots and dogs barking. Wearing bright colors, even blaze orange, in late fall might not be a bad idea.

Jeff Rennicke, in his book *The Smoky Mountain Black Bear: Spirit of the Hills,* estimates that 45-80 bears are poached from the park each year. Black bear gall bladders are sold as Oriental folk medicines for as much as $75 per ounce. Claws and teeth go for $1.50 each and even foot pads are taken. Most poaching occurs near park boundaries, in places like this.

Finally, you will intersect a well-maintained 4-wheel-drive road. From here it's a short, easy hike to the top and the fire tower. With 0.1 mile to go, you will reach the intersection of the Laurel Falls Trail. A nice day hike would be to descend to the Little River Road by way of this trail. It passes through some nice old growth forests and Laurel Falls. Of course, you will have to arrange a shuttle from park headquarters to Fighting Creek Gap where the trailhead is. Our trail, however, continues up a moderate incline to the tower.

By now you have probably noticed another human impact on the park, helicopters. At the time of this writing, the Park Service is studying the issue and the attitudes park visitors have toward the flights. However, local communities who have tried to restrict sight-seeing flights have found these businesses can be pretty resilient.

In the past, hikers have been able to climb the tower to get a great view from above the trees. But today you will have to settle for a view of Wear Cove down the power lines past the tower. A large shed part way up the tower limits access. This shed contains instruments to monitor air quality. Research by the park has shown that more than 100 species of plants are adversely affected by ozone levels in the park's air. Acid rain levels have also been suggested as a cause for the reduced growth of red spruce in the high country. Even the views have been hindered by air pollution. Monitoring in and around the Smokies helps to track the sources of pollution and help the offending parties develop strategies to reduce their impact.

The struggles to protect the park from pollution, poaching, and encroaching development continue, but our trail ends here. You can backtrack to the headquarters—it'll be a lot less tiring going down. Or you might choose to head down the Laurel Falls Trail.

Narrative by Tom Condon

CRIB GAP TRAIL

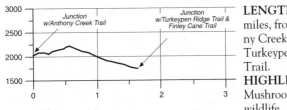

LENGTH: 1.6 miles, from Anthony Creek Trail to Turkeypen Ridge Trail.
HIGHLIGHTS: Mushrooms and wildlife.
CAUTIONS: Crossing Laurel Creek Road.
MAP KEY: 4 D; USGS quads: Cades Cove, Thunderhead.
USE: Horse and hiking trail.
STARTING POINT: Park at or near Cades Cove Picnic Area and walk 0.3 mile on the Anthony Creek Trail to jct. with Crib Gap Trail.

he Crib Gap Trail is not the type of trail you would choose to get away from civilization. This short and easy hike will always be within the sound of a road. Yet the Crib Gap Trail is a nice departure from the bedlam of Cades Cove on a busy summer day.

At the Crib Gap and Anthony Creek trails junction, you will be standing in a hemlock and rhododendron forest. If it is July, the rhododendrons should be displaying their brilliant white flower clusters. There may be no better time of the year to hike this trail, but do not get enthralled by the blossoms or you will miss some of the secrets. Hidden in the cool, damp shade of these forests are a myriad of mushrooms.

The Great Smoky Mountains are home to over 2,100 different species of fungi. As you begin the gently uphill climb to Crib Gap, look about for some. You might spot the beautiful yellow and orange Caesar's amanita mushroom, or its look-alike, the fly agaric. Look, but do not collect, because only an experienced collector can tell the difference between this edible and deadly pair.

The wide gravel path you follow will crest a small hill and drop to a small tributary of Anthony Creek. Jump the stream and begin another climb to the gap. As you climb, the hillside dries and warms. The forest changes from hemlock to pine-oak. Here along the base of some trees you might find a large cauliflower-like mass. This is the cauliflower mushroom. The Audubon Society field guide to mushrooms says that "nothing known to be poisonous even remotely resembles this Elizabethan ruff of a mushroom."

After a few switchbacks up the trail, you will reach a wide opening. There are modest, if somewhat obstructed views of the valleys to the east from here. An old overgrown trail continues ahead, but our trail climbs to the right. It is a short climb up to the 2,200' elevation line, where the trail levels. You now look down upon Crib Gap. This gap marks a drainage divide. The rain which falls on the trail behind you will enter Anthony Creek, Abrams Creek, and ultimately the Little Tennessee River. But the rain which falls ahead of you will enter Laurel Creek, the Little River and eventually the Tennessee River. All water in the Smokies finally makes its way to the Mississippi River and the Gulf of Mexico.

Just ahead you will begin a descent to Laurel Creek Road. The trail is narrow now and requires a little care to traverse. Loose rocks abound. When you reach the road, do not cross immediately. The trail parallels the road for another 500 feet before it crosses. Be very careful here. You have a good view of the road, but most visitors are not expecting you to be here. On a busy summer day, this can be as challenging as crossing a river in the park.

After the crossing, the Crib Gap Trail continues about 30 yards down Laurel Creek Road. The trail is wide again as it descends through an open cove hardwood forest. All around the area, small stone piles can be found. These "foundations" were used by past residents to level their homes.

This young forest with its understory of flowering dogwoods is another great place for hidden secrets. Unknown to the motorists along the road, deer are often seen browsing here in the summer. Squirrels and chipmunks gather acorns here each fall as humans drive to the cove to absorb the colors of the season. Each spring, the bears return to this spot. At least one bear does. She has become known to many as Missy—a Cades Cove regular. She is a small sow and often pretty ragged looking in the spring, but she is also a good mother and is often seen caring for two cubs. She has lived all her life, perhaps 10 years, here in Cades Cove and has learned all about us. She knows how to play the tourist game, often showing amazing tolerance of our ignorance. But she has always remained a wild bear, never panhandling, just foraging about naturally, never raiding the picnic area or campground, just passing through occasionally and always training her young to be like herself—a wild black bear.

The trail enters another hemlock stand as it descends the hillside. The loose rocks in the tread continue, but add to this long sections of mud—making this a difficult path to walk. At **1.6** miles the Crib Gap Trail ends at a complex intersection in a small open field. The trail to the right is Turkey Pen Ridge Trail, but so is the trail to the left. A right will take you to Laurel Creek Road, a left to the Schoolhouse Gap Trail. A third trail enters here as well. It is to the right, too, but not as sharp a turn. This trail has no name. It is just a short, very muddy way to the Finley Cane Trail.

Narrative by Tom Condon

CROOKED ARM RIDGE TRAIL

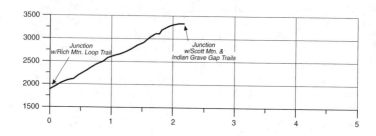

LENGTH: 2.1 miles, from Rich Mtn. Loop Trail to Indian Grave Gap Trail.
HIGHLIGHTS: Views.
CAUTIONS: Loose rocks, rutted trail.
MAP KEY: 4 D; USGS quad: Cades Cove.
USE: Horse and hiking trail.
STARTING POINT: Jct. Rich Mtn. Loop Trail, 0.5 mile from its trailhead at the start of the Cades Cove Loop Road.
NOTE: Part of "Rich Mountain Loop" dayhike.

The Great Smoky Mountains are known for their diversity of plant and animal life. Within this relatively small national park there are at least 8 different recognizable communities. It's been said that within a 2 hour drive you can travel from a gum swamp, similar to coastal Mississippi and Alabama, to a spruce-fir forest, similar to those of southern Canada. Although this short trail cannot provide this great diversity, it will take you through 3 distinct forest types.

At the Rich Mountain Loop trailhead, a field of *Microstegeum* or Japanese grass is surrounded by a hemlock forest. The first half mile to the Crooked Arm Ridge Trail is dominated by this conifer. The Eastern hemlocks grow best in the cool, moist environment this narrow valley provides. The Cherokees, as well as some early settlers, used the needles of the tree in a tea. This hemlock is not the one which Socrates drank to kill himself. He drank a tea made from a flowering plant called water hemlock, a relative to Queen Anne's lace. In fact, the tea from the hemlock tree is rich in vitamin C.

As you pass amongst the hemlocks and other trees, watch the stream for Crooked Arm Falls. This 25' falls is only noticeable during wet weather, and even then can be easily missed. Above the falls you will have to rock hop Crooked Arm Branch. You then begin to climb up the ridge at a steady rate of about 670' per mile. The many switchbacks will help to make the going easier. Don't neglect also to take advantage of the good views along the way. These always provide an opportunity to stop, rest, and get a drink of water. You will want to bring plenty of water as this becomes a very dry trail. At 0.75 mile you will come upon a switchback turning left away from the power line right-of-way. Stop and look back. There is a wonderful view of the east end of Cades Cove. The campground is nestled there at the bottom of the mountains.

You might also notice that the hemlocks have given way to mixed hardwoods. The slope now is drier but still sheltered. This provides habitat for oaks, maples, hickories, and dogwoods. The flowering dogwood is a beautiful compliment to any hike, but unfortunately, this may not last into the future. A disease, dogwood anthracnose, is threatening the dogwoods. Much like the chestnut blight of the early 1900s, dogwood anthracnose is removing an important tree from our forests. We all enjoy the beautiful blossoms of the spring, but dogwood's importance goes beyond the aesthetics. Dogwood berries provide much needed food for birds and mammals during the fall and winter months and the leaves return calcium to the soil.

The disease is the result of a fungus, *Discula*, which generally kills the tree within 5 years of infection. Dead twigs, ragged leaf edges and twigs sprouting from the trunk are all signs of infection.

Climbing still higher, you will move across Crooked Arm Ridge and onto Pinkroot Ridge. The trail now has a much more southern exposure, catching the hotter afternoon sun. The trail is drier and again the vegetation changes with these conditions. The forest is now mostly oak and pine. The predominant oak is chestnut oak, named because its leaves resemble those of the American chestnut. Like the pine, these oaks do well on dry slopes, providing much needed shade on a hot summer's day. In this shade thrive a number of interesting plants. Keep an eye open for Indian pipe. This saprophytic flowering plant has no chlorophyll and relies strictly on its relationship with a fungi to receive its food. The Cherokee claim that wherever you find a patch of Indian pipe, kin argued. Cherokee tradition called for ceremonial pipe smoking only after an agreement was reached. Long ago, clan elders broke this tradition. Their transgression so angered "someone powerful" that he struck them dead. Indian pipe stands today as a reminder to strive to reach common ground after a disagreement.

Lift your eyes up out of the sometimes deeply rutted trail and enjoy the views. A second good overlook occurs at mile **1.75.** Here you have a view down onto Sparks Lane, a gravel road crossing Cades Cove. At about **2.0** miles you will come to a fork in the trail. When the trees are in leaf take the lower trail. After the leaves have dropped you may wish to take the upper trail for a better view of the Smokies' crest. Both trails meet again after a short departure.

Shortly you will come to the junction of Scott Mountain and Indian Grave Gap trails. Backpackers looking for campsite #6 turn right and proceed 500 feet along Scott Mountain. Day hikers doing the Rich Mountain Loop follow Indian Grave Gap Trail to the left.

Narrative by Tom Condon

CUCUMBER GAP TRAIL

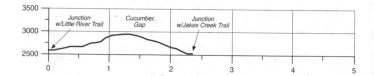

LENGTH: 2.3 miles, from Little River Trail to Jakes Creek Trailhead.

HIGHLIGHTS: Easy family walk, wildflowers

MAP KEY: 6 C-D; USGS quad map: Gatlinburg.

USE: Hiking trail.

TRAILHEAD: From Little River Road, turn in toward Elkmont Campground and Ranger Station. Turn left at the campground entrance and left again at the fork to drive to the Little River Trail (about a mile above Elkmont Campground). Walk 1.3 miles down the Little River Trail and turn right onto the Cucumber Gap Trail.

Combined with the Little River and Jakes Creek trails, the Cucumber Gap Trail makes one of the finest short loops in the park (total loop: 5.1 miles).

The trail takes a gentle ascent through a large grove of second growth tuliptrees, evidence that the Little River Lumber Company continued its operations into this area during the late 1920s. Large banks on the lower part of the trail indicate that it was an old logging road or railroad bed. Park records show that the route was rebuilt as a trail by the Civilian Conservation Corps in the 1930s, connecting it to the Jakes Creek watershed.

After approximately **1.0** mile, the trail crosses the first prominent landmark, Huskey Branch, which is easily forded on numerous flat stepping stones, unless there have been recent heavy rains. This small tumbling stream is named for the Huskey family, one of the first families to settle the Smokies during the 1800s. When the park purchased this land from private owners in the 1920s, 38 parcels in Sevier County were owned by those using the Huskey surname.

After Huskey Branch, the forest understory remains thick with small Eastern hemlock and rosebay rhododendron. In early spring, the entire trail shows off blooms of trout-lily, spring-beauty, bloodroot, and trillium. In summer, the undergrowth at the path's edge becomes thick with dog-hobble, cinnamon and Christmas ferns. Before the trail approaches Cucumber Gap, it crosses two small unnamed branches and several low and damp run-off areas, which in July and August are scattered with patches of scarlet bee-balm. Also, watch for the deer which frequent this area.

Near the top of the gap are a large number of Fraser magnolias (*Magnolia fraseri*), sometimes called "cucumber trees," for which the gap and the trail are probably named. In truth, the cucumbertree is a separate species, *Magnolia acuminata*, but both trees grow a long, bumpy fruit which bears a certain resemblace to a cucumber. Interestingly, hikers say that in May and June patches of Indian cucumber root (*Medeola virginiana*) can be observed on this trail, suggesting another origin for the unusual name.

At the gap, the trail provides a partial vista in late fall and winter of Burnt Mountain (3,373') and the narrow valley created by Bear Wallow Creek. Violets, hepatica, cut-leaved toothwort, and other wildflowers bloom here in spring. At this point the trail makes a gradual, easy descent and levels off into a forest of tuliptrees, mountain maple, hemlock, and basswood trees. Winding through these trees is a great deal of wild grapevine, some as large as six inches in diameter and climbing more than 100 feet into the forest canopy. Also look for turtleheads in bloom during August and September.

About a half-mile after the gap, look for a flat area in the valley below (to the right). This large clearing was owned by Bill Teaster, who had a small cabin on the site and cultivated crops on about 12 of his 41.5 acres. Park archives suggest that Teaster did not want to sell his land to the state commission, which purchased land for the national park. The surveyor, who had estimated the value of the land at $15 per acre, asked Teaster what he thought it was worth, and he said it was worth twice that amount. The case was settled in court in 1930; Teaster received $17.50 per acre and a "lifetime lease." To expedite cases like this one, the federal government offered older residents the opportunity to stay on their land as renters (at a very low rate) until their deaths.

As the trail descends toward the Jakes Creek Trail, it crosses Tulip Branch, called Poplar Branch by the original residents of the area. Both names have as their origin the extremely large tuliptrees that grew along the branch here at the turn of the century. "Uncle" Jim Shelton, who helped build the first railroads into the Elkmont area, recalled seeing a tuliptree so large that it "took two flat cars to carry it out of the mountains." At present there are still many two- and three-foot diameter tuliptrees to admire along this section of the trail.

The Cucumber Gap Trail ends at the Jakes Creek Trail. To return to your car, you can either retrace your steps or walk down the Jakes Creek Trail to the parking area (0.3 miles), then take the first right on the road among the old summer homes and walk up the Little River Road (1.5 miles) to the Little River Trailhead. The trail also may be hiked in reverse, but there is an equal amount of climbing either way.

Narrative by Margaret Brown, Don Davis, and Doris Gove

CURRY MOUNTAIN TRAIL

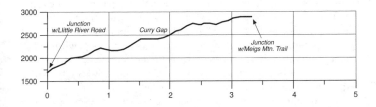

LENGTH: 3.3 miles, from Little River Road to Meigs Mountain Trail.
HIGHLIGHTS: Cultural history.
MAP KEY: 5C; USGS quad: Wear Cove.
USE: Hiking trail.
TRAILHEAD: Drive to and park at Metcalf Bottoms Picnic Area, 9.8 miles west of Sugarlands Visitor Center on Little River Road. Walk 100 yards back toward Sugarlands beside the road until you see the orange gate and trailhead.

The Little River and the road that clings to it swing north to get around two 3,000' peaks, Curry He and Curry She Mountains. Curry Mountain Trail follows an old logging road and access road south past both of these small mountains. It climbs the side of Curry He, crosses a gap between the Curries, and then climbs by Curry She to reach Meigs Mountain Trail and provide access to a small maintained cemetery that once served the Jakes Creek community. The name apparently came from Cherokee *gura-hi*, which means that a particular salad green (*gura*) grows here. Settlers not only corrupted gura to curry; they also named the neighbor hill Curry She.

Just past the gate is a large grassy patch with jewelweed and cardinal flower in late summer. The trail rises into Eastern hemlock mixed with hardwoods and then enters a rosebay rhododendron tunnel as it runs parallel to the Little River Road below. You can peer down through the rhododendron at the roofs of cars and campers racing by. As the tunnel starts to thin, look for squawroot on the sides of the trail. This early spring flower is parasitic on oaks and has fleshy yellow six-inch stalks and yellowish flowers. In late summer, the stalks turn brown and look like thin pine cones poking up through the soil.

The trail becomes both grassy and rocky and then goes through an Eastern hemlock grove so thick that there are almost no ground plants. After a switchback, the forest becomes more open, with maples and other deciduous trees. Look for a patch of crested dwarf iris in and beside the trail after a rocky seep. These flowers bloom in April, and the leaves stay green until late fall.

As you enter the next Eastern hemlock grove, look for stone walls on the sides of the trail and other piles of stones that may indicate house sites or cleared fields. At this point, the noise of Little River Road traffic fades and you can enjoy bird songs and wind music. The trail moves up to a more exposed part of the mountainside with maples, sourwoods, and oaks. Look for gray American chestnut stumps and snags. At **2.0** miles, you cross Curry Gap between Curry He and Curry She mountains and turn left to swing around a ridge that extends down from Curry She. Beyond the gap, the trail climbs steeply for another 0.3 mile and then levels on Long Arm Ridge. The slope after the switchback at the end of the ridge faces southwest and is not sheltered by any other mountain, so it is dry, with pine and oak trees, mountain laurel, and a ground cover of galax, trailing arbutus, and wintergreen. The grass in the trail is replaced by a needle carpet as you ascend through clusters of pine trees. This road has been used for a long time, probably without erosion control or drainage ditches, and in some places the original road bank is as high as your shoulders.

Toward the top, the old road widens a bit, and a forest of sourwoods, oaks, and pines gives way to a tangle of unusually tall mountain laurel. After a small rise and a right curve, the road reaches the junction with Meigs Mountain Trail. Turn right to reach the cemetery (about 50 yards on the right), Meigs Creek Trail, or Lumber Ridge Trail. Turn left for Jakes Creek Trail and Elkmont. If you can arrange a car shuttle or are willing to walk 2.0 miles on Little River Road (not recommended), Curry Mountain, Meigs Mountain, and Meigs Creek Trails together make a nice hike of 8.7 miles.

Narrative by Doris Gove

DEEP CREEK TRAIL

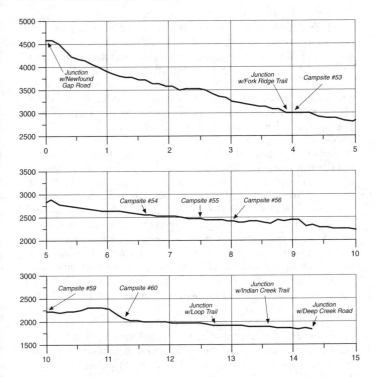

LENGTH: 14.3 miles, from Newfound Gap Road to Deep Creek Road.

HIGHLIGHTS: Scenic stream valley.
CAUTIONS: Stream crossings, muddy stretches, some strenuous terrain.
MAP KEY: 7 D-F; USGS quads: Clingmans Dome, Bryson City.
USE: Horse and hiking trail.
TRAILHEAD: On Newfound Gap Road, 1.7 miles south of Newfound Gap at a marked parking lot and trailhead.

Built to meet National Park Service specifications in 1932, Deep Creek Trail was one of the first trails constructed after the park took possession of the land. Engineer R. P. White considered this trail the loveliest of all those he designed. Although a small lumber operation took out "the large yellow poplar along the main creek and its tributaries during the 1890s," Deep Creek watershed remained largely virgin timber at the time of its acquisition by the park in the late 1920s. Deep Creek is also where *Kituhwa* was located, one of the first Cherokee town sites that botanist William Bartram visited in the early 1800s.

From the trailhead, Deep Creek Trail follows a switchback downhill through Eastern hemlock and rosebay rhododendron. At first, the elevation is high enough for red spruce but too low for Fraser fir; but as soon as the trail drops 300', the red spruce forest ends. Some of the Eastern hemlocks along the first stretch of the trail are quite impressive, especially several individual trees on the right; other species include white oak, Fraser magnolia, yellow birch, and Northern red oak. As it continues to descend towards Deep Creek, the trail winds around two small, lovely coves; small streams ensure lush, diverse vegetation: a carpet of false nettle, orange jewelweed, and wild bergamot on the forest floor, plus a plethora of large trees, including black cherry and Fraser magnolia.

At **1.0** mile, the trail crosses a stream, then proceeds through mixed woodland comprised of Eastern hemlock, yellow birch, and American beech. At times false nettles and smooth blackberry threaten to engulf the trail. By **1.5** miles the trail reaches boggy, level ground and you must hop across a streamlet. Soon the first tuliptrees appear, elevation 3,800', and the trail becomes muddy. You cross several more streams, each of which feeds Deep Creek, roaring off to the right. This is ideal habitat for the red-cheeked salamander, a species endemic to the Smokies.

At **2.0** miles, the trail passes through drier woods where only chestnut stumps and sprouts from old root systems remain of what once was the southern Appalachians' dominant tree. To the right are endless tangles of dog-hobble. While this shrub may have hobbled mountain people's hunting dogs, other animals relish its protection; in spring, you may spook a newborn fawn into it.

By **2.5** miles the trail is several hundred feet above Deep Creek and offers numerous vistas of the creek ecosystem. Rosebay rhododendron and dog-hobble hug the bank, with tuliptree, American basswood, witch hazel, and giant Eastern hemlocks covering the slopes. Soon a creek draining a small cove flows under the trail; you may notice the rock support walls installed by the Civilian Conservation Corps. An impressive tuliptree just to the right showcases that species' height. Also note the Indian cucumber root and false Solomon's seal in spring.

By **3.5** miles the trail nears Deep Creek; with more stream crossings and much wildlife—you may glimpse a Louisiana Waterthrush or a garter snake—this stretch affords close views of the creek, and, as many fishermen will attest, provides good trout habitat.

The junction with Fork Ridge Trail and Campsite #53, "Poke Patch," mark **4.0** miles. The campsite got its name from pokeweed that once grew here. Young green shoots were eaten as a salad green by the mountain people, but pokeweed's deep purple berries and mature leaves are highly poisonous. The berries can be used to make dyes. The site is overused and unappealing. A cucumber-tree and tuliptree grow nearby. The latter's bark features horizontal lines of holes bored by Yellow-bellied Sapsuckers in search of sap and insects. This is good habitat for black bear, whose scat you may see.

At approximately **4.5** miles, after crossing several small feeder streams, you must rock-hop a larger tributary of Deep Creek. The trail climbs to a knoll about 200' above Deep Creek, with a steep drop-off on the right. Another rock-hop across a large feeder creek occurs at **5.0** miles where the trail is both rocky and muddy. By **5.5** miles, the trail maneuvers just to the left of cascading Deep Creek. Now you're moving through dense woods with openings only created by fallen trees. Trilliums thrive. By **6.0** miles, the trail ambles under huge Eastern hemlocks, beside smaller trees like Fraser magnolia. Because of moisture, the pungent odor of decaying vegetation is everywhere.

Deep Creek now moves more slowly than before, causing sand and silt to settle and form sandbars. Park officials have placed drainage culverts and moved the trail uphill away from the creek to prevent and minimize the effects of flooding.

At **6.6** miles, a trail section with a campsite approximately every half mile begins. These sites, numbered 54-59, vary in attractiveness for backpackers. Campsite #55 and #57 are horse camps and may be muddy. The others offer pleasant tent sites.

Throughout this strenuous stretch, the trail weaves up and down knolls, alternately featuring wet and dry habitats of Eastern hemlock, ferns (Christmas, maidenhair, and rock polypody) and white pine. Early on, about mile **7.0**, you pass a sycamore whose whitish bark stands out in the shadowy forest. Referring to this bark, park ranger Cliff Kevill jokingly explained the tree's name: "...at the bottom the tree looks sick; well, as you go up the trunk, it looks sick-a-more."

Campsite #57, Bryson Place, located on a knoll, is the site of Horace Kephart's last permanent camp. Kephart, the author of *Our Southern Highlanders* and an advocate for the establishment of the park spent many years living with and writing about mountain people. His camp is marked with a millstone placed by the Kephart Boy Scout Troop in 1931. The junction with Martin Gap Trail (leading to Sunkota Ridge and Indian Creek Trails) is also at Bryson Place. Further along, campsites #58 and #59 are located along the creek and offer excellent tent sites for backpackers.

By mile **11.0** the trail winds around a small side cove in which American beech, Eastern hemlock, and rosebay rhododendron dominate. You descend, soon reaching Campsite #60 at approximately **11.3** miles, a picturesque flat site strewn with pine needles. Winterberry is one wildflower that prospers in such habitat; so do poison ivy and Virginia creeper (remember, although their leaflets look alike, the poisonous plant has three leaflets per leaf, and the non-poisonous one has five). After crossing Bumgardner Branch on a foot bridge, you climb another knoll and descend into a mixed woodland—American beech, Eastern hemlock, tuliptree, and red maple.

One mile up Bumgardner Branch was the house, barn, and corn crib of W. J. Wiggins, whose farm was still in operation in the early 20th century. Also, near the mouth of Bumgardner Branch was Cindy Bumgardner's house, which was located several hundred yards off the trail. Arvil Greene remembered building barns on Bumgardner Branch. His father taught him to fell trees, hew and notch logs, and rive (or split) boards with a froe and maul. The majority of the barns Greene helped to build in the 1920s and 1930s had four stalls, one each for mules, horses, and milk cows, and one for harnesses, wagons, and sleds in addition to a place to keep hay from rain and snow. Greene emphasized the structures' practicality: "When I was growing up, people laughed at somebody that put paint on a barn, saying he was trying to show off."

At **12.0** miles the trail spills out onto the loop end of a gravel road, the intersection with Loop Trail. Turning right, you set out on a section of four stream crossings, all by bridge. Look for beaver gnawings by the first bridge. This section explains the creek's name since it boasts deep, still pools. At **13.6** miles, you pass a junction with Indian Creek Trail.

Just before you reach Deep Creek Campground and Ranger Station, a side trail on the right leads to Juney-whank Falls, which means "the bear went that a-way" in Cherokee, according to Cliff Kevill.

The center of Deep Creek Campground was the site of Deep Creek Civilian Conservation Corps (CCC) Camp from 1933 to 1936. First, Company 1216 lodged here; then Company 4484 moved in from Mingus Creek Camp to construct several trails in this vicinity, including Deep Creek, Noland Divide, and Thomas Divide Trails.

The mouth of Deep Creek, located several miles from the campground, is the site of a historic Civil War battle, fought on February 2, 1864 between the Col. William Thomas Legion (comprised mainly of Cherokees and western North Carolina mountaineers) and the Union Army, led by Major Francis Davidson and a detachment of the Fourteenth Illinois Cavalry. Davidson, guided by 40 or 50 Union sympathizers, marched his 600 troops up the Little Tennessee River past the mouths of Eagle, Hazel, Chambers, and Forney Creeks, then surprised the Thomas Legion at the mouth of Deep Creek. The battle raged for more than an hour. L. F. Siler, a witness to the fighting, later reported that "The Indians fought nobly until the ammunition ran out" and then retreated into the mountains to fight another day. The Union did not completely capture or immobilize the Thomas Legion, but two of Thomas' men were killed and 18 taken prisoner.

DEEP CREEK CAMPSITE SUMMARY

Site #	Mile	Description
53	4.0	Heavily used, near stream, big trees. 3,000'
54	6.6	Away from creek, good tent sites. 2,600'
55	7.5	Rationed site, horse camp. 2,410'
56	8.0	Horses no longer allowed. 2,405'
57	8.3	Rationed site, Bryson Place, on a knoll. 2,360'
58	8.5	Good tent sites, near creek. 2,360'
59	10.0	Backpacking site, near creek. 2,320'
60	11.3	Flat tent sites on pine needles. 2,120'

Narrative by Ted Olson

DEEPLOW GAP TRAIL

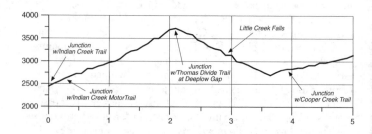

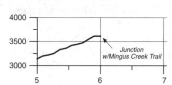

LENGTH: 6.0 miles, from Indian Creek Trail to Mingus Creek Trail.

HIGHLIGHTS: Little Creek Falls.

CAUTIONS: Numerous unbridged stream crossings.

MAP KEY: 8 F; USGS quads: Clingmans Dome, Smokemont.

USE: Horse and hiking trail.

TRAILHEAD: Hike 3.6 miles on Deep Creek and Indian Creek Trails north from end of Deep Creek Road.

The Deeplow area was possibly visited by the naturalist William Bartram in the late 1770s. Bartram, who visited several Cherokee villages in the area during his famous botanical exploration, published a book on his travels through the South. Bartram's *Travels* was popular in England and New England after it was published in 1791. Historians debate the exact route of Bartram's wanderings; nevertheless, it is possible that he crossed into the park in the vicinity of Deeplow Gap.

From its beginning at the Indian Creek Trail, the Deeplow Gap Trail turns to the right opposite a bench on the banks of Indian Creek. The wide roadbed is softened with pine needles from the surrounding pine-oak forest. The trail crosses Georges Branch by bridge at **0.1** mile.

At **0.2** mile you reach a clearing for an old house site, perhaps once belonging to Jim Bumgardner. A large American holly tree grows to the left on the creek banks. An old, ornamental privet hedge has grown to crowd the cleared area. At his home on Georges Branch, Jim Bumgardner set up a pounding mill, a nineteenth-century style watermill used by both Cherokee and early settlers. It could make three cycles per minute and grind two gallons of cornmeal a day.

Above the house site, at mile **0.3,** the trail turns left, while the main roadbed veers right and becomes Indian Creek Motor Trail. Deeplow Gap Trail ascends with Georges Branch on the left. The trail, which is an old roadbed, can be wet and muddy on this section.

After crossing a small branch, the trail enters an area of large trees. The largest are Eastern hemlock and oak. On the left is an enormous dead tree (over 4' in diameter) which could provide a habitat for owls and pileated woodpeckers. Yellow birch grow amid dog-hobble, mountain laurel and galax. The trail continues to be rocky.

At mile **1.0** the roadbed continues straight, but the trail turns right through an Eastern hemlock forest. The trail crisscrosses a small branch all the way up toward Deeplow Gap. Large Eastern hemlocks tower over downy rattlesnake-plantain and partridgeberry. The American chestnut trees which once grew on these slopes lie decaying on the ground. A large Fraser magnolia tree stands near the first switchback. Other Fraser magnolias grow alongside the rocky trail, which steepens after the switchback.

The trail winds up the west side of Thomas Divide to Deeplow Gap (3,715') at mile **2.2.** Here our trail intersects Thomas Divide Trail, which goes 8.2 miles north (left) to the Newfound Gap Road and 5.6 miles south (right) to Galbraith Creek Road. After the gap, you cross Thomas Divide and descend its eastern slope on a graded foot trail. Look for squawroot and downy rattlesnake-plantain among the Eastern hemlocks. Mountain laurel predominates in a mixture of rosebay rhododendron and Fraser magnolia. Galax hugs the sides of the trail.

A switchback takes you to a ford of Little Creek in thick dog-hobble. Follow Little Creek through a lush area where large Eastern hemlocks tower overhead at the top of Little Creek Falls at **2.8** miles. As the trail descends to the base of the falls, it momentarily moves away from the creek by a switchback amid large sandstone boulders. The trail then turns back toward the creek to reach the base of the falls 200 yards below the switchback. Little Creek cascades 95' over hundreds of Thunderhead Sandstone shelves. The falls spreads from 25' to 40' at the base where a log acts as dam and bridge. Rosebay rhododendron and moss-covered logs provide a green frame. Carefully cross the creek via the log in the spray of the falls. A bed of hepatica lines the trail.

The trail continues with a moderate slope. Cross Little Creek again amid rosebay rhododendron and Eastern hemlock. The trail moderates as Little Creek flows on the right. You cross two small branches before a clearing marks an old house site. Little Creek flows right to a junction with Cooper Creek. At mile **3.9**, Cooper Creek

Trail turns south (right), 0.6 miles from the park boundary on Cooper Creek Road.

Deeplow Gap Trail continues north (left) from the unmarked intersection. The trail is a roadbed which follows Cooper Creek. Ferns, striped pipsissewa, and dog-hobble grow under thick rosebay rhododendron. At **4.1** miles, your crossing of Cooper Creek can be wet since few rocks provide stepping stones. Walk through a rosebay rhododendron tunnel before another wet ford of Cooper Creek.

The trail pulls away from the creek and around a large clearing at mile **4.7**. Two chimneys stand to the right of the trail at the site of an old farmhouse. Rotting logs still rest on foundation stones. Yellow birch and flowering dogwood grow here.

When the roadbed splits, the trail bears up and left as you gradually ascend through pine and mountain laurel into a pine-oak forest. Cross Cooper Creek one final time via rock hop at **5.0** miles. The trail becomes steeper but not too difficult and you reach the ridge crest at **6.0** miles.

A trail junction is at the top of the ridge. Mingus Creek Trail goes north 3.0 miles to Newton Bald Trail.

Narrative by Charles Maynard and David Morris

DRY SLUICE GAP TRAIL

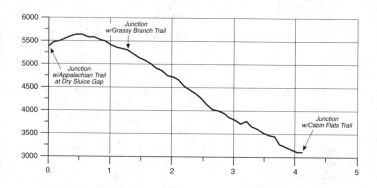

LENGTH: 4.1 miles, from Appalachian Trail at Dry Sluice Gap, (0.4 mile from Charlies Bunion) to Cabin Flats Trail.
HIGHLIGHTS: Old-growth forest with big trees; open ridge on top.
CAUTIONS: Steep, rocky sections.
MAP KEY: 8-9 D; USGS quads: Mt. Guyot, Smokemont.
USE: Horse and hiking trail.
TRAILHEAD: From Newfound Gap, hike the Appalachian Trail north (east) past Icewater Springs and Charlies Bunion to Dry Sluice Gap (4.4 miles). Turn right at trail sign.

D ry Sluice Gap Trail connects the Appalachian Trail with the Smokemont Campground and with Kephart Prong, and you have to hike a little more than 4 miles of other trails to reach any part of it. A car shuttle between Newfound Gap and Smokemont Campground would allow a good day hike on the Appalachian, Dry Sluice Gap, Cabin Flats and Bradley Fork trails. (13.0 miles). A more strenuous day hike or an overnight loop could include the A.T., upper Dry Sluice Gap, Grassy Branch, and Sweat Heifer Creek trails (13.6 miles). The early settlers of Porters Flat didn't have so many choices. Somehow they made their way, with loads of household necessities and livestock, over this gap and down steep shale ledges on the other side like the ones you see exposed on Charlies Bunion.

The trail starts at Dry Sluice Gap with a weedy, brambly climb from the A.T. Notice a big black cherry tree on the left about 50 yards from the junction. The trail levels on a quiet boulevard of red spruce and Catawba rhododendron. After another climb, this one rockier, the trail reaches an open grassy area with good views and, in August, a fine dessert of blueberries, blackberries, and huckleberries. American mountain-ash and pin cherry grow on the edges. Pin cherry, or fire cherry, has long, sharp leaves and usually grows where there has been a disturbance. The ones here probably started after a lumber company fire roared up from Smokemont, destroying habitat and stripping Charlies Bunion of all vegetation and subsequently, soil.

Horse use and erosion have caused the trail to sink below the level of the grassy meadow; in some places the trail banks are knee-high. Long grass can hide rocks in the trail from view. On the right is a grove of curly-barked yellow birches, and on the left, many small Fraser firs crowd the ridge top.

The trail starts down a gully lined with high bush blueberries, trailing arbutus, and three kinds of clubmoss: princess pine, ground pine, and shining clubmoss. Catawba rhododendron closes overhead, and then you reach the junction with Grassy Branch Trail at mile **1.3.** From here it is 2.5 miles to the Kephart Shelter and 7.3 miles on to Smokemont. Non-native Norway spruce, planted by Champion Fibre after the fire, grows around the trail junction.

From the junction, the trail runs to the left of the Richland Mountain ridge. Red spruce and hobblebush are common here, and Rugel's ragwort, a high elevation flower in the aster family, grows along the trail. Its leaves are heart-shaped. Some parts of the trail may be muddy or broken down from horse use. As the trail drops below the ridge line, springs and seeps support meadows of tall summer-blooming flowers: bee-balm, false hellebore, wood-nettle, snakeroot, jewelweed, Joe-Pye-weed, black cohosh, and others. Listen and watch for bees and wasps.

About 0.5 mile from the junction, Eastern hemlock trees mix with the spruce and soon become the dominant evergreen. American chestnut trees used to cover this hillside; you can see decaying snags and logs. The trail descends a very rocky section and then becomes more level and smooth. It enters dry, open woods with tangled mountain laurel, trailing arbutus, galax, a few pink lady's slippers, and some very large oak trees. After another descent, the trail crosses the upper part of the Tennessee Branch of Bradley Fork on stepping stones.

As the trail descends a rocky, eroded section with the branch on the left, look for enormous silverbells, oaks, tuliptrees, and basswoods. This ravine escaped logging and was moist or sheltered enough to withstand the fires, so it is a good example of old-growth forest.

After more rocky trail and two easy side creek crossings, the trail drops to the Tennessee Branch again for another easy rock hop. Look for a huge tuliptree on the right and an oak on the left with a burl the size of a pig bulging out from the trunk. As you continue down with the Tennessee Branch on the right, look for basswoods with crowds of root shoots and a big, mossy nurse log that supports ferns and small trees in its rotting wood. A small yellow birch is perched on the end near the trail with most of its roots exposed, reaching down to find real soil.

A log bridge with a handrail gets you across the Tennessee Branch again, and the trail becomes a high bench above a pretty ravine. As the trail returns to the branch, it becomes rocky and wet, with woodnettle and jewelweed growing along the side. Dutchman's pipe, ferns, and jack-in-the-pulpit grow among the rocks, and, at the base of a large yellow buckeye, another log bridge crosses the branch.

From here the trail is narrow with a few rocks. The creek is on the right but hidden under rosebay rhododendron. Look for big silverbells, oaks, Fraser magnolias, and American chestnut snags.

At mile **4.1**, look for the Dry Sluice Gap Trail sign in a patch of rhododendron. From here, it is 0.6 mile left to Campsite #49. To the right, it is 0.5 mile to Bradley Fork Trail, and 4.5 miles to Smokemont Campground.

Narrative by Doris Gove

EAGLE CREEK TRAIL

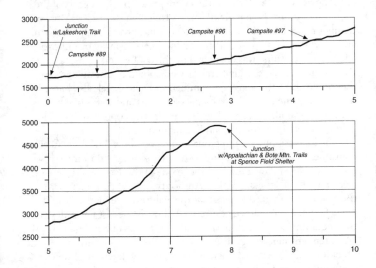

LENGTH: 7.9 miles, from Lakeshore Trail to Appalachian Trail at Spence Field.

HIGHLIGHTS: Spence Field, Eagle Creek.

CAUTIONS: Numerous stream crossings.

MAP KEY: 3 F-E; USGS quads: Fontana Dam, Cades Cove, Thunderhead Mtn.

USE: Hiking trail.

STARTING POINT: Jct. Lakeshore Trail, 6.2 miles northeast of Fontana Dam. Accessible by boat across Fontana Lake to Campsite #90. For commercial shuttle, contact Fontana Village Marina: 1-704-498-2211.

The Eagle Creek drainage has lived many lives. Once its waters were used only by plants and animals. Then came the Cherokee on extended hunting trips. Later they were displaced by white settlers who farmed the land and harnessed the water to run small tub mills and other devices. In 1890, the settlers were joined by the loggers of the Montvale Lumber Company. Between 1890 and the 1930s, Montvale Lumber removed millions of board feet of hardwood lumber from this and nearby valleys. Most of this wood was carried away by railroad engines whose thirst was quenched by the cool waters of Eagle Creek. By the early 1900s, the lumberjacks were joined by another group— the miners. Like the loggers, the miners of Eagle Creek also harnessed the power of the river. It was used to run mills and trains like before, but now it was also used to clean and purify the copper, silver and gold removed from the surrounding mountains.

The loggers, miners, and pioneers are gone now, but Eagle Creek continues to be harnessed by us. Today, these waters flow into Fontana Lake and eventually through one of three generators creating electricity for Tennessee Valley Authority (TVA) customers across the South. Yet in all the lives that this valley has seen, the flow of Eagle Creek has remained constant. Although the last few miles of this mountain stream are lost beneath the waters of Fontana Lake, the creek remains much as it always has been. Its waters begin high in the Smokies at a place called Spence Field. Gravity draws them down, crashing over and carving up the sandstone that is these mountains. Our hike begins at the base of the creek where it still runs free and climbs to the headwaters at one of the most beautiful spots in the Smokies. It is a hike that requires strong muscles and good wet shoes.

The beginning of the Eagle Creek Trail is 0.8 mile east of Campsite #90 on the Lakeshore Trail. At this junction, the Lakeshore Trail crosses Eagle Creek via a footlog with handrail to follow Pinnacle Creek to Jenkins Ridge. Our trail heads north through a cool hemlock forest for about a quarter mile until it too crosses Eagle Creek. Unfortunately, there is no footlog here at this wide and treacherous crossing. You will have to ford the river, so pull out the wet shoes, hitch up the pack, and take very good care in crossing. It is very important that you plan this hike well. If recent rains have brought the creek up, this can be an extremely dangerous crossing; and the trail doesn't get any easier. Between the trailhead and Campsite #97 (4 miles), there are 16 fords, all very swift and deep at high water. This first ford is a good indicator of things to come. If, after crossing, you still can not make up your mind as to continue or not, fret not. Just 1,300' ahead is your next opportunity. This is perhaps even a harder and deeper crossing. Take special care.

If the water levels allow you to continue, you will follow the trail up along the flood plain of Eagle Creek. Here you can really enjoy the beauty of the river; it rivals Deep Creek and Little River as one of the prettiest in the park. At **0.8** miles, the rhododendron and Eastern hemlock give way to a hardwood forest and Campsite #89. This is a large open area capable of supporting 6 or more tents. It even comes complete with a stone table and railroad rails. In the 1890s, when George Wood ran Montvale Lumber Company, his men lived in canvas tents. Perhaps some of those loggers spent a night or two here. It's a good spot: wide, flat, and at the junction of Ekaneetlee Creek and Eagle Creek. There's plenty of water, but remember to treat it before use.

From Campsite #89, the trail immediately fords Ekaneetlee Creek and rock hops a small spur of it. Keep those wet shoes on, because in about a half mile you will be crossing Eagle Creek again—twice in less than 1,000' in fact. These are both swift and deep fords, but not quite as long as the earlier ones. Just ahead is another back to back series of fords; this time the two are within 100' of each other. It hardly makes sense to build a trail this way until you get out here and see how the ridges push right down to the river.

After traveling more than 2 miles, you will reach Campsite #96. To get there however, you will have to ford Eagle Creek again. This is the first short ford. No, the creek isn't any narrower here, it's just that Campsite #96 is on an island. Which means if you camp here, you will have to ford the creek again in the morning. The campsite is nice, with small spots for tents scattered along the island. It can easily accommodate 4 tents, but if you follow park rules, you cannot go to the bathroom here. There is no place more than 100' (or 50' for that matter), from the river or trail as the park requests.

The trail continues to the head of the island and crosses a short, deep, swift ford. Keep those wet shoes on though—just ahead is a small backwash to cross. Then in a short distance you will be back to the big fords. First you will cross to the east shore—rocky and swift.

Then in 1,000' you will return to the creek, but don't cross. Instead, travel upriver—yes, in the river—100' and continue along the east shore for another 900'. Now you can ford the wide, rocky, and swift Eagle Creek. Does this sound familiar?

At just over **3.5** miles, you guessed it, it's ford number 13 and 14 within 600' of each other. Both are long and swift crossings as is ford #15 about 0.5 mile further upstream. But after this crossing, you will walk solid ground for a good distance—about 1,500'. At this point you will reach Campsite #97, the last site before Spence Field. The site sits to the left, between the trail and creek. Like the two lower sites, it sits on the flood plain making for a wide, level spot. There are places for two to three groups here and fortunately someone had hikers in mind when they laid out this site. Just ahead is ford #16, the last, and across it is a another small site. Camping here will put all the fords behind you.

Here at Campsite #97, you will find some old artifacts. Please leave them here for others to enjoy, but let them fire your imagination. Was this wash tub left behind by the loggers or was it the miners; maybe it was Quill Rose who left it? Quill was Eagle Creek's most infamous resident. He was a blockader or what we today call a moonshiner. He was one of the best at his trade which meant he made good, strong corn whiskey and didn't get caught. Least not until he was in his 80s. I guess with his hearing and eyesight fading he didn't know the revenue (law) was about to storm in on him and his still. Nor were his legs strong enough to elude the chase which must have followed. So he was hauled to Bryson City and brought before a judge. Quill's reputation as the best was well known, even to the judge, who before sentencing had one thing to ask. "Quill, I know you're the best blockader there is, so I'd like to know one thing. Wouldn't it make your liquor better if you age it first?" "Well, Judge," Quill responded, "I kept some a week once and it didn't seem to help a bit."

Our hike continues along the shores of Eagle Creek for another 0.5 mile. The trail slowly climbs away from the stream at first, but then becomes steeper. After awhile, the trail drops across a small spring branch. Up and down, over the rises you will go until you again reach the shores of a beautiful mountain stream. This is no longer called Eagle Creek, however. You have climbed to its major tributary,

Gunna Creek. Downriver a short distance, Paw Paw Creek joins Gunna Creek to form Eagle Creek. The change in name may have to do with the change in character. Although Eagle and Gunna Creeks are both mountain streams, they are very different. Eagle Creek is wide and swift, but mostly horizontal. It loses only 1,000' in about 5 miles. Gunna Creek is much more vertical. It crashes and tumbles steeply down the mountains, losing 1,000' in less than half the distance.

And with the change of the river, so changes the trail. You will begin to climb more moderately. You first pass a wide open area in which a small spring branch has usurped the trail. There is also a scattering of wash basins in the area. Intuition tells us that this was once a lumber camp. As you climb past this place, you will begin to notice changes in the forest, too. We are now up over 3,000', the middle elevation of the park. Gone are the sweetgum and sycamore trees of the lower elevations. Now our forest is mostly maples and oaks, cherries and hickories—trees of the northern states. The forests are more open as well. We get views of the cascades on Gunna Creek and the cliffs of DeArmond Ridge to the east. The forest is still too dense to give us good vistas of the valley below—even in winter.

Mile 5.5 sees us cross Gunna Creek for the first time. It is by way of a very challenging rock hop. A few hundred feet ahead is another rock hop. It's challenging, but not as tough as the one before. A sign is strung across the creek here—NO FISHING. From this point on, the creek is closed to fishermen to protect native brook trout.

Perseverance is what you will need now as the trail begins to climb even steeper. After crossing the creek, the trail will take you into an unofficial campsite. Pass through the site to find the trail on a small bench on the hillside beyond. Here you will begin a series of switchbacks. At mile 6.0, you will pass a large sandstone boulder covered with a plant called rock tripe. You will then cross another unnamed stream seeping across the trail. Just ahead is another tripe-covered boulder. This one stands like a monolith left by an ancient civilization. It isn't, of course, just a fluke of nature and gravity.

Continue climbing uphill until the trail turns sharply left and begins to climb very steeply. The waterway you are now following is called Spence Cabin Branch, another name for another change in character. This steep, shallow stream will lead you to the Smokies' crest. The going for the next 1.5 miles is very difficult. The trail is very steep in places and sometimes hard to identify. Your best bet is to remember not to cross the stream until it levels out.

With 1 mile left to go, the trail will pass a large yellow buckeye and rockhop the creek. After that very steep ascent, the trail is much easier going. You pass now through a stand of young American beech trees with occasional large oaks, maples, and birches. Most of the very large trees have been blown over, a testament to the struggles of the high country ecosystems. Finally, you will cross 4,500' in elevation and begin the last steep push to the top. The trail switches back and forth finally crossing a small spring branch just below its source at a small PVC pipe. Here is the water source for the Spence Field Shelter which lies just ahead. There you will find toilets, food storage boxes and a caged sleeping area. So much for the wilderness. Spence Field is very heavily used by dayhikers, backpackers and horseback riders. Make your reservations well in advance of your trip.

Spence Field itself lies another 0.1 mile to the east. This is a large beautiful grassy field sitting on the Smokies' crest. To the north are great views of Cades Cove and the mountains of east Tennessee. To the south is Fontana Lake and the valleys of western North Carolina. The mountains beyond Fontana are in the Nantahala National Forest. Spence Field is a wonderful place to stop, rest, and enjoy. The Appalachian, Bote Mountain, Jenkins Ridge, and of course Eagle Creek trails all converge or diverge here, taking you off into new and challenging directions.

Narrative by Tom Condon

ENLOE CREEK TRAIL

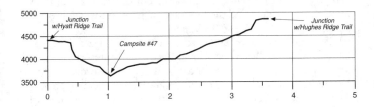

LENGTH: 3.6 miles, from Hyatt Ridge Trail to Hughes Ridge Trail.
HIGHLIGHTS: Old-growth forest, many small waterfalls along a beautiful stream.
CAUTIONS: Muddy trail.
MAP KEY: 9-10 D; USGS quads: Bunches Bald, Smokemont.
USE: Horse and hiking trail.
STARTING POINT: Hike 1.9 miles on Hyatt Ridge Trail from its Straight Fork Road trailhead. Or, hike 5.6 miles on Bradley Fork, Chasteen Creek and Hughes Ridge trails from Smokemont Campground.

Enloe Creek Trail skirts a peculiarly wild area of the park. The area largely escaped logging efforts of competing timber companies, so most of the route is in virgin forest. Most spectacular, however, are the beautiful waterfalls and cascades seen on Raven Fork and Enloe Creek. Unfortunately, the trail is in poor condition in many places due to heavy horse traffic.

Abraham and Wes Enloe were early white settlers of the Oconaluftee region, arriving around 1805. They chose the confluence of Raven Fork and Straight Fork near Big Cove to homestead. An old tale tells of a farmhand named Nancy Hanks who became pregnant while working on the Enloe farm. Wes Enloe helped the young woman move away to Kentucky where the child, named Abraham Lincoln, was born. There is some dispute over which Enloe brother fathered the child, but there was supposedly a strong resemblance between the Enloe family and the former president. Incidentally, folk tales on the identity of Lincoln's biological father abound throughout various parts of the country. Many of the Enloes' legitimate progeny remained in the area, and the Enloes are a noteworthy family of the Smokies.

The trail begins at an unnamed gap on Hyatt Ridge and descends immediately into Raven Fork Gorge. As the trail enters the gorge, the forest changes from young, second-growth mixed hardwoods to old-growth Eastern hemlock, magnolia, yellow buckeye, and tuliptree. The forest was selectively cut for exceptional trees, but it shows little indication of logging.

After about 0.5 mile, the trail passes a cut through a rock outcrop. Notice the speckled appearance of blackish minerals in a lighter matrix. The dark specks are garnets and the rock is called gneiss (pronounced "nice." Closer inspection reveals the garnets' very dark red color. Note that some garnets taper on either end in a characteristic eye shape. These "eyes" are augen, the German word for eye. This type of rock is an augen gneiss. Augen result as minerals form around the garnets in response to pressure. The garnet serves to disrupt the distribution of pressure, and minerals grow in the "lee" of the garnet.

Gneiss is uncommon in the Unaka Range of which the Smokies are part. The Unakas are mostly sedimentary rock of Cambrian and Precambrian age. Gneiss is a metamorphic rock, formed from intense heat and enormous pressures. These metamorphic rocks are over a billion years old. The basement rocks are similar to those found east of the Unakas, in the Blue Ridge and Piedmont. They are found here, in what is known as the Straight Fork Window, due to faulting and later erosion, allowing a view into the heart of the mountain range.

The trail continues its descent into the gorge passing several small tributaries that cascade straight down the fall line toward Raven Fork. At 0.8 mile the old Raven Fork manway once could be found entering on the right. Overgrown by rosebay rhododendron, and with occasional fords of Raven Fork, this route is purely off-trail hiking. The manway leads about 6.5 rough miles to McGee Springs, at the terminus of Hyatt Ridge Trail.

At 1.0 mile, the trail reaches Raven Fork. The roar of this large stream echoes off the gorge walls and gargantuan boulders. Raven

Fork is one of the largest streams in the park that does not have a trail along it. Adding to its grandeur is that most of its drainage is untrammeled wilderness. Boulders in the stream are conspicuously free of mosses, testament to their scouring by periodic flash floods. For example, a torrential cloudburst in September 1992 dumped over 4" of rain here in 1 hour. The resulting flash flood sent a 12' wall of water out of Raven Fork and into Straight Fork that devastated homes and the trout farms on the Cherokee Indian Reservation. Waters were 20' above normal pool in many places. The waters overtopped the wooden base at the bridge across Raven Fork, which is easily 15' above the stream. This bridge was built several years after a backpacker lost his life trying to ford here during high water.

On the opposite side of Raven Fork lies Campsite #47. This small site is often wet and muddy. Although many enjoy sleeping to the serenade of a tumbling stream, the dull roar of the small waterfalls at this site make it almost uncomfortably noisy. Fortunately, the surrounding area is beautiful and interesting, with many large boulders for scrambling and exploration.

The trail then climbs gradually away from Raven Fork to within sight of Enloe Creek at **1.5** miles. The trail passes several cascades that may be obscured from view by summer vegetation, but are worth a closer look. Although a piped spring on the right runs slowly, locating water is hardly a problem on this trail. The trail crosses Enloe Creek on a foot log at **2.0** miles, then enters a muddy stretch of trail through a rosebay rhododendron thicket.

At about **2.5** miles, the trail has climbed away from the creek, and there is a good view of Katalsta Ridge to the north. Note the conspicuous red spruce on the ridge, suggesting upland, old-growth forest. This trailless ridge used to be named Left Fork Ridge but was renamed when the park was established to honor the daughter (Kata'lsta) of the Cherokee chief Yonaguska (Drowning Bear). Kata'lsta was a skilled potter who followed traditional Cherokee methods. She single-handedly maintained this tradition into the twentieth century.

The trail climbs in a southwesterly direction up Enloe Ridge and twists through several switchbacks. Notice that since the trail entered the Enloe Creek drainage, the rocks are sandstone and slate, indicating that the trail has traveled out of the Straight Fork Window. These rocks are typical of the Ocoee Series mentioned earlier. The Ocoee is gray or brown and plain. It lacks the shiny, crystalline appearance of the basement rock.

At **3.4** miles, the trail reaches a sag, and returns to an open forest of second growth hardwoods. The gentle hollow on the left shelters the headwaters of Batsaw Branch, a name which probably refers to earlier lumbering activities. This portion of the trail is often overgrown with briers and nettles in late summer. At **3.6** miles, the trail ends at an intersection with Hughes Ridge Trail. To the right, Bradley Fork Trail is 2.5 miles and Pecks Corner Shelter is 4.5 miles. To the left, Smokemont Campground is 7.9 miles on Hughes Ridge Trail, and 5.6 miles via the Hughes Ridge, Chasteen Creek and Bradley Fork Trails.

Narrative by James Wedekind

FINLEY CANE TRAIL

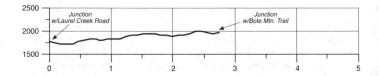

LENGTH: 2.8 miles, from Laurel Creek Road to Bote Mtn. Trail
HIGHLIGHTS: Rhododendron tunnels.
CAUTIONS: Trailhead parking.
MAP KEY: 4 D; USGS quad: Thunderhead.
USE: Horse and hiking trail.
TRAILHEAD: Laurel Creek Road, 5.75 miles west of Townsend "Y".

The Finley Cane Trail is most often used as an access point to Spence Field via the Bote Mountain Trail. Avoiding it because the high country is not your destination is an unfortunate mistake. Finley Cane is an easy and enjoyable hike.

To reach the trailhead you must travel west on the Laurel Creek Road (toward Cades Cove). Watch your odometer because the pull-offs on each side of the road are quite narrow and the trailhead can easily be missed. Travel 5.75 miles west of the Townsend "Y". The parking here serves 3 trails: Finley Cane and Lead Cove on the south side and Turkey Pen Ridge on the north side of the road. You are forced to park parallel to the road and since traffic can be heavy, be careful.

The Finley Cane Trail is the rocky path to the left. It parallels the road for a short distance heading east or downhill. Immediately you will notice that rosebay rhododendrons and Fraser magnolias abound. These trees will line the first half of the trail. Just after passing a large American beech tree, you will turn away from the road and cross Sugar Cove Creek. This is an easy rock hop at low water, but a real wet one when the water is high. Fortunately, the latter is very rare.

This is a great place to do a little salamander watching. The Smokies are renowned for their diversity of salamanders. The park has 27 species of these amphibians, the greatest concentration in the world. You are very likely to stir up a dusky salamander by carefully turning over a few rocks here. They are the most common species at this elevation. It's best not to touch the salamanders and to return the rocks to their original locations.

Continuing along the trail, you will enter a young stand of Eastern hemlock trees. This will take you up to a muddy intersection. The left fork here will take you back toward Laurel Creek Road. It then passes under a small bridge where Sugar Cove Prong passes as well. This very muddy, well-used horse trail will ultimately join the Turkey Pen Ridge Trail.

Finley Cane continues straight ahead at the intersection. Like the other trail, it can be very muddy. It will continue in this way for another short distance until you cross a small spring branch and begin to climb along the north flank of Bote Mountain. Here you will enter a rhododendron tunnel which will open and close on you for more than 0.5 mile. The tunnel is a wonderful place to be on those hot days of summer, particularly in July. The shade will keep you cool and in July the rhododendron explode into bloom. The large white flower clusters are some of the most beautiful in the park, both on the plants and off. As they become pollinated, the flowers drop their petals to the ground, reminding you of snow.

After you rock hop Laurel Cove Creek and Hickory Tree Branch within 200' of each other, the rhododendron will give way to an open cove hardwood forest. At first the forest is young, made up of many small trees. But soon you reach a mature forest where large stately trees abound. Here you will see big oaks, Eastern hemlocks, hickories, and especially tuliptrees. These are not the monsters of the park's virgin timber, but delightful all the same. Be sure to take a moment to marvel at the straight, towering trunks of the tuliptrees. At mile **2.5**, you will pass right between 2 gorgeous pillars, each over 2' in diameter. These majestic columns are draped with purple-red grape vines—a magnificent sight.

Throughout this hike you have been slowly rising and falling. On the mountain side, the trail has been dry and smooth. But occasional spring branches cross the path. They run almost imperceptibly yet the continual flow leaves the trail muddy in places. This mix of wet and dry provides you with a diversity of more than just salamanders. Mushrooms are also plentiful here. Count the varieties you see, but do not expect to see them all. Park researchers estimate over 2,000 species exist here, from the beautiful but deadly destroying angels to the morels, highly prized as a choice edible.

The last mile or so of the trail climbs from a dry crossing of Finley Cove Creek to Bote Mountain Trail. Here you will pass the patch of cane which probably lends its name to the trail. Cane is the only native relative of bamboo in the park. It prefers streamside habitats, but is occasionally found in drier sites like this one. Its nickname, switch cane, probably referred to its use in correcting childhood misbehavior. Or perhaps it was just used to drive cattle up to Spence Field. Continuing along, the going is rocky in places, so watch your footing. When you reach the Bote Mountain Trail, you have many choices. Backpackers can continue up to Spence Field (5.4 miles) or opt for campsite #18 (1 mile) on the West Prong Trail. Day hikers can do the same or return along the Finley Cane Trail to your car. A third alternative is to combine Finley Cane, Bote Mountain, and Lead Cove into a 7.1 miles round trip journey.

Narrative by Tom Condon

FLAT CREEK TRAIL

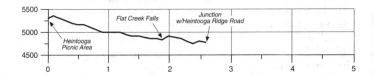

LENGTH: 2.6 miles, from Heintooga Overlook to Heintooga Ridge Road.
HIGHLIGHTS: Flat Creek Falls, mountain vistas.
CAUTIONS: Stream crossings.
MAP KEY: 11 E; USGS quad: Bunches Bald.
USE: Horse and hiking trail.
TRAILHEAD: Take Heintooga Ridge Road north from Blue Ridge Parkway, past Balsam Mountain Campground to Heintooga Picnic Area. The trail starts at the signed Heintooga Overlook adjacent to the picnic area.

Few short trails in the Smokies are as beautiful as Flat Creek Trail. Built in 1934 by the Civilian Conservation Corps, this moderate 2.6 mile trail offers good views, an enchanting, grass-carpeted ridge forest, a lush creek valley, and an energetic two-tier waterfall.

On the short walk to the trailhead, good views of the Great Smokies range (with Mount Guyot prominent on the horizon) are visible to the right of the picnic area's water-fountain. After **0.1** mile, a sign marks the trail, which veers right onto a 5,300' high ridge. You enter a dark "elfin" forest comprised of American beech, red spruce, striped maple, red maple, Eastern hemlock, and yellow birch.

Few large trees grow on this snaking ridge because the region was heavily logged after 1900 when a small lumber company established a camp nearby, bringing with it a portable mill. The logs cut by this company were taken by wagon to nearby Whittier, N.C. This deforestation intensified during the 1920s, when the Suncrest Lumber Company expanded its operations into the region. Suncrest extensively logged the trees near Flat Creek right up to the day the title was transferred to the park. Suncrest "cut everything they could before that date," remembered former logger Dave Wiggins. He explained why he and his peers welcomed the timber companies despite the devastation they brought to the fragile mountain environment: "Work was scarce those days in this country, [with] five or six hundred men and their families depending on the Suncrest operation up here for their livelihood."

Wiggins lived at nearby Black Camp, where loggers and their families resided in shanty cars brought up by railroad. He recalls paying Suncrest two dollars per month to rent a shanty car for himself and his wife, a price that would have been a considerable portion of a logger's income in the 1920s. Other loggers often rented two, one for themselves and one for their families. The site of the company town is known today as Black Camp Gap, back down the Heintooga Ridge Road from the trailhead; a Masonic monument marks the spot—the shanty cars are long gone.

The thick grass growing along the upper-stretch of the trail is evidence of extensive logging: grass historically did not grow in the deep shade of southern Appalachian virgin forests. Those plants that did take root in the shadows of uncut forest generally possessed wide leaves—the wider, the better, to catch the minimal sunlight filtering through the dense canopy. Grass, with its narrow blades, thrived in exposed settings, such as on the handful of southern Appalachian balds.

About 0.5 mile from the trailhead, after a rapid descent down the ridge, you reach Flat Creek. At this point, the forest closes in on you, for the vegetation here, well-watered by Flat Creek, is lush. Many species comprise this dense undergrowth, including the trail's first stand of rosebay rhododendron; the creek's humidity also supports mosses, lichens, and mushrooms. Soon, on the right, you spot an old yellow birch measuring roughly 4' in diameter. Growing larger than other birches, this species is most common in the northeast U.S. and southeast Canada, but it flourishes in the cool, moist upper elevations of the southern Appalachians. The tree's presence is directly attributable to the glaciers that once extended as far south as Pennsylvania and Ohio, bringing to the southeast a far colder climate than that experienced today. As the glaciers retreated northward 10,000 years ago, the climate of North America changed. Many cool-weather species of plants and animals died out in the warming south; but a number of the species that we now associate with the north, such as the yellow birch, survive in the higher elevations and cooler temperatures of the southern mountains.

After several stream crossings by foot log and rock-hop, the trail jogs away from Flat Creek; you enter a mixed second-growth forest of serviceberry, maple, hawthorn, cherry, birch, and American beech. At times these trees form a thicket, creating good nesting habitat for a variety of birds, including the Brown Thrasher and the Rufous-sided Towhee. And then, once you've forgotten about the creek, you hear it cascading quickly down the slope, pounding against the rocks in its way. On the right, **1.5** miles from the trailhead, a short spur trail meanders down to Flat Creek Falls. To obtain the best, most complete view of the waterfall, rock-hop carefully across the creek at the top of the waterfall and climb down the slope on the other side: from this vantage point, you see the lower half of the falls, a steep waterslide. The water spreads in feathery fingers over the flat, sheer rock.

Flat Creek Trail continues another mile, traversing the ridge between Flat Creek and Bunches Creek. At one point, you may see partial views of the valley into which Flat Creek flows. The trail threads a dense, mixed-hardwood forest—birch, American beech, and maple where the Veery's *vee-ur, vee-ur, veer, veer* and the Red-Eyed Vireo's nasal whining *chuway* can be heard. After crossing two forks of Bunches Creek by foot bridge, you reach Heintooga Ridge Road between Black Camp and Polls (Paul's) gaps.

Narrative by Ted Olson

FORK RIDGE TRAIL

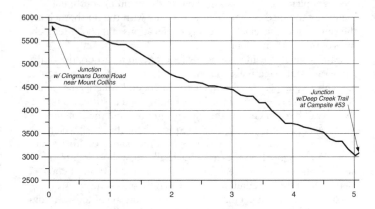

Junction
w/ Clingmans Dome Road
near Mount Collins

Junction
w/Deep Creek Trail
at Campsite #53

LENGTH: 5.1 miles, From Clingmans Dome Road to Deep Creek
Trail.
HIGHLIGHTS: Old-growth forest, transition between forest ecosystems.
MAP KEY: 7 E; USGS quad: Clingmans Dome.
USE: Hiking trail.
TRAILHEAD: From Newfound Gap Road, take Clingmans Dome
Road 3.5 miles to small Fork Ridge trailhead parking area on the left.

From its trailhead, Fork Ridge Trail (beginning elevation 5,880')
gradually progresses downhill through red spruce, yellow birch, mountain-ash, and Fraser fir. The many dead trees along the upper stretches are Fraser firs, which have been killed by a non-native insect, the
balsam woolly adelgid.

The Fork Ridge Trail descends along cool, moist Fork Ridge. At
one point on the right is a spectacular outcrop: vertical layers of rock
with intrusions of quartz; trees grow precariously on top of it. Nearby,
just off the trail on the left, is a vertical boulder, covered with mosses

and ferns like rock polypody.

Along the upper part of the trail, you may encounter bluebead-lily, hobblebush, and false nettle; Dark-eyed Juncos nest by the trail and Black-capped Chickadees and Winter Wrens call from nearby limbs. Soon the trail begins a steep descent through large red spruce, with patches of ferns and Fraser fir seedlings.

By **1.0** mile, after coursing through its first stand of rosebay rhododendron, the trail heads downhill among mountain-ash. To the left, the slope drops steeply. Descending again, the trail skirts a grove of large red spruce and levels briefly at a forest opening where smooth blackberries, mountain maple, and tall meadow rue grow among scattered young Fraser fir. Heading downhill, you step over a spring-fed streamlet into an opening of orange jewelweed, dodder (a parasitic orange vine), and flowering dogwood, as well as yellow birch and American beech.

At approximately **2.0** miles, the trail crosses a small stream near large red spruce. On the left tower some large yellow birches with 3-4' diameters; also note the red, sugar, and striped maples in one clump on the left. In mid-summer, look for the Turk's cap lily. Since by now the trail has descended below 4,500', the minimum elevation for fir, Fraser fir is all but absent and Eastern hemlock takes over.

Just past an area of many downed Eastern hemlock trees—probably victims of lightning—the trail levels out. Shortly afterward, you enter a thick Eastern hemlock grove, with a huge, 5'-diameter tree to the left. Nearby are many American chestnut stumps, a large clump of Fraser magnolia, and a few yellow birch. Soon, the first dog-hobble appears.

At approximately **4.0** miles, you pass an American chestnut still standing even though it has been dead more than 50 years. The ridge becomes much drier—sassafras, mountain laurel, greenbrier, and galax are among the more common plants. Heading downhill again among Eastern hemlock, you reach an oak-maple forest with three parasitic wildflowers: wood betony, squawroot, and Indian pipes.

Far below to the right, you hear the Left Fork (of Deep Creek) downstream from where a smaller stream, Keg Drive Branch, merges into Left Fork. Somewhere in a cave up Keg Drive Branch (below and to the right of Fork Ridge Trail), the Cherokee Indian Tsali was reputed to have hidden from federal authorities in the 1830s to avoid being sent to Oklahoma.

Soon Fork Ridge Trail bends left, where the all-deciduous forest is quite lush. A huge Fraser magnolia tree possesses one main trunk surrounded by many smaller sprouts growing from the same root system; an American chestnut shoot grows next to it, while nearby a clump of black locust stands. Off to the right, note the good view of Noland Divide. Suddenly the trail descends steeply among Eastern hemlock and American beech. This is good black bear habitat: near here, I turned a corner and surprised a bear cub who was 30' up a tuliptree; to escape, it slid down the tree as if the trunk were a fire pole.

The trail descends through a dry ridge environment, first through a mountain laurel thicket, and subsequently through Virginia pine, sassafras, black oak, red maple, and white pine. At 5.0 miles, the trail follows a knife ridge of rosebay rhododendron, mountain laurel, and flame azalea. Creeks flow on both sides of Fork Ridge: Left Fork (of Deep Creek) on the right and Deep Creek to the left. The trail continues across this ridge, with occasional views of Noland Divide to the right. After the trail heads downhill, a clearing opens to the right bordered primarily by chestnut oaks. The sound of the stream is deafening. Pine needles on the trail signal a grove of scrub and white pine. The trail now descends rapidly into a cove, enters an oak-maple forest, then leads into a grove of young tuliptrees where Wood Thrushes are common. In spring, phacelia and spring-beauty carpet the coves.

Finally, the trail takes an abrupt left turn through a rhododendron thicket and then tall tuliptrees; before long, Deep Creek is visible below. After wading through a dense cluster of false nettles, you move toward Deep Creek. Crossing Deep Creek on the wide footbridge, the trail meets Deep Creek Trail. Turning left here, it is 4.0 miles to Newfound Gap Road; just downstream to the right lies Campsite #53.

Narrative by Ted Olson

FORNEY CREEK TRAIL

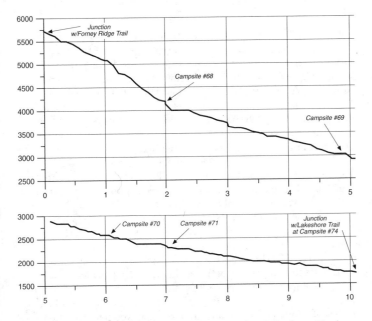

LENGTH: 10.3 miles, from Forney Ridge Trail to Lakeshore Trail on Fontana Lake.

HIGHLIGHTS: Cascades and water slide.

CAUTIONS: Rock-hop creek crossings, hidden nails in cross-tie foot bridges.

MAP KEY: 6-7 E-G; USGS quads: Clingmans Dome, Noland Creek, Silers Bald.

USE: Hiking trail only from trailhead to Jonas Creek Trail junction; horse and hiking trail from this intersection south to Lakeshore Trail.

TRAILHEAD: Park in the parking area at the end of the Clingmans Dome Road. Hike 1.1 miles on Forney Ridge Trail to Forney Creek trailhead to the right. Clingmans Dome Road is closed at the first snowfall or ice storm of each winter, usually in November. It reopens in March.

Forney Creek drains two long ridges that extend southwest from Clingmans Dome, the highest point in the Smokies. This area was heavily settled and logged between 1865 and 1934, when the park was established. The names of the tributaries of Forney Creek are intriguing: Advalorem Branch, Bee Gum Branch, Chokeberry Branch, Bear Creek, Gray Wolf Creek, Steeltrap Creek, White Man's Glory Creek, and Slab Camp Creek. Each one contributes cold, rushing water to make the Forney Creek crossings challenging. During or after very rainy weather, choose another hike.

The Norwood Lumber Company took out as much as 40,000 board feet of timber per day from this valley and caused several fires. One burned from the mouth of Forney Creek up to Clingmans Dome. Most of the trail is along old logging railroads and was built by a Civilian Conservation Corps crew that camped near Bee Gum Branch. Although you will see many signs of logging along this trail, you will also see how well this rich forest has recovered.

The trail goes through a blackberry patch and then out onto a high ridge. The wreck of a Norwood Lumber Company locomotive lies a few hundred yards to the right on an old railroad bed. The trail becomes narrow and rocky and drops quickly. For a moment, there is a view of Clingmans Dome straight ahead, but you need to watch your feet because there are seeps, wet rocks, and mud pockets. Soon the descent gets easier on a packed dirt trail, and you go through a stand of tall red spruce mixed with yellow birch. The trail switches back into a rosebay rhododendron hollow where you can hear a creek.

As you descend rapidly, notice an Eastern hemlock or two mixed with the red spruce. The range of these two trees overlaps between 4,000 and 5,000'; as you go down this valley, you will see more and more Eastern hemlock. There are scars along this upper trail from ball-hooting. When loggers cut trees high above the nearest railroad bed, they cleared a swath and shot or rolled the logs down the slope. You can see some of the eroded gullies, now grown over.

The trail moves down on a graded bench toward Forney Creek,

which has big mossy boulders and white quartz rocks. Don't cross here. Some hikers have, and it looks as if the trail goes on across the creek. The real trail turns downstream over some boulders before leading up and away from the creek. Then the creek noise recedes, muffled by rhododendron.

The trail rises high above Forney Creek and then moves away to cross a side creek where a rail holds rocks in place. As you cross, look up the creek at a series of cascades framed in rhododendron. Just after the creek, there is a large, smooth slanted rock in the trail that could slide you back into the creek if it is wet or covered with leaves.

From here on, the trail clearly follows a railroad bed. After a switchback, it drops down to Forney Creek again and runs along a wide, flat area that may have been a lumber camp or a log loading siding. Cables and buckets lie around, and a metal grate has been absorbed by the trunk of a yellow birch tree. Forney Creek goes down Rock Slab Falls, a spectacular water slide. The water ripples down 50' of rock, pauses in a small pool, and then descends another slide just as long. It must be the best water slide in or out of the park. However, this is not an official camp site.

After the rock slide, the creek is bigger, with more pools and thicker rosebay rhododendron. Look for other signs of former logging: rails converted to waterbars, pieces of pipe, cables, other roadbeds.

At mile **2.0**, the trail forks. The left fork goes to Campsite #68, which has a nice pool and a big, flat tent site with room for 8 people. The creek supplies the water. The right fork just loops up over the camp and rejoins the other fork at the end of the camp. The trail continues down a roadbed. Metal culverts and stonework send creeks and seeps under the trail, and the walking is easy. You cross Steeltrap Creek on timbers and cross ties. Watch out for nails hidden in the moss. This warning goes for all such crossings on this trail.

A 10' high stone wall keeps the old roadbed level across a creekbed. Look for Fraser magnolias, smooth-barked trees with leaves as thin and as long as one page of a legal brief.

After a roadcut, the trail crosses another creek valley on a long, curved stone wall. This is a good place to imagine a huge black steam engine pulling a load of massive logs. At the same time, you have to imagine bare, dirty hillsides with deep erosion gullies. But around you stands a vigorous forest of tuliptrees, American beeches, Fraser magnolias, black locusts, and grapevines.

A common shrub along the trail here is buffalo-nut, or oil-nut. The oil, which is said to be poisonous, was mixed with animal fat to make candles. The plants are parasitic on the roots of deciduous trees; since they can't reach the sun, they associate with someone who does.

The next flat clearing has a no camping sign nailed to a tree. Then there are two side creek crossings on rotting timbers and a sharp switchback. Some hikers have cut across a steep slope. This is not the official trail, and using it causes erosion and trail damage. After the switchback, there are four side creek crossings with varying support from old timbers. Then comes the first major Forney Creek crossing, where a side creek tumbles down through rosebay rhododendron. This crossing has good stepping stones.

The trail moves away from Forney Creek, crosses some more gullies, runs through a rhododendron tunnel, and turns two more switchbacks before rejoining the creek. Then you cross Forney Creek again. A timber stretches halfway, after which you can find stepping stones. The trail continues at creek level, with some nice pools on your left.

Campsite #69 (Huggins) appears at the junction of Forney and Huggins Creeks (more water for your next crossings). Campsite #69 boasts two creeks, cast iron machine parts, pieces of rail in the fire ring, and comfortable sitting rocks. There is room in a large shaded area for 12 people. It is lightly used.

After #69, there's a hard creek crossing and then a pleasant third of a mile on a level roadbed, interrupted once or twice by side creek gulleys. Then, since Forney Creek just can't stay out of the way, you cross it again. This one may require wading. The trail moves away from the creek through a rosebay rhododendron, sourwood, sassafras, hickory, oak, and holly forest. You cross a small side creek and then tackle the next Forney Creek crossing, which may be difficult. There is a deep pool, and the water may cover the best rocks, but there are shallow places to wade across. Then the creek plain widens, and the trail runs along the left side of Forney Creek.

A no horses sign warns people not to take horses where you have just been since only the lower half of the trail allows horses. You cross one more timbered gully where Board Camp Creek joins Forney

Creek, and then the trail runs through thick rosebay rhododendron and dog-hobble.

Another sign and a foot log with a handrail across Forney Creek mark the junction with Jonas Creek Trail, which runs right. You have come 7.2 miles from Clingmans Dome, **6.1** miles on the Forney Creek Trail. It is 1.0 mile farther to Springhouse Branch Trail. Jonas Creek joins Forney Creek here, and Campsite #70 lies between the two creeks. The camp is big and rocky and has its own creek gauge nailed to the base of a sycamore. It has room for 12 people and six horses and receives heavy use. The trail down from #70 is rocky and eroded from Forney Creek overflows. After about half a mile from the trail junction, Slab Camp Creek joins Forney Creek from the opposite side. Near the mouth of Slab Camp Creek, the Woody family had both a tub mill and a grist mill. Many families built water-powered tubmills, which had two legs in the water and two legs on a high bank, to grind corn or sprouted corn for use in their liquor stills. The grist mill was larger and probably for community use in making corn meal for bread. Farther up this creek, there was a hunting camp made of bark slabs.

After passing an open area that may have been a logging camp, the trail climbs a small, steep ridge, levels, and then makes you scramble down a rocky, narrow passage before leveling on the roadbed again. Campsite #71, a horse camp, appears on the left, while Forney Creek is still on your right. The campsite is rationed and overused, so you'll need to reserve a spot from the Backcountry Reservation Office. Because the campsite used to be the location of the Bee Gum CCC camp, this camp has more conveniences than most: a two-story stone chimney with brick fireplaces, a bathtub, a fire ring, a sitting area, waste baskets. However, the building that once enclosed them is gone. Boxwoods, poison ivy, white pine, and periwinkle surround the camp, and metal barrels, a dump, and cement foundations for smaller buildings can be found. Fifty yards up Springhouse Branch Trail is a good spring enclosed in stonework. There is room for 12 people and their horses.

From here, Springhouse Branch Trail leads to Board Camp Gap and the bottom of the Forney Ridge Trail (5.5 miles) and to the Noland Creek Trail (8.3 miles).

The Forney Creek Trail continues with the creek on the right flowing around several pretty creek islands. A logging dump on the left contains rusty pipes and rail pieces. You walk down a road lined with young Eastern hemlocks, mountain laurel, and rosebay rhododendron and cross a side creek on rocks into a fern field. After two more side creek crossings, the trail leaves the road and climbs away from the creek. Horses may have left muddy spots.

The trail eventually drops back to the creekside road. As you hike along an avenue of yellow birch, maple, sycamore, and tuliptrees, look across the creek at a rock jumble and a recent major boulder slide into the creek.

There is a steep detour up to the left, and then you reach the junction with White Oak Branch Trail. From here it is 2.0 miles to Lakeshore Trail and 4.5 miles to Lakeview Drive Parking Area. From the junction, the trail ascends a narrow bench, curves around a muddy switchback, and drops back to creek level. The creek is quiet, with deep pools. Steep canyon sides alternate with broad, ferny creek plains. Hollies and pines grow here.

A trail sign announces the junction with Bear Creek Trail. A recently-closed campsite lies just across the bridge.

The last half mile takes you to Lakeshore Trail along a road bed with hearts-a-busting, bamboo, and many five-leaved jack-in-the-pulpit plants. The trail crosses the creek on a wide bridge and proceeds on a gravel road to Campsite #74 on the lake. This site has picnic tables, fire rings, pit toilet, grassy docking area, fishing regulations sign, and several tent sites along the lakeshore and two in the shade of white pines. This area is heavily used for camping, fishing, and horseback riding.

FORNEY CREEK TRAIL CAMPSITE SUMMARY

Site #	Mile	Description
68	2.0	Steel Trap. Located at Forney Creek by a nice pool. Flat tent sites. Room for 8 people.
69	4.8	Huggins. Between two creeks. Room for 12 people. Lightly used.

70	6.1	Jonas Creek. Big, rocky, and heavily used. Room for 12 people and six horses.
71	7.1	CCC. Rationed, overused horse camp. Room for 12 people and their horses.
74	10.3	Lower Forney. Located on Fontana Lake. Large and elaborate. Heavily used.

Narrative by Doris Gove

FORNEY RIDGE TRAIL

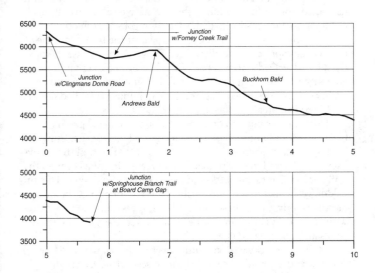

LENGTH: 5.7 miles, From Clingmans Dome Parking Area to Springhouse Branch Trail.
HIGHLIGHTS: Andrews Bald.
CAUTIONS: Steep and rocky trail.
MAP KEY: 6 E-F; USGS quads: Clingmans Dome, Silers Bald, Noland Creek.

USE: Hiking trail.

TRAILHEAD: Drive to the Clingmans Dome Parking Area at the end of the Clingmans Dome Road. Look for a short access trail between the water fountain and the paved trail to Clingmans Dome tower.

The first section of Forney Ridge Trail is eroded and uneven, with huge rock slabs on the left. At mile **0.1**, the Forney Ridge Trail intersects with the Clingmans Dome Bypass Trail which leads to the Appalachian Trail.

Red spruce and Fraser fir cover this ridge top, but most of the firs have died from an infestation of the non-native balsam woolly adelgid, a sap-sucking insect that wraps itself in gobs of protective white wool. Young spruce and fir trees crowd against the trail. On some of the firs, look for brown needles, an early sign of the disease. Before the adelgid arrived, this was one of the best examples of virgin old-growth spruce-fir forest in the park. A 1925 fire, caused by careless timber cutting, destroyed much of the virgin forest that had not been logged, so this area was once especially valuable.

The trail continues to drop, now through a tangled patch of blackberries and raspberries. They ripen in July or August. Stinkbugs love the juicy raspberries; check before you eat. The trail then moves back into spruce forest with many small Fraser firs. Bluets carpet the trail banks with sesame seed-sized leaves and trailing stems. This tiny wildflower, sometimes called Quaker ladies or innocence, blooms mostly in spring, but can send out a few flowers during any month with several days of warm weather. The flowers have four bluish petals and yellow centers.

After more rocky descent with roots to trip you, the trail levels on a broader ridge top that seems to be a nursery for spruce and fir saplings. Hobblebush and American mountain-ash also grow here, and the leaves turn bright colors in fall.

At mile **1.1**, Forney Creek Trail diverts to the right. Keep straight for Forney Ridge Trail. After a level stretch, with perhaps some muddy spots, the trail ascends a steep, eroded rut back into a forest of large spruces. So many dead fir trees stand or lie here that if you stay quiet, you can hear the scritch-scritch of the various bark beetles and wood borers. Look for their beautifully engraved tunnels under the bark of dead trees. The woolly adelgid may also be responsible for a population increase of these beetles, and perhaps also of woodpeckers that feed on them. One beetle that may be heard here is the death-watch beetle. It makes a regular ticking sound by bobbing its head against the wood, probably advertising for a mate. This beetle often bores into furniture, just more dead wood to it; a European superstition (transferred here) holds that it was counting off the time before the death of someone in the house.

The trail rises through quiet forest and then drops down toward Andrews Bald. Look for blueberry bushes along the way. The bald is named for Andres Thompson, with a slight spelling change. He was born in 1823 and herded cattle up to the bald in the 1840s. At that time, Forney Ridge was called Rip Shin Ridge; it must have been a hard trip. Thompson moved his family to the bald in 1850, went off to fight in the Civil War, and returned to live on his bald.

As you enter the bald at mile **1.8**, an interpretive sign explains that this bald and Gregory Bald near Cades Cove are being maintained as balds to favor grasses and native azaleas. Other grassy balds in the park are shrinking as trees move in. Biologists are unsure of the origins of the balds, but it is likely that livestock grazing preserved them. Small spur trails near the sign lead to overlooks and views of the Noland Creek Valley. If it's not socked in, these are some of the most spectacular views in the park.

Flame azaleas and Catawba rhododendrons on Andrews Bald put on a show in mid-to-late June, and the blueberries get ripe in August. Catawba rhododendron has shorter, rounder leaves than rosebay rhododendron, the one that crowds along the creeks at lower elevations. Catawba rhododendron grows on heath balds and high elevation open areas like Andrews Bald, and its flowers are pink.

The trail is a well-worn rut through the grass; follow it down and right through an area of long grass and healthy-looking young fir trees. If the trail gets lost in the grass, look for a sign at the edge of the woods and a fenced hog exclosure. From here it is 3.9 miles to Board Camp Gap on the Springhouse Branch Trail, 9.4 miles to Forney Creek Trail, and 12.6 miles to Fontana Lake. Look into the hog exclosure and see if the plants are doing better inside than out.

The trail drops into spruce-fir forest, goes round a switchback, and becomes rocky. Between here and the gap, the trail plunges down the ridge line, sometimes on top, where it is windy, and sometimes just to the side. After a tangled blackberry patch, it goes by steep rock outcrops. When the trail levels a bit, look for a big oak on the left with a bustle-shaped burl. Mosses, ferns, and oak twigs sprout from the top of the burl. Oaks and spruces dominate, and you may find oak apples on the trail. Each of these brown ping-pong-ball-sized galls once housed and fed a wasp larva; look for a little hole where the wasp left. Judging from the number of stumps and logs, American chestnut was also a dominant tree here.

The trail reaches a narrow, exposed end of the ridge, which drops off steeply on both sides. During the next part of your plunge, notice that American beech trees become common. Eastern hemlock and rosebay rhododendron also appear in sheltered spots. You will cross some seeps from uphill springs; look for toothwort, foamflower, and other flowers in spring, and bee-balm and gentian in late summer.

Boulders litter the side of this ridge, and they support polypody fern on top and rock tripe on the sides. This is one of the best rock tripe displays in the park. This lichen ranges from silver-dollar size to Frisbee size and has a black velvet underside. It is said to be edible in emergencies.

As you continue down, beech forest alternates with rosebay rhododendron and Eastern hemlock. More dead American chestnuts slowly decay on both sides of the trail. About 2.5 miles from the end of Andrews Bald, the trail becomes level and less rocky. Sassafras and chestnut saplings line the trail. Apparently, the old chestnut trees, the ones whose trunks you already passed, were completely killed by the chestnut blight that swept through this area in the 1920s and 1930s. However, the roots of younger trees keep the ability to send up shoots after the tops die. These shoots grow until they are big enough for the bark to split. Then the fungus, which lives on in oaks and other trees, infects them again.

The trail becomes hard-packed dirt, a pleasure to walk on, and you descend to the junction with Springhouse Branch Trail. To the right, it is 5.5 miles down to Forney Creek Trail. These trails could be combined for a long (19.4 miles) day hike or a more relaxing backpacking trip. To the left, it is 2.8 miles to Noland Creek Trail, which you could also use with the Noland Divide Trail for a loop to get back to your car.

Narrative by Doris Gove

GABES MOUNTAIN TRAIL

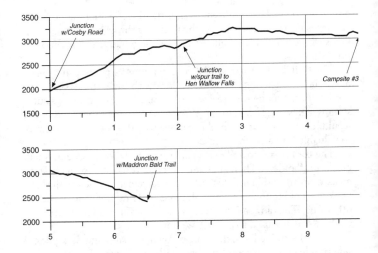

LENGTH: 6.6 miles, from Cosby Road to Maddron Bald Trail. (2.2 miles to Hen Wallow Falls.)
HIGHLIGHTS: Hen Wallow Falls, old-growth forest with big trees.
CAUTIONS: Slippery rocks at falls, some tricky rock hop stream crossings during high water.
MAP KEY: 9-10 B; USGS quads: Hartford, Luftee Knob, Mt. Guyot, Jones Cove.
USE: Hiking trail.

TRAILHEAD: From I-40 take the Foothills Parkway (closed in winter) or the exit for US 321 (#440). Take US 321 south, then TN 32 when US 321 turns right at the Cosby Post Office. 1.2 miles from the 321/32 jct., turn right into the park and drive about 2.0 miles to Cosby Campground registration building. Park behind it in Hiker Parking. The trail starts across the road from the picnic area.

Gabes Mountain Trail runs roughly (very roughly) parallel to the upper parts of Maddron Bald and Snake Den Ridge Trails. It is at about 2,500-3,000' elevation while the other two trails are at about 5,000', so the Gabes Mountain Trail is sheltered by high mountains and faces north. Consequently, the trail runs through moist woodlands where giant trees of almost every variety native to the Smokies flourish.

The trail, built by a Civilian Conservation Corps crew in 1934, moves up through quiet Eastern hemlock with thick stands of rosebay rhododendron along the creeks. Look for massive chestnut logs and stumps. These trees died in the 1920s or 1930s; any other kind of tree would have rotted long ago. You can see why the chestnut wood was so valuable for barns and fenceposts.

The trail twists up and over small ridges and crosses several small creeks on foot logs. Then at about **1.0** mile, you come to an elegant creek crossing with a foot log, culvert, and cement causeway. Just up a bank is an old traffic loop; cross the loop and find the trail on the other side. The old road that makes the loop comes up from the Cosby Road and used to be Hen Wallow Falls Trail.

After the traffic loop, there are many house sites and rock piles. A side trail leads to a pleasant flat area with two former chimneys. The family of M. A. Ramsay settled not far from here. In 1928, the Ramsays received $1,300 from the Tennessee Park Commission for 73 acres, 60 apple trees, a log house, a small barn, and a smokehouse. The family probably smoked coons, possums, and bear meat as well as domestic livestock. Their farmstead was one of the many that had to be bought to form the park. The Smokies was the first national park where land had to be purchased from companies and private individuals. The fundraising efforts took ten years and almost faltered during the Depression. Tennessee school children gave pennies and dimes and John D. Rockefeller Jr. gave $5,000,000.

The trail ascends easily through a rhododendron-laurel tunnel and then follows an old roadbed across another creek. Old posts for a railing show that this road was used by cars, and Hen Wallow Falls was once a fashionable destination for a Sunday drive and picnic. After this creek, the trail rises past rock slabs and boulders. At mile **2.1**, a short, steep spur trail goes right to the base of the falls. On the way down, look for a boulder on the left with two quartz (white crystal) veins across it. At the falls, water cascades down three sections of rock, the lowest bulging and very slippery. A crazy jumble of rocks at the bottom provides places to sit, but observe the warning sign and don't climb on wet rocks. The water trickles and gurgles through the rock pile and then disappears downstream into more rocks and rose-bay rhododendron. This creek is Lower Falling Branch, which runs into Hen Wallow Creek about 1.0 mile down.

To continue on Gabes Mountain Trail, return to the sign and turn right. In about 0.1 mile, you will see a high rock face with rock tripe lichen on the top and patterns of crustose (flat) lichen on the face. You can hear the falls from here, and a warning sign indicates that the old trail behind it is no longer safe or usable. The trail then makes a switchback to allow you to ascend as steeply as the creek is falling. Lower Falling Branch here is just a series of cascades and falls, and you cross another spectacular one soon. Look for a low, wet cave to the right of the main cascade where a side trickle of water comes through.

After a few more easy creek crossings (including Upper Falling Branch and Gabes Creek), the trail climbs alongside Snake Den Mountain. Pines, mountain laurel and oaks live out on the exposed ridges; rosebay rhododendron, Eastern hemlocks, and giant, old-growth hardwoods live in the sheltered coves. Look for silverbells (bluish flaky bark), Fraser magnolias (smooth yellowish-gray bark, lots of root shoots), and American beeches (smooth gray bark with initials carved in it). The white rock seen in some creeks is quartz; in one dry creek bed there is a Volkswagen-sized piece.

At mile **4.8**, you descend into Sugar Cove and Campsite #34 (3,240' elevation). As you get ready to cross the creek, look right for a silverbell tree whose trunk split at an early age (about 10' up) and rejoined later on (about 25' up). This rock hop crossing may be tricky during high water. Across the creek, there are upper and lower tent sites, each with a private waterfall. This site accommodates 15 campers, is open and pretty, and gets heavy use.

The trail continues to wind in and out of creek draws and passes big, old-growth silverbells, Fraser magnolias, American beeches, yellow buckeyes, basswoods, chestnut oaks, maples, Eastern hemlocks, and tuliptrees. In spring, you can find hepatica, bishop's cap, Fraser's sedge, squawroot, Clinton's lily, Indian cucumber, wood-sorrel, and many other wildflowers blooming near the creeks and in moist, open parts of this trail.

At about **6.0** miles, look for chestnut logs and stumps. One large stump sits on the right as the trail makes a sharp left turn. Chestnut heartwood rots first, and a young Eastern hemlock is growing out of the center while mosses and partridgeberry thrive on the rest of the stump. Look for a pile of acorn shells on a high part of the stump ring—squirrels bring nuts to places like this and eat them and watch for predators at the same time. Gabes Mountain Trail crosses one more creek on stepping stones and descends through Eastern hemlock to meet Maddron Bald and Old Settlers Trails.

Narrative by Doris Gove

GATLINBURG TRAIL

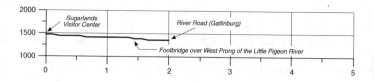

LENGTH: 2.0 miles, from Sugarlands Visitor Center to River Road in Gatlinburg, TN.
HIGHLIGHTS: Lack of hills, homesites.
MAP KEY: 6 C; USGS quad: Gatlinburg.
USE: Hiking trail.

TRAILHEAD: Sugarlands Visitor, 2 miles south of Gatlinburg, TN.

The Gatlinburg Trail is frequented more by "exercisers" than hikers. Many locals walk or jog it daily. Consequently, it's not the best trail for those seeking solitude. It is, however, a very pleasant respite from the hustle and bustle of downtown Gatlinburg.

The first 0.4 mile of this route is a little confusing as it wends its way through the park's sprawling headquarters complex. Once you've parked at Sugarlands Visitor Center, head for the restrooms. From that building, follow the asphalt path that leads into the woods. The tree on the right with the giant leaves is an umbrella magnolia. Its grapefruit-sized white flowers attract a lot of attention in late April and May. The Sugarlands self-guiding nature trail forks off to the left. It's a worthwhile, 1-mile loop that leads past a well-preserved home-site and a vigorous hardwood forest.

That big stone building on the left is the headquarters for Great Smoky Mountains National Park. Inside, administrators, rangers, and resource managers grapple with the day to day business of preserving one of the most significant natural areas in the eastern United States. In fact, the trail leads right past the park superintendent's window.

Before Sugarlands Visitor Center was built in 1960, this building served as the official welcome and information place. It was built by the Civilian Conservation Corps (CCC) during 1939-40. The lobby is a reproduction of the livingroom of the Blount Mansion in Knoxville, TN. There is beautiful wormy chestnut paneling which was salvaged from blight-killed trees. Two iron light fixtures on the ceiling were wrought by a country blacksmith in Wear Cove using parts from a logging skidder which operated in the Little River water-shed. The stone on the outside was quarried by the CCC at Ravens-ford, NC, just inside the park. If you want to take a look, go on through the double doors and you'll be in the lobby.

In 1940, the Park Service recorded 875,000 visits. Recently that number topped 9 million. Hosting so many guests and preserving the natural integrity of the park provides plenty of challenges for the employees inside to think about.

The asphalt trail ends in a small parking area on Park Headquarters Road. Turn left and follow this paved side road for 0.3 mile past

Little River Ranger Station to the park's maintenance area. Don't go out onto the busy Newfound Gap Road to the right.

At the maintenance area, the road ends and our route becomes a gravel path beside the West Prong of the Little Pigeon River. Several species of water-loving trees, including sweetgum, sycamore, Eastern hemlock and ironwood line the riverbank. A quarter mile past the maintenance area, two side channels of the West Prong join the mainstream in a thunderous cascade which is especially impressive during periods of high water. About 0.1 mile beyond the cascade a short side trail leads to an ideal swimming hole. If you are stealthful and look carefully, you can often see rainbow trout holding at the tail end of the pool.

At 0.4 mile from the maintenance area, you walk under the overpass of the Gatlinburg Bypass road. Just beyond here, a handsome stone wall lines the river. Prior to park establishment in 1934, several families, including Trenthams and Ogles, worked the rocky land in this area. Today, many tourist businesses in Gatlinburg carry these same names.

The trail starts up the only hill on its route. Halfway to the top, look to the left to see a homesite with a very unusual and ornate set of semi-circular stairs. Other artifacts at the site include metal from a stove, a few timbers, and a foundation. At the crest of the hill, two impressive fireplaces mark building sites. If you investigate the taller chimney, you'll see its firebox is lined with milky quartz, a common rock in the Smokies.

There is limited information available on who occupied these houses when, but Gladys Trentham, who grew up in the area, recalls a Henry Ebonother from Knoxville who spent his summers in a small, white frame house on this knoll. During the early part of the twentieth century, several wealthy Knoxvillians kept summer homes at various locales in the Smokies.

At 0.8 mile from the maintenance yard you reach a footbridge over the river. Mrs. Trentham recalls a tragedy which took place near here when this large stream was crossed only by a footlog. As Trentham and her siblings watched, a man who was said to have an affinity for moonshine attempted to negotiate the log. When nearly across he slipped and plummeted to his death on the rocks below.

For the rest of the route, you will be between the river and the Newfound Gap Road. Many travel-weary vacationers stop here for their first glimpse of the famed park. Trail's end is at River Road in Gatlinburg. The stone building on the left is the city's waterworks. If you're in need of supplies, the Happy Hiker is just across the road.

Narrative by Steve Kemp

GOLDMINE LOOP TRAIL

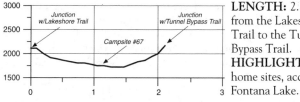

LENGTH: 2.1 miles, from the Lakeshore Trail to the Tunnel Bypass Trail.
HIGHLIGHTS: Old home sites, access to Fontana Lake.

CAUTIONS: Unbridged stream crossings.
MAP KEY: 6 F; USGS quad: Noland Creek.
USE: Horse and hiking trail.
STARTING POINT: Hike Lakeshore Trail 1.0 mile through tunnel from end of Lakeview Drive.

The name Goldmine probably expresses the hope of an early settler rather than the presence of a mine. Limited mining was done, however, along the Eagle Creek watershed 12 miles to the west.

This little-used trail begins on a ridge top in a pine-oak forest, then descends steeply through mountain laurel and American holly. Once it reaches a saddle in the ridge, a moderate descent along the right leads to the site of a farmstead. Turning left, the trail skirts the south side of a clearing surrounded by Fraser magnolia, American holly and rosebay rhododendron.

At 0.5 mile, the remnants of a chimney stand on the right. Many other signs of farm life are scattered about: wash tubs, cans, bottles, crockery and glass. Wild hogs have furrowed the ground as well. A small stream separates the trail from the house site.

Soon the trail becomes an old roadbed and follows Goldmine Branch, a small, sandy-bottomed stream that meanders down to Fontana Lake. The trail proceeds through a tunnel of rosebay rhododendron with oak and Eastern hemlock towering above. Dog-hobble crowds the creek bank.

At **0.75** mile, another home site emerges on the right, across Goldmine Branch. Two large boxwoods mark the location of a house where steps and a rock-lined cellar remain. Assorted relics litter the area, also marred by wild hogs. The trail turns left, up and away from the roadbed for a few hundred yards, joining it again under Eastern hemlock. The understory includes mountain laurel, galax, ferns and dog-hobble. This portion of the trail can be mucky in wet weather.

At **1.0** mile a path on the left leaves the trail to follow Hyatt Branch 300 yards to large, level Campsite #67, which does not appear heavily used. An old chimney and stone piles suggest the remains of a house and farm.

The main trail continues 0.3 mile down Goldmine Branch to where its waters rush into silent Fontana Lake. You circle this embayment, cross a small branch, and turn left, following Tunnel Branch up a moderately steep ascent through hemlock and pine with a mountain laurel understory.

At a level area, the trail turns left (north) away from Tunnel Branch to ascend a ridge. American holly and pipsissewa decorate the trail through the pine-oak ridge forest. The climb regains most of the elevation lost from the trailhead to the lake in 0.6 mile. Mountain views of Welch Ridge to the northeast can be seen through the trees along the spine of the ridge. At **2.1** miles the trail ends at a junction with Tunnel Bypass Trail. Continue ahead 0.5 mile to the parking area at Lakeview Drive.

Narrative by Charles Maynard and David Morris

GOLD MINE TRAIL

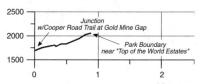

2500

2000

1500

0   1   2

Junction
w/Cooper Road Trail at Gold Mine Gap

Park Boundary
near "Top of the World Estates"

LENGTH: 0.8 mile, from Cooper Road Trail to park boundary.
HIGHLIGHTS: Cultural heritage.

MAP KEY: 2D; USGS quad: Blockhouse.
USE: Horse and hiking trail.
STARTING POINT: Jct. Cooper Road Trail, 2.6 miles from the Abrams Creek Campground.

This road is part of the remains of an old track between Montvale Springs and Cooper Road. According to Charles Pflanze of Maryville, the mine for which it was named was in the flats of the mountain (a relatively level area) and was abandoned because the gold extracted covered only 70% of the cost of mining it.

Montvale Springs was one of the earliest and most popular watering places (resorts with mineral springs) in this part of the country. A log hotel was built there in 1832 by David Foute, and by 1853 there were accommodations for over 300. Poet Sidney Lanier spent time at Montvale in his youth and Lake Sidney Lanier in Georgia was named for him. The site is now a YMCA camp.

Also of interest on this road was a log cabin built in 1886 and still remembered as the Monkey House and its occupant as the Monkey Man. Dr. Felix T. Oswald wrote Household Remedies in his two summers there in 1886 and 1887, but his lasting claim to fame comes not from his writing but from his companion, a strange and fascinating creature to local folk of that time—a monkey. This site lies about a quarter mile west of the park boundary, near the Wilson cabin.

The road ascends through a mixed hardwood forest and soon enters a rosebay rhododendron tunnel which erupts in a splendid display in late June. Later, an acre of the polished leaves of galax blankets the left slope. In four places the road turns rocky, rough and steep for short climbs. Then it's sandy and smooth again. At **0.8** mile is the park boundary, and 0.2 mile beyond that Goldmine Road terminates on meeting the main road of Top of the World Estates at the edge of Park Line Heights.

The geology here is a mixture of various sedimentary formations including Hesse Quartzite and Nichols Shale. The sand in the road-way is from decomposed quartzite and sandstone.

Narrative by Woody Brinegar

GOSHEN PRONG TRAIL

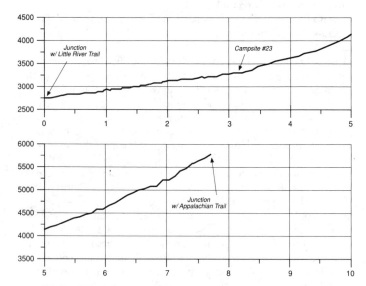

LENGTH: 7.7 miles, from Little River Trail to Appalachian Trail.
HIGHLIGHTS: Beautiful creeks, small cave.
CAUTIONS: Possible major crossing of Little River, rocky sections near top.
MAP KEY: 6 D-E; USGS quad map: Silers Bald.
USE: Hiking trail.

STARTING POINT: Park at the Little River Trailhead above Elk-mont Campground and hike 2.7 miles up the Little River Trail, past Cucumber Gap and Huskey Gap trails.

NOTE: If the gravel entrance road to the Little River Trailhead is still closed due to the 1994 flood, you'll have to walk 1.0 mile to reach the start of Little River Trail.

Goshen Prong Trail follows Fish Camp and Goshen prongs up to trickles and then continues up to the Appalachian Trail near Double Spring Gap, about 2.3 miles from Clingmans Dome. The first part of the trail runs on logging railroad beds and is therefore wide and easy. The upper part climbs nearly straight up to the Smokies crest, and is rocky, steep, and challenging. For maximum aerobic benefit, hike up Goshen Prong as in this description. The other way is to hike 2.3 miles of the Appalachian Trail from Clingmans Dome and then hike down. Either way, a car shuttle might help.

The Little River Lumber Company logged Fish Camp Prong extensively around 1915 and used ground skidders, overhead skidders, and railroads to get the logs out. Champion Fibre Company logged the upper area by coming over the crest, taking out red spruce, Fraser fir, and Eastern hemlock with a flume on the North Carolina side.

Shortly after you leave Little River Trail and begin hiking on Goshen Prong Trail, you come to a crossing of the still very wide Little River. At the time of this writing, a pair of temporary bridges had been erected on what used to be the Little River ford, 25 yards upstream from the old bridge foundation. There is talk of erecting a permanent bridge on the old foundation, but to date that has not been done.

However, if you arrive at the crossing and find the new bridge has not been built and the temporary one has been washed away, you'll need to ford. Some hikers have made a path upstream from the bridge foundation and rock-hopped to an island and then to the other side; some just go across where the bridge used to be. Either way, you will probably take off your shoes and socks or wish you had. This ford is not deep or dangerous except in high water (when it should not be attempted), but it can be tricky. Bring a towel.

On the other side, the trail is less trampled and is carpeted with ferns and mosses. Soon it meets Fish Camp Prong and a mixed forest of witch-hazel, yellow birch, sycamore, rosebay rhododendron, and Eastern hemlock. Signs of the logging days include cinders, bits of coal, stone walls, and drainage ditches for the railroad bed. The trail and prong wiggle beside each other, rising slightly but easily. On a broad plain you can find trilliums, bedstraw, jewelweed, may-apple, violets, wood-nettle, fringed phacelia, iris, toothwort, and Indian cucumber in spring and early summer.

The trail enters a high-walled valley and the creek runs over cascades and chutes. After about mile 1.0, the trail widens into a traffic turnaround and then becomes a narrow, grassy footpath, still along an old railroad bed. Look for two impressive ledge waterfalls, a long rock slide, and large pools. A moist cliff face on the left supports wildflowers on mossy ledges: umbrella leaf, wild ginger, violets, anemone, wood-sorrel, foamflower, Solomon's seal, brook lettuce, trilliums, bee-balm, plantain-leaved sedge, and bishop's cap. Some Jack-in-the-pulpit plants here have five leaves instead of three.

The trail alternates between wide fern fields and rosebay rhododendron tangles, and you start climbing up some rocky and perhaps muddy spots. Then comes an easy walk along an avenue of yellow birch, maple, Eastern hemlock, and American beech. After an open fern field on the left, there is a sandy open area on the creek bank with a black cherry and a birch growing entwined. A sign insists No Camping, but it is a good place to eat lunch, wade, or nap in the sun.

After another fern field and two easy side creek crosses, the spur trail to Campsite #23 goes left. The campsite is 100 yards from the main trail, accommodates 12 people, and is pretty. The creek provides water.

A few yards beyond the campsite spur trail, the main trail angles left and a sign announces that it is 4.4 miles farther to the Appalachian Trail. You have come 3.3 miles from the Little River crossing.

The Goshen Prong trail goes left from the trail sign and away from the side stream (Buckeye Gap Prong) up through a quiet rosebay rhododendron thicket. It then rejoins the old railroad bed and climbs above the prong on a level bench decorated with wood-nettle, poison ivy, and other wildflowers. A lot of ramps grow here; look for their garlicky leaves in April and their baseball-sized flower clusters in late

June. If you are here in April, you can pick one or two ramps for flavoring scrambled eggs or salad, but don't pick more than that (you don't need more, anyway), and leave the bulb for next year. If you are here in the summer, pinch a flower and get a whiff.

The trail drops down to Goshen Prong (having left Fish Camp Prong near the sign) at a ledge cascade and a set of pools. It then turns left and climbs through a rosebay rhododendron thicket to an easy side creek crossing. Then it follows a well-graded level bench up a pretty valley and easily crosses another side creek with a long cascade down slabs of tipped rock. This may be the last water source on the trail.

Just up trail from that creek some other slabs of rock form a small cave on the left. It is big enough to provide shelter in a rainstorm. The cave is at about 4,250' in elevation and is a little more than 2.0 miles from the top.

As you continue up the trail, you can look down into Goshen Prong Valley full of small hardwood trees, but soon, you will notice larger trees as you get away from lumber company land. The trail crosses a dry creek bed full of boulders. Eastern hemlock and red spruce grow together here, along with American beech, dog-hobble, and yellow birch. After a level dirt pack stretch of trail, you climb over rocks and roots up a steep section and pass through a rosebay rhododendron tunnel that serves as a watercourse during heavy rain.

Loose rocks can make the footing rough for the last mile of this hike. Look for hobblebush and mountain maple, and, nearer the top, small Fraser fir trees. Catawba rhododendron, the high elevation variety with deep pink flowers, blooms here in June and the blueberries are ripe in August. Lady ferns and mosses make up a rich undergrowth. On spring and early summer hikes, you can hear Veery, Red-breasted Nuthatch, Dark-eyed Junco, and Winter Wren songs.

At the junction, you will see white blazes for the Appalachian Trail and a trail sign. Double Spring Gap is 0.3 miles to the right, and Clingmans Dome is 2.3 miles to the left.

Narrative by Doris Gove

GRAPEYARD RIDGE TRAIL

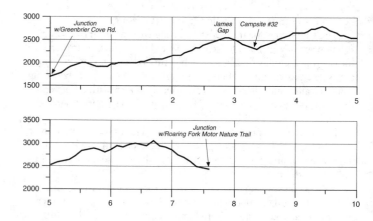

LENGTH: 7.6 miles, from Greenbrier Road to Roaring Fork Motor Nature Trail.
HIGHLIGHTS: Cultural history sites.
CAUTIONS: Unbridged stream crossings.
MAP KEY: 8-7 C; USGS quad: Mt. Le Conte.
USE: Horse and hiking trail.
TRAILHEAD: There is a small parking area on the left at the jct. of the Greenbrier Road and the roads to Ramsay Cascades and Porters Creek. Be sure to pull your vehicle well off the road to leave the access road open.

Just south of the Grapeyard Ridge Trail at Porters Creek was the Greenbrier Civilian Conservation Corps (CCC) camp, 1933-36. The CCC men built this trail and you can see some of their handiwork in a rock wall on the right at the beginning of the trail.

The trail climbs gently for about a quarter mile and then passes over a small ridge to the Rhododendron Creek valley. Watch out for stray roadbeds that intersect the path and may throw you off the trail.

CCC Company 1459, which worked in the valley, recalled the "vast number of rattlesnakes they encountered" in what is today called Rhododendron Creek. Today, this trail still has something of a reputation among locals for copperheads and timber rattlesnakes.

Trees remain small here because the Rhododendron Creek area was heavily populated with many small farms and cultivated corn fields. Avery Whaley and Lewis Messer had homes on this level area where the trail joins Rhododendron Creek. Whaley owned 61.8 acres, 15 of which supported 50 apple trees and a garden. He had a three-room frame house, a woodhouse, smokehouse and corn crib, all of which he sold to the state for the national park for $1,750 in 1929.

The trail winds back and forth across the creek six times. In dry weather rock-hopping is not difficult, but if it's raining count on getting your feet wet, because the creek stretches 10' or more in some places. Walter Parton, country singer Dolly Parton's grandfather, once lived above the creek on the left. "God has blessed most of the Parton family with talent," her great Aunt Tennie Russell Parton wrote. "Some preach and some pick and sing for the Glory of God and some pick and sing in other places, but we are proud of them all."

Eastern hemlocks and tuliptrees dominate the forest above the rhododendron understory. After the fourth creek crossing, look for fence posts with a little barbed wire on them. Near the headwaters of the creek, at the top of the hollow, is a pile of stones which marks the way to the Dodgen-Rayfield cemetery.

The trail moves away from the creek and climbs upward toward James Gap. From his home at James Gap, Andy Rayfield frequently traveled up to Mt. Winnesoka and other nearby peaks to tap Fraser fir trees. At the turn of the century, fir sap sold for 75 cents a pint and was purchased by medicine companies, who bottled it as a remedy for burns and cuts, and for internal use as a kidney medicine. "It took about a day to collect a pint," remembered Rayfield, "but by working extra hard as much as a quart of sap could be gathered."

Cas Rayfield, Andy's mother, was legendary in the Greenbrier valley for her honesty and strength of character. According to Park Ranger Glenn Cardwell, who grew up in the valley, "Aunt Cas" had several chickens that one day wandered into a neighbor's garden. The neighbor shot them. A few days later, however, the neighbor's hog wandered into Aunt Cas' garden. Rather than shoot it in revenge, she tied it up in the barn and fed it. The neighbor felt so badly when he saw how well she cared for his animal that he told everyone he "wished she would have shot the hog."

At **2.9** miles, the trail climbs to James Gap, which was named after Dallas James or his father, who lived above Rayfield. The trail then winds down toward the headwaters of Injun Creek. In the creek below, look for the remains of a steam engine, a Nichols-Shephard No. 4246, which overturned into the creek in the 1920s. According to park sources, the steam engine was brought to Big Greenbrier Cove to saw timber for a new school and crashed on its return trip to Webb's Creek. Glenn Cardwell said that "as the driver of the engine topped over the gap and started downhill, one of the wheels got too close to the edge of the road. The engine tumbled into the creek and the man driving the engine jumped off."

No one was injured in the wreck, and many of the engine parts were salvaged by the owner; the turbine and a couple of wheels remain. Injun Creek derives its name from the wreck, though many people erroneously refer to it as Indian Creek, thinking the name has to do with the Native Americans that once lived here.

The trail goes gently downhill on the west bank of Injun Creek on what appears to be part of the old railroad bed. After roughly a quarter mile, the trail levels off, and the woods are more open with second growth tuliptrees and oaks. Campsite #32 is located off to the right, near Injun Creek. At this point you've traveled **3.2** miles. The trail down to the campsite follows a rock wall that borders on an old farm site settled prior to the turn of the 20th century. The campsite is level and the rushing waters of Injun Creek make it a restful and private spot.

Leaving the campsite, the trail begins a long climb, crosses a wet-weather branch, and zig-zags up Grapeyard Ridge. At last you can see why the trail and ridge are called "Grapeyard," because here tangled vines form large Gordian knots in the hemlocks, cucumber trees, and red oaks. On the ground surrounding the trail are large patches of galax and dog-hobble. Striped pipsissewa can be found near the base of large trees and is identified by its green leathery leaves that are mottled with lighter green veins.

After you descend the west side of the ridge, where a stream crosses the trail, you reach the site of the Preston Ogle place. Look for signs of a stone foundation to the tub mill he built here. His farm consisted of 123 acres, 38 apple trees, a two-room log cabin, and a barn. He was paid $1,900 for his property in 1929 when the state purchased the land for the national park. Several rock walls line the creek. Just past Dudley Creek, a trail forks off to the right to a horse trail that follows the creek down to Smoky Mountain Riding Stables on Highway 321 near Gatlinburg.

Our trail then climbs westward, away from Dudley Creek. Because of areas of loose rock and narrow shoulders, the path can be hazardous in inclement weather. Deeply rutted by horse traffic, this section of the trail is at times a difficult climb. The trail continues to wind steeply uphill, through a more open woods that was once logged or burned over by fire. The trail at the gap is 3,000' in elevation, 1,300' below the top of Mt. Winnesoka. Just beyond the gap, the trail to the right is another unnamed bridle path leading to Indian Camp Branch. There are a number of fence posts nearby suggesting a former property boundary.

Crossing Indian Camp Branch below the gap requires some rock hopping, though this is a relatively easy crossing. The woods here are mixed hardwoods—tuliptrees, oaks, and maples. An underground stream passes beneath the trail before it continues its gradual descent. The trail is still heavily rutted in places and remains miry in wet weather. A long downhill stretch winds through dense rhododendron thickets and at times the high banks on either side of the trail make it seem like you are walking in a ditch. As the trail turns to the left, it passes through a pine woods of shortleaf and pitch pines, and their needles carpet the ground below.

At this point you will begin to hear Roaring Fork, which also means you are nearing the end of the trail. As you cross a small unnamed tributary of Roaring Fork, notice the large boulders on the left side of the trail. Continue downward toward Roaring Fork until the trail comes to an intersection marked by a sign. Roaring Fork Motor Nature Trail is only about 0.1 mile downhill to the right.

The trail ends abruptly in a clearing which contains a 4-stall barn, corn crib, and cabin. The cabin belonged to Alex Cole and his wife, who actually lived in a frame house on 31 acres in the Sugarlands area. For his property, Cole was given $2,100 and a "lifetime lease," or the opportunity to stay on his land after the park took it over. This is probably why the cabin remained in good condition until it was moved here. One day while firing a sorghum evaporating fan, Cole got a splinter in his hand and the resulting infection cost him the sight in one eye and his hand was amputated. During the 1930s he wrote the park requesting employment, saying he was "an old time mountaineer that knows every hole and corner" in the Smokies. It is not known whether the park hired him.

Narrative by Margaret Lynn Brown & Donald E. Davis

GRASSY BRANCH TRAIL

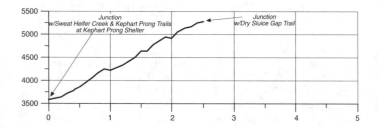

LENGTH: 2.5 miles, from Kephart Prong Trail to Dry Sluice Gap Trail.
HIGHLIGHTS: Grassy woods.
MAP KEY: 8 D; USGS quads: Smokemont, Mt. Guyot.
USE: Horse and hiking trail.
STARTING POINT: Drive 8.8 miles south from Newfound Gap (22 miles from Gatlinburg, or 5 miles from Smokemont) and look for the Kephart Prong parking area on the river side of the road. You cross the Oconaluftee River on a good bridge and hike 2.0 miles on the Kephart Prong Trail to the shelter. The jct. is marked with a sign.

This part of the park belonged to Champion Fibre Company, which built a narrow gauge railroad along Kephart Prong. The company removed spruce trees from 2,200 acres and left brush piles on the hillsides. A 1925 fire started in North Carolina, roared up the mountain, and crossed into Tennessee, burning both dead and green trees. Later, heavy rains removed most of the bare topsoil. After the fire, the company planted thousands of non-native Norway spruces, mostly above 4,000' elevation. As you hike through this area, you will see cables and other signs of the logging, but this forest is again beautiful with vigorous second growth.

From the front of the shelter, turn right and go around it, passing the massive stone chimney. Follow the trail straight back. A few yards from the shelter, the trail turns left up a steep, narrow, rocky shelf along a hillside, almost a cliff. You can see Grassy Branch below and a pretty understory of American beech trees, bright green in spring and bronze or gold in fall.

At mile 0.5, the trail merges with an overgrown roadbed. Note the good stone wall near the edge—this probably supported logging trains. Here the trail is wider and more level, with rhododendron on the right and an open deciduous forest of American beeches, yellow birches, and maples on the left.

The roadbed climbs to the head of a creek, crosses, and ascends the opposite hillside. After skirting a ridge, the trail becomes drier and not so steep. Mountain laurel and pines grow here. Then the trail repeats the same maneuver higher up to cross Lower Grassy Branch, the last creek crossing of this trail. Some of the Norway spruce that Champion Fibre planted and never got to harvest grow here above Lower Grassy Branch. They look like the native red spruce except that their branches hang down like those of a weeping willow.

The trail switches back at a rock pile and continues through a forest of beech, oak, maple, and Fraser magnolia. There are stands of beech trees of all heights alternating with dark Norway spruce groves. A tangled mass of greenbriers politely curves away from the trail on the left, and asters, gentians, and goldenrod can be seen in fall at forest openings. Gaps in the trees offer glimpses of the Smokies' crest with rows of native red spruces silhouetted against the sky.

After another switchback, the trail rises gently to the end of a ridge. The roadbed is somewhat overgrown with mountain laurel. Around the ridge, you enter a dense grove of Norway spruce and proceed on to a blackberry patch. The trail is rough here, sloping and eroding downhill, perhaps damaged by wild hogs rooting.

Soon you will hear a creek on the right and cross high enough in its draw that it is dry most of the year. Look for a gnarled yellow birch on the right with many epiphytes, (non-parasitic plants) growing on it.

The trail crosses another creek draw and ascends through a broad area of open woods with thick grass, which gave this hike its name. The trail then moves up to a shrubby, exposed knob where American beech and oak trees are twisted and stunted by the wind. Look for three kinds of clubmoss beside the trail. These are evergreen ground plants that stand taller than mosses and may look like miniature pine trees. Clubmosses spread by underground runners; a patch is likely to be all one plant. On this trail, you can see shining clubmoss (furry green fingers with minimal branching), ground pine (well-formed tiny Christmas trees), and fan-shaped and scaly ground cedar.

The trail moves into a laurel thicket and becomes so eroded that its banks are at knee level. When you emerge from the thicket into a spruce grove, you will see the Dry Sluice Gap Trail sign. The Appalachian Trail is 1.3 miles to the left. To the right, you can reach Bradley Fork Trail in 3.3 miles and Smokemont in 7.3 miles.

Narrative by Doris Gove

GREENBRIER RIDGE TRAIL

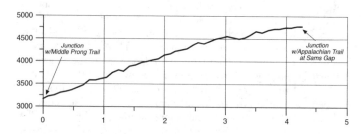

LENGTH: 4.2 miles, from Middle Prong Trail to Appalachian Trail.
HIGHLIGHTS: Mountain streams, wildflowers, views.
CAUTIONS: River crossing at high water.
MAP KEY: 5 E; USGS quad: Thunderhead.
USE: Hiking trail.
STARTING POINT: Middle Prong Trail, 4.1 miles from end of Tremont Road.

The trailhead for this hike is along the Middle Prong Trail. To reach this point, you'll have to hike past the old Tremont lumber town and follow the old rail bed to the trail junction. After 4.1 miles, the Middle Prong Trail turns and climbs sharply to the left, but our journey continues straight. Backpackers may wish to stay at Campsite #28, 1.3 miles along the Lynn Camp Prong Trail, because there is no camping on Greenbrier Ridge. The next campsite along this route is the Derrick Knob Shelter almost 5 miles away. It is quite a challenge to climb to the shelter with a pack in one day, though some hearty backpackers do just that.

The Greenbrier Ridge Trail follows another old railroad bed up and over a small ridge. After a short rockhop across a spring branch, the trail drops from the ridge and follows Indian Flats Prong upriver. The ridge you just crossed has one of the most infamous names in the park — Mellinger Death Ridge.

According to local lore, two brothers one day set bear traps along the ridge, but failed to heed local customs. A trap needed to be set with two large C-clamps. It was common practice to leave a set of clamps by each trap in case someone accidentally stumbled into one. A hunter also marked the trap area and checked it daily. Imagine their surprise when the unscrupulous brothers returned a few days later to find an almost dead Jasper Mellinger in their trap. There was no way they could get Jasper to Elkmont for care before he died and if they came in with a dead man surely they would be tried for manslaughter. So the brothers murdered Jasper, dragged his body to a rocky cliff and pitched him over. A search by authorities found nothing and the mystery surrounding Jasper's disappearance lingered for 30 years. One brother died with his secret, but the second brother needed to clear his conscience. On his death bed he revealed the story. An exact location was given and a quick search turned up Jasper Mellinger's remains.

Our trail passes the base of this ridge and then climbs slowly along Indian Flats Prong. At **0.25** mile, you'll cross the river twice within a few hundred yards. The first crossing is the hardest, especially at high water. It requires some nimble hopping from boulder to boulder. After a good rain there's no choice—this will be a wet crossing through a shallow, swift current. Take special care here. The river, however, is very lovely as it cascades through a dense stand of rhododendron and Eastern hemlock.

The second crossing of Indian Flats Prong is a much easier rock-hop. It too, however, is a wet crossing at high water, but the current is not as difficult to handle. From here the trail begins to climb moderately up Greenbrier Ridge (formerly known as Davis Ridge). This trail is a good choice for early summer hikers who wish to explore the spring wildflowers. The spring-beauties and violets of early spring can be found here even into late June. Many others, including crested dwarf irises, can be found throughout the summer.

The trail grows steeper in places, but offers good views of the mountains to the north in exchange. One large sharp peak that can be seen around mile **1.0** is Blanket Mountain.

Our trail continues uphill at a moderate pace another 0.5 mile to a small stream crossing. These are the headwaters of a stream called Double Trestle Branch, a name which recalls the logging railroads which extended into this area in the 1920s. The branch is the last water until near Sams Gap at the Appalachian Trail. Along this section of trail there are many loose rocks which could easily twist an ankle. The trail climbs steeply in places, adding to the danger as you ascend the ridge. You'll make many turns and as you do so, notice how the forest changes. At one moment you're deep in hemlocks and rhododendrons, but then around a bend and it's all tuliptrees and maples. These are all second growth forests with remarkable diversity.

At mile **2.25**, you will climb around a sharp left turn and in a stand of hemlocks reach the ridgeline. From here the trail gently climbs to Sams Gap. This is a great place to see those early spring wildflowers if you missed them down low. It's also loaded with some very interesting trees. You'll pass lots of maples, oaks, cherries and even yellow buckeyes, but you'll also pass some silverbells and sweet (black) birches. The silverbell has beautiful white blossoms which litter the forest floor like snow in June. The sweet or black birch is a unique taste treat. Chew one of the small twigs. You'll love the wintergreen flavor. In the past, this was used to flavor medicines and stronger beverages. Renowned natural foods expert Euell Gibbons said that birch beer made from these trees' sap had "a kick like a mule."

Around mile **3.0**, the forest begins to open again. There are more views of the surrounding mountains now. First, there are views to the west of Thunderhead Mountain and the upper Middle Prong valley. The trail then passes to the eastern side of the ridgeline and provides good views of Blanket Mountain and Miry Ridge. In late fall and winter there are even glimpses of the high peaks beyond, including Mount Le Conte. With 0.5 mile to go, the trail again moves to the western side of the ridgeline and back into view of Thunderhead and now Blockhouse Mountain.

You are now following the contour lines around Mt. Davis. This peak was named for Willis P. Davis who, with the help of his wife Ann, initiated the movement to create Great Smoky Mountains National Park. The trail climbs very gently past two small springs — nothing more than mere seeps—and on to a larger spring branch. You can get water here or wait until you reach the Derrick Knob Shelter. Continuing up the trail another 300' will take you to Sams Gap and the Appalachian Trail. Turn left on the A.T. for Miry Ridge and Silers Bald. Turn right and you'll be off toward Derrick Knob Shelter (0.2 mile) or on to Thunderhead Mountain.

Narrative by Tom Condon

GREGORY BALD TRAIL

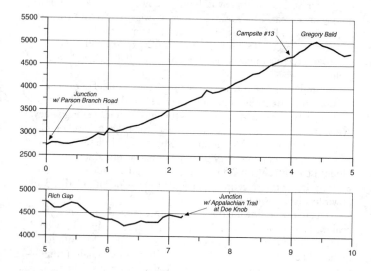

LENGTH: 7.2 miles, from Parson Branch Road at Sams Gap to Appalachian Trail at Doe Knob. (4.5 miles if only going to Gregory Bald.)

HIGHLIGHTS: Sheep Pen Gap, Gregory Bald.

MAP KEY: 2-3 E; USGS quads: Calderwood, Cades Cove.

USE: Horse and hiking trail.

TRAILHEAD: Turn off Cades Cove Loop Road just past the visitor center and Cable Mill area. Follow signs to Parson Branch Road (closed in winter). Sams Gap is approximately 5 miles from start of Parson Branch Road.

NOTE: At press time, Parson Branch Road was closed indefinitely due to flood damage. It's an extra 4 miles if you walk from Forge Creek Road to Sams Gap on the washed-out road.

"It is still insisted there can be nothing finer than this trip to Gregory Bald in azalea time, and the ascent made by moonlight."
—*Smoky Mountain Hiking Club bulletin, 1937*

The trail begins in a gentle grade through pines, then swings in a wide circle west, south, and back to the east around the southeastern knob of Hannah Mountain. Beyond, the path swings around another bulge past a couple of large trailside tuliptrees and oaks. In June, the blooms of Catawba rhododendron brighten this passage.

Galax, that polished, heart-shaped leaf, borders the trailway. It turns bronze when the sun hits it in late fall and was once gathered by mountain people and sold for Christmas decorations. Ascending through an open forest of mixed hardwoods, with northern red oaks predominating, the trail reaches Panther Gap. It is named for Panther Creek, whose headwaters form along the path in several oozing streams, the last being the watering place for Campsite #13 at Sheep Pen Gap.

American Beech and yellow birch become more frequent as the trail border changes from galax to grass. Sheep Pen Gap was named for an enclosure used to gather sheep prior to the drive home in the fall. As sheep and hogs feasted on acorns and chestnuts, they were left in the mountains longer than cattle.

Cades Cove native and author of *The Cades Cove Story*, Dr. Randolph Shields, recalled the giant chestnuts which stood on this broad, grassy flats. "Sheep," he said, "kept close to or on the crests while cattle often drifted deep into hollows. Even exploding bolts of lightning usually failed to drive them from the heights."

Campsite #13, at mile **4.0**, is well-located in a cushion-like grassland under yellow birch trees. It's an excellent camping place, though more frequently used than most, lying between two grassy balds.

At the trail sign here, you reach the original Appalachian Trail which went across Gregory and Parson Balds (until 1948) and on down the Smoky Mountain (North Carolina-Tennessee) ridgeline. The remaining 3.2 miles to Doe Knob are along the old A.T.

Rising steeply, the trail ascends to Gregory Bald at mile **4.5**, long known for its picturesque azalea display in the latter half of June. Flame azaleas, like those on Gregory, were first noted by botanist

William Bartram. He saw them in the Nantahala Mountains in North Carolina in 1775 and wrote in *The Travels of William Bartram*: "The epithet fiery I annex to this most celebrated species of azalea, as being expressive of the appearance of its flowers; which are in general of the color of red-lead, orange, and bright gold, as well as yellow and cream-color."

Gregory is a broad grass meadow with blueberries that ripen in August. Azaleas, blueberries, and broad vistas have long made this perhaps the most visited grass bald in the southern Appalachians. In the high woodlands, shaded azaleas often show their bright colors through July.

The path descends to Rich Gap at mile **5.1**, once a holding area— known as a gant lot, for cattle to slim down a bit before the fall drive to home farms. Their droppings made the gap quite fertile, giving Rich Gap its name.

Moore Spring, a cold and bountiful water source emerging from beneath a boulder, is just south of the bald, and a path leads there southwest from Rich Gap. A popular hiker's shelter once stood near the spring, but wasn't replaced when it burned in the 1970s. Moore Spring is always remembered and visited by old timers when they go to Gregory. Also of interest is a giant flame azalea on the north side of the spring clearing.

From Rich Gap the trace runs east, ascending the north side of the peak of Long Hungry Ridge. Then it descends and swings south of the crest of Forge Knob, named for the Cades Cove Bloomery Forge which was operated from 1827-47.

In places on the ridge crest the north face of the ridge drops steeply toward Cades Cove, so sharply in places it appears to have been chopped away with a giant hoe. Flame azaleas splash this pathway in brilliant color in late June and July.

The forest is yellow birch, although the bark is more gray than yellow. It's an easy, pleasant path running level, then descending and ascending steeply. Blackberry vines are thick in places and gave names to Brier Lick Gap and Knob. Brier Lick means a thicket. However, the briers have been pretty well rooted out of the gap.

As the path swings on the Carolina side of the knob leading to Brier Lick Gap, American chestnut shoots are prolific. Some of these stems are three inches or more in diameter. The unusual feature is the abundance— hundreds of eruptions from the roots of long-dead chestnuts. Their numbers seem to say, "this was a mighty chestnut forest and we persist in our struggle to survive and thrive again."

Ascending Doe Knob, the path moves through brier patches along the old Appalachian Trail until reaching the junction of the new trail turning abruptly south from the western crest of the knob. Rooting hogs keep the soil well-tilled between Rich Gap and Doe Knob.

Narrative by Woody Brinegar

GREGORY RIDGE TRAIL

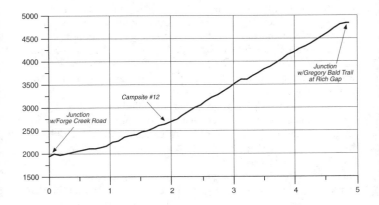

LENGTH: 4.9 miles, from Forge Creek Road to Gregory Bald Trail.
HIGHLIGHTS: Old-growth forest, views, access to Gregory Bald.
MAP KEY: 3 E; USGS quad: Cades Cove.
USE: Hiking trail.
TRAILHEAD: At end of Forge Creek Road. The road starts just past the turnoff for the Cable Mill area halfway around the Cades Cove Loop Road. The trailhead is at road's end just past the turn to Parson Branch Road at a small circle with parking for 6-10 vehicles.

This has been and probably will always be one of the finest hikes in the Great Smoky Mountains. The journey up Gregory Ridge to the bald offers you everything that makes the Smokies such a wonderful place. You get scenic views of course from the bald and Rich Gap, but you also get the little wonders of spring wildflowers. The upper reaches of the trail blaze with flame azaleas in June, but also sparkle with frost in the winter and shower you with color in the fall. The azaleas are a sight to see, but so is the old-growth forest you pass to get there. Of all the trails in the park, this has perhaps everything you could wish for.

Forge Creek Road, which leads to the trailhead, is an interesting road historically. It runs through an area known in the 1800s as Chestnut Flats. The Flats was a notorious place. It was sort of the skid row of the Smokies. Fights, stabbings, and shootings happened all too frequently as arguments over the main commodity—moonshine—got out of control. According to Durwood Dunn, moonshining continued in the Flats well into the 1900s. Often, the families of the moonshiners lived in desperate poverty while the distiller served time in prison or was laid to rest in a graveyard.

The Gregory Ridge Trail, however, will climb out of this valley and its infamous history. It starts with a short climb over a ridge and then levels off as it follows Forge Creek through a second growth hemlock forest. At **1.4** miles it crosses the creek on a foot log. Perhaps the original forest here was cut to fuel the furnaces at the creek's namesake. Certainly other forests in this area were used for such a purpose. To the west is Coalen Ground Ridge, named for all the charcoal made here to fire the Cades Cove Bloomery Forge along this creek. Daniel D. Foute built this simple style of forge in 1827 to produce iron. Iron ore was mixed basically in a large chimney with limestone and charcoal. The limestone floated the impurities as the iron was tapped from below. Unfortunately for Foute, the iron was too poor to be profitable, yet not before the ring of the 500 pound hammers had scared all the wolves from the cove.

Campsite #12 is ahead along Forge Creek. It is a bit of an uphill climb to the site. Sometimes the trail follows the creek, as it rumbles down to the cove, filling your ears with its persistent roar. Other times the trail will lead you away from the creek and the forest will fill your mind. In season, wildflowers carpet the forest floor. The majesty of the trees lead your eyes to the sky. The chipping of the junco, the squeaking wheel song of the Black-and-White Warbler or the *zee-zee-zee-zoo-za* of the Black-throated Green Warbler will fill the air.

A second crossing of Forge Creek along a footlog leads you into a large uncut stand of tuliptrees. Many of these giants reach diameters of over 50". This is the beginning of the old growth forest that will accompany you to the high country. A majority of all the old-growth forests in the eastern United States exist in Great Smoky Mountains National Park. Yet only about 20% of the park qualifies as untouched.

After crossing Forge Creek a third time, you will reach Campsite #12 (Forge Creek, 2,600'). The campsite has plenty of water and a clear view of the evening sky for 3-4 tents, but no easy places to hang your food out of the reach of bears. You will have to be creative here. The campsite marks an important change. You have come about two miles to this point, mostly following Forge Creek. Now you will begin the 2,400' climb up Gregory Ridge to Rich Gap. At an average slope of 800 feet per mile, this is a challenging climb. It is also a dry climb, so carry plenty of water. The first few switchbacks will give you a good idea of what lies ahead—steep and beautiful.

After a 0.75 mile climb through dry oak forests and their understory of huckleberries and greenbriers, you will reach a large sandstone outcrop. Stop for a snack and enjoy the partially obstructed views of the park's western end.

One-quarter mile ahead, you will pass through a laurel tunnel—where the mountain laurel branches close in above you. Notice the sourwood trees and trailing arbutus along the trail. At **3.5** miles you will come to a huge tuliptree on the left. A long lightning streak scars the side of this 57" diameter giant, but it goes on living. Lightning is just one of the hazards that make it hard for any tree to make it to old age, especially if it pushes its crown so high along these ridges.

Climbing along sometimes moderately, sometimes steeply, you will start to get some obstructed views of the mountains to the east and cove to the north. Be patient as you climb. Listen and watch for the brilliant Scarlet Tanager and its "chick-burr" call or the "I am laaa-zeeee" call of the Black-throated Blue Warbler. Your patience will be rewarded at mile **4.0** as the views begin to open. At **4.75** miles, the views to the east are superb, particularly at the peak of fall color in mid-October. You will be peering along the backbone of the Smokies. Take notice of the rises in the foreground called knobs, including Forge, Brier Lick and Doe. Trace the ridge line to the lower gaps—Mud, Ekaneetlee, and Little and Big Abrams. The large open field in the distance is Spence Field and the peak looming above it is Thunderhead Mountain. At 5,527', it is the highest peak in the.western end of the park.

After you have taken in the views, continue along the last 0.25 mile of trail. It is a level hike to Rich Gap and the junction with the Gregory Bald Trail. The trail junction is in an open stand of oaks with groundcover of wild grasses and snakeroot. Taking the trail to the left will bring you to the Long Hungry Ridge Trail in 0.1 mile and its access to the Twentymile portion of the park. This is a rather remote area and for backpackers not prepared it could mean a long hungry journey. A left hand turn can also take you to the Appalachian Trail at Doe Knob in 2.1 miles.

A right turn takes you 0.5 mile up a small rise to Gregory Bald. It is named for one of Cades Cove's most prominent citizens, Russell Gregory. The bald has been a large open field for as long as white settlers have been in these mountains. No one is sure as to how grass balds were formed. Theories suggest Indian development, lightning strikes, and even animal grazing. When the first surveys of these mountains were done in 1821, this and Parson Bald were both noted. Today, the National Park Service maintains Gregory and Andrews Balds to preserve the historic and biological uniqueness. A trip to either of these balds in late June will easily show you why—the fields blaze in color from the flame azalea blossoms. On Gregory Bald, the azaleas are so genetically mixed that these small trees bloom in every color from white and pink to yellow and red. The British Museum of Natural History in London has even collected a few because of their uniqueness.

As an alternative to backtracking, day hikers might wish to return to their cars by crossing the bald and descending the Gregory Bald Trail 4.5 miles to Parson Branch Road at Sams Gap. This one-way gravel road will take you 4 miles to Forge Creek Road and your car to the right. Just before the junction of Parson Branch and Forge Creek Roads is a small jeep trail to the north. A short 150' detour up this trail will bring you to the Boring cemetery. Here the family of William Boring, a Baptist preacher, is buried. His wife and three daughters died during a typhoid epidemic in the late 1800s.

Narrative by Tom Condon

GUNTER FORK TRAIL

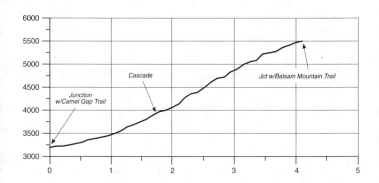

LENGTH: 4.1 miles, from Camel Gap Trail to Balsam Mountain Trail.

HIGHLIGHTS: Forest variety, pleasant creek scenes, dramatic cascade.

CAUTIONS: Several unbridged stream crossings.

MAP KEY: 10 C; USGS quad: Luftee Knob.

USE: Hiking trail.

STARTING POINT: Follow the Big Creek Trail for 6.1 miles from its trailhead.

The Gunter Fork Trail begins at Walnut Bottom, a short distance beyond the end of Big Creek Trail at Campsite #36. A sign warns hikers to avoid Gunter Fork Trail during high stream flow and recommends the Swallow Fork Trail as an alternative. Hikers must cross Big Creek once and Gunter Fork several times without benefit of footlogs. Normally, these crossings are not difficult, however, high water can make them hazardous.

Gunter Fork offers a pleasing blend of fine ingredients, making it a gem among Smoky Mountain trails. Open forest, fine stream views, a unique cascade and high mountain vistas are part of the trail's appeal. Footing is good throughout.

From its beginning, the trail bears left and immediately reaches a crossing of Big Creek. There is a picturesque view of the stream at this crossing. Water swirls around moss covered boulders forming pleasant runs and pools. With patient observation, trout may be seen in the pool above the crossing. Beyond the crossing, the trail joins an old railroad grade and ascends gently through a pleasant cove forested with second growth maple, tuliptree and birch with an understory of rhododendron.

This well-engineered railroad grade was constructed in the early part of the century by the Crestmont Lumber Company to enable it to log the virgin timber on Gunter Fork. Graded trail constructed by the Civilian Conservation Corps continues beyond the rail grade offering a steeper but comfortable ascent to the crest.

The trail fords Gunter Fork at **0.3** mile and a side stream at **0.4** mile, ascending through open forest comprised mainly of second growth tuliptree. The stream may be viewed on the right as it splashes downward in runs and small cascades. The trail fords Gunter Fork again at **0.9** mile and becomes steeper. In April, these slopes provide a fine display of trillium which bloom later along the higher reaches of the stream.

A delightful surprise awaits you a short distance above a stream crossing at **1.4** miles. A large pool is reached by descending a few feet to the right of the trail. Gunter Fork cascades 10' into a deep blue-green, fan-shaped plunge pool which is framed on two sides by dark, moss-covered stone walls. This is a mandatory stopping point because the beauty of the setting cannot be fully realized from the trail.

At **1.7** miles the trail reaches an exquisite cascade approximately 150 feet high. A thin film of water streams from a small falls at the crest and glides down the moss-covered face of the cascade to a small pool at its base. An interesting geological feature is exposed in the Thunderhead sandstone formation over which the water flows. A diagonal layer of sandstone forms the base of the cascade. Above this is a layer of conglomerate which is composed of irregular rocks fist-sized and larger. While different in appearance, both types of stone are part of the same geologic formation.

Carson Brewer, in his book, *A Wonderment of Mountains: The Great Smokies*, describes a visit to this spot on a cold autumn day.

"The water made its final descent down the rock wall eight or ten feet in front of us. Most of the water was falling free from the right side of the wall. But a generous portion was sliding over the steeply sloped left side—and it was doing it under ice. Just the thinnest glaze of ice that followed the contours of the rocks under it. And in that thin space between rock and ice hurried a thousand trickles of water. It was a psychedelic sight no drugs and lights could match."

The trail makes a final creek crossing beyond the cascade before climbing away from it on switchbacks. It is possible to view "laurel slicks" or "hells" on adjacent side ridges from the first switchback at approximately 4,200'. These places which look smooth at a distance are actually a thick growth of shrubs, including rhododendron, which appears pink when it blooms in June. A good view of Seven-mile Beech Ridge is obtained a short distance beyond a second switchback at 4,400'. This ridge extends from Big Cataloochee Mountain to Walnut Bottom. Be sure to note three large Eastern hemlocks—one on the right and two on the left—with trunks 4' in diameter near the upper vista. In autumn, hearts-a-busting bears fruit along the trail. The pink outer cover, which looks like a strawberry, opens to reveal bright red seeds.

The trail continues ascending more steeply along a side spur of Balsam Mountain in northern hardwood forest. Maple, yellow birch, black cherry and Eastern hemlock will be noted through here. Near the crest, tall red spruce trees are present, adding their rich green to the forest, a particularly pleasing contrast to the rich hues of autumn. A thick bed of feathery sphagnum moss covers the forest floor adding to its beauty.

The trail grade moderates at **3.5** miles and continues more gradually until reaching the crest of Balsam Mountain and the Balsam Mountain Trail at **4.1** miles. Signs at this junction indicate the Mount Sterling Ridge Trail is 0.9 mile to the left and Tricorner Knob is 4.9 miles to the right. Laurel Gap shelter is 1.4 miles to the left.

Narrative by William A. Hart, Jr.

HANNAH MOUNTAIN TRAIL

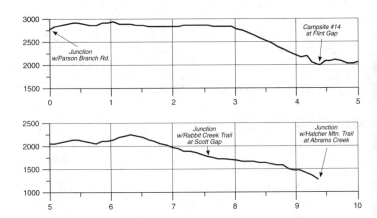

LENGTH: 9.4 miles, from Parson Branch Road to Abrams Creek ford and the jct. with the Hatcher Mountain and Abrams Falls trails.
HIGHLIGHTS: Ridge walking, Flint Gap.
CAUTIONS: Abrams Creek crossing.
MAP KEY: 2 E; USGS quad: Calderwood.
USE: Horse and hiking trail.
TRAILHEAD: Sams Gap, on Parson Branch Road. Turn off the Cades Cove Loop Road just past the Cable Mill area and visitor center. Follow signs to Parson Branch Road (closed in winter). Sams Gap is approximately 4 miles from the start of Parson Branch Road.
NOTE: At press time, Parson Branch Road was closed indefinitely

due to flood damage. It's an extra 4 miles if you walk from Forge Creek Road to Sams Gap on the washed-out road.

According to veteran Smokies' hiker Robert Lochbaum, this route has "the best footing of any trail in the Smokies. It is smooth with much of it softened by a…pine needle carpet."

From the trailhead, the path gradually ascends the northwest slope of the ridge, then runs the ridgeline before moving onto the east slope. Open woods enhance the pleasure of this path.

After approximately mile **2.0**, a massive tuliptree borders the trail on the right. At least 6' in diameter, the trunk swells with large bulges, unlike the normal column-like trunk of the tuliptree.

This is a pleasant, ridge-running, gently graded trail along a path built in the 1840s by David Foute with Cherokee labor to connect his Montvale Springs Resort on Chilhowee Mountain to scenic Gregory Bald and its azaleas. This path was long known as the Foute Trail, or the Dug Trail by local people. "Dug Trail" was an apt description, meaning shaped by tools in contrast to a manway or a game trail. This term is also used by old-timers to designate the graded, dug trails in the park. Montvale Springs was a resort which attracted summer visitors with its cool breezes and mineral baths. It was in operation from 1832 to 1933.

The highest peak on Hannah Mountain is Mount Lanier, named for poet Sidney Lanier, whose kin operated Montvale Springs from 1857 to 1862. Sidney spent time as a young man at Montvale Springs and in Cades Cove and would have used this path to visit Gregory Bald.

Descending along the flank of Mount Lanier above Bell Cove, the forest changes from principally pine and oak to mixed hardwoods with tuliptrees, maple, black locust, sourwood, hemlock, and hickory. Wood ferns are present and occasionally the lovely northern maiden hair fern.

Soon the trail circles around the north end of Hannah Mountain and down to Flint Gap and Campsite #14, which straddles the broad gap. This site has lots of fresh breezes, but the nearest water is several hundred yards east on the trail. During dry weather, even this source may dry up.

According to Dwight McCarter, long time backcountry ranger in this section, the gap name came from the blue flint found here. An old Indian trail leading to the Little Tennessee River runs south-southwest. The Indians chipped arrow and ax heads at this location. Dwight reported having found flint arrowheads and chips in or near the gap.

He further reported that there was once a good spring just below the gap, but this water source is questionable now as wild hogs often wallow there. The flow is also negligible except in wet weather.

Blue-gray flint shows up on down the trail, but very little appears in the gap. Sourwood tree sprouts can be seen along the path. They begin showing scarlet fall leaves in late August.

Again the trail curves back, this time to go around the north end of Deadrick Ridge. Just short of this gap are 30" thick remnants of the mighty chestnut which once comprised about 30% of Appalachian forests. Dead since the 1930s, this hardy trunk is slowly returning to the soil. Beyond the chestnut are some black trunks of the appropriately named black locust. This too is a tough, hardy wood, which according to one old timer, "Changes to concrete 20 years after being planted as a fence post."

In the gap beyond the downed chestnut and locusts there used to sit a log cabin. Several families lived there over the years. The last was that of John Boring, according to Clayton Whitehead of Happy Valley, who remembered the old dwelling. The old fields (farmland) were in the gap and on the west slope where it declines on a slight grade, all completely reclaimed by the forest.

Leaving this quiet and remote homesite, the trail gently climbs the slope of Polecat Ridge. It tops the crest and moves from the left to the right and back to the left flank of the ridge to descend to Scott Gap at mile **7.6**. The gap is named for farmer George Scott who lived near where the 8-man shelter cabin to the left of the trail stands today. The shelter was built by the Youth Conservation Corps in the 1970s and is located 100 yards below Scott Gap in a pleasant, quiet hardwood forest. During dry weather, the water source here may vanish. Reservations are required. The shelter is popular on weekends.

Large tuliptrees and hemlocks stand near the gap, including a tuliptree 13' in circumference, standing beside the path at the gap.

The trail to the Abrams Creek ford runs through laurel and rhododendron and a mixed hardwood and pine forest with the principal trees being white pine and hemlock. Many of the trunks are from 18 to 30" in diameter. The steepest part of the Hannah Mountain Trail is the last 100 yards where it drops sharply to Abrams Creek. To cross requires wading—extremely hazardous in high water.

The trail geology begins with Cades Sandstone and changes to the coarser sandstone of the Wilhite Formation. Variety is also abundant, including the blue-gray flint and considerable conglomerate stones in which milky quartz pebbles are embedded. An example is a rock in Scott Gap at the right of the path to the shelter. Several more of these stones lie along the way to the shelter.

Prior to park establishment, the timberland on Hannah Mountain was owned by the Morton Butler Lumber Company. It was logged in sections by several contractors early in the twentieth century.

Narrative by Woody Brinegar

HATCHER MOUNTAIN TRAIL

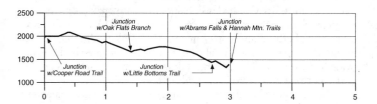

LENGTH: 3.0 miles, from Cooper Road Trail to jct. Abrams Falls and Hannah Mountain trails.
HIGHLIGHTS: Fringed polygala blooms in May.
MAP KEY: 2 D; USGS quads: Calderwood, Blockhouse.
USE: Horse and hiking trail.
STARTING POINT: 4.9 miles along the Cooper Road Trail from Abrams Creek Campground.

This is an easy and delightful trail rising slightly from Cooper Road Trail along the south slope of Hatcher Mountain through a reasonably open, mixed pine-hardwood forest of Virginia and pitch pine, oak, maple, hickory, sourwood, and flowering dogwood. It soon crosses the crest onto the north side, where it is shaded and cooler.

Hatcher Mountain is reported to have been named for Alex Hatcher, who once lived a few miles to the north in a place known as Hatcher Flats (now known as Top of the World Estates, a residential development).

An occasional large, gnarled, misshapen chestnut oak, spared the logger's saws, appears along the way. A few large pitch pines stand beside the path as it leaves the ridge and turns back to descend into the closed-in hollow of Oak Flats Branch. Flats is a term for fairly level mountain land. Nothing flat, however, appears in this secluded rhododendron hollow. When the leafy curtain falls in winter, the flat area opens up to the northeast, from which the branch flows. Large Eastern hemlocks and white pines are abundant in this shaded hideaway.

The trail ascends out of this depression into open woods again and down the north slope to the junction with the Little Bottoms and Abrams Falls trails. On the lower half of this path are a couple of small patches, easily overlooked, of a lovely flower. Quite small, only 2" to 5" high, this plant sports a midget-sized pink-reddish bloom with wings. Fringed polygala, it's called here, and gay wings or bird-on-the-wing in some areas. This delightful flower blooms also in spots on the Little Bottoms and Beard Cane trails in May.

The geology of Hatcher Mountain is a coarse-grained sedimentary rock with the occasional appearance of milky quartz. However, rocks are not much in evidence along this path.

Hatcher Mountain is one leg of a 10.9 mile loop beginning on the Cooper Road Trail out of Abrams Creek Ranger Station area and circling to the Hatcher Mountain Trail and back along the Little Bottoms Trail to complete the loop.

Narrative by Woody Brinegar

HAZEL CREEK TRAIL

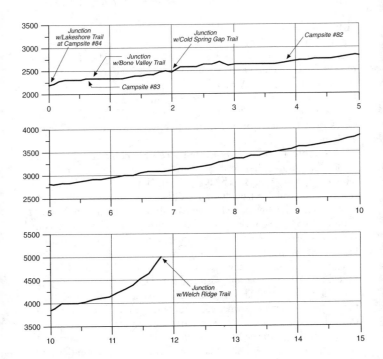

LENGTH: 11.8 miles, from Lakeshore Trail near Campsite #84 to Welch Ridge Trail.

HIGHLIGHTS: Cultural history, diverse plantlife, trout fishing.

CAUTIONS: Stream crossings above Proctor Creek.

MAP KEY: 4-6 F-E; USGS quads: Tuskeegee, Thunderhead, Silers.

USE: Horse and hiking trail.

STARTING POINT: Jct. Lakeshore Trail at Campsite #84.

NOTE: The section of the Lakeshore Trail between Campsite #86 on

Fontana Lake and Campsite #84 is often called "Hazel Creek Trail" as well. See Lakeshore Trail, Campsites #86-84, for that narrative.

The Hazel Creek watershed has a rich and varied history. Once the haunt of Indians, pioneer farmers, timber barons, miners, wealthy sportsmen, writers, and twentieth century townspeople, Hazel Creek has seen a lot of change. A trip up Hazel Creek will not only take you through this gamut of Appalachian history but also through most of the ecological zones represented in the park.

The most complete historic record of Hazel Creek to date is *Hazel Creek from Then til Now* by Duane Oliver. This interesting volume is available at most park visitor centers.

A few hikers and most horsemen access Hazel Creek via the Lake Shore Trail from either Fontana Dam or Twentymile Ranger Station. The most popular access is by boat and the Lakeshore Trail. Boat shuttles are available from Fontana Village Marina (704)-498-2211.

Cross the short wooden bridge over Haw Gap Branch and pass Campsite #84 on your right. The campsite accommodates hikers but is not available to horsemen. The site is in relatively good condition but is a bit on the small side. Its proximity to a number of trails makes it a good base camp for day hikes into the surrounding area. From here on up, bears commonly visit the Hazel Creek campsites so proper care and storage of food is well advised. An abandoned road that turns upstream at the downstream end of the fifth bridge leads about 0.7 mile to the most impressive waterfall on Hazel Creek.

Follow the main road past Campsite #84 for 0.7 mile to arrive at Bone Valley Creek and Campsite #83. Just before reaching Bone Valley Creek you will cross a small flat knoll with a massive white oak on your right. This was the site of the Bone Valley Baptist Church. A quarter-mile long trail to the left from here leads to the Bone Valley cemetery (82 graves). It is interesting to note that all graves in these cemeteries face east so that on Resurrection Day, everyone interred there would be facing in the proper direction. Examination of the headstones reveals the tenuous life deep in the Smokies—many infant and child graves, evidence of the 1919 influenza epidemic.

Campsite #83 accommodates 20 hikers and 10 horses and is arguably the nicest campsite on Hazel Creek. The camping areas are well spread out in the level area at the confluence of the two creeks. Its proximity to both Hazel and Bone Valley creeks and its distance from the more heavily-fished lower section of Hazel Creek make it an excellent choice as a base camp for a trout fishing expedition. An intermittent spring is located near the campsite and water from the streams is also readily available.

Cross the wooden bridge over Bone Valley Creek and turn right to continue up Hazel Creek. The road to the left is the Bone Valley Trail.

About 1.0 mile from Bone Valley a faint trail to the left leads 0.5 mile up a steep ridge to McCampbell Gap cemetery (6 graves). To the right, across Hazel Creek, was the site of the Burlingame Home. Called by many the finest home on the creek, this three story frame structure had about twenty rooms, each paneled with a different species of wood. Orson Burlingame came to Hazel Creek as the civil engineer for Ritter Lumber Company. Like many other Ritter imports, he became enamored with the area, married a local girl and stayed on after Ritter left. He is buried at Bone Valley cemetery.

At **2.0** miles you will cross a small spring branch and arrive at the Cold Spring Gap Trail and the Park Service bunkhouse. The Cold Spring Gap Trail turns right and leads 3.6 miles to the Welch Ridge Trail. To the left is a frame building maintained as a bunkhouse for Park Service personnel working in the area. Members of the Cable family lived here in the 1930s.

About 1.5 miles from the bunkhouse you will pass the old Calhoun fields and rock foundation of the Josh Calhoun house on your right. There is a wooden post with a small metal tag on the right of the road near here that marks the original park boundary (pre-1943 agreement). Just past the upper end of the Calhoun fields, you will reach Campsite #82 (Calhoun). It's situated in a rather small but level area near the creek and is surrounded by rock outcrops. It accommodates hikers and horses. Horses should be quartered in the larger, level area across the trail from the campsite. Calhoun is the most deteriorated campsite on the creek and can get muddy in wet weather. Its location in a boulder and bluff landscape, however, can make it an interesting place to spend some time. There is no spring nearby, but water is available from the creek.

The complexion of the forest changes somewhat above campsite #82 as you are now approaching 3,000' in elevation. About 0.5 mile above #82 you will rock hop across Walkers Creek. Just past this ford the Walker's fields lay off to your left. Walker cemetery (6 graves) is about 0.5 mile up Walkers Creek on the side of a knoll on the south side of the creek. A fairly large settlement was located in and around the Walker's fields. Many members of the Brooks family lived here. Homesites abound. A county school operated here 1908-26.

Just above Walkers Creek the trail fords Hazel Creek twice. A foot trail on the left bank avoids these fords and has some very interesting rock bluffs. One half mile above Walkers Creek you will cross Proctor Creek and reach the point where horses are no longer permitted on the trail. This level opening was the site of Ritter's camp #7, the uppermost in the string of Ritter logging camps. A forked tuliptree grown around a metal water pipe to the left of the trail gives evidence of this industrial penetration into what Horace Kephart called the "Back of the Beyond." An outstanding view of the confluence of Hazel Creek and Proctor Creek can be seen looking back downstream from here.

The Hazel Creek Trail bears right from the clearing and quickly fords the main creek. Chimneys, foundations, and terraces mark one of the furthest upstream settlements on Hazel Creek. Old apple and persimmon trees now frequently attract wildlife.

The trail from here on up to the Welch Ridge Trail is an entirely different hiking experience from what you have enjoyed so far on Hazel Creek. Although the trail is along the old railroad grade for much of the distance, it soon becomes narrow and somewhat overgrown. You ford the creek numerous times before starting the climb up Welch Ridge. These upper sections are home to the brook trout, the only trout native to the Smokies. It is against regulations to kill a brookie, so if you catch one it must be carefully released.

The forest now reflects the considerable elevation you have attained. Upland plant species that have been uncommon so far become more prevalent. In summer, Turk's cap lily, putty root orchid, Michaux's saxifrage, and grass-of-Parnassus are added to the wild-flower show. The transition from a cove hardwood forest to a northern hardwood forest is marked by the disappearance of flowering dogwood and tuliptrees and the dominance of yellow birch and American beech. As a grand finale, the trail, in its last mile, climbs nearly 1,000'. The first sightings of witchhobble, red spruce, and American mountain-ash confirm that you have really arrived in the high country and are approaching the trail's end at the junction with the Welch Ridge Trail. From the ridgetop junction it's 1.8 miles to the Appalachian Trail near Silers Bald.

Narrative by Lance Holland

HEMPHILL BALD TRAIL

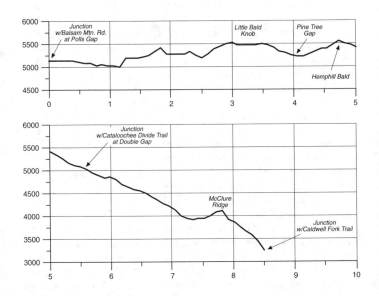

LENGTH: 8.5 miles, from Polls (Paul's) Gap to Caldwell Fork Trail.
HIGHLIGHTS: Good views.
CAUTIONS: Fallen trees, wash-outs.
MAP KEY: 11 E; USGS quads: Bunches Bald, Dellwood.

USE: Horse and hiking trail.

TRAILHEAD: From Blue Ridge Parkway, follow signs toward Balsam Mountain Campground (Heintooga Ridge Road) and park at Polls Gap.

Many hikers use Hemphill Bald Trail as the first part of a 14-mile loop hike starting and ending at Polls Gap, a loop that also takes in the uppermost sections of Caldwell Fork and Rough Fork trails. Of the three trails that embark from the parking area at Polls Gap (elevation 5,130'), you take the trail to the right, which descends along an old logging railroad through yellow birches. The grass alongside Hemphill Bald Trail reminds you that the Cataloochee region was extensively logged by Suncrest Lumber Company before the establishment of the park. Nearby ridges eroded rapidly once their forest cover was gone. Grasses were the first plants to grow back. Although second-growth forest now secures the soil of these high ridges, some grass remains in less densely shaded areas.

To the left of the trail are good views into Caldwell Fork Valley. You soon enter Sugartree Licks, whose name reflects the surrounding sugar maples. Christmas ferns and may-apples line the trail banks, while fallen American chestnut trunks remain unrotted more than half a century after their deaths. Mountain people greatly valued American chestnut: they used its bark for tanning, its leaves for home remedies, and its fruit for food. After crossing a small rivulet, the trail climbs slightly up Whim Knob.

At 1.0 mile, the trail descends to join the park boundary, punctuated by a split-rail fence built in the 1930s by the Civilian Conservation Corps, in part to keep out stray livestock. Members of the CCC had no way of knowing that the fence they erected might one day keep out an animal who once claimed the Smokies as home, but that is what happened. After escaping from a nearby wildlife reserve, a herd of buffalo ended up on an area golf course. A local sheriff and his "posse" took off on golf carts to "round up" the herd. Two animals eluded the officials and moved toward the park. It took weeks to catch the last two renegade buffalo. Ironically, the buffalo, former Smokies residents, were seen as threats to the park's environment.

The trail climbs the side of Buck Knob among yellow birch,

mountain maple, and yellow buckeye. False Solomon's seal, Jack-in-the-pulpit, and wild geranium grow beside it. Descending from Buck Knob, you pass a spring that is actually "gurgling." By **3.0** miles, you have passed Maggot Spring Gap and climbed up Little Bald Knob. Here, the trail courses through a fairly thick rosebay rhododendron grove; other plants include squawroot (a parasitic wildflower that, because it contains no clorophyll, takes nourishment from the roots of trees), bluebead lily, bluets, and wood betony.

By **4.1** miles the trail is climbing Hemphill Bald. From this point on, a thick second-growth forest of yellow buckeye, pignut hickory, shadbush, and sugar maple flourishes to the left, while to the right the vista frequently opens up. Instead of being cloaked with trees, much of Hemphill Bald is grassy, having been logged before the park's founding, then kept cleared for sheep and cattle. Not only does the trail provide sweeping views of rolling pasture, it also offers good bird-watching. This environment, where a forest meets a field, is called a "margin." Red-eyed Vireos and Veeries, species of the deep woodland, and field birds like Eastern Bluebirds and American Robins are present. Climbing steadily up Hemphill Bald, with the fence-line immediately to the right, you pass several black locusts which mountain people used for rot-resistant fence posts in so many split-rail fences. In this section, you will see common buttercup, bull thistle, Turk's cap lily, wild geranium, as well as a number of mints, including wild bergamot and heal-all. Members of the mint family can be identified by their distinctive scent and square stems.

By **4.7** miles, you reach the summit of Hemphill Bald (5,540' elevation), where cool-loving trees proliferate, including red spruce, Northern red oak, and yellow birch. At **5.5** miles, the trail meets Cataloochee Divide Trail at Double Gap. Hemphill Bald Trail abruptly turns left, heading downhill toward Caldwell Fork Trail, while Cataloochee Divide Trail continues straight ahead, following the Cataloochee Divide toward Cove Creek Gap.

Heading downhill from Double Gap, you enter a second-growth forest of yellow birch, mountain maple, sugar maple, American basswood, and Eastern hemlock. You might see a Red-tailed Hawk soar overhead, riding the updrafts at Double Gap. Patches of grass at the base of several yellow birches suggest that this now-wooded slope was once pasture. To the left, the trees are small, perhaps stunted—the soil is quite shallow here, a consequence of the erosion caused by pre-park logging. Umbrella-leaf, a wildflower distinct for its two-foot wide leaves, thrives. In winter, Caldwell Fork Valley becomes visible on the downhill slope.

At approximately **6.0** miles, the trail swings gradually right. Soon you cross Double Gap Branch for the first of several times. The trail winds down both sides of the branch. A good habitat for salamanders, Double Gap Branch courses over several small waterfalls. Wildflowers along this section include bluebead-lily and trailing arbutus (the latter species is a tiny member of the heath family).

At **7.0** miles the trail passes a boulder field, with many rocks exposed by extensive erosion. Nearby, the old root systems of American chestnut stumps send up new sprouts. The trail descends steeply away from the branch, where you enter a dry ridge environment; black locust and greenbrier dominate. Soon, you enter a mountain laurel thicket interspersed with Eastern hemlock as well as red and striped maple. At **8.0** miles, the trail returns close to the branch within a rosebay rhododendron glade. After walking across Double Gap Branch, you enter a grove of large Eastern hemlock. Nearby, on the right, is a huge Northern red oak with a 6' diameter trunk. You cross a feeder creek and then recross Double Gap Branch; to the right is a "slick" (a rhododendron and mountain laurel thicket). Descending through mixed second-growth hardwoods, you follow the rushing branch to one more crossing, which requires rock-hopping. Beautiful cinnamon fern grows on the bank among Eastern hemlocks. This area is quite moist: at one point, rosebay rhododendron saplings sprout out of a decaying Eastern hemlock trunk. At **8.5** miles, Hemphill Bald Trail reaches Caldwell Fork Trail. Before the park existed, this was the site of a house belonging to J.L. Sutton. Park records say that he and his family not only built a house here, but also a barn, smoke-house, and shed.

Nearby on Caldwell Fork is Campsite #41, which is beautifully situated for hikers wanting to explore the upper end of Caldwell Fork Valley, despite the fact that it is heavily used by fishermen.

Narrative by Ted Olson

HUGHES RIDGE TRAIL

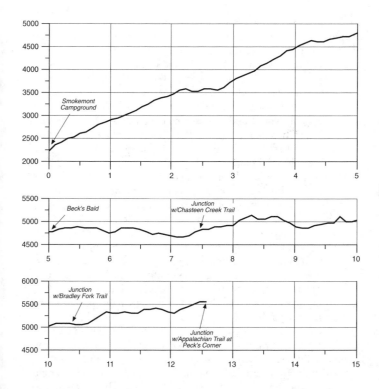

LENGTH: 12.6 miles, from Smokemont Campground to the Appalachian Trail.
HIGHLIGHTS: Summer wildflowers.
CAUTIONS: Unmaintained trail section outside park boundary.
MAP KEY: 9 C-F; USGS quads: Mt. Guyot, Smokemont.
USE: Horse and hiking trail.
TRAILHEAD: Turn off Newfound Gap Road onto the side road to

Smokemont Campground. Just after crossing the bridge, turn right into the gravel parking area. Cross the road and look for the trail sign.

Built in 1934 by the Smokemont Civilian Conservation Corps Camp, Hughes Ridge Trail climbs from Smokemont up to Hughes Ridge and follows it all the way to Pecks Corner on the Appalachian Trail. The ridge was named for Rafe and Lizzie Hughes, who settled there before 1814. Their descendants lived at the foot of the ridge until the park was established. Other landowners in this area were 49 Cherokee families who lived on land ceded by a treaty of 1819, which allowed them to own land and become US citizens. They successfully resisted the Cherokee removal of 1838, and were joined by fugitives from the Trail of Tears. These groups became the Eastern Band of the Cherokee. They did not receive US citizenship until 1924 and North Carolina did not allow them to vote until 1930.

Hughes Ridge Trail is beautiful, but there is one problem: it goes outside the park boundary and crosses a corner of the Cherokee-owned lands. The section of trail outside the park, about 1.5 miles, is not maintained by the park, and rangers cannot recommend it. They can, however, tell you current conditions. Before hiking this trail, check with rangers at Sugarlands or Oconaluftee visitor centers for information about new logging roads or other changes. Also, you need to carry plenty of water on this mostly ridgetop trail.

From the trailhead, the white Smokemont Chapel is uphill to your left, partly hidden by trees. Turn right on a heavily-used horse trail which curves left up to a left turn for Hughes Ridge. There are several new signs and new trails for concession horses in the first mile. The trail is a dirt pack bench with a few rocks. Twisty mountain laurel grows on the trail bank, and you can hear a small creek on the right.

After mile 0.3, Hughes Ridge Trail forks left. The trail is an easy grade uphill, but may have some muddy seeps. At the next junction, after open woods and a rosebay rhododendron tunnel, you take the left fork again. Hughes Ridge Trail crosses dry, open woods with poison ivy, Virginia creeper, and buffalo-nut bushes. After a left switchback, the trail is somewhat overgrown with small trees. At the next trail junction, take the right fork, which goes uphill beside a grassy creek. After a left turn across the creek, the trail becomes weedy and winds through brush and saplings with oversized leaves. A sandy road signals that you have left the park. At the time of this writing, the trail was easy to follow, but you should carry a compass and topo map. Trail switchbacks correspond to the ones on the map and are the best landmarks. New roads and logging may obscure the trail.

Cross the road; the trail climbs right and reaches a sandy ridge top and then dips into a sheltered cove with sassafras, striped maple, and wildflowers. It crosses another ridge top logging road where you can see the deep valley to your right and Hughes Ridge ahead. Two switchbacks take you into the park, in a big patch of rosebay rhododendron, and then back out again to a drier area. After crossing another road, the trail passes a boundary stake, orange paint marks on trees, and a USNPS boundary sign, all assuring you that you are back in the park.

The trail climbs gently up a nice ridge, shaded by oaks, hickories, maples, and a few Eastern hemlocks. After several hundred yards, the trail slips to the right of the ridge, where spiderwort, bee-balm, rue-anemone, fire pink, bowman's root, false hellebore, evening primrose, geranium, mandarin, umbellate clintonia, and other spring and early summer flowers grow. The trail runs almost straight north until it swings east to go around Becks Bald (5,053' elevation).

A gurgly creek at the base of Becks Bald might be a water source and provides moisture for even more flowers, ferns, and a few brambles. Flame azaleas flourish here and bloom in late June. After Becks Bald, the trail runs on the other side of Hughes Ridge and looks like an old road or railroad bed. It crosses a very rocky, wide creek bed and rises into another bramble patch. The chestnut saplings are big here and some bear chestnuts before succumbing to the blight. Interrupted fern, fly poison flowers, and silverbell trees all grow along this section, and yellow strands of dodder, a parasitic flowering plant, twine up the stems of other plants.

The trail crosses a four-branched seep of water coming down from Becks Bald. After the seep you enter a rosebay rhododendron and mountain laurel thicket, then open deciduous woods with giant oak trees. The trail drops down to a small gap and may be rough with roots and rocks. After the gap, it crosses another rich fern and flower field and climbs back to the ridge top. Look for American chestnut logs and snags, and soon you reach the junction with Chasteen Creek Trail. You have hiked **7.4** miles since Smokemont and 5.2 miles more will take you to the Appalachian Trail. If you take the Chasteen Creek Trail 5.3 miles back to Smokemont, you will come out at the upper end of Smokemont Campground, about 1.0 mile from the chapel.

From this junction, the trail climbs through yet another outstanding wildflower patch: flame azalea, mountain laurel, bowman's root, tall bluets, whorled loosestrife, evening primrose, wood betony, St. Johns-wort, fire pink, spiderwort, and more. Then, after the junction with Enloe Creek Trail, Hughes Ridge Trail descends a long slope with some forest openings created by windthrow of big trees. On this slope, you will see the first red spruces of this hike, but at the bottom, the main evergreen will be Eastern hemlock. After a small gap, the trail rises to a spruce-covered ridge. The next ridge has the plants characteristic of high elevation ridges: American beech, catawba rhododendron, Fraser magnolia, hobblebush, wintergreen, mountain laurel, painted trillium, and trailing arbutus.

At the next trail junction, 2.5 miles from Enloe Creek Trail, Bradley Fork Trail drops off to the left, and you could use it to return to Smokemont in 7.3 miles. Hughes Ridge Trail continues north along a wide jeep track. Look for a shaggy, big maple. The trail becomes steep and rocky as it climbs through dark red spruce forest. At the ridge top is a beautiful stand of tall spruces with ferns, blue-bead lily, Canada mayflower, a needle carpet, and a nice forest smell. There may be hog wallows in the dips along this jeep track; look for tracks in the mud. A few American beech trees on the right support crowds of epiphytes—ferns, mosses, lichens and flowers that establish themselves in branch angles.

The trail passes a small utility shack on the right, once used for horse patrol, and climbs through more red spruce forest. After it dips down and up, it comes to a clearing with a horse rail on the left. The path down to Pecks Corner Shelter is to the right, just before a gnarled, leaning yellow birch. The stone shelter has a wire front, wire bunks, a fireplace inside and a fire ring in front. The water source is about 100 yards in front of the shelter. A sign points to the right for the toilet area. Treat all water.

The trail above the shelter is steep, rocky, and possibly wet through typical high elevation spruce-fir forest. Most of the Fraser fir trees are either dead or small because of the balsam woolly adelgid infestation. After climbing for about 0.2 mile, the trail drops to meet the Appalachian Trail at Pecks Corner.

Narrative by Doris Gove

HUSKEY GAP TRAIL

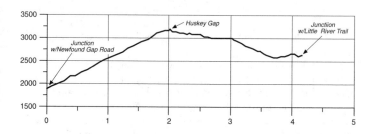

LENGTH: 4.1 miles, from Newfound Gap Road to Little River Trail.
HIGHLIGHTS: Pleasant forest.
MAP KEY: 6 C-D; USGS quad: Gatlinburg.
USE: Hiking trail.
TRAILHEAD: Take the Newfound Gap Road 1.5 miles south from Sugarlands Visitor Center and park at the second Quiet Walkway on the left. The trail begins across Newfound Gap Road.

Not long after you begin the trail, notice an obvious road bed and a rock wall about 20 yards below the trail on the right. This is a home-site. The road once linked this farm to the Sugarlands community that prospered just east of here, across Newfound Gap Road. In fact, during the late 19th and early 20th centuries, each of the drainages leading to the West Prong of the Pigeon River had communities of a dozen families or more—Sugarland Branch, Fighting Creek, Forks of the River, and Bullhead. The Sugarland Branch valley, which you can see below at several points along this trail, had families with the surnames Whaley, Ogle, Huskey, and Parton living there before the park purchased their property in the 1920s. A check of the local telephone directory will reveal that these families continue to have a strong presence in the area.

For the first quarter mile, crested dwarf iris lines the trail in several spots. These lovely, purple wildflowers bloom in late April and early May, but their distinctive leaves are visible throughout the warmer months.

As you begin your climb upward, the trees immediately get larger—some tuliptrees here are more than two feet in diameter. Running water can be heard on the right, a sign that you are approaching Flint Rock Branch. During summer, pale jewelweed grows abundantly along the trail.

After crossing Flint Rock Branch, the trail gently ascends and the somewhat open forest permits, in almost every season, a vista of Mount Harrison to the immediate right and English Mountain and Mount Le Conte to the extreme right, over your shoulder. Smooth Solomon's seal is common on both sides of the trail as well as numerous spring wildflowers: trilliums, bloodroot, bellwort, and phlox.

The heavy vines climbing the trees along this trail are grape vines. Note how in some cases they have broken off branches or even trunks of their host trees.

Not quite halfway to the gap you will start seeing boulder fields, or block fields as they are called by geologists. Many were formed by the intense freezing and thawing action which occurred here during the last ice age, 15,000-20,000 years ago.

As you get closer to Huskey Gap, on your right across the valley is a view of Gatlinburg and its many homes and chalets. Further in the distance is the Cumberland Plateau, a faint level line on the horizon. Fraser magnolia trees become more prevalent as you approach the gap, a common species in mid-elevation mountain passes.

Below the gap on the right is the old Huskey Gap Road, an old settlers road still faintly visible from the trail. According to a map drawn by Carl M. Ownby and Jack L. Ownby, the Huskey Gap school house was located just below the gap on the left side of the old road.

The school was in operation between 1893 and 1922 and served the Sugarland Branch community.

At mile **2.0**, as you approach the gap, mountain laurel and other heath shrubs become thicker along the trail's edge. Elevation at the gap is about 3,200'.

Huskey Gap was the route taken by many who lived in the Sugarlands and Gatlinburg area who worked in the Little River Lumber Camps, particularly Three Forks, a camp a short distance below Clingmans Dome. Olin Watson, who grew up in the Three Forks Lumber Camp, remembered being caught in a snowstorm on the way to visit his family in Gatlinburg. "It snowed so hard Mom took her scarf and fixed it around my head so I could breathe easier and she pulled her coat around her head. Mom finally scouted some hemlocks growing against a cliff and she dragged me under them," Watson said. Then, as luck would have it, a neighbor was seen in the distance. Olin and his mother couldn't immediately catch the neighbor, but followed his tracks in the snow to safety.

If you pass over the gap in the early fall, you should be greeted by isolated stands of black gum trees, easily identified by their brilliant red leaves. Here also is where the Huskey Gap trail intersects the Sugarland Mountain Trail. Travel to the right 3.1 miles to reach Fighting Creek Gap on the Little River Road or 9 miles to the left along the top of Sugarlands mountain to the Appalachian Trail near Mount Collins.

About a half mile below the gap, the trail crosses Big Medicine Branch. Look closely at the stone foundation under the trailbed there. It was most likely built in the 1930s by the Civilian Conservation Corps who constructed the majority of the trails in the park. Below Big Medicine Branch, the trail levels off and begins a more gradual descent toward Little River. In warmer months, Eastern chipmunks can be seen or heard on the trail, their high pitched "chip" serving as a warning alarm to other ground squirrels.

A half mile from Big Medicine Branch the trail crosses Phoebe Branch, most likely named for the Eastern Phoebe, a small gray flycatcher that was commonly found here when the park was settled (Phoebes prefer more open woodland near streams). There are several enormous boulders at the Phoebe Branch crossing, and a bench rest nearby. Further along are some large grape vines—one specimen is six inches in diameter where it twists and rises from the forest floor.

As you begin your approach to Little River, the trail levels off considerably (total drop in elevation from the gap is 600'). As you get to Little River, you cross a road or dry stream bed. The trail gradually veers off to the left into a large clearing that was a homestead owned by Ben Parton in the late 1920s. After crossing the Parton place you walk through a beautiful wooded glade of large tuliptrees and sugar maples.

Passing through the wooded glade, the trail closely follows the left bank of Little River for several hundred yards over an old road bed. At the end of the trail, you can go right to the Little River Trailhead, which is 1.7 miles away or go left to the Goshen Prong Trail, 1.0 mile away. In order to return to your original starting point on Newfound Gap Road, a car must be left at the Little River trailhead. Starting the hike there is another possibility, but there appears no clear advantage to doing so, as both approaches require an equally steep climb to the gap.

Narrative by Margaret Lynn Brown & Donald E. Davis

HYATT RIDGE TRAIL

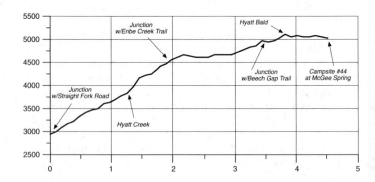

LENGTH: 4.5 miles, From Straight Fork Road to Campsite #44.

HIGHLIGHTS: Mature hardwood and virgin forest; McGee Springs.
MAP KEY: 10 D-E; USGS quads: Luftee Knob, Bunches Bald.
USE: Horse and hiking trail.
TRAILHEAD: From the Oconaluftee/Cherokee entrance to Great Smoky Mountains National Park, drive about 8 miles northeast on Big Cove Road. Continue on Straight Fork Road 2.5 miles inside the park boundary. The trail will be on the left.

Hyatt Ridge rises out of Big Cove and forms a jagged connection to the high country on Balsam Mountain near Tricorner Knob. The trail covers only a couple of miles on the ridge and reaches the ridge top after climbing from Straight Fork to an unnamed gap. The trail then continues to dead end at McGee Springs Campsite #44. This route once continued up the ridge to intersect Balsam Mountain Trail at Mount Hardison.

At the trailhead, the trail leaves the road and climbs along Hyatt Creek as an old road or railroad grade. This area was logged by Parsons Pulp and Lumber Company, primarily for red spruce. Demand for the softwood species multiplied during World War I to build airplanes for the fledgling U.S. Air Force. These hills once supplied up to 200,000 board feet of timber a day to the sawmill at Ravensford. Since the red spruce and Fraser fir were removed, the forest is now almost wholly mixed hardwoods.

The trail climbs steadily beside Hyatt Creek. It becomes rocky, and crosses several intermittent drainages, then the main stream and a major tributary at 0.7 miles. All these crossings are easy rock hops. The rocks here consist of light yellow sandstone, and white or gray banded gneiss. These widely different rock types found in the same vicinity are evidence of the nearby Greenbrier Fault system. The fault has pushed the oldest rocks in the Smokies up over younger ones.

The banded gneiss is part of the so-called basement complex. The basement makes up the foundation upon which the rocks of the North American continent rest. In the Smokies, the basement is estimated to be about one billion years old. The sandstone was deposited on top of the basement about 600 million years ago. The sandstone found here is part of the Snowbird Group. These rocks are named for exposures in the Snowbird Mountains north of the park. During the Appalachian Orogeny (an orogeny is a mountain-building event), the basement was pushed (or slid) up and over the Snowbird along the Greenbrier Fault system. When older rock has been thrust over younger rocks, and then slides overtop, it is termed an overthrust, or, simply, a thrust fault.

The Greenbrier Fault is not a simple overthrust. You can see this clearly by looking at a geologic map. The fault is found all along the base of the Smokies on the Tennessee side, twists around Mt. Cammerer and Mt. Sterling, then cuts through Cataloochee and trends north. Another piece of the fault rims a large area of basement rocks that stretches from Cherokee, North Carolina, to Balsam Mountain. This portion generally follows Straight Fork and includes much of this trail.

The odd twists seen in the Greenbrier Fault are the result of later folding of the faulted rocks. That is, the Smokies did not rise all at once. An earlier phase of their history saw great masses of the older rocks thrust up and over younger rocks along great faults that included the Greenbrier. Later, a second phase of mountain building bent the faults and their accompanying strata into folds. Erosion has removed the tops of the folds, revealing their ancient core.

Hyatt Ridge Trail enters the basement rocks at about **1.5** miles. This piece of basement is named the Straight Fork Window. Here, the window reveals the inner mechanics of mountain building. Many are familiar with the Cades Cove and Tuckaleechee Cove windows, where erosion allows you to "view" the younger limestone in the valley floor through the older rocks of the mountains. The Straight Fork Window is quite different. This window affords a view of much older, intensely folded basement and later Precambrian sedimentary rock (including the Snowbird) within a mass of the younger Ocoee Supergroup.

Hyatt Ridge Trail continues its ascent of the ridge, passing into deep time. The trail reaches an unnamed gap (sometimes referred to, as are many low places in the Appalachians, as Low Gap) at **1.9** miles. Enloe Creek Trail begins here and descends to Campsite #47 on Raven Fork, and connects with Hughes Ridge Trail. Hyatt Ridge Trail turns right, climbing out of the gap.

Past the gap, the trail levels in a small laurel slick, and skirts a mature forest of large Eastern hemlock, tuliptree, American beech, and yellow birch. Apparently, this portion of Hyatt Ridge marks the end of the old logging operations. It is fascinating to view the contrast of the younger second growth and virgin timber as the trail follows this wide ridge top. You can imagine the scene in the 1930s as the loggers reached this ridge top. Behind them was a massive scar, the result of twenty years of clear-cutting. The forest they faced was peaceful and scenic, just as it appears today.

The trail climbs steadily around the summit of Hyatt Bald (elevation 5,153'), which is wooded and grassy, and it is hard to imagine that this may once have been a bald. After a short descent, Beech Gap Trail intersects on the right, having climbed 2.8 miles from Straight Fork. Hyatt Ridge Trail continues along the ridge, passing a sign that indicates the way to McGee Springs (Campsite #44) at **4.5** miles and the trail's end.

McGee Springs Campsite is located in a wide area on Hyatt Ridge, where Breakneck Ridge enters from the west. It is in an enchanted glade among dense trees and undergrowth of the old growth forest. In the past it has been closed because of bear activity, so store food carefully. Most tent sites are in damp areas; since this clearing is the headwaters for the Right Fork of Raven Fork, and there are many small springs and seeps. The main spring boils clear, sweet mountain water from beneath a mossy rock. Water from the springs may be associated with the Greenbrier Fault, which cuts across Breakneck Ridge at this location. Springs are often associated with faults in the Appalachians, for water accumulates in the many fractures along the fault trace.

It is not known for certain, but the spring may be named for Bishop Francis Asbury's traveling companion, Reverend John McGee. McGee and his bishop braved many hardships to bring the gospel to mountain settlers in the early 1800s. In 1810, McGee accompanied the aging Asbury along old Indian trails into the newly settled Pigeon River Valley of western North Carolina. Hardy as these circuit riders were, it is doubtful they ventured deep enough into the mountains to visit this spring. Perhaps the name was provided in tribute to this largely forgotten figure of pioneer history.

Hyatt Ridge Trail once continued and joined Balsam Mountain Trail near Tricorner Knob. The old trail is now thoroughly overgrown and obscured by a maze of blowdowns and undergrowth high on Mount Hardison. McGee Springs is also the terminus of the old Raven Fork Trail. It used to lead down a spur of aptly-named Breakneck Ridge to Three Forks on Raven Fork.

Narrative by James Wedekind

INDIAN CREEK MOTOR TRAIL

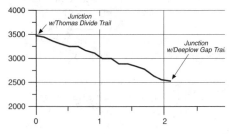

LENGTH: 2.1 miles, from Thomas Divide Trail to Deeplow Gap Trail.

HIGHLIGHTS: Lush, second-growth forest.

CAUTIONS: Overgrown trail sections.

MAP KEY: 8 F; USGS quads: Bryson City, Clingmans Dome.
USE: Horse and hiking trail.
STARTING POINT: Take NC Highway 19 south from Cherokee; in Bryson City, follow the signs toward Deep Creek Ranger Station and Campground. Drive 1.0 mile up Tom Branch Road and park on the left at the start of Thomas Divide Trail. Hike 3.2 miles up Thomas Divide Trail.

The Indian Creek Motor Trail connects Thomas Divide Trail with Deeplow Gap Trail. It was first constructed as part of a scenic auto road, a project that was later abandoned. Currently it is little-used and not well maintained.

The first part of the trail is obscured by low-growing plants, particularly during summer. Entering a second-growth forest, the trail heads downhill among tuliptrees, pignut hickories, white pines, Eastern hemlocks, yellow birches, and red maples; Christmas ferns and ground pines grow beside the trail. White snakeroot, also called "pioneer killer," flourishes. The plant was a hazard because pioneer children would unknowingly drink poisoned milk from cows who had eaten it. To the right, between Thomas Divide Trail and Indian Creek Motor Trail, was the site of the Randall farmhouse, barn, and corn crib.

Continuing steadily downhill, you enter a grove of large oaks, with American chestnut stumps scattered beneath. At one point along the trail is a ground cover familiar to many urban and suburban dwellers: periwinkle. This non-native plant—brought to the New World from Europe—was originally planted by early mountain settlers around homes and in cemeteries (a local name for this species is "graveyard grass"). But the plant naturalized and lingers in the forest.

The trail flattens then heads downhill through a grove of tulip-trees. A small creek flows on the left; on the right by the creek, a "wolf" tuliptree spreads—its growth has been stunted, perhaps because of lightning. Instead of standing straight, the tree spreads, shadowing an unusually wide area and "devouring" so much sunlight that few other plants can compete with it.

To the left are several flowering dogwoods clearly suffering from dogwood anthracnose. After a grove of young tuliptrees, you walk left of a large dry cove, where scrubby trees and poison ivy are common. Descending down a dry slope cloaked by black oaks, you enter lush woods then step across a stream that cascades among large Eastern hemlocks. On the left, huge rotting American chestnuts lie, while Christmas and maidenhair ferns cover the right trail bank.

Soon, Indian Creek can be heard far below on the left. You may see a White-breasted Nuthatch climbing headfirst down a tree trunk, uttering its distinctive nasal call, "yank-yank." The trail enters a more mature (though still second-growth) forest of tuliptree, Eastern hemlock, sourwood, red maple, white pine, and yellow birch. At mile **2.1** the trail reaches Deeplow Gap Trail. Indian Creek Trail is only 0.3 mile to the left.

Narrative by Ted Olson

INDIAN CREEK TRAIL

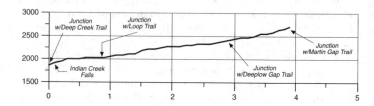

LENGTH: 3.9 miles, from Deep Creek Trail to Martin Gap Trail.
HIGHLIGHTS: Indian Creek Falls, farmstead sites, scenic stream valley.
CAUTIONS: Slippery rocks around waterfall.
MAP KEY: 7-8 F; USGS quads: Bryson City, Clingmans Dome.
USE: Horse and hiking trail.
STARTING POINT: Follow signs through downtown Bryson City, NC to Deep Creek Ranger Station, Campground, and trailhead. Hike 0.7 mile on Deep Creek Trail to the Indian Creek trailhead.

From its trailhead, Indian Creek Trail heads up an old road on the east side of Indian Creek. Indian Creek Falls, a high, steep waterslide, is 200' on the left; you may get a closer look by taking a side trail down to the creek below the falls. Shortly after the falls, the trail crosses Indian Creek by bridge and continues upstream. Rosebay rhododendron veils the creek on the right, while on the left, the forest is dry, choked by poison ivy. Also left is an old stone wall with a seedling growing out of it. The trail, now moderately level, courses through Fraser magnolia, yellow birch, Eastern hemlock, sugar maple, and American beech. White pine saplings grow beside the trail, as do spiderwort and common blue violet. At **0.5** mile, Stone Pile Gap Trail branches to the right and ascends 0.9 mile to Thomas Divide Trail. Indian Creek Trail follows the roadbed among tuliptree, red maple, and scarlet oak, with an understory of flowering dogwood and wild hydrangea. You soon approach the creek, where the trail enters a grove of white pines; daisy fleabane and Virginia creeper grow alongside while Carolina Wrens sing in the brush.

At 0.8 mile, the trail meets Loop Trail, a connection to Sunkota Ridge and Deep Creek Trails. Indian Creek Trail continues into a grove of huge Eastern hemlocks where downy rattlesnake-plantain grows. At approximately 1.0 mile, somewhat below the trail to the right, Queen Branch flows into Indian Creek. It was named for the Queen Family who once lived 0.5 mile up the branch. Park records state that, when the park was being established in the late 1920s, Joe T. Queen owned several houses and a barn, as well as a corn crib, chicken house, springhouse, and privy.

By 1.5 miles, the trail passes a section of cleared land adjacent to Indian Creek, tell-tale signs of pre-park homesteads. Walking upstream, you pass four in a row: the Beard farmstead, which once had a house, corn crib, and barn; the Widow Styles place, which boasted house, barn, and two smokehouses; the Hardy Styles place, which possessed a house; and the William Laney place, which featured a house, barn, and corn crib. None of these buildings remain; even the clearings are disappearing. In one site a stately black walnut grows; on the edge of another stands an arrow-straight tuliptree. Black walnuts, an old hedge, red clover, oxeye daisy, daisy fleabane, and black raspberry reign in another site. These clearings are interspersed with patches of forest—American basswood, sassafras, and scrub pine.

At one point between the clearings, the trail rejoins Indian Creek, which now cascades into a chasm lined by rosebay rhododendron and Eastern hemlock. The stream's mist fosters a lush forest of Fraser magnolia. Soon on the right, Indian Creek flows through whirling pools and tumbling waterslides; later flowing around a large boulder, it forms two small waterfalls.

At 2.0 miles, the trail turns uphill. Nearby, flowering dogwoods are dying from dogwood anthracnose. Soon the next clearing appears on the right, after which the trail levels and veers from the creek into scrubbier forest. Then the trail passes the last farmstead and plunges back into the forest where it meets and crosses Indian Creek by bridge. Near the bridge sits a bench. Eastern hemlocks and yellow birches tower over the creek while dog-hobble straddles its banks.

Nearby, Georges Branch flows into Indian Creek. Here a small forest clearing marks the site of Nancy Jenkins' farmstead that once had a barn, corn crib, and smokehouse. The buildings are long gone—yellow buckeye rapidly closes the opening.

The trail's last mile is punctuated by four more bridged crossings of Indian Creek; you tread slowly uphill through a forest of American basswood and yellow buckeye. At **2.9** miles the trail reaches Deeplow Gap Trail which climbs 2.2 miles to Thomas Divide Trail. You soon cross Estes Branch, a small feeder creek. The trail ends at Martin Gap Trail, just past the old road turnaround.

Narrative by Ted Olson

INDIAN GRAVE GAP TRAIL

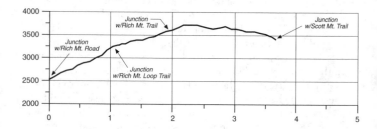

LENGTH: 3.6 miles, from Rich Mountain Road to jct. Crooked Arm Ridge and Scott Mtn. trails.
HIGHLIGHTS: Scenic views, flame azaleas.
MAP KEY 3-4 D; USGS quads: Cades Cove, Kinzel Springs.
USE: Horse and hiking trail.
TRAILHEAD: 2.2 miles up the Rich Mountain Road. This one-way gravel road begins along the Cades Cove Loop Road across from the Missionary Baptist Church. It is a seasonal road, usually closing from November through March. Take the road up the flanks of Cades Cove Mountain, crossing Tater Ridge and Branch. The Indian Grave Gap Trail leaves the road to the right. Since it angles back away from the road, it may be difficult to spot. Watch for the trail sign and the small parking area to the right. There's room for two cars at the most.

There is perhaps no other trail in the park with such an impressive name. Unfortunately, the reason for the trail name is a mystery—no signs of Indian graves now exist. Fortunately, dramatic views and beautiful forests do lie ahead.

Indians certainly did frequent this area, however. To the Cherokees, the Smokies were a sacred place used for ceremonies and hunting. Although they never built permanent settlements here, they did spend enough time to establish well worn trails and leave many place names. To reach the trailhead you will have to pass through a wide valley the Cherokee called "Tsiyahi" or "the otter's place." Today we call it Cades Cove.

This trail also serves as the power company's access road to the power lines serving Cades Cove. It is therefore a wide, seldom-driven jeep road as the locked gate at the trailhead will testify. We start the hike by passing a small outcropping of phyllite partially hidden by many young maples. Here is the bedrock of this portion of the park. It is an old, soft stone which erodes very easily.

Continuing past the gate, the trail climbs moderately through a pine-oak forest. At 0.5 mile, you drop through Indian Grave Gap and pass an old road. Was this the original Rich Mountain Road, the old Indian trail and place so many of the early settlers passed? It's hard to know for sure, but today we'll take the high road and begin to climb more steeply to the ridge line. In the next mile, we will gain nearly 1,000' elevation. If you look up as you hike, you'll notice that now the pines are gone and the trail is passing through a hardwood forest. Here you will see a wide variety of trees, including oaks, maples, tuliptrees and silverbells.

After a steep climb, you'll reach the intersection with the Rich Mountain Loop Trail near the top of Tater Ridge. You have hiked 1.1 miles to this spot. Just a few feet to the right is a small clearing which offers outstanding views of Cades Cove and the Smokies' crest. It's a great place to look out and understand a little about the forces which build and shape mountains. Below in the valley, the soil covers a layer of limestone, a sedimentary rock formed on the ocean floor. The mountain you stand upon is underlain by phyllite, while the mountains across the cove are built of sandstone. Both these latter rocks were also formed beneath a shallow sea, but much earlier than the limestone below. So how did these much older rocks wind up on top? Tectonic activities hundreds of millions of years ago pushed and bent the sandstone and phyllite into the mountains you see. Shifting continents then pushed these mountains up and over the younger limestone. Water, ice, and wind have ever so slowly re-exposed that limestone in what geologists call a "fenster" or window. From our vantage point, the window is open allowing us a great peek into the geologic past.

If for no other reason than this view, the climb to here was worth it. But there's more to come. Turning left, you will continue to climb, but more gently, as you pass blankets of galax and a scattering of flame azaleas. Flame azaleas erupt with large orange blossoms in June and July—a wonderful time to hike this trail. You are ascending a ridge known as Double Mountain, because of its twin peaks beyond the intersection with the Rich Mountain Trail.

At **1.9** miles, the trail reaches the Rich Mountain Trail. To the left, about 100 yards, is the Rich Mountain Shelter and spring. Backpackers may wish to take advantage of this small wooden shelter safely snuggled in a tiny cove on Double Mountain. Day hikers will likely wish to push on to Cerulean Knob (3,686'), 0.2 mile further. The knob is marked by a small spur trail leading steeply past the site of an old cabin and on to a level opening marked with cement blocks. These blocks were the foundation for the Rich Mountain fire tower. Today, the small clearing marks the highest point on Rich Mountain, but the views are not what they used to be. Russell Edward Whitehead was one of the first fire guards to be stationed here. From the tower, he said that in the fall, "I could stand up there and see every color of the rainbow just as far as I could look."

Return to the main trail and continue east. From here you will gradually descend in an up and down fashion to the trail junction 1.5 miles further on. The trail retains all its character. Azaleas, wildflowers, and mushrooms are scattered all along the way. Occasionally, the trail will also walk a narrow ridge providing good views to the valleys below. First, there will be a great view down into Dry Valley and Townsend. If you are hiking after the leaves have fallen, you will also get some nice views back into Cades Cove.

As you walk along the ridges, you will be tracing the park boundary. At mile **3.0**, a small overgrown side trail continues along the boundary as Indian Grave Gap Trail drops deeper into the park. Continue along the Indian Grave Gap Trail until you see a small clearing ahead. This is the power line clearing and just 150' ahead is the three-way trail junction at mile **3.6**. Indian Grave Gap runs straight into Crooked Arm Ridge Trail. Crooked Arm will take you down into Cades Cove. To the left is another trail, Scott Mountain. This trail runs back to the park boundary and follows it to Schoolhouse Gap. Backcountry Campsite #6 is just 500' down this trail. It's a good spot for two small or one medium sized group and has a small spring for water.

Narrative by Tom Condon

JAKES CREEK TRAIL

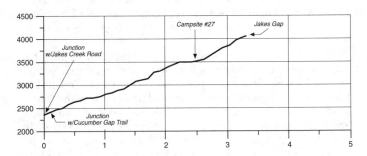

LENGTH: 3.3 miles, from Jakes Creek Road to Jakes Gap.
HIGHLIGHTS: Abundance of Fraser magnolias.
MAP KEY: 5-6 D; USGS quads: Gatlinburg, Silers Bald.
USE: Horse and hiking trail.
TRAILHEAD: From Sugarlands Visitor Center, drive west on Little River Road, and at mile 4.9 turn into Elkmont. After another 1.4 miles, just before the campground, turn left for Jakes Creek and Little River Trails. Where the road forks 0.6 mile farther, stay to the right for 0.5 mile and park at the gate.

Selective logging and settling occurred in this valley in the 1800s, but in 1901, the Little River Lumber Company bought the land for $3 an acre. In 1909, the company built a railroad up Jakes Creek. On June 30 of that year, a locomotive and several cars broke loose and sped down steep grades toward Elkmont. In the crash, engineer Daddy Bryson and another man were killed. This accident inspired at least two Tennessee folk songs. A fire burned the Jakes Creek Valley in 1925 when sparks from a log skidder ignited stumps and brush debris. It burned from June to September and destroyed houses, saw logs, and equipment. When the lumber company had taken all the trees they could, they sold small plots to new settlers, and 17 families lived in Jakes Creek when the land was repurchased by the park commission.

One group of settlers, the vacation home owners of Elkmont, did not have to leave the park in 1934. They negotiated extended leases for their cabins along the Jakes Creek and Little River Roads. Most of these leases terminated in 1992, as did the lease for the Wonderland Hotel. At the time of this writing, the controversy over what to do with the vacated buildings continues; they may be gone by the time you hike Jakes Creek.

The Jakes Creek Trail follows the route of the railroad. After the gate, the gravel road rises through a forest of small tuliptrees, maples, and black locusts. Fraser's and plantain-leaved sedge grow on the left bank. These two plants look like oversized tufts of grass with blades an inch or more wide. Fraser's sedge blades are dark green, smooth, and thick, while plantain-leaved sedge blades are lighter green, slightly crimped, and papery. The flowers, which bloom on stalks from the center of the tuft and look like fuzzy Q-tips, appear in April and May.

At mile **0.3**, Cucumber Gap Trail exits left, and at mile **0.4**, Meigs Mountain Trail goes right. Then the trail approaches noisy Jakes Creek, and you might see rusted cable left from logging. On the left are some rock outcrops with trees perched on them. After about **1.4** miles of gentle rise, the trail crosses Waterdog Branch, an easy rock hop. Then it rises over a steep ridge and drops down to cross Newt Prong, just as easily. After a switchback, the trail rises gradually with Jakes Creek on the left. Some hikers have cut across the switchback, causing erosion. Please don't use these illegal trails.

After the switchback, the most common tree is Fraser magnolia, with huge leaves, multiple trunks, and absurdly magenta fruits. In early spring, the leaves pop out of inch-long buds and grow until they are 1-2' long. Sometimes a late frost withers the first leaves and the tree has to start over. This is the only tree in the park with eared leaves, that is, lobes where the blade of the leaf meets the leaf stem, or petiole. In late April or May, look for creamy white magnolia petals. Occasionally, squirrels knock down an entire magnolia flower, and you can smell the fruity aroma. Higher on this stretch of trail, you may be level with the tops of some Fraser magnolias that grow in the creek valley, and you may be able to see the flowers or later, the fruits.

At mile **2.5** and 3,520' elevation, Campsite #27 appears between the trail and the creek. It is high, flat, and heavily used, with room for eight people and their horses. After the campsite, the trail climbs the right side of the draw, and the creek dwindles and disappears. At the head of the draw at mile **3.3** is Jakes Gap (4,055' elevation) with two trails to choose: Panther Creek straight down to the Middle Prong Trail and Miry Ridge left up to the Appalachian Trail.

Narrative by Doris Gove

JENKINS RIDGE TRAIL

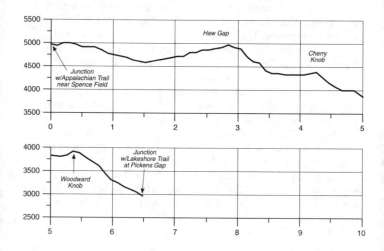

LENGTH: 6.5 miles, from Appalachian Trail to Lakeshore Trail.
HIGHLIGHTS: Scenic views, variety of vegetation.
CAUTIONS: Steep trail, creek crossing.
MAP KEY: 4 E; USGS quad: Thunderhead.
USE: Horse and hiking trail.
STARTING POINT: Appalachian Trail at Spence Field.

The Jenkins Ridge Trail begins on the Tennessee-North Carolina state line high on the crest of the Smokies at Spence Field. The vista from Spence Field includes many scenic views. Looking south-south-east, Jenkins Trail Ridge runs to the south with Eagle Creek just west of it. The trail leaves the Appalachian Trail 0.25 miles east of the Spence Field Shelter. It traverses the full gamut of vegetation types in its descent from high grassy bald to lower elevation pine forest.

The trail winds through the grasses, blueberries, and serviceberry of Spence Field. Bear and deer feast on the berries in September when they ripen. The trail passes through catawba rhododendron, mountain laurel, and flame azalea which bloom in late spring and early summer. The first 0.1 mile is often overgrown.

Soon you enter a wooded area of American beech and other hardwoods. The trail climbs 200 yards through the forest which has a grassy ground cover. This area was once a part of the bald but has been taken over by the forest. The rocky trail bed can make walking difficult. Wild hogs have damaged the forest floor rooting for food. Through an open forest of American beech, yellow birch, and other northern hardwoods the trail levels a bit before beginning a slight, easy descent. Rocky Top is above the trail to the north.

On the descent the vegetation is rich and varied. Look for white snakeroot, umbrella leaf, wild hydrangea, beech, and maples. Several types of ferns and fern allies line the trail. Notice the fine-grained metasandstone of the Thunderhead formation.

At **1.5** miles rock hop across Gunna Creek which is a major tributary to Eagle Creek. Although this creek crossing is a level spot beside a pretty mountain stream, it is not a campsite. It has been used illegally but should not be further destroyed. Linger but don't stay.

The trail ascends moderately around the flanks of Blockhouse Mountain. Wood-sorrel, Fraser magnolia, and witch-hobble stand out in the surrounding forest. Notice the change in the rocks. The metasandstone has given way to a slate similar to the Anakeesta formations elsewhere in the park.

After a slight descent, the way ascends steeply. Haw Gap is at **2.8** miles. This area is overgrown with blackberry, black-eyed Susan, beebalm, greenbrier, wild phlox, and serviceberry. Haw Gap, which lies between Blockhouse Mountain to the north and De Armond Bald to the south, once had a backcountry campsite. It's no longer a campsite, although old firerings can still be seen, so again don't camp here. The area will require a long time to recover from past abuses.

The trail begins a steep descent through galax, mountain laurel, trillium, and ferns through a drier forest. Walking is difficult on this stretch which is straight down the ridge with no switchbacks.

At a saddle gap along the ridgetop, Paw Paw Creek is to the west (right). Just below this gap, Will Myers of Eagle Creek had a mountain shack which was used by those tending cattle in the high country. A grist mill was on the site as well. The trail continues to follow the ridge crest as it moves south. It is fairly moderate and almost level for 0.4 mile.

To the west, in the Eagle Creek drainage, Montvale Lumber Company logged in the early years of the 20th century. An extensive network of narrow gauge rails were laid for the logging operations. Logs were ball-hooted down to the railroads from the higher ridges. Operations ended around 1925 after an estimated 100,000,000 board feet (enough to build 10,000 homes) were cut. The small town of Fontana, from which the lake and village are named, was built by the Montvale Lumber Company for its employees.

Cherry Knob (4,455') is gained at **4.3** miles. This elevation is only slightly lower than the beginning altitude of 4,958' at Spence Field. The trail has simply moved out Jenkins Ridge. The major part of the descent is in the last 2 miles. The trail drops steeply off Cherry Knob through oak, mountain laurel, and hardwoods. It is a different type of forest from the northern hardwood forest near Spence Field. Again, no switchbacks break the steepness of the downward journey.

A slight rise precedes the crossing of Woodward Knob (3,940'). In the next 0.4 miles the trail descends 800', which is the steepest part of the Jenkins Ridge Trail. Depending upon whether one is going up or down, this stretch is a lung buster or knee breaker. Take time to notice the change in the forest type. White pine and oak predominate with mountain laurel and galax in the understory.

The headwaters of Sugar Fork are to the east on this final leg of the trail. Horace Kephart, writer and early park advocate, first lived in the area in a small log cabin on Sugar Fork from 1904-1906. Kephart's writings were an important factor in establishing the Great Smoky Mountains National Park.

The trail terminates on the Lakeshore Trail at Pickens Gap after a descent of a steep bank. Eagle Creek is 3.6 miles to the west and Hazel Creek is 2.4 miles to the east. This portion of the Lakeshore Trail was constructed by the County Line Company of the CCC in 1935. The Jenkins Ridge Trail is a long dry trail which is strenuous in either direction.

Narrative by Charles Maynard & David Morris

JONAS CREEK TRAIL

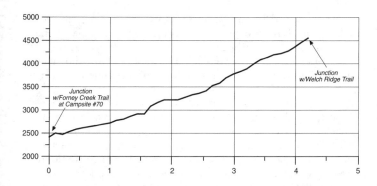

LENGTH: 4.2 miles, from Forney Creek Trail to Welch Ridge Trail.
HIGHLIGHTS: Scenic views, cascades.
CAUTIONS: Unbridged creek crossings, mud.
MAP KEY: 6 F; USGS quad: Silers Bald.
USE: Horse and hiking trail.
STARTING POINT: Hike Forney Creek Trail to the starting point 3.7 miles north of jct. with Lakeshore Trail.

The Jonas Creek Trail travels through the upper regions of land that was logged by the Norwood Lumber Company in the early 1900s. Norwood's logging of the abundant spruce reached a zenith during World War I. It was later estimated that fifteen thousand board feet of spruce per acre were taken from the area. By 1925, the major logging of the Forney Creek watershed was over.

The trail begins on the Forney Creek Trail 4.2 miles from its southern terminus at Fontana Lake and 7.2 miles below the Forney Ridge (Clingmans Dome) parking area. The trail crosses Forney Creek on a foot log. Some of the bridge has been washed away, but enough is intact to permit a safe crossing. Bear to the right through the woods to reach Campsite #70 (Jonas Creek). This campsite, which accommodates horses, is at the base of Suli Ridge, the junction of Jonas and Forney Creek Trails. It is heavily used and often has trash strewn about its several fire rings.

Amid some of the garbage are remnants of the logging days: iron spikes, rails, even a door to a stove. Today, rosebay rhododendron, mountain laurel, yellow birch, and American beech grow where the large red spruce were once logged. Jonas Creek Trail runs through the middle of the campsite, which is sandwiched between Jonas and Forney creeks.

The trail, which is an old logging railroadbed, follows Jonas Creek through a thick rosebay rhododendron tunnel. Sycamore trees grow along the creek banks. A wet crossing of Jonas Creek is reached at mile **0.3**. Take extra care on the damp, moss-covered rocks which make fording the stream difficult. The surrounding forest is a northern hardwood forest with many yellow birch and American beech. On the other side of the creek, the roadbed becomes rocky. A picturesque waterfall is to the right of the trail. Thick moss carpets the large boulders that squeeze the creek to a 4' width. The creek falls 5' into a large plunge pool.

A second crossing of Jonas Creek is 0.1 mile from the first and just beyond the small waterfall. This crossing is on an old foot log. The roadbed narrows as it extends through Eastern hemlock, American beech, birch, and Fraser magnolia. For a short distance the creek takes over the roadbed. You must skirt around the water or walk through it.

Even though the roadbed soon becomes more defined, it can be very wet and muddy. A third creek crossing again requires rock hopping. The trail next passes through an open area beside the creek. This is not a campsite, even though others have used it for one. The next (fourth) crossing is less than 0.1 mile from the previous one. The remains of a foot log can get you across dry. Sourwood, oak, American beech, and tuliptree populate this area. A patch of downy rattlesnake-plantain grows alongside the trail above the crossing.

Cross Jonas Creek for the last time just above its junction with Little Jonas Creek at mile **1.2**. An old foot log was present at the time of this writing. However, it may be safer to rock hop across. The trail now follows Little Jonas Creek toward its headwaters on the flanks of Welch Ridge. You cross Little Jonas Creek near the confluence of

Yanu Branch about 0.5 miles from the last crossing.

The trail now follows Yanu Branch up the eastern slopes of Welch Ridge. Yanu is the Cherokee word for bear. Many creeks in the Smokies were named Bear Creek when Great Smoky Mountains National Park was created and the nomenclature committees were struggling to find appropriate names which would not duplicate other features. Oftentimes Cherokee words were selected.

Sassafras, sourwood, American beech, oak, American holly and Fraser magnolia are some of the many trees in this area. The bed of the old road resembles a ditch at one point where the wear and tear of travel have worn the soil away. Yanu Branch is crossed on a foot log amid large boulders.

A beautiful stair-step cascade of over 100' is to the right of the trail after a switchback. The trail winds through a boulder field of talus caused by sandstone breaking free during the hard winters of the last Ice Age. A series of four switchbacks punctuate the ascent. Rosebay rhododendron closes in on the trail before it breaks out into a more open northern hardwood forest. Two more switchbacks are 225 yards above the first set.

One last switchback moves the trail away from Yanu Branch to climb Yanu Ridge. Downed American chestnut trees lie amid maple, black locust, and oak. The ridge top is reached at mile 3.4. The drier crest has oak, beech, and mountain laurel. The trail moderates into a fairly level walk for a short distance. Catawba rhododendron is mixed with the larger-leafed rosebay rhododendron.

Jonas Creek Trail ends at a junction with Welch Ridge Trail on the side of Welch Ridge. The state line and the Appalachian Trail are 2.5 miles to the right (north), while High Rocks is 4.7 miles left (southwest).

Narrative by Charles Maynard and David Morris

JUNEY WHANK FALLS TRAIL

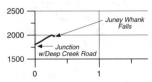

LENGTH: 0.3 mile, from Deep Creek Road to Juney Whank Falls.
HIGHLIGHTS: Waterfall.
CAUTIONS: Slippery rocks around falls, unsigned trail junctions.

MAP KEY: 7 G; USGS quad: Bryson City.
USE: Horse and hiking trail.
TRAILHEAD: Follow the signs through downtown Bryson City, NC toward Deep Creek Campground. Drive all the way to the end of Deep Creek Road. Do not cross Deep Creek at either bridge. Park at the large parking area at the end of Deep Creek Road and walk back (downstream) 0.1 mile to the beginning of the trail.

Juney Whank is a Cherokee phrase which has been translated to mean "place where the bear passes." Your chances of encountering a bear along this trail are not much greater than on other park trails, however. Some 400-600 black bears live in the national park and their population is fairly evenly distributed. In fact, The branch and its falls may actually be named for a Mr. Junaluska "Juney" Whank, who is said to be buried near the falls.

Where the trail leaves Deep Creek Road, look for maiden-hair fern and Solomon's seal. The latter sports dainty flowers along its underside in April and May. One hundred twenty-five yards from the start of the trail, an unmarked roadbed joins the trail from the left. Stay to the right. Sixty yards further, another roadbed diverts to the right and you need to stay to the left. Soon you will know you're on the right track, as the roar of Juney Whank Falls is heard in the distance. A narrow path leaves the graded roadbed and leads down to the falls and a footlog bridge across Juney Whank Branch.

The footbridge makes an excellent place to view the scenic falls. Water cascades across bedrock for 40' above the bridge and 50' below. The official trail ends at the falls, though several unofficial routes continue in several directions. Most are used by the horse concession

near Deep Creek Campground and may not be desirable for hikers.
Narrative by Steve Kemp

KANATI FORK TRAIL

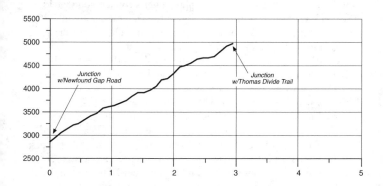

LENGTH: 2.9 miles, from Newfound Gap Road to Thomas Divide Trail.
HIGHLIGHTS: Lush cove forest, spring wildflowers.
CAUTIONS: Rock hop stream crossings, mud.
MAP KEY: 8 E; USGS quads: Smokemont, Clingmans Dome.
USE: Hiking trail.
TRAILHEAD: Newfound Gap Road, just north of Kephart Prong Trail parking area (where foot bridge crosses Oconaluftee River), 8 miles north of Oconaluftee Visitor Center.

According to Cherokee legend, Kanati and his wife Selu were the first people. At first, Kanati, Selu, and their sons, the Thunder Boys, lived on Pilot Mountain (in what is today Transylvania County, NC), but they moved westward after Selu's death. Since most of the Kanati stories recorded by James Mooney, a nineteenth-century ethnologist, took place in what is now the Tuckasegee River Valley and not in the Smokies, it is unclear how the name Kanati came to be applied to this stream.

Starting up the trail, you walk steadily up Kanati Fork through a lush forest of tall, straight tuliptrees, Fraser magnolia, and yellow birch, with rosebay rhododendron forming much of the understory; to the left, dog-hobble lines the creek. Forest ground cover includes ground pine and various ferns as well as downy rattlesnake-plantain and false Solomon's seal. After stepping over a rivulet, good views of the creek valley appear to the left. Soon the trail climbs among tuliptrees, Eastern hemlock, and sassafras, and near such wildflowers as wood betony, bee-balm, and hog-peanut.

Continuing uphill, crossing another rivulet and a seepage, the trail winds higher through Eastern hemlocks and red maples. After crossing and recrossing another of Kanati Fork's feeder creeks, the trail climbs a switchback; then, at **1.0** mile, recrosses the creek and continues through sugar maple, Fraser magnolia, and American basswood. Nearby grow Dutchman's pipe, a vine with big heart-shaped leaves that often climbs over 100' up some of the forest's tallest trees; and dodder, a parasitic orange vine that winds itself around other plants, then draws nourishment out of their stems. The trail, muddy in places, continues climbing and passes rosebay rhododendron and mountain laurel, with dead American chestnut stumps all around. At one point, you gain a great view into the cove below. In April and May the flowers of the silverbell trees are spectacular.

Soon Thomas Divide looms ahead. After crossing another feeder creek, you walk among American basswood, yellow birch, and Eastern hemlock. At **2.1** miles, the trail levels. Eventually, the trail ascends a ridge, passes through a second-growth forest, and climbs a switchback toward Thomas Divide. Toward the crest of the ridge, you may see Jack-in-the-pulpit, spiderwort, Turk's cap lily, wild bergamot, and hobblebush, among other wildflowers. At **2.9** miles, Kanati Fork Trail meets Thomas Divide Trail.

Narrative by Ted Olson

KEPHART PRONG TRAIL

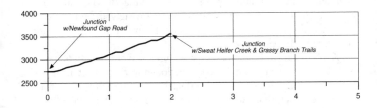

LENGTH: 2.0 miles, from Newfound Gap Road to Kephart Prong Shelter.

HIGHLIGHTS: Remains of a Civilian Conservation Corps Camp, fish hatchery, and narrow gauge railroad.

MAP KEY: 8 D; USGS quad: Smokemont.

USE: Horse and hiking trail.

TRAILHEAD: Drive on Newfound Gap Road about 8.8 miles from Newfound Gap or 5.0 miles from Smokemont Campground. The parking area, a small crescent on the east side, will be on the left from Newfound Gap or the right from Smokemont. Watch for the large footbridge over the Oconaluftee River.

A riverine stroll. The translation of the Cherokee word "Oconaluftee"—by the river— accurately describes this trail along a branch of the Oconaluftee River. The trail follows Kephart Prong from its confluence with the Oconaluftee up toward the Appalachian Trail. It provides access (via Grassy Branch and Dry Sluice Gap trails), particularly for day hikers wanting to avoid Newfound Gap crowds, to Charlies Bunion, an outcrop offering panoramic views of both the Tennessee and North Carolina sides of the park. Kephart Prong Trail gains only 830' elevation, and your ascent is so gradual that you rarely sense a climb.

The prong, trail, and mountain above them are named to honor Horace Kephart, author of *Our Southern Highlanders*, a classic portrait of mountain culture during the first decade of the twentieth century.

An author, scholar, and librarian from St. Louis, Kephart came to the Smokies in 1904 after a nervous collaspe, which seems mostly to have been a mid-life crisis and shift in values. Leaving his wife and family, he lived alone in the mountains and wrote lovingly and honestly about the Appalachian settlers and land. He was also a leading park advocate in the 1920s.

Kephart Prong Trail crosses Oconaluftee River immediately on a wide bridge surrounded by rosebay rhododendron and Eastern hemlock. The trail is wide, flat, and surfaced with gravel. It was once a paved jeep road; that's why you'll see patches of broken asphalt throughout. Maidenhair and Christmas ferns, daisy fleabane and black-eyed Susan decorate the gentle slope.

None of the trees here are very big because this trail was logged and later became the location of a Civilian Conservation Corps Camp from 1933-1942. During World War II, the camp housed conscientious objectors. The compound included barracks, officers' quarters, latrine, mess hall, educational and recreational buildings, and a woodworking shop. You'll see evidence of the camp at 0.2 mile where large boxwoods mark a front yard on the right. Behind them stands a 6' x 5' hearth made of stream-rounded and now moss-covered stones under an oak tree. A stone water fountain, well-preserved except that it doesn't work, is a few steps ahead, just before another, much larger hearth and chimney in the center of an Eastern hemlock stand. Constructed of brick and stone with a cook surface in front, this one is about 15' wide.

After the camp, the trail narrows to about a yard's width. In short succession, two offshoot trails lead you to the creek, the second to a small pebble "beach." The trail itself is surrounded by tuliptrees and oaks, with lots of may-apples underneath. Also called mandrake, English folk wisdom maintains that if pulled out of the ground, the plant will scream like a human since the roots supposedly look like a man's body. Would that all wildflowers were so alarmed. Blooming may-apple plants have two prominent leaves under which a small white flower blooms in early spring and from which the "apple" grows afterwards. Non-blooming plants have only one leaf. Both grow anywhere from 18"-30" tall.

Soon you reach a fork in the trail. Take the left one; a burned oak trunk blocks the right option to a spur trail that peters out on a hill-side. In a couple of minutes, you'll round a curve to the first prong crossing; you can wade across or take the railed footbridge a bit fur-ther up. The bridge itself is sturdy although you might test the rail before you depend on it. It wobbles. You'll walk through a second-growth tuliptree forest with lots of wood betony, a spring wildflower whose leaves look very mcuh like a fern's, growing below. Other com-mon names for this plant are lousewort and, logically, fernleaf. Look up to the left to see a grass-covered roadbed.

At **0.5** mile, you'll see a cement platform with a two-foot square well in one corner up a steep bank on the left. To the right, you'll spy another cement platform. These platforms may be the remains of a cistern to a fish hatchery run by the Works Project Administration in the 1930s. The hatchery supplied trout and bass to overfished park streams. A successful project, in December 1936, 50,000 trout eggs were hatched here. An archive photograph shows dozens of round, stone-encircled rearing pools spaced along the slope of a grassy streambank, but no vestige of these pools remains in the rebounding forest.

At **1.0** mile the trail becomes a corridor of tall, slender American beech trees with ferns below on the stream bank. The trail moves at a slow incline, its surface pebbles and rocks. When the bank becomes steep, the corridor veers in and out of Eastern hemlock groves and heath slicks. A nice view of Kephart Prong appears on the right with cascade falls. Within the next half mile come four stream crossings; wade across or continue 30 paces up the trail to the foot bridges, some buttressed by CCC stonework.

During the final 0.2 mile, you'll notice lichen-covered railroad irons scattered alongside. They are the remains of a narrow gauge rail-road that Champion Fibre Company built up the prong for removing spruce lumber from the 2,200 acres it clear-cut in the 1920s. Now del-icate rue-anemone lines the trail. In July crimson bee-balm and its white cousin, wild bergamot, add bright blooms to the understory. At one point a rivulet runs alongside then through the trail and ulti-mately finds the prong. It's a good place to see dusky salamanders.

As the trail rises a bit, it becomes eroded and dominated by roots, rocks, and mud. Then it dries, the pebbles change to flint, and the shelter, once the location of a logging camp, comes into view under American beech trees. It has two sleeping platforms and an indoor fireplace.

A signed trail junction connects to Grassy Branch Trail. Sweat Heifer Creek Trail can be found around the left of the shelter and across a foot log.

Narrative by Beth Giddens

LAKESHORE TRAIL

INTRODUCTION

The Lakeshore Trail is an amalgamation of old roads, trails, and man-ways. It is not shown on USGS topographic maps but is on newer park trail maps. There are limited brown paint blazes and small square brown metal tags on trees at some points along the trail. Care must be taken to stay on the correct route, since some side trails appear more used than the Lakeshore Trail. Vehicle access is available only at Fontana Dam or the end of Lakeview Drive near Bryson City, NC. Access by boat can be arranged through Fontana Village Marina (704) 498 2211 ext. 277 to either end of the section detailed here.

Because use of this trail is usually confined to short segments, we have broken the trail into sections and run the narratives in the direction most often traveled by hikers. The long segment of this trail between Lakeview Drive and Campsite #86 (Proctor) is accessed by boaters and some horseback riders, but only infrequently by hikers.

Some segments of what is officially called the Lakeshore Trail are better known by colloquial names. The section from Campsite #86 (Proctor) to Campsite #84 (Sugar Fork) is often referred to as part of the Hazel Creek Trail. The segment from Campsite #90 (Lost Cove) to the Jenkins Ridge Trail is referred to as Pinnacle Creek. However, all Park Service trail signs use the Lakeshore name.

The lakeside portions of this trail are most scenic when the lake is full (May-October). During low water, you may have to walk an extra half mile or so to reach the trail after crossing the lake by boat.

LAKESHORE TRAIL

LAKEVIEW DRIVE TO CAMPSITE #77

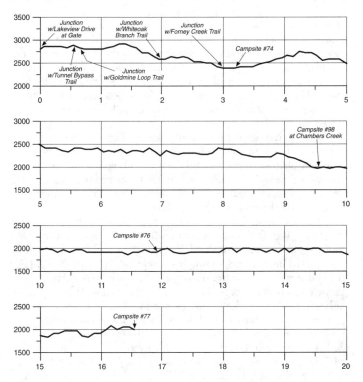

LENGTH: 16.6 miles, from the end of Lakeview Drive to Campsite #77.

CAUTIONS: Unbridged stream crossings.

HIGHLIGHTS: Fishing, old homesites, solitude.

MAP KEY: 6-5 F-G; USGS quads: Noland Creek, Tuskeegee (trail not marked on quads).

USE: Horse and hiking trail.

TRAILHEAD: From Bryson City, drive northwest about 9 miles on Lakeview Drive to its end.

The Lakeshore Trail begins at the end of Lakeview Drive, often called the "Road to Nowhere." The construction of this road was begun in the 1960s to fulfill a promise made by the government when a strip of land north of the Little Tennessee River was incorporated into the national park upon the construction of Fontana Dam in the 1940s. The road, which was never completed, now ends at the trailheads for the Tunnel Bypass and Lakeshore Trails. These trails access the Forney Creek area.

From the trailhead at the end of Lakeview Drive, walk on the paved road to the tunnel. Built in the early 1960s, the tunnel was originally planned to connect Bryson City with Fontana Dam via Lakeview Drive. However, the government scrapped the project because of budget constraints, environmental problems, and the presence of a good highway south of the lake.

The paved tunnel, wide enough for two lanes of traffic, is 375 yards long. It is similar in construction (i.e. stone and mortar) to the tunnels on Newfound Gap Road. You may want to carry a flashlight through the unlit tunnel, or simply stumble through with the light at the end as your guide. After the tunnel, the headwaters to Hyatt Branch flow to the left and Tunnel Bypass Trail passes below, although you will reach its trail junction in about 0.2 miles. From the junction, you can take Tunnel Bypass Trail 2.1 miles back to the parking area. Tunnel-shy horses often use the bypass route.

Lakeshore Trail then travels 0.3 mile to another trail junction, which is the western end of the Goldmine Loop Trail. After the junction with Goldmine Loop, the trail descends through a pine-oak forest with a mountain laurel understory. A small trail with red-orange painted markings veers to the right. Stay on the main trail which continues a descent to the lower left.

After a gap, the trail descends beside a small branch through a tangle of rhododendron to a junction at an old homesite. At mile **2.0**, the White Oak Branch Trail leaves the Lakeshore Trail to the right to travel 2.0 miles to the Forney Creek Trail. The Lakeshore Trail passes through a grassy area with the remnants of a fruit orchard and a chimney. Flowering dogwood, pine, and American beech populate the area which is frequented by wild boar and deer.

The trail crosses a small branch onto a roadbed just below the homesite. The way becomes a little confusing in this area. The trail runs into another old roadbed that looks well traveled. Turn to the right to pass over Gray Wolf Creek on a bridge. This low area is often wet and muddy. The trail turns to the left off the roadbed onto a foot trail about 30 yards past the bridge.

The ascent of the ridge is a moderate one to a gap. The Gray Wolf Creek watershed is to the east while Forney Creek flows to the west. Woody Cemetery is near the gap to the south of the trail. Hickory and maple are among the hardwoods which surround the trail as it descends to Forney Creek.

At mile **3.0** the trail joins the Forney Creek Trail which has come almost 10 miles down from its terminus high on Forney Ridge below the Forney Ridge Parking Area at Clingmans Dome. The Lakeshore Trail, which has been a foot path, now shares a wide roadbed with the Forney Creek Trail.

The wide roadbed was used for logging by the Norwood Lumber Company which began logging in the Forney Creek area in 1910. During World War I, Norwood Lumber Company was cutting spruce at the rate of 40,000 board feet per day. By 1925 Norwood Lumber had ceased its operations.

Forney Creek and Lakeshore Trails cross Forney Creek on a bridge. One hundred yards below the bridge the Lakeshore Trail turns to the right. Backcountry Campsite #74 (Lower Forney Creek) is just beyond the trail junction where picnic tables are on the banks of the creek. Several fire rings indicate good places to camp. A pit toilet is another convenience at this wide flat site which is heavily used. White pine and hemlock shade the area which has much doghobble in the understory. Campsite #74 is the first contact point of the Lakeshore Trail to Fontana Lake when traveling from east to west.

The Lakeshore Trail turns to the right off the Forney Creek Trail to ascend a ridge in a moderate but steady climb. You will gain 400' in elevation as the trail climbs through American beech, mountain laurel and chestnut oak and leaves the rushing sounds of Forney Creek behind. The top of the ridge is in a drier forest of mixed hardwoods.

For the next approximately 5 miles the trail will skirt the lower flanks of Pilot Knob which is a peak to the north. The trail descends from the gap through maple, oak, and tuliptree. Rock hop across Glady Branch to ascend again a smaller ridge to another gap. Old fence posts with rusted strands of barbed wire still stand but no longer mark the boundaries of small farms which once covered the area.

Some of this land was once owned by Jack Coburn, who lived at the mouth of Bone Valley on Hazel Creek. Coburn was a lumber dealer who moved to Tennessee and then North Carolina from Michigan as a young man. He made his money buying land and timber. When Horace Kephart first came to the mountains in the early years of the century, Jack Coburn befriended him and helped him find a cabin. Later the two worked to help establish Great Smoky Mountains National Park.

When the trail narrows once again to a footpath, the steep slope tends to make walking difficult. Erosion has claimed several short sections of the trail in this part. Try to stay on the trail so that further damage isn't done to the forest.

Cross another small ridge on several switchbacks on the ascent and descent. Jenny Branch is reached at the foot of the ridge. Rock hopping again will do the trick to continue to yet another low ridge. The forest is mainly a mix of hardwoods with oaks predominating. Wild turkey inhabit the region. Look for signs of their search for food along the trail. Turkeys scratch away the ground cover of dead leaves.

A couple of branches with a rise in between are within a half mile of each other. Galax and rhododendron crowd both runs which dry to nearly nothing in the late summer and autumn months. One fourth mile beyond the second branch, Gunter Branch is crossed. Rock walls were used to terrace the land into a more usable form. Hemlock and rhododendron cool the area in the hot summer.

The trail continues to rise and fall along finger-like ridges which reach out from Pilot Ridge. An old roadbed is crossed but the trail does not follow it. The trail descends past it to reach another roadbed. Two more small branches are crossed within one half mile of each other. Rhododendron, holly, and Fraser magnolia green this area that is well above the lakeshore. The trail runs along the 2,000' contour.

Ascend a ridge with the trail twisting into several switchbacks. The walk on the ridge crest is through mixed hardwoods with mostly oak and hickory. However, notice the change in the forest as more pines mingle with the oaks in a drier area. The trail descends to cross the upper reaches of Welch Branch. The Welch name is on many features in the area. It comes from one of the families that settled and worked this region. Welch Creek flows into the Fontana Lake near where the Little Tennessee River and the Tuckasegee River join.

After crossing Welch Branch at mile **8.7**, the trail comes to an open grassy area where it is more difficult to follow. Numerous signs of human habitation abound. Terracing, stone piles, rusty tubs, and even pieces of an old stove are the tell-tale evidence of those who once lived here.

A large holly tree grows on the right of the trail. It is ten to twelve inches in diameter and thirty to thirty-five feet tall. The trail winds past it through the open area then skirts the edge. It turns up the ridge to the right to head west up the northern slope through a pine-oak forest. Old fence posts again mark fields which are long gone. The trail now travels on an old roadbed. A maze of old roadbeds force many decisions. Continue on the most worn bed to a saddle in the ridge. Bear to the right to descend the ridge.

An old homesite is marked with a privet hedge, rock wall, and many rusting artifacts. The naked chimney, which is no longer clothed with a house, reveals a curved lintel made of a low arch of stones. A large hemlock grows beside the chimney.

Follow a small tributary down a moderate descent to Chambers Creek. The trail turns to the left off the roadbed to cross the creek on a bridge. Avoid the temptation to camp where others have beside the creek. Campsite #98, Chambers Creek, is to the right of the trail at mile **9.5**. The small pathway leads over Anthony Branch about 200 yards to an old homesite. A chimney stands amid oaks and large dogwoods. The campsite is not as heavily used as the illegal spot near the lake.

Lakeshore Trail is only 50 yards above Fontana Lake at this point. Much trash along the shore shows the heavy use this spot suffers. Ascend the trail along a footpath up from the lake through hardwoods which are mainly oak.

The trail now parallels the shoreline of Fontana Lake through land that was once worked by several families. The Brewers in their book, *Valley So Wild*, quote a TVA report which states, "With all the handicaps and hardships of mountain farming, the typical Fontana region farmer is satisfied with his environment and prefers not to be disturbed. He likes the isolation and does not take kindly to life in the more densely populated areas located out of the mountains. He is frugal, hardy, and self-sustaining, and likes to hunt and roam at will."

Most of the farms were worked by hand or animal power. At the time of the construction of Fontana Dam there were no tractors in Graham County and only ten in Swain. Nearly six hundred families were removed due to the construction of the TVA dam in 1944. More than half of these were from the area through which the Lakeshore Trail passes.

A cleared area appears about 1.2 miles from Campsite #98. A stone stack on the right indicates that a house once stood here. The remnants of a springhouse that once was refrigerator and faucet to the household is to the right of the trail. Buckets and other artifacts are littered about the clearing. The trail continues over two more small branches which flow into an embayment of the lake.

A foot trail leaves the roadbed to the right to go to several old housesites above the trail. A chimney on the right stands amid what is left of several outbuildings at a farmstead. Cans and other signs point to the hard life that was once scratched out in this area.

Campsite #76 is to the right of the trail at Kirkland Branch at **11.9** miles. The creek flows past a rock wall through hemlock, rhododendron, and beech at this little used campsite. Plenty of room for tents, combined with the cool waters of Kirkland Branch, make this a nice spot to camp. The campsite is far enough away from the lake that only hikers and horseback riders frequent this place.

Continue to follow on the old roadbed which was the major road through the area before the waters of the Little Tennessee were dammed up. Several roads come down to the main road which is now the Lakeshore Trail. A 1930s vintage car body remains on the road as if it had been left only a few years ago rather than the more than fifty years that this area has been in the park.

At times stone walls line both sides of the trail. The roadbed eventually follows the shore of the lake high above the water through a forest composed mainly of tuliptrees. One large tuliptree grows in the middle of the road. This shows how quickly trees can reclaim an area that has been farmed or logged.

Clubmoss often crowds the trail. The plant is one of the more primitive plants in the park. About 250 million years ago these plants, which grew to heights of over 100', dominated the land. The clubmoss, along with the fern, were the first plants to develop roots, stems, and leaves.This small evergreen plant resembles cedar or juniper. Another old car body lies off to the right of the trail by a small branch. The roadbed continues through hickory, oak, tuliptree and other hardwoods.

The road moves away from the lake up through a pine forest with Table Mountain and shortleaf pines amid mountain laurel and holly. The trail gently descends to a small embayment of the lake where the roadbed splits. One branch goes to the left to cross a manmade embankment. The Lakeshore Trail stays to the right to pass another old housesite. Much trash from the lake has collected in this area which also has artifacts left from those who lived here.

The trail climbs away from the lake through white pines whose needles soften the pathway. Many disturbances indicate the presence of wild hogs in the area. The boar destructively root through the forest, leaving the ground ripped up.

At a small branch the roadbed is left behind. The trail becomes a foot path through a pine-oak forest. At the top of the ridge grow several large holly trees. Descend the western side of the ridge toward Pilkey Creek. The water of Fontana Lake can been seen ahead. The trail reaches another old roadbed near the creek. Turn right and go upstream for 50 yards. Pilkey Creek is crossed on a bridge which can be very slick when wet.

The Lakeshore Trail turns southward (to the left) to run along Pilkey Creek. Large picnic tables are 100 yards to the south and about 100 yards from the lake. Another old car body lies on its side between the trail and the creek.

The trail turns up away from the creek to moderately ascend a ridge southward. The trail then turns north to descend the ridge through a pine-oak forest to Campsite #77 at Clark Branch. This campsite was once a homesite. Rock walls and piles are under the pine trees in this beautiful area. The lake is about 0.25 mile to the south. The Lakeshore Trail continues on toward Fontana Dam.

Narrative by Charles Maynard & David Morris

LAKESHORE TRAIL

CAMPSITE #81 TO CAMPSITE #77

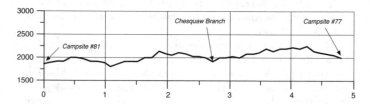

LENGTH: 4.8 miles, from Campsite #81 to Campsite #77.
HIGHLIGHTS: Lakeside views and old homesites.
CAUTIONS: Numerous creek crossings.
MAP KEY: 4-5 G; USGS quad: Tuskeegee (trail not marked on quads).
USE: Horse and hiking trail.
STARTING POINT: Campsite #81 (North Shore), 3.5 miles from Campsite #86 (Proctor) on Hazel Creek.

The Lakeshore Trail, which basically follows the north shore of Fontana Lake, tracks through land that was not originally in Great Smoky Mountains National Park when it was established in 1934. The park boundary was a little farther to the north. The Lakeshore Trail traverses land which was added when the Tennessee Valley Authority flooded Fontana Lake with the construction of Fontana Dam in 1944. Many small farms dotted the region just north of the Little Tennessee River. The Lakeshore Trail passes through the remnants of many of these farms.

Campsite #81 is on the banks of Mill Creek 200 yards above the Calhoun Branch embayment of Fontana Lake. The campsite, which is at an old homesite, is in a level area with mountain laurel, white pine, Eastern hemlock and Fraser magnolia. Few fire rings and no trash indicate the campsite is little used. The trail above #81 is through Table Mountain and white pines whose needles soften the tread along an old roadbed. Striped pipsissewa and clubmoss surround the trail.

The trail turns eastward away from its northerly track to pass through a pine grove mixed with flowering dogwood and American holly. Only a few hundred yards above Campsite #81 is an old homesite with the remains of a chimney and root cellar. When the old roadbed divides, the trail follows the lower course. Follow the trail down and to the right to cross a small branch at a large boxwood. After the crossing, signs of former habitation such as rusted wash tubs and other implements (along with a chimney pile) are on the opposite side of the rock wall-lined creek.

A moderate ascent through mountain laurel, striped pipsissewa, and galax climbs into a pine-oak forest. As the ridge top is gained, Table Mountain and pitch pine predominate. A small creek crowded with dog-hobble is crossed on the descent.

At mile **1.0**, stone terracing has leveled the land around Calhoun Branch. A farmer, now unknown, used the stones which were cleared from the fields to even the terrain. Dogwood, beech, paw paw, shortleaf pine, white pine, and American holly are in this area which has a chimney pile above the trail to the left.

A large chimney with daffodils and boxwoods is 50 yards above a second small branch. Extensive stonework here terraced the uneven ground for better farming. The trail climbs away from the creek up the side of another small ridge through rhododendron, oak, beech, and mountain laurel. A switchback breaks the ascent as the trail heads southward. An embayment of Fontana Lake is west (right).

A lone chimney stands to the right at **2.3** miles in a cleared area with dogwood and pine mixed with many hardwoods. The trail levels out on the opposite side of the ridge to travel through mostly oaks of varying types. Cane grows along the side of the ridge above and below the trail.

The trail becomes a wider roadbed with occasional holly trees spread throughout the forest. Large gray sandstone boulders crowd the area. The sandstone is probably that of the Thunderhead Formation which is common in the park. A beautiful cascade slides 35' down a 40 degree slope of this sandstone at Chesquaw Branch (mile **2.8**). Mitchell Cemetery is higher up the ridge on the west side of Chesquaw Branch. Hemlocks green this picturesque spot all year round.

The trail narrows to a small, little-used path. The lake is to the south as the trail traverses the south end of a ridge. A couple of small branches are hopped in the next mile. Several types of ferns grow under the hardwood canopy. After the trail crosses the second branch at **3.9** miles, a dense pine forest extends down the ridge below.

Clark Branch is crossed in a flat area which was once a clearing. Campsite #77 is on Clark Branch below the trail (to the right). The fire rings are in a pine forest with ferns scattered about. Pine needles cover the ground making this a nice campsite. A stone pile indicates that a house once stood here. The lake is a quarter mile to the south. Several paw-paw trees populate the area along Clark Branch. The Lakeshore Trail continues to the east along the shores of Fontana Lake to reach Lakeview Drive nearly 16 miles away.

Narrative by Charles Maynard and David Morris

LAKESHORE TRAIL

CAMPSITE #86 TO CAMPSITE #81

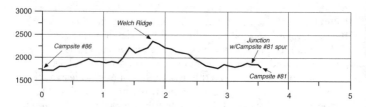

LENGTH: 3.5 miles, from Campsite #86 to Campsite #81.

HIGHLIGHTS: Historical artifacts, interesting and varied terrain.
CAUTIONS: Trail can be difficult to follow.
MAP KEY: 4 F; USGS quad: Tuskeegee (trail not marked on quad).
USE: Horse and hiking trail.
TRAILHEAD: Near Campsite #86 (Proctor) on the Lakeshore Trail, at the first bridge.

A walk of one-half to one mile, depending on lake levels, is needed to get from the boat at Fontana Lake to the first bridge on Hazel Creek. On the way, you will pass Proctor Campsite #86 on your left. Vehicle access is available only at Fontana Dam or the end of Lakeview Drive near Bryson City. Access by boat can be arranged through Fontana Village Marina (704) 498-2211 x277 to either end of the section detailed here.

Before crossing the first bridge, proceed straight ahead on the Lakeshore Trail down what was once known as Struttin' Street when the town of Proctor prospered here. Many artifacts such as bottles, bedframes, and parts of tools can be seen, but remember all artifacts are federally protected and should not be disturbed. About 50 yards past the remains of a concrete cold storage house to your right, the Lakeshore Trail leaves the level area on an old road heading up the hill. Care must be used to find this old road.

The old road traverses a boulder-strewn hillside with an impressive second growth forest which includes tuliptree, American beech, and oaks. Deer are often seen in this area. A quarter mile from the bridge you will reach an intersection. Turn sharply right. The road straight ahead parallels Hazel Creek and leads to Rowan Branch. You will soon reach the gap in this finger ridge and head downhill. At the bottom of the hill, an old road turns right and comes out on Fontana Lake. Continue straight.

After crossing another finger ridge, you will arrive at Laurel Branch and the homeplace of Uncle George and Elvira Welch at mile 1.1. Known as the "prayin'ist" man in the country, Uncle George is buried at Proctor cemetery. Their large homesite is to the left of the trail. Part of a wheelbarrow can be seen here that was left behind when the Welches left in 1944 as a result of the Fontana Dam Project. Jimmy Birchfield lived on up the holler past Uncle George.

Just past the boggy crossing of Laurel Branch, the remains of a chimney on your right marks the home of Minnie Lynn.

Now ascend rather steeply for a half mile to reach the top of Welch Ridge or River Mountain as it was known by some former residents. The trail you are walking was the main road from Hazel Creek to the town of Wayside on the Little Tennessee River and the outlet to the rest of the world prior to the construction of NC Highway 288 in the 1920s. Just before reaching the gap, an old fence row can be seen on the right of the trail. To the left, just past the gap, an almost pure stand of straight, tall, and even-aged tuliptrees that sprouted when the field was abandoned marks the farm of Ott Curtis.

Soon you will come into another gap on a side ridge. Just ahead and to the left is an outstanding old-field tuliptree stand. The evenly spaced trees with their lowest branches 50' from the ground give the illusion of a gray ghost army standing silently in ranks. Former resident Gene Laney remembers Old Man Garrett Holloway plowing this field where he grew corn and potatoes. Look for the fence row on the left of the trail past the gap that bordered the field.

About **2.8** miles from Hazel Creek you will reach Whiteside Creek and the Garrett Holloway homeplace. Across the creek from the trail the running gear from an old car can be seen. Garrett's barn was here; his home was up the creek in the existing opening. The name Whiteside Creek was probably derived from some early residents calling it Wayside Creek since they followed it down to the river on their way to Wayside, NC. Most local people today call it Millsaps' Branch after J.C. (Jess) Millsaps who owned and lived on the lower section of the creek. This is but one example of the colorful yet sometimes confusing nomenclature of the Smoky Mountains.

Leave the homesite and immediately rock hop Whiteside Creek. Within 0.25 mile you will reach an intersection on top of a low ridge. Take the trail to the left; the trail straight ahead out the ridge leads about a half mile to Fairview cemetery and Fontana Lake. You will soon cross another low ridge. Cook cemetery is off to your right.

Next you will reach a trail intersection marked by a square wooden sign reading #81. The Lakeshore Trail continues straight ahead. Turn sharply right on the side trail to reach Mill Branch, Campsite #81, and Fontana Lake. Campsite #81 is located in a level area near the branch. It is shown only on the newer maps and is available to hikers and horses. A good spring is located just down from the campsite right below the benched homesite of Sanders and Margaret Calhoun. A second benched area on down the branch was the site of their barn.

Sanders operated a store that was located at the high water mark of the lake. Many times when Gene Laney and his dad patronized the store, Sanders would give them a mess of catfish from the river which they would load on their wooden land sled and then head back home to Hazel Creek. Fairview School, a consolidated county school, was located at the confluence of Mill Branch and Calhoun Branch, now under the waters of the lake.

When Fontana Lake was created (1942-45) to supply the nation's wartime demand for electrical energy, about 30 miles of the rather narrow but lush Little Tennessee River was flooded. The Southern Railway line, Highway 288, and towns such as Wayside, Bushnell, and Judson are now only a memory to those people who gave up their homes for the good of the country.

Narrative by Lance Holland

LAKESHORE TRAIL

CAMPSITE #86 TO CAMPSITE #84

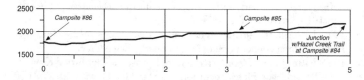

LENGTH: 4.7 miles, from Campsite #86 to Hazel Creek Trail at Campsite #84
HIGHLIGHTS: Cultural history, trout fishing.
MAP KEY: 4-6 F-E; USGS quad: Tuskeegee
USE: Horse and hiking trail.

TRAILHEAD: Campsite #86 (Proctor) on the Lakeshore Trail.
NOTE: This section is sometimes called lower Hazel Creek trail.

The Hazel Creek watershed has a rich and varied history. Once the haunt of Indians, pioneer farmers, timber barons, miners, wealthy sportsmen, writers, and twentieth century townspeople, Hazel Creek has seen a lot of change. A trip up Hazel Creek will not only take you through this gamut of Appalachian history but also through most of the ecological zones represented in the park.

The most complete historic record of Hazel Creek to date is *Hazel Creek from Then till Now* by Duane Oliver. This interesting volume is available at most park visitor centers. A brief chronology of Hazel Creek is as follows:

1830 Moses Proctor, his wife Patience, and young son William "cross over" from Cades Cove to build their cabin at the site of the present Proctor cemetery and become the first white settlers on the creek.

1860 Hazel Creek had at least four families: the Proctors, Cables, Welches, and Bradshaws.

1884 Fonzie Hall discovers copper on Sugar Fork. Mine opened by W. S. Adams in 1889.

1892 Taylor and Crate Lumber Company build three splash dams on Hazel Creek and harvest about one million board feet of timber.

1902 The W.M. Ritter Lumber Company sends timber cruisers to Hazel Creek and begins eight years of preparations and construction to "wage war" on the forests of Hazel Creek.

1904 Horace Kephart, author of *Our Southern Highlanders*, published in 1913, arrives on the creek.

1910 Ritter starts cutting timber and changes the watershed forever.

1927 Fontana copper mine opens on nearby Eagle Creek.

1928 Ritter Lumber Company, referred to as "the Hardwood King of the World," completes operations on Hazel Creek with 201,000,000 board feet of lumber (enough to build approximately 20,000 homes) cut from the watershed.

1929 J. G. Stikleather buys most of Ritter's holdings and establishes the Hazel Creek Outing Club. The Kress family, owners of the dimestore chain, builds a private hunting and recreation club in Bone Valley.

1932 Civilian Conservation Corps (CCC) camp opens near site of the Ritter sawmill.

1941 TVA moves in to build Fontana Dam and Lake.

1943 An agreement is signed to condemn 44,000 acres of land between the new lake and the existing park boundary for inclusion in Great Smoky Mountains National Park.

1945 TVA reports that 1,319 families had vacated the North Shore area. About 600 of these families were land owners.

A few hikers and most horsemen access this section of the Lakeshore Trail from either Fontana Dam or Twentymile Ranger Station. The most popular access is by boat. Boat shuttles are available from Fontana Village Marina (704) 498 2211 x277.

About 0.5 mile after departing the boat on Fontana Lake (the point of departure will vary with lake levels), you will arrive at Campsite #86 and the site of the town of Proctor. The campsite has picnic tables and pit toilets and accommodates hikers and horses. The schoolhouse spring is about 100 yards back down the trail toward the lake on a short side trail between the road and the creek. Although it is the most heavily used campsite in the area, it is not badly deteriorated. Tables and fire pits are well spaced beneath the CCC-planted white pines.

Campsite #86 was once the site of the Proctor School ballfield. The big pool in the creek on the west side of the campsite was the school swimming hole and occasionally served as a baptismal pool. The school itself, an impressive structure accommodating several hundred students, was located on the knoll across the road from the campsite just west of the existing horse hitching rack.

At the first bridge you will intersect the eastbound Lakeshore Trail; straight ahead and to the right will lead you to Whiteside Branch and eventually Lakeview Drive near Bryson City. During the Ritter era, the railroad and Struttin' Street were straight ahead. The street featured a boardwalk, sugar maple trees, picket fences, and a row of neatly painted houses. Today, deer and wild turkey are often seen here.

Cross the bridge. To the left you can see the Calhoun House, actually built by the Higdon family. The house was later home to the

"Squire of Hazel Creek," Granville Calhoun. Turn right at the end of the bridge to continue along the Lakeshore Trail. To the left, about 0.5 mile past the house, is the Proctor cemetery with 198 graves.

The next 4.7 miles to Sugar Fork Creek and Campsite #84 are locally referred to as the lower Hazel Creek trail. You are now walking along Calico Street, a repeat of Struttin' Street across the creek but with no railroad and smaller houses. Less than 0.25 mile from the first bridge, look for concrete foundation blocks on both sides of the road. This was the site of the Proctor Baptist Church. The railroad crossed the creek here and the road over Clubhouse Hill turned left. About 0.3 miles from here you will pass a large depression on your left that once was the log pond. Across the pond you can see the remains of the dry kiln. When the land was purchased for the national park, all the remaining structures other than the Calhoun House were burned. The concrete and brick construction of the kiln and adjacent valve houses saved them for us to see today. The sawmill itself was located at the upstream end of the log pond.

About 0.5 mile above the sawmill you will reach North Proctor. On the way you will pass a cylindrical concrete river gauging station on your right. North Proctor today is a rather open flat area with a fine stand of black walnut trees. This area was home to a contingent of African-American workers that Ritter had brought in for his logging operation. One of these men succumbed to the influenza epidemic in 1919 while helping afflicted families and is buried at the Higdon cemetery on Sugar Fork. A simple marker placed by the North Shore Cemetery Association reads "A Black Man."

Cross the second and third bridges while paralleling the boisterous creek well-known for many years as a mecca for trout fishermen. The second growth forest is impressive and small pockets of virgin timber can be found that were saved from Ritter by landowners who would not sell their timber rights for "no amount of money." You will pass Campsite #85 (Sawdust Pile). The campsite accommodates hikers and horses. The actual camping area is rather small but is in good condition. The adjacent large, flat area gives Sawdust Pile a feeling of openess not often found at backcountry campsites. There is no spring nearby, but water is readily available at the stream. A small private sawmill operated here cutting logs that were not available to Ritter.

Deer are often seen browsing in the level area near the campsite.

About 1.0 mile above the third bridge you will reach a fork in the road. The road to the left known as the "Dirt Road" by former residents for its lack of gravel and was the main Hazel Creek Trail from the 1970s until 1992. The fourth bridge and the infamous Wilson Span Steel Bridge at Sugar Fork had become unsafe so this old route up the creek was resurrected. You may take the dirt road as an alternate route. It wanders steeply above and away from the creek and traverses some very interesting boulder-strewn landscape with sections of mature hemlock forest and rejoins the main road at Sugar Fork. Five new bridges were built on Hazel Creek in 1991-1992. This complicated construction job required barging 72 loads of heavy equipment and materials across Fontana Lake.

Take the right fork and continue paralleling Hazel Creek. Cross the fourth and fifth bridges to arrive at Sugar Fork and the site of the former community of Medlin.

Medlin became a place name in 1887 when Marion Medlin convinced the postal officials in Bryson City that there were enough residents here to establish a post office in his store, which became the second post office on the creek. Marion was not only the storekeeper and postmaster but also the doctor, Justice of the Peace, and minister of the Gospel.

The Medlin post office was the place that Horace Kephart, author of *Our Southern Highlanders,* sometimes posted his own mail (in the absence of the postmaster) during his 3½ year sojourn in the Hazel Creek watershed. For most of that period "Kep," as he was called by his neighbors, resided in a small log and frame cabin about 2.5 miles up Sugar Fork Creek at the closed-down Adams-Westfeldt copper mine. The timber barons made the world aware of the lumber riches in the Smoky Mountains, but Horace Kephart, through his writings in popular outdoor journals of the day, made the world aware of the area's recreational and environmental riches. (See the Lakeshore Trail, Jenkins Ridge Trail to Hazel Creek Trail, narrative.)

After the fifth bridge you pass the other end of the old "Dirt Road" which you previously encountered between the third and fourth bridges. The road to the right is the Hazel Creek Trail which tracks for some 10 miles to the junction with the Welch Ridge Trail.

The Lakeshore Trail continues to the left. Across the short wooden bridge over Sugar Fork Creek is Campsite #84. It's pleasant and the only campsite in the Hazel Creek watershed which doesn't allow horses.

Narrative by Lance Holland

LAKESHORE TRAIL

JENKINS RIDGE TRAIL TO HAZEL CREEK TRAIL

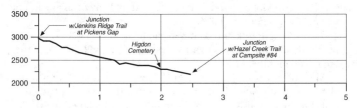

LENGTH: 2.4 miles, from Jenkins Ridge Trail to Hazel Creek Trail near Campsite #84

HIGHLIGHTS: Horace Kephart and Adams Westfeldt copper mine legacies.

MAP KEY: F 4; USGS quads: Tuskeegee, Thunderhead Mtn.

USE: Horse and hiking trail.

STARTING POINT: Jct. Jenkins Ridge Trail.

NOTE: This trail is sometimes referred to as Sugar Fork.

Access to this section of the Lakeshore Trail, known to many as the Sugar Fork Trail, is best accomplished via Eagle Creek or Hazel Creek. Boat shuttles across Fontana Lake are available from Fontana Village Marina (704) 498-2211 x277. Access from the Appalachian Trail at Spence Field is via the Jenkins Ridge Trail.

From Pickens Gap, at the junction of the Jenkins Ridge Trail and the Lakeshore Trail, you will follow a well-graded roadway downhill for the entire length of this route. This road was built in the late

1930s by the workers from the Civilian Conservation Corps camp located on Hazel Creek.

One mile from Pickens Gap you will pass the confluence of Little Fork and Sugar Fork creeks. Little Fork is notable for two reasons; the Adams-Westfeldt copper mine and author Horace Kephart.

While prospecting for mica on Little Fork Ridge in 1883, Fonzie Hall found what he thought was gold. Fonzie took his ore to Benson Cook who declared the find was actually copper. Due to low copper prices and inaccessibility, Fonzie's find lay dormant for several years. Around 1889, W.S. Adams, a mineral developer from New York who was in Western North Carolina developing a kaolin deposit, heard of the copper vein. He procured 25 pounds of ore, and after having it assayed, headed immediately to Sugar Fork. Upon his arrival he purchased 200 acres for $750 and made preparations to open the mine. Storage sheds, a compressor house, dwellings, and a wagon road down Hazel Creek were built to facilitate the operation. The miners sunk shafts as deep as 75 feet with hammer and steel, picks, shovels, and dynamite. In 1901 the mine was closed due to a lawsuit brought by George Westfeldt of New Orleans who had purchased 640 acres of land on Hazel Creek in 1869 and claimed the mine was on his property. The litigation lasted for 26 years, the longest court case in the history of the United States, and cost the litigants over a half million dollars. Both Adams and Westfeldt died before the case was resolved.

The Adams side won the case in 1927, but the heirs were not interested in reopening the works. In 1942 the Kalb family from New York bought and reopened the mine, removing thousands of tons of incredibly rich ore before TVA bought the land for inclusion into the Fontana Dam project and subsequently the national park.

Horace Kephart was born in East Salem, Pennsylvania and grew up on the Iowa frontier. A highly educated man, he was a career librarian at Rutgers and Yale Universities and St. Louis Mercantile Library. He was recognized as an authority on the lore of the Old West. In 1904 Kephart left his wife and six children and retired to the backwoods of the Great Smoky Mountains to regain his failing health. The first three and one-half years of this sojourn were spent in a lonely caretaker's cabin at the closed Adams copper mine where Kephart became interested in his mountain neighbors. His most famous work, *Our Southern Highlanders*, first published in 1913, was no doubt conceived during this period. Many of the episodes in the book are about his Hazel Creek friends.

Kephart was a conservationist long before that role became fashionable. He campaigned tirelessly for the establishment of a national park in the Great Smoky Mountains. Horace paid the rent by writing articles on life in the outdoors for the sporting journals of the day. These articles revealed to the world the recreational opportunities the Smokies had to offer. He personally established the route for much of the Appalachian Trail through the new park. Describing his time on Little Fork, Kephart once wrote, "It was almost as though I had been carried back, asleep, upon the wings of time, and had awakened in the eighteenth century, to meet Daniel Boone in flesh and blood." Kephart died in 1931, three years prior to the establishment of the national park. His grave overlooks Bryson City and is marked with a boulder from the park.

About one quarter mile on down the road from Little Fork you can see the remains of a tub mill in the creek on the right side of the road. This mill supplied corn meal for about 40 families that lived in the district and is pictured in *Our Southern Highlanders*.

The entire length of this trail parallels Sugar Fork and traverses a mixed second growth forest. The hillsides are dominated by tuliptree, maple, oak, flowering dogwood, sourwood, and an occasional American beech. Along the stream you can expect to see white pine, Eastern hemlock, sycamore, mountain laurel, and rhododendron. In summer, cardinal flower and bee-balm bloom in the boggy areas on both sides of the trail.

The rock outcroppings along the creek contain schist, slate, mica, and bits of their more valuable relatives: copper, gold, and silver.

At **2.0** miles from Pickens Gap a faint trail to the right leads a quarter mile to the Higdon cemetery (20 graves). Haw Gap Branch comes in from the left here and was also the site of early prospecting. At **2.4** miles you will reach Hazel Creek, the Hazel Creek Trail and the old settlement of Medlin. Campsite #84, Sugar Fork, is near the junction. It's pleasant and the only campsite along the Hazel Creek watershed which doesn't allow horses.

Narrative by Lance Holland

LAKESHORE TRAIL

CAMPSITE #90 TO JENKINS RIDGE TRAIL

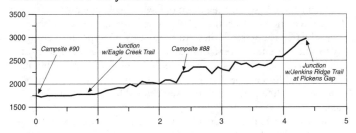

LENGTH: 4.4 miles, from Campsite #90 to Jenkins Ridge Trail.
HIGHLIGHTS: Pinnacle Creek.
CAUTIONS: Numerous stream crossings.
MAP KEY: 4 F: USGS quads: Thunderhead Mtn., Fontana.
USE: Horse and hiking trail.
TRAILHEAD: Campsite #90 on Fontana Lake. Campsite #90 is a
5.4 mile hike from Fontana Dam along the western end of the
Lakeshore Trail. If you choose to boat, you can use your own boat or
arrange transportation from the Fontana Village Marina (704) 498-
2211 x 277. They provide boat shuttles as well as the best place to
put in your own boat to cross the lake. There is a fee for both of these
services.
NOTE: This trail is sometimes referred to as Pinnacle Creek.

To many long-time residents and hikers of the North Carolina side
of the Smokies, the Lakeshore Trail is broken down into many sections each with a separate name. This portion is known locally as the
Pinnacle Creek Trail. This also happens to be an uncanny description of the trail. Running from Fontana Lake at Campsite #90 to
Jenkins Ridge Trail, this trail will give you an exceptional understanding of Pinnacle Creek. In fact, by the time you reach Campsite
#88 you will probably feel like the creek: wet and cold in the winter,

cool and refreshed in the summer. There are 15 fords to cross on this trail. So before you take this hike you might want to dig up an old pair of sneakers to use as wet shoes. There is no way to keep your boots dry here.

Campsite #90 sits at the mouth of Eagle Creek, at least where Eagle Creek flows into Fontana Lake. The lake was created in the 1940s by the Tennessee Valley Authority (TVA) to produce electricity for the war effort. Crews worked round the clock to complete what would become the highest dam, not only in the TVA system, but in the eastern United States. In January 1945, the first of three generators came on line powered by the water stored in the 29-mile-long lake.

In winter, when TVA draws down the lake for flood control, be aware that the lake will not reach Campsite #90. You will have to traverse the mud and gravel lake bottom to reach it. At the height of the lake's capacity though, Fontana easily pushes up beyond the campsite. Campsite #90 is at the point where Lost Cove and Eagle creeks join. It is a large, open, heavily-used site. Its easy access, good fishing, and lake swimming probably account for its popularity.

The Lakeshore Trail continues from Campsite #90 by crossing Lost Cove Creek via a short footlog with handrail. The trail then continues wide and flat along the banks of Eagle Creek. At 0.5 miles, the trail turns and crosses the river. Here a wide metal-framed bridge reminds us of the history of the area. The bridge may look old, but don't be fooled. The NPS constructed this miniature railroad bridge in 1991, but left it unpainted to allow it to blend into the history and environment. Continue to follow Eagle Creek upstream and cross it again in a quarter mile. This time you will have to make do with a footlog with handrail. This crossing though is not for the faint of heart when the water is high. The crossing is wide and the river very swift, so take some extra care when crossing.

By now the trail has narrowed and passes beneath a young hemlock forest. At mile 0.8, you will reach the junction with the Eagle Creek Trail. This trail continues along this river and its tributaries to Spence Field. Our trail turns east and crosses Eagle Creek one last time. Again we have use of a foot log and although the river is a bit narrower, remember that it is swift and powerful. Take your time and be safe when crossing.

Now our trail takes us away from Eagle Creek and on to Pinnacle Creek to enjoy its beauty and challenges. It is very important that you plan your trip at a time of low water. This trail is best from summer to early winter because along it you must cross Pinnacle Creek 15 times. There are no bridges or footlogs. In less than a quarter mile you will reach your first crossing. This ford is about 15 yards wide and the current is very swift. Use it to help you decide to continue or turn back. The remaining fords are very similar and if this one feels uncomfortable or dangerous, turn back. You will not enjoy the trail.

Put on a good pair of wet shoes before you cross and keep them on until you reach Campsite #88. From this ford, the trail climbs up and away from Pinnacle Creek. Below, you will hear the roar of the rushing waters. The heavy rhododendron growth around the trail keeps you from getting all but a fleeting glimpse of the river. A half mile from the Eagle Creek footlog, you will drop down again to Pinnacle Creek, pass through a thicket of dog-hobble bushes, and reach the second ford. This crossing is much the same as the first, but it begins a series of 14 fords in less than 0.75 mile.

After wet crossing number 15, Campsite #88 (Pinnacle Creek) is on the north side of the trail in a young second growth stand of hardwoods. There are two spots open and level enough for a tent and lots of good trees to hang your bear bag between. Backpackers may wish to aim for this site rather than Campsite #90 as it puts all the fords behind you. The Lakeshore Trail continues from the campsite by beginning an easy climb through a stand of mountain laurel and other hardwoods. You will be leaving Pinnacle Creek behind, at least for a mile. By mile **3.2**, the trail becomes a more moderate climb, cresting a small ridge before dropping to a small spring branch. Up and down past patches of club mosses or fields of quartz the trail goes, finally opening to a wide boulevard lined with trees. This is one of the places that Montvale Lumber pushed a railroad into to haul the lumber from the mountains. Keep a watchful eye and you may spot other evidence of the logging. That "grapevine" on the ground to the right might really be an old skidder cable used to pull logs to the rail sidings. Take a second look: the forest is slowly hiding the artifacts, but they are still here.

At mile **3.8**, you will reach the upper end of Pinnacle Creek. Fear not, this time the creek can be crossed with an easy rockhop. This crossing marks the beginning of the steepest part of the hike. The trail now climbs through a series of long switchbacks up the side of Jenkins Trail Ridge. As you climb, enjoy the open views below. It's a lovely climb through a second growth hardwood forest. The tall straight trees are tuliptrees or "poplars" as the loggers called them. For many years, their lumber built not only the homes of the mountain pioneers, but the homes of many Americans. It wasn't until most of these tuliptrees had been cleared out and many areas replanted with pines that the lumber companies retooled their mills and tuliptrees lost favor. Fortunately, no pine plantations were created here and the "poplars," oaks, maples, and other hardwoods again dominate the land.

At mile **4.2**, you will pass a wild hog trap used by the park to capture and remove wild hogs from the park. Traps like this one are left in permanent locations and only set when evidence indicates a hog's presence. Hogs turn or root up the ground looking for any kind of food, from rootstocks to salamanders. This behavior has damaged many areas in the park, so in the 1970s a program was put in place to remove these animals. By 1992, more than 7,000 hogs had been removed from the Smokies. Park officials estimate that more than 500, possibly as many as 1,000, animals still remain. With a reproduction rate which allows each sow to have two litters of up to 12 piglets each year, constant control of the population will be needed for years and years to come.

The trail climbs further up the ridge until at mile **4.4** it passes another hog trap and reaches the junction with the Jenkins Ridge Trail. From here you can ascend by way of Blockhouse Mountain to the eastern end of Spence Field (6.5 miles). You may also chose to stay on the Lakeshore Trail and continue on to Hazel Creek (2.4 miles) on the section known locally as the Sugar Fork trail.

Narrative by Tom Condon

LAKESHORE TRAIL

FONTANA DAM TO CAMPSITE #90

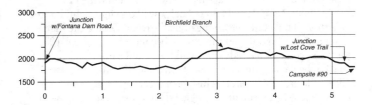

LENGTH: 5.4 miles, from near Fontana Dam to Campsite #90.
HIGHLIGHTS: Historical artifacts, views of Fontana Lake.
CAUTIONS: Several small stream crossings.
MAP KEY: F 3; USGS quad: Fontana.
USE: Horse and hiking trail.
TRAILHEAD: Fontana Dam Road, 0.6 mile north of (across)
Fontana Dam.

This trail begins along an old road bed, then drops off on a well-worn sidehill trail through a rather pleasant second growth hardwood forest. The original timber was harvested by the Whiting Manufacturing Company in the early 1900s. After crossing Payne Branch at **0.7** mile, the route follows old NC Highway 288. Now is the time to watch for artifacts such as old bottles, farm implements, and car parts, but remember all artifacts are federally protected and should not be disturbed. At mile **1.5** you pass an old homestead marked by small open fields and fruit trees. Most of the land you will cross on this hike was purchased by the Tennessee Valley Authority (TVA) from J.E. and Bland Coburn for the Fontana Project and subsequent inclusion in the national park. The Coburns were land speculators who purchased vast tracts of land after the lumber companies had finished with it.

As you walk along old Highway 288, imagine what life was like when this road was the main highway and virtually the only link with the outside world. You will pass several old abandoned cars in this section. Although missing many parts now, some of the cars abandoned on the North Shore were in good running order—except for tires. Tire rationing during the war and the abrupt evacuation of the area resulted in folks just parking the flivver and moving on.

At about **2.5** miles, old State Highway 288 swings right, but the Lakeshore Trail continues along a small stream. During the high water season, the trail and this stream become one for about 100 yards. As you climb beside this small brook and throughout this hike, you will be passing the Nantahala Formation. It consists of slate, mica, chlorite schist, sandy schist, greywacke, and fine conglomerate. From 1926-44 this formation yielded the most significant mineral production in what is now Great Smoky Mountains National Park. Over a half million tons of very high grade copper ore were shipped from the Fontana Copper Mine, located just across Eagle Creek from here, to the smelters at Copperhill, Tennessee (on the Tennessee/ Georgia border). Old-timers say that copper was just a byproduct of the mine—gold was the real money maker. Assays and company records show that over 250 pounds of gold and 14,500 pounds of silver were processed from the Fontana ore body.

You will now begin to rise and fall over the finger ridges of Little Shuckstack Mountain. A gentle, but steady climb of about a half mile will take you through a mixed hardwood hillside. Oaks and pines dominate the forest canopy, while rhododendrons and huckleberries compete for sunlight below. Springtime brings the forest floor alive as violets, trilliums and rue anemones dot the trailside. Just past mile **3.0** Birchfield Branch is crossed. At high water, this could be a very wet crossing. Birchfield Branch cuts a deep path through a small valley. About a half mile beyond this creek, you will cross another small stream. Here a 4' falls spills from beneath a thicket of rhododendron and Eastern hemlock.

Contouring along the mountainside, you will be treated to several views down to inlets of Fontana Lake as this trail gently rises and falls. The second growth forest is mostly pine and oak, becoming quite attractive in early autumn with its fine array of sourwoods, flowering dogwoods, and scarlet oaks.

Near mile **4.0** you cross a small stream and follow it downhill a couple of hundred feet before turning away to cross a finger ridge of the larger Snakeden Ridge. Blueberries abound here under the mixed hardwood forest. At mile **4.5**, you drop down close to Fontana Lake, but then ascend away on another ridge. Finally you will crest a rise to hear Lost Cove Creek rushing below you. Watch for the wildflower little brown jugs as you make your descent. This relative to the wild ginger uses a musky odor to entice fungus gnats to lay their eggs in the blossom. Pollen is deposited on the unsuspecting gnats which fly off to the next plant. The poisonous flower tissue kills any gnat which might be unlucky enough to hatch here. In this manner, the flower survives to produce seeds for a new generation.

At **5.2** miles, intersect the Lost Cove Trail and turn right. The trail parallels Lost Cove Creek, a rough and tumble mountain stream sporting moss-covered boulders, and traverses a hemlock forest with rhododendron and mountain laurel understory. Soon you will arrive at Lost Cove Campsite (#90). Lost Cove is the most heavily used campsite on Eagle Creek but is not too badly deteriorated. There is no spring at #90 and horses are allowed.

The proximity of Fontana Lake and Eagle Creek offer swimming opportunities not generally available at park campsites. Permits are required for all overnight stays in the park but no reservations are needed at #90. Permits are available at self-registration stations located at Fontana Marina, the Appalachian Trail shelter at Fontana Dam, and Twentymile Ranger Station.

Narrative by Lance Holland

LAUREL FALLS TRAIL

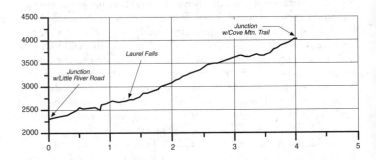

LENGTH: 4.0 miles, starting at Laurel Falls Parking Area and ending at Cove Mountain Trail. (1.3 miles to Laurel Falls.)

HIGHLIGHTS: Waterfall, big trees, air quality monitoring station.

CAUTIONS: Rocks around falls are slippery and many people are injured here each year.

MAP KEY: 5-6 C; USGS quad: Gatlinburg.

USE: Hiking trail.

TRAILHEAD: Drive on Little River Road to Fighting Creek Gap between Sugarlands Visitor Center and Elkmont Campground. The parking area is also the trailhead for the Sugarland Mountain Trail. On weekends it's hard to find a parking place at the gap.

Laurel Falls Trail is one of the most popular in the park—short, paved, and spectacular. It runs north, or right, if you are coming from Sugarlands. It was built by a Civilian Conservation Corps crew in 1935 and is a wide bench cut into a rocky hillside. Up to the falls, it is excellent for baby strollers, possible for wheelchairs (though the pavement is rough on the edges and steep in spots), and generally as accessible as any hilly sidewalk.

From the road it runs gently uphill through dry woods with pines, maples, dogwoods, and mountain laurel. Look for galax and trailing arbutus on the right bank. The round, shiny galax leaves last all year, and each plant sends up an 8-10-inch stalk with tiny white flowers all along it in late July. Arbutus plants flower in February or March; the delicate pink flowers hide under the leathery leaves and have a surprisingly strong, sweet smell. But you have to kneel to smell them.

At a resting bench after a bit of climbing you can look through an opening in the trees and see far down the Laurel Creek and Little River Valleys. Fighting Creek Gap, where this trail started, divides the Little River drainage from the Little Pigeon River drainage.

Beyond the view, the route passes rocks that the CCC crew had to blast through to make this wide graded trail. This rock work provided not only a beautiful trail, but also some prime real estate for two species of spiders that you can find all along these rock faces. Lampshade spiders live underneath flat overhanging slabs of rock. The webs look like a round lampshade with a small top ring (about the size of a silver dollar) attached directly to the rock and the larger bottom ring held taut by support web strands to surrounding rock. The webs are visible all year, and the spiders are in residence during most of the warmer months. They sit quietly in the middle of the small ring of the lampshade, but if disturbed, they either scamper away on long legs or vibrate in their webs. Try looking for one in its lampshade web with a flashlight.

The other spider here is a funnel web spider, which chooses flat or slanted rock surfaces with deep cracks. Each spider builds a sheet web with a funnel extending down into a safe crack. It waits in the funnel and runs out when it feels the vibrations of an insect. Funnel web spiders are timid, but sometimes you can coax one out by stroking the edge of its web with a grass blade.

The trail continues to rise, with higher rock faces on the right and steeper drop-offs on the left. Be careful in icy weather and watch small children in any weather. Many kinds of lichens grow on the rocks. One is as yellow as a dandelion flower. The forest here is mostly cove hardwood, with tuliptree, maple, flowering dogwood, and oak. This area was logged, and the fires that started on the dry piney slopes near the beginning of this trail probably spread up into this valley, so the trees are small. But they are big enough to shade the trail, making it cool in summer.

At **1.3** miles, you reach Laurel Falls, a vigorous 75' waterfall divided in the middle by the trail and a pleasant pool. Rock slabs are well placed for crossing, but they can be slippery when wet. There are always lots of people here—parents dangling babies' feet in the pool, teenagers climbing down to the lower falls, families having picnics. As you continue up Laurel Falls Trail, the solitude will be a contrast. At first, the trail is rough, rocky, and steep as you climb around a small ridge and double back above the falls. Three creeks, named Jay Bird, Red Bird, and Tanager, join Laurel Creek just to the right. Then the trail enters quiet Eastern hemlock woods as you climb steadily on packed dirt. You pass two giant tuliptrees on the right. The second is riddled with holes of Yellow-bellied Sapsuckers, while the first is untouched by these small woodpeckers. Big buckeyes, Fraser magnolias, and basswoods with crowds of root sprouts line the ascent.

Fires and loggers did not come up this far, so much of the rest of this hike is through virgin forest, changing gradually from cove hardwood to exposed ridges as you climb.

The trail turns away from the creek valley and starts up a drier ridge, with red and white oaks, sourwoods, and huckleberries. Look for a tree on the left with a hole right through it at head level—a good place to startle the hikers behind you or take a bark-framed photograph of someone.

At mile **3.1** from the beginning and mile 1.8 from the falls, the trail meets Little Greenbrier Trail, which goes left to Wear Cove Gap. Laurel Falls Trail continues straight and starts up Chinquapin Ridge. American chestnut saplings, striped maples, and Dutchman's pipe vines with enormous heart-shaped leaves grow here, but no chinquapins (a type of tree). At the end of the ridge, the trail joins the Cove Mountain Trail that runs along the park boundary to Sugarlands. Turn left and walk along the jeep road. On your right, a gravel road runs parallel to the trail; look for metal NPS boundary signs on trees. A gentle climb takes you to the grassy top of Cove Mountain (4,077') and the fire tower.

The tower is no longer available to hikers because its third stairway has been converted to an air quality monitoring station, a cooperative venture of the Tennessee Valley Authority and the national park's Twin Creeks Natural Resources Center. The station measures regional ground level ozone, hydrocarbons, and oxides of nitrogen, industrial pollutants that contribute to acid rain and damage ecological communities. Clingmans Dome and Look Rock also have monitoring stations. Air quality information will be correlated with systematic vegetation sampling to determine how changes in pollutants affect plants. One of the sampling areas is along Laurel Falls Trail on Chinquapin Ridge, where you just hiked. It seems fitting that old fire towers are being remodeled to watch for new dangers.

Narrative by Doris Gove

LEAD COVE TRAIL

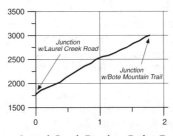

LENGTH: 1.8 miles, from Laurel Creek Road to Bote Mountain Trail.

HIGHLIGHTS: Old cabin site, old fields (reforested cropland).

MAP KEY: 4 D; USGS quad: Thunderhead Mtn.

USE: Horse and hiking trail.

TRAILHEAD: Big Spring Cove on Laurel Creek Road to Cades Cove (5.5 miles west of the Townsend "Y" and about one mile east of Crib Gap). Look for a trail sign on the east side of the road. There is parking for 5 or 6 cars on the east side and space for 3 more on the west.

The trail begins with a rough path bordering Laurel Creek Road. Within a few hundred feet, it turns sharply left onto a broad, gentle trail. This was an old road through fields (former cropland) now reforested in Eastern hemlock, tuliptree, and mixed hardwoods.

On crossing Sugar Cove Prong, the trail steepens above and parallels the singing brook. Soon the rockpile remains of an old chimney and stone foundation appears on the left. Dr. Randolph Shields, a native of Cades Cove, reported this to have been the cabin of Gibson Tipton. The Tipton family is known for being some of the first white settlers in the cove (1821).

Rising on a sharp grade until making a 90 degree left turn, the trail begins its swing around the north face of the rising slopes. It goes through rhododendron, through mixed hardwoods, and dips into moist, cool hollows where small streams cross. A delightful path it is. In the open woods, several spring flowers bloom, including trillium, bloodroot, violets, and Solomon's seal. It is a popular route to Spence Field and as the upper leg of a 7-mile loop hike which also involves Finley Cane and Bote Mountain trails.

Neither the Lead Cove or Finley Cane trails appear on the 1964 USGS Thunderhead quad map quadrant as they were abandoned (not maintained) from after WWII until around 1970, when they were re-opened.

The only view point is near the Bote Mountain Trail junction where grapevines or a strong wind burst has opened the forest canopy below the trail. Across the Laurel Creek Valley stands Scott Mountain, where the park boundary runs the ridge line. A few hundred yards beyond this opening is Sandy Gap and the Bote Mountain Trail.

The trail name comes from the galena, or lead ore, once extracted in small amounts from the area. Dr. Shields remembered having heard that one or more wagon loads of the ore were taken out during the Civil War. However, he didn't know the exact location of the ore bed.

This short trail crosses three geological formations beginning with the limestone window of Big Spring Cove, where the older Metcalf Phyllite Formation has eroded to expose the underlying limestone. (The actual "big spring" is a sinkhole which lies beside the Finley Cane Trail.) The path then moves across a thin strip of the Metcalf Phyllite to the prevalent Elkmont Sandstone.

Narrative by Woody Brinegar

LITTLE BOTTOMS TRAIL

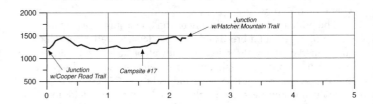

LENGTH: 2.3 miles, from Cooper Road Trail to Hatcher Mountain Trail.

HIGHLIGHTS: Abrams Creek.

CAUTIONS: High water will cover a portion of trail. Trail is not graded.

MAP KEY: D 2; USGS quad: Calderwood.

USE: Hiking trail.

STARTING POINT: 1.4 miles up Cooper Road Trail from Abrams Creek Ranger Station.

Although frequently used, this trail is recommended only for those who are sure of foot. It generally follows an old man-way shaped more by 150 years of walking feet than by shovel and mattock. This path is as much a relic of the past as Cable Mill and rail fences. It retains characteristics of mountain footpaths of the old days before the uniform graded trails were built.

Little Bottoms Trail gets considerable use as the most convenient route to Abrams Falls from Happy Valley and also as one leg of several dayhike loops (see map). Unlike graded trails, it turns sharply up and down in places, and its width isn't consistent. Generally it's about 2' wide, but narrows to 12" in places along some slopes. Bottomland is choice farmland, and the trail name comes from a secluded bottomland on both sides of the creek a mile and half in at the junction of Mill Branch. It's reforested principally in Eastern hemlock and white pine.

This was the only farmland along Abrams Creek between the upper reaches of Happy Valley and Cades Cove. The Anderson farm was on the west side and Jim and Kate Johnson lived on the east side where the trail runs.

The principal product raised here and on most mountain farms was corn, essential for bread and livestock feed, as well as for selling on the market. They also raised virtually all of their own foodstuffs other than such items as salt and pepper. Meat came from hogs and hunting. Self-sufficient they were and had to be.

Popular Campsite #17 is on the east edge of the old fields in a hemlock forest, not far from sleep-inducing Abrams Creek. The creek or a nearby branch is the water source. Ruins of an old homesite are visible here.

Just beyond Cooper Road Trail, a small spring emerges from beneath the base of a hemlock tree. Known as the Tom Hearon Spring, it is no longer a dependable source of water. Hearon farmed the old fields nearby, now returned to hemlock forest.

The trail immediately climbs a pine ridge and passes at the crest an unusually large patch of fragile Indian pipes. They bloom now and then from June through August. Indian pipe appear in small clusters along the path, as do the white blooms of striped pipsissewa. On reaching the south fork of this ridge, you're suddenly joined by the murmuring music of Abrams Creek. The pleasing sound of the stream is shaped by its chattering with the Cades Sandstone and coarse-grained rocks known as Whilhite Formation which lie in its path.

Time and erosion cut the Abrams Creek Gorge through Cades Sandstone, a resistant, sedimentary rock. Near Hatcher Mountain runs the Rabbit Creek Fault where the rock changes to a coarser grained sandstone.

Even though the total change in elevation is negligible, the trail ascends and descends 200' several times between beginning and end through a mixed, low-level forest of pine and hardwood. A few big hemlocks and white pines border the path. At **2.3** miles the Little Bottoms Trail ends upon meeting the graded Hatcher Mountain Trail. It is 0.2 mile to the intersection with Abrams Creek Trail and the Hannah Mountain Trail.

In the 1.7 miles beyond the ford to Abrams Falls, the Abrams Falls

Trail continues more gradually up and down but is fairly level for a time a hundred feet above the creek. It's seldom that the sound of Abrams Creek is out of hearing. A choice and constant companion for this low elevation walk on the slopes which shoulder the stream, Abrams Creek and the old manway make this hike memorable.

Narrative by Woody Brinegar

LITTLE BRIER GAP TRAIL

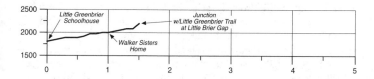

LENGTH: 1.5 miles, from Little Greenbrier School to Little Greenbrier Trail.
HIGHLIGHTS: Walker Sisters' cabin and farmstead
MAP KEY: 5 C; USGS quad: Wear Cove.
USE: Hiking trail.
STARTING POINT: Little Greenbrier School.

> There is an old weather bettion house
> That stands near a wood
> With an orchared near by it
> For all most one hundred years it has stood
>
> It was my home in infency
> It sheltered me in youth
> When I tell you I love it
> I tell you the truth.

Louisa Susan Walker wrote the above as part of a poem called "My Mountain Home." Louisa was the poet amongst five women who lived at this "small house that stands near a wood." This trail will bring you to that house today.

To reach the Walker Sisters' home, you will first have to travel to the Little Greenbrier School. You can reach the school by either of two methods. From spring to fall, a narrow, twisting dirt road allows you to drive right to the school. It is however, closed in winter. This small road begins at the paved road between Metcalf Bottoms Picnic Area and Wear Cove, just a short distance north of the picnic area. The more interesting alternative to driving is to hike the 0.6 mile Metcalf Bottoms Trail from the picnic area to the school.

From the school, the Little Brier Gap Trail starts as a gated access road. It is up the hill from the school's parking area.

As you walk the one-mile gravel road to the site, try to prepare your mind for what is at the homesite. What should be used for the home's construction? How much land would need to be cleared? Wylie King probably asked these questions as he walked this land. This Little Greenbrier Cove was to be his home for nearly 30 years. He and his wife, Mary Jane (Adair), would raise 10 children to adulthood here. Their grandchildren would be amongst the last to live in the Smokies.

The trees along the trail were the raw materials used to build a home. Tuliptrees were cut and hewn for the walls. Each was carefully notched to fit together tightly so no nails or even pegs were needed. White oak was split with a froe for shingles. Red oak, maple, and beech were burned for heat.

As you approach the **0.75** mile mark, a grassy road will continue straight as the gravel road switches back. This grassy road is a continuation of the Little Brier Gap Trail as it climbs 0.5 mile to its terminus at the Little Greenbrier Trail on the park boundary. The gravel road leads to the Walker Sisters' cabin in less than a quarter mile.

As you near the homesite, the springhouse will be the first structure you encounter. Perishables like milk, eggs, and cheese were stored here. Notice how it is not built directly above the spring, but just downstream. This was to ensure that the spring was never fouled. To the right is the house. It is actually two homes. Look closely and you will see where they were placed side by side. The smaller room was probably built by Brice McFalls in the 1840s. Originally, it sat nearly 400 yards away. Wylie started his family in that cabin, but as it grew, he constructed the larger building. After Wylie's death, John N. Walker, Wylie's son-in-law, moved his growing family into the larger house in the 1870s, sharing it with his aging mother-in-law. By the late 1870s, John's family was growing too large, so he dismantled the old McFalls' cabin and placed it here as the kitchen.

John and Margaret Jane (King) raised 11 children to adulthood here. This was quite an accomplishment for the late 1800s and is probably attributed to Margaret Jane's great skill as an "herb doctor." John, in fact, bragged that in all his life he had only spent 50¢ on doctor bills.

John Walker was an independent and industrious man. Luxuries were never found here, nor would they have probably been wanted. Indulging oneself was seen by the Walkers as sinful. If you couldn't do it or make it yourself, it wasn't necessary. At a time when most men were their own carpenters and blacksmiths, John was seen as a real craftsman.

As a result of this hard work, many outbuildings were established. Today the springhouse and corn crib/gear shack are all that remain. If you use your imagination, you might picture where the barn sat, or maybe the pigpen, smokehouse, applehouse, poultry yard, blacksmith shop or even the grist mill with wood-turning lathe. There was no outhouse: women went to the woods downhill and men uphill. The Walker Sisters once refused to let their kin put one in because of the odor and "embarrassment" it would cause.

Maybe you can even imagine the rail and stone fences, ash hopper, tar kiln and charcoal making pit. Can you spot an old apple, peach, plum or cherry tree which indicate where the orchards sat?

Now imagine five old women living here and working the land. Often this valley is called the "Five Sisters Cove" in honor of the daughters of John Walker who forsook the "good life" of modern society and stuck by their tradition of hard work and humble living. Each day they worked hard to collect, prepare and preserve their food, spin and weave their own clothing, tend their livestock, work in the fields, and attend to the daily chores. "Use it up, wear it out, make it do or do without" was the code the sisters lived by. The sisters—Margaret Jane, Mary Elizabeth (Polly), Martha Ann, Nancy Melinda, Louisa Susan and Hettie Rebecca lived here as spinsters until one by one they passed away. The last, Louisa Susan, died in 1964.

The greatest change to their lives came in the 1930s when the national park was formed. The park wanted to purchase their land but the sisters did not want to go. Finally, the sisters agreed to sell if the park would let them live out their lives on their land. Hesitantly, the park agreed, and so was created the "life-time lease" which helped many farmers agree to sell their land to create this national park.

Today, the cabin remains as a sort of symbol of the dedication to the land which made farming in the Smokies possible. The land here is not prime, but as John and his daughters proved, a little perseverance and love is what really makes a home.

If, instead of backtracking to Little Greenbrier School, you wish to continue on to the junction with the Little Greenbrier Trail, you have a 0.5 mile climb through open hardwood forest to Little Brier Gap. This is the route the Walker Sisters' father, John, probably walked to court their mother. From the gap, an unofficial trail leads 0.5 mile steeply down to Robeson Road in Wear Cove. The Little Greenbrier Trail leads east to the Laurel Falls Trail or west to the Wear Cove Road 1.25 miles above Metcalf Bottoms Picnic Area.

Narrative by Tom Condon

LITTLE CATALOOCHEE TRAIL

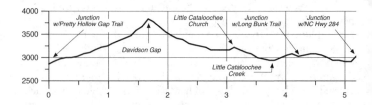

LENGTH: 5.2 miles, from Pretty Hollow Gap Trail to NC Route 284.

HIGHLIGHTS: Historic area with old structures, varied forest scenes.

MAP KEY: C-D 11; USGS quad: Cove Creek Gap.
USE: Horse and hiking trail.
STARTING POINT: Pretty Hollow Gap Trail, in the Cataloochee Valley.

The Little Cataloochee Trail begins 0.8 mile from the Cataloochee Road on the Pretty Hollow Gap Trail and follows old roads through the historic Little Cataloochee Valley, so identified to separate it from its neighboring valley—Cataloochee, or Big Cataloochee. Little Cataloochee may be considered an "island community," typical of the loosely-connected rural settlements which made up much of the United States a century ago. As such, it provides an interesting study of settlement and community life in a remote mountain setting.

The Cataloochee area was the last portion of Haywood County to be settled because of its rough topography. Permanent settlement of Big Cataloochee did not occur until the 1830s. Settlement of Little Cataloochee occurred between 1854 and 1860 as the sons and daughters of the original Palmer, Caldwell, Hannah and Bennett settlers established their own homesteads in the valley. By 1910, there were 1,251 people living in Cataloochee settlements. Farming and cattle raising were the sources of income for area residents and apple growing significantly stimulated the economy in Little Cataloochee after 1910.

From Pretty Hollow Gap Trail, the Little Cataloochee Trail ascends gently along an old road passing overgrown fields on the left which were previously farmed. At 0.3 mile the trail crosses Little Davidson Branch on rocks and reaches Davidson Branch at 0.4 mile, which it follows for the next 0.6 mile. After crossing Davidson Branch, the trail ascends more steeply, making several additional easy crossings of the stream. Frequent horse use and seepages in the trail make this segment quite muddy in places, requiring hikers to pick a route along its margin.

The trail ascends through a hemlock forest with many fine specimens. This is a distinct forest type which also includes tuliptree, maple, American beech, yellow birch and silverbell. An understory of rosebay rhododendron shades the branch and provides a display of pink-white flower clusters in June. A wide variety of wildflowers may be observed along this section in spring.

A switchback to the right at **1.0** mile follows a fork of Davidson Branch through second growth forest which replaced slopes cleared for agricultural use. A remnant of an old log structure with three courses of saddle-notched chestnut logs is left of the trail at about **1.4** miles, marking the remains of an old farmstead. Beyond is a fine wall constructed of stones cleared from former fields.

Davidson Gap is reached at **1.6** miles after a very steep climb. Davidson Gap, Davidson Branch and Little Davidson Branch are named for William Mitchell Davidson and his sons, who hunted and ran cattle in this area. A faint trace leads right out of the gap and across Bald Top to Bald Gap. This path intersects with an old trail which connected the two valleys and served as a mail route.

Having reached Davidson Gap, you can easily understand Raymond Caldwell's comments about travel between Big Cataloochee and Little Cataloochee as quoted in *Cataloochee: Lost Settlement of the Smokies*. He said, "Well, it was quite a chore to go through Davidson Gap...it would take more than a day to go over to Little Cataloochee and back...so, in one respect, it was separated about as much as New York City and California are today [by airplane]."

The delightful and historic trail segment which lies beyond the gap is made even more interesting by imagining the valley as it existed in 1920. Then, cleared fields extended to Davidson Gap. Houses, barns and outbuildings dotted the valley, apple orchards were planted on the slopes, corn grew in the bottoms, and sleek livestock grazed in the fields. The community store, church and school completed the fabric of a settlement made up of hard-working families.

The trail descends moderately, passing a rock wall on the right before making a switchback into the head of the valley where the trail becomes a road. At **1.9** miles it reaches the site of a farm complex erected between 1895 and 1905, by W. G. B. (Will) Messer, a leading citizen of the valley. The complex consisted of a one and one-half story log house, barn, springhouse and apple house. The apple house is now part of the Mountain Farm Museum at Oconaluftee and the barn, known as the Messer Barn, was moved and restored beside the Cataloochee Ranger Station.

Still descending, the trail continues along the headwaters of Coggins Branch, reaching the Dan Cook place at **2.3** miles. Dan Cook, whose daughter, Rachel, married Will Messer, built the earliest and finest log house in Little Cataloochee between 1856 and 1860, using native wood and stone. This house stood left of the road across from the foundation of the Dan Cook apple house, which is all that remains of the original farm complex. Near the apple house ruins is the terminus of an old road which crossed Noland Mountain at Noland Gap, connecting Big and Little Cataloochee. Beyond, our trail descends through hardwood forest, with an understory of thick rhododendron, before reaching a relatively level stretch which passes through old fields. Rock work, fence posts and a few apple trees mark man's presence here. An easy climb leads to Little Cataloochee Baptist Church at **3.1** miles.

The church was built by area citizens in 1889, including Will Messer, who built the pulpit and steeple. Services were held twice a month by "circuit riders" with a lot of socializing before and after services. Grave markers in the cemetery below the church contain family names familiar in Cataloochee and western North Carolina, although the earlier graves are simple unmarked field stones.

The trail winds down the forested hill beyond the church and passes a fine rocked-up spring on the left at the bottom. The community of Ola was located in the level area beyond the spring. Will Messer purchased this area, a 100-acre tract on Little Cataloochee Creek, and moved his family here from the upper end of the valley sometime after 1905. About 1910, Mr. Messer built the largest and finest house in Little Cataloochee. It consisted of 11 rooms, had hot and cold water, and was illuminated by an acetylene lighting system. On this portion of his property he developed several barns and mills, a general store, a blacksmith's shop and several other structures. The post office was given the name Ola, after the Messers' daughter Viola.

Although Will Messer was a shrewd businessman, he was mindful of community needs and earned a reputation for being "helpful, generous, and honest." He accepted eggs and honey in exchange for needed supplies and extended credit during hard times.

Little remains of Ola except a few fragments of tin, some stonework along the creek and a few apple trees. The site of the Will Messer house can be located approximately 75 feet right of the road near the spring by looking for two tall, pyramid shaped ornamental shrubs.

The trail crosses Little Cataloochee Creek at **3.5** miles and begins ascending. At **3.8**, miles a trail leads 220 feet left to the John Jackson Hannah Cabin. Mr. Hannah moved here with his bride in 1857 and lived in a smaller board cabin until he built the present structure in 1864. Mr. Hannah lived by farming the slopes about his cabin. The cabin was restored in 1976 by National Park Service workers who used the broad ax, foot adze and other period tools to duplicate both the original construction practices and appearance.

A side trip to this fine old structure is recommended. It has a beautiful puncheon floor with puncheons up to 29" wide. Fragments of newspapers, which once papered the walls to seal out cold air, still cling to interior logs. Stone piles above the house are left from field clearing. Once bee gums sat in a corner of the front yard, a garden was nearby and rail fences marked field boundaries. To the southwest was an orchard which once boasted the world's largest apple tree.

The Long Bunk Trail exits left at **4.2** miles, leading 3.7 miles to the Mount Sterling Trail. The Hannah Cemetery, a worthwhile side trip, is 0.2 miles along the Long Bunk Trail. Beyond the junction, the Little Cataloochee Trail curves around the end of the ridge and descends through mature forest with several large tuliptrees and Eastern hemlocks to reach a bridged crossing of Correll Branch at **5.0** miles. The Little Cataloochee Trail ascends 0.2 miles beyond Correll Branch to reach N.C. 284 at **5.2** miles.

Narrative by William A. Hart, Jr.

LITTLE GREENBRIER TRAIL

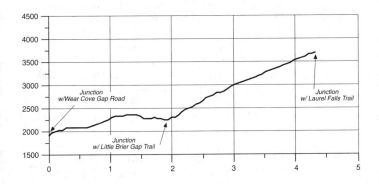

LENGTH: 4.3 miles, from Wear Cove Gap Road to Laurel Falls Trail.
HIGHLIGHTS: Scenic views, wildflowers.
MAP KEY: 5 C; USGS quads: Wear Cove, Gatlinburg.
USE: Hiking trail.
TRAILHEAD: Wear Cove Gap Road at park boundary. From the Little River Road, turn into the Metcalf Bottoms Picnic Area. Proceed straight across the bridge for 1.25 miles. The trailhead is to the right just before the top of the hill (park boundary). There is very limited parking here at a small pulloff.

Even though this trail features many beautiful views, it actually receives little use. It's therefore a perfect choice for those looking to get away from the constant activity of America's most visited national park.

The first quarter mile climbs through a pine-oak forest before turning left and entering a mixed hardwood forest. This is how the trail will be almost the entire time, mostly pine-oak and all uphill. But fear not, the uphill may be continuous, but it is never hard. I like to hike this trail in the late summer and fall, because that's when the blueberries are at their peak. And this trail is loaded with them.

Climbing along, you will begin to catch glimpses of Wear Cove from the ridge. But save your film, they'll keep getting better. You're now walking the park boundary. This will become apparent quite quickly. At **0.75** mile, you will see your first boundary marker. Today, you'll be in and out of the park a number of times. Watch for the posts and tree markers on both your left and right.

Now, don't concentrate too hard on finding the best views of the valley, or you'll miss the views at your feet. This trail holds a number of real treats. Scattered along the trail and through the seasons are some of the loveliest wildflowers in the park. Springtime has an abundance of course, but the show continues through the summer and into the fall.

Look for orchids of all types, especially the tiny downy rattlesnake-plantain. Long ago, scientists and physicians believed in a theory called the "Doctrine of Signatures". This theory assumed that cures to diseases or illnesses could be found by looking for plants that resembled the diseased organ or its cause. In the case of rattlesnake-plantain, because the white lines on the leaves resembled the scales of a snake, this little orchid was considered a cure for all snake bites, including the rattlesnake's. Fortunately for the plant world, and perhaps unfortunately for us, this doctrine lacks all merit. Thus the rattlesnake-plantain survives and we struggle to find cures in other ways.

After **2.0** miles of hiking, you will have climbed 400' to Little Brier Gap. See it isn't that steep. Here the trail crosses the Little Brier Gap Trail. A left turn will take you out of the park and into a section of Wear Cove formerly known as Buckeye Springs. A right turn leads 0.75 mile down to the Walker Sisters homesite, a small farm where five strong-willed sisters subsisted by simple means until 1964. The short side trip to it is well worth the effort.

Continue straight to remain on the Little Greenbrier Trail. The character of the path remains the same, climbing steadily along the park border. You are now climbing Chinquapin Ridge. It is named for a relative of the Amercian chestnut tree. However, according to the park's official tree checklist, no chinquapins occur in the Smokies. American chestnuts and chinquapins are difficult to tell apart, but, look for long, thin, deeply toothed leaves of the later species. The chestnut's are dark green above and smooth gray green below. The chinquapin's have small gray hairs on the underside.

As you approach mile **3.0**, you will notice a small outcropping of Metcalf Phyllite. This metamorphosed shale tells the story of these mountains. Once this land sat at the bottom of a shallow sea where sand and mud formed thick layers and cemented themselves into rocks. The phyllite is from those mud layers. Great upheavals hundreds of millions of years ago pushed and folded these stones into the mountains you see today. Once taller than the Rockies, the southern Appalachians have been worn down by wind and water over time.

The trail winds around the corner and opens into a spectacular view of these magnificent mountains and the picturesque valleys they hold. This is Wear Cove, a hole in the fabric of the mountains. Once this valley was covered by ridges like the one you stand upon, but phyllite is a soft stone and it wears away quickly; quickly by geologic standards anyway. This erosion has opened three large valleys along the edge of the Smokies—Wear, Cades and Tuckaleechee (Townsend) Coves.

Moving along, the path continues up Chinquapin Ridge. An interesting sight greets you at mile **3.5**. Here a large vine has woven a basket. Using red maples as its staves, the vine has worked itself in and around these trees' trunks. The large heart-shaped leaves in the basket, however, are not grape. These belong to the Dutchman's pipe vine. In June, look for the little pipe-like flowers of this plant.

Just 0.5 mile ahead the forest opens a bit more as you cross the ridge and grasses invade the trailside. Presently, you reach the junction with the Laurel Falls Trail. Turn right and it's downhill (1.8 miles) to the most visited waterfall in the park. Turn left and you will climb another 0.9 miles to the top of Cove Mountain. The summit features a fire tower which once provided spectacular views, but now is closed to the public. Only very limited views are now available from the open summit.

Narrative by Tom Condon

LITTLE RIVER TRAIL

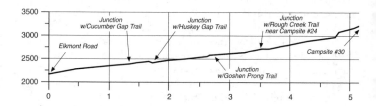

LENGTH: 5.1 miles, from the barricade on the sideroad upstream from Elkmont Campground to Campsite #30.
HIGHLIGHTS: Easy, wide trail, beautiful river.
CAUTIONS: Three river crossings near the end.
MAP KEY: 6 C-D; USGS quads: Gatlinburg, Silers Bald.
USE: Hiking trail.
TRAILHEAD: Drive to Elkmont Campground 4.9 miles west of Sugarlands Visitor Center. Near the entrance to the campground, turn left. Bear left again 0.6 mile later to reach Little River parking area via a gravel road.

Little River is actually pretty big. It drains a large area of the Tennessee side of the Smokies, carries a lot of water, and has branches from the highest ridges. Over millions of years, Little River carved out a wide valley that leads right to the base of the Smokies' crest, and it was this easy access that attracted Little River Lumber Company.

The company bought out the few farms and built a base camp with a sawmill at Elkmont. Then crews moved up the rivers and branches with road and rail lines, set up temporary camps, cut all the trees, and moved on. Rail lines went up steep areas such as Rough Creek and Goshen Prong, and when the terrain was too steep even for the railroads, loggers pulled the logs down with overhead cable skidders, mule teams, or wooden chutes. In extreme cases, men ballhooted the logs—they cleared an area below where the logs had been cut and rolled or shot them down the steep hillsides toward a rail siding. This was dangerous work and made even worse gashes in the mountains than routine logging. Evidence of logging can still be found along the road; look for cables, pullies, and railroad ties.

In the late 1920s, Little River Lumber Company agreed to sell its large holdings to park organizers only if it could continue logging for five years. Edward J. Meeman, the editor of the Knoxville News, ridiculed this "conservation with an axe," and a painful controversy went on for months among Tennessee park supporters. However, park organizers felt they had no choice; it was an amazing accomplishment that they raised the money at all during the Depression. Meeman finally, if reluctantly, added his editorial support. As a result of the sale agreement, the park was established in 1934 even though the company continued to lay track and clear-cut virgin timber until 1938. Though it is sad we cannot see the magnificent virgin forests, a new, beautiful forest now fills this area.

Gold was discovered in Little River in the early 1920s, but the gold rush was short-lived when someone calculated that you could only earn $1.27 in gold for each ton of rock crushed.

Two famous visitors to Little River Trail were Clarence Darrow and John Scopes in 1925. Park organizers in Knoxville invited them, knowing that the Scopes "monkey" trial had brought national and international reporters to Tennessee. Publicity about Darrow's visit helped nationalize the park movement. William Jennings Bryan was also invited, for a different weekend, of course, but he suffered a fatal heart attack after the trial. Carlos Campbell writes in *Birth of a National Park* that Bryan's phone call of July 26, 1925, to accept the invitation may have been his last official act.

Little River Trail starts at a locked gate and proceeds up a good gravel road along the river. The wet rocks on the right harbor mosses, liverworts, and walking fern, and many wildflowers grow at the base of the rocks. The moss and fern experts at the University of Tennessee use this trail for field trips. In mid-summer look for Ruby-throated Hummingbirds feeding on the nectar of crimson bee balm, also known as Oswego tea. A few steep fishing trails on the left lead to the river.

At mile 0.3, there is a bench and a big, deep, green swimming hole. A little farther is another bench with a view of rapids on a curve of Little River. Notice a bunch of yellow birch trees just up-trail from the bench with their bark curled in perfect ringlets. On the right is a patch of umbrella leaf, a dinner-plate-sized leaf with jagged edges on a stalk about 18" tall. This plant is related to may-apple and is relatively rare, growing only in wet rocky places like this. It blooms in April or May, and the leaves last until late fall.

The road swings away from the river, but soon they rejoin as Huskey Branch cascades in from the right and flows under a wide, flat bridge. The swimming is even better here than before, though not much warmer. At mile **1.3**, Cucumber Gap Trail merges with Little River Trail and is marked by a bench at the base of a big sycamore. Then the road crosses Little River on a bridge that, according to a sign, is damaged; repairs have made it strong enough for foot traffic. Soon the road looks more like a trail, with plants creeping onto the sides and middle. The Huskey Gap Trail veers left at mile **1.7** and leads up to Sugarland Mountain Trail and then down to Newfound Gap Road.

Little River is now on the right, lined with sycamore trees. You will probably see sycamore bark peelings on the trail, looking like pieces of camo cloth. At mile **2.7**, right after a bridge over Lost Creek, the trail forks. Goshen Prong Trail goes right and reaches the Appalachian Trail after 7.7 miles and an elevation gain of 3,000'. Little River Trail goes left and then crosses Rough Creek on the last bridge of this trail. Little River spreads out into several channels, and the trail crosses two of these on a rocky island. At mile **3.5**, Campsite #24 appears on the right. This site is heavily used, has room for 15 people, and enjoys frequent bear visits. The elevation is 2,860'.

Just beyond Campsite #24, Rough Creek Trail forks left to another route to Sugarland Mountain Trail that can be combined with the Huskey Gap Trail for a nice loop. Little River Trail continues straight, rises a bit, becomes rocky in spots, and suddenly turns tricky with three rough creek crossings. There is evidence that some campers surveyed the first crossing and decided that, sign or no sign, they had already reached Campsite #30. The official #30 does have a sign. The second creek crossing has rotten bridge timbers with slippery moss and hidden nails; the timbers are tempting, but it might be safer to rock hop. After the third crossing, you will find Campsite

#30, and it is worth the effort. The tent sites are on a high, flat bank at the confluence of several creeks (with names like Spud Town, Rattler, Devil, Snake Tongue) that rush down from the Mt. Collins-Newfound Gap basin. This site has room for 12 people and is much less used than #24. You are only two miles from the Appalachian Trail, but an elevation gain of 3,000' (off trail) lies between you and the ridge. You can understand why the lumber company and the Civilian Conservation Corps crew stopped here.

Narrative by Doris Gove

LONG BUNK TRAIL

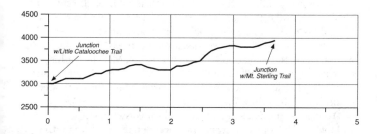

LENGTH: 3.7 miles, from Little Cataloochee Trail to Mt. Sterling Trail.
HIGHLIGHTS: Historic areas, beautiful forest vistas.
MAP KEY: 11 C; USGS quad: Cove Creek Gap.
USE: Horse and hiking trail.
STARTING POINT: Little Cataloochee Trail at 4.2 miles; 1.0 mile from NC 284.

Long Bunk Trail, which provides a connection between the Little Cataloochee and the Mount Sterling trails, offers a delightful walk through a former settlement which comprised part of Little Cataloochee. It passes along the lower reaches of Long Bunk, a mountain extending from the slopes of Mount Sterling. This trail is also known as the Pig Pen Trail, so named for a pig pen which once stood near the trail's upper terminus.

During the 1820s, before permanent settlement in Cataloochee had occurred, the meadows near Long Bunk were used as summer pasture by residents of Haywood County. Herders turned out their animals to roam the forests from early spring until October. Hogs would be left out until they had received the full benefit of the nuts and acorns. All animals were marked with slits in their ears to distinguish the livestock of each owner. Their markings were registered in the Range Master's record at the county court house to provide a means of settling ownership disputes. Herders visited the mountains to check on their livestock and provide salt for them in natural depressions or hewn logs called "licks" or "licklogs."

According to Elizabeth Powers' *Cataloochee: Lost Settlement of the Smokies*, Ned McFalls was a legendary herder who ranged cattle on Long Bunk with the assistance of a young man named Allen Davidson. On one occasion they searched for lost cattle on Long Bunk without success. In an effort to locate the cattle, McFalls put his hands to his mouth and shouted, "Low, Dudley, Low." In an instant they heard Dudley, the lead bull, bellow from where the cattle were grazing more than three miles away.

Young Allen Davidson went on to distinguish himself as a Colonel in the Confederacy, but he never outgrew his love for the Cataloochee slopes. At 80 he returned to view the scenes of his youth and with tears in his eyes said, "good-bye, world, this is the last time." The beauty of Long Bunk makes these feelings understandable.

Long Bunk Trail exits the Little Cataloochee Trail at 4.2 miles from Pretty Hollow Gap Trail; however, it is most easily reached by walking 1.0 mile from Little Cataloochee Trail's terminus at route 284. Footing is generally good, although several areas are miry during wet periods due to horse traffic. The area through which the trail passes was formerly settled with small farms dotting the valley to the trail's upper terminus. Mac Hannah, Dude Hannah, A.R. Hannah, Janea Smith, Bill Seay, Henry Grindstaff, Will Johnson and W.H. Messer were among those who lived in the area. Signs of the past are still evident to careful observers.

Initially, the trail ascends moderately along an old road, reaching the Hannah Cemetery at 0.2 mile. The cemetery has approximately

50 graves. Grave markers reflect many pioneer names, including John Jackson Hannah and his wife, Martha Ann, whose restored cabin is nearby on Little Cataloochee Trail. According to Mark Hannah, native of Cataloochee and long-time ranger, a bell was rung when anyone died in Little Cataloochee. Everyone would stop and listen, silently counting the number of peals—one for each year of the deceased's life.

The trail continues climbing more gently beyond the cemetery, passing large oak trees on the right and left at **0.4** mile. It then descends to an old homesite at **0.5** mile. To the left are fence posts and the tumbled remains of an old building with rived shingles. After crossing a small branch, you will notice on the right a large white oak tree which is dying. A few feet to the right of the tree are the rotting remains of a log structure with hand hewn, dovetail-notched logs.

After a gentle ascent, the trail levels, then makes a short steep ascent before passing through mixed hardwoods to reach Dude Branch at **1.2** miles. Dude Branch was named for Dude Hannah who lived not far from this crossing. Dude and his brother, Ras Hannah, fooled a judge once by switching their clothes. A witness who had accused Dude of moonshining was completely discredited when he pointed to Ras. Ras and Dude contributed a certain liveliness to their community as musicians, dancers and balladeers as well as distillers.

The old road which has served as the trail narrows and generally ascends, crossing occasional small seepages at **2.2** miles. At **2.9** miles the trail crests a ridge forested with large oak trees, some with trunks 4-5' in diameter. In a good season, the ground here is covered in acorns. Beyond the crest, the trail gently descends through second growth forest into a pleasant cove with lush grass growing beneath the trees. Two crossings of forks of Correll Branch follow at **3.2** and **3.3** miles. Rock work beside the stream at the first crossing confirms agricultural activity here. This inviting area beckons the hiker to pause and fully savor this idyllic setting.

While contemplating the trail, imagine the children of Mr. and Mrs. David B. Nelson, who lived one mile north of Mount Sterling Gap and hiked this route five miles to Little Cataloochee school, arriving there daily at 10:00 a.m.

The trail ends at the Mount Sterling Trail at **3.7** miles. A sign here indicates Mount Sterling Gap is 0.5 miles to the right and Mount Sterling is 2.3 miles to the left.

Narrative by William A. Hart, Jr.

LONG HUNGRY RIDGE TRAIL

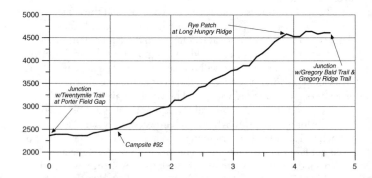

LENGTH: 4.6 miles, from Twentymile Trail to Gregory Bald Trail.
HIGHLIGHTS: Rye Patch.
CAUTIONS: Crossing Twentymile Creek in high water.
MAP KEY: 3 F; USGS quads: Fontana Dam, Cades Cove.
USE: Horse and hiking trail.
STARTING POINT: Twentymile Trail at Proctor Field Gap, 3.0 miles from Twentymile Ranger Station.

The name of this ridge and trail came from an event early in the twentieth century. Rain and high water kept a party of bear hunters marooned for days. They couldn't cross the creek and nearly starved before getting out.

The path follows an old railbed built by Kitchin Lumber Company when they logged this area in the 1920s. Rhododendron borders a straight length of trail. It crosses Proctor Branch, which can be a problem in high water.

Across this stream the railbed goes west around the end of a ridge which was burned in the 1980s. Dead stems of mountain laurel reach starkly above the emerging green beneath. Gray boles stand among surviving trees in the burned forest.

White rocks called milky quartz, one of the hardest and most common minerals in the Smokies, occasionally catch your eye along the path. Old log beams cross small streams and display giant nails which once fastened bridge planking.

Campsite #92 (elevation 2,520') appears to the left where the trail leaves the railbed. An open area adjacent to a small boulder field, the site is shaded by cherry, maple and tuliptree. The creek runs nearby, and at the edge of the clearing a 3' length of railroad track leans against a dogwood. A circle of rocks encloses a much-used firepit.

Past the campsite and the crossing of Twentymile Creek, the path threads an open hollow forested with tuliptree. Then it turns east on crossing Rye Patch Branch.

It's an excellent, graded trail, often curving along the southern slope of this rib of the ridge. The path ascends the eastern side of Long Hungry Ridge, which was known by natives as Killpecker Ridge. An old manway once followed the ridgecrest, for a lengthy and exhausting climb.

The climb is about over on reaching the crest, which is a broad expanse of level land extending a quarter of a mile. So appealing was this mountain top that Richard Russell planted rye there before the Civil War. Since then it has been known as the Rye Patch, an open, mixed hardwood forest with a ground cover of grass and weeds.

Horsemen sometimes make trails through the lush growth which may confuse the hiker, especially for those coming from Gregory Bald in summer.

The forest changes to yellow birch near the state line. On the crest, the path meets the Gregory Bald Trail. West about 250 yards is Rich Gap.

Narrative by Woody Brinegar

LOOP TRAIL

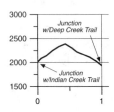

LENGTH: 1.0 mile, from Indian Creek Trail to Deep Creek Trail.

HIGHLIGHTS: Access to south end of Sunkota Ridge Trail, good loop route for those camping at Deep Creek Campground.

MAP KEY: F 8; USGS quad: Bryson City.

USE: Horse and hiking trail.

STARTING POINT: On Indian Creek Trail 0.8 mile from its junction with Deep Creek Trail, and 1.5 miles from Deep Creek Campground.

In combination with small sections of Indian Creek and Deep Creek Trails, Loop Trail makes an excellent short loop hike for those embarking from Deep Creek Campground. Also, Loop Trail provides the only access to the south end of Sunkota Ridge Trail.

From its intersection with Indian Creek Trail, Loop Trail parallels a small creek, which has carved out a narrow ravine through rock. As the trail climbs steadily uphill, the ravine, below and to the left, widens. At one point, the creek disappears under leaves for a dozen yards or so, then reappears. Vegetation on the forest floor along this stretch consists largely of Christmas fern and Virginia creeper. Halfway up the ridge lies the spring feeding the creek; near that stands an old stone wall. Further up the trail are many dead and dying white and Virginia pines, victims of the Southern pine beetle. Near the top of the ridge you enter a maple-pine forest with an understory of sourwood and flowering dogwood.

At **0.5** mile, at the top of the ridge, Loop Trail meets Sunkota Ridge Trail. From a thicket of rosebay rhododendron, mountain laurel, and dog-hobble, you descend the west side of the ridge through white pine, Eastern hemlock, sugar maple, and flowering dogwood. Soon Deep Creek, flowing below, becomes audible. Among tuliptrees, the trail joins Deep Creek Trail. Deep Creek Campground is to the left, 1.7 miles.

Narrative by Ted Olson

LOST COVE TRAIL

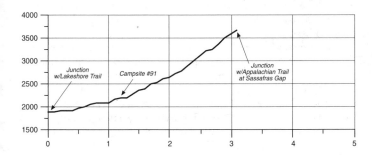

LENGTH: 3.1 miles, from Lakeshore Trail to the Appalachian Trail at Sassafras Gap.

HIGHLIGHTS: Outstanding variety of plantlife as trail ascends, remnants of logging railroad.

CAUTIONS: A total of 13 stream crossings, ranging from simple stepovers to a few that are dangerous in times of flood.

MAP KEY: F 3; USGS quad: Fontana Dam.

USE: Horse and hiking trail.

TRAILHEAD: Lakeshore Trail near Campsite #90.

Many hikers think that Lost Cove got its name due to the cloverleaf of short, unnamed trails near campsite #90. The actual origin of the name "Lost Cove," however, has itself been lost to time.

Lost Cove Trail provides the opportunity for a loop hike without the necessity of a boat shuttle. Starting at the trailhead on the national park side of Fontana Dam and following the Appalachian Trail over Shuckstack to Sassafras Gap, then down Lost CoveTrail to the Lakeshore Trail for the return leg to the Fontana Dam trailhead results in a 12-mile sampling of what the south side of the park has to offer.

The more popular and direct access to Lost Cove Trail is to arrange a boat shuttle from Fontana Marina (704) 498-2211 x277.

Fontana's shuttle service will drop you off at the appropriate trailhead and pick you up at a prearranged time. One-way shuttles are also available so you could do a portion of the aforementioned loop hike. The appropriate trailhead for Lost Cove Trail depends on the level of Fontana Lake.

In summer, when the lake is full, the boat can drop you off at Campsite #90. Now you must negotiate the cloverleaf of short trails around Campsite #90. Generally proceed uphill and to the left of the campsite itself. Soon, you will reach a well-defined, side-hill, old rail-road grade. Continue gradually uphill on the railroad grade on the left side of Lost Cove Creek. At **0.4** miles, at a signed junction, the Lakeshore Trail turns left (southwest) and the Lost Cove Trail continues straight ahead up Lost Cove Creek.

In the fall, winter, and spring, when lake levels are lower, the boat shuttle will drop you off at the alternate trail around the bend before you get to Campsite #90. The alternate trail is actually the simplest way to get on the Lost Cove Trail. Once on the alternate, just keep generally to the left and you will end up on the Lost Cove Trail.

Lost Cove Creek is a rough and tumble mountain stream, its banks lined with moss-covered rocks. From elevation 1,720' at Campsite #90 to about elevation 2,760', well above Cold Springs Branch, you will become well acquainted with Lost Cove Creek. About half of the stream crossings are rather insignificant and in low water conditions most of the rest can be rock-hopped. Periods of rainy weather will require you to take your boots off and ford at main creek crossings. Heavy rains can make some crossings treacherous.

Avoid becoming so preoccupied with the creek that you miss the outstanding forest that surrounds you. Much of this section of the trail is lined with partridgeberry, dog-hobble, and rhododendron. There is a wide variety of hardwoods, including maples, umbrella and cucumber magnolia, hickories—notably shagbark, and oaks. In the spring, the wildflower show along this section has been described as "magnificent" by veteran Smoky Mountain hikers.

As you walk along you will pass massive Eastern hemlock trees that were left standing by Montvale Lumber Company when they logged this watershed around 1915. Although some hemlock was used for bridge stringers, trestle beams, and pulp, it was often passed over by timber cutters. Therefore, you find today virgin trees within this second growth forest.

Montvale Lumber Company's base of operations and sawmill were located at the original town of Fontana, situated where Eagle Creek emptied into the Little Tennessee River (see Eagle Creek Trail). Montvale constructed a narrow gauge railway up Eagle Creek and a spur up Lost Cove Creek. Climax and Hiesler locomotives were used to pull or push the log trains. The remnants of a trestle can be spotted near the second ford above Campsite #91. Other logging artifacts such as cables may also be spotted along the trail.

About **1.1** miles from Campsite #90 the trail makes a sharp left turn and crosses Coldspring Branch. Campsite #91 (Upper Lost Cove) will be to your left. The campsite is in a pleasant level area and accommodates both hikers and horses. There is no spring at #91, but water may be obtained from the nearby stream. There is evidence of an old homeplace.

A short distance above the thirteenth and final ford, the trail leaves the creek and the old railroad grade and ascends steeply on switchbacks to reach the Appalachian Trail at Sassafras Gap. The intersection is well signed. The Appalachian Trail to the left will lead you over Shuckstack and to Fontana Dam. The trail continuing west from Sassafras Gap will take you down Proctor Branch to Twentymile Creek and Ranger Station. The Appalachian Trail to the right takes you to Doe Knob at the intersection with Gregory Bald Trail.

Narrative by Lance Holland

LOW GAP TRAIL I

BIG CREEK TRAIL TO APPALACHIAN TRAIL

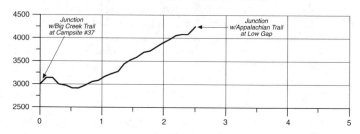

LENGTH: 2.5 miles, from Big Creek Trail at Walnut Bottom to Appalachian Trail at Low Gap.
HIGHLIGHTS: Forest scenes, signs of early settlement.
MAP KEY: 11-10 C-B; USGS quad: Luftee Knob.
USE: Horse and hiking trail.
STARTING POINT: Big Creek Trail at Lower Walnut Bottom.

Low Gap Trail begins at 5.1 miles on the Big Creek Trail and 0.1 mile above the bridge at Walnut Bottom. The route receives moderate horse use and is miry and rocky in places. Otherwise, footing is good.

The trail bears sharply right and ascends away from Walnut Bottom. It crosses Chestnut Cove Creek on rocks at **0.1** mile and becomes relatively level as it parallels Big Creek on the slopes above the stream for the next 0.7 mile. At **0.3** mile the trail crosses an unnamed stream flowing over green, mossy stones. This segment offers fine views of Big Creek and the pleasant flats along its border. These scenes are worth admiring as are the fine stands of tuliptrees and mixed hardwoods through which the trail passes.

The gentle slopes to the right and left of the trail beyond Chestnut Cove Creek were inviting to early settlers, who cleared them for farming. A few stone piles evidence field clearing efforts, although these fields are now dominated by second-growth tuliptrees. It's difficult to visualize settlement here now. However, Mrs. Zelphie Sutton of Chestnut Branch described the Walnut Bottom area in pre-park days this way: "It was thick of houses, thick of people up thar then."

At 0.7 mile the trail passes through hemlock and maple trees, the latter turning brilliant pink-red in autumn. Then it bears left to climb, with Low Gap Branch paralleling it at a distance. To the right are views of a broad cove, forested primarily by tuliptree. Occasional Dutchman's pipe vines reach to the top of these tall, straight trees. In spring, the cove through which the trail passes offers a rich variety of wildflowers. Spring-beauty, chickweed, hepatica, bloodroot, trillium and violets are among the flowers found here.

More signs of farming activity will be observed on the ascent of Low Gap Branch. At about 1.0 mile the trail crosses a small drainage in the vicinity of the Dan Gunter homesite. Immediately to the left of the crossing is a fine spring protected by dry-laid stone walls and a flat stone cover. Often spring houses were built over springs to protect the water source and food stored there. A short distance past the spring, the remains of an old chimney is a few paces to the right of the trail. Remnants of a cast iron wood stove lie at its base. Past the homesite there are fragmentary rock walls and stone piles easily viewed from the trail.

The trail climbs left at 1.2 miles and continues through the cove in a fine stand of tuliptrees, including several large specimens. Beyond, the trail passes a field of moss-covered boulders on the left and reaches an easy crossing of Low Gap Branch at 1.8 miles. After this crossing, the trail steepens.

After a sharp switchback at 1.9 miles, the trail climbs along a spur of the main ridge before beginning a final climb to Low Gap. Fine views of the Low Gap Branch drainage and Cosby Knob, which looms to the left, are worth pausing to admire. Silverbell trees are magnificent through here when in bloom in late April and May.

At 2.5 miles the trail reaches Low Gap and the Appalachian Trail. The trail continues straight ahead 2.5 miles to Cosby Campground. Cosby Knob Shelter and the Camel Gap Trail are left 0.8 and 2.4 miles, respectively. And the Mt. Cammerer Trail is 2.1 miles to the right.

Narrative by William A. Hart, Jr.

LOW GAP TRAIL II

COSBY CAMPGROUND TO APPALACHIAN TRAIL

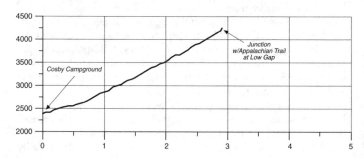

LENGTH: 2.9 miles, from Cosby Campground to Appalachian Trail at Low Gap.
HIGHLIGHTS: Big trees, signs of early settlement.
MAP KEY: B 10; USGS quads: Luftee Knob, Hartford TVA.
USE: Horse and hiking trail.
TRAILHEAD: Cosby Campground, at the hiker/picnic parking area

The Low Gap Trail begins at Cosby Campground and offers a short, but steep route to the Appalachian Trail at Low Gap. Originally, William Profitt, Lucinda Bryson and Virgil Messer had homes in the area now occupied by the campground. Also, Mountain Grove School was located here, providing education for families scattered throughout the area on small mountain farms.

Near the trailhead was the site of the Cosby Civilian Conservation Corps (CCC) camp, in operation nearly five years during the 1930s. The entire length of this trail was constructed by the young CCC men in Company 1462, which was comprised of 212 members in 1934.

The Cosby area had an element of notoriety. It was known as the "moonshine capital of the state," according to P. Audley Whaley, one of the first park wardens in the Cosby area in the 1930s. Making white liquor was something of a necessity for some mountaineers. In hard times, Whaley said, "they didn't have much way of feeding their families except that." But Whaley didn't have much difficulty with moonshiners. When he found a still, he just left a note telling them to move it. Evidence of stills can still be found along some remote streams. Relics often include broken glass, jar lids, fire rings and barrel hoops.

The Low Gap Trail begins at the hiker parking area which is located just to the left of the campground registration booth. The trail bears right from the parking lot and skirts the campground amphitheater to reach a paved loop road. Continue left on the loop road, passing the Lower Mount Cammerer trailhead, to reach a second Low Gap trail sign at **0.4** mile, which indicates it is 2.5 miles to the Appalachian Trail.

The trail ascends along a gated road through a nice stand of second growth tuliptrees which occupy old fields. Stone piles and stone work confirm farming activity here. The trail continues past water supply reservoirs on both sides of the road and at **0.6** miles crosses the Cosby horse trail which leads right 0.4 mile to the Snake Den Ridge Trail. Soon the trail reaches a turn-around and passes between two small boulders. A thick bed of partridgeberry grows just beyond the boulders. In winter the bright red berry of this plant brightens the drab winter woods. Also, a dense growth of hepatica grows in the same area. This plant can be identified by its three-lobed, somewhat leathery leaves. Hepatica is one of the earliest wildflowers to bloom, appearing in March and early April.

A footlog spans a small cascade of Cosby Creek at **0.8** mile. This visually pleasing stream is closed to fishing to protect the native brook trout which inhabit the upper reaches. This is a pleasant place to pause and enjoy the stream or even cool hot feet in the cold water during summer. A short distance above this crossing is a trail leading left 0.4 miles to the lower Mount Cammerer Trail. This offers a pleasant walk back to Cosby Campground for those not interested in climbing to the crest.

The trail ascends more steeply, generally paralleling Cosby Creek. At **1.2** miles the trail bears left on the first of several switchbacks and passes several large Eastern hemlocks and tuliptrees. It climbs through a forest of hemlock at **1.6** miles. At **1.8** miles a small boulder field lies left of the trail. Many such boulder or "block" fields in the park were created during the last Ice Age (lasting until 15,000-20,000 years ago) when extreme freezing and thawing crumbled rock faces. Geologists believe that during this period, the highest elevations of the Smokies were above timberline.

Throughout this segment the trail offers interesting and varied forest vistas. The upper slopes of Cosby were only selectively cut, and many very large trees can be seen.

A distinct change in forest type occurs at about **2.2** miles with a transition to closed oak forest. Oak trees predominate, with a thick understory of rhododendron in places. The closed oak forest also contains red maple, yellow birch, sourwood, hickory, tuliptree and black gum. The rhododendron is nature's thermometer. Its leaves curl in reaction to the cold—the tighter the curl, the colder the weather. With experience, hikers can approximate the temperature using rhododendron leaves as guides.

At **2.5** miles, after a steep climb, the small headwaters of Cosby Creek are crossed on rocks at the head of a pleasant cove. Beyond, the trail moderates and makes a steady side-hill climb to reach Low Gap at **2.9** miles. Ahead, the trail continues 2.5 miles to Walnut Bottom. Cosby Knob Shelter and the Camel Gap Trail are right 0.8 and 2.4 miles, respectively; and the Mount Cammerer Trail is 2.1 miles to the left.

Narrative by William A. Hart, Jr.

LOWER MT. CAMMERER TRAIL

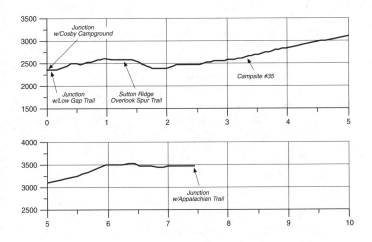

LENGTH: 7.4 miles, from Cosby Campground to the Appalachian Trail.

HIGHLIGHTS: View from Sutton Ridge, many creeks.

CAUTIONS: Rocks and crossings of small creeks on second half of trail.

MAP KEY: 10-11 B; USGS quad: Hartford.

USE: Horse and hiking trail.

TRAILHEAD: Enter the park at Cosby entrance on TN 32 and drive 2.0 miles to the camper registration building. Park in Hiker Parking. Enter the woods at the trail sign and turn right toward the campground.

Imagine a giant cupcake plopped upside down. To hike around it, you need to go in and out of all those hills and valleys of the cupcake paper. The Lower Mt. Cammerer Trail dips in and out of creek valleys as it swings half way around Mount Cammerer to connect the Cosby Campground with the Appalachian Trail near Davenport Gap. A

Civilian Conservation Corps crew worked on this trail, and you will appreciate their stone culverts, well-placed water bars, and foot bridges. These conveniences are found on the first half of the trail, until Campsite #35. After that, the trail is rougher and may be wet.

In 1925, Arno B. Cammerer, then associate director of the National Park Service, drew the boundaries of the proposed new park. Cammerer also enlisted the help of his good friend John D. Rockefeller, Jr. when the park commission needed more money for land purchase. The result was a $5 million trust fund that Cammerer administered while wrestling with the legalities of land purchase from Champion Fibre Company. Cammerer succeeded Horace Albright as director of the National Park Service. He really should have three or four mountains named after him.

From the parking lot, a pretty nature trail winds through an Eastern hemlock grove on the left. Beyond the amphitheater, look for another trail sign for Sutton Ridge, Campsite #35, and the A.T.

Follow the gated gravel road for about 0.2 mile to a wide area with picnic tables, toilet facilities, and a horse rail. The nature trail also spills out here. The Low Gap Trail goes right and also provides a connection to the Snake Den Ridge Trail. Lower Mount Cammerer, still a gravel road, goes straight and rises gently through a forest of small Eastern hemlocks, tuliptrees, maples, and flowering dogwoods. Look for a walled spring on the right with a dipping pool. Liverworts, looking like soggy green cornflakes, grow near the water line. The spring water flows through a matching stone culvert under the trail.

At mile 0.5, there is a former traffic circle. The trail goes to the right through thick rosebay rhododendron, deciduous woods, and groves of small Eastern hemlocks. After an easy creek crossing, the trail gets rockier and then forks, but it's just another old traffic turnaround. The left fork passes a double stone wall leading to the creek, perhaps an old bridge foundation. The forks rejoin and the trail crosses a branch of Toms Creek on a foot log.

You climb out of Toms Creek drainage, leaving house sites and roadbeds behind, and rise along a sandy, well-graded bench. Sutton Ridge, at mile 1.4, is the first Mount Cammerer ridge, and is dry and exposed. A steep spur trail leads 200 yards up to an overlook, and there is a horse trail at the bottom in case your horse would rather rest than see the view. Along the spur trail, arbutus, galax, mountain laurel, gentian, and greenbrier grow, and at the top, you will see maple, sassafras, chestnut oak, sourwood, and Fraser magnolia. To the left of the clearing there is a clump of American chestnut saplings; some of the larger ones may show signs of chestnut blight such as withered leaves, bark splits, or orange spots on the bark. From this ridge clearing you can see Foothills Parkway to the north, Cosby Valley, and Gabes Mountain to the west.

Scramble down the Sutton Ridge spur and continue right on a wide trail with rhododendron on the right and many striped maples on the left. Notice the pretty striped bark on the younger trees. Here is where you start the cupcake maneuver—out around the nose of a ridge and then back into a tiny creek draw. Some of these quiet little creeks probably sheltered moonshiners in the 1930s. P. Audley Whaley, one of the first park wardens, called Cosby the "moonshine capital of the state… They didn't have much way of feeding their family except that." The moonshiners hired a guard, he said, who would shoot a stick of dynamite for the whole valley to hear when he saw an IRS car coming up the only road from Cosby. Then all the residents would get into their cars and follow the agent. "There'd be so many cars…look like a funeral procession behind the law…following to see whose still he's gonna raid." Whaley himself didn't hassle the moonshiners; when he found a still, he just left them a note and asked them to move.

The next creek is Riding Fork; stop and look up the creek at the water rippling down hundreds of tiny mossy steps—as impressive as any Roman fountain. Stonecrop, or sedum, grows on the stonework at this creek. It blooms in April or May.

Out to another ridge nose, in to a creek, and so on. From one grassy open ridge, you can look across at Sutton Ridge. At mile **3.3**, you come to Campsite #35 (2,680' elevation), which you can see across the creek long before you can put your pack down and rest. Sites A, B, and C are level spots along the creek marked by logs and fire rocks and receive heavy use. Sites D and E, 50 yards farther along the trail, are grassy, secluded, and away from water; camping impact on these sites is low. Orange ribbons show the way, and there is a horse rail near Site D.

After #35, you plunge back into rosebay rhododendron and then hop across a rocky creek (no more culverts) lined with nettles and jewelweed. From the next ridge, you might get a glimpse of the Mount Cammerer fire tower if the trees are not full of leaves. The trail continues to undulate, but you will notice that it is rising also. Look for larger trees, chestnut stumps and logs, and views of the other side of the valley. After a serious climb of about half a mile, the trail levels. Here, at about 3,500' elevation, the creeks are much smaller, but you still have to cross them. The trail becomes rocky, narrow, and weedy near the creeks. Great rock slabs appear on the right. Look for a pair of big maples on the left as the trail enters a weedy creek draw—this is the last one. The trail rises gently to the junction with the Appalachian Trail. From here, it is 2.9 miles to Davenport Gap and 2.3 miles to Mount Cammerer Trail. You could return the way you came or increase the distance by less than a mile with a loop over Mount Cammerer and down the Low Gap Trail.

Narrative by Doris Gove

LUMBER RIDGE TRAIL

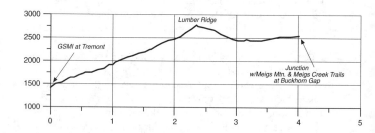

LENGTH: 4.0 miles, from Tremont Road to Meigs Mtn. and Meigs Creek trails.

HIGHLIGHTS: Hardwood forests, winter views of Tuckaleechee Cove.

MAP KEY: 4-5 D; USGS quad: Wear Cove.

USE: Horse and hiking trail.

TRAILHEAD: Turn off the Laurel Creek Road, just west of the Townsend "Y" (intersection of Little River, Laurel Creek and Townsend entrance roads) onto the Tremont Road. Travel the paved road for 2 miles and turn into the Great Smoky Mountains Institute at Tremont and park.

The Great Smoky Mountains Institute at Tremont is on the Tremont Road, 2 miles upstream from its intersection with the Laurel Creek Road. Now don't get this Tremont confused with the town of Tremont, because the town no longer exists. The town of Tremont was built by the Little River Lumber Company just 3 miles from the Institute. In fact, the Tremont Road you travel today was the route of the railroad which took loggers upriver and logs down. You can visit the former logging days and Tremont by picking up the logging tour brochure across the road from the Institute's entrance.

To hike Lumber Ridge, pull in and park at the Institute. According to the facility's director, the goal of this education center is to use the uniqueness of the Smokies' resources to bring people closer to nature. Bringing folks closer helps them to build a love and respect for the natural world which in turn helps us all to protect the environment. Stop in at the small visitor center here to find out more about their programs and to browse the book store.

Climb the gravel road the short distance to the two-story dormitory, for this is where the Lumber Ridge Trail begins. Although the trail is used by horses, it is in excellent shape for hiking. You will start by climbing fairly steeply along the western slope of Mill Ridge. Here you will pass large outcrops of Metcalf Phyllite, a metamorphosed shale. Between mile 0.25 and mile 0.5, rocky outcrops provide excellent views of the Middle Prong of the Little River and Walker Valley. The valley was once owned mostly by one man—William Marion Walker. "Big Will" came to this valley with his wife Nancy Caylor about the time of the Civil War. Together they cleared the land and built a productive farm in the valley. Nancy, and Will's two common-law wives—Mary Ann Moore and Mol Stinnett—also helped populate the valley by providing Will with over two dozen offspring.

Will Walker protected his valley from the big saws and skidders of the lumber companies all his life. Had he lived but a few years longer, the forests here might still be old growth, but as the name of this trail implies, the land was ultimately harvested. On December 30, 1919, Will died. Two years later Nancy died and the land passed to three of Walker's daughters by Mol Stinnett. They finally sold the forests to Colonel W.B. Townsend whose Little River Lumber Company harvested the land in the 1920s. Ironically, in 1927, Col. Townsend sold the land to the Tennessee Park Commission, but not the timber rights. So harvesting continued until 1938, making this valley the first purchased, but last protected.

The trail continues past more rock outcrops until at **0.5** mile the path turns right and leaves the tumbling noise of the Middle Prong behind. To your left now is the little valley cut by the Pigpen Branch. Its sounds are soft and muted. The remainder of the hike will reflect the Pigpen's quiet peace. Auto noise and helicopter passes are yet unheard here.

At mile **1.0**, and elsewhere on this trail, you will pass through a stand of pitch pines devastated by the Southern pine bark beetle. This insect bores through the bark to feed on the nutrient-rich inner bark. Find an old piece of bark on the ground and you will see the tunnels carved by these beetles. Outside the park, the infestation is seen as an economic disaster. Here it is just another natural cycle, since the beetles are native species which have co-existed with pines here for many thousands of years. Older trees removed by natural infestations give the next generation a place to grow.

You will continue climbing fairly steeply up the north side of Mill Ridge, weaving into and out of small spring branch valleys. The forest changes back and forth as you move from the sheltered areas to the exposed ridges. The cool, moist valleys harbor cove hardwood forests with plenty of spring wildflowers, while the warm, dry ridges are homes to pines, oaks, and berry bushes. Ecologists call the cool wet areas mesic zones, the dry ridges are referred to as xeric. These changing environments account for much of the diversity of life here in the Smokies. Wildflowers you may see on this section include crested dwarf iris, spring-beauty, and wood-sorrel.

Your climbing will end at mile **2.4** when you reach "the saddle." This is the low point between Lumber and Mill Ridges. It is a nice place for lunch here under the large oak trees. The trail now follows the edge of Lumber Ridge, still weaving between the mesic and xeric slopes.

At mile **2.75** there is a big stand of mountain laurel which is beautiful when it blooms in May and early June.

After a short descent from the saddle, the trail levels off. The final mile to Buckhorn Gap will give you plenty of opportunity to look up and around. The oaks and huckleberries which abound here make this a great place for squirrels and bears, birds and deer, so keep your eyes and ears open. The occasional stands of hemlocks also provide cover for Ruffed Grouse, a ground bird which explodes into flight if one gets too near. You may hear the "drumming" of the male grouse as he attempts to establish territory and attract a mate. He accomplishes this by rapidly beating his wings, which sounds almost like an engine starting up as he begins slowly then increases in speed steadily.

Although it might have seemed that the saddle was never going to come, the last mile and a half will quickly pass. The trail ends at Buckhorn Gap where it intersects the Meigs Mountain and Meigs Creek Trails. Meigs Mountain continues on to Elkmont (6.4 miles) and Meigs Creek drops 1,000' to The Sinks (3.5 miles) and Little River Road.

Narrative by Tom Condon

LYNN CAMP PRONG TRAIL

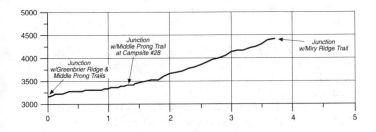

LENGTH: 3.7 miles, from Middle Prong Trail to Miry Ridge Trail.

HIGHLIGHTS: Mountain streams.
MAP KEY: 5 E; USGS quads: Thunderhead, Silers Bald.
USE: Horse and hiking trail.
STARTING POINT: At the end of the Tremont Road (closed in winter), follow the Middle Prong Trail to its terminus 4.1 miles ahead. The Middle Prong Trail ends at the intersection of Lynn Camp Prong Trail and Greenbrier Ridge Trail.

Named for a lumber camp operated by the Little River Lumber Company in the 1920s, Lynn Camp Prong Trail slowly climbs through a formerly logged watershed. "Lynn" is a nickname for the white basswood tree, which makes excellent lumber. The Little River Lumber Company, owned by Colonel W.B. Townsend, moved their operation from one watershed to another as the forests were depleted. From 1926 to 1929, the company removed more than 90 million board feet (enough to build 9,000 good-sized homes) from the forests of the Tremont valley.

As you drive and hike to the trailhead for Lynn Camp Prong, you will pass through one of the last and most heavily harvested areas. The drive along the Tremont Road will take you past Spruce Flats Branch, where the last tree was commercially harvested in the Smokies. This occurred in 1939, a few years after the valley was included in the national park. An auto tour guide for this road relates the history of logging in the Smokies.

The first two miles of Lynn Camp Prong are relatively easy, level and lined with Fraser magnolia, silverbell, tuliptree, sourwood, American beech, and black cherry. You can hear Lynn Camp Prong to the left, and there is one easy crossing of a side creek that flows down from Mellinger Death Ridge. Then you come to a large, flat clearing and can see the prong and Campsite #28. Its elevation is 3,490', and it holds 20 people and 20 horses. Though it gets fairly heavy use, the tent sites are spread over a wide area. Water is available from a creek.

Campsite #28, also known as Marks Cove, sits on an old railroad bed, which insures that the campsite is wide and flat, but not too attractive.

Pass through the first tent site and you will come upon Buckeye Cove Branch. This small tributary was once crossed by the logging railroad, as the level grade across the way proves. The bridge no longer exists, probably removed by the company when the trees ran out, but some more attractive campsites sit over there. You will have to rock-hop across if you wish to use them.

The trail continues by heading south into a stand of black birch and rhododendrons. After a long hike on a level, well-graded old railroad bed, the hazards of this trail become quite obvious. The footing here is no worse than many backcountry trails used by both horses and hikers, but you may not adjust to it quickly enough. Force yourself to pay attention to the rough footing so as not to twist an ankle or knee. The trail is also muddy in places.

Our trail begins to climb easily toward Miry Ridge. At **1.6** miles, you will cross the first of many small streams. This is Buckeye Cove Branch again and it is easily rock-hopped in all but the wettest weather. The small stream cascades down a valley strewn with boulders. It's very pretty, framed by hemlocks, rhododendrons, and a variety of hardwoods. Ahead, you leave all but the hardwoods behind. One of the park's many interesting trees can be found in the next stretch. The Fraser magnolia, with its yellow-orange knobby bark, likes these hillsides. There is plenty of moisture, but not too much heat here. Mixed in with all the other species, you will find a few of these wonderful trees.

Continue climbing at an easy pace to **1.8** miles where you can view Buckeye Cove Branch below. As you round the bend ahead and leave this small stream behind, look down to the right. At your feet are ferns and club mosses. In days gone by, club mosses were harvested on a commercial basis. These primitive plants reproduce with spores. In the 1800s, the spores were collected and sold to photographers, who used them as flash powder. As you move on, you will notice lots and lots of ferns, mosses, lichens, and wildflowers carpeting the forest floor. You will also hear the roar of Lynn Camp Prong below. You will never see the river, however. You pass well above its headwaters as you climb moderately to Miry Ridge.

Miry Ridge would be a good name to describe the next mile or so of trail. You will be continually crossing small spring branches and seeps from the hillside. The small streams are all very pretty, cascading down through boulder fields, and require only easy rock hops to cross. The seeps, however, can really turn the trail into a mess. Watch your footing through here, but keep your ears tuned to the woods, too. You might find yourself being scolded by a boomer. A boomer is what the mountain folks called a red squirrel. These little guys, who feed on the seeds of pines and hemlocks, can really make a racket when disturbed.

At about **2.8** miles, you will cross your last stream. It's a short rock hop over a shallow stream flowing down from a nice stand of hemlocks. The trail climbs around a corner and into a very nice stand of black cherry trees. If it is August, watch for bears above, they love the cherries. Biologists estimate the bears can put on as much as three pounds per day just by eating cherries in season.

The trail now climbs more moderately up the slope. It's drier now too, but occasionally a small seep will muddy your path through the young forest. The Little River Lumber Company may have harvested these trees with some devastating techniques, but given time, the forests will return. It is fortunate for all the animals and plants which live here that the soil was not completely lost. For trees may take tens of years to return, but soils take centuries. As the soil again gets damper, the hardwoods disappear and a small stand of hemlocks takes over. This marks the trail's end at the line of Miry Ridge. A right here will take you to the Appalachian Trail in just 2.5 miles. A left will take you down past Campsite #26 and on to Jakes Gap (2.4 miles). Campsite #26, like #28, sits smack in the middle of the trail less than 0.1 miles away. Water is not easily available here, so come prepared.

Narrative by Tom Condon

Maddron Bald Trail

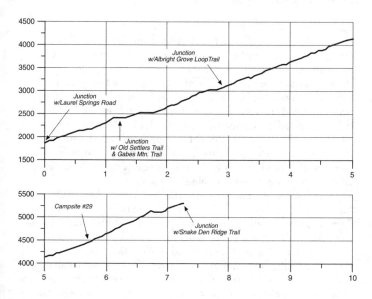

LENGTH: 7.2 miles, from Laurel Springs Road off Highway 321 to Snake Den Ridge Trail.

HIGHLIGHTS: Virgin forest, views from the bald.

CAUTIONS: Creek crossings, rocky trail on upper part.

MAP KEY: 9 B; USGS quads: Jones Cove, Mt. Guyot, Luftee Knob.

USE: Hiking trail.

TRAILHEAD: Drive US 321 15.4 miles from Gatlinburg or 2.9 miles from Cosby to Laurel Springs Road. Coming from Cosby, turn left after Yogi Bear Campground onto the Laurel Springs Road, pass some trout ponds on the left, and cross Indian Camp Creek on a minimal bridge. At mile 0.2, look for the park sign and gate on the right. There is only room for two or three cars, and they may not be safe; several vehicles have been stolen from here and recycled at a local chop shop. Safe parking (for a fee) may be available at nearby businesses on US 321. Do not park on private property without permission.

The first 3.0 miles of Maddron Bald Trail are along an old road and offer pleasant, easy walking with Buckeye Creek on your left. At first, the right side of the trail is dark with young Eastern hemlocks, so thick that there are no ground plants, but soon the forest opens up with small American beeches, maples, and tuliptrees. This area was heavily farmed and had large corn fields and apple orchards. In 1929, the Tennessee Park Commission paid landowner Marshall Justus $4,750 for 109 acres near Albright Grove. Justus had a barn, a five-room frame house, an apple house, 685 apple trees, a tenant house, two corn cribs, and a woodshed. This was one of the 6,600 separate land purchases necessary to establish the national park.

A Civilian Conservation Corps crew lived at the base of this trail from 1933-35 and built most of the trails and bridges in this area. Their culverts, waterbars, and trail engineering efforts make this trail a delight to hike; the trail to Albright Grove is dry and well graded.

The trail rises above the creek and at about 0.5 mile, it levels as it passes the Willis Baxter cabin on the right. This one room cabin, built in 1889, has a shake roof, two doors, and a healthy population of mud wasps. At the turn-of-the-century, Alex and Sara Baxter and their four sons lived in this cabin. They raised pigs, apples, corn, and sweet potatoes. All the original wood for this cabin was American chestnut, possibly all from one tree. American chestnuts with circumferences of 33' were recorded in this area before the blight.

The present cabin has been restored with some pine and tuliptree, but the walls, ceiling joists, and rafters are the original chestnut. Most cabins built at this time had at least one window, usually a small granny window beside the fireplace. From this window, the granny of the house could keep in touch with family members outside without leaving the warmth of the fire. But the Baxter cabin doesn't even have that and must have been pretty dark on cold winter days. However, as Horace Kephart wrote in *Our Southern Highlanders*, "no mountain cabin needs a window to ventilate it: there are cracks and catholes everywhere, …the doors are always open except at night."

Plants that probably came up this valley with the settlers are still here in front of the cabin: clover, heal-all, plantain, dandelion, and poison ivy. The poison ivy is native, but it couldn't venture into woodlands without the help of farming disturbances. Beyond the cabin is a large field of second growth tuliptrees mixed with a few maples and locusts. Arthur Stupka, park naturalist from 1935 to 1964, states that this kind of forest, with 80% tuliptree, usually marks the site of a former corn and potato field.

The trail crosses Cole Creek, which supplied the cabin with water, and then rises, entering Eastern hemlock and rosebay rhododendron forest again. Look for patches of Indian pipe, or ghostflower, in this area. This parasitic plant flowers in July, and the grayish stalks may be visible until October.

The trail rises again and levels at a wider place at mile **1.2**. Here Gabes Mountain Trail goes left and Old Settlers Trail goes right. Maddron Bald Trail continues straight through a row of three boulders that looks more like a roadblock than a natural geological formation. It becomes narrower and mossier and crosses several small creeks, but the CCC culverts will keep your feet dry. Open woods near these creeks encourage wildflower growth. Then the trail continues on a long level stretch with dense Eastern hemlock and rosebay rhododendron on the left and open deciduous woods on the right. After a sharp right switchback, you climb away from Maddron Creek drainage and toward Indian Camp Creek drainage.

The trail seems to fork, but it is just an old traffic turnaround. Either fork leads to the next Maddron Bald Trail sign. Before you step off the old road bed onto the forest trail, look around at the skinny trees, mostly tuliptrees with a few maples and small Eastern hemlocks. This is the end of the settlement road and the end of the cut-over look.

Now you proceed on a real trail, rising gently from the end of the road. There are a few roots and rocks, but it is still easy walking. Bigger trees, mostly Eastern hemlock at the beginning, appear, and the deeper woods muffle the creek sounds and your footsteps. A tree fall and a creek crossing have made a wild garden with foamflower, blue cohosh, violets, hepatica, Fraser's sedge, and clubmosses. Farther along there are American beech trees and beech drops (brownish many-branched six-to-ten-inch-tall flowering plants that are parasitic on beech roots), a big patch of Fraser's sedge, and several decaying nurse logs. When competition for land and light is fierce, saplings on nurse logs get a boost. And later, when the nurse log rots, successful saplings look as if they are standing up on their roots.

The trail climbs a small ridge and finally you can see Indian Camp Creek through the rosebay rhododendron. You descend to the creek with a view of a large creek island and then cross the creek on a good, bouncy foot log. After passing another big patch of Fraser's sedge, the trail rises sharply and then levels at the junction of Maddron Bald and Albright Grove Loop trails. Maddron Bald Trail goes left and ascends rather steeply through a forest of big Eastern hemlocks, maples, Fraser magnolias, and more wonderful nurse logs. At 0.3 mile from the junction, you pass the other end of Albright Grove Loop Trail, and then the trail looks less traveled.

This upper part of the Maddron Bald Trail makes you appreciate the excellent work of the CCC crews; culverts, bridges, and trail drainage systems are all behind you. In less than half a mile, you cross Indian Camp Creek and a few small side creeks on stepping stones. Indian Camp Creek cascades on your right; look for a big stump on the left with a rosebay rhododendron growing out the top. The trail uses the Indian Camp Creek valley to gain about 500' of altitude, but you have to cross it and its tributaries several times. Some of these crossings may be hazardous in wet weather. After the third crossing of Indian Camp Creek, the trail moves away and follows contour lines, rising some on each ridge. Elevation gain is steady, but not steep.

The trail crosses Copperhead Branch and then becomes rocky, narrow, and possibly wet. It rises to a drier area out at the end of a ridge. A small spur trail on the left gives a view of Maddron Bald and Greenbrier Pinnacle. After the spur, the trail rises through a jumble of boulders and then crosses Otter Creek at Campsite #29 at elevation 4,560'. This campsite has room for 10 people. The upper tent site is rocky, but two lower ones are smoother and reasonably level. Near the trail is a rope, pulley, and cable system to hang food bags out of the way of bears who are often seen here. The user's manual for this camp appliance has grown into the tree.

After Campsite #29, the trail is rocky, narrow, and wet as it crosses sheltered coves and dry where it noses out on ridges. But then it leaves the contour line and turns up through Eastern hemlock and rosebay rhododendron until it comes out onto Maddron Bald, with sand myrtle, mountain laurel, pines, and red spruces.

Maddron is a long, sloping heath bald, and the trail climbs up it. It levels in a large patch of sand myrtle where you can climb up some rocks to get a better view of Old Black, Inadu Knob, and everything else for 360 degrees. The trail then descends, enters a red spruce forest, crosses a few muddy patches, and then rises to the junction with Snake Den Ridge Trail. From here it is 0.7 mile up to the Appalachian Trail at Inadu Knob, and then, with an investment of only 1.9 miles more, you can reach the second highest peak of the Smokies, Mount Guyot (6,621' elevation). Maddron Bald Trail could be combined with Snake Den Ridge Trail if you can arrange a car shuttle to Cosby Campground. Add to that the Gabes Mountain Trail for a loop—a little long for a day hike, but a good two or three day backpack.

Narrative by Doris Gove

MARTINS GAP TRAIL

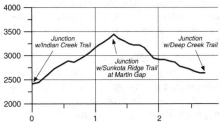

LENGTH: 2.7 miles, from Indian Creek Trail to Deep Creek Trail.

HIGHLIGHTS: Diverse vegetation.

MAP KEY: 7-8 E; USGS quad: Clingmans Dome.

USE: Horse and hiking trail.

STARTING POINT: From Deep Creek Campground, hike 0.7 miles on Deep Creek Trail to Indian Creek Trail. The Martins Gap Trail begins at the end of Indian Creek Trail after an additional 3.9 miles.

Martins Gap Trail handily connects 3 of the 5 major north-south trails in the Deep Creek area and consequently can help you plot loop hikes. The trail climbs over Sunkota Ridge connecting Indian Creek, Sunkota Ridge, and Deep Creek trails. From its trailhead at the end of Indian Creek Trail, Martins Gap Trail crosses Indian Creek twice by foot bridge. Climbing uphill through dense dog-hobble and rosebay rhododendron, you pass several moss-covered, decaying American chestnut logs. The trail continues steadily uphill, entering a mixed woodland of Eastern hemlock, American basswood, red maple, and striped maple; soon it rises approximately 40' above the creek which roars below. In season, the flute-like song of the Wood Thrush resounds through the dense woods. You cross Indian Creek by foot bridge, then climb among Eastern hemlock, dog-hobble, witch-hazel, and rosebay rhododendron.

Finally, the trail rises out of the creek valley toward Martins Gap; a streamlet crosses the trail. Coursing through a dry second-growth forest of scrub pine, Eastern hemlock, and mountain laurel, the trail crosses more streamlets and passes by rosebay rhododendron, galax, trailing arbutus, and, near Martins Gap, pink lady's slippers.

On Martins Gap, at **1.2** miles, the trail intersects Sunkota Ridge Trail then heads down the other side of the ridge in a moderately steep descent through Eastern hemlock, white pine, red maple, mountain laurel, sourwood, and scarlet oak. Yellow-fringed orchids and trailing arbutus flower along this dry section. The trail enters a grove of Eastern hemlock, then continues downhill through sourwood, white pine, and several species of oaks. By **2.0** miles, Deep Creek roars loudly below; a good view of the valley is possible at one point. Beside the trail, a number of tree trunks are covered with Yellow-bellied Sapsucker holes, and the orchid downy rattlesnake-plantain appears, its white-veined basal leaves distinctive.

After crossing a log bridge spanning a cascading streamlet, you descend via switch-back through white pine, chestnut oak, and American basswood. With a stream on the left, the trail approaches Deep Creek through large Eastern hemlocks, red maple, and, finally, American holly. At **2.7** miles, the trail reaches Deep Creek Trail junction and Campsite #57, also known as Bryson Place. This site was

Horace Kephart's last permanent camp. Kephart spent many years exploring the Great Smoky Mountains and wrote *Our Southern Highlanders*, a classic portrait of mountain people and their culture.

Narrative by Ted Olson

McKEE BRANCH TRAIL

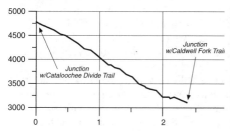

LENGTH: 2.3 miles, from Purchase Gap on Cataloochee Divide Trail to Caldwell Fork Trail.
HIGHLIGHTS: Rushing streams.
CAUTIONS: Mud.
MAP KEY: 11-12 D;
USGS quad: Dellwood.
USE: Horse and hiking trail.
STARTING POINT: From Cove Creek Gap, hike Cataloochee Divide Trail 4.6 miles, or from Polls (Pauls) Gap hike Hemphill Bald and Cataloochee Divide Trails 7.3 miles to Purchase Gap.

Although on older maps McKee Branch is called Long Branch, that appellation was not its first. A nineteenth-century lawyer, Allen Davidson, mourned the loss of its Cherokee name: "How much I wish I could remember the Cherokee name for Long Creek. There is another jewel of a name lost to the world because of the want of music in the soul of an ordinary landgrabber, as most of our early settlers were. 'Long' Creek was substituted for some Cherokee liquid to designate a regular necklace of a stream which sparkles in the sunlight or glooms in the shadows more perfectly than the rubies and diamonds of fashion." Somewhere along the way, the creek's name was changed from "Long Branch" to its current name; yet "McKee Branch" might be more accurately named "McGee Branch" for the

McGee family who lived and are buried nearby on Caldwell Fork, in Cataloochee Valley.

McKee Branch Trail was heavily used by mountain people traveling from their homes along Caldwell Fork to communities on the other side of Cataloochee Divide. Today it is used most often by horseback riders and fishermen from nearby resorts.

From its trailhead at Purchase Gap (on Cataloochee Divide Trail), McKee Branch Trail descends from the high Cataloochee Divide ridge through a dry, second-growth forest: Eastern hemlock, red maple, and Northern red oak, with an understory of rosebay rhododendron and mountain laurel. After crossing a few seeping springs, the trail weaves among patches of flame azalea, striped maple, and Juneberry.

Because the Cataloochee Valley is heavily used by horseback riders, the trail is muddy in places despite the placement of water-diversion logs to prevent erosion. Continuing steeply downhill, you enter a stand of Eastern hemlocks interspersed with American beech seedlings. A creek becomes audible to the left; soon you see it rushing downhill through a tangle of rosebay rhododendron.

After stepping across three spring-fed streamlets, you enter a rosebay rhododendron glade then descend via switchback through a second-growth hickory/oak/maple forest. A dry cove appears on the left, where American chestnut trunks litter the dry, open forest floor.

After crossing a small seepage, you enter lush woods, which feature tuliptree and Fraser magnolia; sundrops, hog peanut, and Christmas fern line the trail. After leveling briefly, the trail heads downhill again through an Eastern hemlock grove and a second-growth forest. On the right are downy rattlesnake-plantain and flowering dogwood; the latter suffers visibly from dogwood anthracnose. A creek emerges on the right, which you soon step over. Walking among white pines here, you may glimpse a red squirrel carrying a pine cone; the Smokies is just about as far south as this northern species lives.

Continuing less steeply downhill among Eastern hemlocks and mountain laurels, you pass a large clearing—the former homestead of Jim Sutton. A cabin, barn, and blacksmith shop all once stood here. Although he was the mail carrier for the nearby Little Cataloochee community, Sutton also kept bees and picked a banjo. Today, black walnuts and daisy fleabane grow in Sutton's field.

At **2.0** miles, after crossing a small rivulet, you hop across McKee Branch. The trail levels and continues through a second-growth forest of Eastern hemlock and red maple, with a witch hazel understory. The next clearing, where J.L. Sutton once built a house and barn, is returning to forest; several pioneer tree species—black walnut, red cedar, and black locust—are taking hold. After passing through young tuliptrees where John Caldwell's house, barn, and smoke house were once located, McKee Branch Trail reaches Caldwell Fork Trail at **2.3** miles.

Narrative by Ted Olson

MEIGS CREEK TRAIL

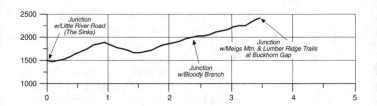

LENGTH: 3.5 miles, from The Sinks parking area on Little River Road to Meigs Mountain and Lumber Ridge trails.
HIGHLIGHTS: Pretty creek, wildflowers.
CAUTIONS: 18-20 creek crossings.
MAP KEY: 5 C; USGS quad: Wear Cove.
USE: Hiking trail.
TRAILHEAD: Drive to The Sinks parking area, 12 miles west of Sugarlands Visitor Center on Little River Road, or 6.0 miles east of the Townsend "Y" on the same road. The trail begins on the right of the parking area.

If you need rock-hopping practice, this is the trail for you. Meigs Creek Trail runs up the narrow, rocky valley of Meigs Creek, which flows into Little River just below The Sinks.

Mr. Return Jonathan Meigs was a revolutionary war hero, an early surveyor of these mountains, and a government agent working with the Cherokees. Return was his given name, given in honor of his father's successful persistence in courting his mother.

The Meigs Creek watershed was logged by the Little River Lumber Company, which built railroads up the creeks and extended their reach with steam-powered skidders. The road you drive on to get to The Sinks was once the company railroad. A branch railroad on Meigs Creek had a swinging inclined suspension bridge, said to be the only such bridge in the world. The steel cables under the ties held it up, and the engine pulled cars back and forth with a steam-powered winch. But by 1926, there were no trees left within reach, and the lumber company recycled cables, rails, and ties over to the Middle Prong of Little River (Tremont).

The trail begins by climbing the high rocks over The Sinks pool. After the rocks, the trail rises over a small ridge on rock and root steps and descends to a low swampy area, a former Little River channel. You will see native bamboo (cane) on the right, some friendly mosquitoes, and a paw-paw patch just beyond a muddy seep. Paw-paw leaves are nearly a foot long, tapered at both ends, and have a smell of burnt tires when rubbed. The larger bushes produce maroon flowers in April about as big around as a quarter. The famous fruits are edible in September, but usually the squirrels get them first.

The trail turns sharp right and ascends the side of a ridge. The mossy banks support maidenhair and Christmas ferns, dog-hobble, foamflower, jack-in-the-pulpit, plantain-leaved sedge, and violets. You are climbing the hip and shoulder of a ridge that extends west from Curry He Mountain, and in spots, you will see and hear the Little River on the right. As the trail switches back around the ridge, the soil becomes dry and sandy. Shortleaf pines, white pines, mountain laurels, huckleberries, oaks, and maples live here, and you have a soft needle carpet to walk on. As you walk, scan the sunny spots of the trail for timber rattlesnake throughout this section. This kind of dry south-facing ridge is an ideal habitat for timber rattlesnakes, and Adopt-a-Trail volunteers have reported seeing these snakes in this section. Rattlesnakes usually just rest in a sunny spot and watch the hikers go by.

The trail now descends first through pine and then Eastern hemlock, crosses a creek, and enters a rosebay rhododendron tunnel. At about 1.0 mile, you meet Meigs Creek and begin the first of 18-20 stream crossings, depending on how you count. The crossings are all easy in low water. Some are easy at moderate water levels, and all can be tricky if it has rained all week. You may wish to change into old sneakers or water sandals. Taking hiking boots off at every crossing will become tedious. A walking stick may help.

After the fourth crossing, the trail gets squeezed even closer to the creek by the rocky walls of the narrow valley. Look for a rock slab on the right with lampshade spider webs on the underside. The trail gets a little steeper and passes a beautiful cascade and pool on the right. Between the sixth and ninth (surely you're still counting) crossings, look for cardinal flower on the creek banks or on rocks in the creek. It blooms in August and September. Each plant has several 18" stalks lined with deep red blooms.

Logging must have been difficult on this creek, and soon you see bigger trees that have been spared. Massive Eastern hemlocks grow on both sides. On the left, in a rare flat area, look for a big American beech tree with buttress roots, smooth gray bark, and no branches lower than 25'. Bloody Branch joins Meigs Creek from the right near here. The name comes from a story about settler William Walker, who let his pigs forage wild in the woods. One year, he and his dogs went out to drive the pigs home. They found the herd of pigs here and slaughtered them on the spot; presumably it was easier to carry them out of this valley than to herd them home. It must have startled folks downstream.

The trail hugs the creek through a rock slab area; a rock overhang on the right might offer shelter from rain. At the fifteenth crossing, Meigs Creek is quite small and the trail moves higher in the valley. By now, you will feel as if you know Meigs Creek intimately—you have seen it as a trickle, a young stream, a teenager, and a mature creek. The few remaining crossings are of side creeks and a spring. After a short climb, the trail comes to Buckhorn Gap and the junction with Lumber Ridge and Meigs Mountain Trails.

Narrative by Doris Gove

MEIGS MOUNTAIN TRAIL

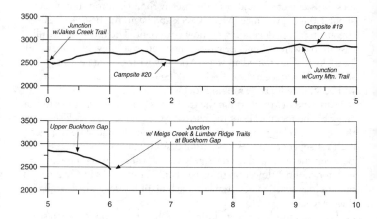

LENGTH: 6.0 miles, from Jakes Creek Trail to Meigs Creek Trail.
HIGHLIGHTS: Easy family walk.
CAUTIONS: Many stream crossings, but all easy.
MAP KEY: 5-6 D; USGS quads: Gatlinburg, Wear Cove.
USE: Horse and hiking trail.
STARTING POINT: Drive toward Elkmont Campground from Little River Road and follow the signs for Jakes Creek. On Jakes Creek Trail, hike past the junction with Cucumber Gap Trail at 0.3 mile and continue 0.1 mile further. Meigs Mountain Trail turns right.

The Meigs Mountain Trail connects Elkmont and Tremont. The side of Meigs Mountain has the distinction of being one of the first parts of the Smokies to be logged by a company. The J. L. English Company went up Blanket Creek before 1900 and removed 3,300 board feet of cherry and basswood. The later lumber companies cut everything they could and then sold the land to settlers in the 1920s. Seventeen families lived along Jakes Creek and many more lived here on the gently sloping side of Meigs Mountain.

The Meigs Mountain Trail starts by descending to Jakes Creek. You can rock hop across or find a camouflaged foot log downstream. The creek is lined with Eastern hemlock and rosebay rhododendron. The second hemlock downstream from the beginning of the foot log has many horizontal rows of Yellow-bellied Sapsucker holes. These small woodpeckers run a trapline. They make holes in favored trees, and, after the sweet sap attracts insects, the birds come back to harvest the bugs. Eastern hemlocks, tuliptrees, and Fraser magnolias seems to get a lot of attention from Sapsuckers, while oaks and beeches rarely do.

After the creek, the trail skirts a raised house site with a stone wall and a fine spring. It then forks; the left fork is Meigs Mountain Trail, and the right goes down to a grassy fenced area where horses are kept for park rangers' use.

The trail ascends from the creek through open woods of matchstick tuliptrees mixed with a few small maples. The settlers had just enough time to drag out rocks and establish their corn and potato fields here before they had to sell their land to the park commission. The Smokies was the first U.S. national park in which private land was purchased for inclusion; it was also the first park where eminent domain was used to force land sales.

Look for stone walls and a spring house foundation on the left and flat house sites on the right. Then the trail enters a sheltered cove, ascends to a dry gap covered with oaks and American beeches, and drops down to a creek valley. Campsite #20 (elevation 2,520') sits at the confluence of several small creeks that make up Kiver Branch of Blanket Creek. This campsite has room for 10 people and is in a broad, open hollow with plenty of flat tent sites. It was a garden and orchard.

After the campsite, you might get a glimpse of Meigs Mountain (4,004' elevation) on the left. It is named for Return Jonathan Meigs, who surveyed this area in 1802 to establish boundary lines for treaties with the Cherokee Indians. The trail here is a road that probably ran through fields and is now lined with sassafras and sourwood trees, which both turn scarlet early in fall. The settlers probably brought their beehives here in July, after the orchard trees stopped blooming, so the bees would collect sourwood nectar. Sourwood flowers grow at the tops of the trees and look like white bells hanging from twiggy up-turned fingers. If you find a sourwood flower stalk on the ground, smell it to see what attracts the bees. Sourwood honey has a distinctive taste, and beekeepers harvest that honey before the bees find nectar from other sources and dilute it.

The Meigs Mountain Trail crosses two more creeks easily, but the crossings could be muddy. Just up the trail from the second crossing are some rusted iron pieces of an engine, perhaps a tractor. A little farther along, look for a big chestnut stump on the left.

At mile **4.1**, the trail rises to a small gap and meets Curry Mountain Trail, which goes 3.3 miles down to Little River Road at Metcalf Bottoms. Buffalo-nut (oil-nut) bushes, with long, dark green leaves and greenish stems, grow around the trail sign. The larger bushes might have tiny yellow-green flowers in spring or an olive-sized green waxy nut later in the year. Settlers used the oil in the nuts to harden the tallow in candles. The oil from oil-nuts is poisonous, which may have been another reason it was useful in candles, making them less attractive to hungry house mice. Near this junction was the Henderson place, with two cabins, a barn, and a chicken house.

Just past the junction, a spur trail leads right to a small maintained cemetery. Most of the stones are unmarked; some headstones are for members of the Huskey family.

Campsite #19 (Upper Henderson) is a few hundred yards beyond the cemetery. In 1934, the house, barn, and smokehouse of Andy Brackin stood here. The campsite is small, with room for two or three tents in a clearing. Tangled grapevines line the trail.

About 1.0 mile from the junction, the trail enters a forest of large Eastern hemlocks and a few Fraser magnolias growing in clusters. Then you start a long descent through Eastern hemlock to a dry, sandy gap where Meigs Mountain Trail meets Meigs Creek Trail. Meigs Mountain Trail changes its name to Lumber Ridge Trail, which continues to Tremont (4.0 miles).

Narrative by Doris Gove

METCALF BOTTOMS TRAIL

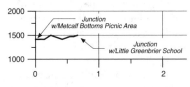

LENGTH: 0.6 mile, from Metcalf Bottoms Picnic Area to Little Greenbrier Schoolhouse.

HIGHLIGHTS: Little Greenbrier Schoolhouse.

MAP KEY: 5 C; USGS quad: Wear Cove.

USE: Hiking trail.

TRAILHEAD: Metcalf Bottoms Picnic Area. The picnic area is located between Elkmont and the Townsend "Y" on Little River Road. Park at the picnic area and cross Little River on the bridge. The trail begins at the barricade just across the bridge.

For many visitors to the park, the only way to reach the Little Greenbrier Schoolhouse is by turning off Wear Cove Gap Road and onto the park's access road. This twisty-turny, two-way, one-lane dirt road is truly an experience in itself. But on a busy summer's day, it is by no means the best way to visit the school. Most of the visitors who come this way will arrive at a small isolated log cabin out in the middle of nowhere. Hiking the Metcalf Bottoms Trail will give you a better understanding of this one-time school and church.

Today, many students see attending school as an albatross hung around their neck. Each day their parents load them onto a bus and send them off to have learning inflicted upon them. But 100 years ago, school was not something everyone could attend. Prior to the 1880s, schooling was not available to the children of this area. With the world changing so quickly, this left many people behind and in poverty. So the folks in this valley decided to act. They petitioned the Sevier County government for a school and a teacher. Proposals were made by each side and finally in 1882, an agreement was reached: the community would provide the schoolhouse and the county would provide the teacher for at least as long as the poll tax ($1.25 per student) would allow.

As you walk this short trail, try to imagine life at this time. The trail turns left and begins climbing away from the picnic area and river. As you reach the water tower, look to the left. Notice the stone wall. Behind the wall are signs of past lives in the valley. Yucca plants and an old pile of rocks, perhaps from a chimney, are all that remain to tell us of an old home. Did the children reared here attend the school we are traveling to? Did the entire family walk this way to church each Sunday? Chances are they did.

The trail will quickly reach the top of this small hill and turn right into a rhododendron tunnel. The children of the area might have walked this way. Richard Walker might have passed here early every morning—probably before sunrise. Richard lived up on Indian Camp Branch above Elkmont. He had to get to school early as it was his job to build the fire each morning. The school paid him a nickel for his trouble.

By now you will be walking along Little Brier Branch. The trail is flat from here on, but you will be crossing the creek, fortunately along a couple of foot logs with handrails. Did the students of the school have it this easy? George Melton remembers his hikes to school, "I've come here barefooted...frost on the ground...when our toes would be as red as turkey snouts when we got here." For many years school was only held when the frost was on the ground, when it was "too cold for the boys to be needed in the fields." Sometimes school was only held for two months each year. This is all the poll tax would pay. In 1900, there was no school at all. There were not enough children (i.e., poll taxes) to pay for a teacher, make needed repairs, and buy firewood. Only repairs were made that year.

Over the years to come, school would become a regular part of the community. The school year continued to increase until it resembled that of today's school year.

At **0.6** mile you will finally cross your last foot log and climb a small slope to the school.

Like many communities, the people of this area saw school as a way into the future. So together they built it, each family giving what they could. William Abbott donated the land, Ephriam Ogle the tuliptree logs for the walls, William Walker and his oxen were hired to do the hauling. Others helped too. John Walker, (father of the Walker Sisters) was one of 3 skilled cornermen—a great testament to his skill. And even Billie Ogle, an old man at the time, helped by splitting shingles for the roof. Back breaking labor and love built this school. It opened on January 1st, 1882, with Richard Perryman as the teacher.

A school was a community building much too valuable to leave unused, so the school also functioned as the community church until 1924 when a building exclusively for this purpose was placed nearby. Again it was a community project: the men built the frame structure, the women brought food to the "workin'" and the children hauled boards here and there during school recess.

The church is gone now—sold and moved in 1936. The school too is gone—for it is the students and teacher who make up a school. The cabin here looks much as it did when Herman G. Matthews dismissed his last class early in 1936. But memories remain. These are what this building is about. These are what you can't get along a dirt road with your air conditioner on high. These are what make the buildings of the Smokies so special. They are a place of memories: memories of good times and hard; memories of struggles for life and love for the land; but mostly, memories about what it meant to be part of a community working for the future.

Narrative by Tom Condon

MIDDLE PRONG TRAIL

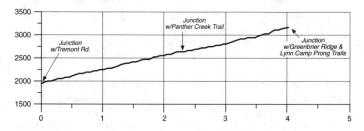

LENGTH: 4.1 miles, from the end of the Tremont Road to jct. Lynn Camp Prong and Greenbrier Ridge trails.

HIGHLIGHTS: Wildflowers, cascades.
MAP KEY: 5 D; USGS quad: Thunderhead Mountain.
USE: Horse and hiking trail.
TRAILHEAD: Follow the signs from the Townsend "Y" toward Cades Cove. In 0.2 mile, turn left onto the Tremont Road. At 2.3 miles, you will see the entrance to the Great Smoky Mountain Institute at Tremont, an environmental education camp, on your left. Continue on the main road, which quickly becomes a gravel road, and follow it for 3.1 miles to a gate and parking circle. The last three miles of this road are closed in winter.
NOTE: At press time, the Tremont road was closed at the Institute due to extensive flood damage.

Middle Prong Trail follows the railroad bed that carried the last logs out of the Smokies in 1939. Because of negotiations that made land purchase possible during the Depression, the Little River Lumber Company continued to log for five years after the establishment of the park in 1934. The company removed one billion board feet of lumber (enough for 10,000 homes) from this area between 1903 and 1930, and probably used almost as much for fuel and building. The top yielding tree species were tuliptree, American chestnut, and basswood.

So you will see signs of recent disturbance: road cuts, second-growth forest, cables, and bridges. However, you will also see how wonderfully this land is rebounding. For more information about logging history, pick up an auto tour booklet where the pavement ends on the Tremont Road.

The trail starts on a high bridge just below where Lynn Camp Prong and Thunderhead Prong join to form Middle Prong of Little River.

The flat area around the bridge used to be a lumber camp, with a company store where the currency was script or coins made by the company that could not be spent anywhere else. A hotel and post office also stood here. Temporary logging camps were transported to higher valleys by the logging trains. A family house fit on a flatcar and could be lifted off by a crane. The instant town made by a row of these boxes was called Stringtown.

The trail is a wide, graded roadbed with rock faces on the right and the Lynn Camp Prong down a bank to the left. Mosses and ferns grow from cracks in the rocks, and some trees perch on top with their roots snaking down. Toothworts, jack-in-the-pulpits, foamflowers, anemones, violets and other flowers bloom on the banks in spring. Rosebay rhododendron and dog-hobble hang over the rocks.

As the trail rises higher over the river, bigger rock faces appear, broken into great chunks with deep cracks. Trees, ferns, and flowers have anchored in the cracks. A small drainage ditch on the right provides a moist place for flowers. The prong and the road turn left together, and there is a bench to rest and look at a rock slide and pool. Tall jewelweed and wild ginger crowd a wet spot, and sycamores, tuliptrees, and yellow birches line the prong.

Above the curve, the whole prong is forced into a fast chute, and the middle of the prong is occupied by a smooth rock mound. Two overlooks on the left provide views of the top of that chute and of a strong, short waterfall just upstream. Above the falls, the prong is a jumble of rocks with water zig-zagging and tumbling through. Then the trail becomes level and the prong becomes less violent, with some clear, deep pools.

There is a bench near a three-step waterfall composed of three solid ledges across the prong. This is the remains of a splash dam. Before the railroad was built, loggers built dams on creeks to get the big timber out. As the creek valley filled with water, loggers cut and trimmed big trees and rolled them into the growing lake. When the lake surface was jammed with logs, they blew up the dam with dynamite and flushed the logs downstream to a sawmill, in this case, to Townsend. Sometimes they dammed side creeks also and timed the dynamite explosions to provide extra water.

The trail runs level with the prong for a while. Look for an old bridge foundation; you'll see a log on the far side and stone near the trail. Soon there is another bench in a dip. It is mossy and moist, with jack-in-the-pulpit, wild ginger, doll's eye, trillium, sweet cicely, woodsorrel, and other spring wildflowers. Goldenrod and asters bloom here in fall. The trail moves away from the prong after passing a housesized rock flanked by yellow birches. It ascends a bit and then levels out in a wide, flat area. At mile **2.0** look for a narrow trail to the right and follow it about 50 yards to an old car frame. It is rusty and missing just about everything, but it must have been elegant once. According to someone who worked at the Middle Prong Civilian Conservation Corps camp, this is an old Cadillac that belonged to the supervisor. One day it quit running, and camp members just pushed it off the road and left it.

Continue on the spur trail to get back on the Middle Prong Trail. Look for a Witness Post sign on a maple on the left. A piece of white quartz lies at the base of the tree, and on a mound of granite to the left, you can find the brass US Geological Survey benchmark. The elevation here is 2,515'.

Shortly after the benchmark, at mile **2.3**, Panther Creek Trail goes left and crosses Lynn Camp Prong. Middle Prong Trail goes straight, narrows a bit, and rises. On the left stands an old chimney, probably the remains of a cabin owned by William Walker, a farmer and patriarch who fathered 27 children. You can also see a foundation to a storage building built by Little River Lumber Company if you look for it. An open grassy area on the left may have been a parking lot when this trail was a road. After the grassy place, several sassafras trees grow on the left. One cluster stands in a circle with all the trunks curved out as if they are holding a giant beach ball. All these trunks are probably stump sprouts from the same root. Look for the rounded sassafras leaves in three shapes: standard leaf, mitten (try to find a right and a left) and three-lobed (or a glove for a three-fingered person). Usually, small sassafras saplings have the most variety, while the big trees produce mostly standard leaves.

The Middle Prong CCC Camp was near here. A crew of 172 men built trails, bridges, and roads between 1933 and 1937.

The trail becomes rocky and a little steeper as it swings up around a switchback. Small Eastern hemlocks, a few black locusts, and one white ash grow in the angle. In a few yards, there is another switch-back and a good example of the erosion damage hikers can do when they make a shortcut across switchbacks. The trail is now quite high over the river, and both Fraser and umbrella magnolias grow here. Then it rises into drier woods with oaks and hickories. Soon you cross a side creek and drop down to cross Indian Flats Prong on a fine flatbed bridge. Look for old bridge timbers on the right. After the bridge, there are some muddy spots, but the trail turns away from the creek and climbs steeply through grapevine and Dutchman's pipe vine. You turn around three switchbacks in quick succession. The long extensions on these switchbacks allowed the lumber trains to switch direction—if the engine was pushing, it pushed the whole train out the extension and then switched to pulling. On the smooth, gray rock faces on the left of this section, look for dynamite bore holes.

At a junction of three trails, the sign points right for Sams Gap via Greenbrier Ridge Trail (4.2 miles) and Derrick Knob Shelter (4.4 miles). To the left is Marks Cove Campsite (# 28, 1.3 miles), the Miry Ridge Trail (via the Lynn Camp Prong Trail, 3.7 miles) and Buckeye Gap along the Appalachian Trail (6.2 miles).

Narrative by Doris Gove

MINGUS CREEK TRAIL

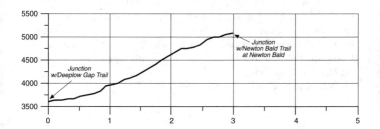

LENGTH: 3.0 miles, from Deeplow Gap Trail to Newton Bald Trail.
HIGHLIGHTS: Pine-oak forest.
MAP KEY: 8 E; USGS quad: Smokemont.
USE: Horse and hiking trail.
STARTING POINT: At the end of Deeplow Gap Trail, 2.4 miles from its jct. with Cooper Creek Trail or 6.0 miles from Deeplow's jct. with Indian Creek Trail.

This trail begins at a somewhat confusing intersection. An unmaintained trail runs 2.8 miles down to Mingus Mill and the Newfound Gap Road. Use is not encouraged because the stream which the trail follows is the water supply for the Oconaluftee area. Another unmaintained trail once led 0.5 mile to Adams Creek Road.

Our trail weaves from side to side of the ridge, dipping occasionally just below its crest. Pine and oak predominate the ridge's crest with mountain laurel underneath. The latter shrub blooms from early May through June. It's a steady climb along the ridge until six switchbacks zig-zag up a steep part. Fortunately, after the switchbacks, the trail moderates.

One-half mile beyond the switchbacks and through a rhododendron tunnel, a live American chestnut stands on the right, having survived a blight that killed most of the species. The 30' tall, 6" diameter tree is 6-8' off of the trail. Although it bears fruit, which is quite rare today, the seeds are probably not fertile since American chestnut requires cross pollination from other trees.

Newton Bald (5,080') is reached at mile **3.0**. Because this bald has been reclaimed by American beech, oak, and other hardwoods, no spectacular vistas are possible. Newton Bald Trail runs east 4.7 miles to the Newfound Gap Road at Smokemont and 0.5 mile west to Campsite #52. Thomas Divide Trail is 0.7 mile west of Newton Bald on Newton Bald Trail.

Narrative by Charles Maynard and David Morris

Miry Ridge Trail

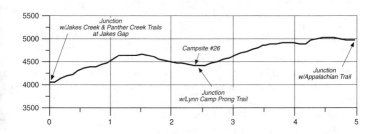

LENGTH: 4.9 miles, from Jakes Gap to the Appalachian Trail near Buckeye Gap.

HIGHLIGHTS: Views, windy ridge top.

MAP KEY: 5-6 D; USGS quad: Silers Bald.

USE: Horse and hiking trail to jct. Lynn Camp Prong Trail; hiking trail only from there to the Appalachian Trail.

STARTING POINT: The trail starts at Jakes Gap, which is a 4.5 mile hike from the Middle Prong trailhead on Tremont Road, or a 3.3 mile hike from the Jakes Creek trailhead near Elkmont.

The Miry Ridge Trail is an easy hike up the ridge that separates the drainages of the main Little River and the Middle Prong of Little River. When a Civilian Conservation Corps crew built the trail in 1935, they had to remove or crush huge boulders and build retaining walls.

From Jakes Gap, turn south (left from the Jakes Creek Trail) and start up an open slope with cherry, basswood, silverbell, and maple trees. The trail enters a grove of young Eastern hemlocks with ferns and clubmosses growing among rock slabs. It becomes wet and rocky, and you may get a few quick views of the Lynn Camp Prong valley and Blanket Mountain to the right. The trail switches back around the end of Dripping Spring Mountain and becomes drier, with laurel, galax, small American chestnuts, wintergreen, and trailing arbutus growing on both sides. This switchback shows the difference between north-facing (moist and dark) and south-facing (dry and open) exposed slopes. In the Smokies, vegetation and microclimate are affected by slope exposure and the presence of deep sheltered coves; ecological studies are wonderfully complex here.

Dripping Springs Mountain is named for a series of slatey ledges on the other side (not chosen by the CCC as a trail route) that drip and ooze constantly. Harvey Broome, a Knoxville lawyer, was 15 in 1917, and was, in his own words, "undersized and weakly." His father and uncle decided that a hike in the Smokies was just the thing for the sickly boy. They took the train to Elkmont (two hours and fifteen minutes, via Townsend) and hired a guide to lead them up Dripping Spring to Silers Bald, 12 miles with no trail and a 3,500' elevation gain. Broome later described Dripping Spring as "slippery and inhumanly steep." However, he gained weight on the trip and went on to be an ardent Smokies hiker, a park advocate, and an organizer of the Wilderness Society.

After moving through a mountain laurel tunnel mixed with sourwoods and oaks and a solid rosebay rhododendron tunnel, the trail levels at an overlook where a spur trail leads left to give you a view to the right. You can stand on a rocky knob (elevation 4,801', the highest point of Dripping Spring Mountain) and look across the valley of Lynn Camp Prong to Mellinger Death Ridge, straight out, and to Cold Spring Knob on the Smokies crest, just over 5,000' elevation. In the winter you can see Lynn Camp Prong Trail in the valley. A shorter view to the rocks around your feet will reveal ground pine, a kind of clubmoss.

After the overlook, the trail descends into another rosebay rhododendron tunnel and then a dark Eastern hemlock forest. Look for chestnut stumps and logs. Indian cucumber, a summer flower, grows along this part of the trail. Look for a whorl of leaves around a 6-10" stem. Young stems have a single whorl, but those old enough to take on the responsibility of blooming and pollinating have a second, smaller whorl above the first. Sometimes these upper leaves are streaked with red. The roots really do taste like cucumber.

The trail continues down through Eastern hemlock to an open gap with a meadow of grass and flowers. Yellow buckeye, American beech, black cherry, and big maple trees surround the meadow, and there is a deep Eastern hemlock grove on the right. It looks like a good place to camp, but a Park Service sign reminds you that this is not a designated campsite. It wouldn't be as pretty with fire rings and bare, hard soil. The trail heads right into the Eastern hemlock, goes around a knob, and joins the narrow top of Miry Ridge. Campsite #26, the legal one, appears at mile **2.3**, or about 0.3 a mile beyond that open gap. This site is right on the ridge top with lots of big cherry logs to sit on. It can be windy, and the tent sites slope. Bring a rope to tie things down and don't sleepwalk.

In 0.1 mile from #26, Miry Ridge Trail meets Lynn Camp Prong Trail, which comes up from the Middle Prong Valley. If you are staying at Campsite #26, the Middle Prong is your water source, so you may follow this trail 0.5 mile or so to the creek. From here to the Appalachian Trail, you are hiking on or near the breezy ridge top. Look for bluets, spring-beauty, beech drops, and dodder in spring. About 0.5 mile beyond the junction, look for the Ben Parton Lookout on the left, where you can get a view of Clingmans Dome. Ben Parton worked for Little River Lumber Company and built a platform here to watch for fires or trespassers.

Soon you start to see high elevation plants along the open trail: mountain-ash, viburnum, and red spruce. Blackberries ripen in late summer. Gentian blooms here in fall. The beetles that pollinate this deep blue flower pry it open to get at the pollen; this is probably a good adaptation for living in windy places. The yellow birches, maples, and cherries that live here are gnarled and covered with lichens. Look for a large yellow birch on the left with a rosebay rhododendron growing 20' up in a crotch. A wide part of the ridge top is popular with the non-native wild hogs, whose rooting causes erosion, water pollution, and habitat destruction. If a place beside the trail looks as if it has been rototilled, the hogs have been there. In wet weather, some of those spots become miry, that is, filled with black, sticky mud because the ridge bedrock forms a basin with no drainage. This mire hampered loggers and settlers who gave the ridge its name, but you can find similar boot-snatching mires on many ridge tops.

The trail slides left of the ridge top through a typical American beech gap. Beech gaps form on ridge tops like this apparently because beech trees are able to withstand wind damage better than other trees at this elevation. The billowy grass here looks as if it has just been washed and blow-dried, and it probably has. To the left, you can see up to Buckeye Gap. The trail rises steadily and crosses a rocky, dripping outcrop with ferns, moss, and a thicket of dog-hobble. From here, the trail is steep and rocky, sliding off the steep side of the ridge, but soon it hooks into the Appalachian Trail. To the left is Silers Bald (2.9 miles); to the right is Derrick Knob (1.8 miles).

Narrative by Doris Gove

MOUNT CAMMERER TRAIL

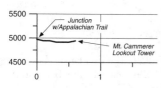

LENGTH: 0.6 mile, from the Appalachian Trail to the summit of Mt. Cammerer.

HIGHLIGHTS: Unobstructed views from the summit, historic fire-tower.

CAUTIONS: Partly exposed cliffs, eroded trail.

MAP KEY: 10 B; USGS quad: Hartford.

USE: Horse and hiking trail to 0.4 mile; hiking trail only for last 0.2 mile.

STARTING POINT: Hike 5.2 miles from Davenport Gap or 2.1 miles from Low Gap.

For the Appalachian Trail hiker, a side trip to Cammerer is essential. The trail mostly passes through mountain laurel with many fine views. At 0.4 the trail switches through some rocks (tricky footing due to erosion) and arrives at a hitch rack. Horseback riders must leave their horses here. An impressive sandstone outcrop shelters the hitching area. Climb through the rocks and enter a grove of tall rose-bay rhododendron with the lookout tower in sight. The trail is a quagmire of strong-smelling humus and bare roots. A series of tilted rocks then protrudes through the vegetation. In fair weather, scramble up the rock—the view is immediate and expansive.

Clear days reveal the Tennessee Valley, including the low, narrow ridges that trend up the valley. These include Webb Mountain in the foreground (just left of Newport), the Bays Mountains (further north, in the distance) and Clinch Mountain (further still, but a little west). Beyond, is the rim of the Cumberland Escarpment, about 60 miles away. The ridges follow the trace of ancient thrust faults, where older strata slid over younger rocks. The characteristic long ridges and intervening valleys give the topography its name of Valley and Ridge. This geographic province stretches from northern Alabama to Pennsylvania and is a characteristic of the southern and central Appalachians.

The mountain immediately to the north is Stone Mountain in Tennessee (note the gleaming white quartzite on some slopes). To the east is Snowbird Mountain (elevation 4,263'), across the Pigeon River gorge. It is distinguished by the white aviation tower on its summit. Just right of Snowbird is the grassy dome of Max Patch, the sharp, cleared top of Naked Place, then (turning east) Mary's Knob, which is bald on one side. These peaks are almost 5,000' in elevation. Beyond, are the Unakas to the northeast and the Blue Ridge east of them. The orange fire tower on Mount Sterling is prominent to the south, as are Balsam Mountain and Mt. Guyot. In all, it is a 360° view worthy of contemplation, and a good topographic map.

Mt. Cammerer's precipitous slopes allow the viewer to see into the heart of the mountain and gain an understanding of the makeup and origin of the Smokies. Erosion has highlighted the rocky prominence of Cammerer. The peak is surrounded by the Greenbrier Thrust Fault. Here, the hard sandstone once slid along the fault. The faulted rock later was squeezed and bent under further tectonic stress. Rock on Mt. Cammerer was pinched in the center of the fold, and squeezed even more.

Viewed from Interstate 40 at the Waterville Exit, the mountain top is seen edge-on. The pinnacle of rock, once called Sharp Top or White Rock, points westward into Tennessee and reflects the tilt of the rock in the core of the synclinal fold. The first survey of the state line in 1799, started in Virginia and ended here, at a "high pinnacle of the Smokey mn." The steepness of this landmark probably did little to warm the spirits of the survey crew and they quit. The Tennessee-North Carolina boundary to the south remained a rough estimate for over 20 years.

Arno Cammerer was Director of the National Park Service around the time the Smokies became a national park. A likable and trusting man, Cammerer was diligent in generating federal support and private funding to add the Smokies to the system of national parks. Unfortunately, he was too amiable and unskilled at political posturing. Cammerer was badgered into submission and ridiculed by then Secretary of the Interior Harold Ickes. Ickes took pleasure in badgering his subordinates and particularly disliked Cammerer. In *Strangers in High Places*, Michael Frome states that Ickes moved to oust Cammerer as Director for no apparent reason, other than the need for "new blood and a strong man." Suffering from repeated public embarrassment, Cammerer resigned after a sudden heart attack, and died in 1941. To honor his devotion to the Smokies, the Park Service named the mountain for him in 1943.

The historic stone fire tower adds a medieval quality to this already engaging scene. The Civilian Conservation Corps constructed the tower in the late 1930s, soon after completion of the trail. Built according to the "Yosemite model" of fire towers common in western states, the CCC used native timber and stone. Not used since the 1960s, the tower has seen better days. It once housed living quarters, and a catwalk ringed the outside. Local organizations and the Appalachian Trail Conference are soliciting funds to restore the structure.

Narrative by James Wedekind

MOUNT LE CONTE TRAILS

Five trails lead up the slopes of Mt. Le Conte: Alum Cave, Bull Head, Rainbow Falls, The Boulevard, and Trillium Gap. This section serves as an introduction to all five.

Call it charisma. Or mystique or magnetism. Whatever you call it, Mt. Le Conte has it in abundance, enough to lure thousands of hikers each year up its rocky trails to its lofty summit.

Nobody knows the who or the when of the first person ever to look east from Le Conte's Myrtle Point to watch the sun rise out of the mists and mountains, or who was first to see a sunset from Cliff Top. Hunters probably were first to go to Le Conte. But people began climbing the mountain early in the twentieth century simply for the challenge and beauty it offered.

In a 1963 essay, John O. Morrell, a Great Smoky Mountains National Park management assistant, wrote of his first hike to Le Conte in August 1913. The way he and his father and another Knoxville father-son pair did it, it took seven days to reach the top of Le Conte.

They spent the first six days riding a train to the mountains, finding a guide, setting up camp and taking three daily conditioning hikes. Finally, on day 7, they headed up Bearpen Hollow to the top of Le Conte. Nearing the top, they missed the "faint trail," which would have taken them to Cliff Top; they reached West Point instead. They saw the "faint trail" on their return down the mountain. It's significant that there was a "faint trail" in 1913.

In a 1964 letter, Paul Fink of Jonesborough recalled a week he and two friends spent atop Le Conte in June 1921. He said there "was not much sign of previous visitors at all. The rudimentary trail out to Myrtle Point was so obscure that we spent part of our time chopping it out."

By late 1921, enough hikers were going to Le Conte to give some unidentified person the idea of nailing a Prince Albert tobacco can to a post; hikers were invited to leave their names on a piece of paper in the can. C. L. Baum of Knoxville attached a copper can to a Le Conte tree in 1922, and in it he left a book for names to be recorded. He wrote:
"This book was placed on top of Le Conte Mountain for records on June 6, 1922, by C. L. Baum, at this time said to be the oldest man to climb to the top. Age 61."

Hugh Davis of Knoxville later put another copper can on Le Conte for the same purpose.

In the middle 1940s, when Jack and Pauline Huff were operating Le Conte Lodge, their son Philip found the so-called Walker Stone. On this hard blue piece of slate, unearthed during some excavation work around the Basin Spring, were carved the names of J. N. Walker, L. L. Houser, and T. F. Walker. Also scratched onto the stone were likenesses of a hunter, a deer, and a hunting dog. And there was a date, July 27, 1880. Much later, in 1962, Mel Walker of East Tennessee and Florida told The Knoxville News-Sentinel that it was his father, Thomas Walker, who carved the hunter, dog, and deer on the stone. He thought Houser had carved the names. Mel Walker said he went to Le Conte with his father in 1925 to search for the stone, but they didn't find it. He said his father told him that he and his brother, John Walker, each killed a deer on that trip.

Houser and the Walkers probably were not the first hunters on Le Conte; they were just the first to leave a record of it.

Surely those two scientists, Profs. Samuel B. Buckley and Arnold Guyot, climbed Le Conte when they were surveying and giving names to the southern mountains in the late 1850s. It was Buckley's idea to give his friend Joseph Le Conte's name to the mountain. But the name must not have stuck at first, for Morrell said it was known locally as "the Big Balsam" when he climbed it in 1913. It is generally believed that Joseph Le Conte never climbed Mt. Le Conte.

But these scientists probably were not the first people on Le Conte. Curious, adventuresome settlers were living down in the lowlands within sight of Le Conte's peaks. But the closest people, starting in the late 1830s, were the employees of the Epsom Salts Manufacturing Company who were mining Epsom salts at Alum Cave Bluff. These men were only two or three miles from the top of Le Conte. Wouldn't some of them have found time to go to the top on a sunny Sunday?

But wouldn't some Cherokee, living along the Little Tennessee River or its tributaries, have reached the top even earlier?

Le Conte stands about four miles north of the main ridge of the Great Smokies. Narrow-crested Boulevard ridge joins the two. It is as if the Maker of Mountains first created the main mountains and then decided to add a delightful annex.

The east-west crest of Le Conte runs about 1.3 miles between Myrtle Point on the east end and West Point on the west. Its north-south width probably is no more than a half-mile at the widest point. It has four high peaks. West Point is 6,344' above sea level. Myrtle Point is about 6,440', Cliff Top 6,555', and High Top is the highest at 6,593'. But High Top is not impressive. It is a small forested dome, not much unlike the two Great Smokies higher mountains, Clingmans Dome and Mt. Guyot. West Point is a little-visited wooded knob. The geographic features for which Le Conte is famous are the great stone cliffs of Myrtle Point and Cliff Top. On clear days they offer views of miles of mountains. Myrtle Point was named for sand myrtle, the low-growing evergreen heath plant that grows in the company of catawba rhododendron at Myrtle Point and also at Cliff Top.

The Great Smoky Mountains Conservation Association in the 1920s was plugging for a national park to be established in the Great Smokies. Interior Secretary Hubert Work had appointed a committee to recommend which of several suggested places in the southern Appalachians would be best for such a park. When two members of that committee came to look at the Great Smokies in August 1924, it was to Mt. Le Conte that Great Smokies boosters took them.

Paul Adams was one of those in the group that headed up the trail along Le Conte Creek to Rainbow Falls and then the mountain top. Years later, in his book, *Mt. Le Conte*, Adams said, "The 'trail' went up a leaning tree near the bluff, about 100 feet west of the (Rainbow) falls." He said that helpers at the base of the tree "helped some of the less agile guests to reach the first tree branches." Above Rainbow Falls, the trail then continued right up the creek until it dwindled to a trickle near the mountain top.

The visitors stood on Myrtle Point and saw the sunrise the next morning. "We were small spectators, awe-struck by the vast, primitive beauty of an extra-special Myrtle Point sunrise," Adams wrote.

Later that day, the group went down the mountain by way of Alum Cave Bluff. A path from Le Conte to the bluff had been hacked out only a few days earlier, but the trail from the bluff on down the mountain was many years old.

The following year, Adams, then an employee of the conservation association, established a camp on top of Le Conte, just a few yards west of the Basin Spring. In all the years since, that spring has never gone dry. The camp was for important conservation association guests and for any wandering hikers willing to pay for food and a place to sleep in a tent. Adams spent that winter on the mountain and built a small log cabin.

The next year, 1926, Jack Huff took over from Adams and started Le Conte Lodge, which has been there ever since. Jack and Pauline Huff were married at sunrise on Myrtle Point April 29, 1934. Pauline said recently that the wedding party started up the Bearpen Hollow route at 10 p.m. the night before.

The Huffs operated the lodge through 1959. Herrick and Myrtle Brown took it over in 1960. The lodge is now operated as a National Park Service concession by Le Conte Lodge Ltd. Partnership.

Le Conte's crest has become such a popular hiking destination that it's nearly impossible to get a weekend reservation at the lodge unless you start trying the year before. It's not much easier to get a weekday reservation. Oct. 1 is the date the lodge starts accepting reservations for the following year. The number to call is 615-429-5704. Good luck.

If you aren't able to get a lodge reservation, you can try through the National Park Service for a reservation in the 12-person shelter that stands in a clearing between the lodge and High Top. The number to call for that is (615) 436-1231. Failing in that effort, you can always hike up and down the mountain the same day. Many do that. In fact, 31-year-old Bill Sharp of Andersonville, Tennessee, on a June day in 1992 made four round trips to Le Conte in one day. He did it by way of the Alum Cave Trail. He figured that he walked 41.6 miles up and down the mountain.

Sharp's friend Paul Dinwiddie of Knoxville had made 744 hikes to Le Conte by late July 1993. That's probably the record for recreational hikes to the popular peak. But Dinwiddie says some of those who worked at the lodge — Jack Huff and Herrick Brown, for instance — probably made more trips.

And C. L. Baum, who in 1922, at age 61, thought he was the oldest person to hike to Le Conte, has lost that distinction to thousands of older hikers. Rufus Morgan, the late long-walking Episcopal minister from Franklin, North Carolina, made his 174th and last hike to Le Conte on his 93rd birthday. Margaret Stevenson of Maryville, Tennessee, who has hiked every trail in the Great Smokies and had recorded 607 Le Conte hikes by early August 1993, is 81 and still going strong.

—*Carson Brewer*

MOUNT STERLING RIDGE TRAIL

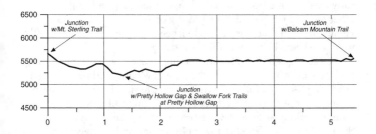

LENGTH: 5.4 miles, from Mt. Sterling Trail to Balsam Mtn. Trail.
Elevation Change: 351 Feet
HIGHLIGHTS: Spruce-fir forest scenes, pleasant high country walk-
ing.
MAP KEY: 11-10 C; USGS quad: Luftee Knob.
USE: Horse and hiking trail.
STARTING POINT: Mount Sterling Trail, 2.3 miles from NC 284.

The Mount Sterling Ridge Trail offers a pleasant walk along Mount
Sterling Ridge, which extends from Balsam Mountain to Big Creek.
From its beginning, the trail descends almost 500' to Pretty Hollow
Gap and regains 351' before ending at the Balsam Mountain Trail.
The last three miles of the trail are almost level, offering what is prob-
ably the longest relatively level high-country trail segment in the
Smokies! The trail is regularly used by horse parties and has extensive
muddy areas. Despite the trail's moderate grade, the hiker will experi-
ence significant elevation gain to reach either end.

Early settlers in Big Creek and Cataloochee ranged their livestock
on Mount Sterling Ridge and on "Far Old Indian Field" and "Near
Old Indian Field", grassy areas on Mount Sterling. These were locally
called the "Nigh Field" and "Fur Field." During the months the herds
roamed the mountains, the herders would visit to check on them and
to provide salt in natural depressions or hewed logs called "lick logs."
Also, hunters regularly pursued the black bear whose haunts were the

ridges above Cataloochee and Big Creek. In earlier times both wolves and mountain lions were common to Big Creek and Cataloochee, but early residents methodically killed these animals by hunting and other means to stop them from preying on livestock. Turkey George Palmer, whose home was in Cataloochee, used poisoned meat to kill wolves to keep them from killing his sheep.

Before beginning the Mount Sterling Ridge Trail, you may wish to make a worthwhile side trip to the crest of Mount Sterling. This can be accomplished by following the Mount Sterling Trail, which bears sharply right at the trailhead, for 0.5 mile. This trail leads past the Mount Sterling backcountry campsite (#38)and ends at the Mount Sterling fire tower. The fire tower offers commanding views of the main crest of the Smokies, Balsam Mountain, Mount Guyot and the surrounding mountains. These views should not be missed.

Our trail begins in spruce-fir forest made up of Fraser fir and red spruce interspersed with yellow birch, oak and American beech trees. It descends moderately along a sometimes rocky trail for the first 0.5 mile. At **0.7** mile the trail climbs gently, crossing a knoll at **0.9**, and then descends into Pretty Hollow Gap and a small, inviting grassy clearing at **1.4** miles. The Swallow Fork Trail bears right in the gap and leads 4.0 miles to Walnut Bottom on Big Creek. The Pretty Hollow Gap Trail bears left and leads 5.3 miles to Cataloochee Valley.

Our trail climbs out of Pretty Hollow Gap for 0.2 mile and then undulates for 0.4 mile along the broad shoulder of Mount Sterling Ridge in a nice stand of yellow birch. The trail is extremely muddy through this area, forcing the hiker to detour to the trail margin, or into the woods for solid footing. Lush grass grows beneath the trees creating a pleasant prospect. In winter, when the forest is cloaked in snow, this area and the trail beyond is exceptionally beautiful.

At **2.0** miles the trail ascends again, climbing to the left of the ridge and at **2.5** miles it reaches an elevation of 5,540'. From this point, the trail generally follows the contour to its end with little variance.

The remainder of the trail is especially pleasant to walk as it passes around Big Butt and the slopes of Big Cataloochee Mountain. Fraser fir, yellow birch, hobblebush and American beech trees contribute to a rich forest panorama. Winter views of Pretty Hollow Gap, Balsam

High Top, Shanty Mountain, and the Balsams are available at a number of places. Also, the trail crosses the headwaters of a number of streams. In spring and summer, these "beauty spots" are lush with a variety of wildflowers. Finally, the trail itself offers a continuous change, ranging from sunlit stretches passing through thick beds of ferns, to shaded segments beneath arching rhododendron and Fraser fir trees. This is backpacking at its best.

The small headwaters of a number of streams are crossed, including tributaries of Cooks Creek at **3.1** and **3.7** miles and Lost Bottom Creek at **4.9** miles. Just before crossing Lost Bottom Creek, note several partially earth-covered logs to the right of the trail. These are associated with early logging operations and probably were part of a slide to facilitate movement of logs to a railroad grade 0.6 mile below. This grade was extended into the area by the Ravensford Lumber Company.

The trail ends at the Balsam Mountain Trail at **5.4** miles. To the left is Laurel Gap Shelter at 0.5 mile. The Beech Gap Trail and Pin Oak Gap are reached at 2.0 miles and 4.3 miles, respectively. To the right, the Balsam Mountain Trail continues on to terminate at the Appalachian Trail at Tricorner Knob.

Narrative by William A. Hart, Jr.

MOUNT STERLING TRAIL

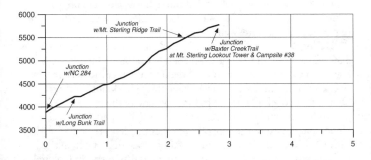

LENGTH: 2.8 miles, from NC 284 to Mt. Sterling (campsite 38).

HIGHLIGHTS: Transition from hardwood to spruce-fir forest, dramatic views from crest.

MAP KEY: 11 C; USGS quad: Cove Creek Gap.

USE: Horse and hiking trail.

TRAILHEAD: Mt. Sterling Gap. Access to the trailhead via I-40: In North Carolina use exit 20 onto route 276. Immediately turn right onto Cove Creek Road (Old 284) and proceed 15.7 miles. In Tennessee use exit 451 (Waterville Road) off I-40. Turn left after crossing the Pigeon River and left again after 2.3 miles at the village of Mount Sterling. Follow old NC 284 for 6.7 miles.

The Great Smoky Mountains form a rugged barrier between western North Carolina and eastern Tennessee. This barrier has influenced travel, transportation, settlement patterns and even politics. Subsequently, the infrequent gaps in the Smokies have figured prominently in regional history.

Mount Sterling Gap is one of the most historic in the Smokies. The buffalo probably made the earliest paths through the gap, instinctively seeking the easiest route between pastures. From prehistoric times, Indians passed through here on their way to trails in the Waynesville, NC area.

Methodist Circuit rider Bishop Francis Asbury crossed here in 1810 on one of his many missions and recorded his impression in his journal: "But O, the mountain-height after height, and five miles over!" Parts of the route which led through the gap were improved as a cattle road in the late 1820s to make it easier to drive cattle to the high mountain pastures and to market.

During the Civil War, the route took on special significance. Toward the close of the war, Confederate Captain Albert Teague of Haywood County, NC captured three union sympathizers in the Big Creek section and marched them back through Mount Sterling Gap. On the Cataloochee side, a Mr. Grooms, one of the prisoners, was told to play a tune on the fiddle. He played "Bonaparte's Retreat." Upon completion of the song, he was shot and left beside the roadside with the bodies of his companions. Afterwards, the song he played was known as Grooms' Tune. In another Civil War event, Colonel George W. Kirk led a federal force of some 400 cavalry and 200 infantry from Newport, Tennessee through Mount Sterling Gap to Haywood County in April, 1865 as part of a three pronged thrust into western North Carolina. Ultimately, his forces were driven through Soco Gap and back into Tennessee.

The Mount Sterling Trail begins at a small parking area in the gap. It offers a steep side ridge ascent to the crest of Mount Sterling along an old roadbed which provides solid footing. The fact that the trail is well graded compensates somewhat for its steepness. Across the road is a sign marking the Asbury Trail. Hikers contemplating walking the Asbury Trail should be aware that it may entail some difficulty due to irregular maintenance.

The Mount Sterling Trail ascends steeply at first, passing through closed oak forest with a number of large individuals. At 0.5 miles the Long Bunk Trail exits to the left where the grade moderates briefly. Cataloochee Valley may be viewed through the trees here. Also, there are a few other limited views on the ascent.

This section provides a pleasant display of fall wildflowers, including purple asters, yellow coneflower, starry campion, Joe-Pye-weed, pale jewelweed and dodder. Dodder is a parasitic vine with small white flowers which grow on a fragile orange vine. According to folklore, if one places a strand of this vine on a plant, and it grows, this is a sign of their sweetheart's love. Not surprisingly, dodder is also known as "love vine." Blackberry plants are also present along the trail, providing fruit during late August and early September.

At 0.7 and 1.2 miles, the trail makes switchbacks crossing and recrossing the ridge. The forest begins to reflect a change with the appearance of tall, straight red spruce and hobblebush, the later identifiable by the gold, purple and bronze color of its roundish leaves in autumn. Thick moss along the trail provides nesting sites for the Dark-eyed Junco which sometimes flits from the bank in front of the hiker during nesting season.

The trail continues ascending the side of the ridge, passing a water source at 1.7 miles. Faint game trails cross the old road along this segment. Occasionally deer may be observed near the trail, sometimes appearing quite tame. At 2.3 miles the Mount Sterling Trail reaches the beginning of the Mount Sterling Ridge Trail marked by signs.

The Mount Sterling Trail bears sharply right at this junction, passing an overgrown grassy area on the left which is an inviting place to rest on a sunny day. The trail crests a knoll in a corridor of Fraser fir, decends gently, and then climbs with increasing steepness to reach the crest of Mount Sterling at **2.8** miles. You will pass a hitching rack and the Mount Sterling backcountry campsite (#38) a short distance below the crest. The Baxter Creek Trail terminates in the small clearing on the crest, having climbed 6.2 miles from Big Creek. Water is located 0.4 mile down this trail along a 700 foot side path which exits left.

Indians apparently visited the Mount Sterling area, because along a hunter's trail on the ridge of Mount Sterling early settlers found a one acre clearing with Indian campsites and fireplaces. Beginning in the 1820s, herders ranged cattle on Long Bunk Mountain and Mount Sterling. At that time the crest of the mountain was more open than today, allowing sufficient grazing land to cause residents to refer to the fields on top as the Near Old Indian Field and Far Old Indian Field.

In 1933, the Civilian Conservation Corps' Big Creek Camp erected the 60 foot steel firetower on the crest of Mount Sterling. They also built a sturdy log cabin for the fire warden which sat in the small flat area to the north of the tower. This cabin had a cistern water system which stored rain water from the roof. The water was then pumped into the cabin with a hand pump.

The fire tower affords magnificent 360° views on a clear day. Balsam Mountain and Luftee Knob lie to the west. Mount Guyot and the main Smoky Mountain divide are viewed to the northwest. Max Patch, a grassy mountain top, is east, and Cataloochee Valley lies to the south. These are but a few of the myriad blue peaks which stretch to the horizon in a seemingly endless panorama. Mount Sterling is located in a spruce-fir forest in which the Fraser fir and red spruce predominate. Note the extensive spruce-fir growth on the high peaks to the northwest. The dead evergreens are Fraser firs destroyed by the balsam woolly adelgid, a tiny, non-native insect.

Narrative by William A. Hart, Jr.

NEWTON BALD TRAIL

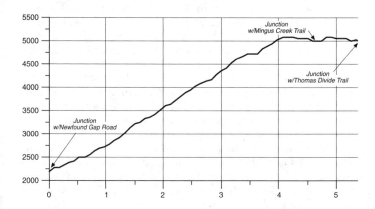

LENGTH: 5.4 miles, from Smokemont on Newfound Gap Road to Thomas Divide Trail.

HIGHLIGHTS: Wildflowers, flame azaleas at top of ridge.

MAP KEY: 8-9 E; USGS quad: Smokemont.

USE: Horse and hiking trail.

TRAILHEAD: Turn off the Newfound Gap Road onto the side road to Smokemont Campground. Immediately after crossing the bridge, turn into the parking area on the right. Cross the Newfound Gap Road and walk on the mowed grass upstream for 250 yards. Look for a Newton Bald trail sign at the edge of the woods.

At the end of this trail is a former bald. It was probably cleared by burning and then kept clear by grazing. When the park was established, the grazing stopped. Some grass and a few high bush blueberries are the only evidence of the former bald. Don't plan on a view.

The trail heads west up a cutover area of small tuliptrees, dogwoods, and maples. Poison ivy creeps along the trail and climbs the trees. A seep crosses the trail where a piece of black culvert rests in the weeds. The moist hillside supports Christmas ferns, lady ferns, dog-hobble, and rosebay rhododendron.

At 0.2 miles, a horse trail joins from the left. Many oaks have fallen here, leaving an open area for young trees to compete in. The trail is sandy and dry, with oaks, tuliptrees, Eastern hemlocks, and hickories. About 0.1 mile farther, Newton Bald Trail turns right while the horse trail goes left, but they rejoin after looping around a small hill. Look for Indian cucumber, a plant in the lily family with a single 6-12-inch stalk and one or two circles of leaves. Plants with two circles, like an umbrella on top of an umbrella, bloom in June and have purplish berries on the top circle later in summer. Plants with only one circle of leaves are youngsters, not ready to bloom. The white tuber tastes like cucumber.

The trail crosses a muddy seep and climbs into a dry forest of thin maples and sourwoods. Ferns, tangled mountain laurel, and buffalonut bushes will brush your legs. At the end of a ridge, you can hear Newfound Gap Road traffic and see across the Oconaluftee River Valley. Trailing arbutus and galax grow here in the sandy soil, but around the corner is a north facing slope, moister and more sheltered. The trail rises through cool rosebay rhododendron and then into open woods again. Squawroot, harebells, maidenhair fern, Christmas fern, yellow mandarin, and sweet cicely grow here. After another rhododendron tunnel and a rocky seep with nettles, you can add blue and black cohosh, Dutchman's pipe, anemone, jack-in-the-pulpit, foamflower, hepatica, bellwort, and more to the spring wildflower list. A left turn takes you into shady rhododendron again, where scattered galax and downy rattlesnake-plantain are the only plants on the ground. Silverbell, Fraser magnolia, and cucumber tree trunks stand with the rhododendron.

The next two rocky seeps support patches of umbrella leaf. This relative of may-apple blooms in April, and the platter-sized leaves with jagged edges last until fall. The trail moves out to the ends of ridges and back into seeps, some of which are weedy with tall beebalm, coreopsis, nettles, and jewelweed. The seeps may be muddy if there has been rain and horse traffic. A big seep, almost a creeklet, at about 2.5 miles, is very rocky with more water, but there should be enough stepping stones.

The trail rises through large oaks and maples and, at about 3.0

miles, reaches a small gap where a chestnut snag rests in the fork of another tree as if it were propped there to hold a giant sorghum kettle over a fire. The trail crosses the gap and climbs a steep, rough section with mountain laurels, striped maples, chestnut oaks, American chestnut saplings, and large patches of flame azaleas, which bloom in May and June.

The trail goes through rhododendron tunnels, crosses two more weedy seeps, and then approaches the ridge top. The packed dirt surface has few rocks but could be muddy. A moist section of woods below the ridge supports cinnamon ferns and other tall ferns as the trail curves right onto the ridge top. Look for a pair of tall American chestnut snags. The trail runs along the ridge top and then slips down to the right, giving you the first descent since Newfound Gap Road. Flame azaleas are thick here.

After a muddy, brambly climb, the trail makes a wide U-turn onto a drier ridge and descends to the junction with Mingus Creek Trail. You have come **4.7** miles from Newfound Gap Road. Around the junction, look for white oaks, red oaks, sassafras, American chestnut saplings, flame azaleas, and highbush blueberries.

As you leave the junction, you might get a view to the left of Thomas Ridge as you make the easy climb up the side of Newton Bald. The former bald is to your right, and the grasses, goldenrods, and black-eyed susans along the trail are evidence that the bald was here. Now you see small beeches on the ridge top with a crowd of Canada mayflowers on the ground. You might spot a pink lady's slipper or two in May or their dark, flat leaves in summer.

Campsite #52 straddles the ridge top. It has three or four tent sites and a spring about 50 yards down to the left. The trail then crosses a dry, piney ridge to the junction with Thomas Divide Trail. One red spruce near the trail sign confirms that you really have climbed to 5,000'.

Newton Bald Trail could be combined with Thomas Divide Trail for a nice loop (with car shuttle) or could be the starting place for any number of backcountry camping routes.

Narrative by Doris Gove

NOLAND CREEK TRAIL

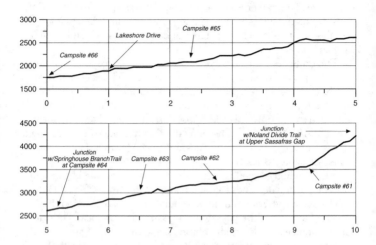

LENGTH: 10.0 miles, from Fontana Lake to Noland Divide Trail.
HIGHLIGHTS: 6 backcountry campsites, fishing along the creek.
CAUTIONS: 4 unbridged creek crossings.
MAP KEY: 6-7 F-G; USGS quads: Noland Creek, Bryson City, Clingmans Dome.
USE: Horse and hiking trail.
TRAILHEAD: Drive 8.0 miles on Lakeview Drive northwest from Bryson City. Take the access trail from the parking lot at the bridge over Noland Creek.

The Noland Creek valley takes its name from the Noland family who once settled in it. However, many others lived alongside the rushing waters of Noland Creek and its tributaries. The trail runs north-south from Fontana Lake to the crest of Noland Divide at Upper Sassafras Gap with its trailhead 1.0 mile from the southern-most point at the lake. In 1934, 10 men from the Deep Creek Civilian Conservation Corps Camp were "kept busy drilling solid rock for one month" to construct this trail. Despite the grueling work, the superintendent reported that "the boys as a whole have done excellent work. There hasn't been a single discharge for failure of anyone to do as requested."

From the trailhead, the trail travels left on a good roadbed one mile south to Fontana Lake. Four bridges cross Noland Creek as it spills into Fontana Lake.

Be on the lookout for beaver signs, like trees gnawed near their base. Slate of the Anakeesta Formation is visible along the side of the trail. Campsite #66 is located on the backwaters of Fontana at the Noland Creek embayment. It is heavily used by fishermen, horsemen, and boaters.

The main part of the trail runs north (uphill) from the trailhead. Walk under the bridge which carries Lakeview Drive high over Noland Creek. The trail soon crosses Noland Creek on a wide, sturdy bridge. Campsite #65 is **1.3** miles north of the trailhead. A narrow trail travels 150 yards up Bearpen Branch to it. Three picnic tables and fire grates are nestled among American beech, oak, and Eastern hemlock. Moderate use has worn the site, but it is still a nice spot to camp.

Continuing beyond the side trail to the campsite, the trail passes through a boulder field of talus, or blocks of rock pried loose by frost wedging at the base of a slope, caused by the Ice Age over 10,000 years ago. Indian Creek tumbles down from the slopes of Forney Ridge 0.5 mile from Campsite #65. At mile **1.8** is a beautiful grove of tall, straight white pine. The understory consists of American beech, American holly, rhododendron, and Eastern hemlock. Noland Creek is crossed a second time via foot bridge beyond the white pine grove.

About 100 yards past the second bridge is an old house site marked by non-native boxwoods and privet, plus a stone pile. A little further, at a small branch, grows Spanish bayonet, a yucca plant named for its tough sword-shaped leaves, at the mouth of Horse Cove. There are many signs of the people that once inhabited this beautiful valley. A large stone foundation with a chimney pile sits at the end of a boxwood-lined walk. The steps are still standing, ready to carry the hiker up to a front door and a welcome that are long past.

The trail descends into Solola Valley which was well populated before the park. Solola Valley is probably named for a post office that once served the area. The name is derived from the Cherokee "salali" meaning squirrel. Also, Salali was a famed Cherokee inventor, metal worker, and storyteller, as well as the first Cherokee to make a rifle on his own. In 1940, a park committee named a creek farther up the valley "Salola" in an attempt to find "short and musical" Cherokee names that were "spelled in such a way as to suggest their proper pronunciation by English-speaking people." Local residents called Salola Branch, Big Branch.

A foundation on the right precedes an open area populated with black walnut trees. The remnants of a grist mill stand on the left. It is possible to see where the water wheel rested on a foundation to catch the fast waters of Noland Creek as they churned by.

Cross Noland Creek a third time on a wide bridge at mile **4.0.** Campsite #64, Mill Creek, is at the junction of Mill Creek and the Springhouse Branch Trail, **4.2** miles from the trailhead. The campsite is a large, heavily used area with six picnic tables, a food storage bin, and a horse rack. The Springhouse Branch Trail climbs 2.8 miles up Forney Ridge to the Forney Ridge Trail before going 5.5 more miles to the Forney Creek Trail. The Mill Creek School, which once served the children of the area, stood opposite Noland Creek from the junction of Mill and Noland Creeks.

Beyond the campsite, the trail crosses Noland Creek again, this time by foot log. A sandstone overhang with shaley layers crowds the trail into the creek just before the crossing. On the other side, the site of an old ranger station is on the right. Foundations and ruins of several buildings are still visible among sycamore, yellow birch, and white pine.

The trail follows the creek away from Solola Valley through a cove hardwood forest. A large quartzite boulder rests on the left of the trail. A very narrow foot log recrosses Noland Creek at **5.0** miles. Campsite #63, Jerry Flats, straddles the trail in an open area on the west side of Noland Creek. This heavily used site provides racks for horses. The cove hardwood forest has yellow birch and Fraser magnolia in particular. A small branch which drains the eastern side of Jerry Bald Ridge flows across the trail near the campsite.

The Eversole Lumber Company removed hardwoods from the Noland Creek watershed in the 1880s, using oxen to slide logs down to a circular mill at the creek's mouth. Another operation, Harris-Woodbury, built a flume on the creek to a portable mill. "We manufactured nine or ten million feet of hardwoods between 1905 and 1908," wrote one of the partners. Champion Fiber later acquired the land, but had not logged it when it was purchased for the park.

You ford Noland Creek twice in less than 0.5 mile. Both crossings are wet ones since the creek is wide and sometimes deep with no foot logs or bridges. At mile **6.8** you find Campsite #62, Upper Ripshin, a moderately used horse camp. Above the campsite, you ford Upper Ripshin Branch and then immediately ford Noland Creek for the last time.

The trail is rocky and can be quite muddy. It is surrounded with pipsissewa and partridge-berry. You rock hop across three small branches before the trail ascends the ridge on an old road bed high above Noland Creek. Sassafras Branch, which flows down from Upper Sassafras Gap, is crossed at **8.3** miles.

Campsite #61 (Bald Creek) is at the junction of Noland Creek and Bald Creek. This horse camp is moderately used and quite pleasantly situated beside the waters of the two creeks. Fifty yards ahead, the trail turns sharply right and ascends the western slopes of Noland Divide. This steep stretch follows Sassafras Branch through Eastern hemlock and oak for about .8 mile. Several switchbacks break the steep ascent. A fire ring at a level spot on the banks of Sassafras Branch is NOT a legal campsite.

Upper Sassafras Gap (elevation 4,240') marks the junction with Noland Divide Trail, which runs 3.7 miles north (left) to the Clingmans Dome Road and 7.9 miles south (right) to Deep Creek Campground.

(see campsite summary, next page)

NOLAND CREEK CAMPSITE SUMMARY

SITE #	MILE	DESCRIPTION
66	1.0 south of trailhead	On backwaters of Fontana Lake. Heavily used as a fish, horse and boating camp.
65	1.3 north of trailhead	Along Bearpen Branch. Moderate use, pleasant, traces of old school.
64	4.2 north of trailhead	Mill Creek. Large, heavily used horse camp.
63	5.6 north of trailhead	Jerry Flats. Heavily used horse camp.
62	6.8 north of trailhead	Upper Ripshin, moderately used horsecamp.
61	8.3 north of trailhead	Bald Creek. Rationed, moderately used horse camp. Pleasant location between two creeks.

Narrative by Charles Maynard and David Morris

NOLAND DIVIDE TRAIL

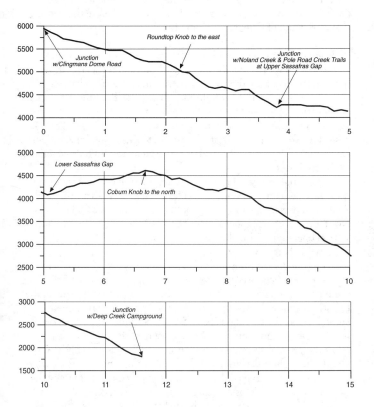

Roundtop Knob to the east

Junction w/Clingmans Dome Road

Junction w/Noland Creek & Pole Road Creek Trails at Upper Sassafras Gap

Lower Sassafras Gap

Coburn Knob to the north

Junction w/Deep Creek Campground

LENGTH: 11.6 miles, from Clingmans Dome Road to Deep Creek Campground.

HIGHLIGHTS: Large elevation change, diversity of forest types, beautiful spruce-fir forest; views, especially in fall and winter.

CAUTIONS: Snakes in summer; yellowjackets in fall.

MAP KEY: 7 E-G; USGS quads: Clingmans Dome, Bryson City.

USE: Horse and hiking trail.

TRAILHEAD: Drive 5.5 miles up Clingmans Dome Road from Newfound Gap. The trail is on the left, 1.5 miles before the parking area at the end of Clingmans Dome Road.

Although hiking it generally requires two vehicles, the Noland Divide trail is well worth the effort. One of the most scenic all-day hikes in the Smokies, the trail offers the largest elevation change of any trail on the North Carolina side of the park. Because it begins at an elevation of 5,929' (amid a lush spruce-fir forest) and ends at an elevation of 1,780' (just after a pine forest), Noland Divide Trail is best hiked from top to bottom. To facilitate this route, hikers should leave one vehicle at Deep Creek Campground and then drive another to the trailhead.

Beginning on a gated primitive road, the trail descends among red spruce, American mountain-ash, yellow birch, and mountain maple. Soon, you pass by a tower. A sign at its base announces "Please Do Not Disturb," then explains that the tower is an acid rain monitoring station operated by the National Park Service and the Oak Ridge National Laboratory.

The trail diverts from the road and becomes a footpath where it enters a magnificent stand of red spruce, which was not logged during the heyday of lumbering in the Great Smokies (the early years of the twentieth century). Another conifer, the Fraser fir, can be seen among red spruce on ridges above 5,000'; both are remnants from the Ice Age when many "northern" species spread their range south. After temperatures warmed, most "northern" species disappeared from all but the highest elevations of the southern mountains. The park's spruce-fir forests survived. Later, many stands were left alone by the timber companies, whose railroads could not gain access to the highest ridges. Fraser firs have recently died in great numbers, the result of the balsam woolly adelgid infestation. Probably brought to the New World by turn-of-the-century nurserymen importing European conifers for Christmas and ornamental purposes, the balsam woolly adelgid flourished by feeding parasitically on a number of North American firs. The adelgid was first detected in the southern Appalachians on the slopes of Mt. Mitchell in the 1950s; by the early

1980s extensive die-back was occurring on the park's high ridges such as Noland Divide. Because it reproduces prolifically and asexually and because it has no natural predators in the New World, the adelgid kills adult fir trees by forming colonies on their trunks and sucking out the trees' water and minerals, thereby starving them. The adelgid has devastated the Fraser fir stands in the southern Appalachians—roughly 95% have been adversely affected. Since the 1980s, the park has sprayed stands of young Fraser fir to kill off colonies of the adelgid; although this process is time-consuming and expensive, to date the park has been successful in maintaining healthy stands along the Clingmans Dome Road. The more inaccessible forest along the Noland Divide trail, however, is not managed, so you will see the aftermath of infestation: dead trunks, some still standing, some fallen. You will also see young fir seedlings rising up, still too hardy to be damaged; sadly, as these seedlings mature, the adelgid will attack them.

Yellow birch is also common on this section of Noland Divide Trail. In fact, the park and North Carolina state record yellow birch appears within the first mile on the left, about 10' off the trail. The bluebead-lily is the most visible wildflower. Sometimes deep furrows are visible in the trail bank, usually an indicator of non-native wild hogs "rooting" for food.

By **1.0** mile, the ridge narrows. The trail now follows the crest of Noland Divide among never-logged and second-growth trees, including Eastern hemlock, various oaks and maples, and Juneberry. American chestnut stumps, fallen trunks, and saplings abound. In fall the saplings' amber leaves glow, a distinct attraction for this trail. As you near **3.0** miles, the ridge dries—a far cry from the moist spruce/fir forest near the start of the trail. Often literally in the clouds, the higher elevations in the Great Smoky Mountains receive much of the precipitation; lower elevations get considerably less rainfall.

Early summer is an ideal time to experience Noland Divide Trail since it is frequently lined by flowering heath bushes like mountain laurel, flame azalea, and rosebay rhododendron. At times the rosebay rhododendron is so thick that almost nothing grows in its shade. Frequently, the only plant that can tolerate the deep shade is galax. Found only in the southern mountains, galax once provided an important source of extra income for mountain people who sold the leaves to florists. Even before hikers see the plant, they may first detect it by its sweet, sweaty odor.

At **3.7** miles, a trail junction appears. To the left is the Pole Road Creek Trail, and Noland Creek Trail forks off to the right. Noland Divide Trail continues straight, at first climbing slightly, then leveling among numerous pignut hickories, so named because mountain settlers often let their pigs roam through the ridge forests to feed on the mast (nuts and fruits).

Far below in the valley on the right, Noland Creek roars. At one point on the left, a large rock outcrop is covered with lichens. Close inspection reveals that the lichens are slowly dissolving the rock, "weathering" the mountains in collaboration with wind, rain, frost, and snow. One of the oldest extant mountain ranges in the world, the southern Appalachians stood as high as the Andes 200 million years ago, but constant weathering has eroded them. Another kind of weathering can be seen in this same outcrop where a mountain laurel grows in a rock crevice originally caused by ice and frost.

A boulder field appears on the left, also the result of weathering. By now, the trail no longer follows the ridge crest but rather runs on its side. Downy rattlesnake-plantain, actually a member of the orchid family and named for the leaves' resemblance to a snakeskin, grows along the trail.

At **5.0** miles, the trail weaves along the upper edge of a cove. In this area, look for the distinctive, furrowed bark of black locust, as well as many fallen chestnut trees. Birds nesting along this stretch include the White-breasted Nuthatch and Pileated Woodpecker. By **6.0** miles, the trail courses through a black cherry, northern red oak, and tuliptree forest with black-eyed Susan, goatsbeard, and Indian pipe below in summer. Indian pipe, or ghost plant, has a single, white nodding flower; oddly, it lacks chlorophyll but feeds off of decaying vegetation.

Shortly after crossing a soppy spot created by a small stream, Noland Divide Trail abruptly turns left through rosebay rhododendron, flame azalea, and mountain laurel, following Coburn Knob. At **7.0** miles the trail continues down through a drier forest, passing a cove on the left. In spring, pink lady's slippers and trailing arbutus grow nearby, as do hop clover and numerous sunflowers. At **8.0** miles the trail follows the knife crest of Beaugard Ridge into a large open area, Lonesome Pine Overlook. Blueberry bushes proliferate on the many exposed rocks. The rocks provide grandstand seats for outstanding views. Below to the right, toward Fontana Lake, lies Lands Creek Valley, straight ahead is Bryson City, and Deep Creek Valley falls to the left.

The trail drops steeply around the east side of Beaugard Ridge, quite dry at first, with sassafras and chestnut oak. Next, the trail enters a rich cove forest comprised of various maples, oaks, and hickories. At **10.0** miles, the trail crosses puddles near a small waterfall, traverses a spur into a dry cove, then drops quickly toward Deep Creek Campground through sandy soil and parched, stunted vegetation where scrub and white pine dominate. At **11.0** miles, you reenter a forest of tuliptrees, red maples, oaks, poison ivy, and multi-flora rose. A footbridge over a small branch at **11.5** miles leads to Deep Creek Campground.

Narrative by Ted Olson

OCONALUFTEE RIVER TRAIL

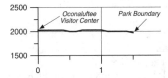

LENGTH: 1.5 miles, from Oconaluftee Visitor Center to the park boundary at Cherokee, NC.
HIGHLIGHTS: Easy, accessible trail along river.
CAUTIONS: Abundant poison ivy.
MAP KEY: 9 F; USGS quad: Smokemont.
USE: Hiking trail.
TRAILHEAD: Park at the Oconaluftee Visitor Center and follow the path to the mountain farm museum. Look for a trail sign on the right just before the entrance to the farmstead.

There were several Cherokee towns along this beautiful river, and they were called Egwanulti, or By-the-river Towns. White settlers filtered in around the 1800s and took over completely after the Cherokee were removed in 1838. The settlers corrupted Egwanulti to Oconaluftee and spelled it various ways. The river drains the wide valley between Thomas Divide and Hughes Ridge and runs along a major geologic fault.

The trail starts between two large Eastern hemlocks and is level and smooth enough for strollers and wheelchairs. It runs between a hayfield and several styles of mountain farmstead fencing. Life form sightings include cows, ponies, chickens, corn, tobacco, and sorghum. But soon you swing left into riverside woods. Flowering dogwood and tuliptrees frame the entrance to the woods, and three large butternuts, or white walnuts, stand on the right with their branches stretching out over the hayfield. In fall, look for their sticky, spicy, elongated nuts. Another low elevation tree to look for all along this trail is the American hornbeam, or blue beech. This small tree has smooth gray bark that usually supports scraggly colonies of mosses and lichens. The leaves are oval like elm leaves with toothy margins, and the branches often have tangles of twigs. Fruits appear in summer and look like dangly earrings made of many tiny pagoda roofs. To complete their scruffy image, hornbeams never grow straight.

The river on the left runs fast and shallow over a jumble of rocks. Big sycamores line the river, and big, hairy poison ivy vines climb them and the tuliptrees. Stonecrop, violets, may-apple, and other spring wildflowers grow beside the trail along with devils walkingstick, a 10' woody stalk with a tuft of compound leaves on top. This plant has thorns on every part of its surface: leaves, stalk, leaf stalks, flower stalks. Maybe you know some people like that.

The trail rises over a small, steep hill that would be no problem for strollers, but someone in a wheelchair might need help. It then passes under the Blue Ridge Parkway. After the underpass, look for a large patch of shrub yellowroot on the left. This plant looks like an annual wildflower, but it has bark and is a shrub, though barely more than knee-high. The leaves are compound and jagged. Beneath the thin bark, the stem is bright yellow.

Several rocky spur trails lead left to the water, one to a deep pool with boulders. Then the main trail turns right and follows a small creek into deeper woods. In late summer, look for tall spikes of cardinal flower in the creek. After three small hills, the trail runs beside Newfound Gap Road and the turn-off for Big Cove Road. It crosses Big Cove Road and enters woods of tuliptree, American hornbeam, and champion poison ivy vines. After 0.1 mile from the road, the trail ends on a grassy area just across the river from Chief Saunooke's Trading Post and Bear Park.

Narrative by Doris Gove

OLD SETTLERS TRAIL

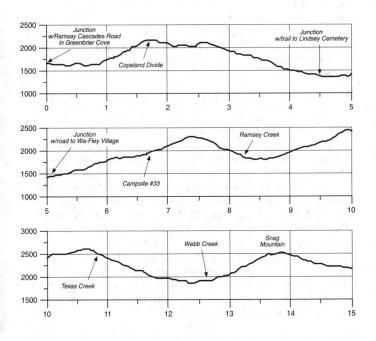

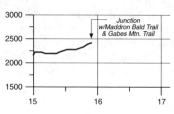

LENGTH: 15.9 miles, from Ramsay Cascades Road to the Maddron Bald Trail.

HIGHLIGHTS: Myriad of historic sites.

CAUTIONS: Unbridged small stream crossings.

MAP KEY: 8-9 C-B; USGS quads: Mt. Le Conte, Mt. Guyot, Jones Cove.

USE: Hiking trail.

TRAILHEAD: Take US 321 5.9 miles east of Gatlinburg, TN and turn onto the Greenbrier Road at the park entrance sign. Continue past the ranger station and picnic area. Turn onto the road leading across a bridge to the left toward Ramsay Cascades trailhead. Cross two bridges, then look for the Old Settlers trailhead immediately on the left.

Traveling the Old Settlers Trail, a hiker can see more traces of l9th and early 20th century mountain community life than any place else in the park. Solitary chimneys and crumbling rock walls are common along this trail as are non-native plants such as daylily, daffodil, privet, boxwood, and lilac that mountain people planted around their homes. Passing through the headwaters of more than a dozen creeks, you'll get a good idea how heavily populated the Smokies were and how these rural families organized their communities along each watershed. Although the trail is relatively easy to follow, the number of small stream crossings makes it difficult at times to determine exactly where you are on the trail.

This trail can provide a challenging two-day backpacking trip, if you camp at site #33 (6.7 miles from Greenbrier trailhead). If you are an experienced hiker and go for the entire length (15.9 miles plus the 1.2 mile entrance on Maddron Bald Trail), be sure to start early on a long summer day and arrange for a shuttle.

As you begin following this fairly level trail by the Little Pigeon River, you are walking into the heart of what was once the Greenbrier community. Although it is not known exactly how many people lived along the watershed, more than 250 children attended school here at the turn of the century and the community supported a general store and two churches. Several hundred families made their living here, primarily as small farmers, until Tennessee began purchasing their land for a national park in the late 1920s.

After the communities were removed, the Greenbrier Civilian Conservation Corps (CCC) Camp was located here in 1933, and that company wove together footpaths and wagon roads to create much of this trail. Because of the number of small farms, the area was not heavily logged, but watersheds such as Webb Creek and Dunn Creek were culled of the best tuliptrees and other hardwoods in the early 1900s.

After a quarter of a mile, the trail crosses Bird Branch and then begins to climb up the ridge and down again, crossing an unnamed branch. The trail reaches Little Bird Branch and ascends alongside it. Look for the rock walls that used to enclose the homeplace of Chriss Parton in the 1800s. Lona Mae Parton Tyson, Chriss Parton's granddaughter, was born here in Greenbrier. She and her seven brothers and sisters were charged with repairing and building these stone fences—not to keep farm animals in, but to keep the hogs, cattle and horses out of the garden. Most animals roamed the fields and woods, where fence laws did not apply. So many Partons grew up along Little Bird Branch and this general area that it was referred to as "Partontown" by community members. The Parton Cemetery rests along Little Bird Branch.

At the top of Copeland Divide, stop for a nice view of rocky Greenbrier Pinnacle to the east. Tyson, a great aunt to the country singer Dolly Parton, remembered climbing to the base of the Pinnacle to pick blueberries for canning or to make a cobbler pie. "We would always take the dog for protection for there were plenty of rattle snakes and copperheads on those mountains…But we never got bit."

In winter you might get a glimpse of the Cat Stairs, stair-like cliffs on the mountaintop to the east of the trail. According to Isham Profitt, who grew up in Greenbrier, foxes used the series of steep cliffs to get away from pursuing dogs.

After following the ridge for a short distance, the trail crosses at the headwaters of Copeland Creek, which flows to the Little Pigeon

River. In the 1920s, Copeland Creek was home for more than a dozen families.

The trail climbs gently around the divide, then twists downward and crosses a fork of Snakefeeder Branch. The trail follows the branch downstream, then crosses another fork of Snakefeeder Branch. Here the landscape flattens and opens, exposing a single chimney, draped in Japanese honeysuckle, an exotic species common around homesites.

The trail continues along Snakefeeder Branch and then goes to the right toward Soak Ash Creek. After crossing several tributaries of Soak Ash Creek, the trail levels off considerably. Conley Huskey, the mayor of Pittman Center for many years, grew up on Soak Ash. He said you always had to be careful when pronouncing the name of his birthplace!

At **4.5** miles, the trail forks. Take the right fork to remain on the Old Settlers Trail. The trail continues upward, following Evans Creek. Along this section of the trail the forest floor is thickly covered with galax, various mosses and the small evergreen plant known as striped pipsissewa. Southern mountain residents once gathered great quantities of galax and sold it to commercial florists, who commonly used it in decorative arrangements. Above the trail, small Eastern hemlocks dominate the forest understory.

The trail then climbs up a short but steep ridge toward Timothy Creek. Look for another nicely preserved rock wall as you reach the banks of the creek. Fording this shallow creek is relatively easy, even though it is 12' wide in places. On the opposite bank, notice the rock wall designating a former homesite. Immediately uphill stands a well-preserved chimney surrounded by numerous spiked yucca, a native species planted by homesteading settlers. To the right of the chimney is a corn crib or hog pen.

Crossing Darky Branch, the trail again curves upward. You climb to a clearing and in the distance to the west should see the town of Pittman Center. Continuing along the trail, you come to Campsite #33, a heavily used, often relocated site marked by a single chimney among a grove of large hardwoods. Below the campsite bubbles Redwine Creek, a wide but shallow crossing along smooth stepping stones.

Descending quickly toward Ramsey Creek on the trail, you pass several homesites before crossing the creek above a beautiful rock chimney. Ramsey Creek was named for the Ramsey families who farmed this area prior to the formation of the park. According to land records, 17 farms in the Smokies were owned by mountaineers with the surname Ramsey. The trail crosses the creek five more times, all easy rockhops, passing several homesites. Watch for a small waterfall on the right of the trail upstream at the last stream crossing.

After the last stream crossing, the trail turns away from Ramsey Creek on an old roadbed. You'll pass numerous rock walls and several former homesites. Look for a tall narrow chimney on the right, one of the best preserved chimneys on the entire trail. Continuing eastward, at **9.3** miles, the trail joins an unmaintained trail that leads out to highway US 321 in 0.5 mile. To continue on the Old Settlers Trail, turn right on the roadbed.

Just below here, on land between Old Settlers Trail and US 321, W.A. Ramsey and Mack Reagen had two good-sized farms. Ramsey had a 77.5 acre farm, including 97 apple trees. Reagen owned 138.8 acres, half in timber and half cultivated. Both men and their families lived in frame houses, which were very common in the mountains during the early twentieth century. The older log cabins (the chimneys of which comprise many of the ruins seen along the trail) were rented to tenant farmers or served as newlyweds' homes, or simply stood vacant.

The trail continues along Noisy Creek, passing through mountain laurel as it ascends upward. The left bank of the trail is very steep as the creek passes below the trail in a deep ravine. The trail then crosses a small branch, before reaching Noisy Creek at an old ford. At the stream crossing rests a rock wall following the trail to the stream's edge. A rock hop with some shallow wading may be required to cross the creek. Directly below the crossing is a crumbling half chimney with hearth intact.

The trail turns left away from the creek, ascending gradually. After crossing a small branch, the trail continues upward, following Noisy Creek. The trail crosses Noisy Creek again, a more difficult crossing in wet weather. Immediately upstream the trail crosses the creek again, then continues upstream, passing several rock walls and more moss-covered rock piles.

Continuing upward, look closely for a row of fence posts on the left side of the trail, indicating this was once a corral. Here the trail turns left and away from Noisy Creek and begins a steeper ascent. Over the ridge, the trail finally begins to descend toward Tumbling Branch. The trail winds among large fallen logs and passes directly through one before crossing the waters of Tumbling Branch. After rock-hopping across the branch, you climb a steep bank and zig-zag upwards through a large grove of rhododendron. Here the trail follows the contour of the ridge before entering a mature hemlock forest on what local people call Chestnut Ridge.

Throughout Chestnut Ridge, there are uprooted American chestnut trees, many at least 6' in diameter at their base. Once the dominant tree species in the Appalachian forest, the American chestnut grew as large as 12' in diameter and 120' in height. However, it has been all but eliminated by a non-native fungus which struck the region in the early part of this century.

"The mountain people," recalled Martin Tipton, "needed those chestnuts. They ate them themselves, of course, but they depended upon them to feed their hogs." The sturdy, rot-resistant wood of the chestnut provided mountain residents framing lumber, siding, shingle roofing, doors, paneling, furniture, farm fencing, and tannin extract for leather. "We used to come upon the skeletons of those trees when we'd be out walking," said Tipton. "Dad said it looked like a third of the mountain was dying."

From the ridge, the highest point on the trail (elevation 2,600 feet), the trail switchbacks downward toward Texas Creek. As the trail levels, you will see a half chimney, a rock wall and a clearing just before crossing Texas Creek at **10.7** miles. Rock hop across the creek and descend along its bank. For the next mile, the trail passes many small waterfalls on Texas Creek. There is evidence of as many as four home sites. One homesite is recognizable by cabin remains and two fallen chimneys, one with an attractive v-shaped opening above the hearth. According to *Mountain Press* columnist Ev Sherrick, this is the Fletcher Lunsford place. Park archives show that the Lunsfords owned 35 acres on Texas Creek, with 200 apple, peach, and cherry trees in their fruit orchard. They lived in a four-room box house, had a cabin, barn, and a corn-crib on their land. As many as a dozen families lived in the Texas Creek valley at one time.

Continuing down the old road bed, you come to a fork where you should bear to the right. The trail crosses at least 3 small branches as it winds through a hemlock and rhododendron thicket, and then follows another old road bed. A fine example of an old rock wall lines the road, eventually on both sides. The wall stands an impressive 4-5' tall and 2-3' wide, and continues more than 100 yards. As the trail approaches Webb Creek, look for a homesite on the opposite side of the creek as you cross. Although 19th Century farmers built their homes very close to the creeks without fear of flooding, flash floods did happen. According to the park superintendent's report, on August 5, 1938, in the early morning, five successive cloudbursts dumped 11 inches of rain, creating a flash flood on Webb Creek that drowned eight persons. One home, along with sleeping parents, four children, and two visitors was swept away.

The trail continues right, following Webb Creek upstream. After a half mile, you pass directly through a rock wall and several homesites along the creek.

Continuing upward on the trail through rhododendron thickets, you can see Webb Creek deep in the valley below. Near the top of the ridge, the trail enters an old road bed, levels off, and then crosses a spring branch. The trail turns sharply left at the remains of an old cabin, a "double pen" outbuilding with half dovetail notching, a construction style common on east Tennessee outbuildings. After turning left, the trail goes around a knoll, passes the spring branch again, and then continues to the ridge atop Snag Mountain. Along the ridge grows mountain laurel and Fraser magnolia, both common species at mountain gaps of this elevation. On a clear day, look to the south; you can see Greenbrier Pinnacle from this vantage point.

From here the trail descends gradually into a small cove, where it enters the Dunn and Indian Camp Creek watersheds. The trail turns sharply left as you approach Snag Branch, a small tributary of Dunn Creek. You cross this creek twice, continuing through a forest of tall tuliptrees and third-growth hardwoods.

As you approach Dunn Creek, watch for more signs of settlement and exotics such as common privet and multiflora rose in the overgrown clearings and rockpiles. After crossing Dunn Creek, the trail curves, making a gradual descent to Indian Camp Creek. The Park Service has recently erected a new foot log to cross this stream, but if it has been washed away by the flash floods common to this drainage, this can be the most challenging crossing on the trail.

The trail undulates a quarter of a mile through mountain laurel, then descends to a small homesite with a half chimney. Rock-hop over Maddron Creek, the last stream crossing, then follow the trail upward through a grove of hardwoods to the trail terminus at the Maddron Bald Trail. From here, take a left onto the Maddron Bald Trail, which takes you 1.2 miles to the Laurel Springs Road, then to US 321.

Automobiles parked at the Maddron Bald Trailhead on Laurel Springs Road are occasionally vandalized or stolen. Alternative parking may be available (sometimes for a fee) from businesses on US 321.

Narrative by Margaret Lynn Brown and Donald E. Davis

OLD SUGARLANDS TRAIL

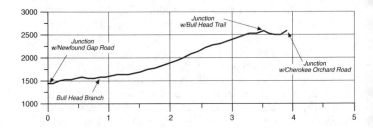

LENGTH: 3.9 miles, from the Newfound Gap Road to Cherokee Orchard.
HIGHLIGHTS: Historic sites.
MAP KEY: 6-7 C; USGS quads: Gatlinburg, Mt. Le Conte.
USE: Horse and hiking trail.
TRAILHEAD: Park at park headquarters by turning in unmarked

road 200 yards north of Sugarlands Visitor Center on the Newfound Gap Road (Highway 441). Walk across Newfound Gap Road and then cross the river on the road bridge.

Although this trail starts near the popular Sugarlands Visitor Center, it receives relatively light use and is an undiscovered treasure, especially for history buffs.

The trail forks immediately: the Old Sugarlands Trail is the right fork that closely follows the left bank of the river (The trail to the left is the Twomile Branch Trail, a bridle-path). Even though the trail is close to a major highway, the roar of the river eliminates noise from the road, making you feel you are in deep woods. Immediately on the left, a large rock cliff rises more than 70' above the trail. This was the site of a quarry used by the state of Tennessee to build the first paved roads over the mountains. According to geologists, the rock face is a gray feldspathic sandstone that represents one of the oldest rock types in the Appalachian mountains.

As the trail climbs up and away from the river, it becomes steep and narrow in places, with rhododendron and doghobble lining it. Then it abruptly leaves the main trail—a trail sign indicates a "hard" right—and winds down a bank to continue following the river upstream. (The steeper trail to the left is a short spur which connects with the Twomile Lead Trail.)

From the embankment, the Old Sugarlands Trail descends along a narrow path, fords a small branch, and passes an old homesite. The telephone poles lying off the trail are reminders that this section of the trail follows what was once Tennessee State Highway 71, one of the first paved roads over the mountains. The trail follows the level floodplain of the river through a grove of small hardwoods, Eastern hemlock and sugar maple saplings.

Highway 71 and the wagon road that preceeded it were once the center of the Sugarlands community. Named for the numerous sugar maple trees that grew here, the Sugarlands included homes, farms, and families that stretched from Bull Head Mountain to Sugarland Mountain. There were two or three blacksmith shops and five grist mills in the valley.

During the 19th century, most farmers here raised corn, vegetables, and grain for hogs, cows, and chickens. They also harvested Winesap, Starks Delicious, White Limbertwig, Blackben, Golden Pippin, Sour John, Milam, and Shockley apples for market. And, because of the plentiful sugar maples, they often collected and sold maple syrup as well. Rock walls visible along the trail indicate where Sugarlands farmers fenced their gardens to keep out deer and roaming livestock.

During the 1900s, the community became more devoted to the growing tourist trade. Sam Newman opened the Sky-u-ka hotel. Fred Newman installed the first pump and sold the first gasoline at his store in 1927. He took chickens and eggs in trade for meat, lard, shoes, cloth, salt, coffee, condensed milk, and canned vegetables.

The trail crosses Bullhead Branch over a small bridge at 0.8 mile. A closer look on the left side of the bridge reveals a benchmark that reads "U.S. Coast and Geodetic Survey, 1934." The trail continues, following the right bank of Bullhead Branch for several hundred yards. Just before the trail turns left is a stand of young sweetgum trees. During the summer months, look for heal-all, used medicinally by early settlers. Heal-all, trailing arbutus, bloodroot, and spring-beauty are some of the many native wildflowers that bloom along this trail.

The trail turns sharply to the left, where it crosses a tributary of Bullhead Branch, the site of an old grist mill. The trail continues for a short distance before coming to a "T." Turn right here to continue on the Old Sugarlands Trail.

Past a straight row of Eastern hemlocks, the Old Sugarlands Trail again turns left, where it follows the route of the old Bullhead or Cherokee Road to Cherokee Orchard. The level trail that continues straight leads to the Sugarlands Cemetery and to the site of the Pi Beta Phi Settlement School, built out of the old Brackins Log School. During the turn of the century, Pi Beta Phi, founded at William and Mary College, extended aid to the people near Gatlinburg. According to one brochure, these college women (or do-gooders, as they were called in the mountains) were devoted to "scientific, humanized service."

On the main trail, notice rock walls, an abandoned garbage dump, and the ruins of foundations and bridges. This area is the site of two Sugarlands CCC Camps (NP-2 and NP-10) that operated here from

June 1, 1933 to July 18, 1942. According to records in the park archives, the Sugarlands CCC crews had a strong sense of community and even published a newsletter of jokes and songs. The company built the stone arch bridge over the West Prong of the Little Pigeon River, which you crossed at the beginning of the hike. A sketch of the bridge was presented to President Franklin Roosevelt.

The young men, many of them driving trucks for the first time, suffered quite a few accidents. From the Sugarlands CCC newsletter:

COP: Why are you racing through town at this speed?

CCC enrollee: My brakes are out of order and I want to get back to camp before I have an accident.

After passing the CCC ruins, the trail begins a gradual ascent along a wide macadam roadbed. Signs of former settlement continue though are much less frequent. Rock walls and occasional forest clearings, designating former homesites, can be seen as you continue the two mile ascent to the trail's end. Before reaching the top of the ridge, the trail again turns to the left. Here the trees are visibly smaller in size, with mountain laurel dominating the undergrowth along the trail's edge. At the 2,400' elevation mark, Sugarland Mountain becomes visible, particularly in the fall, winter, and spring. The trail makes a right turn and continues through a tall rhododendron grove. Just beyond this point, the Two Mile Lead Trail, a well-worn bridlepath, enters from your left.

Continuing further, Two-mile Branch Trail is at **3.3** miles. This is an alternative 2.9 mile return route to Sugarlands Visitor Center. Straight ahead, the Bull Head Trail is at **3.5** miles and finally the trailhead on Cherokee Orchard Road at **3.9** miles. If a shuttle can be arranged from Cherokee Orchard back to the the Sugarlands Vistor Center, this trail is an ideal morning or afternoon day hike.

Narrative by Margaret Lynn Brown & Donald E. Davis

PALMER CREEK TRAIL

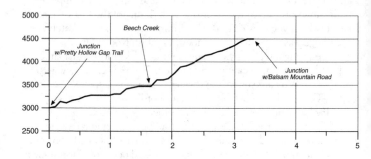

LENGTH: 3.3 miles, from Pretty Hollow Gap Trail to Balsam Mtn. Road.
HIGHLIGHTS: Cove hardwood forest, scenic creek views.
MAP KEY: 11 D; USGS quad: Luftee Knob.
USE: Horse and hiking trail.
STARTING POINT: Pretty Hollow Creek Trail, 1.3 miles from the end of the Cataloochee Road.

The Palmer Creek Trail begins with a picturesque footlog crossing of Pretty Hollow Creek. The trail ascends steadily, gaining 1,500' by the time it reaches the Balsam Mountain Road near the crest of Balsam Mountain. Footing along most of the trail is good, although regular horse use has caused some miry sections.

The flat area near the footlog crossing was once known as Indian Flats. Turkey George Palmer and his father, who visited the area prior to 1875, found evidence of Indian activity in the form of a small cleared field growing up in briers and an old fireplace with pottery pieces nearby.

According to *The North Carolina Gazetteer*, Palmer Creek was named for Turkey George Palmer who lived near the junction of the two streams. Turkey George, a respected citizen of Cataloochee, acquired his name from an adventure trapping wild turkeys. Mr.

Palmer explained that he had trapped nine big gobblers in a pen to keep them from eating corn he had planted. When he got in the pen to kill the turkeys "they riz up an' mighty nigh killed me instead."

Initially, the Palmer Creek Trail climbs through a cove hardwood forest which occurs at lower and middle elevations where rich soil fosters growth of tuliptree, yellow buckeye, silverbell, Eastern hemlock and maples.

In mid-July, clusters of pink-white rosebay rhododendron blooms may be observed along the length of the trail. Bright yellow and orange flame azaleas bloom here from April through June. The forest floor provides its own rewards. Bergamot, Solomon's seal, partridgeberry, trillium, doll's-eyes, squawroot, lousewort and a variety of other plants and ferns provide a source of continuing interest.

Pleasant creek views also abound along this trail, particularly on the lower portion. And even when the runs, pools and small cascades are not visible, the whisper of the creek is a constant reminder of its presence.

The trail crosses a pronounced rock formation just before the footlog crossing of Lost Bottom Creek. The strata exposed in the stream is part of the Thunderhead Sandstone Formation, the thick unit that holds up much of the main range of the Smokies. This strata was carried by the Greenbrier fault when it moved.

Lost Bottom Creek is crossed on a footlog at **1.1** miles. In *Cataloochee: Lost Settlement of the Smokies*, Flora Palmer describes Lost Bottom as a pretty green place with no trees. Ms. Palmer gives another account of a herder who was sent by his father to find lost cattle and caught 97 brook trout from the stream instead. Today, the creek is closed to fishing to protect the declining brook trout.

According to former ranger and Cataloochee resident Mark Hannah, a tragedy once occurred near Lost Bottom Creek. About 1922, Will Camel and a companion camped in early spring under a rock ledge a few hundred yards upstream from where Lost Bottom and Palmer creeks join. They built a fire under a rock overhang for warmth. The heat of the fire caused a large rock slab to break and fall during the night, killing Mr. Camel. The next day the survivor summoned the men of the community to pry the slab off Mr. Camel's body so he could be removed. This event suggests the inspiration for the name Falling Rock Creek, a nearby tributary.

Beech Creek is crossed on a footlog at **1.7** miles. The trail becomes steeper beyond this crossing as it ascends Trail Ridge. Views of Shanty Mountain are visible to the left through the trees. This mountain was named for a shanty built on the opposite side of the mountain, on Shanty Branch, by an African-American slave, Old Smart, who herded cattle for one of the original Cataloochee land owners in the early 1800s.

A change in forest growth becomes quite apparent at the higher elevation as the cove hardwood forest is replaced by closed oak forest which includes oak, sourwood, hickory, mountain laurel, and rhododendron. Galax, trailing arbutus and wintergreen are common plants along the trail margin. The trail passes through a 300-foot-long rhododendron tunnel near its upper terminus, providing an unexpected pleasure for the hiker.

The remains of an earlier trail along Trail Ridge will be noted on the right near the rhododendron tunnel. This earlier trail led from Straight Fork through Pin Oak Gap to Cataloochee Valley.

Flora Palmer, who grew up in Cataloochee, mentioned another old trail in the area. She remembered that Cherokee women sometimes walked through Pin Oak Gap and down Beech Ridge to sell woven baskets for 25¢. According to Ms. Palmer, every child carried lunch in such a basket

The Palmer Creek Trail reaches the one-way Balsam Mountain Road at **3.3** miles. Pin Oak Gap is 0.7 miles to the right and the Spruce Mountain Trail 1.8 miles to the left. During the logging era, a railroad grade extended along Balsam Mountain with a short siding extending out Trail Ridge. Bits of coal, cinders and cable attest to logging activity along the high slopes above Cataloochee. The Parsons Pulp and Lumber Company (later Ravensford) cut hemlock and spruce in the Lost Bottom Creek watershed in the early 1920s and removed the logs through Pin Oak Gap.

Narrative by William A. Hart, Jr.

PANTHER CREEK TRAIL

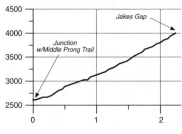

4500 — Jakes Gap

4000

Junction
w/Middle Prong Trail

3500

3000

2500

0   1   2

LENGTH: 2.2 miles, from Middle Prong Trail to Jakes Gap.
HIGHLIGHTS: Panther Creek, rhododendron.
CAUTIONS: Unbridged crossing of Lynn Camp Prong.
MAP KEY: 5 D; USGS quads: Thunderhead Mtn., Silers Bald.

USE: Hiking trail.
STARTING POINT: Middle Prong Trail, 2.3 miles from end of Tremont Road. The Tremont Road begins just west of the Townsend "Y" on the Laurel Creek Road (the road to Cades Cove).

Panthers, "painters", catamounts, whichever you choose to call them, mountain lions haven't been officially documented in the park for years. Are they here? Some biologists believe they are, but most have their doubts. Perhaps a future project will help to restore them to these mountains, much like the reintroduction of the red wolves.

But the only panther you are likely to see today is the creek. And you will see it often. In just over two miles, the Panther Creek Trail crosses this small stream nine times. A tenth crossing, this one of Lynn Camp Prong, is the most difficult and dangerous of the hike. Many trails have one place that most hikers will start from, but the Panther Creek can be reached from either Elkmont, via Jakes Creek Trail, or Tremont, via the Middle Prong Trail. Elkmont hikers must ascend to Jakes Gap and then drop down Panther Creek to the Middle Prong Trail. If you hike this way, you will have to read this description backwards, for it assumes the hiker will start from the Tremont area. We had to make a decision (or make this book twice as long).

From the end of the Tremont Road, you must travel 2.3 miles up the wide, well-graded Middle Prong Trail. This trail follows Lynn

Camp Prong, past many beautiful cascades, to the Panther Creek trailhead and the first of many stream crossings. Turning left onto Panther Creek, the hiker is immediately faced with a cold and powerful river. At high water level, this crossing can be extremely dangerous. Reschedule your hike if you have to. At low to moderate stream levels, this crossing is at best challenging. Large boulders sit in the river, but each year floods shift them about. Take time to study the river and plan the best rock hop. Or if it's a nice summer day, shed the boots and wade across the ford for horses.

From the north side of Lynn Camp Prong, the trail begins to climb moderately on an old railroad bed. This tread is one of many left behind by Little River Lumber Company when the park was created. The bed continues straight into a rhododendron thicket at 0.1 mile. After a short walk, the trail rounds the small ridge and leaves the roar of Lynn Camp Prong behind. Now you will be listening to the gentle crashing of Panther Creek.

At about 0.5 mile, the trail crosses Panther Creek for the first time. It's actually a double crossing. The first, tricky rock hop is followed by a second, easier one. This is a good indication of how the trail will proceed. As you ascend higher up Panther Creek, the crossings will become easier and easier. The final crossing requires but a short jump. From the first crossing, the trail climbs moderately up the flanks of Timber Ridge. At a sharp right turn, the trail levels and widens. If you look closely, you will notice that this too is an old railroad bed. To the left, the bed drops into a rhododendron thicket, its original path erased by this large shrub. We will follow the bed up to the right. It brings you along a bench to a point well above the creek. From here you get some very nice views of the cascades below. A really beautiful cascade can be seen, framed by rhododendrons, at 0.7 mile. After this point, the trail begins to narrow.

The second crossing of Panther Creek comes at mile 0.9. It is a wide crossing, but compared to the two before, it's a piece of cake. This rock hop does, however, mark the beginning of an almost constant crossing and recrossing of Panther Creek. In the next mile, you will cross the creek eight times. A trail this wet in a valley this sheltered—look how narrow it is—can only mean one thing: rhododendrons. At this elevation, the rosebay rhododendron dominates the slopes. Look around, they are everywhere. And although it's an ever-green, the most beautiful time to observe them is in July. This is when the flowers blossom. Each brilliant white flower is part of a larger cluster resembling huge snowballs carefully placed on the tree. Between crossings five and six, the rhododendrons grow so thick as to almost form a tunnel for the trail to pass through.

Continue crossing Panther Creek back and forth. Notice the tiny waterfalls and the special beauty they give the area. But watch your feet, too. Besides stream crossings, there are a number of little seeps which turn the trail to mud. After the final crossing, at mile **2.0**, these disappear. And the scattered hemlocks become fewer and farther between. You have left the cool, sheltered valley for the dry open hardwood forests of Jakes Gap. From this gap, you are faced with a number of decisions. You may simply return the way you came. Or you may choose to turn right and push on up Miry Ridge. Some great views await you along that trail. Or you may wish to push on to Elkmont along the Jakes Creek Trail directly ahead.

Narrative by Tom Condon

POLE ROAD CREEK TRAIL

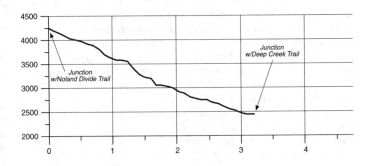

LENGTH: 3.2 miles, from Noland Divide Trail to Deep Creek Trail.
HIGHLIGHTS: Rock outcrops, spring and summer wildflowers,

scenic stream valley.

CAUTIONS: Frequent stream crossings, foot log crossing of Deep Creek.

MAP KEY: 7 E; USGS quad: Clingmans Dome.

USE: Horse and hiking trail.

STARTING POINT: From Clingmans Dome Road, hike Noland Divide Trail 3.7 miles to jct. Pole Road Creek Trail.

Connecting Noland Divide and Deep Creek Trails, Pole Road Creek Trail begins at Upper Sassafras Gap and descends a dry ridge through a second-growth forest of black locust, red maple, Eastern hemlock, and chestnut oak. The primary wildflowers near the top are rosebay rhododendron and wood betony; the latter, partly parasitic, leaches nutrients from other plants' roots. Continuing downhill, you encounter tuliptree and Fraser magnolia, species indicating a transition into a cove environment. Ravines appear on both sides of the trail, with a small stand of Eastern hemlocks populating the left-hand one. Rosebay rhododendron, trailing arbutus, galax, Christmas fern, and wintergreen line the trail banks, while at one point on the left, yellow-fringed orchids and Turk's cap lily grow.

At approximately 1.0 mile, the trail enters a grove of large Eastern hemlock and Fraser magnolia trees with much striped maple nearby. Look for the rock outcrop with its vertical banding, a sign that this particular sheet of rock was tilted on its side in the collision of two continental plates during the creation of these mountains millions of years ago. After walking downhill through a grove of yellow birch, you cross Pole Road Creek, a small stream shrouded in dog-hobble. Several branches of the creek converge into small cascades. The trail descends on the left past a boulder field.

Soon a good vista of a waterfall emerges on the right. After passing a grove of American basswood and yellow buckeye, and a stand of large Eastern hemlock, you step over the creek twice. Winding downhill, the trail enters a stand of huge tuliptrees at 2.0 miles. After another easy crossing of Pole Road Creek, the trail enters a grove of American basswood and then mature Eastern hemlocks.

After rock-hopping across Pole Road Creek again, you descend on the left of the main creek and soon cross feeder creeks. Fraser magnolia and dog-hobble thrive along the creek, while Christmas ferns line the trail banks. The valley widens and the trail levels, then ends by crossing a long footlog over Deep Creek.

Narrative by Ted Olson

POLLS GAP TRAIL

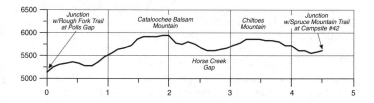

LENGTH: 4.5 miles, from Polls Gap to Spruce Mountain Trail.
HIGHLIGHTS: High elevation vegetation.
CAUTIONS: Steep trail, loose rocks on trail, thick blackberry brambles.
MAP KEY: 10 E; USGS quad: Bunches Bald.
USE: Horse and hiking trail.
TRAILHEAD: Take the Blue Ridge Parkway to Heintooga Ridge Road. Follow this road north about 4.0 miles to Polls (Paul's) Gap. Look for the parking area on the right.

Constructed by Black Camp Gap Company of the Civilian Conservation Corps in 1935, Polls Gap Trail climbs two mountains: Cataloochee Balsam and Chiltoes Mountain. Steep and blocked by fallen trees and overgrown blackberries, Polls Gap Trail makes for strenuous hiking. The trailhead at Polls Gap, sometimes misspelled as Paul's Gap, was where Polly Moody's husband took her favorite milk cow for summer pasturing. The cow was calving, and the calf soon died. Polly became so angry that she wouldn't let anyone forget about it, so her neighbors named the gap after her.

Despite the settler name, the logging history of this area had a lasting effect on the forest and the trail itself. In 1916 the New York-based Suncrest Lumber Company purchased approximately 94,000 acres in and near the Smokies for $1 million. After building a railroad through Polls Gap into the Cataloochee watershed, Suncrest logged extensively. For example, when park formation in 1929 forced the company to stop operations, Suncrest had cut about 7,500 acres in the Cataloochee area (even though it claimed to have cut only 500) and was reluctant to sell out. According to Michael Frome, author of *Strangers in High Places*, Suncrest Lumber Company "made it clear that it would fight for the highest dollar, demanding a total of $2,000,000 for the 26,000 acres [the company's remaining park holdings]. Litigation in Superior Court in Buncombe County [N.C.] set the value at $600,000." This price dispute culminated in a 1932 Supreme Court ruling, which the park won. Suncrest, of course, was not alone in its resistance; Frome, referring to all logging companies in the Smokies, wrote that "The companies were defiant. They did not want to sell and would yield only to condemnation. They wanted to cut timber and would have decimated the virgin stands if they had not been stopped by law." Frank Miller, a Suncrest logger until 1929, corroborated Frome's interpretation, recalling how the company worked as fast as possible to log spruce in Cataloochee because "they were stopped from cutting."

From its trailhead, the trail winds uphill through second-growth forest of American beech and yellow birch. Soon, the trail levels in a stand of red spruce. Coursing among yellow buckeye, mountain maple, sugar maple, and young Fraser fir, the trail rises and levels again. At this point the surrounding forest is half deciduous and half coniferous. During a downhill stretch, a partial view of Cataloochee Valley opens to the right. A number of dead trunks, perhaps Fraser firs, have begun to rot, with young maples filling their places. This windswept ridge, the base of Cataloochee Balsam, supports mainly scrubby mountain-ash and yellow birch, as well as many Fraser fir saplings.

At approximately **0.8** mile, the trail is eroded, with 2-3' deep gulleys exposing shale below; loose pieces shift under your step. Black-capped Chickadees sing from nearby blueberry bushes. As the trail climbs Cataloochee Balsam, larger red spruce appear. Soon, blackberries grow beside the trail, as do many red spruce and Fraser fir seedlings; and though you pass a few yellow birch, the hardwoods thin. For a time, the trail levels among hobblebush and smooth gerardia; then it climbs again and erosion resumes. Because the shallow, rocky soil prevents plants from setting roots deeply, many trees have fallen across the trail.

You continue uphill until, at 1.6 miles, the trail flattens and the forest diminishes on top of Cataloochee Balsam (elevation 5,970'). As you walk across the mountain crest, many dead Fraser fir trunks reveal the damage rendered by the balsam woolly adelgid. Waist-high smooth blackberry brambles are replacing the dying firs.

The trail heads downhill toward Horse Creek Gap, becoming a gully. By approximately 2.5 miles, the trail enters a forest of red spruce, yellow birch, red maple, black cherry, and pin cherry. Many tree roots run across the trail, and furrows in its banks reveal where wild hogs have dug for herbaceous roots. Approaching Horse Creek Gap, the trail enters a level grove of American beech, in which both Rufous-sided Towhees and Dark-eyed Juncos nest and where dodder, a parasitic orange vine, proliferates.

At 3.2 miles the trail climbs Chiltoes Mountain and reenters a dead Fraser fir forest with occasional hobblebush and yellow birch. Smooth blackberry and rocks slow your passage. Reaching the crest (elevation 5,888'), you walk through a level forest of red spruce and yellow birch, then head downhill. The trail levels, weaving among red spruce, yellow birch, American beech, and a thick understory of mountain maple and hobblebush. At 4.4 miles, a short downhill side-trail on the right leads to Campsite #42, one of the highest elevation backcountry campsites in the park (5,480'). Sheltered by large red spruce and yellow birch, this campsite is remote, picturesque, cool, and damp. Just past the side trail, you reach Spruce Mountain Trail junction at 4.5 miles.

Narrative by Ted Olson

PORTERS CREEK TRAIL

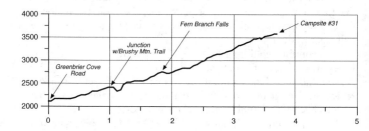

LENGTH: 3.7 miles, from Greenbrier Road to Campsite #31.
HIGHLIGHTS: Wildflowers, waterfall.
MAP KEY: 8 C; USGS quad: Mt. Le Conte.
USE: Hiking trail.
TRAILHEAD: Take US 321 5.9 miles east of Gatlinburg, TN and turn onto the Greenbrier road at the park entrance sign. Pass the ranger station and two picnic areas. At mile 4.1, park on a traffic loop and look for the gate and trail sign.

Greenbrier Cove was heavily settled, and the established farmers and selective logging saved this area from big logging companies. In the early 1800s, the Whaley family is thought to have migrated from North Carolina through Dry Sluice Gap and found this sheltered, fertile valley. By the end of that century, 26 families lived here and, at one point, sent 225 children to the local school, which stood on the site of the present ranger station. The cove had four grist mills, three cemeteries, two churches, two stores, and two blacksmith shops. In 1925, Kimsey Whaley and James West Whaley built the two-story Greenbrier Hotel where Porters Creek joins the Middle Prong near the present picnic area. By this time, there were so many Whaleys in Greenbrier Cove that they needed distinctive nicknames such as Booger Bill, Whiteheaded Bill, and Humpy John.

This trail is famous for its wildflower displays in April and May. If you like to keep lists of what you see in bloom, you might get 30-40 species here. Consequently, the trail gets a fair amount of use. But there is plenty of parking near the trailhead.

After the gate, the trail rises gently; look for mosses, ferns, and lots of wildflowers on the right bank. At mile **0.4**, the foundation of the Cantwell house stands on the right and the John Whaley house and farm site is across the creek. Other house sites, stone walls, and spring house foundations can be seen along this trail.

The trail crosses Long Branch on a good bridge. Up the hill from the bridge, look for a large patch of crested dwarf iris, the Tennessee state wildflower, on the left. They bloom in April and the leaves stay green for the rest of the spring and summer. Then on the right, you will see cement block steps up the bank to the Ownby Cemetery. The gravestones date from the early 1900s, but the families still maintain this cemetery and occasionally place new headstones.

The old road ends in Porters Flat, the open area where the Whaleys first settled. The Brushy Mountain Trail and the historic farm site are to the right and the Porters Creek Trail goes left.

Porters Creek Trail is narrow but easy walking. It descends through a forest of large Eastern hemlocks and Fraser magnolias to the creek. Painted trillium blooms here in late April. The creek itself is deep and rushing, tumbling over great boulders. You will cross on a very long paved foot log that is ingeniously perched on two boulders with little cement platforms to make it level.

Shortly after the foot log, you step into a different world—a moist, sheltered cove with massive yellow buckeye trees and flowers carpeting the ground between them. In early-to-mid April, the fringed phacelia look like a new snowfall. Through a hand lens, each phacelia flower looks like a snowflake. Toothwort, trillium, spring-beauty, hepatica, bloodroot, blue cohosh, phlox, bishop's cap, foamflower—this is just the beginning of the flower list for Porters Creek. The trail turns right and ascends evenly, and as you go up, new flowers in each section brush against your ankles.

Soon the trail is high above the creek on your right, and you pass rock faces on the left. At this level you can find Dutchman's pipe vine, wild ginger, speckled wood lily, and Indian pink, all blooming in May or June. As the trail levels at **1.9** miles, a tiny creek crosses it after plunging and sliding over a 40' waterfall called Fern Falls. Look to your left to see it. Watch for wild ginger and brook lettuce on the creek bank. A steep, nettle-lined side trail leads up to the waterfall, and a large fallen tree makes a good viewing spot.

After the falls, the trail runs along a bench high above the creek. You will see black cohosh (which blooms in June or July and persists until September), plantain-leaved sedge, and more speckled wood lily. But as the trail rises, there are more Eastern hemlocks, and the wildflowers are replaced by a lush moss and fern ground cover. Fraser magnolias and yellow buckeyes grow among the hemlocks. The creek and the trail converge, and you can glimpse cascades and crystal pools. Note the big log jams created by flash floods which frequently roar down from the steep headwaters of this drainage.

At mile **3.7**, the trail turns right toward the creek and comes to the Campsite #31 signpost. A small spring just left of the signpost supplies water, and the campsite is ahead. Beyond the spring, an unmaintained path continues up to the Appalachian Trail at Dry Sluice Gap. Not only is it unmaintained, but it rises 2,000' in just over a mile, mostly up rocks.

Campsite #31 sits in a flat Eastern hemlock grove high above the creek and has several level tent sites. It accommodates 15 people and has infrequent bear visits. There are many large fallen logs to sit on, but don't count on finding much firewood. The creek below, which can be reached by a scramble through rosebay rhododendron, is posted with no camping signs.

Narrative by Doris Gove

PRETTY HOLLOW GAP TRAIL

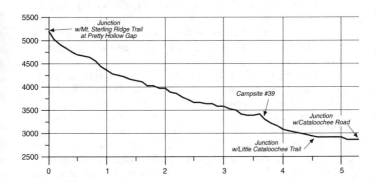

LENGTH: 5.3 miles, from Mt. Sterling Ridge Trail at Pretty Hollow Gap to Cataloochee Road.

HIGHLIGHTS: High elevation forest, historic sites.

MAP KEY: 11 C-D; USGS quad: Luftee Knob.

USE: Horse and hiking trail.

STARTING POINT: Pretty Hollow Gap at jct. of Mt. Sterling Ridge and Swallow Fork trails or (if hiked uphill) the end of the paved road in the Cataloochee Valley.

The Pretty Hollow Gap trail descends through three ecosystems: a spruce-fir forest, a hemlock and rhododendron ecosystem, and a hardwood forest. Each habitat contains some older trees and the trail provides an excellent chance to see how forests change with elevation.

Pretty Hollow Gap Trail begins on Mount Sterling Ridge at Pretty Hollow Gap, 4 miles from Walnut Bottom. Standing at the gap, on clear sunny days, you can see Mt. Sterling above and Indian Knob below. Many high altitude species reside here—look for stands of red spruce, Fraser fir, and yellow birch. Cinnamon and Christmas ferns carpet the forest floor on these higher slopes.

The trail skirts below Indian Ridge about a mile to Pretty Hollow Creek. Horse travel has eroded the trail here so that footing can be difficult in wet weather, and the ridge drops off steeply on the left. As the spruce-fir forest begins to give way to hemlock and pine, look for a stand of mature yellow birch—some a foot in diameter. Ferns and mosses line the edges of the trail, keeping the forest floor a deep green even in winter. Further down the trail, about one-half mile above the creek, notice the trio of very large hemlocks—less than 50' apart—the largest at least 5' in diameter.

At the bottom of the ridge, the trail crosses a tributary of Pretty Hollow Creek, before turning left and following Pretty Hollow Creek for the next 2 miles. According to Mark Hannah, who grew up in Cataloochee, a man once froze to death on Pretty Hollow Creek. In 1915, Robert Caldwell and Bob Forester rode horseback, following the rugged mountain trail that formerly existed on the creek. Bobby Caldwell then headed home to Caldwell Fork Creek. Nothing was heard of Forester, but everyone assumed he went over the mountain to his home. A man trapping in the area later found his body, which was lifted onto a homemade stretcher, placed in a wagon, and transported 22 miles to the Tennessee and North Carolina Railroad Depot.

Along the creek, the trail is lined with rhododendron and large mature hemlocks. You may notice partridgeberry on the trail's shoulder, especially in fall and winter when the plant bears deep red berries. The second stream crossing is a relatively easy rock hop across Onion Bed Branch, a smaller tributary of Pretty Hollow Creek. The trail follows on the right side of the creek before crossing the creek on the first of three well-built foot bridges.

Before the trail crosses the creek the last time, the hemlock forest begins to fall away as oaks, tuliptrees, and maples begin to dominate the landscape. Pretty Hollow Creek continues on the right, carving its way into the narrow valley below the trail. A quarter mile below the last stream crossing, watch for Good Spring Branch entering in a beautiful cascade on the right side of the creek.

As the trail continues, it passes through several large block fields or boulder fields. These were probably created from intense freezing and thawing action during the Ice Age some 15,000-20,000 years ago. As you pass through the block fields, look for Butt Mountain, visible through the trees on the right.

The trail gradually descends closer to the creek bed, following the flood plain all the way to the end of the trail, now less than two miles away. As it begins to widen into a road bed, the trail passes horse stalls and hitching posts and then, on the left, Campsite #39, marked by logs placed in rectangular formation. The campsite is level and near water. It receives heavy use, especially by horse parties.

From #39 the trail begins its final descent to the valley floor, passing a few large trees—a tuliptree approximately 3' in diameter can be seen on the left. After the campground notice a low rock wall and the many small beech trees in the forest understory.

Where Pretty Hollow Creek and Palmer Creek join, the Palmer Creek Trail heads off to the right, following Palmer Creek 3.3 miles to the Balsam Mountain Road. At this point you've gone **4.0** miles from the Pretty Hollow Gap trailhead. The road becomes very wide as it approaches the Cataloochee Valley, a once thriving mountain community. To the left is the Little Cataloochee trailhead, which passes over Bald Top Mountain into the Little Cataloochee Valley.

Just a half mile further on the left is a horse camp with rest room facilities. Cataloochee residents called this Indian Flats, and it was popular with local fisherman and then tourists even before the Park Service acquired the land. Continue straight along the left bank of Palmer Creek.

Here the trail follows what looks like an old road bed. A wide, open field several hundred yards on the right dotted with yucca plants suggests a former homesite. Apple trees are another sign that a farm once prospered here. At the turn of the century, "Turkey George" Palmer and his family lived near here and according to park records, his place included a house, spring house, smokehouse, barn, and sheep shed. Cataloochee history is filled with stories about the life of Turkey George. His daughter, Flora Palmer Medford, recalled that her father's coffin was a steel casket bought in Waynesville. A famous bear hunter, Turkey George requested this security because he wanted to make sure that the bears would not dig him up after his death in revenge—he killed 106, according to one source.

Toward the end of the trail, Beech Grove School is visible across Palmer Creek on the right. Built in 1901 to replace an older log building, the school served the Cataloochee community until the 1930s.

From November through January, school was held from 8 a.m. to 4 p.m. with two recesses and a lunch hour. Gudger Palmer, who attended, remembered buying his own books from the teacher, as well as penny pencils and five cent tablets of rough paper.

The trail ends at the parking area adjacent to the Palmer Creek bridge. A car should be left here in order to shuttle back to your original destination. Of course you could start your journey here, but the hike up to the gap makes the trip a much more difficult one.

Narrative by Margaret Lynn Brown and Donald E. Davis

RABBIT CREEK TRAIL

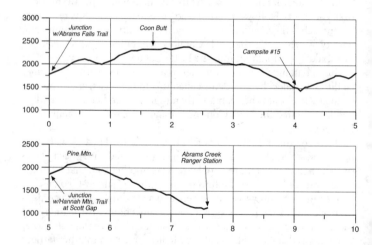

LENGTH: 7.6 miles, from Abrams Falls trailhead off the Cades Cove Loop Road to Abrams Creek Ranger Station.

HIGHLIGHTS: Cleft where time stands still, large tuliptree at Scott Gap.

CAUTIONS: Crossing Mill and Rabbit creeks.

MAP KEY: 2-3 D-E; USGS quad: Cades Cove, Calderwood.

USE: Horse and hiking trail.

TRAILHEAD: Take side road off Cades Cove Loop Road between numbered posts 10 and 11. There is a larger parking area at the end that serves for both Abrams Falls and Rabbit Creek trailheads. (Don't worry, the crowds are headed to Abrams Falls.)

Your journey begins by wading the broad and shallow stretch of Mill Creek at the Abrams Falls trailhead. Later you will wade or rock-hop Rabbit Creek and finish up by passing over Abrams Creek on a long, picturesque footlog.

This trail follows an old mountain track crossing low ridges (below 2,400'), long used by Indians between Cades Cove and their villages on the Little Tennessee River. By 1830 it was used by whites. In the "History of Blount County," an old map calls it the Gourley Trail. Gourleys over time lived at both ends of this old trace.

Now it's a wide, fine trail in good condition, having been vastly improved in the 1930s by the Civilian Conservation Corps (CCC) boys as a fire road. The hard clay surface and Cades Sandstone base have resisted erosion except on a few short, steep sections.

After crossing Mill Creek, the trail sharply climbs the right flank of a V-shaped hollow in Boring Ridge. The ridge is not named for mundaneness, but rather for the Boring family that farmed the area. Today the Boring family is still quite well represented locally, with several on the Happy Valley end of this trail. Rosebay rhododendron closely borders the upper side and its white blooms with a shade of pink, display postcard beauty on the opposite slope in late June and early July.

The trail moves over the broad, gently rounded crest of Boring Ridge through an open, mixed forest of pines and hardwoods. Later on, where the trail curves to lessen the grade, the narrow old road climbs to the right more steeply. It appears to have been too narrow for a wagon and more suited to land sleds. Narrow sleds with smooth sourwood runners were the principal means of transport over short distances for mountain farmers.

It's a relatively easy and lightly used path, excellent in all seasons, where deer are often seen. Colorful crow-sized Pileated Woodpeckers, "woodhens" to the natives, are heard more frequently than observed. Their call sounds something like a soundtrack from a Hollywood jungle film. The trail passes several large white pines on the slight drop to More Licker Branch (a name, suggesting rather strongly, that corn whiskey was brewed there). Ascending again, the trace goes over Coon Butt through pines and oaks.

Coon Butt ridge joins the broad, farmable crest of Andy McCully Ridge. It was the most level portion of Andy McCully's fields. He was the major farmer on the Cades Cove end of this ridge road. There were a half dozen other farms between Abrams Creek and Scott Gap, including those of the Borings and the Gourleys.

Saucer-sized white mushrooms grow at the trail's edge. A spur of the McCully Ridge turns northwest and ascends and runs this crest for a mile before descending for a mile into a hemlock forest at Rabbit Creek. Campsite #15 sits at mile **4.1**, clean and inviting under hemlocks, within earshot of the soothing murmur of the creek. The "Blizzard of '93" knocked down many trees which for a time obscured the path to the best sites 150' from the trail. The sites are still there, however. A Geographical Survey marker is embedded in a large stone on the east edge of a line of stepping stones crossing the creek and reads 1,448' elevation.

The Rabbit Creek Fault line is at or near this stream crossing and runs northeast and southwest. It is the leading edge of the Cades Sandstone which lies north and southwest of Cades Cove. The Wilhite Formation, which includes a range of rocks from siltstone to conglomerates, quartz, and dolomite, borders the Cades Sandstone. This bedrock extends from Rabbit Creek to the north slope of Pine Mountain.

Unusual rocks soon appear, a conglomerate stone with the striking feature of embedded milky quartz pebbles. A large sample of this rock is at Scott Gap.

Not far beyond Rabbit Creek is one of the most delightful trail features in all of the Smokies. It's a narrow, dark, sheltered passage flanked by sharply rising slopes. The sun slips in at noon only, and then is excluded by the thick forest canopy. The rocky bed in this crack in the mountain serves for both stream and trail, absolutely unchanged since the first human passed through. Time stands frozen.

Soon the path ascends the sharp north flank of the mountain and passes increasingly large white pines, Eastern hemlocks, and tuliptrees as you approach Scott Gap. In spring, the forest floor here is carpeted with bloodroot, ferns, and rue anemone. On the left at the gap is a tuliptree of almost 13' in circumference. Just beyond, on the left side of the Hannah Mountain Trail, is a large white pine.

An 8 person shelter is west of the gap and near the homesite of George Scott who farmed the land sloping toward Abrams Creek. The shelter was built by the Youth Conservation Corps in the 1970s and is located 100 yards below Scott Gap in a pleasant, quiet hardwood forest. It's a log structure with wire bunks and is popular on weekends. In dry weather the water source is undependable here and you may wish to camp at #15 instead.

The trail rises for 0.5 mile to the top of Pine Mountain and then descends more slowly along a beautiful pine needle pathway, sometimes on the ridgeline, toward the waters of Abrams Creek. In the bottomland are the old fields, still not reforested, of Leason Hearon on the north side and Charlie Boring on the south. Jonquils bloom here in the spring. Also, the flowers of the purple-flowering raspberry are there in late summer. This plant is unusual in that it often displays blooms and ripe fruit at the same time.

A long footlog runs across a wide and deep span of Abrams Creek. Although quite high above the stream, flood waters lift it off its moorings every few years. If this is the case, the old ford is just above. Beyond that is the terminus of the Rabbit Creek Trail.

Narrative by Woody Brinegar

RAINBOW FALLS TRAIL

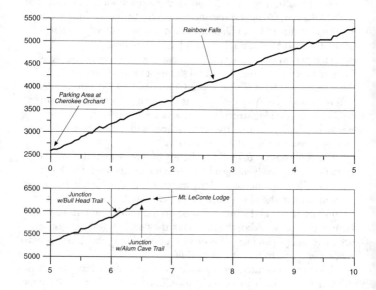

LENGTH: 6.6 miles, from Rainbow Falls Parking Area on the Cherokee Orchard Road to the summit of Mt. Le Conte. (Rainbow Falls is 2.7 miles from the trailhead.)

HIGHLIGHTS: Rainbow Falls, panoramic views, spring and summer wildflowers.

CAUTIONS: Trail may be icy in winter.

MAP KEY: 7 C; USGS quad: Mt. Le Conte.

USE: Hiking trail only.

TRAILHEAD: Take Airport Road (traffic light #8 in Gatlinburg) into the park. At mile 3.4, just after the road becomes one-way, turn right into the Rainbow Falls Parking Area. Find the trail by following a path a few yards south into the woods, opposite the paved road.

This trail to Mt. Le Conte starts close to the same spot where a group started walking to Le Conte in 1924 to ascertain whether the Great Smokies was a fit place to establish a national park.

Though the park was established in the early 1930s and the orchard was bought for inclusion in it, orchardist M. M. Whittle didn't harvest his last crop of apples until autumn 1960. Because the orchard was fairly new, the owners were given a 15-year lease to continue operating after the time of purchase. That lease was extended several times. Whittle grew 47 varieties of apples on 800 acres of land here. A few of the old trees still bloom and produce apples. Morel mushroom hunters search the orchard in April.

The apple house stood slightly east of the present parking area but on the opposite side of the road. Near it was a barn where Jack Huff, Le Conte Lodge operator, stabled pack horses which carried supplies up the Rainbow Falls Trail. (The present lodge operators use llamas as pack animals and they travel another trail. Llama hooves are not as damaging to the trail as horse hooves.)

The trail goes up the left (east) side of Le Conte Creek. Notice the rocks, from the size of marbles to great boulders. They're on the trail, beside the trail and, especially, in the creek. How would you like to cultivate a garden here? Some did. People lived along the creek and cultivated this rocky land. Before the park was established, these lowlands were logged approximately half way up to Rainbow Falls.

Gatlinburg old-timer Lucinda Ogle remembers when Le Conte Creek was called Mill Creek, because it had so many small gristmills on it. She says there were 14 mills on the main creek and two others on small tributaries. The mill she remembers being farthest up the creek was about a quarter-mile upstream from the parking area and about a quarter-mile downstream from the home of Indian Bill. Indian Bill was an herb doctor and the last Cherokee to live in the Gatlinburg area.

The big tree trunk sections decaying on the ground probably are Eastern hemlocks. Look for one of these old logs which is the "nurse" tree for several rosebay rhododendrons growing out of it. Also growing on it is a mat of partridgeberry, the little evergreen ground-hugging vine that produces tiny twin trumpet-shaped flowers and small red berries. The berries are rather tasteless but not unpleasant, something like wet wheat.

After a mile or more, the trail temporarily switches left from the creek and goes through an area where grow rosebay rhododendron, galax, trailing arbutus, teaberry and mountain pepper-bush. Pepper-bush is a shrub that grows a dozen or more feet tall and blooms in mid-summer. Look in this area for pink lady's slippers. You won't find many but you might find one.

The trail switches to the right again and you travel in the general direction of the creek, which you reach and cross on a footbridge about 2.0 miles from where you started walking. Within a quarter-hour or less, you'll cross, without help of a bridge, a small tributary of Le Conte Creek.

Then will come the second and third bridges across Le Conte Creek. The third is just below the falls. If you're here in mid-summer, look for the blooms of pink turtlehead. It's a pretty, high-altitude wildflower. If you're here in mid-winter during a period of prolonged extreme cold, look for the falls to be frozen into an hour-glass shape. This is one of the spectacular sights of the Great Smokies, but it occurs only infrequently.

The "leaning tree" that hikers climbed to get above the falls in 1924 is no longer part of the trail. Instead, the trail follows a reasonable grade to the right, up and around the bluff.

Along this section in July and August, look for the bright blooms of crimson bee-balm and the big yellow blooms of coneflower. You also will see the white blooms of wild hydrangea and white snakeroot. And you will begin seeing Rugel's ragwort, whose blooms are no more attractive than its name. They slightly resemble a small floral hammer, or perhaps the head of a snake poised to strike. They are tan to brown and common in the high Smokies, but not known to grow elsewhere.

The old trail—the one that made use of the "leaning tree"—determinedly followed the creek; its rugged route went above the falls to the last spring and continued to the mountain top. But the new trail, built by young men of the Civilian Conservation Corps in the 1930s, takes a hiker on a long tour of Rocky Spur, the stony divide between the valleys of Le Conte Creek and Roaring Fork Creek. Above the falls, this trail recrosses the creek to the north and then veers west back more than a half-mile toward Cherokee Orchard.

Among the plants that bloom along this section are mountain laurel, rosebay rhododendron, fetterbush and mountain St. John's-wort. You may be able to snack on serviceberries and blueberries in August and hazel nuts in autumn.

At one point, you can stand on a natural stone lookout and see, surprisingly close, the Space Needle and the Park Vista Hotel in Gatlinburg. If seeing the Park Vista and the Space Needle is not enough to make you happy, you can look for witch-hobble. It's a gangling-looking shrub that produces lovely white blooms in May. Its big roundish, leaves are among the first to change color. Starting in early August and lasting into October, they show colors ranging from orange to dark wine.

The trail crosses the Rocky Spur crest at about 4,880' elevation and swings abruptly eastward along the north slope of the ridge. Listen for the songs of Winter Wrens. Down to your left is the valley of Roaring Fork.

The trail climbs gradually—5,000', 5,200'. At about 5,400', it curves south and then west and soon crosses the crest to the south side near the 5,450' elevation. After two or three more direction changes, you come to a side trail on the left. It's worth walking, provided you aren't about to be late for dinner at the Lodge. It's about 0.2 mile long and rejoins the Rainbow Falls Trail at a higher elevation. Its main attraction is great pincushions of mountain myrtle. It's worth seeing any time of the year, but it's especially good when the tiny pink and white myrtle blooms appear, usually in June. At open spots, you can see Brushy Mountain to the northeast and Le Conte's West Point to the south.

Back on the main trail, you move quickly across the upper valley of Le Conte Creek, a very shallow valley at this point. It is so high that in dry weather, you may find no water at the crossing. But in August you will find the blooms of many pink turtleheads.

And soon after that, you will reach the point where the Rainbow Falls and Bull Head Trails meet, just under West Point. After the two trails intersect at mile **6.1**, the single trail continuing uphill to the left, toward the Lodge, still carries the Rainbow Falls name. You still have more than a half-mile of walking before you reach the Lodge, and the first part of it is pretty steep.

Up on top, as well as down the high slopes, you see a great many dead trees. These are Fraser firs, killed by a tiny insect called the balsam woolly adelgid. This exotic pest (brought into this country from Europe in 1908) has killed most of the large firs since it invaded the park in the early 1960s.

About a half-mile beyond the Bull Head Trail intersection, you will see another trail coming in from the right. This is the Alum Cave Trail. Continue on the Rainbow Falls Trail a little more than 0.1 mile and you will reach the Lodge. You also will reach the intersection of the Trillium Gap Trail, coming up from the north. At that point, the name of the trail you've been walking changes from Rainbow Falls to The Boulevard Trail.

Taking off to the right, just opposite the Lodge, is the trail you will walk after dinner to Cliff Top to see the sunset. Enjoy.

Narrative by Carson Brewer

RAMSAY CASCADES TRAIL

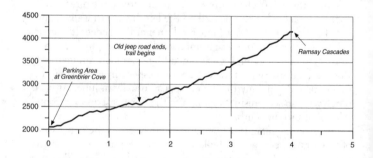

LENGTH: 4.0 miles, beginning at Ramsay Cascades parking area and ending at Ramsay Cascades.
HIGHLIGHTS: Cascades, virgin forest.
CAUTIONS: Rocky trail segments; slippery falls (do not climb).

MAP KEY: 8-9 C; USGS quad: Mt. Guyot.
USE: Hiking trail only.
TRAILHEAD: Drive 5.9 miles east from Gatlinburg on US 321 and enter the park on the Greenbrier Road to the right. The paved road ends and narrows just past the ranger station; heed the warning signs while on the gravel road. At mile 3.2, turn left at a sign for Ramsay Cascade on to a bridge that crosses the Middle Prong. Drive 1.5 miles to the parking area at the end of the road.

Ramsay Cascades Trail provides two kinds of hiking—easy road hiking along the Middle Prong of the Little Pigeon River and then slightly harder, narrow trail hiking along the Ramsay Prong. The early settlers of this area, many of whom were named Whaley, also noticed this difference. They cut most of the mature forest along the Middle Prong and saved the rest for later. Fortunately, by the time Champion Fiber Company had bought the land and planned access railroads to harvest Eastern hemlocks and red spruce, the national park took over. Local settlers had selectively cut tuliptrees, basswoods (lindens), and yellow buckeyes for the lumber companies, but record-size trees still stand along this trail.

Not long after the trailhead, the first stream crossing is on a long, bouncy footbridge where the Middle Prong plunges over huge boulders into green swimming holes. From there you climb gradually along the old road through cove hardwood forest. The presence of black locust trees just across the foot bridge and many small, straight tuliptrees throughout the woods indicates that this area was cut over and probably farmed. The rock slabs and boulders that now support caps of polypody fern and wildflowers must have made for hard plowing. Dutchman's pipe vine (a smooth curvy vine with large heart-shaped leaves) climbs up many trees on this lower part of the trail. During summer hikes, watch out for bald-faced hornet nests hanging out over the trail at just about head level. They look like gray paper cantaloupes. If you see one, just walk by carefully and take a quick look at the guard hornets patrolling the entrance at the bottom.

At mile **1.5**, you come to the old traffic circle and get the first view of Ramsay Prong as it meets Middle Prong. The old Greenbrier Pinnacle Trail used to start here, but since the park no longer maintains it, it may be difficult to follow. Peregrine Falcons have been raised and then released by volunteers on Greenbrier Pinnacle; with luck, the falcons and their offspring are now established in the park.

To the right of the Ramsay Cascades trail sign is a three-trunked witch-hazel tree at the stream edge; behind it a black cherry leans precariously out over the water. To the left of the sign a tunnel of rhododendron and mountain laurel signal where you start the serious climb.

The Ramsay Cascades Trail is narrow and steep in some places but in excellent condition. Credit for that must go to the trail crews who installed rock steps and several fine footbridges. One good set of trail stairs on the upper part of the trail leads past a small cave, just big enough to crawl into if a rainstorm blows up. You will have to cross Ramsay Prong a couple of times on rocks, but the footing is usually good.

Two themes to notice along this trail are big trees and an amazing variety of exposed roots. Some trees have sent out roots to hang on to the shallow, rocky soil, and others started their lives on fallen logs that rotted long ago. Yellow birch roots look like claws clutching at the ground. Eastern hemlocks hang at the edge of a boulder or stream bank and reach back for solid earth with thick, dark roots.

About a mile up the trail, you walk between two huge, straight tuliptrees, as majestic as Roman columns. Even the selective loggers didn't come up this far. Just around the bend on the left side of the trail is the real giant—another tuliptree with roots like elephant toes. Ahead on the right are several large silverbell trees. Their bark is bluish-black and flaky. Though small compared to the tuliptree, they are near record size for their species. Another big tree along this trail is basswood, or linden, which can be identified by clusters of shoots growing up around the base of the tree.

The trail crosses Ramsay Prong and loops away from it for a while. A recent storm knocked down several big tuliptrees and Eastern hemlocks on part of this section, opening up large spaces in the forest canopy. Young trees will compete for those spaces over the next few years, and new trees will grow on some of the dead logs. Bright red bee-balm blooms here in mid to late summer. Pinch the flower gently and smell the refreshing lemon scent.

Suddenly, when you're beginning to wonder just how long 2.5 miles can be, you'll come out on the right of Ramsay Cascades. Water splashes more than 90' from ledge to ledge, and the cool spray feels wonderful on a summer day. You might have to take your shoes off to wade across to the flat rock at the base, but heed the warning signs and do not climb on the falls. Ramsay Cascades is the highest waterfall accessible by trail in the park. Most of the water comes from the slopes of Mt. Guyot, two thousand feet higher.

Look for salamanders and tadpoles in the pools at the base of the falls, and don't leave your lunch sitting out unless you want to share it with red squirrels and yellow jackets. This is a popular destination in summer; even if you don't see another hiker on the trail, the cascades may be a bit crowded.

Hiking time is 2-4 hours going up and 1½-2½ hours coming down, depending, of course, on how many swimming holes you visit.

Narrative by Doris Gove

RICH MOUNTAIN LOOP HIKE

INTRODUCTION

There are essentially two ways to hike a trail if you hope to return to your vehicle where you left it. You can be a yo-yo, hike out and back on the same trail, or you can try to combine the trail with others to create a loop hike. For those of you visiting the Cades Cove area, a wonderful 8-mile loop can be created by combining three trails on the slopes of Rich Mountain. This day hike is generally considered a moderate hike as it does climb about 1,600' from the floor of the cove to the top of Cerulean Knob (3,686'). The three trails involved are the Rich Mountain Loop (appropriately), Indian Grave Gap, and Crooked Arm Ridge trails. Although a loop is technically the same in both directions, there is a preferred way to travel this one. It is not simply for ease of travel, but also for better understanding of the area in which you hike.

Begin your hike on the Rich Mountain Loop Trail and stay on it until it ends. Crooked Arm Ridge Trail, which begins just a half mile along the Loop, is a steep and rocky trail. It receives a huge amount of horse use, and as such, has also become quite rutted. It is much more enjoyable to come down this trail than to try to scale it. Rich Mountain Loop will be steep and rocky in places, but not to the same extent. It also allows you to learn of the history of the cove for soon you will pass the John Oliver Cabin and climb along the old road which he used to enter and first settle the Cove.

—*Tom Condon*

RICH MOUNTAIN LOOP TRAIL

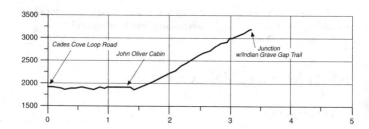

LENGTH: 3.4 miles, from Cades Cove Loop Road to Indian Grave Gap Trail.

HIGHLIGHTS: John Oliver Cabin, scenic views.

MAP KEY: 3 D; USGS quad: Cades Cove.

USE: Horse and hiking trail.

TRAILHEAD: Park at the large parking area at the beginning of the one-way Cades Cove Loop Road, near the orientation shelter. Cross the road and walk along it in the direction of traffic flow a short distance to the trail sign.

This trail begins at the entrance to the 11-mile Cades Cove Loop Road where there is plenty of parking at the orientation shelter. It crosses three creeks a total of six times and then climbs up to Indian

Grave Gap. The crossings—once over Crooked Arm Branch, twice over Harrison Branch, and thrice over Marthas Branch—are all insignificant except in the highest of spring floods. The climb, however, is not. The trail does all its climbing in the last two miles, making for a respectable 670 foot per mile climb.

The first mile and a half meanders up and down along the base of Rich Mountain. The earliest settlers lived along this edge. Their cleared fields are maintained today by Park Service leasees to give you the sense of the settlers' efforts in opening these forests to farming. You will pass along the edge of these openings in the first part of your hike. That large mound across the field at **0.25** mile is not an "Indian mound" as many are inclined to believe. According to park historian Ed Trout, two archeological digs of this impressive little hill found no evidence of human burials or even influences in creating this hill.

Moving along you will pass over Crooked Arm Branch and come quickly to the junction with the Crooked Arm Ridge Trail. Rich Mountain Loop and Crooked Arm Ridge are often used as part of an 8-mile day hike across the face of Rich Mountain, hence the term loop. If these are your plans, stay with this trail and use Crooked Arm Ridge for your descent.

Pressing on, you will cross Harrison Branch twice. Although you will find scattered wildflowers along this section, they will never be numerous. Cades Cove has been invaded by aliens. No, not from outer space, but from Japan. The major ground cover you find here is a plant known as Japanese witch grass. This alien, or non-native, was unknowingly introduced into the area in the 1960s. Keith Langdon of the Park Service's resource management division says that aliens pose the greatest threat to the park. These plants and animals take away space from the native species or damage the remaining habitat. Although research continues, no effective control of witch grass has been found.

As you approach **1.3** miles, you will see evidence of another invasion. This one took place around 1818 when the builder of the cabin before you came to Cades Cove. At the request of his friend Joshua Jobe, John Oliver, having forsaken his training as a collier (charcoal maker), gathered his courage and belongings and moved here. He brought with him his young wife, Luraney, and his daughter, Polly, to try their hand at frontier farming. Their first winter was hard; clearing the land and building a home had kept them from "putting by" enough food for the winter. The Cherokees of the valley provided small gifts of dried pumpkin to these trespassers. Without these gifts, the Olivers would have surely perished, but they survived to see Jobe's return in the spring. He brought with him new settlers and a bribe for Luraney. Two milk cows kept Luraney in the cove and set the Olivers up as the catalyst to push the Cherokees out. By 1819 the Calhoun Treaty had been signed forcing the Cherokee to relinquish their claim to this land. The cove's white population now continued to grow until it reached a peak in 1850 of 137 families or about 700 people.

Turn south now and head up Marthas Branch. This little creek is probably named for John and Luraney's second daughter. In a quarter mile you will see a chimney to the right. No records tell of whose home this was, but it can safely be assumed it was constructed around the 1850s. The heavy settlement of the cove had pushed people away from the quality bottom lands and up the hillsides. This farmer may have grown crops in the "holler" (small valley) behind his house. The view from here must have been incredible then. The forest would have been cleared from the cove floor to half way up the mountains. This farmer's success may have been marginal and he might have migrated to Missouri or other "western" states as many others had just prior to the Civil War, leaving behind a small dream marked only by this old chimney.

The trail now really starts to climb, but it does so in "fits." A steep climb is followed by a short flat section and then a steep climb again. You are climbing Cave Ridge named for the Joe Gregory Cave to the southwest. At first the rocks underfoot are Metcalf Phyllite, a soft metamorphosed shale, but they give way to Cades Sandstone which caps the mountain. Geologists believe that these rocks were pushed up and over the limestone which covers the valley floor approximately 300 million years ago. The Great Smoky Fault, a huge thrust fault, resulted from the collision between Africa and North America. In the years since, the softer phyllite has eroded away re-exposing the limestone beneath. This "hole" in the mountains is what geologists call a window or fenster. Wear Cove and Townsend sit in similar fensters.

Although steep, the climb can be enjoyable at all seasons. Wild-flowers grace the trail in the spring, flame azaleas and rosebay rhododendrons bloom in the summer, autumn has the beautiful colors of sourwood, black gum, oaks, and maples and of course, winter has the expansive views. At mile **3.0** you will get a great view of the cove at any season. In 1890, Reverend Isaac P. Martin recorded a similar view: ". . . presently I came to a cliff from which I could see the entire cove which nestles there among the crests of the great mountains. I had never seen anything quite so beautiful. Cades Cove is the dream of the Smoky Mountains. "

One-third mile further and you will intersect Indian Grave Gap Trail. Turn back here or continue on to Cerulean Knob and loop back to where you started via Crooked Arm Ridge Trail.

Narrative by Tom Condon

RICH MOUNTAIN TRAIL

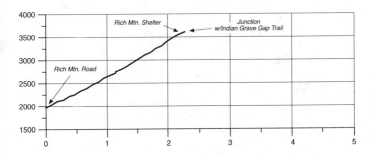

LENGTH: 2.3 miles, from Rich Mtn. Road to Indian Grave Gap Trail.

HIGHLIGHTS: Cascades on Hesse Creek, interesting trees, solitude.

MAP KEY: 3 D; USGS quad: Kinzel Springs.

USE: Horse and hiking trail.

TRAILHEAD: Rich Mtn. Gap, along Rich Mtn. Road (see paragraph 2).

NOTE: This trail is not part of the Rich Mtn. loop hike.

I think the best way to describe this trail is that it's upside-down. Most trails in the park which climb from a low elevation to a higher one tend to start along a creek bed and climb to a dry ridge. On this trail, you will start dry and climb to a creek bed.

To reach the trailhead, you have two choices. For those staying in Cades Cove, the easiest access is to drive up Rich Mountain Road to its end at the park boundary. Except for Saturday mornings in the spring and summer, this road can be reached via the Cades Cove Loop Road. For those traveling from outside the park, it is far easier to approach the trailhead through Dry Valley. Heading south on US 321, turn right after the Kinzel House Restaurant, a few miles west of Townsend. Follow this road to the Tuckaleechee Cove Methodist Church. Turn right here onto Old Cades Cove Road. This will take you through Dry Valley and to the park boundary at Rich Mountain Gap. At the gap, the Old Cades Cove Road runs headlong into the one-way Rich Mountain Road. A small area here provides parking for both the Ace Gap Trail and Rich Mountain Trail.

Rich Mountain Trail begins about 100 yards south of this parking area. The trail is very obvious as it leaves the road from the southeast side. You will immediately begin to climb along Rich Mountain. The trail quickly turns right. All around you will be hundreds of Christmas ferns. Rising above the ground are the fern leaves or fronds, each connected to the other by underground stems. One interpretation for the name Christmas fern is that the leaflets (or pinnae) resemble a Christmas stocking. Others say it looks more like Santa in his sleigh. Still others claim the fern simply takes its name because it is an evergreen—even around Christmas time.

The trail continues to climb steeply along the flanks of Rich Mountain, passing beneath dry pine-oak forests. All around you for the first quarter mile are large locust trees. The field guides call these black locust, but many locals traditionally call them yellow locust. Around here, you can see that the locals are at least better at describing. The deeply fissured bark of these trees is far more yellow than black. The early settlers of Cades Cove and these mountains used the locust for anything that would be wet for long periods because of its ability to resist rotting. Around the area, fence posts are still almost all locust. The drive shaft for the wheel at Cable Mill is locust as well.

You are still climbing, but at **0.25** mile you will switch back away from Rich Mountain Road. To the inside of the turn is a nice example of devil's walking stick. Look at the huge leaves - the largest in North America. What might appear to be a branch is actually a compound leaf, sometimes up to 4' long and containing dozens of leaflets. The small tree's menacing thorns account for its demonic name.

More climbing will bring you to a partially obstructed view of the western end of the park at **0.75** mile. You can see the ridges of Short, Beard Cane, and Hatcher Mountains. At **1.0** mile you will reach the park boundary line and gain some partial views of Dry Valley. Here too is another unusual tree—a large sassafras. Like the devil's walking stick, this tree has strange leaves. In fact, it has 3 different leaf shapes. They come in an oval shape with no lobes, mitten-shaped with 2 lobes, and 3 lobes in almost a bird foot shape. Like the locusts, these trees were also sought by the early settlers. The durable lumber was used for barrels and buckets, the bark could make a pleasant tea, and an orange dye. The wood was also a good fuel.

By now you will be hearing a small creek below you. This is Hesse Creek. It is still far in the distance, but if recent rains have fallen, it will be getting louder. As you walk along on a slope that is no longer very steep, the creek will get closer. Finally at **1.75** mile the trail will reach the creek, just below this junction is a small cascade of about 10'. After a good rain, this is a lovely falls, but difficult to get a good view of. Be careful.

This is where the trail has turned upside-down. Now, after climbing a dry slope for 1.75 miles, you have reached a typical bottomland cove. At 2,000', you would expect this cool moist valley, but not here at 3,000'. It is a little strange, but that is what makes these mountains so interesting and diverse.

Follow the creek back and forth, rock hopping occasionally, for another quarter mile until you begin to climb a small ridge. As you reach the top, the trail will open out into a small dry cove. Here is the Rich Mountain Shelter—a small open front lean-to. Unlike the

Appalachian Trail shelters, Rich Mountain has no chain link fence to lock you in. It does not get the use of the A.T. and therefore has not become well known to bears and other critters. Don't let down your guard however. Take the necessary precautions and hang your food. There is a perfect bear bag tree 100' to the shelter's right.

If you are just day hiking, the junction with Indian Grave Gap Trail is just ahead at mile **2.3**. You can use this to reach Cerulean Knob or drop down into Cades Cove. Or you can spin around and walk the trail outside-in, from a wet valley to a dry ridge.

Narrative by Tom Condon

ROAD PRONG TRAIL

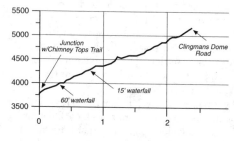

LENGTH: 2.4 miles, from Chimney Tops Trail to Indian Gap on Clingmans Dome Road.
HIGHLIGHTS: Small waterfalls, big trees.
CAUTIONS: Rocky trail, one moderately difficult creek crossing, wet feet.
MAP KEY: 7 D; USGS quads: Mt. Le Conte, Clingmans Dome.
USE: Hiking trail.
STARTING POINT: Drive to the Chimney Tops parking area, 6.7 miles south of Sugarlands Visitor Center (or 6.3 miles north of New-found Gap) on Newfound Gap Road. Look for the large parking area between the tunnel and the "loop." Then hike the first 0.9 mile of Chimney Tops Trail to the starting point.

Road Prong Trail is wet, rocky, steep, and beautiful. It splits left off the Chimney Tops Trail a little less than a mile from the Newfound Gap Road. In this description, you start hiking at the Chimney Tops parking area, but you could also start this trail at Indian Gap on the Clingmans Dome Road (1.3 miles from Newfound Gap), and hike downhill.

Starting from the Chimney Tops Trail, Road Prong Trail is a single file path through grass, sunflowers, bee-balm, and other flowers. In late April, the trail junction is surrounded by a patch of white fringed phacelia so thick it looks like fresh snow. After this open junction, the trail moves up into thick rosebay rhododendron along the creek.

This trail is an old roadbed, now little used, rocky and eroded. It curls around Mount Mingus, named for a North Carolina physician who helped Arnold Guyot, a Swiss geographer, survey the mountains and establish elevations of the peaks. At one time, this route was the main route between Sevierville and Cherokee and it was called the Oconaluftee Turnpike. Tolls were charged for wagons (25-75¢), pigs and sheep (1¢ each), cows (2¢ each), and horse and rider (6 ¼¢).

Jarvis Conner, of Bradleytown, North Carolina (now Smokemont), recalled buying hogs in Tennessee and trying to drive them home: "They'd get so they couldn't travel, you see. They just lag along…They get too bad we just leave 'em." Harvey Broome wrote in 1944 that one of the hazards of camping near this trail in the 1920s was a cattle stampede. The road was first a trade road and later a strategic route for the Civil War. Confederate Colonel William Thomas, a white man raised by a Cherokee family, led a group of Cherokees on a mission to improve the road for access to alum from Alum Cave and as a route of cannons and ammunition. Thomas later studied law and helped the Cherokees who had been removed to Oklahoma repurchase some of their native lands.

As the trail ascends through rosebay rhododendron, you can hear a large cascade to the left, and you will get two quick views of it. The pool below is sometimes filled with a log jam. It is too steep and slippery to explore. A little farther up the trail is a car-sized rounded boulder with a yellow birch growing out of the back. Go left at this boulder and rock hop across Road Prong to pick up the trail on the other side. This is Road Prong's first chance to get your feet wet. In high water you may have to scramble upstream to find logs and rocks to cross on. Just up from this crossing is a vertical slab of lichen-covered rock, as if a giant had sunk a hatchet blade here. Then come several impressive waterfalls and cascades. One looks like a fan as water sprays out from a narrow cleft.

After more ascent, the trail and Road Prong draw even with each other and you enter a fragrant spruce-fir forest with a thick understory of lichens and mosses. Here in this more open forest you can imagine the old road with herds of pigs and cows, a few oxcarts, and deep, muddy ruts. Look for tight oval spruce cones on the ground and for the tall dark green trees. Many of the young Fraser fir trees along this part of the trail have patches of brown needles that are possibly a sign of infestation by the balsam woolly adelgid. Most of the mature fir trees from this elevation on up have already died, and you can see their naked trunks and branches.

The Road Prong gets smaller, but then the trail joins the prong and you either make 10-12 crossings or just accept wet feet and walk up in the middle of the prong until the trail finally decides that left is the way to go. Turtlehead and bee-balm grow in and along the creek. After climbing through a little more spruce-fir and then a patch of skinny yellow birch, you will suddenly emerge onto mowed grass, cross the Appalachian Trail, and watch the Clingmans Dome traffic racing by at Indian Gap—if it is summer. In winter, there is no traffic since Clingmans Dome Road is closed.

Narrative by Doris Gove

ROUGH CREEK TRAIL

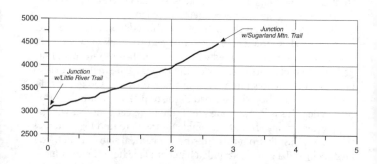

LENGTH: 2.8 miles, from Little River Trail to Sugarland Mountain Trail.
HIGHLIGHTS: Beautiful creek, logging camp sites.
CAUTIONS: Steep and rocky trail sections.
MAP KEY: 6-7 D; USGS quads: Silers Bald, Gatlinburg.
USE: Hiking trail.
STARTING POINT: Hike 3.4 miles from the Little River trailhead or (0.7 from the Goshen Prong/Little River trails jct).

How rough is Rough Creek? The creek's name probably came from the difficulties of timber operations, but the trail is now a pleasant walk with just a few steep or rocky spots.

The Little River Lumber Company built a railroad up this creek in the 1920s. One runaway train crashed at the mouth of Rough Creek, and another locomotive exploded at the same place. Trees too far from the track were pulled out by a Clyde overhead skidder. The dragging caused more damage to hillsides and watersheds than the tree cutting itself. Curt McCarter, a skidder operator on Rough Creek in 1921, said later, "Everything was gone... I'd say ninety-five percent of it were all tore off and torn away." But with the establishment of the park, everything started growing back. The Civilian Conservation Corps built this trail in the 1930s over the former railroad bed.

A few yards up, the trail curves left and away from the Little River Valley. Small American beeches and yellow birches grow in an open area. A large (21" around) American holly stands in the curve of the trail, flanked by dog-hobble and an especially shaggy yellow birch. The trail rises gently and passes several smaller hollies and then enters a grove of straight, tall tuliptrees. Soon it becomes level, cool, and dark with Eastern hemlock and rosebay rhododendron. You can hear Rough Creek down on the left. When you finally see the creek, it's not rough at all, just murmuring through a small plain full of spring flowers. The trail rises a bit more and then descends to cross the creek.

The north side of the creek is drier and more open, with most of the trees deciduous. Look across at the north-facing side of the creek, sheltered from the sun. The dominant plants are Eastern hemlock and rosebay rhododendron, with few wildflowers. As you rise up on the north side of the creek, the hill across from you gets higher and shelters both sides of the creek, and the hemlock and rhododendron converge with the trail. Farther to your left, you can still see the open deciduous woods.

The trail moves away from the creek and rises to meet a definite roadbed with a drainage ditch on the side. A flat area here may have been a logging camp or a loading place for the railroad. Near the trail you can find rusty cable, barrel hoops, galvanized wash buckets, and rusty machinery parts. Look for a tuliptree on the left that seems to have split a large quartz boulder as it grew. Just left of the base of that tree is a dump of rusty cans. Be careful; they are sharp.

The roadbed goes on straight; the trail drops back to the creek, crosses on stepping stones and goes up into rosebay rhododendron, Eastern hemlock, and dog-hobble. Partridgeberry and downy rattlesnake plantain grow on the banks. The trail rises and enters a more mature forest of big Eastern hemlocks, American beeches, maples, and silverbells. Look for a basswood on the left with a hollow base that you could crawl through. Mountain folk used such hollow basswood and black gum logs for cisterns, bee hives, and food storage bins.

Once more the trail turns toward Rough Creek, crosses a feeder creek, and then crosses Rough Creek for the last time. The trail ascends a steep ridge side and crosses several former stream beds of huge boulders. In some places, the trail is eroded and slipping down the hillside; some parts are rocky. Look for chipmunk holes under rocks or roots in the trail. Plenty of oak trees and silverbells provide food for the chipmunks and squirrels that you may hear and see.

When you see some grass in the trail (often a sign that you are reaching the top of something) and a reinforcing stone wall, you are almost to Sugarland Mountain Trail. You come around a massive rock face on the right, admire a cluster of Fraser magnolia, and then reach the trail. Chestnut stumps stand on both sides.

You could return the same way you came, giving you a roundtrip mileage of 12.4 from the Little River trailhead. Or you could follow Sugarland Mountain Trail to Huskey Gap Trail (4.2 miles) and drop into Little River Valley. This will give you a loop of 14.2 miles.

Narrative by Doris Gove

ROUGH FORK TRAIL

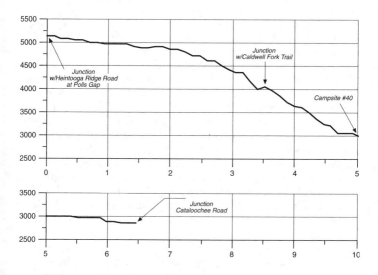

LENGTH: 6.5 miles, from Polls Gap to Cataloochee Road.
HIGHLIGHTS: S. L. Woody homestead.
CAUTIONS: Mud. ·
MAP KEY: 10-11 E; USGS quad: Bunches Bald.
USE: Horse and hiking trail.
TRAILHEAD: Take Blue Ridge Parkway to Heintooga Ridge Road, then drive north toward Balsam Mountain Campground about 4.0 miles to Polls (Paul's) Gap. Take the middle trail and walk around the gate to the trailhead.

Rough Fork Trail follows an old railroad grade gradually downhill; you may occasionally spy railroad spikes alongside. Tall grass indicates that much of the area was once open pasture. Trees include many yellow birch and a few red spruce and Fraser fir. Dark-eyed Juncos nesting in the bank beside the trail sometimes fake injury to lure you from their nests. Veeries and Red-eyed Vireos call from the treetops, while Winter Wrens and Rufous-sided Towhees sing and feed closer to the ground. Common buttercups and bluets are only a few of the spring wildflowers that bloom beside the trail; smooth blackberries and false nettles are also quite common in this section. Not far down the trail, are sugar, mountain, and red maples. A few misshapen, older trees line the trail; they escaped logging precisely because they were misshapen. Shortly after the third bend a clearing suddenly appears in an otherwise seemingly endless forest—evidence of a lightning strike.

At 1.0 mile, the woods thicken; you enter the watersheds of Caldwell Fork, which rushes far below to the right. The canopy overhead features the distinctive leaves (each of which has five leaflets) of the yellow buckeye. After a boulder field at 2.0 miles, the trail descends more steeply into Caldwell Fork Valley where you leave a ridge environment and enter a cove with moss-covered logs and lichen-cloaked trees. At occasional breaks in the forest, you view Cataloochee Divide. At 3.0 miles, the trail has descended below the lowest elevation for Fraser fir and red spruce; instead, Eastern hemlock, American basswood, red maple, white oak, Northern red oak dominate. On the forest floor, flame azalea, galax, and wood betony flourish. Soon you walk past numerous large oaks and Eastern hemlocks, never cut because of the steep slope. At 3.5 miles, the trail reaches Caldwell Fork Trail, which descends downhill to the right into Caldwell Fork Valley.

Rough Fork Trail heads down Little Ridge into the Rough Fork Creek Valley at first through a rosebay rhododendron thicket then into mixed hardwoods, including Fraser magnolias, red maples, and American beeches, as well as many fallen chestnut trunks. At about 4.0 miles, the trail reaches a drier slope featuring American beech then steadily drops through Eastern hemlock and occasional clumps of yellow birch, oaks, and maples.

At 5.0 miles, after passing through a heath thicket, the trail flattens and becomes muddy. On the left Campsite #40 appears, carved out of a laurel slick; huge trees tower on one side, Rough Fork Creek rushes by on the other. After an easy crossing of Hurricane Creek by foot, you pass under large Eastern hemlocks and oaks, several with big burls. In this muddy stretch, the trail meanders through a reemerging forest of witch-hazel, tuliptree, black locust, hemlock, and Juneberry.

Soon, near where Messer Fork flows into Rough Fork, the trail crosses several fields that have not grown back into forest because the National Park Service mows the grass to intentionally frustrate forest succession. Sycamore grows by the creek and black walnut in the field. This is the S.L. Woody Place, which consisted of a house, barn, chicken house, tool house, canning house, spring house, and wood shed. The house, still standing but occupied by Barn Swallows, is a study in architectural design by expansion. Beginning humbly as a one-room cabin in the mid-1800s, Woody enlarged it periodically to accommodate his growing family. Several bedrooms, two porches, and a kitchen were added between 1901 and 1910. Nonetheless the pragmatic original design was never compromised: aligned front and back doors cool the structure via cross-ventilation. The spring house, the only other remaining structure, stands about 50 yards to the side of the house.

From **5.5** miles onward, the trail features several footlog crossings of Rough Fork, which rushes swiftly toward its confluence with Palmer Creek. The trail, now an old road bed, bypasses white pines, whose needles blanket the ground.

Nearby is the place where, on July 13, 1976, summer ranger Charles Hughes encountered the "Wild Man" of Cataloochee. Hughes was checking up on fishermen by Rough Fork when he met a man with a heavy beard. Asked his name, the man replied, "I've got no name, I've lived in these woods all my life." When Hughes demanded his fishing license, the man reached into his canvas coat for a gun. During a scuffle, the ranger succeeded only in punching the man in the face. Hughes then ran to the nearby ranger station for help; a group of rangers tracked the man down Rough Fork by bloodhound well into the night but never found him. The Wild Man became the subject of much discussion in the local press. A song commemorating the event, "The Cataloochee Wild Man" by Sam Parsons, a Texan, was popular throughout the region. Sightings and tales of the Wild Man continue around Cataloochee to this day.

At **5.7** miles, the trail meets Big Fork Ridge Trail. Rough Fork Trail concludes at **6.5** miles, at the end of the Cataloochee Road.

Narrative by Ted Olson

ROUNDTOP TRAIL

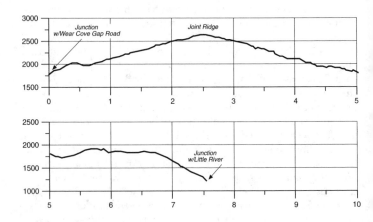

LENGTH: 7.6 miles, from Wear Cove Gap Road to the Townsend "Y."

HIGHLIGHTS: Solitude, scenery, spring wildflowers.

CAUTIONS: Solitude, river crossing, narrow trail.

MAP KEY: 5-4 C-D; USGS quad: Wear Cove.

USE: Hiking trail.

TRAILHEAD: Turn into Metcalf Bottoms Picnic Area from the Little River Road between Elkmont and Tremont. Cross the bridge and continue for approximately 1 mile. The trail is on the west side of the road, just below the crest of the hill and the park boundary. There is no parking here. A small pull off just over the hill (park boundary) provides space for up to 2 cars, but you may choose to park at the picnic area and hike up the road.

In choosing to hike this trail, you are making a decision to enjoy the solitude of one of the least-used trails in America's most popular national park. Of the 9 million visitors to the Smokies each year, only a handful will experience this trail.

The trailhead sign makes a very important point—Townsend "Y" 7.6 miles (No Bridge). Unless you plan on hiking out and back, you are going to get wet, but fortunately not until the very end. During high water, this crossing is absolutely unsafe without a boat. At an average flow rate, you may wish to carry a rope to assist some forders. During warm weather and a dry spell, the crossing is refreshing. When you drop your shuttle car at the Townsend "Y," make sure to take a good look at the river and assess its flow and your abilities.

The trail begins by climbing easily up the eastern flanks of Round-top Mountain. Here you will climb through a pine-oak forest, which will accompany you all the way to the "Y." These forests occur on the dry south facing slopes of the Smokies. As this trail is almost always on the southern exposure of Roundtop and Little Roundtop, the pine-oak forest dominates. As you climb you will notice many dogwoods and laurels, and occasionally American holly. This leathery-leaved evergreen has really found a way to keep the deer at bay. The edges of the holly leaves have formed into sharp spikes. Not easily eaten!

This trail is also notable for wildflowers in spring and early summer. Favorite species include pink lady's slippers and flame azalea.

Shortly you will crest a small ridge and find fine views of Chinquapin Ridge and Cove Mountain (4,077') to the east. If you proceed ahead you will turn right and get your first glimpse of Roundtop (3,071'). The trail never crests Roundtop, climbing only to 2,500', but the mountain will shadow you for the first half of the hike.

At 0.5 mile you will reach the park boundary. In fact, the trail leaves the park for a short time—notice the surveying post and boundary sign to the left. From the small clearing there is a nice view down into Wear Cove and across to the Foothills Parkway. The large bridge is still unused, as this section of the parkway has yet to be completed. But you came for solitude, so turn back to the trail and follow it along as it skirts Roundtop.

The next mile will give you a bit of insight into how the Smokies were formed. Soon you will cross two small spring branches. These are the headwaters of Indian Camp Branch. Over the years, these little seeps, too small to even fill a canteen, have carved the deep valleys they flow through. Water is an indomitable force which slowly seeks out weaknesses in the underlying rocks and carves away our mountains. Geologists estimate that these mountains once stood taller than the Rockies but water has worn them down.

Ahead a quarter mile the trail passes an outcropping of Metcalf Phyllite. This Precambrian stone gives us more clues to the history of these mountains. Phyllite is a metamorphosed stone made of ocean deposits of mud and silt. Millions of years ago these rocks sat beneath a shallow ocean, but tectonic forces lifted, twisted, heated and bent these stones into mountains like Roundtop and Little Roundtop. Because it is a soft rock, the water which seeps across it here at the headwaters of Puncheon Branch quickly wears it away. Mosses, lichens, ferns and other plants grow in the cracks, pushing their roots deeper and adding to the speed of the erosion. But water and plants are slow and so these mountains have stood for eons. Ice is a quicker force and evidence of its presence is also here. At mile 2.0 the trail gains Joint Ridge and turns right past large sandstone boulders. Sandstone is a harder rock for water to erode, but ice seeps into microscopic cracks and pushes the rocks apart allowing gravity to carry the boulders to the valleys below. Ice works here every winter, but some 20,000 years ago the winters were longer and most of these block fields of sandstone boulders were formed. The view from here will give you a complete effect of how these slow forces over time can sculpt magnificent monuments.

The 2.5 mile climb which has brought you to the top of Joint Ridge has been easy. You started at about 1,800' and have now climbed to 2,600'. Now you will begin a long gradual descent to the Townsend "Y" (1,200'). Except that at one point the trail drops quickly and steeply one quarter mile to a small cove at the head of Cane Creek. The cove today is overgrown with laurel, but it doesn't take much imagination to see a small mountain farm here. Two small spring branches which cross the trail join below to create a larger fork of Cane Creek. Was it large enough to support a family and their livestock? It must have been, for a family did live here up until the park's creation in the 1930s. Look carefully and you may see other evidence of their existence.

The trail climbs gradually up and around a small ridge offering good views of Townsend in the distance. Then the trail again drops dramatically. This is the most dangerous point of the hike. A false step here could result in a twisted or broken ankle. To make matters worse, the trail also becomes very narrow—one boot width in places. Take special care as you descend steeply through a set of switch backs before the trail crosses another ravine and levels out.

At **5.5** miles, after an easy climb, the trail again reaches the park boundary. For the next mile you will be in and out of the park—as park and private signs will remind you. Here you are walking a ridge which separates the Little Rivers and Brickey Branchs watersheds. Along the ridge you will pass through a stand of dead pines. Pick up a piece of old bark and you will see the tell-tale signs of Southern pine bark beetles. These native insects bore through the pine bark and feed on the nutrient-rich inner bark eventually killing the tree. Although commercially these insects are a disaster, biologically they are just a part of the plan. The death of these older pines will allow younger trees the chance to grow and spread their seeds. Just like fire, native insect infections are a disaster the trees have adapted to.

Finally, the trail will turn south and begin to drop off the ridge top. Now you will be moving deeper into the park and closer to the "Y". At first the trail climbs up and down over unnamed ridges or skirts around unnamed knobs, but ultimately the trail will become a gradually descending pathway. At mile **6.5** your solitude will be broken by the sounds of man. As the trail becomes steeper and passes by wall after wall of Metcalf Phyllite, the sounds of water and road will fill the air. Then after passing a beautiful overhanging wall of phyllite—loaded with poison ivy—the trail bursts to the edge of a rocky slope directly above the "Y".

Because the river changes over time, it is impossible to tell you where to cross. It may be best to cross directly to the parking area at the "Y", but maybe you should cross the river to the left. Take some time to scout out the best spot, string a rope if you have to, roll up your pant legs, change into sneakers and cross the river back into the world of cars and pavement, leaving behind the birds and leaves and seeps along the slopes of Roundtop.

Narrative by Tom Condon

RUSSELL FIELD TRAIL

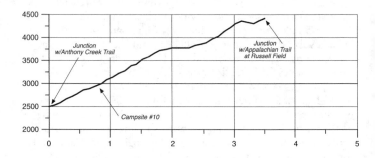

LENGTH: 3.5 miles, from Anthony Creek Trail to Appalachian Trail at Russell Field.
HIGHLIGHTS: Russell Field, big trees, views, wildflowers.
CAUTIONS: Muddy areas, stream crossings at high water.
MAP KEY: 4 E; USGS quad: Cades Cove.
USE: Horse and hiking trail.
STARTING POINT: Jct. Anthony Creek Trail, 1.6 miles above Cades Cove Picnic Area.

In the 1800s, settlers were drawn from other parts of East Tennessee and North Carolina to the fertile lands of Cades Cove. Over time, they completely cleared the forests of the valley floor and the lower reaches of the mountains. The valley was planted in corn and orchards were established at its perimeter. But the biggest cash crop was raised on the mountain tops. Cattle were grazed in the open fields along the Smokies crest. These areas were known as balds. It is unknown whether they were created by fire set by Indians or by some other means, but the settlers ultimately used and enlarged them. One such field is the terminus of this trail—Russell Field.

The Russell Field Trail begins at its junction with the Anthony Creek Trail 1.6 miles from the Cades Cove Picnic Area. The trailhead is in a large stand of tall, stately tuliptrees. They each measure 20-24" in diameter. For us, this is only the beginning of our trail and a journey into some of the last remaining old-growth forests in the west end of the park.

The trail turns right here and follows along the Left Prong of Anthony Creek. You will begin climbing moderately with a small jump over a spring branch after 100 yards. Another 100 yards will bring you to a second easy crossing of a spring branch. But at **0.25** mile, the trail's character changes. You will have to rock hop a small branch of Anthony Creek and begin a steeper climb through a cool rhododendron and hemlock stand. The old timers often referred to these places as "jungles" or "hells." Imagine trying to move through here without a trail and you will know why.

As you approach Campsite #10 at **0.75** mile, you will have to cross the Left Prong twice. The first crossing is along a footlog with handrail, but requires a bit of a rock hop to reach the log at high water. About 100' up trail of this crossing is an impressive 40" diameter hemlock tree. We are entering the old growth. About 200 yards up trail is the second crossing. This is a bit more tricky especially at high water. A ford for horses exists, but no footlog for hikers, requiring a rock hop of slippery rocks and logs.

After crossing, you will climb past a massive 46" diameter hemlock on the left. Campsite #10 is just ahead. The campsite is nicely placed between a small spring branch and the Left Prong. It is a small site, with room for only a couple of tents, and does require a reservation. The site offers plenty of water and views to the sky above. It is a wonderful place to lie back on a starry night and follow the silhouettes of the maples and others up to the constellations. The trees are tall and straight which makes for good contemplation and company, but not for hanging your food beyond the reach of bears. Bring plenty of rope because you will have to be creative here.

For hikers pushing on, the trail continues to climb, but now the path becomes more difficult. The combination of heavy horse use and rain can quickly turn the trail into a quagmire of mud. If such is the case when you hike, you might just walk by that 50" diameter Northern red oak on the right without seeing it. You might even miss that 38" diameter tuliptree at the head of the valley by the second switchback. Although you might notice this one because the trail is starting to dry. You have begun climbing a set of switchbacks which will take you steeply to the top of Leadbetter Ridge.

The next mile is steep and difficult, so you might as well plan on frequent stops to catch your breath and admire the surrounding forest. At an elevation of 3,700' you finally reach the ridge line. The trail now levels out for about a half mile.

The more moderate climb of the ridge line takes you through dry stands of oak and pine. You will walk through a large stand of Table Mountain pine. This unique tree is an endemic to the southern Appalachians, meaning it is found nowhere else in the world. The pine is also referred to as a serotinous tree, meaning that it requires fire as part of its life cycle. It is a remarkable adaptation to the frequent fires of these dry slopes.

Ultimately the trail will leave the moderate climb of Leadbetter Ridge and climb steeply to Russell Field. Along this half mile climb, the quagmires return, making travel through these rhododendrons a real hell even on the path. In the winter and late fall, you will get a few good views of Cades Cove and as far as Maryville, Tennessee. At last you reach Russell Field.

Russell Field today is part grassy bald and part forest. It does not take much imagination to see why the settlers grazed their cattle here. But try to imagine the views they must have had: to the north is Cades Cove, to the west is Gregory Bald, to the east is Spence Field and to the south is Eagle Creek. These would all have been open to the herders back then. Today, the forest obscures the views. But on a sunny day, you can't beat the grassy fields of the high country.

The trail does not end here. It pushes on for another 1.2 miles to the Russell Field Shelter and the Appalachian Trail. Halfway to the shelter you will pass through a laurel patch with a 50 yard intensive quagmire. Push on, for the shelter is absolutely lovely. The small rock structure sits in an open stand of oaks, maples and serviceberry trees. The understory is of grass and flowers, particularly white snakeroot. For those camping here, water can be found at a small spring 500' down the trail to the north. For others, the AT can take you east to Spence Field or west toward Gregory Bald. Or you may just want to return to the old-growth forests along the Russell Field Trail.

Narrative by Tom Condon

SCHOOLHOUSE GAP TRAIL

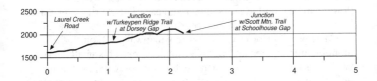

LENGTH: 2.2 miles, from Laurel Creek Road to Scott Mtn. Trail.
HIGHLIGHTS: Birding and wildflowers.
MAP KEY: 4 D; USGS quad: Wear Cove, Kinzel Springs.
USE: Horse and hiking trail.
TRAILHEAD: From the Townsend "Y", proceed toward Cades Cove on the Laurel Creek Road for 3.9 miles. The trailhead is a large, paved parking area on the right.

Dr. Isaac Anderson, first President of Maryville College, had a life-long dream to "educate young men for the missionary." The trail on which you now walk is just one part of this dream.

In the 1840s, the Hazel Creek area of the Smokies was beginning to develop. Copper mining was bringing more and more men and their families into the area. Dr. Anderson saw the need for a road to connect East Tennessee to this area for commerce and missionary work. So with an energy only he could muster, Dr. Anderson pushed forward a plan. The North Carolinians would build a road up and over Haw Gap to Spence Field. He would build a road from School-house Gap up Bote Mountain to connect with them. Paying Chero-kees still living in the area one yard of calico cloth for each day of labor, Dr. Anderson completed his road. However, the North Caroli-na road was never completed. And so the "Anderson Road" was abandoned.

The trail today looks much more like a road than perhaps Dr. Anderson's ever did. From the trailhead, you gradually climb up Spence Branch, a small, tranquil mountain stream, to Dorsey Gap at mile **1.1**. Here the trail intersects Turkeypen Ridge Trail which heads west toward Cades Cove. A marshy area to the right of the trail just before the gap is a good birding spot. All along the creekbed and the trail edges is good for wildflowers. Spectacular patches of cardinal flower can be found in late summer and early fall. At the same time, keep your eyes open for its blue cousins, downy and great lobelias.

After passing Dorsey Gap, a narrow manway leads off to the west, dropping into an area known as Whiteoak Sink. This small sunken valley was once home to as many as 10 families. It is now home to many non-native wild hogs, several rare plants, and an assortment of caves. Written permission must be obtained from the park service to enter any of the caves.

The trail continues uphill for 1.1 miles to Schoolhouse Gap and the park boundary. Along the way you will pass through fields of Japanese witch grass and patches of Japanese lespedeza, both exotic plant species. According to Keith Langdon, a Park Service resource manager, exotic plants like these threaten the native species in the park. Exotics often grow uncontrolled due to a lack of natural predators and parasites, hence they take away resources native species require. In the case of lespedeza and witch grass, which often grow along roadsides and other disturbed areas, they out-compete rarer native plants for this important habitat. Experimental efforts have been made to control these exotics, but little success has been made. Efforts do continue.

Just before Schoolhouse Gap, the trail passes through some nice stands of pine-oak forest. Here a late summer hike will find the sourwood tree already in its spectacular fall display. This small tree's leaves turn crimson red as the drier, cooler fall weather arrives. Later in September and October, the oaks, maples, hickories, and others will join the sourwood in the displays of color which blanket these mountains.

Was there a school at Schoolhouse Gap? All my local sources say no. The name may relate to the practice of children walking through the gap to and from school in Townsend.

The Chestnut Top Trail meets this trail just a quarter mile before Schoolhouse Gap. In April of 1901, an ill-fated cattle drive topped Schoolhouse Gap headed for Bote Mountain and the summer pastures on Spence Field. Of the 500 cattle involved, some 450 never made it.

A spring blizzard dumped several feet of snow on the mountains, starving the cattle and discouraging future large scale drives in the Smokies.

At the gap you reach the park boundary. The private home is actually just outside the park. The Scott Mountain Trail arrives from the west. Chestnut Top Trail leads east 4.3 miles to the Townsend "Y", while Scott Mountain meanders 3.6 miles west into the Cades Cove area. Enjoy either, or return to your car the way you came here, along Dr. Anderson's and the cattle drovers' dreams.

Narrative by Tom Condon

SCOTT MOUNTAIN TRAIL

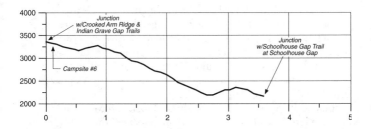

LENGTH: 3.6 miles, from jct. Indian Grave Gap and Crooked Arm Ridge trails to Schoolhouse Gap Trail.
HIGHLIGHTS: Hardwood forests.
CAUTIONS: Narrow, steeply pitched trail.
MAP KEY: 4 D; USGS quads: Cades Cove, Kinzel Springs.
USE: Hiking trail.
STARTING POINT: Jct. Indian Grave Gap and Crooked Arm Ridge trails.

While many people are drawn to the high mountains and waterfalls of the Great Smoky Mountains, there are many lesser-known trails which offer the hiker as pleasant an experience. Scott Mountain Trail is one of these. There are no big peaks or grand vistas on this trail. Nor are there any tumbling streams to keep you company. Instead, Scott Mountain offers you a quiet hike through a forest in transition. It's a place to get away from the crowds and noise of the park.

The trail begins at the top of Crooked Arm Ridge where it joins not only the Crooked Arm Ridge Trail, but also the Indian Grave Gap Trail. The two mile climb up this ridge is along a steep rocky trail. Do not underestimate the time it will take you to reach the trailhead, especially if you are backpacking.

From the 3-way trail junction, you will immediately cross beneath an old series of powerlines which supplied Cades Cove before underground utilities were installed. You will pass into a rhododendron jungle which will be a refreshing break if it's a hot summer day. As the jungle starts to thin a mere 500' ahead, you will come upon Campsite #6 (Turkeypen Ridge). Backpackers might choose to use this lovely site atop the small ridge to the left. It's a good choice if you're forced into a late start. There is enough room here for two small parties and there is a good, though somewhat meager, spring over the ridge. The trail continues down and around this small ridge. It will soon pass over the spring branch which supplies the campsite with water. The trail then drops into an open oak forest.

Like many forests in the park, those along Scott Mountain were harvested in the early 1900s. Even though some of the logging practices of those days were extremely damaging, nature has found a way to replant itself. And so it is on these slopes. The oak forest here is young, with many small to average trees. Occasionally, though, a larger tree can be found. To the right of the trail, just a short distance from the spring crossing, is a chestnut oak tree with a diameter of over 30". Maybe someday this forest and this oak will develop into the giants of the uncut stands which were once common here.

The trail continues downhill until at 0.5 mile it begins to climb toward the park boundary. The hillside here is very steep and unfortunately, the trail is very narrow. Erosion of the slope has also pitched the trail with the hillside. This requires that you take extra care with your footing, but don't fail to notice the large sheets of Metcalf Phyllite scattered along the hillside. Phyllite is an old, but soft stone. This characteristic has allowed water and ice to carve away vast amounts of this metamorphic rock. This is most noticeable when we look at Cades and Tuckaleechee (Townsend) coves. These coves are the result of the weaker phyllite eroding away faster than the sandstones which make up the higher mountains.

Today, our trail continues around this slope. At **0.8** mile, it turns and drops into another rhododendron jungle or what some old-timers called "hells." Imagine trying to climb up this hillside without a trail and you'll know why. Ahead there is a nice outcropping of phyllite, which creates a small grotto. And as you continue past it, you will begin to lose the rhododendron in favor of ferns and mosses. Wood fern and Christmas fern are the most dominant. Also note the two very large silverbell trees. Both measure over 20" in diameter, virtual giants for their species. Perhaps there is hope this forest will become an old-growth stand again.

Cross the spring branch ahead and continue downhill until you reach a small gap at mile **1.2**. A large tuliptree sits off to the right. Like the oak and silverbells before, this 50" diameter tree may some-day be a common sight in the park. Presently you will begin a series of switchbacks taking you off the ridgeline. Again you will pass through rhododendron, but hidden amongst them are the smooth gray-barked Fraser magnolias. Some of these trees are as large as the species can get. Take note of their leaves. They were named for a famous natural-ist, Dr. Fraser, and have two earlobe-like protrusions at their base.

As you continue descending, you will pass a spring branch seeping from the hillside and dropping off the rocky outcrop. This is probably the best place to get water and to get your feet wet if you're not care-ful. The seep turns about 100' of the trail into a muddy mess. Contin-ue descending past oaks and tuliptrees, silverbells and rhododendrons. If you're here in mid-summer, you might even get to collect a blueber-ry or two. At mile **2.5**, the rocks change from phyllite to limestone. This younger rock, geologically speaking again, underlies the large coves in the area. The phyllite of the hills above was pushed up and over these rocks hundreds of millions of years ago. Slowly it was erod-ed away, re-exposing the limestone. To the right, down that steep slope, is a secluded valley known as Whiteoak Sink and its famous cave opening called the "blow hole." Like Cades and Tuckaleechee coves, this valley is called a fenster or window by geologists. As you stand on this hillside, you are looking down through a hole into younger rocks.

By **2.75** miles, the limestone dominates the hillside. Here you finally reach the park boundary, which you will follow 0.5 mile to the trail's end at Schoolhouse Gap. As you pass along the ridge, you'll catch glimpses into Dry Valley—a small arm of Tuckaleechee Cove. You will also pass a most unusual tree—the red cedar. In the Smokies, the red cedar is often found near old homesites, but not often in the deeper forests. The early settlers cultivated these trees for chicken roosts. It was believed the tree could keep lice out of their poultry.

Enjoy the cedars as you climb the small rise. As you reach the crest at mile **3.1**, you will enter a pine forest which will accompany you almost to the end. The trail takes you so close to the park's edge that a dirt road passes within 100' of you. It's the first intrusive sign of civilization since you started and marks the final push to trail's end. Soon you will see a small cottage and reach Schoolhouse Gap. A right turn will take you back into the park on the Schoolhouse Gap Trail. It leads 2.2 miles to Laurel Creek Road or 0.2 mile to Chestnut Top Trail. The latter trail winds just over 4 miles through pine-oak forests to the Townsend "Y". Either trail will offer you more opportunities to experience the quiet forests of the Smokies.

Narrative by Tom Condon

SMOKEMONT LOOP HIKE

If you are making the 5.7 mile Bradley Fork/Smokemont Loop trails loop, it is slightly easier to hike the Bradley Fork Trail first. Park in the hikers' parking area near the entrance to Smokemont Campground. Walk the 0.5 mile to the trailhead at D Loop.

SMOKEMONT LOOP TRAIL

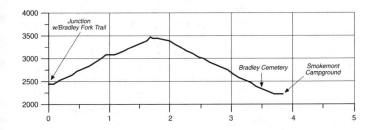

LENGTH: 3.8 miles, from Bradley Fork Trail to Smokemont Campground.

HIGHLIGHTS: Cemetery access, spring and summer wildflowers.

MAP KEY: 9 E; USGS quad: Smokemont.

USE: Hiking trail.

STARTING POINT: Hike 1.7 miles on Bradley Fork Trail from Smokemont Campground, or find the trailhead at the old concrete bridge at Smokemont Campground.

At the starting point on Bradley Fork Trail, the trail begins by crossing the fork on a long, skinny foot log. This is one of the longest foot logs I have ever used in the Smokies, and it is a bouncy, narrow experience. You'll be grateful for the hand rail. Across the fork, the trail immediately heads south for about 100 yards before turning sharply right and uphill. An unmarked trail continues along the water, but it is not the "true path."

You climb steadily through a mixed hardwood forest. The area is rather wet and supports lots of spring and summer wildflowers like crested dwarf iris, spotted wintergreen, and Indian pipe. Both spring and fall are pleasant seasons for this route—the former offering wildflower color, the latter featuring a mix of fall color from maples, flowering dogwoods, and tuliptrees. A summer hike might be muddy and buggy, though still pretty.

The trail soon veers away from the fork and into a higher, drier forest. While most of the trees are young, occasional giant tuliptrees allow for a more open understory. After about 0.75 mile, pine trees, hickories, grasses, and briers signal a dry slope and provide some good views to the east and northeast before the trail switches back to the west side of the ridge.

At this point, you're likely to hear auto noise from Newfound Gap Road. The slope steepens here too, and you embark on a long uphill pull of about 1.0 mile, bringing you finally to a knob at the top of the ridge 1.7 miles along. Next comes a 180 degree switchback that turns back east toward Chasteen Creek and, mercifully, downhill. This side of the ridge features more and older hardwoods. Within a quarter mile the trail passes through a distinct saddle between two ridges that would make a nice picnic spot. It is gently sloped and grassy under a grove of big, mixed hardwoods.

The trail winds its way down the ridge uneventfully until about a half mile from the campground. Growing under a canopy of mixed oaks and pines, sweet peas, wild roses, and sawbriers signal the site of a homestead. More evidence of former habitation appears a few hundred feet ahead when you encounter an old cemetery down the slope. People have climbed down to the graveyard at numerous spots, creating steep and eroded side trails, but better access is provided a few hundred yards further along via a maintained spur trail.

This cemetery is commonly known as the Bradley Cemetery, named for a family that settled in the region during the beginning of the nineteenth century. It contains 30-50 graves that date from the late 1800s to 1925. Some are weathered to the point that no inscription can be read. Those that are still legible have Bradley, Wilson and Reagan family names.

Bradleytown was the name for the Smokemont region before the establishment of organized logging activities in the early 1900s. Smokemont acquired its current name when a town grew up around a saw mill used by Champion Fibre Company.

Smokemont Campground is only a short walk beyond the cemetery. The trail joins with a service road and crosses a bridge into the campground 0.3 mile from the Bradley Fork trailhead to your left.

Narrative by Bill Beard

SNAKE DEN RIDGE TRAIL

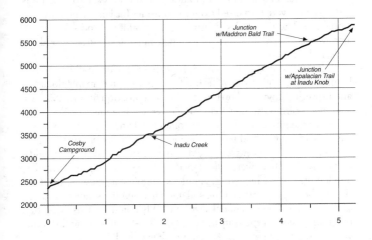

LENGTH: 5.3 miles, from Cosby Campground to the Appalachian Trail.
HIGHLIGHTS: Small waterfall, views, old-growth forest.
CAUTIONS: Some steep sections.
MAP KEY: 9-10 B; USGS quads: Hartford, Luftee Knob.
USE: Horse and hiking trail.
TRAILHEAD: Enter the park at Cosby, drive 2.0 miles, and park behind the camper registration building for Cosby Campground. Walk up into the campground, turn right at the pay phone, walk to Campsite B-55, and look for a trail sign.

There may well be snake dens here, since snakes often choose rocky, dry, south-facing slopes to hibernate, and the part of this trail above Inadu (snake in Cherokee) Creek fits that description. But once the snakes come out of hibernation, they tend to distribute themselves all over the park, so don't worry about them. If you do see one on a trail, just say hello and move on.

Before the park, the lowlands around Cosby Campground support-ed several small farms and a community. In the 1920s, ferns and East-ern hemlock were harvested from the hillsides for landscaping in Knoxville. Though the local farmers cut trees for use and sale, this area was spared the intrusion of logging companies, railroads, skid-ders, and splash dams.

The trail starts as an old road through a grove of small Eastern hemlocks which give way to a thin forest of tuliptree, maple, locust, and flowering dogwood. It rises steadily to a junction at mile 0.2 with a connector from the Low Gap and Lower Mt. Cammerer trails.

After the junction, the trail becomes level and passes through a patch of 15-20-year-old Eastern hemlocks. These young trees are part of a successional regrowth of the original forest. When the cornfields and house sites here were abandoned in the 1930s, tuliptrees, maples, and locusts eagerly moved in. Hemlocks didn't start growing until these other trees improved the soil and provided the shade that their saplings need. These hemlocks will probably dominate this forest by overtaking most of the tuliptrees and maples. Farther along the trail, you can see black locust trees (their dark gray bark has deep furrows that look braided together) that are dying out as the habitat becomes unfavorable to them.

Good culverts shunt the next three creeks under the trail, which then rises again. On the right is a small graveyard. Most of the burials date from the early 1900s, but one granite stone marks the 1982 grave of Ella V. Costner, identified on the stones as a W.W.II POW and Poet Laureate of the Smokies. Costner was born in 1894 in Cosby and grew up on Crying Creek, near the beginning of the Gabes Mountain Trail. She served as an Army nurse in Pearl Harbor and Guam, and then returned to live in Newport, Tennessee. She pub-lished three books of poetry and one of essays and poems called *Lamp in the Cabin* (1967). One legend she tells is that of Tater Hill, a high potato-shaped rock mound above the Gabes Mountain Trail. An Indian maiden, distraught when settlers killed her lover, leaped to her death on Tater Hill. Later, men called up to fight the Civil War hid their gold there, and most never came back. So Tater Hill is both haunted and treasure-laden. Another story she told is of a revenuer who was so drunk after a raid on the stills of the hollows that he couldn't walk. Costner's father took him in and let him sleep it off. The families whose stills the revenuer destroyed, she said, had little food and were left without a way to buy more.

The trail climbs to an old traffic circle. From a cement slab on the right you can look down at the creek. Just left of the cement slab, the trail passes three big boulders and becomes rocky as it rises above the creek. After it descends through a rocky old stream bed and approaches Rock Creek, you'll need to look for a new foot log upstream. After the creek, larger trees indicate that you have moved out of the settled area. Tuliptrees, silverbells, and Eastern hemlocks line the steep, rocky trail as it turns away from the creek. Look for a shattered Eastern hemlock stump on the left.

The trail swings around a switchback. A big silverbell tree stands in the angle; look for flaky bluish bark. In April, silverbells carpet the trail with their flowers, and in September, they drop light brown winged nuts that are hard for anyone except squirrels to open.

After the switchback, the trail enters a jumble of boulders and an old stream bed. Foamflower, violets, nettles, and Fraser's sedge bloom here in spring, and jewelweed, goldenrod, and Indian cucumber bloom later.

After more steep climbing and another dry stream bed, the trail finally drops a little to cross Inadu Creek at about **1.8** miles. It is an easy crossing and has upstream and downstream waterfalls and a quiet pool with water striders.

The trail again heads away from the creek, supported by a strong rock wall on the right. But this time, the trail reaches the nose of the ridge. Through Eastern hemlocks, you can get a view into the valley, and then the vegetation changes to that characteristic of exposed ridges: mountain laurel, American beech, oak, maple, pine, with a ground cover of trailing arbutus, galax, wintergreen, and flat mosses. As the trail turns back to a more sheltered cove, rosebay rhododendron, Eastern hemlock, and Fraser magnolia dominate. Shining clubmoss, which looks like furry green fingers, grows below. The trail alternates between exposed and sheltered habitats. From one ridge nose, you can see Cosby Valley and Foothills Parkway, and if you lean out carefully, you can get a glimpse of Mt. Cammerer to the right.

By now you are above 4,000' elevation, and you start seeing small red spruce trees beside the trail, though Eastern hemlock is still the dominant conifer. After another switchback, the trail runs along the top of a dry ridge with a steep drop-off on both sides. Mountain laurel, catawba rhododendron, wintergreen, ground pine (another clubmoss) and reindeer moss (a lichen) grow here. Then a mountain laurel and rosebay rhododendron tunnel closes over you as the trail slips off to the side of the ridge.

When you emerge from the tunnel, you will see more red spruce than Eastern hemlock. Hemlock needles are flat with a white line underneath; spruce needles are square in cross section with no white line. Other high elevation plants, such as hobblebush and mountain maple, grow here, along with large yellow birches.

The trail becomes level in a large grassy spot with a yellow buckeye tree in the middle; not a campsite, but perhaps a place to tie a horse. The trail is rocky, narrow, and steep for the last half mile up to a trail junction at mile **4.5**. To the right, Maddron Bald Trail drops to Campsite #29 in 1.5 miles, to Albright Grove in 4.0 miles, and to the trailhead near US 321 in 7.2 miles. To the left, Snake Den Ridge Trail continues up to the Appalachian Trail in 0.7 mile. It climbs through a spruce-fir forest with bluets, ferns, and jewelweed along the sides. Mountain-ash, mountain maple, and hobblebush grow in open spots. The trail becomes steeper and rockier and may be wet; as it levels a bit, look for maple-leafed viburnum, bee-balm, blackberries, and huckleberries. As you come over the crest and start down, you see the end of Snake Den Ridge Trail. Mountain-ash grows to the right, red spruce to the left. There is a grassy patch for a nap and some views if the leaves aren't too thick.

The Appalachian Trail to the right reaches Mt. Guyot, the second highest peak of the Smokies, in 1.9 miles. To the left, it goes to Low Gap in 4.7 miles.

Narrative by Doris Gove

SPRINGHOUSE BRANCH TRAIL

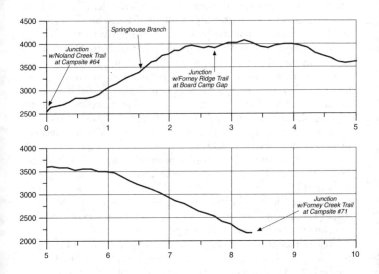

LENGTH: 8.3 miles, from Noland Creek Trail at Campsite #64 to Forney Creek Trail at Campsite #71.

HIGHLIGHTS: Variety of spring wildflowers.

MAP KEY: 6-7 F; USGS quads: Noland Creek, Silers Bald.

USE: Horse and hiking trail.

STARTING POINT: Hike 4.2 miles north on Noland Creek Trail from Lakeview Drive.

Springhouse Branch Trail begins at Campsite #64, a horse camp on the Noland Creek Trail 4.2 miles up from Lakeview Drive, and just up from Solola Valley, a flat meadow that used to have a post office and trade center. The campsite is large and sloping, with horse rails, fire rings, picnic tables, a food storage barrel, and creekside tent sites.

To find the trail, cross through the campsite with picnic tables on your left and enter the woods just to the right of a tent site and the creek. After about 100 yards, the trail crosses Mill Creek to an island and then crosses back, so the creek is again on your left. The trail then runs directly south, steadily uphill into Eastern hemlocks. It is an old trail, sunk deep in the hillside with earthen water bars. The forest opens out with yellow birches and grape vines, and the trail crosses the first of many muddy seeps. A house site on the left has rock piles, stone walls, and poison ivy. For the next mile or two look for signs of a large farming settlement—rock piles, old fields, rusted metal. Greenbrier, black locust, sourwood, tuliptree, yellow birch and sassafras all compete for sun. After a log bridge with a new handrail, there is a pretty fern field with a No Camping sign. Virginia creeper twines on the stone walls, and buffalo-nut bushes line the trail.

The trail leaves the settlement area and climbs to a dark Eastern hemlock grove. Ground pine grows here, first on the right and then on both sides. Listen for Ovenbirds and Wood Thrushes as the trail leaves the hemlock and enters open deciduous woods with oak, maple, sassafras, and tuliptree. This area was cleared for corn or pasture, and you will see locust fence posts on the left.

The trail continues to climb through a patch of smaller Eastern hemlocks and then open woods again. You can still hear Mill Creek on the left, and, as you enter the narrow valley of Springhouse Branch, larger trees appear. Wood betony, or lousewort, a plant with ferny leaves and orange flowers in May, grows on both sides of the trail in front of chestnut snags and logs.

The trail crosses the creek on stepping stones once at a large yellow buckeye (notice the ripply bark) and again at a big Eastern hemlock stump and log. Then the trail twists back to the right and enters a fine, moist old-growth forest with huge trees and some spring and early summer wildflowers: bee-balm, blue and black cohosh, violets, golden Alexanders, geranium, jack-in-the-pulpit, trillium (several kinds), foamflower, sweet cicely, phlox, may-apple, pipe vine, bloodroot, anemone, sedum, speckled wood lily, plantain-leaved sedge, loosestrife, mandarin, Indian cucumber, squawroot.

The trail is rocky in spots and crosses several muddy seeps. Flame azalea, striped maple, and American beech saplings appear on the ridge tops between the seeps. At a grassy curve to the right, look for speckled wood lily on both sides of the trail. From here, the trail goes through tangled mountain laurel, dark Eastern hemlock and rosebay rhododendron, and then more mixed deciduous forest to reach Board Camp Gap. From here you can take Forney Ridge Trail up to Andrews Bald and Clingmans Dome parking area or you can continue on Springhouse Branch Trail. Or you can sit on a chestnut log and eat lunch and listen for Ravens.

After Board Camp Gap, Springhouse Branch Trail climbs a narrow ridge covered with flame azalea, striped maple, red maple, American chestnut stumps, and vigorous chestnut saplings. Look for clusters of chestnut saplings with leafless upper branches, recent victims of the chestnut blight. The fungus that causes the blight came here in the 1920s, but it still lives on oaks and other trees. As soon as a chestnut shoot gets big enough to have bark cracks, the fungus gets in. It doesn't infect the roots, which can send up more shoots.

After a small dip at **3.6** miles, the trail climbs another dry, open ridge. Listen for the *grock...grook...groak* of Common Ravens as they soar on thermals from the valley on your left. The trail drops to the right of the ridge line, narrow at first and overgrown with mountain laurel. It descends more and then follows another ridge line down to a small gap.

From here, you descend into Forney Creek Valley. The trail is narrow and your uphill foot will get tired. After another switchback, the trail plunges into Eastern hemlock and rosebay rhododendron, crosses muddy seeps, and comes to mixed deciduous ferny woods with the creek noise of Bee Gum Branch on the left. A 2-3 story rock on the right supports rock tripe (a lichen), witch-hazel, rosebay rhododendron, and Eastern hemlock, and may be where you meet your first Forney Creek mosquitoes. After an overgrown ridge and more muddy seeps, the trail enters rich woods of chestnut oak, maple, locust, hickory, flowering dogwood, ash, and Fraser and cucumbertree magnolias. Cucumbertrees have light, furrowed bark much like that of tuliptrees. Look for cucumbertrees along this trail with thousands of Yellow-bellied Sapsucker holes.

The trail descends rapidly, crossing more muddy seeps and stretching along one more dry ridge top. After a left switchback, you will hear the authoritative murmur of Forney Creek in the distance. After a right switchback, look for a spring just before a wide, shallow crossing of Bee Gum Branch. The spring makes a dipping pool in a square rock basin. It was covered by treefall and rock slide in the 1993 blizzard and may be hard to find.

After the creek is an open field with holly bushes and cement house foundations on the left. A little farther on is Campsite #71, a horse camp with a chimney, a bathtub, and a large, heavily impacted tenting area. An old pre-park dump of rusty metal pieces has collected plastic drink containers and other modern trash. From #71, it is 8.2 miles up to Clingmans Dome parking area and 5.7 miles back to Lakeview Drive via several connecting trails.

Because Springhouse Branch is a narrow trail, and rocky in parts, you will be looking down for most of your hike. And it's a horse trail. So you may have opportunities to study a trail commodity: horse dung. Snails, centipedes, wasps, and flies all make use of horse dung, but the real volume customer is the dung beetle. The dung beetles here are black and shiny, about the size of a lima bean, and related to the sacred Egyptian scarabs. They deserve to be worshipped. Without them, some parts of the trail would be knee deep. During hot weather, dung beetles hustle out on the trail and collect balls of dung. They eat some of it, but most they bury as a food supply for their larvae. Neither adults or young eat the most fibrous part of the dung, so if you see a dry patch of what looks like chewed grass fibers, it is what the beetles have already worked over. Males help females provide for the young, a type of paternal care almost unheard of among insects. And, of course, where there are valuable resources, there is crime: some beetles steal balls of dung from others who have done all the work of collecting it, and some females use the Cowbird trick. They wait until another female finishes a nest and then they crawl in and lay their own eggs in the dung ball.

Another thing to consider—if you have the opportunity to observe many dung beetles on this hike—is that dung beetles remove dung from the trail before flies can lay their eggs on it. Also, if the horse has parasitic roundworms or flatworms, the dung beetles will remove them too. So try not to step on those scuttling black beetles, who always look clean and elegantly dressed.

Narrative by Doris Gove

SPRUCE MOUNTAIN TRAIL

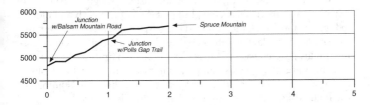

LENGTH: 2.0 miles, from Balsam Mountain Road to top of Spruce Mountain.
HIGHLIGHTS: Evidence of geological processes, high elevation vegetation.
CAUTIONS: Steep trail, blackberry brambles, fallen trunks across trail.
MAP KEY: 10 D; USGS quad: Bunches Bald.
USE: Hiking only from Balsam Mountain Road to Polls Gap Trail. Horse and hiking use from Polls Gap jct. to the mountain top.
TRAILHEAD: Take Blue Ridge Parkway to Heintooga Ridge Road, then drive north about 6.0 miles to reach Balsam Mountain Road, a one-way, unpaved road. Drive 5.9 miles to the trailhead.

The trail climbs straightaway up Spruce Mountain through rosebay rhododendron, yellow birch, and, of course, red spruce. Beside the trail are false nettles, spotted touch-me-not, and Joe-Pye-weed.

The trail itself is a lesson in geology. On the right lies a mossy boulder field—fragments of rock broken from the mountain's crest; off to the left a steep drop-off suggests a wedge failure landslide, the result of two planes of weakness folding, faulting, and crushing the rock. Nearby, a stream cascades downhill, carving away at the mountainside. Add to these factors the dramatic shifts in weather and the heavy precipitation that these upper slopes endure, and you can understand how the southern Appalachians, in their 250 million years, have eroded from a height estimated to equal the Andes' to their current elevations.

After crossing the aforementioned stream, the trail levels briefly, then ascends. Here, white snakeroot and foamflower grow. You climb a switch-back, then persevere uphill past American beech and more red spruce. On a rock formation to the left, a red spruce clings tenaciously, its roots clawing into a crevice. The trail is quite rocky. Nearing the lush gap between Chiltoes Mountain and Spruce Mountain, you encounter two species that play major roles in the higher peaks' ecology: smooth blackberry and Fraser fir. Once, Fraser fir dominated the high peaks, but the non-native balsam woolly adelgid has attacked the Fraser fir and allowed the blackberry to replace it.

At the gap between Chiltoes and Spruce Mountains stand huge red spruce and large yellow birches; spruce seedlings are growing out of birch roots. At **1.0** mile, you reach the junction with Polls Gap Trail; a 0.2 mile walk to the right takes you to Campsite #42. Continuing left up Spruce Mountain Trail, you encounter heavy vegetation (mostly smooth blackberries) overgrowing the trail, as well as fallen Fraser fir trunks blocking it. Hobblebush grows alongside as do many Fraser fir seedlings. Chunks of quartz litter the forest floor.

At **2.0** miles, you reach the clearing on top of Spruce Mountain, which is the trail's end. Once the site of a fire tower built in 1930s, this summit now cultivates smooth blackberry, with some yarrow and Joe-Pye-weed. Red spruce, pin cherry, yellow birch, and a few Fraser fir saplings slowly advance on the clearing. Only vestiges of the fire tower remain—the old stone chimney of the ranger's cabin and, at the far edge of the clearing, fragments of the tower's support posts.

Narrative by Ted Olson

STONE PILE GAP TRAIL

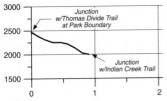

LENGTH: 0.9 mile, from Thomas Divide Trail to Indian Creek Trail.
HIGHLIGHTS: Crossing of Indian Creek via 25' footbridge.
CAUTIONS: Stream crossings, slippery rocks.

MAP KEY: F 8; USGS quad: Bryson City.
USE: Horse and hiking trail.
STARTING POINT: Hike 1.1 miles on Thomas Divide Trail north of Galbraith Creek Road, or hike 0.5 mile on Indian Creek Trail from its junction with Deep Creek Trail.

Stone Pile Gap Trail is useful for hikers who wish to take a direct route from Thomas Divide Trail to Deep Creek Campground. It heads downhill from the trailhead into a lush cove. Eastern hemlock and yellow birch grow here, as do flowering dogwood and mountain laurel; less noticeable is the heal-all, a small member of the mint family often used as a remedy for various ailments. After rock hopping a shallow creek, you descend among pignut hickory, sassafras, flowering dogwood, and mountain laurel. To the right, a stream gurgles and the trail angles downhill on a switchback. After two more stream crossings, the trail courses down the middle of the streambed over slippery rocks and through an Eastern hemlock grove. Amid yellow buckeye and yellow birch, you cross two more creeks then descend to cross Indian Creek, which is about 25' wide at this point and spanned by a foot log. A short stroll through tuliptrees leads you to Indian Creek Trail, 1.2 mile from Deep Creek Campground.
Narrative by Ted Olson

SUGARLAND MOUNTAIN TRAIL

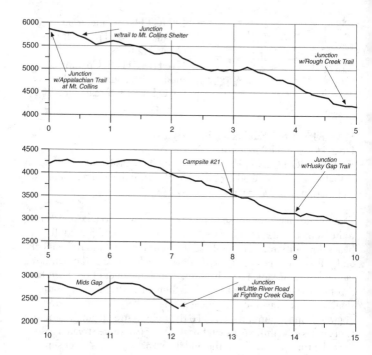

LENGTH: 12.1 miles, from the Appalachian Trail to Little River Road at Laurel Falls parking area.

HIGHLIGHTS: Great views, a variety of forest types, and large trees at the upper reaches.

MAP KEY: D-C 7-6; USGS quads: Clingmans Dome, Mt. LeConte, Gatlinburg.

USE: Hiking trail.

TRAILHEAD: Park at the Fork Ridge trailhead on the south side of the Clingmans Dome Road (closed in winter), 3.6 miles from Newfound Gap. Cross the road and walk 0.2 mile on the Appalachian Trail to the top of the Sugarland Mountain Trail.

Hiked from top to bottom, the Sugarland Mountain Trail is a long, leisurely delight. It is only occasionally steep and rocky and is nowhere very muddy. There are exceptional vistas from several points along the way, as well as some old-growth forest and a splendid diversity of forest types. Hiking the trail for its entire length is a wonderful way to spend a whole day outdoors in the Smokies.

The first half mile of the Sugarland Mountain Trail leads you through a fragrant spruce-fir forest. Although the larger Fraser firs have all been killed by the balsam woolly adelgid (an insect from Europe), it is worth noting the numerous small, seemingly healthy firs here. Perhaps some of these youngsters will prove to have a resistance to the adelgid and will pass this propensity on to their offspring.

At **0.5** mile you reach a 50-yard long, signed side trail to the Mt. Collins shelter (elevation 5,870'). The 12-bunk structure is set in an attractive open area surrounded by stately red spruce trees. Like all shelters, reservations are required. Being so close to a road, it is usually crowded (and sometimes raucous) on summer weekends.

Two hundred rocky yards past the shelter on the Sugarland Mountain Trail you will reach a meager spring. Ironically, this mountaintop spring is the only water along the entire length of the trail.

At approximately mile **1.0**, note a huge yellow birch tree on the right of the trail with red spruce trees growing on one of its limbs. Such "epiphytic" growth is common in rain forests and is a clue to the heavy rainfall which the upper portion of this ridge receives. Growing on the limb of a tree doesn't leave much opportunity for a large root system, but with lots of rain, humidity, and frequent cloud baths, the small spruce don't need extensive roots. Along the next couple of miles of trail you may also see epiphytic rhododendron and ferns.

The next 3.8 miles (to the Rough Creek Trail junction) are the most spectacular of the entire trail. The ridge will narrow to 8-10 feet wide at several places with sheer drops on both sides. Much of the forest on the ridgeline was left uncut or was only selectively cut and you will see a good deal of large yellow birch and red spruce. To the right you will catch glimpses of Mt. Mingus and Mt. LeConte, to the left watch for Goshen Ridge.

Besides birch and spruce, you will also see many pin cherry trees along this upper section. They are easily recognized by the horizontal lines on their otherwise smooth, reddish bark. When the brilliant red fruits of this species mature in late summer, black bears are quick to take advantage. In fact, Sugarland Mountain has one of the higher bear populations in the park and you will likely see their scat frequently along the trail.

After a little over 3.0 miles you will pass a steep, unmaintained, and dangerous side trail which descends precipitously to the right. Just beyond here you have an unusual opportunity to look down on the Chimney Tops. From subsequent view points you can also see the Newfound Gap Road, Mt. LeConte, the West Prong of the Little Pigeon River, and Gatlinburg.

Before reaching the Rough Creek Trail junction, the character of the forest gradually changes. You will begin to notice Eastern hemlock trees as the trail descends into a cove forest populated with red maple, yellow buckeye, white basswood, Northern red oak, and other hardwood species.

At approximately 4.4 miles you reach one of the trail's best lunch spots. A large, rocky outcrop populated with Table Mountain pine and mountain laurel provides fabulous views across the Little River valley and low ridges beyond.

After a couple more knife-edge ridges and some impressively large hemlock trees, you reach the Rough Creek Trail junction. From here the Rough Creek Trail descends the side of Sugarland Mountain to join the Little River Trail in 2.8 miles. This point also marks a drastic change in the character of the Sugarland Mountain Trail.

From mile 4.8 to Huskey Gap at mile 9.0, the forest is definitely second growth. In many places the woods are pleasantly open and the topography broad and flat, a striking contrast to the narrow ridgetops you have been tightrope walking so far. Mountain laurel is common along this section, making it a colorful walk when the shrub blooms in May and June. During early autumn, you should notice the blood-red leaves of the many black gum trees that thrive here.

Around mile 7.0 an extensive bouldery area is home to a bustling community of Eastern chipmunks. Listen for their sharp calls as they dive for cover in the rocks. This rough section may be where the Civilian Conservation Corps (CCC) trail builders had to cut "through solid rock" in 1934. Twenty-five CCC men built the trail during that summer, doing "considerable drilling and blasting" on sections like this. Most of the rock is Thunderhead Sandstone, a coarse-grained variety containing blue-tinted quartz, feldspar, and small quantities of granite and quartzite.

Near mile **8.0** you reach Campsite #21, one of the oddest campsites in the park. It's dispersed along a boulder field, at the headwaters of Big Medicine Branch, and looks like it could become a stream during heavy rains. There are level spots for three tents, but all are very close to the trail. This site's numerous boulders, however, are convenient for sitting. Water is usually available 200 feet downhill from the site. During dry times you may have to go a bit further. The site receives fairly heavy use.

Descending steadily to Huskey Gap, you will pass some of the runtiest trees in the park. Relatively light precipitation, acidic soils, or recent fires may be behind the small size of the second growth chestnut oak, scarlet oak, and Northern red oak.

At **9.0** miles you reach Huskey Gap and one of the major crossroads on the Tennessee side of the Smokies. From the gap, the Newfound Gap Road is 2.0 miles, the Little River Trail is 2.1 miles, and the Little River Road is 3.1 miles.

The path below Huskey Gap is pleasantly smooth and narrow. Notice that many of the pines in this area and along spots above the gap are dead or dying. The native Southern pine bark beetle is the culprit here. Flare-ups occur every few decades, killing lots of pines but never all. The National Park Service considers the actions of the native beetle part of natural processes in the park and pretty much lets nature take its course. Part of that course will probably be wildfire, followed by a healthy regeneration of new pines and other species.

At about mile **9.8** you reach a breathtaking vista of the Sugarlands Valley, Mt. LeConte and Bull Head. This view is worth walking up the trail from Little River Road for (2.3 miles), especially in autumn.

Around mile **10.8** you arrive at a broad, smooth saddle called

Mids Gap. The gap is said to be named for a man who lived in the area whose last name was Middleton. Mr. Middleton, and others who lived in the Sugarlands area, frequently tapped sugar maple trees for their sweet sap. Hence the name Sugarlands Valley and Sugarland Mountain which rises out of it.

Mids Gap is the namesake for the Mids Gap Fault, which runs right through it. The fault is responsible for the gap, as the broken and crushed rock along it erodes faster than surrounding, more intact rock. An unmaintained manway cuts down from Mids Gap to Mids Branch.

From the gap you have the longest uphill climb of the entire trail (about 0.4 mile). This area is rich with root shoots of American chestnut trees. Although their boles were killed over 40 years ago by a non-native fungus, some shoots along here reach over 12' tall, keeping the hope alive that someday these "redwoods of the East" will find a way to survive.

The forest becomes richer as you descend toward the Little River Road at Fighting Creek Gap. Note several chestnut oaks and tulip-trees of impressive size. Also note the damp seeps, the first moisture seen on this long, lovely mountain since Mt. Collins.

The trail ends at the large Laurel Falls parking area. Finding a parking spot can be difficult here during summer and on some off-season weekends. Fortunately, 99% of the parkers are walking the Laurel Falls Trail. You can have Sugarland Mountain almost all to yourself just about any day you choose.

Narrative by Steve Kemp

SUNKOTA RIDGE TRAIL

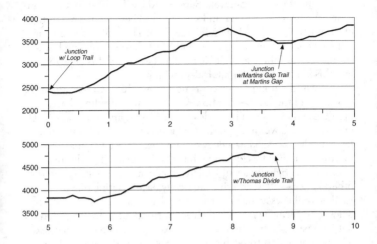

LENGTH: 8.6 miles, from Loop Trail to Thomas Divide Trail.
HIGHLIGHTS: Diverse vegetation, good fall vistas.
MAP KEY: 8 E-F; USGS quads: Bryson City, Clingmans Dome, Smokemont.
USE: Horse and hiking trail.
STARTING POINT: Hike Loop Trail 0.5 mile from its junction with Indian Creek Trail.

In the heart of the ancestral Cherokee territory and near the historic Cherokee township of *Kituhwa*, Sunkota Ridge is a low, moderately dry ridge wedged between and parallel to Noland and Thomas Divides. The trail's name derives from a garbled version of the Cherokee word for apple since apple trees once grew along the ridge. The trail meanders along the ridge crest. Not much used, it is often only 1' wide, a humble footpath compared to more popular routes.

The Sunkota Ridge trail also offers subtle beauty. Although most of the ridge was logged before the coming of the park, its vegetation has recovered impressively. A diverse, shadowy forest now covers most of the ridge; you can walk Sunkota Ridge Trail without encountering the heavy poison ivy and smooth blackberry undergrowth that clogs much of nearby Thomas Divide Trail. The trail also offers partial views of the higher ridges on both sides. In the winter and early spring, many of these are full views. And because of this ridge's variety, this is a good trail for fall leaf-watching.

At first, the trail is level, coursing among white pines on the dry south end of the ridge; soon, however, it climbs. Winding slowly uphill, the trail passes a large, dead yet still-standing tree—woodpecker holes are all over it. Soon the woods become dense; at one point large maples overshadow a dogwood understory. At **1.0** mile, the trail narrows in a mixed second-growth forest dominated by tuliptrees. Soon, on the right, you will see large boulders, one stacked upon the other; lichens and weathering are slowly disintegrating them.

The trail rises among rosebay rhododendron, oaks, and flowering dogwoods; decaying American chestnut trunks litter the floor. On the left, far below the trail, is a narrow wooded gorge formed by a creek. The trail meanders through a mixed second-growth hardwood forest. Continuing uphill, the woods become more dense and the trail levels on the ridge among pignut hickories, scarlet oaks, and tuliptrees. With little undergrowth, you can view Thomas Divide off to the right through occasional breaks in the trees. At **2.0** miles, the trail climbs the east slope via a switch-back through an oak grove with rosebay rhododendron and trailing arbutus. Good views of Noland Divide are to the left.

The trail continutes uphill among Northern red oak, white oak, Eastern hemlock, and black locust then runs level on a breezy, 30'-wide knife ridge. Next it skirts the southeast side of the ridge through pale, low-bush blueberry, wood betony, and giant chickweed then courses past tuliptrees, mockernut hickories, and maidenhair fern. One thousand feet below, Indian Creek roars. Downy rattlesnake plantain, hop clover, American holly, and pink lady's slippers grow on the left. By **3.0** miles at an elevation of 3,805', the trail drops toward Martins Gap through a dry forest of sassafras and sourwood.

At mile **3.8**, the trail joins Martins Gap Trail. While the first section of the Sunkota Ridge Trail (Loop Trail to Martins Gap Trail) was constructed by the National Park Service in the 1970s, this second section (from Martins Gap Trail to Thomas Divide Trail) was built by a Civilian Conservation Corps group (based at the Deep Creek CCC Camp) in the 1930s. Like the first, it offers good views, diverse vegetation, and solitude.

At a moderate grade, the trail passes through rosebay rhododendron, mountain laurel, red maple, scarlet oak, sourwood, and white pine. You soon pass a spring, but be sure to treat any water before you drink from it. Nearby are several impressive Eastern hemlocks. At **4.6** miles, the trail enters a rosebay rhododendron glade. After passing another spring and skirting many chestnut logs, at **5.5** miles, the trail meanders across the ridge top for a couple of miles through mixed second-growth forest. Along the ridge you can see good eastward vistas of Thomas Divide and Indian Creek valley. By **8.0** miles the trail levels and at **8.6** miles reaches its junction with Thomas Divide Trail (elevation 4,780').

Narrative by Ted Olson

SWALLOW FORK TRAIL

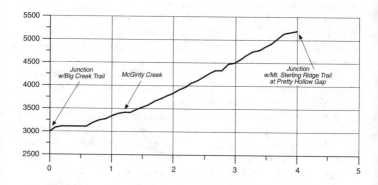

LENGTH: 4.0 miles, from Big Creek Trail to Mt. Sterling Ridge Trail.

HIGHLIGHTS: Pleasant forest and stream vistas, overgrown mountain farmstead, high mountain views.

MAP KEY: 11 C; USGS quad: Luftee Knob.

USE: Horse and hiking trail.

STARTING POINT: 5.0 miles on the Big Creek Trail at Walnut Bottom.

Swallow Fork Trail begins at 5.0 miles on the Big Creek Trail a few hundred feet below the bridge crossing at the Lower Walnut Bottom campsite (#37). Although miry in places due to horse traffic, footing is generally good along Swallow Fork.

The Crestmont Lumber Company, operated by Champion Fibre Company, logged the Big Creek watershed early in the twentieth century. In order to reach the high slopes of Mount Sterling Ridge, the Company built a railroad track with nine switchbacks and cut hemlocks and hardwoods in 1911 and 1912. In 1934 the Civilian Conservation Corps' Big Creek Camp rebuilt the old rail grade as a motorway. Beyond the old grade, the CCC constructed the well designed, graded trail which hikers enjoy today. Swallow Fork has been popular with hikers since the earliest days of the park. It was a featured hike of the Smoky Mountains Hiking Club of Knoxville, Tennessee in September, 1934.

The first mile of the Swallow Fork Trail is both interesting and pleasing to walk because of the easy grade and pleasant, open forest. The trail ascends away from the Big Creek Trail and parallels Big Creek at a distance on the shoulder of a gentle mountain slope, offering occasional views of Big Creek. At 0.1 mile a medium sized yellow birch is growing on stilt roots to the left of the trail. The seeds of this tree germinated on a rotten log and its roots grew over the log into the earth. At 0.2 and 0.5 miles the trail crosses tributaries of Swallow Fork which flow through a forest consisting primarily of second growth tuliptree.

These gentle slopes did not go unnoticed by early settlers. And although not apparent now, the area through which the trail passes was once cleared as part of a mountain farmstead. Look for scattered piles of stone, the result of field clearing efforts, and a large apple tree to the left of the trail which are remnants of past activity. A number of apple trees were noted when the writer visited this area in November, 1976. The limbs of these trees had been bent and broken by bears which had congregated to eat apples which still grew in the remains of the old orchard.

The trail crosses Swallow Fork on a footlog at 0.8 mile, offering a good view of the stream's small cascades, pools and runs. McGinty Creek is crossed on rocks at 1.1 miles. McGinty Creek and John Mack Creek, major tributaries of Swallow Fork, drain opposite ridges and flow into the main stream within 0.1 mile of each other. Both streams contain brook trout, while Swallow Fork contains both brook and rainbow trout. Despite their small size, streams such as these were regularly fished in pre-park days and it was not uncommon to keep large numbers of small "speckled trout." The trout were fried and eaten "head and all." Today the brook trout is protected in the Smokies.

The trail ascends more steeply beyond McGinty Creek, passing through open forest with areas of moss-covered logs and stones and rich fern growth. These same slopes offer a rich variety of plants and flowers in the spring including Fraser's sedge, jack-in-the-pulpit, wild leek (called ramps by mountain people), trout-lily, spring-beauty, and trillium. At **1.5** miles the old Crestmont rail grade is evident across the creek on the left. After a side stream crossing at **1.9** miles and a final crossing of one of Swallow Fork's seven tributaries, the trail bears left and climbs away from the stream.

As the trail ascends, it is possible to view a side ridge extending from Mount Sterling. On a bright autumn day, the pastel reds, yellows, crimsons and greens of the northern hardwood forest contrast with the dark green of scattered sharp-topped fir on the distant crest to create a breath-taking scene. The trail bears sharply to the right at **3.3** miles and begins a steady ascent to Pretty Hollow Gap. It is possible to observe Mount Guyot, the second highest peak in the Smokies, through the trees along this segment. At **3.6** miles the trail crosses the old Crestmont logging grade which continues right about 2.5 miles to end at Sevenmile Beech Ridge. The Swallow Fork Trail terminates in a small grassy clearing at Pretty Hollow Gap on the Mount Sterling Ridge Trail at **4.0** miles. The Pretty Hollow Gap Trail is straight ahead, leading 5.3 miles to Cataloochee Valley. Signs indicate the Mount Sterling and Baxter Creek Trails are left 1.4 and 1.9 miles, respectively.

Narrative by William A. Hart, Jr.

SWEAT HEIFER CREEK TRAIL

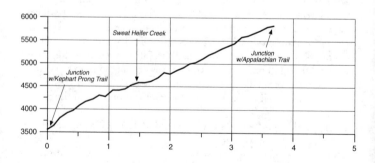

LENGTH: 3.7 miles, from Kephart Prong Trail to the Appalachian Trail.

HIGHLIGHTS: Cascading creek, partial views through open northern hardwood forest, solitude.

CAUTIONS: The upper portion may be overgrown with blackberry brambles. Upper portion is also steep and rocky.

MAP KEY: 8 D; USGS quads: Smokemont, Clingmans Dome.

USE: Hiking trail.

STARTING POINT: Hike 2.0 miles on Kephart Prong Trail to the shelter. Sweat Heifer Creek Trail forks left from that point.

Before Champion Fibre Company bought a huge parcel of land between Smokemont and the Smokies crest, North Carolina farmers drove some of their cattle up for summer grazing. Perhaps they chose the young, strong cows and left the older ones down in the valley. They may have followed the creek that you come to about half way up; by the time you reach the top, you will understand the odd name for this trail, even if you hike it in winter.

From the shelter, continue toward the creek. You can rock hop across or turn right for a foot log. Immediately after the log or rock hop, turn left and walk along the creek bank for a few yards. Then turn right and climb away from the creek onto a flat area. Usually this trail is easy to follow, but if a lot of leaves have fallen, it might be tricky.

Look for a big yellow birch with three trunks on the right about 0.1 mile from the creek. In a mature forest, yellow birches germinate best in rock cracks or on nurse logs; their roots don't pierce the soil litter. However, this part of the park has been both logged and burned, and this lone birch is just one sign of the disturbances that occurred early in the twentieth century.

At a tiny creek, bear left to cross it and walk along an almost dry creek bed with big boulders and big Eastern hemlocks. The trail swings right through a forest of American beeches and then left and up the side of a hill. It passes between the cut trunks of two American chestnut trees. Small American beech trees grow along the trail here; find a tree with smooth, light gray bark and feel the sharp bud at the end of a twig. Also look for a big candelabra Eastern hemlock on the left. Sometime in its youth, this tree lost its terminal bud, and side branches grew up straight.

The trail rises around the contours of the mountain. This section is hard packed dirt with few rocks, narrow, but well maintained. On a drier slope, you start seeing Norway spruce trees that the Champion Fibre Company planted here after a disastrous fire in 1925. Eastern hemlock, a few big Fraser magnolias, and mountain laurel also grow here. Through gaps in the trees you can see the stateline crest ahead and to the left.

The trail becomes narrower, steeper, and rockier for a while. Tangles of greenbrier and wet seeps may make footing difficult. Then, after crossing a usually dry creek bed, the trail joins an old railroad bed. Notice a road cut between the mountain on the right and a five-story mound on the left. The logging trains had a curve here instead of a switchback on the end of the ridge. You will welcome level ground as the trail follows the roadbed.

Great boulders fill the next dry creek bed, and the following road cut has a big American chestnut stump on the left. Rosebay rhododendron, mountain laurel, and Eastern hemlock darken this ridge, but they give way to an open American beech and birch forest. From a large, flat rock on the left, you can hear a new creek and again see the crest that you are trying to reach.

As you approach that new creek, which is Sweat Heifer, you go back into Eastern hemlock and rosebay rhododendron, but just as you start to cross the creek, look for a spectacular stand of tall yellow birches, with their yellow bark curled into ringlets.

The creek has ledges, pools, slides, and cascades. You may feel a rush of cool air as you come down to creek level, and there are some boulders to scramble over before crossing. If you haven't had lunch yet, this is a good place. From the shelter, you've come 1.5 miles.

The trail rises diagonally up the other hillside. Look back at the creek for another view of the cascades. Around the end of the ridge is the first of many blackberry patches. The trail drops a little to a tributary of Sweat Heifer Creek. It also has a beautiful cascade with rock slabs and a vein of quartz right above the crossing. If you have any lunch left, stop here, too.

At 4,800' elevation, the trail leaves the railroad bed and climbs a sheltered, flowery hillside. Ferns, toothwort, crested dwarf iris, and many other spring flowers grow here. As you continue the unrelenting climb to the Appalachian Trail, blackberry brambles grab your clothes. Rather suddenly you emerge onto a dry ridge top and turn right. Logs on the ground mark the trail, which becomes overgrown and rocky. Red spruces, the native ones, grow on this ridge.

At a switchback, you will see a big, gnarled yellow birch and some big red spruces. You might get a view of the crest, and it still looks pretty high. There are root surprises and mud traps where the trail is eroded below the soil surface. After some more rough footing, rocks, and brambles, you turn right toward a grassy ridge top with stunted American beech trees. Finally, the trail becomes level as you approach the Appalachian Trail sign. Red spruces and Fraser firs stand to the left of the sign and Siamese twin yellow birches with a tangle of stilt roots stand to the right of the sign. Newfound Gap is 1.7 miles to the left; The Boulevard Trail (1.0 mile) and Mount Katahdin, Maine, (1,800 miles) are to the right.

Narrative by Doris Gove

THOMAS DIVIDE TRAIL

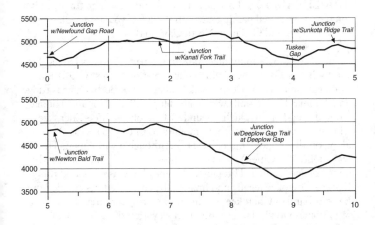

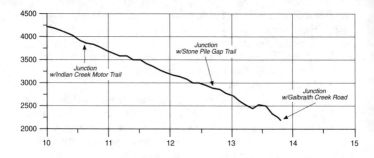

LENGTH: 13.8 miles, from Newfound Gap Road to Galbraith Creek Road.

HIGHLIGHTS: Good views in fall, diverse vegetation.

CAUTIONS: Extensive blackberry brambles and poison ivy in summer.

MAP KEY: 8 D-F; USGS quads: Clingmans Dome, Smokemont, Bryson City.

USE: Hiking trail only along the ridge 4.7 miles to Sunkota Ridge trail junction. Horse and hiking use from Sunkota Ridge trail junction south to Galbraith Creek Road.

TRAILHEAD: 3.0 miles south of Newfound Gap. The trailhead is a long, narrow, paved parking area (on the left if you are heading toward Newfound Gap from North Carolina).

One of the longer individual trails in the park, Thomas Divide Trail was built in 1934 by the Civilian Conservation Corps (CCC) stationed at what is now Deep Creek Campground. Both Thomas Ridge and Thomas Divide trails were named for William Holland Thomas, a noted friend of the Qualla Boundary Cherokee (those Cherokee who did not leave the southern mountains in the 1830s for Oklahoma along on the tragic "Trail of Tears.") Although a white man, Thomas was adopted by Chief Yonaguska and became chief himself in 1839 after Yonaguska died. Throughout his life, Thomas supported the Eastern Cherokee legally and financially, and his efforts enabled the Eastern Band of Cherokee to remain in North Carolina.

Thomas Divide Trail begins at an elevation of approximately

4,650' and courses up and down through a forest of Eastern hemlock, yellow birch, American beech, and sugar, red, and mountain maple. Several large Eastern hemlocks and a few 4'-wide white oaks are the only trees to have escaped extensive pre-park logging. You will notice many fallen chestnut logs on the forest floor. They have not rotted even though the trees died more than fifty years ago. The tannic acid in their bark makes American chestnut hardier and more weather-resistant than many other trees, a quality that led pioneers to prefer chestnut wood for barns and houses. Also, the tannin from chestnut bark was widely used for tanning hides. While sprouts of saw-toothed leaves continue to grow from old root systems, they invariably die before they reach a height of 20'.

Depending on the season, you may see rosebay rhododendron, fire pink, wild bergamot, spring-beauty, Turk's cap lily, and galax. Dodder, a parasitic vine with white bell-like flowers and orange trailing stems, is especially noticeable during mid-summer. Mountain people called dodder strangle-weed and love vine. Nearby grows squawroot, another parasitic flowering plant that taps tree roots for food and whose stalks look like pine cones.

At **1.8** miles Thomas Divide Trail reaches Kanati Fork Trail, which descends 2.9 miles through the steep valley of Kanati Fork to Newfound Gap Road. Thomas Divide Trail follows the crest of Thomas Divide through thick vegetation, including trees such as Juneberry, chestnut oak, scarlet oak, red maple, and Eastern hemlock, and wildflowers which include flame azalea, trailing arbutus, spider-wort, Indian cucumber, butter-and-eggs, wood betony, and Joe-Pye-weed. Although common today, a flower you would not have seen in the Smokies two hundred years ago is the heal-all. Brought to the New World by European settlers for its medicinal qualities, heal-all was widely used as a home remedy. Another non-native species along this trail is the black-eyed Susan, originally a prairie wildflower which gradually spread into the Eastern U.S. as wagons and trains accidentally carried its seed eastward. You may also spot signs of black bear, such as scat or claw marks in the trail's banks.

At **2.8** miles the trail traverses Nettle Creek Bald, which is the highest point on the trail but is too heavily forested for good views. It then descends toward Tuskee Gap, after which it climbs again. At **4.7** miles, the trail meets Sunkota Ridge Trail. In 0.4 mile, at the Newton Bald Trail junction, Thomas Divide Trail turns right and continues along the ridge. During the summer, the trail from this point on is overgrown with blackberry bushes. The blackberries' dominance results from extensive logging of this ridge; they thrived in the direct sunlight that other species could not tolerate after logging. Fortunately, trees have managed to regain a foothold at many points along the Thomas Divide, and in these places you get a clearer sense of what a dry ridge environment looks like. Cinnamon, lady, and hay-scented ferns grow in clumps beside the trail; you may see pink lady's slippers. Semi-shaded areas harbor flowering spurge and white snakeroot, named for the relief it offered Indian snakebite victims, according to park naturalist Arthur Stupka. During early summer, many heaths bloom, including flame azalea and mountain laurel. In semi-wooded areas, Rufous-sided Towhees scratch for food among leaves; they call "chewink" (as the sound was transliterated by the Indians), "towhee" (as eighteenth-century naturalist Mark Catesby identified it), or the infamous song, "drink your tea!."

Proceeding down the ridge past several dry creek beds, you will notice that not all tree species have declined since the days of logging; the black locust and sassafras actually prosper in this eroded soil. Because black locust is one of the first species to grow back in a disturbed area, foresters and naturalists call it a "pioneer" species; because its wood rots slowly, the early mountain settlers used black locusts as posts for split-rail fences. Sassafras is likewise tenacious—the folk adage that "if you pull up one sassafras seedling, two will grow back" is no exaggeration. Mountain settlers used its roots to make soap and tea.

Descending among pignut hickories and tuliptrees, the trail reaches, at **8.2** miles, Deeplow Gap Trail. Continuing through second-growth forest of Northern red oak and American beech, Thomas Divide Trail climbs up and down several knolls. Goatsbeard, bouncing bet, and Solomon's seal bloom alongside in spring. Less pleasing is poison ivy, which at times is so thick that you must hold it back with a walking stick.

The trail follows the crest of the Thomas Divide among red maple, black locust, Eastern hemlock, and tuliptree. You may hear the loud *croak* of the Raven, a northern species whose range reaches its southernmost point just south of the Smokies, or the Black-billed Cuckoo, a species seldom seen but occasionally heard rhythmically calling *cucucu* three or four times.

At **10.6** miles, the trail merges onto an old road originally created to be part of the Indian Creek Motor Nature Trail, a project that has since been abandoned. The trail junction with Indian Creek Motor Trail is marked with a sign. Heading downhill to the left on Thomas Divide Trail, you descend among tuliptrees, whose straight, tall trunks display the qualities that make this the most stately tree of the southern Appalachians. The forest understory consists of flowering dogwood and multi-flora rose. As the trail weaves its way downhill on the old road, it passes a variety of trees—red maple, black cherry, sweet birch, white pine, Eastern hemlock, and American basswood. To the right, far below, roars Indian Creek, while the park boundary lies immediately to the left. At **12.7** miles, the trail reaches Stone Pile Gap Trail, a 0.9-mile trail that descends to Indian Creek Trail. Maidenhair ferns grow on the left bank of the trail, along with Christmas ferns and dog-hobble. A beautiful cove forest appears to the right, but as the trail approaches its end at Galbraith Creek Road, it enters a scrubby forest dominated by Virginia pine, sassafras, and black locust. A side trail off to the right leads to a pioneer cemetery. The trail ends at a small parking lot next to Galbraith Creek Road. Deep Creek Campground lies about 1.0 mile to the right down an unsurfaced stretch of Galbraith Creek Road.

Narrative by Ted Olson

TRILLIUM GAP TRAIL

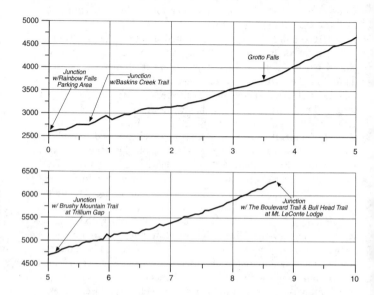

LENGTH: 8.7 miles, from Rainbow Falls Parking Area to the summit of Mt. Le Conte.

HIGHLIGHTS: Grotto Falls, views, diversity of plant life.

CAUTIONS: Rocky, wet trail near the top; some difficult creek crossings in rainy weather; ice in winter.

MAP KEY: 7 C-D; USGS quad: Le Conte.

USE: Horse, llama (for Le Conte Lodge), and hiking trail.

TRAILHEAD: Take Airport Road (traffic light #8) from the main street in Gatlinburg (441). Drive to the park boundary, past the Twin Creeks Resource Center Road and Ogle home site, and into Cherokee Orchard. At mile 3.4, just after the road becomes one-way, turn right into the Rainbow Falls Parking Area, park on the left, and look for a trail sign on the right near the entrance to the parking area.

There are three distinct sections of this trail to Mt. Le Conte: a 2.4 mile stretch from Cherokee Orchard; a 2.8 mile easy climb to Trillium Gap; and a 3.6 mile strenuous climb to the lodge at Mt. Le Conte. During three seasons, you can drive past the first section and park at the Grotto Falls parking lot on the Roaring Fork Motor Nature Trail, but in winter, that road is closed. This trail description includes all three sections. If you prefer to skip the first section (which we recommend), continue driving about 2.0 miles into the one-way Roaring Fork Motor Nature Trail to the Grotto Falls parking area.

Cherokee Orchard was a 796-acre commercial orchard and nursery that operated on this hillside in the 1920s and 1930s, with 6,000 fruit trees and thousands of boxwoods, azaleas, Eastern hemlocks, and andromedas for landscaping. The owners fought state and national bills that allowed condemnation privileges for the park commission; consequently, this land was not included in the original park boundaries. However, the company sold the land to the commission and turned it over to the park in 1942. The signs of settlement along this trail are quite recent: glass bottles, shells of electric appliances.

Just a few yards into the woods on the Rainbow Falls Trail, Trillium Gap Trail goes left and Rainbow Falls Trail continues straight. From here, it is 3.5 miles to Grotto Falls and 5.1 miles to Trillium Gap. The trail runs parallel to Cherokee Orchard Road through a tangled forest of grapevines, greenbriers, locusts, maples, and tuliptrees. As the trail turns away from the road, a large building site appears on the left. Non-native periwinkle covers the ground, and a spring and creek provide water. Several spicebushes grow along the trail here. This bush is about as tall as a person, thin, with small leaves. It is most easily recognized in late February, when its small yellow-green flowers are the only blooms in sight. The twigs have a pleasant, spicy smell when bruised.

The trail rises and then crosses a tiny creek. The one-way Roaring Fork Motor Nature Trail is just below, and you will see it from time to time for the next 2 miles. Several spur trails lead to the road.

Look for chips of quartz, a sharp white crystalline rock, in the trail. Uphill to the left are stands of Eastern hemlock all the same size mixed with tall, skinny tuliptrees. All of this area was cleared for the orchards or cut for timber. Those young hemlocks couldn't colonize the ground as quickly as the deciduous trees could, but as soon as the tuliptrees improved the habitat, the hemlocks got started. To show their gratitude, they will probably shade out most of the tuliptrees in a century or two.

The trail drops to cross a pretty creek and swings around a dry hillside with galax, trailing arbutus, and pine trees. It then crosses a moist slope with silverbells, yellow buckeyes, and flowering dogwoods. American chestnuts and many other dead trees have fallen down the slope. Toothwort and hepatica, which both bloom in March, are scattered about these open woods. Also look for squawroot, putty root orchids, striped pipsissewa, and downy rattlesnake plantain.

After the next creek crossing, you move into old-growth forest with larger trees. Look for a big silverbell on the left with a bad case of warts and burls. American beech, Fraser magnolia, and basswoods also grow here, with an understory of dog-hobble.

In a dark Eastern hemlock grove, you come to the intersection with the Grotto Falls Trail from Roaring Fork Road. Turn right onto a wide, packed dirt trail. Large American beeches, silverbells, and maples share space with the Eastern hemlocks in this mature forest, and you can find rotting trunks that support little trees and shrubs. You might also see more recently dead snags and stumps that have been worked over by Pileated Woodpeckers. If fresh splinters of wood have been scattered on the ground and if there are rectangular holes big and deep enough to stick your hand into, this woodpecker—the largest of the region—has probably been there. You might hear its crazy laughing call or glimpse a flash of a black and white crow-sized bird flying from trunk to trunk. It doesn't bother healthy trees, just dead or dying ones.

The trail rises steadily, following a typical Smokies hiking pattern: in toward a creek, cross, out around a ridge, in again. All of the crossings are easy, but some might be muddy because of horse or llama traffic—this is the route for llamas to carry food and laundry to Le Conte Lodge. From the trail high above a creek valley, you can look down into the tops of Eastern hemlocks, basswoods, and Fraser magnolias. After a little more than 1.0 mile from the trailhead, the trail rounds one more ridge, and you can hear a louder, more insistent creek. This is Roaring Fork, which roars and tumbles from near the top of Mt. Le Conte down to Gatlinburg, where it joins the West Prong of the Little Pigeon. As you approach Grotto Falls, look down to the left and watch the white water. A straight downhill section of trail takes you to Grotto Falls, with a little sign in case there's any doubt. There are rocks to rest on; Grotto Falls draws crowds on some days.

Liverworts grow in the rocks within the spray zone, and if it's warm, you should be able to see salamanders basking in misty showers. Upstream and down you can see massive boulders and throngs of rosebay rhododendron. You can cross Roaring Fork on some slippery stepping stones, or you can walk behind the water in the grotto. In very high water, either crossing may be difficult or impossible; you may want to check the weather if you are planning to use this route down from Mt. Le Conte.

Trillium Gap Trail after the falls is narrower and rockier, but still a good trail, climbing through mature forest. Near the seeps that cross the trail, giant yellow buckeyes and shaggy yellow birches grow. About 1.0 mile beyond the falls, a boulder field starts—great fractured rocks with polypody ferns and fabulous mosses. Trees and shrubs growing on these rocks have developed wild designs as their roots searched for soil. These boulders came from the extreme cold of the glacial periods. Though the glaciers apparently did not reach the Smokies, cold weather did, and water and deep freezing fractured off boulders from the bedrock.

A creek running through part of the boulder field is easy to cross but could be slippery. After the creek, the trail continues to rise and passes a wonderful rock face on the right decorated with white, yellow, and green lichens. Soon you might see a few red spruce cones on the trail and find red spruce among the Eastern hemlock. Then grass appears, and soon the open forest of gray, lichen-covered American beech trees. Look for a big gnarled silverbell tree on the left with clusters of root sprouts. Ahead, you can see the Trillium Gap sign and trail junction.

To the left is a short climb to Brushy Mountain, a heath bald with good views. Straight ahead, Brushy Mountain Trail leads down to Porters Flat and Greenbrier Cove. Trillium Gap Trail turns right and starts the 3.6 mile climb to Mt. Le Conte.

Trillium Gap is a typical American beech gap, with beech trees and grass as the dominant plants. They thrive here because they can withstand the constant wind. If you stand at the entrance of the spur trail to Brushy Mountain and look south toward Mt. Le Conte, you can see that the beech gap is roughly triangular, and you are standing in the center of one side. The triangle extends down both sides of the gap and ahead up the slope. However, the sharp rise of Brushy Mountain behind you offers some protection, and Eastern hemlocks, rosebay rhododendrons and a few young red spruce trees grow there.

As you start up the last section of the Trillium Gap Trail, note that mosses gradually replace the grasses on the trail edge as you leave the gap. The trail slips to the right of the ridge, and Eastern hemlocks and yellow buckeyes appear with the beeches. Ferns and mosses take over as ground cover. Look for spruce cones in the trail and small spruces mixed with the hemlocks. This trail is a high bench alongside a Le Conte ridge, and through gaps in the trees, you get glimpses of a higher ridge with a line of big red spruces that look like sentinels on duty. Frequent tree falls on this steep slope provide views.

Look for a boulder on the right about 0.5 mile from the gap with a crop of polypody fern on top. This fern looks a little like Christmas fern with shorter fronds, and it almost never grows on the ground.

The trail climbs constantly, and there are roots and rocks to trip over. A Civilian Conservation Corps crew built this trail with great difficulty, and they had an even harder job when they were asked to go back and widen it to make it safe for horse travel. Several small creeks and seep crossings are usually no problem, but the rocks can be slippery or icy. One creek bubbles down a small, mossy waterfall on its way to meet Roaring Fork. Rosebay rhododendron lines the trail, and the presence of hobblebush, or viburnum, should assure you that you're gaining elevation.

After a swing west, the trail turns south to run along the 5,200' contour line and then switches back to make a steep climb. The trail is rocky, and during rain, water stands in the trail. In some spots, the trail slopes down the steep hillside, and you have to be careful about footing. You will understand why Le Conte Lodge employs llamas. In the next mile, you gain another 600' to another switchback. By this point, the Eastern hemlocks are all below you, and the dominant evergreen is red spruce. Young Fraser fir trees, waist-to-head high, line the trail, but most of the adult fir have died from infestations of the balsam woolly adelgid, a type of sap-sucking aphid. Throughout the woods here you see the dead trees, and as you go higher, the proportion of dead trees increases. Spruce trees are also having problems at high elevations, but not so severe as the Fraser fir.

You can distinguish between spruce and fir saplings because fir needles are flat and blunt at the ends, while spruce needles are square in cross section (you can roll them between your fingers if your fingers aren't stiff with cold by now) and sharp on the ends. On larger (head-high) fir saplings, you can also look for blisters of sap on the trunks. Some early settlers thought this sap resembled milk and named fir she-balsam. Spruce, fir's companion on these high peaks, became he-balsam. It was a long hike up here for the settlers, too. If you find a patch of young firs, look for yellow or brown needles that indicate the beginning of disease.

Finally, after a particularly rocky trail section, the lower buildings of Le Conte Lodge will loom, probably out of the fog, before you. Water from a spring on the left (Warning sign: Boil all water) trickles down and across the trail and eventually joins Roaring Fork. With just another 50-yard climb, you reach the lodge and junction with the other Le Conte trails.

Narrative by Doris Gove

TUNNEL BYPASS TRAIL

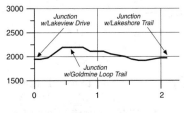

LENGTH: 2.1 miles, from end of Lakeview Drive to Lakeshore Trail.

HIGHLIGHTS: Few people, opportunities for making loops.

MAP KEY: 6 F; USGS quad: Noland Creek.

USE: Horse and hiking trail.

TRAILHEAD: From Bryson City, drive northwest about 9 miles on Lakeview Drive to its end.

Tunnel Bypass Trail begins at the end of Lakeview Drive, often called the "Road to Nowhere." The construction of this road was begun in the 1960s to fulfill a promise made by the government when a strip of land north of the Little Tennessee River was incorporated into the national park upon the construction of Fontana Dam in the 1940s. The road, which was never completed, now ends at the trail-heads for this trail and Lakeshore Trail. These trails access the Forney Creek area.

Tunnel Bypass Trail begins across the road from the lower end of the parking area at the end of Lakeview Drive. The trail ascends through hemlock and rhododendron 0.4 miles to a saddle in the ridge. Pass through a mixed hardwood forest to a trail junction at **0.5** miles. The Goldmine Loop Trail turns to the south (left) to travel 2.1 miles to connect with the Lakeshore Trail.

Ascend Tunnel Ridge in a moderate climb. The trail then descends to pass over the headwaters of Hyatt Branch. This stream crossing is below the western end of the tunnel. The roadbed can be seen above the trail to the right. At mile **2.1** the trail ends at a junction with Lakeshore Trail which runs 0.7 mile back to the end of Lakeview Drive and the parking area.

Narrative by Charles Maynard & David Morris.

TURKEYPEN RIDGE TRAIL

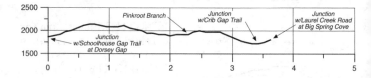

LENGTH: 3.6 miles, from Schoolhouse Gap Trail to Laurel Creek Road.

HIGHLIGHTS: The level in and out weaving of the trail along the eastern face of Turkeypen Ridge.

MAP KEY: D 4; USGS quads: Wear Cove, Thunderhead Mtn.
USE: Horse and hiking trail.
STARTING POINT: Jct. with Schoolhouse Gap Trail 1.1 miles from Laurel Creek Road OR Laurel Creek Road, 5.5 miles west of the Townsend "Y."

There are two likely starting points for this path; one is across from the trailhead of the Lead Cove and Finley Cane trails, 5.5 miles west of the Townsend "Y" on the Laurel Creek Road. The nearer one is at the start of the Schoolhouse Gap Trail, 3.5 miles west of the Townsend "Y" on the Laurel Creek Road. This description is from the Schoolhouse Gap Trail junction.

After walking northwest 1.1 mile on the gentle grade of Schoolhouse Gap Trail, the Turkeypen Ridge Trail appears on the left at Dorsey Gap. This gap has no marker but was named for Anderson Dorsey, a Civil War veteran who farmed some of the old fields beyond the gap to the west of the trail.

This popular path is convenient to get to and easy to walk. After the gap, the trail passes through a thicket of rhododendron, then ascends through a mixed hardwood forest. Mountain laurel also appears on occasion. On moving to the south side of the ridgeline, the forest changes to a mixture of pine and oak.

Soon the canopy on the right opens up as the result of the pines having been devastated by an invasion of the native Southern pine bark beetle some 15-20 years ago.

Before reaching the top of the ridge, if you're lucky enough to pass when azaleas are in bloom, there are several, quite small, flame azaleas with blood-red blooms. Among other flowers along this trail are galax, wood vetch, trillium, and big patches of crested dwarf iris in the moist hollows.

The trail runs briefly along the top of a level ridge, northwest of which lies a large and unusual depression, known as Whiteoak Sink. No graded or officially maintained trail enters that area.

The path swings left and runs level, in and out, around each descending spoke of the eastern face of Turkeypen Ridge. The path moves out and around the dry flank of each bulge, then back into the cool, moist havens next to the heart of the mountain. In and out the trail weaves, going deepest where it crosses two prongs of Pinkroot Branch.

Pinkroot is the local name of a beautiful flowering herb, Indian pink, which grows in limestone soil.

At the last crossing of Pinkroot Branch is a picturesque ledge, or outcropping of layered rock. It's a moist and cool place to pause and relax and enjoy the quiet seclusion and enchantment.

The trail leaves the level, passes through a small gap, and gradually descends and drops into the old fields (reforested cropland) of Big Spring Cove. Several small piles of rock can be seen from the path. These are common on old mountain farms, piled by the farmers to enable them to more easily work the rocky land. An old saying was, "This land grows more rocks than anything else."

Toward the bottom of the descent another branch of Laurel Creek is heard, then seen, to the right. Just before crossing the branch, an old home site is to the right. There are stove remnanats near the trail and cane is growing along the creek.

Two-tenths of a mile before reaching the trail's end at Laurel Creek Road, the Crib Gap Trail crosses and the sound of traffic soon creeps in to dissolve the quiet comfort of Turkeypen Ridge Trail.

Narrative by Woody Brinegar

TWENTYMILE LOOP TRAIL

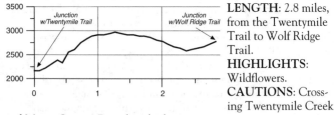

LENGTH: 2.8 miles, from the Twentymile Trail to Wolf Ridge Trail.
HIGHLIGHTS: Wildflowers.
CAUTIONS: Crossing Twentymile Creek and Moore Springs Branch in high water.
MAP KEY: 2-3 F; USGS quad: Fontana Dam.
USE: Hiking trail.

STARTING POINT: Twentymile Trail, 3 miles from Twentymile Ranger Station.

This loop trail is the upper link in a 6.3 mile triangle which includes the lower Wolf Ridge Trail along Moore Springs Branch and the Twentymile Trail.

The Kitchen Lumber Company, which logged this whole area between 1921 and 1929, built railroads up Twentymile Creek and Moore Spring Branch as well as a connecting line on a portion of this loop trail. The trail leaves the old roadbed at the crossing of Twentymile Creek and runs higher on the slope than the rail route.

The trail begins at the point where the Twentymile Trail starkly diminishes in width and maintenance. This is Proctor Field Gap, named for John Proctor who settled there.

This route is gently sloped and an easy walk. A spiderstick comes in handy to brush aside the dozen or so single strands of invisible spider web which usually cross the path at various spots. It descends into a shaded hollow with hemlocks, oaks, maples, and white ashes providing the canopy.

Soon a level patch of land opens up and under a stand of hemlocks is a patch of pink lady's slippers (usually these flowers are in pine and oak forests). They delight the eye with their lovely blooms in May.

Beyond is a covering of wood fern prior to the crossing of Twentymile Creek. High water is a serious problem here. For example, Long Hungry Ridge, around whose lower edge this trail circles, got its name from hungry hunters who spent several winter days waiting to cross this creek in flood.

After the crossing, the trail gradually ascends through a mixed pine and hardwood forest. The trail swings around the rounded fingers of the ridge and back into the creased recesses between. Midway, a long-dead American chestnut trunk 30" thick crosses the path. The path width of the trunk has been removed. These giants of the Appalachians are becoming less frequently seen as they are rapidly melting into the soil.

The highest point of this low elevation trail is reached just after passing through a gap. Not far beyond is a slightly higher gap. Then the trail descends like a wiggling worm to Moore Springs Branch. This branch, incidentally, carries about the same amount of water as Twentymile Creek.

The trail crosses Moore Springs Branch and meets the Wolf Ridge Trail in a very short distance. This wide stream is also a hazard when in flood stage.

Narrative by Woody Brinegar

TWENTYMILE TRAIL

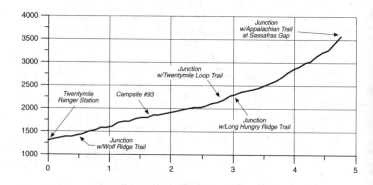

LENGTH: 4.7 miles, from Twentymile Ranger Station to the Appalachian Trail.
HIGHLIGHTS: Opportunity to see bears, unusual logging history, easy walking.
MAP KEY: 2-3 F; USGS quad: Fontana Dam.
USE: Horse and hiking trail.
TRAILHEAD: Twentymile Ranger Station.

Twentymile Ranger Station is one of the most remote ranger stations and once was the site of one of the most unusual logging operations in the park. Kitchens Lumber Company moved into the area in 1921. Charles and John Kitchens persuaded the Southern Railway to extend their standard gauge railway down the Little Tennessee River from its terminus at the original town of Fontana, situated at the mouth of Eagle Creek, to their new town and mill. Kitchensville was located on the shore at the upper end of the newly constructed Cheoah Reservoir near the present day N.C. Highway 28 river bridge just downstream from Fontana Dam. Still five miles short of their timber bonanza on Twentymile Creek, the Kitchens boys devised a unique solution to their transportation dilemma. They constructed a 50' steamboat from the finest timbers and powered it with a coal-fired sawmill engine. They christened the boat "Vivian" after Charles' wife. Barges were also constructed to haul the logs and equipment, and one barge was outfitted with an American log loader to create a floating crane. They loaded their narrow gauge Hiesler locomotive, rail cars, rails, and all other equipment required by a large-scale logging operation on the barges and steamed them down the lake to Twentymile Creek. It was said that when the "Vivian" and Southern Railway's massive rod-engine "Big Junaluska" arrived simultaneously at Kitchensville, the resulting salute from their dueling steam whistles reverberated through the mountains for miles.

Stone retaining walls of the original railroad grade can be seen just uphill from the paved driveway to the ranger station. Parking is available at the station and up the road from the station near the bunkhouse. Proceed around the locked gate to begin your hike. You will be walking along the old railroad grade for the entire length of this hike. This road was improved by the Civilian Conservation Corps after inclusion in the park to provide access to the Shuckstack fire tower. The rock cuts on the first part of the trail exposed some of the geologic makeup of the area. Veins of white quartz run through the schist and gneiss rock. Large boulders are evident on the mountainside and in the creek as a result of water, ice, roots, and time breaking the boulders from solid rock. Many varieties of mosses and lichens cover parts of the exposed rock.

At 0.3 miles you will pass the park service horse barn and corral. There are usually several traps stored here which are used to trap the wild hogs that were imported into the area in the early 1900's by an English sportsman. At the first bridge the Wolf Ridge Trail bears left and runs 6.4 miles to the state line at Parson Bald. Notice the large nurse-log sycamore tree at the northwest corner of the bridge. This tree sprouted on top of a downed tree and sent roots down both sides of the log. Later the log rotted and created the hole at the base of the sycamore. Follow the main road to the right. About 100 yards from the first bridge a small foot trail leads off to the right and will take you to Twentymile Cascade. Caution should be exercised around this and all waterfalls. A fine stand of partridgeberry is evident along this short side trail.

Continue up the main road paralleling Twentymile Creek through a typical south slope second growth forest. Tuliptree, maples, magnolias, basswood, and occasional hemlock and white pine can be seen here. Just 1.7 miles from the ranger station you will come to Twentymile Creek Campsite (#93). The campsite is in a level grove of trees that was once a field. No horses are allowed and there is no spring, but water may be obtained from the creek. This campsite makes a good base to fish the pocket waters of Twentymile and Proctor Creeks.

At 3.0 miles you will arrive at Proctor Field Gap. The Long Hungry Ridge Trail turns left here and leads 4.6 miles to the state line Ridge at Rich Gap. From there the Gregory Ridge Trail leads directly to Cades Cove. This is probably the route that members of the Proctor family "crossed-over" from the Cove to settle at Proctor Fields. Remnants of stone walls and foundations can be found in the large level areas here. Follow the old road in an easterly direction up through old fields. You are now traveling along Proctor Branch, a series of cascades and pools that hide a population of very wily rainbow trout. The trail soon leaves the branch and follows a contour through a south slope mixed forest to arrive at Sassafras Gap and the Appalachian Trail. Many bear sightings have occurred on the upper reaches of this trail. Watch for clawed trees, game trails, droppings, dug-out bee's nests, wallows, and other bear sign.

Narrative by Lance Holland

TWIN CREEKS TRAIL

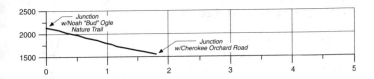

LENGTH: 1.8 miles, from Noah "Bud" Ogle Nature Trail to Cherokee Orchard Road near the park boundary.

HIGHLIGHTS: Easy walk; good children's nature hike.

MAP KEY: 6 C; USGS quad: Gatlinburg.

USE: Hiking trail.

TRAILHEAD: From US 441 in Gatlinburg, turn at traffic light #8 onto Airport Road. After you enter the park, drive 1.8 miles and park at the Noah "Bud" Ogle place parking area on the right. As you approach the cabin, turn right. Cross two creeks, and at about 0.3 mile, look for the #6 signpost. Forty yards downhill from #6, turn right onto Twin Creeks Trail. At the time of this writing, there is no sign, but the trail is obvious.

This easy trail parallels Cherokee Orchard Road from the Noah "Bud" Ogle Nature Trail to the park border. It runs through old fields and house sites and along a pretty creek. The hardest part of hiking it is finding it, but once you do, it is a good hike for families and children.

It starts as a gentle descent through Eastern hemlock mixed with cucumber trees and umbrella magnolias. Both of these magnolias bloom in late April, and their fruits turn bright red in August. Cucumber tree fruit is shaped like a short, crooked pickle, and umbrella magnolia fruits look like fleshy pine cones. Squirrels or wind often knock them down before they ripen, so you might find one or two on the trail. Scratch and sniff the spicy smell. If you find one of the orange seeds, scratch and sniff it for a different smell. Then pull the seed gently away from the fruit to see the elastic strand like chewing gum that connected the seed to its food source.

The trail then levels out in a drier area of small oaks, hickories, and American beeches. You are not far from the road on this hike and can hear, see, or smell cars. Soon you come to a stone wall on the left and a boxwood hedge on the right. Most of the trees here are thin and scraggly, possibly because of exhausted soil. But after another length of stone wall, you come to a large sycamore on the left with a wide three-forked trunk. The bark pattern around the fork is unusual; you might ask children what sort of face or animal they can see in it.

The creek on the left is Le Conte Creek, and the water you see along this trail went over Rainbow Falls just a few minutes earlier. Here the water tumbles over small cascades into dark pools before dividing to go around a small island.

After passing an old chimney, the trail descends and swings away from the creek into a grove of larger Eastern hemlocks. You pass through a rocky section then a side creek where there might be salamanders. Look for a large white oak tree on the left that appears to have split a refrigerator-sized boulder into pieces as it grew.

A flat place near a side creek has rock piles, foundations, and other signs of settlement; you might ask a child to describe what it looked like when people lived here, or what those people might have been doing this time of day or year.

The best stone wall yet appears at mile **0.6**, and you go through a gap and cross the road for the Twin Creeks Resource Center. Cherokee Orchard Road is 30 yards to the right. Continue straight across and look for holly and poison ivy on the other side. The trail winds through more scraggly woods, home sites, and piles of rocks that were probably beside old cornfields. A few black locust trees, with deeply furrowed bark and compound leaves like fern fronds, live here, but they don't look healthy. They became established when farmers left this land, and they can't compete with tuliptrees, Eastern hemlocks, oaks, and other trees. By a process of succession, or gradual changes in the types of plants and animals that live here, the mature forests of the last century will reestablish themselves. The poison ivy, boxwoods, honeysuckle and most of the black locusts will be replaced by the tuliptrees and Eastern hemlocks.

The trail detours onto a grassy road to the left, where you will see an electric cable box. The trail then almost immediately turns right back into the woods. Look for straight, gray tuliptrees with great, furry poison ivy vines. It looks as if the trees are being climbed by skinny orangutans.

A foot log with a handrail spans a small side creek. Look for the old bridge foundation that the foot log rests on and imagine farm carts rumbling across. The trail curves left to follow the creek and passes a tall, square chimney on the right covered with a tangle of honeysuckle. The trail then uses another piece of that old grassy road, leaves it near a boulder wall, and leads down through a stand of Eastern hemlocks to Cherokee Orchard Road. From here you can return to the Noah "Bud" Ogle place, making this a four-mile hike. Or you could send one person back for the car and let everyone else walk down to Gatlinburg for ice cream cones.

Narrative by Doris Gove

WELCH RIDGE TRAIL

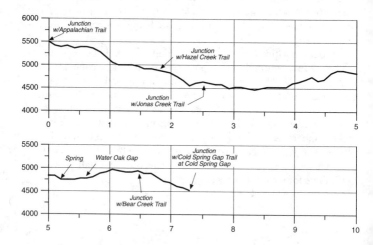

LENGTH: 7.3 miles, from Appalachian Trail to Cold Spring Gap Trail.

HIGHLIGHTS: High Rocks, easy grade, many trail connections.

MAP KEY: 5-6 E-F; USGS quads: Silers Bald, Noland Creek.

USE: Horse and hiking trail.

STARTING POINT: Drive to Forney Ridge parking area at the end of Clingmans Dome Road. Hike west on the Appalachian Trail 4.5 miles to Silers Bald.

The Welch family settled around Alarka Creek in the 1810s. From there, they spread through the mountains, including Forney Creek, where Joseph Washington Welch was raised. It is not known whether the Welch Bald and Ridge refer to the Joseph or Joseph Washington Welches. These men were cousins by marriage, but not directly related. Joseph Washington arrived in Hazel Creek in 1852, married the daughter of the original settlers and started the second family in the valley. Joseph Welch arrived about ten years later, and his family settled on the lower end of Welch Ridge, then known as River Mountain.

Welch Ridge forms a long rib off the spine of the main range of the Smokies, separating Hazel and Forney Creek drainages. Constructed by the Civilian Conservation Corps in 1934, Welch Ridge Trail runs along the crest of this ridge. The route apparently followed earlier paths used to drive cattle up to high pastures on Silers Bald. Evidence of former trails is still visible along the present route.

Welch Ridge Trail provides access to a secluded area of the park. Since the closest access to the trail is from Clingmans Dome along the A.T. and most hikers use this access, this description follows the trail downhill, from its high point near Silers Bald to Cold Spring Gap. The route follows the wide ridge as it gradually descends toward Fontana Lake. Formation of the lake in 1945 effectively isolated this area, which formerly was home to many families and supported lumber and mining activity. Today, you have to hike at least a day in any direction to reach the southern trailhead.

The trail, marked with a sign on the A.T., is 0.2 mile from Silers Bald. It skirts around the bald through a young forest of yellow birch and American beech. The trail is overgrown by thornless blackberry and passes through old fields that suggest the earlier extent of the bald. The trail joins the ridge top at a faint trail that climbs back up to the A.T. near Silers Bald Shelter.

After following the ridge a short distance, the trail passes a small grassy meadow where a cabin once stood. The U.S. Geological Survey referred to this cabin as the Franklin Place when they mapped the area in 1929. This cabin may have been owned by W.A. Franklin, who operated a store on Hazel Creek (in Franklin Town) from about 1912 until 1943. Mountain families used such high country cabins while tending cattle during the warmer months and for hunting camps in the fall and winter. You'll notice signs of old trails that served these former residents.

Descend through switchbacks to Mule Gap (elevation 4,990') after about 1.2 miles. An obscure trail enters from the right at the gap, and water may be found after a steep descent to the left. These springs are the headwaters of an unnamed branch of Little Jonas Creek. Prospecting for copper was once conducted here and on Silers

Bald. Columnist Carson Brewer reported (*Knoxville News-Sentinel* 5/30/76) that Granville Calhoun (a noted Smokies mountaineer from Hazel Creek who lived to be 105) said he helped excavate several prospect pits in 1905, which uncovered traces of the ore minerals galena and chalcopyrite. But a dispute erupted over ownership of the mineral rights by competing miners, and a lawsuit followed that dragged on for over a quarter century. Both parties were dead by the time of the decision. The ore remains in the mountains. The dark specks of garnet and biotite in the slaty rock that you see as you descend into Mule Gap attest to some of this mineralization.

The trail begins a level stretch, passing the junction with Hazel Creek Trail on the right at **1.8** miles. Descend gently, skirting a knob, then a trail sign indicates Jonas Creek Trail entering on the left.

Welch Ridge Trail continues on a level grade through second growth oak, hickory, magnolia, and yellow buckeye. As the ridge narrows, you begin a gentle climb. A rocky ledge at **3.2** miles provides a good exposure of the Thunderhead Sandstone, the rock that makes up the backbone of the Smokies. Old-timers called such exposures "greybacks" for their gray, weathered appearance.

The trail then climbs around Mt. Glory and Hawk Knob, passing a piped spring at **5.2** miles. This spring is the head of Hawk Ridge Branch that flows into Hazel Creek. Water Oak Gap follows. The water oak (*Quercus nigra*) is adapted to swampland in the southeastern coastal plain, not the high ridge tops of the Appalachians. Although the Smokies support 11 species of oak, the water oak is not one of them. Water Oak Gap probably refers to the oak grove at the nearby spring, instead of an exotic tree.

After a climb over Bearwallow Bald, the ridge broadens, and the trail drops gently. Bear Creek Trail enters on the left, having climbed Jumpup Ridge from Forney Creek. The trail is wide from increased horse traffic, broadening to the side trail to High Rocks at **6.8** miles.

A path to High Rocks leads to the right, as an overgrown road. The trail winds up the narrowing ridge, entering a young forest of American beech and rosebay rhododendron. The trail curves around two beech trees with right-angle bends in their trunks, then climbs some stone steps. The route gets confusing as it enters a thicket of mountain laurel and rhododendron, but the top is just ahead, 0.4 mile from the main trail.

High Rocks, at an elevation of 5,188', was the site of a fire tower removed many years ago. Even without the tower, there is a good view from the rocky bluffs. The tower's foundation and the lookout's cabin remain. The Park Service typically removed these cabins when the lookout towers were disassembled, with this exception. This one should remain for it is of beautiful construction, and serves as a memorial to a forgotten craft. The rough-hewn timbers are chinked with clay (notice the native quartz pebbles in it), largely hidden by hand cut chestnut shake siding. The old green paint on the window frames is still visible. A cistern which once collected rainwater for drinking is at the rear of the cabin and still holds water. Note how the cabin was placed precariously on a rocky bluff, adding to its charm.

The rock exposures on the bluffs are worth exploring. Although they are composed of Thunderhead Sandstone, this rock is distinct from earlier exposures. The many quartz pebbles suspended in sand matrix are called a conglomerate. This conglomerate formed as submarine channels carried coarse sediment away from an ancient mountain range about 800 million years ago. Similar environments today are found along the escarpment of continental shelves, where sediment periodically races through submarine canyons during phenomena called turbidity currents. Such events are not "currents" as commonly known. A turbidity current is like a tremendous flash flood or mudslide on the ocean floor where literally square miles of sand, silt, and mud rocket into the abyssal depths adjacent the continent.

Other geologic features on the cliffs tell a later story. A nearly vertical vein of white quartz cuts through the bluff in front of the cabin. Such veins formed as the rock was folded and thrust westward as the Appalachians formed. As the rocks were bent, they often cracked and pulled apart. The resulting fractures are now filled with smoky quartz. The veins formed as silica-enriched fluids served to "heal" the open fractures by precipitating quartz.

Past the trail to High Rocks, Welch Ridge Trail descends steadily as an old road. The trail becomes rocky as it passes through a rock field populated from the bluffs above. Several small springs emerge from the rocks, and the trail is muddy in places. You'll reach Cold Spring Gap at **7.3** miles, where the trail ends. Cold Spring Gap Trail also ends here, having climbed 3.6 miles from a wet ford across Hazel Creek.

Narrative by James Wedekind

WEST PRONG TRAIL

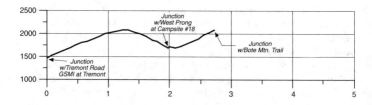

LENGTH: 2.7 miles, from Tremont Road to Bote Mountain Trail.
HIGHLIGHTS: Walker Valley Cemetery, hardwood forest, pretty creek.
CAUTIONS: Foot log stream crossings.
MAP KEY: 4 C-D; USGS quads: Wear Cove, Thunderhead Mountain.
USE: Horse and hiking trail.
TRAILHEAD: From the Townsend "Y," turn toward Cades Cove. In 0.2 mile, turn left toward the Great Smoky Mountain Institute at Tremont. At mile 2.0, look for the West Prong Trail on the right, just before the entrance to the Institute. Turn right and park in a gravel lot. From here, you can see a pump house uphill to the left, at the end of a paved drive. The trail starts behind the pump house.

West Prong Trail provides a hiking connection between the Tremont-Elkmont trails and Cades Cove trails and begins along the banks of the Middle Prong. To the old timers, a fork of a river was called a prong. Both the West and Middle Prongs are part of the Little River, which drains most of the western end of the park from Elkmont to Cades Cove. These prongs join just west of the Townsend "Y" at the road intersection leading to Tremont.

After a good rain, the beginning of the trail may be a bit muddy, but don't let that turn you back. The trail will climb along the flanks of Fodderstack Mountain and remains very dry. Immediately, you will come to an intersection. One choice is to follow the trail, which swings left. Another is to go right from the trail sign and visit the maintained cemetery, which appears in about 100 yards. Moore, Stinnett, Carlyle, and McCarter are some of the names here, with several recent burials. Two new-looking stones mark the graves of an infant who died in 1882 and his mother, born in 1862 and died in 1882. In fact, you will see the graves of many children. High childhood mortality was common in the 1800s and early 1900s. To many religious people, infant mortality meant that God had other plans for their babies: children were God's gifts and He could take them back whenever He wanted. The epitaph "born on earth to flower in heaven" was often used on children's graves.

Look for one grave in particular while you are here: Vannie Cook's. It lies in the back corner of the cemetery. Vannie died when a large tree fell upon her while she and her sister watched a forest fire. The fire was the result of a short-lived feud, which, like many arguments, got out of control. Vannie's father, Sam Cook, and a group of men set out to suppress the fire and used the children as fire spotters to watch slow-moving flames while the adults attacked the faster moving sections. Vannie and her sister Eva were stationed in a spot that seemed safe, but the fire burst into life and quickly surrounded them. A large tree, engulfed in flames, dropped a limb which crashed down on the two girls. Eva escaped but Vannie did not. She was seriously injured when the men arrived. Broken and burned, she was brought to Will Walker's cabin just down the hill. As Vannie was laid on the bed, a dove flew by and landed on the window sill. The women of the community tried desperately to save her. For 2 days they struggled and the dove stayed nearby. On the third day, Vannie breathed her last and the dove flew off, convincing her nurses that the dove had been an angel sent to take Vannie to God in heaven.

A rough but fairly clear trail goes up from the cemetery to meet the West Prong Trail in progress, or you can go back to the trail sign and pick up West Prong Trail at the beginning. The trail is in three roughly one-mile segments—one up, one down, and then another up.

It is wide and level, ascending first through a cut-over forest of small tuliptrees and maples.

At 0.25 mile, look down the slope to the right for a wild hog trap. The wild hog is a non-native animal and was brought to a private hunting camp in North Carolina in the 1940s. Because of the war and economic hardships, no one wanted to pay to hunt, so the camp failed. Its fences deteriorated and the hogs escaped. Soon they had made their way to the Smokies where they began to cause extensive damage. Not only do they root up the ground, they also damage native vegetation, spread the seeds of exotic plants such as Japanese witch grass, kill and trample ground nesting birds, eat salamanders, and even compete with the black bears for those all important fall acorns. As early as 1959, the Park Service began removing them from the Smokies. By 1992, over 7,000 animals had been removed, with 1986 as the record year when 1,146 hogs were taken. (Trivia: the park record for the number of hogs caught in one trap at one time is 17—piglets of course.)

At mile 0.3, the trail forks. Take the left fork to continue; the right forks leads back down to the cemetery. At about 1.0 mile, an unmaintained trail joins West Prong Trail from the right.

West Prong Trail climbs the side of Fodderstack Mountain (2,550') to about 2,000' elevation. The trees are bigger here, and there is a fine view through open woods down into the creek valley. The trail ascends steadily to dry woods with pines, sourwoods, and chestnut oaks. You can hear the West Prong below. Then you start a mile-long descent to the prong through open woods alternating with thick patches of rosebay rhododendron. Several seeps cross the trail, and wildflowers can be found beside them.

The trail crosses a side creek, an easy rock hop, and then passes a beautiful fractured rock face on the left. Rosebay rhododendron, ferns, and yellow birch grow out of rock cracks. Just around a bend from this creek, the trail reaches Campsite #18 at 1,700' elevation. There are two tent sites close to the river, and this campsite receives heavy use.

The West Prong Trail turns sharply right, and you have to follow it across some rocky seeps to get to a foot log across West Prong. Big sycamores line the prong here, and campers have built an informal dam that provides a fairly deep swimming pool.

After the foot log, turn left, back-track up the other side of the West Prong, and look for the trail starting up on your right. The trail goes uphill for over a half mile; it is never steep, but never relenting either. Eastern hemlock and mountain laurel tunnels alternate, and pine trees grow on the drier, more exposed sections. At mile **2.7**, West Prong Trail joins Bote Mountain Trail. From here, you can hike down to Laurel Creek Road (1.2 miles), up to Spence Field (6.0 miles), or back to your car.

Narrative by Tom Condon and Doris Gove

WET BOTTOM TRAIL

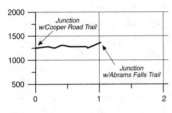

LENGTH: 1.0 mile, from Cooper Road Trail to Abrams Falls Trail.
HIGHLIGHTS: Tranquil setting.
CAUTIONS: Mud.
MAP KEY: 3 E; USGS quad: Cades Cove.
USE: Horse and hiking trail.

STARTING POINT: 0.2 miles west of Cades Cove Loop Road on Cooper Road Trail.

Designed primarily for horse use, this trail in dry weather offers the hiker a chance to get away from the hustle and bustle of the Cades Cove crowds. But the Wet Bottom Trail is indeed wet. It connects Cooper Road Trail with Rabbit and Abrams Creeks trails by cutting across the Abrams Creek flood plain. Rainy weather combined with horse use makes this area a quagmire, so hike this trail only after a few days of sunshine.

Approximately 0.2 miles from the junction of the Cooper Road Trail and Cades Cove Loop Road, the Wet Bottom Trail begins. It heads south down a dry pine-oak hillside. At **0.25** miles, you come upon a large red barn. Originally built by John W. Oliver in the early part of the 1900s, it is now used by the Park Service to store wood used to maintain the numerous historic structures in the cove.

At the barn, Wet Bottom Trail joins the main walkway from Cades Cove Loop Road to the Elijah Oliver Place. A left turn here will take you out to the loop road. A right will allow you to continue along the Wet Bottom Trail or to the post-Civil War home of Elijah Oliver. This site preserves a farm as it might have been at the end of the 19th century. The farm house and all its out buildings remain, but the fields are gone. The forest that now shelters you has replaced the rows of corn, sorghum, tobacco and other crops.

In wet weather, backpackers wishing to return to their cars at the Abrams Falls trailhead might wish to continue all the way to Elijah Oliver's Place and the follow the other major walkway to the trail-head. In dry weather, the Wet Bottom Trail cuts the corner of these two trails. Watch the woods to your left. About 300 yards west of the red barn, Wet Bottom Trail again turns south. The trail is difficult to spot. It is about half way through a pine flat, appearing more like a small water diversion than a trail. Watch for hoof prints for your clue.

The trail continues south about 0.25 mile before reaching a sturdy wire fence. This is the Abrams Creek flood plain exclosure used by the National Park Service to protect this special area from the rooting of the non-native wild hog. The wetland protected within its confines is home to some interesting plant and animal species. Here is one place you might find the colorful spotted salamander.

At the fence, the trail turns right. As you follow along the fence line, watch for clubmoss, a species of *Lycopodium*. The spores of this tiny pine-like plant were once collected to be used as flash powder by photographers. Eventually, a small spring branch joins the trail for nearly 100 yards. At the fence corner, this tiny creek turns left, while our trail continues straight. Presently, you will join Abrams Creek for a peaceful stroll along its banks. Here's a good place to look for spring wildflowers, deer or even river otters. Otters were released into these waters in the early 1990s as part of a National Park Service program to re-establish these native creatures to the Smokies. More than 100 otters were released throughout the park.

Ahead a short distance, the trail fords Abrams Creek. You may choose to do this as well and pick up the last few hundred yards of the trail on the southern bank. It turns down river, before climbing a small ridge to the Abrams Falls parking area. An alternative trail meanders along the north bank before joining the major walkway between the parking area and Elijah Oliver's Place. For those who haven't found this trail living up to its name, you may wish to stay dry by taking this alternate trail. It's about 0.25 mile to the trailhead.

For those interested in hiking this trail the opposite direction, starting from the Abrams Falls parking area, make an immediate right upon entering the woods between the parking area and the trail bridge. Follow the small path over the small ridge to reach the river ford just upstream. The drier alternative is to cross the trail bridge and turn right toward Elijah Oliver's. Watch the river carefully as you head upstream. The meandering north bank path leaves the major trail when the river bends away as well. Follow this path until you reach the ford, watch for hoof prints, and turn left to continue along Wet Bottom Trail. Enjoy your reprieve from the summer crowds.

Narrative by Tom Condon

WHITEOAK BRANCH TRAIL

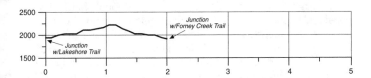

LENGTH: 2.0 miles, from Lakeshore Trail to Forney Creek Trail.
HIGHLIGHTS: Spring wildflowers, house sites, trail connections.
CAUTIONS: Unbridged stream crossings.
MAP KEY: 6 F; USGS quad: Noland Creek.
USE: Horse and hiking trail.
STARTING POINT: Hike Lakeshore Trail 2.5 miles from Lakeview Drive.

Whiteoak Branch Trail is a short, connecting trail between the Lakeshore and Forney Creek trails beginning at a former farmstead 2.5 miles from Lakeview Drive. The house once stood below the trail junction in a grassy clearing surrounded by a forest of American beech, American holly, tuliptree, and flowering dogwood. In the spring, daffodils planted by former residents grow in clumps. Furrows in the ground indicate where non-native wild hogs have rooted for herbaceous plants.

The trail slowly ascends a low ridge through mountain laurel and oak as it follows a tributary of Gray Wolf Creek to a crossing. The trail courses through a pine/oak forest with an understory of mountain laurel and a ground cover of ferns. The trail is sandy with tiny quartz pebbles. At 0.8 mile an old roadbed veers off to the right just before the trail crosses Gray Wolf Creek via rock hop, climbs another low ridge, and levels.

At 1.25 miles the trail reaches a clearing in a forest of tuliptree and flowering dogwood. Only a pile of chimney rocks remains of the house that once stood here. A small spring is nearby. White quartz lies about the area, created when cracks formed in rock far below the surface. Water flowed through the cracks, depositing minerals, which formed quartz.

The trail climbs to its highest point, a 2,260' saddle in the ridge, populated by short-leaf, Table Mountain, and white pine. As it descends by switchback, the sounds of Whiteoak Branch and Forney Creek become increasingly audible, and the vegetation changes to dog-hobble and rhododendron. Accompanied by Whiteoak Branch, the trail becomes a rocky, old roadbed which can be wet and muddy. You cross Whiteoak Branch just before meeting Forney Creek Trail.

Narrative by Charles Maynard and David Morris

WOLF RIDGE TRAIL

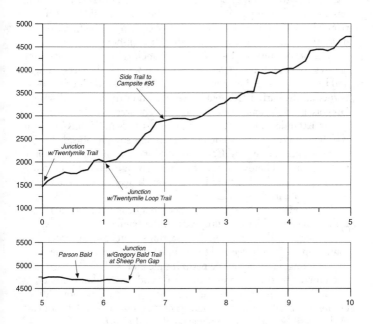

LENGTH: 6.4 miles, from Twentymile Trail to Gregory Bald Trail
HIGHLIGHTS: Ferns, blueberries, partial views.
CAUTIONS: Moore Spring Branch crossing in high water.
MAP KEY: 2 F; USGS quads: Fontana Dam, Tapoco, Calderwood,
Cades Cove.
USE: Horse and hiking trail.
STARTING POINT: Jct. with Twentymile Trail, 0.5 mile from its
trailhead.

The trailhead for the Wolf Ridge Trail is at the left fork of the road
just past the first bridge on Twentymile Trail. It's a jeep trail on an

old railroad bed running beside Moore Springs Branch. The railroad was built by the Kitchen Lumber Company in the 1920s. This stream has a strong flow, especially in wet weather. In the mile to the Twentymile Loop Trail junction there are five crossings. The first three are by footlog, and the next two by wading or rock-hopping.

The headwaters of Moore Springs Branch is Moore Spring on top of Gregory Bald. It has provided cold, clear water to herders, campers, and hikers for more than 150 years. The popular herder's cabin burned in the early 1970s, but those who know the area don't visit Gregory Bald without a side trip to drink the waters of Moore Springs.

At 1.0 mile you should see a trail junction sign. Wolf Ridge Trail goes left and the Twentymile Loop Trail runs straight ahead. The grade is quite gentle until Campsite #95, about a mile above the junction, in a mixed hardwood forest. Water is readily available from a small branch beyond or from Dalton Branch nearby. This is an excellent campsite in an appealing location.

This portion of the route was once a public road of sorts across Dalton Gap from Parson Turnpike to Twentymile Creek.

Just beyond the campsite, the trail turns right to swing around the south end of Wolf Ridge and then climbs the west flank. Fraser magnolia saplings grow along the path. It's pleasant walking through an open mixed hardwood forest where oaks and maples dominate.

At 3,000' elevation, the path zigs left to reverse direction. After climbing for half a mile to a slight gap, it zags right then left just east of the crest. Sassafras saplings appear along the path.

Ferns can be seen here and there and blanket one small hollow. The trail hits the ridgecrest a mile short of Parson Bald and passes through a forest fernland mixed with a few blackberry bushes.

At the edge of Parson Bald are blueberry bushes whose fruits ripen in August. In July and August, colorful crimson bee-balm blooms here as well as another member of the mint family, the smaller and subdued blue blossoms of heal-all. Trees are gradually diminishing the bald and closing off views. Unlike Gregory Bald, Parson is not being maintained by the National Park Service in an open condition.

Flame azaleas grace the fringes of this once heavily grazed mountaintop meadow, named for Joshua Parson, whose influence was such in the early 1800s that Parson Turnpike and Parson Branch Road perpetuate his name. He lived at the confluence of the Little Tennessee River and Abrams Creek, and, along with John Isbell, was contracted to build a road from Abrams Creek to the North Carolina state line.

The remainder of the trail, from Parson Bald to Sheep Pen Gap, is a delight. It's downhill on a gentle grade through an open forest. Sheep Pen Gap also features an open forest and Campsite #13 is a favorite among backpackers. Water is available from a small seep down the Gregory Bald Trail.

Underlying the relatively thin layer of soil on Wolf Ridge is the hard, sedimentary bedrock of Elkmont Sandstone. However, few outcroppings appear.

Gray wolves were a part of the wild environment when the Smoky Mountain hollows were first settled. "Wolf Ridge" preserves a permanent reminder of their presence.

Narrative by Woody Brinegar

SMOKIES' BUSIEST TRAILS

If it's solitude you seek, you'll want to avoid these trail sections during summer and on weekends throughout the year. Good off-times to hike busy trails are weekdays during the school year or early (before 10 a.m.) or late (after 4:00 p.m.) in the day.

Abrams Falls Trail (to the falls)
Alum Cave Trail (to the bluffs)
Appalachian Trail (from Newfound Gap to Charlies Bunion)
Chimney Tops Trail
Forney Ridge Trail (to Andrews Bald)
Laurel Falls Trail (to the falls)
Trillium Gap Trail (to Grotto Falls)
Rainbow Falls Trail (to the falls)
Ramsay Cascades Trail

TRAILS GROUPED BY AREA

CADES COVE AREA TRAILS

Abrams Falls
Ace Gap
Anthony Creek
Beard Cane
Bote Mountain
Cane Creek
Cooper Road
Crib Gap
Crooked Arm Ridge
Finley Cane
Gold Mine
Gregory Bald
Gregory Ridge
Hannah Mountain
Hatcher Mountain
Indian Grave Gap
Lead Cove
Little Bottoms
Rabbit Creek
Rich Mountain Loop
Rich Mountain
Russell Field
Schoolhouse Gap
Scott Mountain
Turkeypen Ridge
Wet Bottom

CATALOOCHEE/BIG CREEK AREA TRAILS

Balsam Mountain
Baxter Creek
Beech Gap
Big Creek
Big Fork Ridge
Boogerman
Caldwell Fork
Camel Gap
Cataloochee Divide
Chestnut Branch
Flat Creek
Gunter Fork

Hemphill Bald
Little Cataloochee
Long Bunk
McKee Branch
Mt. Sterling
Mt. Sterling Ridge
Palmer Creek
Polls Gap
Pretty Hollow Gap
Rough Fork
Spruce Mountain
Swallow Fork

DEEP CREEK AREA TRAILS

Cooper Creek
Deep Creek
Deeplow Gap
Fork Ridge
Indian Creek Motor Trail
Indian Creek
Juneywhank Falls

Loop Trail
Martins Gap
Noland Divide
Pole Road Creek
Stone Pile Gap
Sunkota Ridge

ELKMONT/TREMONT AREA TRAILS

Bote Mountain
Chestnut Top
Cove Mountain
Cucumber Gap
Curry Mountain
Goshen Prong
Greenbrier Ridge
Huskey Gap
Jakes Creek
Laurel Falls
Lead Cove
Little Brier Gap
Little Greenbrier

Little River
Lumber Ridge
Lynn Camp Prong
Meigs Creek
Meigs Mountain
Metcalf Bottoms
Middle Prong
Miry Ridge
Panther Creek
Rough Creek
Roundtop
Sugarland Mountain
Turkeypen Ridge

FONTANA LAKE-CLINGMANS DOME AREA TRAILS

Andrews Bald
Bear Creek
Bone Valley
Clingmans Dome Bypass
Cold Spring Gap
Forney Ridge
Hazel Creek

High Rocks
Jonas Creek
Lakeshore
Springhouse Branch
Welch Ridge
Whiteoak Branch

GATLINBURG/LE CONTE AREA TRAILS

Alum Cave
Baskins Creek
Boulevard
Brushy Mountain
Bull Head
Cataract Falls
Charlies Bunion
Chimney Tops
Cliff Tops
Cove Mountain
Gatlinburg
Grotto Falls

Huskey Gap
Jumpoff
Myrtle Point
Old Sugarlands
Panther Ridge
Rainbow Falls
Road Prong
Sugarland Mountain
Trillium Gap
Twin Creeks
West Prong

GREENBRIER/COSBY AREA TRAILS

Albright Grove Loop
Brushy Mountain
Camel Gap
Gabes Mountain
Grapeyard Ridge
Henwallow Falls
Low Gap

Lower Mt. Cammerer
Maddron Bald
Mt. Cammerer
Old Settlers
Porters Creek
Ramsay Cascade
Snake Den Ridge

NOLAND CREEK AREA TRAILS

Goldmine Loop
Lakeshore

Noland Creek
Noland Divide

OCONALUFTEE AREA TRAILS

Beech Gap
Bradley Fork
Cabin Flats
Chasteen Creek
Dry Sluice Gap
Enloe Creek
Grassy Branch
Hughes Ridge

Hyatt Ridge
Kanati Fork
Kephart Prong
Mingus Creek
Newton Bald
Oconaluftee River
Smokemont Loop
Sweat Heifer Creek
Thomas Divide

TWENTYMILE AREA TRAILS

Eagle Creek
Jenkins Ridge
Lakeshore
Long Hungry Ridge

Lost Cove
Twentymile
Twentymile Loop
Wolf Ridge

ABOUT THE HIKER/WRITERS

Bill Beard is a counselor at Pi Beta Phi elementary school in Gatlinburg, TN. He has spent many of his recent summers collecting data for park researchers on trail use in the Smokies.

Carson Brewer is a columnist for the Knoxville News-Sentinel. He is the author or co-author of several books, including: *Valley So Wild*, *Just Over the Next Ridge*, *A Wonderment of Mountains: The Great Smokies*, *Great Smoky Mountains National Park*, and *Hiking in the Great Smokies*.

Woody Brinegar is a past president of Great Smoky Mountains Natural History Association and has written about history and the out-of-doors for the Maryville Times. He is the author of *Old Burt: Sage of the Smokies* and has contributed to *Walks in the Great Smokies*.

Margaret Lynn Brown is currently writing an environmental history of the Great Smoky Mountains, a work which will also complete her Ph.D in history from the University of Kentucky. She has written about the out-of-doors for *Backpacker*, *The Utne Reader*, *The Christian Science Monitor*, and other publications.

Tom Condon works as a Park Ranger in the Cades Cove area of the Smokies. He is at work on a manuscript about the wildflowers of the park.

Donald E. Davis teaches teaches sociology at Dalton College in Dalton, Georgia. He is the author of *Ecophilosophy: A Field Guide to the Literature* and is presently completing *Where There Be Mountains*, a history of man's impact on the southern Appalachians from pre-history to the present.

Beth Giddens is Publications Editor for the Southern Regional Education Board in Atlanta. She earned a Ph.D in English from the University of Tennessee, taught writing at Auburn University for several years, and is co-author of *Crafting Prose*.

Doris Gove has a Ph.D in zoology from the University of Tennessee and has worked as a naturalist at nature centers in Knoxville, TN and Highlands, NC. She is the author of several children's books, including *Miracle at Egg Rock: A Puffin's Story*, *A Water Snake's Year*, *One Rainy Night*, and *Red-Spotted Newt*.

William A. Hart, Jr. is Director, Member Services, for Western Carolina Industries, a regional association of employers headquartered in Asheville, NC. He has hiked 3,000 miles in the Smokies and pursues an avocational interest in the history, lore, music, flora, and fauna of Great Smoky Mountains National Park.

Lance Holland works as Special Projects Director for Fontana Village in Fontana, NC and as a location scout for most films shot in the region, including *The Fugitive*, and *Nell*. He has led hundreds of groups on hikes in the Fontana Lake area and is an expert on the lore of Hazel and Eagle creeks.

Steve Kemp is Publications Specialist for Great Smoky Mountains Natural History Association. He has worked as a Park Ranger in Yellowstone and Denali national parks and is author of *Trees of the Smokies*.

Charles Maynard is Executive Director for Friends of the Smokies and has also worked as a storyteller and as a United Methodist Minister. He is co-author of *Time Well Spent: Family Hiking in the Smokies* and *Waterfalls & Cascades of the Smoky Mountains*.

David Morris works as a nurse anesthetist in Knoxville, TN and is an Adopt-a-Trail volunteer. He is co-author of *Time Well Spent: Family Hiking in the Smokies* and *Waterfalls & Cascades of the Smoky Mountains*.

Ted Olson has worked many summers as a Park Ranger on the Blue Ridge Parkway in North Carolina. He is pursuing a Ph.D in English and Southern studies at the University of Mississippi where he serves as Founding Editor of *CrossRoads: A Journal of Southern Culture*.

James Wedekind is an Environmental Scientist for CDM Federal Programs in Oak Ridge, TN. He has a Masters degree in geology and is a contributing author of *Wilderness Trails of Tennessee's Cherokee National Forest*.

TRAIL INDEX

OTHER BOOKS & MAPS

From Great Smoky Mountains Natural History Association

BIRDS OF THE SMOKIES
by Fred J. Alsop, III
This extraordinary guide includes 100 color photos of park birds and a detailed text which reflects over 25 years of birding in the Smokies. It tells where to find birds, includes suggested birding trips, a bird song guide, a complete checklist, and a special "how to" section on the park's 12 most sought after species. 167 pages, 4.5" x 6" **$9.95**.

TREES OF THE SMOKIES
by Steve Kemp
A delightful, pocket-sized field guide to the trees of the area. Features 80 color photographs of the most common species along with over 100 line drawings. Text covers virgin forests, record trees, blooming times, fall colors, plus a complete key and checklist. 128 pages, 4.5" x 6" **$8.95**.

THE SMOKY MOUNTAIN BLACK BEAR
by Jeff Rennicke
This beautifully-written book examines the relationships between bears and humans in the Smoky Mountains from the days of the Cherokee Bear Dancers through the pioneer period to the present. Includes color photographs and exquisite line art. 60 pages, 9" x 8.5" **$7.95**

EARTHWALK PRESS HIKING MAP
Topographic map with trails and backcountry campsites. 1:62,500 scale. **$4.50** (paper) **$7.95** (plastic).

TO ORDER CALL (615) 436-7318. *Free Catalog Available.*
GSMNHA 115 Park Headquarters Road, Gatlinburg, TN 37738